56 VICHY DR.
SARATOGA SPGS N.Y.
Phone 587-2851

SOCIOLOGY

SOCIOLOGY

David Popenoe

Douglass College, Rutgers University
The State University of New Jersey

Second Edition

PRENTICE-HALL, INC., Englewood Cliffs, New Jersey

PRENTICE-HALL INTERNATIONAL, INC., *London*
PRENTICE-HALL OF AUSTRALIA, PTY. LTD., *Sydney*
PRENTICE-HALL OF CANADA, LTD., *Toronto*
PRENTICE-HALL OF INDIA PRIVATE LIMITED, *New Delhi*
PRENTICE-HALL OF JAPAN, INC., *Tokyo*

CONTENTS

PREFACE

PURPOSE

This text is designed for introductory sociology courses at the college level. It includes systematic and comprehensive coverage of basic concepts and principles, terminology, and elements of important social institutions, processes, and trends. The book also functions as a survey of sociological subject areas, so that students who later wish to take advanced courses will be familiar with the major fields of specialization.

Every textbook writer must start with the realization that there is no one "right" way to teach a course; a good teacher will adapt his material to suit his own special abilities and interests and his students' needs. To limit a book to only one school of sociological thought—functionalist, evolutionist, conflict—is to limit its usefulness. This book, therefore, introduces many different sociological points of view. An inclusive approach seems especially valuable in a field such as sociology, which is changing and developing rapidly, for this approach gives the student a broad framework with which to handle the new concepts and viewpoints that will arise in the next few years. A special effort has been made to use many current resources which will help keep the reader abreast of recent developments with significance for the future. For example, we include readings on the phenomena of student activism, inner-city ghetto problems, social class structure, religious pluralism today, problems of modernization in Turkey, and the movement for equal rights among Mexican-Americans in the southwestern United States.

The scope and variety of sociological study are introduced. Basic concepts are presented here, in a manner that points out that not all sociologists agree on how to define them. We discuss the results of studies and research projects conducted by eminent men in the field today. Charts, graphs, and tables found throughout the book present statistical data. The intent of this wide variety of information is to give the student the opportunity to develop a viewpoint of his own regarding the subject matter. Hopefully, it will also give the professor wide latitude with which to develop his own ideas.

As do most introductory books, this text introduces and discusses many different societies, both past and present. But it concentrates on the student's own social environment, modern American society, thus providing him with a tool to help him develop a new understanding of his own society and his position in it.

THE PLAN OF THE BOOK

The book begins with a discussion of basic concepts of sociological study and elements of social life; it moves on to social patterns and institutions, and concludes with the processes of maintenance and change in societies.

The focus of Part I: *Elements of Social Life* is the conceptual basis of sociology, as seen in three important elements of social life—individuals, social groups, and culture. The first chapter in Part I deals directly with the central concern of sociological study, social structure or organization, giving the student a framework for subsequent analysis of all other aspects of society. The following chapters discuss culture, socialization, and social groups, showing how these elements interrelate and how they contribute to overall organization.

In Part II: *Social Patterns and Social Insti-*

tutions, concepts and terminology developed in Part I are applied in analyzing communities and societies. This section deals with the social patterns of stratification and inequality, and ethnic and racial pluralism; it discusses three major institutions—the family, education, and religion. The last chapter in Part II is devoted to the environmental backdrop of social life—population and ecology.

Part III: *Order and Change in Society* looks at the important processes of maintenance and change, with special reference to the major trends of contemporary society. Chapter 12 focuses on deviance and the functions of social control; chapter 13 discusses collective behavior. The next two chapters deal with the twin processes of urbanization and industrialization, and developments in government and politics in modern and newly emerging nations. Social and cultural change are discussed in Chapter 16.

WHY ANOTHER SOCIOLOGY TEXTBOOK?

We are putting this new book on the market because teachers have indicated that certain improvements might be made in sociology textbooks—improvements such as increased readability and the inclusion of resource materials seemed especially necessary to make a book that is more interesting and useful to students and a better teaching tool for professors.

Readability

The only good textbook is one that students can and will read, yet the complaint most frequently made by teachers and students alike about introductory textbooks is that they lack readability. A first step in producing this book, therefore, was to define "readability" in the context of the teaching situation, and determine how it might be achieved. After much discussion and analysis, and with the help of professionals, it was decided that readability depends essentially on organization, language, and relevance.

Good organization makes a book readable.

Students learn best when material is clearly presented one step at a time and the sequence of presentation indicates important interrelationships. The chapters in this book are broken down into from two to five "topics," each of which is a separate and virtually self-contained unit of study. This style of organization makes the material easy for the student to comprehend and at the same time allows the teacher considerable latitude in arranging reading assignments in the text to suit his own curriculum.

Clear and familiar language make a book readable. Students often find it difficult to learn a whole new vocabulary in order to understand their text. Fortunately it is often possible to introduce even the most complicated concepts in simple language. This book, therefore, uses only the amount of professional terminology which a student must know in order to comprehend his outside reading, or to prepare for a more advanced course. When new terms are introduced, they are set off in italics and clearly defined. A glossary at the end of each chapter serves as a convenient reference and study aid; it also notes the page of the text where the term is discussed in more detail. The *Modern Dictionary of Sociology*[1] served as a guide for many of the definitions.

Relevance makes a book readable, because it provides a motivation to read. Therefore, in this book sociological theories and concepts are illustrated not only with the results of published studies, but also with examples drawn from the students' own social environment—the daily behavior of friends, parents, classmates, and neighbors.

Readings

Most teachers assign readings to supplement and illustrate the textbook they have chosen. This book includes such readings in each chapter. The material, drawn from pub-

1. George A. Theodorsen and Achilles G. Theodorsen, *Modern Dictionary of Sociology* (New York: Thomas Y. Crowell, Apollo Edition, 1970).

lished books and articles, has been abridged to make the length and subject matter appropriate for the introductory student, but the style of the original author has, of course, been retained.

In keeping with the current trend toward interdisciplinary study, the selection of readings includes items by sociologists and writers in related fields, such as anthropology, psychology, and education. Some are written in an academic style, others in a more popular vein; some concentrate on small specific studies, and others formulate broad principles and concepts. Each was chosen because of its significance to the subject of the chapter in which it appears and its interest to introductory students.

Research exercise

Since the study of sociology involves both knowledge of concepts and a familiarity with methods of research, many introductory courses feature at least one student research project. Chapter 7 outlines a suggested project of this type. It is presented in sufficient detail to serve as a guide for the student working on his own; it could also be used as a model from which the class could make its own project or as a reading to illustrate the problems and techniques of actual research in the field.

Graphs, charts, and tables

Since sociology depends heavily on empirical evidence, it is important for the new student to be able to understand statistical data. All the statistical material in this text has been designed by a specialist, to make it attractive, graphic, and comprehensible. The book includes samples of many different types of graphs or charts in frequent use.

Boxed-off inserts

Other supplementary materials have been included where appropriate to clarify and illustrate the text. Among these are short excerpts from books of general interest (for example, R. C. Townsend's *Up the Organization*) that illustrate a point under discussion;

short summaries of important textual material, which serve as additional study aids; and clarifications of difficult concepts used in sociology, such as correlation or mode.

Illustrations

Sociologists were among the first to point out that modern society is increasingly oriented toward visual images. This book contains a large number of photographs which give visual impact and support to the text.

Bibliographies

Each chapter of this text contains its own bibliography, annotated to describe for the student the values, uses, approach, and subject matter of the books listed. Each bibliography begins with sociological works, both classic and modern; the listing is up-to-date and is heavily weighted with paperbacks. To stimulate student interest, the bibliography includes a list of related resources, such as films, novels, and popular nonfiction, which deal with the chapter subject. Each entry was chosen both for its subject and its readability. Some students may wish to become familiar with the kind of research that is reported in journals or carried out for advanced degrees. Although these materials are sometimes difficult to locate, we have included a small sample of specific articles.

SUPPLEMENTS

Accompanying the text are a Study Guide and ACCESS® Workbook, and an Instructor's Manual. The workbook is designed to help students interrelate concepts from various sections and chapters and to review the important points of the text. (The self-test sections of the workbook utilize ACCESS®, a process in which an answer printed in invisible ink is revealed by rubbing it with the ACCESS® activator. The student thus receives immediate verification of his self-test responses.)

The Instructor's Manual includes not only suggestions for quiz and exam questions, but also background resources, suggested illustrations for lecture use, and topics for class discussions for many of the major points of the text. In addition to the Instructor's Manual, a separate Test Item File is also available. For each chapter there are also suggestions for research papers and projects, and for essays or essay-type exam questions.

ACKNOWLEDGMENTS

To achieve readability, and to assure the text's usefulness to teachers and students, a team of specialists have cooperated with me in the development of this book. They have included market specialists, research assistants, professional writers and editors, designers, and photo researchers—experts in different areas who know and understand the interests and needs of the beginning student of sociology. I would like to take this opportunity to express more than the usual gratitude of an author for professional assistance I received in writing the book, especially from Miss Judith Davis, and to Miss Sally Saunders, who was the chief editor. If we have achieved clarity of expression and a felicity of style, which I hope we have, it is primarily due to their great contributions. Next, I would like to express great thanks to two research assistants who did much of the background research and legwork, Mr. Mathew Greenwald and Mr. Tony Vice; to two colleagues who read and commented on portions of the manuscript, Dr. Donald F. Heisel and Dr. Robert Parelius; and to two other colleagues whose consultations with me regarding the text, and sociology in general over the years, have been of enormous help to me, Dr. Robert Gutman and Dr. Harry C. Bredemeier. Finally, a very special word of gratitude must be extended to my wife, Kate. She not only "made it all possible," but she read fully and criticized in detail, both substantively and editorially, every chapter in the book. Her breadth of knowledge and sense of good judgment were a tremendous asset to me.

SPECIAL NOTE ABOUT THE SECOND EDITION

This textbook first appeared on the American college and university scene in early 1971. I am very thankful for the suggestions for improvement which have come since then from many students and faculty members in all parts of the United States. As a result of these suggestions, the following major changes have been made in the Second Edition:

1. A new section on sociological methodology has been added to chapter one, enabling the student to develop a general understanding of both sociological methods and "substance" in the opening chapter.
2. A new chapter on the family has been added to Part II, providing much more coverage of this major social institution.
3. The materials covering broader and more theoretical aspects of social and cultural change have been consolidated into a new final chapter of the book. It is felt that this positioning will make the materials more meaningful to the student, since he will have a greater understanding of concrete social and cultural changes developed in the preceding chapters.
4. A chapter summary, which provides a useful study and review aid, has been added to each chapter.

Several other changes have also been made: the materials on primary groups and organizations have been consolidated into a single chapter (chapter 5); the illustrations which accompany each chapter have been considerably updated; new abridgments have been added, and those which proved to be less informative to students have been deleted; the chapter bibliographies and footnote references have been updated; general revisions have been made in the body of the text itself, especially the updating of examples; the supplements to the text—Study Guide, Instructor's Manual, and Test Item File—have been thoroughly revised and updated.

All of these changes, I feel, add significantly to the strength of this textbook as an educational tool. The book has been praised as one of the very few now on the market which is sociologically "solid" and accurate, yet at the same time highly readable and interesting to the student. This, at least, has been our goal, and it is hoped that the Second Edition achieves it even better than the First Edition.

D.P.

Princeton, New Jersey
1973

SOCIOLOGY

1. Sociology: The Field and Its Methods

When a beginning student of sociology tries to
discover exactly what it is that he will be studying
for the next term, he runs into a perplexing question:
What is sociology? To judge from the variety of
courses offered in the field, sociology seems to
include the study of drug addiction, methods of
child raising, Haitian voodoo rites, the problems
of bureaucracies, and the political climate in obscure
African countries. What could be the common
denominator of such widely varied fields of
investigation?

Sociology is the disciplined and objective study of
human social interaction. Sociologists study
individual social acts, such as a friendly wave over
the back fence to a neighbor; social relationships,
like those of husbands and wives, teachers and
students, and buyers and sellers; organizations
large and small, from the High School Photography
Club in a little Nebraska town to the federal
government of the United States; and the total social
system of communities or nations. Social structures
(the family, state, or church) and social processes
(conflict, change, and communication) are both
included. Specific factual studies of these subjects
are carefully conducted within the framework of
systems and theories.

1 THE FIELD OF SOCIOLOGY

Because the sociologist is interested in all kinds of human interactions, his field of study overlaps many other disciplines. Like the historian, he wants to learn about the wars that destroyed cities in ancient Greece. Like the politician, he tries to predict the way citizens will vote in an election. Like the doctor, he asks questions about the effects of a stay in the hospital on a sick man. But the sociologist focuses on an aspect of each of these areas which is different from those of interest to the other specialists. His interest is not in the physical health of the hospitalized patient, but in the patient's relationship with the doctors, nurses, and other members of the staff. The sociologist does not see the man as a case of appendicitis but as a person who must suddenly adjust to a whole new social environment under conditions of emotional stress. We might say that sociology is not so much a unique matter as a way of looking at and analyzing topics which are often familiar. To study sociology is to look for the underlying social meanings that give significance to ordinary human actions.

SOCIOLOGY AS A SCIENCE

An important aspect of the sociological viewpoint is that it is basically scientific in character. Sociologists try to study human social behavior by using objective techniques; it is this commitment to the scientific method that makes sociology a scientific discipline rather than a branch of the humanities. Scholars, philosophers, and men of letters have speculated about sociological

subject matter for centuries. The plays of Shakespeare, the novels of Charles Dickens, the essays of Voltaire, all contain brilliant insights into social systems and relationships. Folk proverbs—"Love your neighbor but don't pull down your hedge"; "The innkeeper loves the drunkard but not for a son-in-law"—also contain much social wisdom. But sociologists do not accept insight or intuition or common sense alone in answer to their questions. They seek scientific evidence.

Sociologists gather this evidence in ways not unlike those used by physical scientists. They collect and analyze verifiable data; they keep careful records of their observations; they try to control the conditions surrounding the subject under study. Above all, they maintain a position of moral neutrality toward the subject and their conclusions. As sociologists they try not to label either individual behavior or social systems as "good" or "bad," but attempt to remain objective and impartial. Their final goal is to analyze their carefully collected data and arrive at a precise and accurate conclusion, a scientific truth.

To a scientist, truth is not absolute—it is not an unchanging, all-encompassing eternal law—but is relative to the special circumstances in which it was discovered, demonstrated, and formulated. This principle is particularly applicable to sociological truths, which are almost always generalizations based on incomplete evidence; the conscientious sociologist, therefore, will always indicate the limitations of his dis-

Reinhard Bendix

University of California at Berkeley

Jessie Bernard

Penn State University

Peter Blau

Columbia University

Herbert Blumer

University of California at Berkeley

coveries. He does not say, "All women want to get married"; instead he says, "The majority of American women now living who are between the ages of 20 and 55 have expressed a favorable attitude toward the possibility of marriage." Although this habit of qualifying and modifying statements sometimes makes sociological writing hard to read and comprehend, it is this very insistence on qualification and the careful definition of the relativity of its own truths that makes sociology a scientific, useful, and illuminating field of study.

SOCIOLOGY AS A SOCIAL SCIENCE

When scientific methods are applied to the study of human behavior, rather than to the nonhuman "natural" world, we call that study a social science. Sociology is related to the physical sciences through its methodology; it is closely related to other social sciences because their subject matter overlaps. The divisions between sociology, economics, psychology, anthropology, and history are sometimes arbitrary and artificial. The investigation of problems of inner-city residents with incomes below the poverty level could easily be classified as a study in urban sociology, or family economics, or political issues of government. But we can make some general distinctions regard-

ing the subject matter of each of the major disciplines of social science.

Economics studies the ways in which goods and services are produced and distributed. For the most part, economists have concentrated on such topics as the effect of supply and demand on prices, the ratio of savings to investment, and the speed with which money changes hands. But there is a clear connection between economics and sociology. Money does not move in and out of banks all by itself, or at the dictate of impersonal forces. It is deposited there by people who have made social decisions about accepting a job and saving for the education of their children or a house in the suburbs; it is withdrawn by people who want to buy a new car because their neighbor got one last week or start their own business instead of taking orders from a boss. Thus economic activities are often influenced by people's social activities, and the sociologist can help the economist understand the social basis of economic behavior. In turn sociologists have found that many of the social relationships they study are based on, or influenced by, economic considerations. We will discuss this interaction in chapter 14, Community and Economic Change.

Political science focuses on both the abstract theories and the practical operation

Albert Cohen

University of Connecticut

James S. Coleman

Johns Hopkins University

Barry Evans Photograph

Kingsley Davis

University of California at Berkeley

Otis D. Duncan

University of Michigan

of government. The student of political science looks at the ideas behind systems of government and the way those systems function. The political sociologist, on the other hand, is more interested in questions of political behavior—the reasons people join political movements or support political issues—and the relationships between political and other institutions. When sociologists look at the government, they see it as it relates to other institutions and to the larger society, rather than as an isolated political and administrative mechanism. Chapter 15, Politics and Power, is devoted primarily to the topic of political sociology. In recent years, political science and sociology have grown even closer together in methods, subject matter, and concepts, and it is increasingly difficult to draw firm lines between them.

History looks backward in an effort to determine the causes, sequence, and significance of past events. A sociologist would tend to focus on the relationship of those events to the larger societies of which they were a part. Formerly some historians were content merely to list the dates of battles and reigns of kings. Today they are turning to sociological methods of analysis for help in discovering the underlying social forces that may have influenced the events being chronicled. The focus of historical inquiry

has shifted from obtaining anecdotes about persons and places to tracing broad social movements. In their turn, sociologists have found the accounts of historians a valuable resource. They can, for example, draw on these to compare the social effects of industrialization in the West in the 1800s with the effects observed today in modernizing countries of Africa and Asia, or to outline the development of American social ideals from colonial to modern times. We will use historical references in this text to clarify social phenomena.

Psychology deals with human mental processes. It studies the way we receive and process information and the emotional responses that certain kinds of information may evoke. Psychology originated as a branch of biology; it features a greater stress on laboratory experiments and clinical procedures than does any other social science. It differs markedly from sociology in focusing on the individual experience, rather than the generalized experiences of an entire social group. But social psychology—the study of the ways in which personality and behavior are influenced and shaped by the individual's social setting—is closely related to sociology and draws from the knowledge and methods of both disciplines. Chapter 4, Socialization, is based heavily on the work of social psychologists.

Anthropology is concerned primarily with the study of primitive man. Physical anthropology, using techniques borrowed from biology, studies the story of man's physical and biological development by investigating ancient bones and artifacts. Cultural anthropology studies the social organization and development of primitive societies all over the world. By contrast, sociology specializes in the study of advanced and modern civilizations; but many anthropological concepts and approaches have been borrowed by sociologists, and in a number of universities the two fields are combined in one department. Chapter 3, Culture and Society, incorporates the anthropological approach to the study of culture. Anthropology is faced with a built-in limitation of material; there are few primitive societies left to study, and virtually none of these has remained untouched by civilization. This is one reason twentieth-century anthropologists have widened their field of study to include modern communities and societies, thus bringing their field closer to sociology in subject matter.

Culver Pictures, Inc.

Auguste Comte (1798-1857) is often referred to as the father of sociology. He suggested that sociologists might use the tools of research developed by the natural sciences, although he himself was primarily a theorist, not a researcher. His broad division of sociology into social statics (social structure) and social dynamics (social change) is still widely followed today. Many of his specific ideas, such as his "law of three stages" (that all societies develop through theological, metaphysical, and positivist stages), are now considered outdated, but sociologists continue to be interested in the perspectives and analyses contained in his works, *The Positivist Philosophy* (1830-1842) and *The System of Positive Polity* (1851-1854).

THE HISTORY OF SOCIOLOGY

The history of sociology is the story of the gradual differentiation of that discipline from the natural sciences, from philosophy, and from the other social sciences. It was Auguste Comte (1798–1857), a French social philosopher, who first conceived the idea of turning speculation about human society into a scientific discipline; Comte was also responsible for coining the name "sociology" to describe the new field of study. His own writings were often noticeably lacking in empirical foundation, but his vision of sociology as a factual study of social structures and processes inspired other men, many with more scientific training and background, to enter the field. Another important figure in the early development of sociology was the English philosopher and naturalist, Herbert Spencer (1820–1903). Spencer made numerous contributions to the theoretical foundations of sociology. One of the most significant was his suggestion that societies, like natural species, are constantly changing to adapt to their environment.

The earliest sociologists were theoreticians; the job they performed was to establish the outlines of the new study. They were followed by a second generation, men who began to collect the facts and undertake the research needed to support *grand theories*. Among the most notable were Emile Durkheim (1858–1917) in France, who introduced the use of statistical method in sociological study and ways of scientifically studying social interaction in whole societies; the

The New York Public Library Picture Collection

Emile Durkheim (1858-1917) was both a social theorist and a social researcher. He was especially interested in social organization and sought to answer the question, "How is social order achieved?" Durkheim rejected many of the answers of earlier workers in the field and developed new views which stressed the importance of broadly shared moral values and collective institutions, such as government. His views were considered quite radical at the time. Today he is perhaps best remembered for his research methods and use of statistics. His pioneering book, *Suicide* (1897), was the first major scientific study of a social problem; it developed the concept of *anomie,* or normlessness. *The Elementary Forms of the Religious Life* (1912) combined careful research of many different primitive religions with a conceptual framework which stressed religion as a powerful force that binds a society together.

American William Graham Sumner (1840–1910), who collected volumes of data on the customs and moral laws of many different societies; and Max Weber (1864–1920), a German sociologist who stressed the role of values and ideas in social life.

By the second decade of the twentieth century, the scientific study of social interaction was no longer just an idea, but a reality. Sociology consisted of both abstract theories and empirical studies. During the past several decades, the pure and applied branches of sociology have worked closely together to help solve social problems. The relationship between sociological research and social planning is rather like that between science and engineering.

The majority of sociologists work as teachers, conducting scientific research as a part of their academic duties. Grants from foundations, universities, and the federal government may make it possible for professors to spend one or two semesters away from the classroom, developing sociological knowledge. The results of such research efforts are published in books and scholarly journals, making them available to everyone.

A growing number of sociologists, however, are departing from this teaching-research career pattern and entering the field of applied sociology. They serve as policy consultants to businesses and governments. For example, when legislators consider the possibility of changing the laws to abolish the death penalty for murder, they may ask sociologists for a prediction of the effect this step might have on the murder rate. Sociologists would then draw on their knowledge of the social causes of deviance and their comparative studies of other societies which have tried passing such a law. They would come up with a well-researched and reasoned observation: for example, abolishing the death penalty probably would have no substantial effect on the murder rate. This information would assist the legislators in making their decision.

Sociologists also work as technical experts, helping large organizations manage their social environment. A large corporation might hire a sociologist to help it resolve conflicts between the production and the management staffs, or to plan a program to make executive relocation as easy as possible for the men and their families. Although Comte's dream of a society guided by a ruling class of sociologists working to achieve the public good has not come true, sociology does play an important part in helping to plan modern society.

SOCIOLOGICAL CONCEPTS

Defining sociology has not been an easy task; the student may wonder if the subject will be as hard to study as it is to define. The first step in a sociological education is to learn the basic concepts of the discipline. A *concept* is a generalization, an abstraction, a way of classifying similar things. When man creates a concept, he invents a broad category that may cover a large group of specific examples. We learn to handle many concepts even before we go to kindergarten. A four-year-old boy already understands the concept of "car," for example, and knows that it includes his father's new red Dodge, his brother's dilapidated 1964 Mustang, and the neighbor's big black Cadillac. Later he discovers that it also applies to a dune buggy and a Formula IV racer. The concept of "car" channels his attention in certain directions. He learns to disregard color, size, and radiator design, none of which is important to a car's essence. Instead he must look for wheels, an engine, and seats for driver and passenger. His understanding of this concept imposes a pattern on the boy's perception of the actual physical object that is sitting in his driveway.

Concepts in general use are often vague in meaning. "Family" might mean just parents and children, or it could be used to include 193 second and third cousins. Ordinarily, we can guess at the definition of a concept by listening to the context in which it is used. When your mother tells you to go to the grocery store and buy a 25-pound turkey because the family is coming for Thanksgiving dinner, you understand that she must mean the kind of family that includes uncles and aunts, cousins, and grandmothers.

But these poorly defined concepts, adequate for daily use, do not make good tools for sociological inquiry. Students reading a paper on "Communications Systems Within Family Groups Among the Chinese" should not have to guess at the meaning of the author's concept of family. Sociologists,

Culver Pictures, Inc.

Herbert Spencer (1820-1903) had a major impact on the early development of sociology. Paralleling Charles Darwin's theories of evolution by natural selection and the survival of the fittest, Spencer developed an elaborate and unified view of social life. His view was based on the concept of social evolution, the idea that all societies change from simple to complex forms. His belief that societies adapted to change through natural processes led him to oppose all forms of governmental control of social life. In his lifetime, Spencer was highly influential in many different fields of thought. His best-known work, one that aroused much interest in sociology in the United States, was *Principles of Sociology* (1876-1896).

like all specialists, have therefore developed a set of concepts, with agreed-upon definitions, to describe the specific events or relationships or things they must deal with frequently. The first section of this textbook is primarily devoted to the explanation of many important sociological concepts, such as culture, role playing, and primary groups.

In studying these basic concepts, it helps to remember that they are abstractions and generalizations, rather than concrete entities. Like all other ideas, they are subject to frequent change and reinterpretation; they may also be the cause of argument and differences of opinion. Concepts are not

Amitai Etzioni

Columbia University

Herbert Gans

Massachusetts Institute of Technology

Alvin Gouldner

Washington University at St. Louis

Scott Greer

Northwestern University

unvarying rules, like a mathematician's formula; instead they are guidelines to help us in the interpretation and understanding of the realities we study.

SOCIOLOGICAL RESEARCH

In addition to concepts, students of sociology must also develop a basic understanding of sociological methods and problems of social research. Sociological *research* is the systematic and objective attempt to study social life for the purpose of deriving general principles. Sociologists have adopted special research techniques for use in their own field.

Social scientists may have more trouble in arriving at verifiable conclusions than do physical scientists, because they deal with living people instead of inanimate things. The social situations they study can never be perfectly controlled, since no human being will allow another the freedom of completely rearranging his life for the sake of a scientific experiment. The reaction between two chemicals under a given condition can be repeated over and over again in a laboratory, but the reaction between two people, such as strangers meeting at a party, can only be observed once; the next time the two meet, they aren't strangers and the conditions are no longer the same.

Moreover, even people who are sincerely trying to cooperate may mislead the sociologist by making inaccurate statements, hiding some of their feelings, and saying or doing things that are subject to misinterpretation. These difficulties constitute some of the reasons most sociological research conclusions are expressed in generalizations and statements of statistical probability, rather than in laws of behavior.

The formation of concepts and theories and the collection of data through social research are actually two closely related parts of the single process of sociological inquiry. Concepts, and the theories built up from them, serve as a supporting framework for the purposeful examination of facts; research provides raw material from which concepts can be constructed. The sociologist must be familiar with both aspects of his science.

SOCIOLOGICAL PERSPECTIVE

The student of sociology must learn one more important thing—the sociological perspective—for sociology is first and foremost a way of looking at the social world. The sociologist must see into and through man's daily round of activities.

One of the hardest things for the untrained eye to see is simply the routine that un-

George C. Homans

Harvard University

Amos Hawley

University of North Carolina

Philip M. Hauser

University of Chicago

Irving L. Horowitz

Rutgers University

derlies daily social interaction. Everyone has become so accustomed to the fact that he kisses his children, waves to his neighbor, and shakes hands when he meets a stranger that these actions are virtually invisible. The initial task of the sociologist is to teach himself to notice these social relationships with fresh eyes, with as much wonder as if they were exotic rites performed by some far-off jungle tribe. The sociologist specializes in seeing those things to which familiarity has made most of us blind.

After the sociologist has learned to see these little transactions which make up the fabric of human social life, he must next ask himself the question, *why* do people do these things? When a college boy goes home for the Christmas vacation, why does he kiss his mother but shake hands with his father? Why does he go to church services on Christmas Eve? Why does he feel that he ought to spend more on his girlfriend's present than she does on his?

Of course, it does not take sociological training to be able to supply some answers to these questions. Most people would say that a son does not kiss his father because men are supposed to be emotionally restrained—it's the "right" way to behave. The sociologist, however, must look beyond these answers that invoke tradition

or morality. He asks why the custom has become traditional, how people know it is "right," who or what conferred this "rightness" upon it. He might point out that an action which is one society's sacred custom may be another's immoral vice.

In other words, the sociologist will look beyond the generally accepted explanations for social behavior and seek more scientific and definitive answers. This is what Peter Berger, in his popular and widely read book *Invitation to Sociology: A Humanistic Perspective,* calls the "debunking" function of sociology.[1] When sociologists "debunk" traditional explanations, many of their answers become sources of public controversy, because people are upset and offended by even a brief glimpse behind the social facade. For example, most people would say that they attend church service on Christmas Eve for reasons of religious observance; they are angered by the suggestion that their attendance might also be motivated by a desire to enhance their social standing or exhibit their new clothes. Berger also points out that a sociologist must be willing to accept classification by other people as "unrespectable," precisely because

1. Peter Berger, *Invitation to Sociology* (New York: Doubleday, 1967).

WHERE SOCIOLOGY IS APPLIED
Numbers and Percentages of 7,658 Sociologists Registered with the National Government According to:

As the science of sociology develops, more and more sociologists are applying the basic concepts of the field to study specific social phenomena and to participate in social planning. This table gives some idea of how varied the areas of application are.

Primary Work Activity, 1970	No.	%
Teaching	3,921	51.2
Research and Development	1,426	18.6
Management and Administration	1,056	13.7
Exploration, Forecasting, Reporting	83	1.0
Consulting	39	0.5
Other	200	2.6
Total	6,725	87.6

Note: The percentages do not sum to 100% because retired, unemployed and those who did not report primary work activity are not included in this table.

Type of Employer, 1970	No.	%
Educational Institutions	5,674	74.0
Nonprofit Organizations	346	4.5
Federal Government	224	2.9
Other Government	300	3.9
Industry and Business	129	1.6
Self-employed	57	0.7
Military	49	0.6
Other	56	0.7
Total	6,835	88.9

Note: The percentages do not sum to 100% because retired, unemployed and those who did not report type of employer are not included in this table.

Type of Research Undertaken, 1970 (receiving federal support)	No.	%
Health	886	38.5
Education	677	29.4
Urban Development	282	12.2
Agriculture	166	7.2
International	114	4.9
Rural Development	118	5.1
Housing	121	5.2
Defense	75	3.2
Natural Resources	65	2.8
Transportation	47	2.0
Public Works	25	1.0
Space	14	0.6
Atomic Energy	3	0.1
Other	568	24.7
Total	3,161	136.9
Total no. of individuals receiving support	2,297	

Note: The percentages do not sum to 100% because many social scientists who are active in research hold more than one research grant at a time.

SOURCE: National Register of Scientific and Technical Personnel, National Science Foundation, *American Science Manpower 1968* (Washington, D.C.: U.S. Government Printing Office, 1969) Table A-10, pp. 85–87.

he is lacking in respect for the force of tradition and the explanation of custom which serve to answer most people's questions about the workings of society.

THE RELEVANCE OF SOCIOLOGY

The beginning student of sociology may also wonder about the relevance of his classroom work to the broader concerns of his life. What is the use of studying sociology?

The most immediate benefit of a knowledge of sociology is the acquisition of a new viewpoint, a new way to look at one's own world. Many of the most perplexing and distressing problems a person faces are problems of social relationships. It is helpful to be able to view these problems through the clear and unemotional perspective of sociology. It enables the individual to step for a moment outside the social network of his own world, and to exercise his own judgment about his place in that world.

Some of the wider benefits of sociological knowledge are suggested in the excerpt from C. Wright Mills. Among the most significant benefits is the assistance sociology may give to the members of a society in seeing clearly what their society is, and what it may become. Society is a creation of man, but without the help of trained specialists, men may not realize what they have created and thus may be unable to alter it when it no longer serves their needs or advances their goals. Sociology provides necessary information for those who are responsible for guiding and maintaining society. Some of the results of sociological inquiry may be used by community leaders, and by businesses and governments in planning future activities, but perhaps even more important is the use ordinary people will make of this information in personally evaluating society and their own place in it.

C. WRIGHT MILLS
The Promise of Sociology

From *The Sociological Imagination* by C. Wright Mills. Copyright © 1959 by Oxford University Press, Inc. Reprinted by permission.

Introduction

A question that students of introductory sociology often ask is, "What relevance has this subject matter I am studying to my life?" It is this important question which Mills attempts to answer in his book. He points to the ways in which the information contributed by sociologists can illuminate many facets of daily life. Even more important is the way a sociological outlook, or perspective, can serve as a tool with which to interpret and understand one's own life. A sense of one's own position in the web of society is a necessary part of the search for an individual identity and an awareness of what is truly the self.

The Promise

Nowadays men often feel that their private lives are a series of traps. They sense that within their everyday worlds, they cannot overcome their troubles, and in this feeling they are often quite correct: What ordinary men are directly aware of and what they try to do are bounded by the private orbits in which they live; their visions and their powers are limited to the close-up scenes of job, family, neighborhood; in other milieux, they move vicariously and remain spectators. And the more aware they become, however vaguely, of ambitions and of threats which transcend their immediate locales, the more trapped they seem to feel.

Underlying this sense of being trapped are seemingly impersonal changes in the very structure of continent-wide societies. The facts of contemporary history are also facts about the success and the failure of individual men and women. When a society is industrialized, a peasant becomes a worker; a feudal lord is liquidated or becomes a businessman. When classes rise or fall, a man is employed or unemployed; when the rate of investment goes up or down, a man takes new heart or goes broke. When wars happen, an insurance salesman becomes a rocket launcher; a store clerk, a radar man; a wife lives alone; a child grows up without a father. Neither the life of an individual nor the history of a society can be understood without understanding both.

Yet men do not usually define the troubles they endure in terms of historical change and institutional contradiction. The well-being they enjoy, they do not usually impute to the big ups and downs of the societies in which they live. Seldom aware of the intricate connection between the patterns of their own lives and the course of world history, ordinary men do not usually know what this connection means for the kinds of men they are becoming and for the kinds of history-making in which they might take part. They do not possess the quality of mind essential to grasp the interplay of man and society, of biography and history, of self and world. They cannot cope with their personal troubles in such ways as to control the structural transformations that usually lie behind them.

Surely it is no wonder. In what period have so many men been so totally exposed at so fast a pace to such earthquakes of change? That Americans have not known such catastrophic changes as have the men and women of other societies is due to historical facts that are now quickly becoming "merely history." The history that now affects every man is world history. Within this scene and this period, in the course of a single generation, one sixth of mankind is transformed from all that is feudal and

backward into all that is modern, advanced, and fearful. Political colonies are freed; new and less visible forms of imperialism installed. Revolutions occur; men feel the intimate grip of new kinds of authority. Totalitarian societies rise, and are smashed to bits—or succeed fabulously. After two centuries of ascendancy, capitalism is shown up as only one way to make society into an industrial apparatus. After two centuries of hope, even formal democracy is restricted to a quite small portion of mankind. Everywhere in the underdeveloped world, ancient ways of life are broken up and vague expectations become urgent demands. Everywhere in the overdeveloped world, the means of authority and of violence become total in scope and bureaucratic in form. Humanity itself now lies before us, the super-nation at either pole concentrating its most coordinated and massive efforts upon the preparation of World War Three.

The very shaping of history now outpaces the ability of men to orient themselves in accordance with cherished values. And which values? Even when they do not panic, men often sense that older ways of feeling and thinking have collapsed and that newer beginnings are ambiguous to the point of moral stasis. Is it any wonder that ordinary men feel they cannot cope with the larger worlds with which they are so suddenly confronted? That they cannot understand the meaning of their epoch for their own lives? That—in defense of selfhood—they become morally insensible, trying to remain altogether private men? Is it any wonder that they come to be possessed by a sense of the trap?

It is not only information that they need—in this Age of Fact, information often dominates their attention and overwhelms their capacities to assimilate it. It is not only the skills of reason that they need—although their struggles to acquire these often exhaust their limited moral energy.

What they need, and what they feel they

Everett Hughes

Brandeis University

Mirra Komarovsky

Barnard College

Paul Lazarsfeld

Columbia University

University of North Carolina Photo Lab

Gerhard Lenski

University of North Carolina

need, is a quality of mind that will help them to use information and to develop reason in order to achieve lucid summations of what is going on in the world and of what may be happening within themselves. It is this quality, I am going to contend, that journalists and scholars, artists and publics, scientists and editors are coming to expect of what may be called the sociological imagination.

The sociological imagination enables its possessor to understand the larger scene in terms of its meaning for the inner life and the external career of a variety of individuals. It enables him to take into account how individuals, in the welter of their daily experience, often become falsely conscious of their social positions. Within that welter, the framework of modern society is sought, and within that framework the psychologies of a variety of men and women are formulated. By such means the personal uneasiness of individuals is focused upon explicit troubles and the indifference of publics is transformed into involvement with public issues.

The first fruit of this imagination—and the first lesson of the social science that embodies it—is the idea that the individual can understand his own experiences and gauge his own fate only by locating himself within his period, that he can know his own

chances in life only by becoming aware of those of all individuals in his circumstances. In many ways it is a terrible lesson; in many ways a magnificent one. We do not know the limits of man's capacities for supreme effort or willing degradation, for agony or glee, for pleasurable brutality or the sweetness of reason. But in our time we have come to know that the limits of "human nature" are frighteningly broad. We have come to know that every individual lives, from one generation to the next, in some society; that he lives out a biography, and that he lives it out within some historical sequence. By the fact of his living he contributes, however minutely, to the shaping of this society and to the course of its history, even as he is made by society and by its historical push and shove.

The sociological imagination enables us to grasp history and biography and the relations between the two within society. That is its task and its promise. To recognize this task and this promise is the mark of the classic social analyst. It is characteristic of Herbert Spencer—turgid, polysyllabic, comprehensive; of E. A. Ross—graceful, muckraking, upright; of Auguste Comte and Emile Durkheim; of the intricate and subtle Karl Mannheim. It is the quality of all that is intellectually excellent in Karl Marx; it is the clue to Thorstein Veblen's brilliant and ironic insight, to Joseph Schumpeter's many-sided constructions of reality; it is the basis of the psychological sweep of W. E. H. Lecky no less than of the profundity and clarity of Max Weber. And it is the signal of what is best in contemporary studies of man and society.

No social study that does not come back to the problems of biography and of their intersections within a society has completed its intellectual journey. Whatever the specific problems of the classic social analysts, however limited or however broad the features of social reality they have examined, those who have been imaginatively aware of the promise of their work have consistently asked three sorts of questions:

(1) What is the structure of this particular society as a whole? What are its essential components, and how are they related to one another? How does it differ from other varieties of social order? Within it, what is the meaning of any particular feature for its continuance and for its change?

(2) Where does this society stand in human history? What are the mechanics by which it is changing? What is its place within and its meaning for the development of humanity as a whole? How does any particular feature we are examining affect, and how is it affected by, the historical period in which it moves? And this period— what are its essential features? How does it differ from other periods? What are its characteristic ways of history-making?

(3) What varieties of men and women now prevail in this society and in this period? And what varieties are coming to prevail? In what ways are they selected and formed, liberated and repressed, made sensitive and blunted? What kinds of "human nature" are revealed in the conduct and character we observe in this society in this period? And what is the meaning for "human nature" of each and every feature of the society we are examining?

Whether the point of interest is a great power state or a minor literary mood, a family, a prison, a creed—these are the kinds of questions the best social analysts have asked. They are the intellectual pivots of classic studies of man in society—and they are the questions inevitably raised by any mind possessing the sociological imagination. For that imagination is the capacity to shift from one perspective to another— from the political to the psychological; from the examination of a single family to comparative assessment of the national budgets of the world; from the theological school to the military establishment; from considerations of an oil industry to studies of contemporary poetry. It is the capacity to range from the most impersonal and remote transformations to the most intimate features of the human self—and to see the relations between the two. Back of its use there is always the urge to know the social and historical meaning of the individual in the society and in the period in which he has his quality and his being.

That, in brief, is why it is by means of the sociological imagination that men now hope to grasp what is going on in the world, and to understand what is happening in themselves as minute points of the intersections of biography and history within society. In large part, contemporary man's self-conscious view of himself as at least an outsider, if not a permanent stranger, rests upon an absorbed realization of social relativity and of the transformative power of history. The sociological imagination is the most fruitful form of this self-consciousness. By its use men whose mentalities have swept only a series of limited orbits often come to feel as if suddenly awakened in a house with which they had only supposed themselves to be familiar. Correctly or incorrectly, they often come to feel that they can now provide themselves with adequate summations, cohesive assessments, comprehensive orientations. Older decisions that once appeared sound now seem to them products of a mind unaccountably dense. Their capacity for astonishment is made lively again. They acquire a new way of thinking, they experience a transvaluation of values: in a word, by their reflection and by their sensibility, they realize the cultural meaning of the social sciences.

Conclusion

The key to the sociological imagination is the ability to see how the whole historical sweep of society relates to individual lives at one time in history. Many people have some sociological knowledge and an understanding of some aspects of social life, but they lack the sociological imagination to see their own places in society. The science of sociology, at its best, can make this connection and give us not only a knowledge of society, but also a greater understanding of ourselves, for each of us is in many ways a product of our social surroundings.

TOPIC

2 THE METHODS OF SOCIOLOGY

Like all scientists, sociologists must study the specific in order to understand the general. The true concern of the geologist is not the peculiarity of the rock he holds in his hand; the concern of the botanist is not the fate of the flower he finds in a field; the concern of the sociologist is not the specific event he observes and records. All science is concerned with the order and pattern of its subject matter—those things that rocks or flowers or persons or societies have in common.

One aspect of moving from the specific to the general is the use of statistical averaging. A chemist observes the reactions of millions of atoms; although he cannot predict with certainty the behavior of any single hydrogen atom, he can say with assurance that most hydrogen atoms behave in a certain way. Similarly, although a sociologist can never predict the political opinions of any particular blue-collar worker, he can say that most members of a given socio-economic class have a certain kind of political opinion.

A second aspect of moving from the specific to the general is the development of intellectual frameworks. Raw data can be organized into the framework of concepts; relationships between concepts can be organized into the framework of *generalizations;* generalizations can be developed into *theories,* or explanations of causality; theories are sometimes expressed in schematic outlines called *models.* Each level in this hierarchy of abstractions represents another step away from the concrete reality of the raw data, and, therefore, it becomes more open to misinterpretation and misunderstanding, more ambiguous, and more debatable. Yet the benefits conferred by this process of abstraction are enormous, and the relationships and patterns thus revealed form the body of sociological knowledge.

THE SCIENTIFIC METHOD

The general guideline for all scientific research is the *scientific method*. Although it is possible to outline a series of steps called the scientific method, its real importance is not as a body of rules but as an attitude toward the work of observation and generalization. It has often been said that many scientific discoveries were due to a lucky accident; Galvani, for example, discovered that nerves transmit electrical impulses when one of his assistants left a freshly dissected frog on the lab table near an unrelated experiment in electrical conduction. But it is not the element of chance that should be stressed in such an occurrence; the key element was Galvani's trained powers of observation, his ability to derive a possible explanation for what he saw, his knowledge of the way to test that explanation. Galvani's assistant, who observed this lucky accident with him, dismissed it as a curious coincidence; it was Galvani the scientist who saw the implications of the coincidence.

How can one learn to observe and generalize in a scientific manner? The following steps serve as a general guideline to the application of the scientific method in sociological research.

First, make a careful statement of the problem to be investigated and frame a hypothesis. A sociologist begins by defining precisely what it is he wants to know. He generally states the problem so that it fits into existing theoretical frameworks and is related to the relevant findings of previous research; this insures that knowledge will be cumulative and that one researcher's findings can be easily utilized by others. The problem must also be formulated as a verifiable *hypothesis,* one that can be tested

before it is accepted or rejected. Many provocative hypotheses can never be tested. For example, one might hypothesize that God exists, but no one has found a way to test this hypothesis. The scientist must modify the original hypothesis to one he can test, such as, "The majority of adult Americans believe that God exists."

An illustration of the way this first step of the scientific method is applied in sociological research can be seen in the case of a researcher who suspects a correlation between urban residence and mental illness. The researcher would begin by defining a city: How big is it? What are its social characteristics? How does it differ from a nearby suburb? With this definition in mind, he looks for the aspects of a city that might be associated with mental illness: population size and density, quality of housing, prevalence of low income groups, availability of free recreational facilities. After examining existing theory and research findings in this area, he would frame a hypothesis that stated an expected relationship between some specific urban variable and mental illness. For example, he might hypothesize that the incidence of mental illness increases in proportion to the size of the city, with the largest cities having the highest rates of mental illness.

In the search for ways that these variables (characteristics that are present in varying amounts or degrees) could be measured, the hypothesis might be further refined. The researcher might choose to limit his study to those patients actually hospitalized with a diagnosis of mental illness, thus eliminating all those mentally ill urban residents who have not been diagnosed and are not being treated. Although this refinement makes the hypothesis easier to test, it also introduces an additional problem, that of the number of institutions that can diagnose and treat mental illness. Thus, the rates of mental illness might appear higher in some cities simply because they have the facilities to

Seymour M. Lipset

Harvard University

Robert K. Merton

Columbia University

Wilbert Moore

Princeton University

Talcott Parsons

Harvard University

treat all the mentally ill, whereas in other cities, a large percentage of the mentally ill population goes untreated. Each choice of a specific measure brings with it new possibilities of error and bias, yet the general hypothesis must be reduced to specifics if it is to be tested at all.

Second, develop a research design, *or plan for the collection, analysis, and evaluation of data.* This involves deciding how facts are to be selected, how they are to be evaluated and classified, and how they are to be analyzed to uncover relationships and patterns that bear on the original hypothesis. The major goal of the research design is to insure that the evidence gathered to test a hypothesis will be trustworthy, and that extraneous factors that might falsify the results will be controlled. The classic *controlled experiment* in a laboratory is the ideal scientific research design: an experiment designed in advance and conducted under conditions in which it is possible to control all relevant factors while measuring the effect of an experimentally induced variable.

In a controlled experiment the subjects are divided into two closely matched groups. The variable whose effect is to be tested, or the *independent variable,* is then introduced into the experimental group while it is withheld from the control group. The

two groups are subsequently compared to determine whether there are any significant differences between them regarding the factor that is expected to change, or the *dependent variable.* On the basis of this comparison, the original hypothesis, proposing a specific relationship between the independent and dependent variables, can be confirmed or rejected.

It is seldom possible to test sociological hypotheses in controlled laboratory conditions. The typical social research design is therefore developed with this limitation in mind. Since sociologists normally must use as their data base the daily activities of ordinary people, the control in most social research must be drawn from this data, rather than being applied artificially through the manipulation of a laboratory environment. For example, suppose a sociologist wanted to test the hypothesis that co-ed college dormitories foster male sexual promiscuity. Obviously he would not be permitted to set up control and experimental dormitories for this purpose alone; no addition to scientific knowledge could justify such a blatant exploitation of young people's lives and emotions.

One approach would be to locate a "natural" experiment: a college with a very homogeneous student body that was in the process of instituting some co-ed dorms. The researcher could then use the students who remain in men's dormitories as the control group and those who move to co-ed dormitories as the experimental group. However, the chances of stumbling across this situation are relatively small. It is much more probable that the researcher will have to assemble his control and experimental groups on a statistical basis. He would have to find a number of men similar in many relevant aspects: socio-economic background, educational history,, attitudes toward women, sexual histories, beliefs regarding sexual morals. About half of these men should be living in co-ed dorms and the other half in all-male dorms. If a single college or university does not provide a large enough sample, the researcher might add students from a second school, carefully chosen for its similarity to the first; for example, he might compare students from the University of Minnesota and the University of Wisconsin, or Yale and Princeton.

The independent variable in this experiment would be the presence of women in the dormitory. The dependent variable would be sexual promiscuity. Some quantitative measure (indicator or index) of promiscuity would have to be agreed upon; for example, it might be having sexual contact with more than three different women in one month. The control group and the experimental group would then be compared in regard to this dependent variable. If it is found that men living in co-ed dorms have a higher rate of promiscuity than men living in all-male dorms, the results suggest that the hypothesis might be valid. But further information would be required before a firm conclusion is warranted. If the controls and measuring instruments used in the experiment hold up under further scientific scrutiny, and, most importantly, if the same difference between the two groups is found in repetitions of the experiment (*replication*) by other scholars, then a significant scientific conclusion or empirical generalization can be drawn.

Third, collect data in accordance with the research design. There are three general ways of getting information about human behavior and social life. (1) Observe the way people actually behave: how they act in a given situation, what they do on a daily and regular basis. Accurate and objective observation by trained observers is a fundamental distinguishing feature of all the sciences.

(2) Ask people about their actions, their attitudes, and their beliefs. The answers to such questions reveal subjective reality, the meanings and thoughts, or "reasons," which lie behind a person's behavior. This is a distinguishing characteristic of the social sciences as distinct from the natural sciences, which focus only on objective reality, or that which can be seen to happen. Some sociologists question the scientific *validity* of this subjective reality, however, and concentrate exclusively on the observation of objective reality. They maintain that the only valid evidence for scientific purposes is what we can observe about human behavior, not what people tell us. But because observation of people in real life is more complex and difficult than observation in the world of nature or in the laboratory, much social science research involves asking people how they behaved in a given situation, rather than directly observing their behavior. People are asked, for example, whether or not they voted in the last election, how often they go to church, how much time each day they spend with their children. Thus, in the social sciences, objective reality is often determined through indirect means.

(3) Examine the cultural products of thought and behavior: books, houses, clothing, laws, cities. To find out how a factory is organized, for example, we can look at the organization chart and the layout of offices, rather than observing people in their daily routines, or asking them about their place in the hierarchy of command. To find the

things that are valued in a society, we can examine art forms and literature rather than taking a poll of public opinion.

The fourth step in the scientific method is to analyze the data and draw conclusions. It is at this step that the initial hypothesis is accepted or rejected, and the conclusions of the research are related to the existing body of theory, perhaps modifying it to take account of the new findings. The findings are usually presented in articles in scholarly journals, monographs, or books.

By no means do all, or even most, sociological research investigations closely follow this outline of the scientific method. Many sociologists are simply interested in accurate description, others do not develop precise hypotheses or elaborate research designs, most do not formally go through the step of either accepting or rejecting a hypothesis. But this model of the scientific method, nevertheless, is highly influential as a guideline for both the planning of research, and the evaluation of research findings. It represents the ideal that all scientists strive to attain.

APPROACHES TO SOCIAL RESEARCH

The *methodology* of social research of necessity differs from that of research in physical sciences. The chemist conducts a laboratory experiment in which he fractionates a protein and then subjects it to varying kinds of controlled analysis; the sociologist takes a survey of people's opinions and statistically analyzes the results. Although the methodology differs, the underlying goals and attitudes are much the same. Both the chemist and the sociologist are interested not in the unique occurrence but in the statistical average; not in the specific events but in the generalizations that can be drawn from them. All methods in both physical and social sciences are designed for this purpose.

Probably the best way to develop an understanding of the special techniques and problems of sociological methodology is to look at the major types of sociological research in which sociologists are engaged.

Systematic Observation. Careful and systematic observation of human behavior can take place either in the laboratory or in

---

UNDERSTANDING CHARTS AND TABLES

1. Begin by reading the title. It will tell you precisely what you can expect to learn from the table or chart.

2. Check for other explanatory notes. Sometimes there is a headnote, explaining how the data was gathered, or the conditions under which it was collected, or the reason that certain classifications were chosen. Footnotes also contain explanations of the data, such as its source, or possible instances in which it is incomplete or inaccurate.

3. Read the column headings across the top of the chart or table, and the stubs down the left-hand side. These tell you precisely what data are contained in the chart.

4. Find out what units of measurement are used. It is easy to become confused, for example, when figures are presented in thousands or millions. Rates are even more troublesome, because they can be expressed to a variety of bases—the number of times something happens per 100, or 1,000, or 1,000,000 people.

5. Estimate the range of variability in the data. Look for the highest figure, the lowest, and the average. This gives you a basis of comparison for each of the individual entries.

6. Draw conclusions about the significance of the chart. Did the source of the data sound reliable? Was it gathered scientifically? Is there enough difference in the figures to make the results significant? Can you rule out chance as a factor in causing the apparent results? Could there be any bias in the way the figures are reported? Answers to questions like these will help you to judge for yourself the significance of the chart or table you have studied.

the field. The most common form of laboratory observation in the social sciences has been small group research. In a typical example, a group of undergraduates is brought together and assigned various tasks. Investigators systematically record and analyze their behavior as the group members interact. The observation of laboratory groups has yielded a vast amount of useful information, though care must always be taken in generalizing from laboratory to real life conditions, and from college students to people in general.

An example of systematic observation in the *field study* — the type of research in which the subjects of investigation are observed under their usual environmental conditions — is the examination of children's play activities in different types of housing developments. Playgrounds and play areas are studied over a period of time to see how and when they are used, the number of children that use them, and the ways in which playgrounds of different types may shape children's play. Much valuable information has been gained in this manner, contributing to the design of better play facilities.

One of the most famous observational studies in the social sciences is the Hawthorne study.[2] The management of Western Electric's Hawthorne works wanted to find out if environmental factors, such as the intensity of illumination, were associated with workers' productivity and morale. A team of social scientists was allowed to experiment with a small group of workers who were set apart from their co-workers where they could be closely observed, and where the environmental conditions of their work could be systematically controlled. To the great surprise of the experimenters, the productivity of these workers continually increased in response to any change in the environment, even when the changes seemed

to be disadvantageous. It was finally concluded that a unique element had unwittingly been introduced by the social researchers into the work life of the experimental group; this is what accounted for the change in productivity, not the controlled modifications of the work environment. Because of the presence of the observers the workers in the experimental group began to feel that they were something special; they came intimately to know and trust one another; and they developed a strong belief in the importance of their work. From the management's initial point of view, the experiment was a failure, but within sociology it marked the start of a long line of research into a newly discovered social phenomenon: that bonds of friendship and small group solidarity are very important factors in accounting for worker motivation. The study also contributed the term "Hawthorne effect" to the language of the social sciences: the effect in which the subjects of an experiment are changed by the mere fact that they are the subject of observation and experimentation.

Experimental and Statistical Control. Controlled experiments such as the Hawthorne study are not common in sociology, for human beings are not ready subjects for experimental manipulation, and human experimentation involves many ethical problems. But some of the basic elements of planned, experimental research are found in a wide variety of social investigations. The goal of experimental design to hold all factors constant except the independent variable can sometimes be partially achieved through the use of contrived experiments in the field. An example is research conducted in the area of family planning for developing countries. In an effort to assess the effects of different ways of getting people to come to birth control clinics for family planning advice, researchers picked two similar areas of a city. In one they put up posters, held meetings with leaders, and

2.   F. J. Roethlisberger, *Management and Morale* (Cambridge, Mass.: Harvard University Press, 1949).

David Riesman

Harvard University

Matilda W. Riley

Rutgers University

Philip Selznick

University of California at Berkeley

Neil Smelser

University of California at Berkeley

conducted a direct mail campaign; in the other they did nothing. After a period of time, the effect of these measures was studied by finding out how many persons in the experimental group came in for advice, and why, as compared with the control group.

A much more typical approach to experimental design in sociology, however, is to control factors statistically and after the fact (*ex post facto*), that is, after the data have been collected. An example of the use of statistical controls in a research design can be seen in an experiment that tried to answer the question, "Why do certain types of educational institutions produce more people who go on to take a Ph.D.?" The researcher knew that some institutions contribute a much higher percentage of their student body to doctoral programs than others; he wanted to find out whether this is due to special characteristics of those institutions, or merely to the fact that their enrollment includes a high percentage of students predisposed to go on to graduate school.

The experimenter, Alexander W. Austin, began with a widely varied sample of 265 educational institutions.[3] He gathered in-

formation on relevant characteristics of all entering freshmen, found out how many Ph.D.s received their bachelors degrees from each of the institutions in his sample, and how many bachelors degrees each institution had granted. From this information, the experimenter computed each school's Ph.D. production rate: from none at all per annum to 23 percent of all graduates.

The experimenter still had to discover whether it was the institutions themselves or merely the enrollment of a certain type of student that accounted for the Ph.D. production rates. He began by determining which of a student's characteristics were strongly related to achievement of a Ph.D.; turning to previous research, he found that a student's I.Q., sex, and the area of his major were among the most significant variables. These, then, were the student traits that he would try statistically to control. The experimenter produced a method of assessing the probable Ph.D. production rate of an institution based on the presence of the following factors in the student body: student intelligence, percent of males, and distribution of majors. Next, he matched each school's probable Ph.D. production rate against its real rate. Thus, given the characteristics of its students, it could be determined whether an institution was pro-

3. Alexander W. Austin, "Productivity of Undergraduate Institutions," *Science* (April 13, 1962), pp. 129-135.

ducing "too many" or "too few" Ph.D.s.

The experimenter's finding ran counter to several common assumptions. He found that, for example, most large state institutions produced more Ph.D.s than was probable. The small colleges, contrary to popular belief, produced fewer than was probable; this was particularly true of church-related institutions. However, regardless of size, most all-male or all-female institutions were poor producers. Harvard, Princeton, and Dartmouth were rated poor producers. Such schools as Brooklyn College, Yeshiva, Brigham Young, Utah, and Utah State, produced more than was probable for them. Since the first two of these high producers have heavy Jewish enrollments and the last three have high Mormon enrollments, there seemed to be religious—and possibly socioeconomic and ethnic—factors at work. Thus, the stage was set for further analysis that would attempt statistically to control these additional factors.

Survey Research. The most common type of empirical, or quantitative, research in sociology is the *survey*, which consists of systematically questioning people about their opinions, attitudes, or behavior. The survey is often called a sample survey, when a sample, or limited number of selected cases drawn from a larger group, is questioned. Sometimes the survey is referred to as a sample interview survey, because information is commonly elicited from people through interviewing them. The sample interview survey is in widespread use, because it provides a manageable way of getting accurate information with which one can generalize about large populations. It has also spurred the extensive use of statistical analysis in sociology because of the large and precise body of data that it generates.

The major steps normally involved in survey research are:

(1) Before a survey is begun, the questions to be asked must be clearly defined. At the same time, the *population* to be interviewed is selected. The population might be all male citizens in Liberia, all working mothers under 35 years of age in Milwaukee, or all fraternity members at a state university—the total number of individuals with the characteristics that the researcher is interested in examining. This first step is crucial, for if the population is not correctly specified, the result of the survey may be meaningless. For example, if the aim of the research is to predict the results of an election, it is very important that the population chosen consist only of those persons who will actually vote in that election.

(2) If the population is large, time and cost will almost always make it impractical to interview the entire population, so the second step in surveying is to pick an appropriate *sample* of the population to interview. Careful procedures have been established for selecting samples. The better the sampling procedure, the more closely the sample selected for study will resemble the entire population, and the more accurate will be the generalizations or predictions.

In simple random sampling, the sample is picked by chance selection, so that every member of the group has an equal opportunity to be selected. Drawing names from a hat is an example of random sampling. In systematic sampling, a certain system, such as choosing every tenth name in a telephone book, is used. A sample may also be stratified, in which case the population is divided, before random sampling, into a number of strata or groups. For example, the student population in a college might be divided into first, second, third, and fourth years, and a simple random sample drawn from each group.

Although random sampling techniques have become very sophisticated, many researchers prefer to use samples that have been carefully selected for their representativeness. For example, the data that is the basis for the Nielsen ratings of television programs come from a relatively small sample that was carefully selected as being representative of the average viewer. A great deal of research sponsored by consumer-products industries has gone into identifying people who are "trend-setters," so that they can be used as a sample to obtain opinions on new products.

(3) Once the sample is selected, the third step in survey research is to interview the selected people and to collect the data. At this point a major consideration is the precision of the questions. Do the questions really pinpoint the issue concerned? Are they phrased in such a way that they will be interpreted correctly and similarly by each person interviewed (the respondents)? When a public opinion poll reports that a certain percentage of Americans favor more civil rights legislation, we assume that the respondents all interpreted the meaning of "more civil rights legislation" in the same way. But did they? A survey question not only must be very precise and unambiguous in meaning, but also neutrally stated. It has been found, for example, that a question phrased negatively (You don't want civil rights legislation, do you?) will get significantly more "no" replies than one put neutrally (Do you want civil rights legislation?) or positively (You want civil rights legislation, don't you?).

For the most accurate results, it is necessary that the entire sample be interviewed, particularly if the sample is small. If some people refuse to answer or if people are unavailable for interviewing, the accuracy of the data may be reduced, because the sample is no longer representative. Nonresponse is frequently a problem when questionnaires are sent by mail, for refusals to respond to mailed questionnaires tend to be high. Replies often come only from those who have some interest in the particular issue, thus introducing a bias into the survey findings.

To assure maximum response, most major attitude surveys and public opinion polls are conducted through personal interviews.

These interviews may range from the highly structured to the highly unstructured. A structured interview consists of a set of questions with checklist answers; the questions and answers are always stated in the same way and in the same sequence. The answers are thus easily compiled and generalized. Most public opinion polls use structured interviews. For other research purposes, where more extensive information about individual attitudes or behavior is desired, the unstructured interview has many advantages.

An unstructured interview may consist of open-end questions (How do you feel about the way students are behaving at the university?) or even just a list of topics to be discussed. The interview can be adapted to the individual respondent; leads can be followed and individual points pursued, and the interviewer can better determine whether or not the respondent really understands the questions. The disadvantage of this type of interview is that the answers are much less precise and, therefore, more difficult to generalize. If the interviewer words the questions differently for each respondent, he may change the meaning of the questions. The responses he collects would be answers to different questions and, therefore, difficult to compare.

It is quite possible for the interviewer to introduce bias into the survey. He may, for example, use expressions or make comments that encourage the respondent to answer in a certain way; in an unstructured interview he may influence the answers by the way he phrases the questions. It is important that interviewers be suited to their task and that they be well trained in the techniques of interviewing.

(4) The final step in survey research is the tabulation, analysis, and interpretation of the data. In all but the smallest surveys, this step normally involves the use of computers.

There are several possible sources of error

in survey results. Sampling error is the degree to which the selected sample is not truly representative of the population as a whole. Other major sources of error arise from problems in observation and measurement, processing the data, and analyzing the findings. A basic problem with all surveys is that what a person says may not always agree with how he acts. A person may not know his true feelings about a subject until he must act; then he may find that the feelings he reported to the interviewer were not quite accurate. People sometimes conceal their true attitudes purposely. A man may be prejudiced against Indians, for example, and act in a discriminatory fashion toward them, but because he knows that this prejudice is disapproved of, he will not admit it to an interviewer. Or someone may honestly say that he is in favor of something—for example, better schools— but when it comes time to vote he may vote against improving the schools because that would require raising property taxes; keeping taxes low may be more important to him than improving the schools, and the research did not explicitly ask for his value judgment in the conflict of these two ideals. Research that is well designed and carried out can help to overcome these difficulties, but the sociologist must be constantly aware that attitudes expressed in interviews are not always perfect expressions of underlying values, and that actions do not always reflect stated attitudes.

Secondary Data and Comparative Studies. It is not always necessary for a sociologist to collect new or *primary* data. A great deal of existing or *secondary* data are often available to him, either the findings of previous research, or data collected by private organizations or governmental agencies. The single most important source of data in the United States is the census. The census is a periodic head count of the population; it also includes additional data about such characteristics as age, sex, marital status, income, family size, and other variables.

Most modern societies have fully entered the statistical age. From birth to death— including such mishaps and benefits as auto accidents, divorces, arrests, political party affiliations, and employment—the census records the major features of each individual's history. While some complaints are heard about invasion of privacy, this kind of public information gathering has become essential to the efficiency of all complex societies.

Though public records are often extensive, they are not always completely accurate. Illegitimate births cannot be counted in the states that have passed laws making such official designation illegal. Family doctors sometimes mask a quiet suicide as "heart failure" or "respiratory failure" to save the survivors public embarrassment. The deaths of derelicts or rural residents may go unrecorded. Police records are usually highly detailed and, therefore, often very useful to a researcher, but they are not without problems, such as those which were uncovered when the President's Commission on Law Enforcement and Administration set out to determine the "true rate of crime" in America. In 1966, the Commission sponsored a national survey of 10,000 households, asking people if they had been victims of crime. This survey discovered that more than twice as much criminal victimization existed in the nation than was shown for the same period by the official reports of the FBI. In several large cities, in fact, a special survey revealed from three to ten times more offenses than were reported officially.

The availability of secondary data is often an important stimulus to *comparative analysis* in sociology. The comparative study is not a special technique in itself, but a particular use of existing research techniques. Sociologists today make considerable use of three basic types of comparative study. One compares differences among populations within

Melvin Tumin

Princeton University

Ralph Turner

University of California at Los Angeles

Robin Williams

Cornell University

one society, at a given point in history. Thus the family structure of working-class persons is compared with that of the middle class, or neighborhood patterns of rural areas and urban areas are compared.

In the second type of comparative study, the focus is the specific differences between groups or institutions that are otherwise highly similar. The sociologist might compare the legal services that a law firm accords to a wealthy individual with the services that a court-appointed attorney provides to a poor person.

A third type of comparative study examines a single similarity shared by two different societies. A researcher might, for example, find that despite the manifest differences between the contemporary American and the Amazonian Indian, both have structured their societies on the premise of male superiority.

A landmark example of comparative analysis was the study of occupational prestige in modern societies by Alex Inkeles and Peter Rossi in 1956.[4] Their hypothesis was that nations become more similar as they become more highly industrialized; one possible aspect of this similarity is a common

prestige rating for various occupations, despite the differences in natural history and culture. Inkeles and Rossi were able to locate roughly comparable data in such countries as Japan, New Zealand, Germany, and the United States. They indeed found a striking similarity of occupational rankings, and concluded that "There is a relatively invariable hierarchy of prestige associated with the industrial system."

Qualitative Methodologies. A significant number of sociologists choose not to use the natural science approaches to the study of human behavior. They prefer to sacrifice a certain precision of measurement and objectivity in order to get closer to their subjects, to examine the social world through the perspective of the people they are investigating. Such sociologists sometimes refer to quantitative researchers as those who "measure everything and understand nothing."[5]

By far the most important of the so-called qualitative methodologies is *participant observation,* in which the researcher participates in the daily life of the people under study, observing things that happen, listening to conversations, informally questioning people. This may be done covertly, as when

4. Alex Inkeles and Peter Rossi, "National Comparisons of Occupational Prestige," *American Journal of Sociology* 61 (1956).

5. William J. Filstead (ed.), *Qualitative Methodology* (Chicago: Markham Publishing Company, 1970), p. vii.

a sociologist becomes a prison inmate in order to study the effectiveness of rehabilitation programs. It may also be done openly, by joining a group in the formal role of observer.

Probably the most celebrated participant observer in modern times was a white Southern novelist named John Howard Griffin. In 1961 *Ebony* magazine hired him to study the life of the blacks in the South. He dyed his skin and spent many months as a participant observer. Through his personal experiences in which he was treated as an ordinary black man, Griffin discovered sharp contrasts with his former feelings and beliefs about their lives. Significantly, he titled his book on the experience *Black Like Me*.[6]

Far more common is the social scientist who is an official observer not pretending to be anything but a scholar who is sincerely interested in understanding a group or a situation. This is the approach that is characteristic of the anthropologist who studies the culture of a primitive tribe. The methods of participant observation have been considerably refined through anthropological field work; careful procedures have been formulated to help maintain objectivity, and to permit other persons to recheck data and conclusions.

One of the pioneering uses of participant observation by sociologists in a modern setting was *Street Corner Society* by William Foote Whyte.[7] Before the Second World War, Whyte studied lower-class, "slum" street corner groups by joining and talking informally with the members. He gained access to the first group through a social worker, became friendly with the group's leader, was introduced to other groups, and finally was accepted as "one of them," though he did not have to "play their game all the

way." By "hanging out" on the street corner for a period of time, Whyte gained much valuable information about the group's goals and structure, and the motivations of its members.

Most participant observation research uses the *case study* approach: a detailed record of a single event, person, or social grouping. Case studies have played a very important role in the development of the social sciences as a source of insights and hypotheses which are later applied to larger populations. Entire communities have often been the focus of a case study, or *community study*. This method usually relies heavily, but not exclusively, on participant observation techniques. Typically, the researcher resides in the community over a period of time, sharing the life of the inhabitants. One of the most famous community studies was Robert and Helen Lynd's 1929[8] and 1937[9] investigation of Muncie, Indiana. A husband and wife team, the Lynds lived in this midwestern town for a number of years just before and during the Depression, to develop an accurate description and understanding of the workings of a small community. They interviewed scores of Muncie citizens, methodically worked their way through newspaper files to discover information about past events, and attempted to enter fully into small town life. Their conclusions about small town life and change remain important in sociology to this day, though many are difficult to verify in any scientific sense.

On the scale of community and society, the approach of the qualitative methodologist shades into what is sometimes called the *impressionistic* (or *interpretive*) *approach*. In a general sense, the impressionistic method of gathering social data is similar to a news-

6. John Howard Griffin, *Black Like Me* (New York: New American Library, 1961).

7. William Foote Whyte, *Street Corner Society: The Social Structure of an Italian Slum* (Chicago: University of Chicago Press, 1955).

8. Robert S. Lynd and Helen M. Lynd, *Middletown* (New York: Harcourt, Brace & World, 1929).

9. Robert S. Lynd and Helen M. Lynd, *Middletown in Transition* (New York: Harcourt, Brace & World, 1937).

paperman's procedure when he is assigned to write an in-depth analysis of a city's Bowery, waterfront, or artists' colony. The process is primarily one of absorption of scenes, images, ideas, and, of course, facts. The work of the social scientist differs from that of the journalist, however, in that the scientist relies heavily on available research findings and on social science theory, and he tries to organize his research so that the information he gains will be cumulative, building on and adding to the existing body of social science knowledge.

The relatively brief history of sociology is studied with excellent impressionistic works of research that have become famous as sources of insights and hypotheses. Some of these have focused on society as a whole, such as David Riesman's *The Lonely Crowd* (1950),[10] or, two decades later on a similar theme, Philip Slater's *Pursuit of Loneliness*

(1970).[11] The impressionistic study provides a fund of ideas that can be tested by more rigorous techniques.

Qualitative methodologies have been gaining renewed attention in recent years by young scientists who view them not merely as a step on the path to a more scientific sociology, but as approaches which have intrinsic worth in their own right. These scientists feel that the quantitative methodologies fail to shed much light on the subjective interpretations and meanings of people's actions. Whether qualitative methods will ever be accorded the same enthusiasm and acceptance now shown for quantitative methods remains to be seen. It will depend, in part, on finding solutions to the considerable problems of objectivity and precision which are posed by all non-quantitative approaches.

10. David Riesman, *The Lonely Crowd* (New Haven, Conn.: Yale University Press, 1950).

11. Philip E. Slater, *Pursuit of Loneliness: American Culture at the Breaking Point* (New York: Beacon, 1970).

LEE RAINWATER
The Sociologist as Naturalist

From *Sociological Self-Images: A Collective Portrait,* Irving Louis Horowitz, ed. (New York: Pergamon Press, 1970), pp. 91–100. Reprinted by permission of the editor.

Introduction

Lee Rainwater, brought up in a small town in the South, is now Professor of Sociology at Harvard University. He is one of a number of sociologists who was asked several years ago to write a brief "sociological self-image." Among the questions put to him were: What do you consider to be the most uniquely defining characteristic of your way of doing sociology? Which of your own writings do you like best and why? What impact would you say your sociological efforts have had on reshaping the field? What

is your view of the current relationship of sociological theory and social application? Though Rainwater is not necessarily a "typical" sociologist, his essay provides an inside look at the way one sociologist views his background and career, his methodology, and his style of sociology.

The principal attitude which directs my work is one of puzzled curiosity. I have always felt that I don't understand the people around me very well, and with that feeling has come a strong curiosity to try to figure out exactly what they are doing and why they are doing it. This attitude is perhaps not particularly distinctive to me, but the form by which I have sought to resolve that puzzled curiosity during my professional life is perhaps more distinctive. I have always been drawn to styles of sociological and psychological work that partake of the naturalist's approach—that is, an approach in which there is an effort to observe the forms and behaviors in which one is interested until one feels one understands how they hang together, and then to depict as accurately as possible what one thinks he has observed so that others may apprehend that reality, and perhaps by replicating the observations validate it. This kind of activity has seemed socially worthwhile, as well as personally gratifying, for three reasons.

The first, and I suspect the most enduring for me, is a belief in the intrinsic, almost esthetic value, of an accurate and penetrating depiction of reality. In this I think perhaps I was influenced by my father, who was an historian, and who, in his own way, impressed me with the effort to see things as they are, just because they are that way. In addition, I have always felt that if men are to achieve their goals, if they are to avoid troubles and construct a society which meets their needs as fully as it might, they need to understand their world better. The particular part of the country in which I grew up can impress an observer with the extent to which men are their own worst enemies. If one for some reason does not become fully socialized to a particular world view, one can never lose the sense of puzzlement and anger at how men in that society hurt themselves and others to no good purpose.

Finally, I have always hoped that if the social naturalist's task is done well, he provides the best kind of grist for the mill of the social theorist. As a person who has neither interest in, nor talent for, doing other than heavily grounded theoretical work, I nevertheless feel that the other fellow, the theorist, would be more successful in his work if he could draw upon good descriptive work. Unfortunately few theorists have pursued this strategy systematically, although I would still feel that the best

correction for much of the nonsense that passes as sociological theory is the use of work in the ethnographic tradition as raw material for theory.

There are any number of ways one might be led by the puzzled curiosity I have described. A further distinctive characteristic of my work has been the reliance on qualitative data—from participant observation, open-ended interviewing, and projective techniques. Such methods have always seemed to me to more closely replicate human life as it is experienced than the more controlling techniques of questionnaires, laboratory experiments, and the like. Since these kinds of data have been the ones that have impressed me most—whether in the psychoanalytic case study, the ethnography of the great anthropologists, or the field studies of men like William F. Whyte, or Howard Becker—it is ironic that I happen to be a rather poor and indifferent field worker. Were it not for an accident of career development I might never have circumvented this impasse—I might have had perforce to become a survey researcher! The accident was that during graduate studies in the Committee on Human Development at the University of Chicago, I became intrigued with the work being done at Social Research, Inc., in Chicago, a private research firm. . . . This organization was devoted to applying the combined techniques of an anthropologically informed sociology . . . and a psychodynamically oriented social psychology to studies of "ordinary social life" for such diverse clients as manufacturers, advertising agencies, the movie industry, and government agencies. (This kind of research some five years later came to be called "motivation research," but at the time we saw it as simply an extension of more academically oriented community studies.) Because Social Research, Inc., carried out numerous small projects in short periods from beginning to completion (ranging from two months to six months) the organization had adapted survey research techniques to the qualitative approach. I was able, therefore, to make use of a staff of interviewers trained to do focused and nondirective interviewing and to administer specially designed projective techniques, and consequently to work with the kind of data that was meaningful to me without having to collect it myself.

As I have worked as a "secondhand" observer, my respect for the field worker's ability has increased year by year. Apparently my ability to analyze this kind of data has also increased, so that I am often flattered by readers of my work who take it for granted that I myself collected the data about which I write and are surprised and a little unbelieving when I say that I have not. (My most recent experience as a field worker, a study of the Moynihan Report controversy, again impressed me with how much better other people are at collecting the kind of data I like to work with; fortunately I had a collaborator who is an excellent field worker.) . . . .

How did I end up in a place like that? The intellectual and organizational coordinates of my career are hardly typical for a sociologist, except perhaps in that I, no more than other sociologists, aspired to that profession as a child—almost none of us knew it existed! From about twelve years of age I had expected to become first an electrical engineer and then a physicist. But by my first semester in college I had changed my mind. I think I now see that such a choice was a constricting defense against the anxiety that accompanied the puzzled curiosity which I felt about the world. It was a defense that didn't work for me, although, of course, it does work for many others, including quite a few men who have shifted from the physical sciences to productive careers in sociology and psychology. So from physics I shifted to psychiatry; that was about the only model of how one might go about making a career

of understanding the what and why of people that penetrated to me in Mississippi. I knew, of course, from having grown up with discussions about history and political science that those, too, were fields that dealt with man, but in the South even an adolescent could get the feeling that such studies were directed more toward justifying the region and its peculiar institutions than to getting at the guts of human behavior. Psychiatry, of course, meant undergraduate work in psychology, but I found that incredibly dull. My interest was sustained only by out-of-class reading of Freud and his followers. Finally, a co-worker at the State Department, where I worked the midnight shift in the code room while studying at George Washington University during the day, told me that given my political and racial views (which put me in a highly argumentative minority against my conservative co-workers who were mostly trainees for the Foreign Service) I should study sociology. George Washington's one sociologist was in the army at the time, so I began reading through the entries that struck my fancy under sociology in the card catalog at the Library of Congress and the Public Library. This sent me eventually to the University of Southern California (Emory S. Bogardus had more entries in the card catalog than anyone else) and finally to the University of Chicago, where I see-sawed back and forth between sociology and psychology, finally settling down for doctoral work in the Committee for Human Development which regarded both interests as legitimate.

If I had been a somewhat less superficial reader while still in Mississippi, I might not have had to take such a circuitous route to sociology. In my senior year I had read the new book, *An American Dilemma,* and had been fascinated to learn that there seemed to be a great many people who didn't share most white Mississippians' views about white supremacy, segregation, and all that. (It must have taken a courageous librarian to buy that book for the Jackson Public Library—fortunately I don't think many people besides myself read it that year.) I knew, of course, from sketchy readings of history, the *Reader's Digest,* and *Time* magazine that I was not alone in believing that there was something tragically destructive about how Negroes had been and were being treated in the South, but I had not realized that there was a scientific way of trying to understand all that and perhaps of doing something about it. Myrdal told me that there was, but somehow I did not realize that the pivotal science involved was sociology, and therefore, had to rediscover it some years later. The book that finally persuaded me to a sociological career was *Deep South,* which led me to *Yankee City,* and eventually to the University of Chicago to study with W. Lloyd Warner, Allison Davis, and Burleigh Gardner. Like many Southerners who become sociologists, the irrationalities of race have been a continuing sociological concern for me. I am pleased, however, that the contingencies of my career took me away from the study of race relations into a broad range of studies of specific aspects of the life styles of Americans of different social classes. These studies ranged from subjects of substantial social importance such as attitudes toward political candidates to trivia such as attitudes toward breakfast cereal. This research experience provided a kind of perspective which I have found extremely valuable during the past five years, when I have been able to return again to the problem of race that initially sparked my interest in sociology. . . .

I like my first book and my last one, but each for quite different reasons. The first book, *Workingman's Wife,* represented a combination of researches conducted over a number of years with my colleagues at Social Research, Inc. . . . I think I like the book most, not for what is unique to it, but for what it shares with the work of a number of other sociologists who were studying the working class at about the same time and without knowing what each other was doing. . . .

The second book, *And The Poor Get Children,* I simply thoroughly enjoyed doing. It represented the application to a particular problem, family planning, of findings developed in previous working-class research and somehow all the pieces fell together right. I think I like the book also because of its shock value, its demonstration that such presumably "sensitive" topics as sexual behavior and contraceptive practice are quite available to qualitative survey methods. Finally, I enjoyed it because I made such a colossal error of prediction— cautioning that large numbers of lower-class women could not be expected to adopt the oral contraceptive because of the demands of the daily pill-taking regimen. That mistake has been a very instructive one for me, and has strongly influenced the way I derive practical implications from social-psychological findings in the research in which I am now engaged.

Finally, I enjoyed the *Moynihan Report and the Politics of Controversy* because it gave my coauthor and myself an opportunity to experiment with sociological journalism and because it represented one of the few occasions on which I have strayed outside the area of the sociology of "private" behavior. It has always seemed to me that one of the most profound divisions within sociology is between those who study private behavior (the family, informal social relations, deviant behavior, and the like) and those who find such concerns trivial and instead concentrate on the larger questions of formal institutional behavior, political behavior, community power structures, etc. Although I have long had an interest in the operation of government bureaucracies and private cause groups, I had never had an opportunity to shift my focus from the private behavior of individuals and families to this level of social organization. The Moynihan controversy study provided an opportunity to test a number of hypotheses which I had been developing over the previous few years about the operation of the government and civil rights groups in connection with an event which had made the people involved highly self-conscious about what they were doing.

The question of impact is a difficult one for the person concerned to assess, particularly in the case of one who is not concerned with the development of theory. I believe that my efforts have had an impact in three areas. In family sociology my studies of lower-, working-, and middle-class family life have helped to break down the stereotype of one dominant American family life pattern. The particular focus of several of my books on contraception and family planning has, I believe, helped considerably to establish this area as a crucial part of any meaningful effort to understand family behavior.

I believe my work has had some constructive effect as an example of the value of qualitative methodologies. Particularly through the early 1960s, qualitative methodology enjoyed very poor standing in sociology. My work has fit in with that of a number of other sociologists who persisted in the use of these methods and who now seem to have captured the attention of an important segment of the younger men in the field. One hears much less often today than ten years ago the notion that qualitative studies are suitable only for the pilot phase of larger investigations.

Finally, I feel that my recent work has begun to have an impact on policy diagnoses concerning the race and poverty problems. In all of these areas it would be presumptuous to consider that my sociological efforts have had an impact in "reshaping" the field, but such information as I can gather concerning how my work is being used does encourage me to believe that it is playing its part in fostering standards of greater naturalistic accuracy and detail in sociological presentations, and more careful and systematic attention to policy implications.

The relationship of sociology to social problems was at the heart of my initial interest; for many years I functioned as an applier of social science knowledge and research techniques to the concerns of highly varied clients, and more recently I have been concerned to develop knowledge into sociologically informed programs for undoing the damage of racial oppression and economic exploitation of the poor. Even so, I value the wide range of styles of work in the field—from the men who do not want to move out of the ivory tower to those who are willing to work actively for change by getting their hands dirty in political movements and bureaucratic organizations. A sociology which strives so hard for relevance and application that there is no play for pure curiosity must inevitably use up its intellectual capital; a sociology in which application is either rejected or considered "dirty work" better delegated to other professions like social work or planning runs the very real risk of losing touch with the reality its theories are supposed to encompass.

I value the increasing sophistication about application and policy relevance that I think the field has begun to show in the past half-dozen years, with the increasing understanding that policy relevance also involves moral commitment on the part of the sociologist which he needs to acknowledge and address consciously.

But I think the central issue has been and will be . . . the autonomy of social science. And it is the autonomy of the practicing sociologist, and not just of the field in the abstract, that is important. Sociology is extremely fashionable these days—with undergraduates, with the mass media, and with government. But, its popularity comes not so much from an understanding of what sociological knowledge has to offer, as from the belief that other branches of knowledge have failed to "solve" our problems and because sociology talks about some of the most obvious ones (race, poverty, alienation, bureaucracy, etc.) it has the solution. The autonomy of the sociologist to pursue knowledge and develop theory will be seriously threatened by this popularity—not only by the threat of co-optation by the powers that be, but also by the threat of ideological co-optation in the service of the powers against the powers that be. Sociological knowledge is potentially extremely embarrassing to all of these forces since it seldom neatly confirms the preferred world view of any of the contenders in the political process. Sociology is in a position today to make crucial contributions to changing society, but it is in that position only by virtue of several decades of empirical and theoretical work which was relatively insulated from *direct* political interference by the society at large or on the campus. Now the pressures to interfere are strong. And the more accurate sociological depiction becomes, the stronger these forces will be. Sociologists will need a strong sense of solidarity no matter how varied their own individual pursuits of sociological knowledge. If they are to

weather these pressures, they will need a deep and sensitive commitment to each other's freedom of responsible inquiry, and an insistent resistance to the distortion of their findings by those who perceive themselves to be adversely affected by "sociological truth."

Conclusion

Several of Lee Rainwater's views are very common among the younger generation of sociologists: the concern for the application of sociology to social policy and problems, and the acceptance of a wide range of methodological approaches, not just those which are close to the methods of the natural sciences. He is probably typical of most sociologists in choosing sociology as a career rather late in life, and in developing an interest in sociology out of an abiding concern for social problems. His essay points up many of the dominant themes and ideals which motivate and guide all sociologists: "puzzled curiosity," "responsible inquiry," and "the autonomy of the sociologist to pursue knowledge and develop theory." At the same time he suggests some of the many obstacles which sociologists face, such as political interference, and candidly admits that, like all other professionals, the sociologist makes his share of mistakes.

SUMMARY

Sociologists do not establish universal laws of human behavior, but rather try to provide a way of understanding human social life through the disciplined and objective study of human social interaction. Their field of inquiry includes individual social acts, social relationships, organizations, and total social systems of communities or nations. They approach their subject scientifically: collecting and analyzing verifiable

data, recording their observations, controlling the conditions surrounding the subject studied, and maintaining a morally neutral position. Sociology often overlaps in terms of subject matter with the fields of economics, psychology, anthropology, and history.

The idea of turning speculation about human society into a scientific discipline was first conceived by Auguste Comte, a nineteenth century French social philosopher. Men such as Emile Durkheim, William

Graham Sumner, and Max Weber helped to build a body of empirical studies that provided a sound scientific basis for abstract sociological theories. Today many sociologists are entering the field of applied sociology as policy consultants to government and industry and as technical experts on social management and planning.

Like all other sciences, sociology tries to develop knowledge through organizing data into *concepts* which are systematically measured; discovering relationships between concepts, or *generalizations;* and formulating *theories* based on generalizations. Research provides sociologists with the raw material from which concepts or abstract interpretations can be constructed. Concepts and theories in turn serve as a supporting framework for the purposeful examination of facts. At the outset of any sociological inquiry, the researcher must carefully define the *variables,* or characteristics that the individuals or groups being studied possess in varying degrees. Some variables, such as age or income, can be directly measured. Others, such as social cohesion, must be analyzed indirectly through measurable and observable factors. Accurate research depends on continually testing the validity of these factors, and on defining all concepts and variables in precise terms that are free of other connotations.

By examining the relationships among two or more variables, the sociologist can form a generalization about his subject, usually involving a cause and a quantitative effect, and often stated in terms of a probability relationship. An empirical generalization is based on factual observation, while a *hypothesis* merely suggests a relationship that must be tested further. *Theories* are constructed when several generalizations, backed by empirical support, are assembled to logically explain the causes of a social event or phenomenon. Theories are built slowly and cautiously. Due to the complexity, mutability, and element of free will in all human behavior, a theory is never proven finally and absolutely, but is always a source of further testing and new hypotheses. Concepts, generalizations, and theories are each a kind of explanation in ascending order of completeness. When the higher order explanations form schematic outlines of social behavior, they are called *models.* These may be verbally stated or plotted quantitatively and expressed in mathematical terms. Some so-called *grand theories* are not built up from data and are not scientifically testable. Rather, they are attempts to explain broad and complex social phenomena through loose-knit verbal models.

In order to assure that research will lead to valid generalizations and theories, sociologists are guided by the rules and procedures of the *scientific method:* (1) careful statement of the problem to be investigated and the framing of hypotheses; (2) the development of a research design or plan for the collection, analysis, and evaluation of data; (3) collection of data in accordance with the research design either through observation of human behavior in a controlled or natural setting; through direct interviews and questionnaires about people's actions, attitudes, and beliefs; or by examining cultural products of thought and behavior; (4) analysis of data and drawing conclusions.

Sociological research may be conducted through a variety of approaches. (1) Careful and systematic observation of human behavior can take place in a carefully controlled laboratory setting or, more commonly, by investigating subjects in their natural environmental setting. In either case sociologists try to hold variable factors constant in order to study the relationship between a *dependent variable* (the change or effect to be studied) and a particular *independent variable* (the presumed cause). Often, however, research is conducted after a cause and effect sequence has already occurred and these factors must be controlled statistically once the data have been collected. (2) The *sample survey,* perhaps the most common type of empirical research, attempts to determine the occurrence of a specific action or opinion within a large group of people. It is based on a randomly or systematically selected sample that is representative of a specific population. Data are gathered through structured or unstructured interviews and are analyzed to determine public attitudes or opinions. Despite the possibility of sampling error, or the fact that people's attitudes may change or may fail to coincide with their actions, opinion surveys have proved generally reliable when carefully administered. (3) Rather than collecting new or primary data, sociologists often rely on existing secondary data such as the census. They may use such data to make different kinds

of *comparative studies:* comparison of differences among populations in one society at a given point in time; comparison of specific differences between otherwise similar groups or institutions; comparison of a single similarity shared by different societies. (4) Qualitative methodologies do not emphasize precise measurement and quantification, and often examine the social world through the perspective of the people who are being investigated. In the *participant observation* method, the researcher participates in the lives of the people he is studying, observes daily occurrences, and questions people informally. This method is often used in the *case study* approach: a detailed record of a single event, person, or social grouping. On the larger scale of community and society, the qualitative methodologist may take a more *impressionistic* approach, providing much of the raw material that can be tested by more rigorous techniques.

GLOSSARY

Case study A research approach which involves a detailed and thorough analysis of a single case. (page 28)

Community study A research approach that focuses on the detailed analysis of a single community; an application of the case study approach. (page 28)

Comparative analysis The comparative study of different types of groups and societies in order to determine the factors that lead to similarities in social behavior; often involves cross-cultural and historical comparisons. (page 26)

Concept A word or set of words that expresses a general idea about the nature of things or events, or the relations between them; it often provides a category for the classification of phenomena. (page 9)

Controlled experiment An experiment designed in advance and conducted under conditions in which it is possible to control relevant factors, while measuring the effects of an experimentally introduced variable. (page 19)

Dependent variable A variable whose occurrence or change is related to the occurrence or change of another variable (or variables). (page 19)

Ex post facto study A research approach which probes past conditions and events in order to find causes for present conditions and events. (page 23)

Generalization A general statement or proposition based on a number of specific observations. (page 17)

Grand theory In sociology, a very extensive but rather loose-knit verbal model which attempts to explain an extremely wide range of social behavior and social institutions. (page 7)

Hypothesis A tentative statement which asserts a certain relationship among variables. (page 18)

Impressionistic approach A relatively informal approach to social investigation in which the researcher relies heavily on his own logic and intuition in making generalizations, rather than on quantitative methods. (page 28)

Independent variable A variable whose occurrence or change results in the occurrence or change of another variable. (page 19)

Methodology   Analysis of the conceptual, logical, and research procedures by which knowledge is developed. (page 21)

Model   A schematic representation or outline of a pattern of relationships found in the real world. (page 17)

Participant observation   A research method in which the investigator participates in the social group which he is studying. (page 27)

Population   (In research) the total number of cases which have a selected characteristic. (page 24)

Replication   The repetition of an experiment or study in order to check its accuracy. (page 20)

Research   The systematic and objective attempt to study a subject matter for the purpose of deriving general principles. (page 10)

Research design   A plan for the collection, analysis, and evaluation of data. (page 19)

Sample   A limited number of selected cases drawn from a larger group. (page 24)

Scientific method   A body of rules and procedures designed to assure that research will lead to valid generalizations and theories. (page 18)

Survey   A research approach which involves the systematic questioning of people about their opinions, attitudes, or behavior. (page 24)

Theory   A set of interrelated propositions that serves conceptually to organize and explain a subject matter in a systematic way. (page 17)

Validity   Correspondence between what a measuring device is supposed to measure and what it really measures; refers to the problem of whether it is measuring what it purports to measure. (page 20)

Variable   A concept which refers to a characteristic common to a number of phenomena (people, groups, events) and that is possessed in varying amounts or degrees. (page 19)

SUGGESTED READINGS

READINGS IN SOCIOLOGY

Bates, Alan P. *The Sociological Enterprise.* Boston: Houghton Mifflin, 1967. Bates discusses sociology as both an academic and an occupational field, including the functions of sociology for society and the nature of sociological knowledge.

Berelson, Bernard, and Gary Steiner. *Human Behavior, An Inventory of Scientific Findings.* New York: Harcourt, Brace & World, 1964. Berelson and Steiner discuss methods of investigation in the social sciences. Note especially Chapter 2, "Methods of Inquiry."

Berger, Peter. *Invitation to Sociology.* New York: Doubleday, Anchor, 1967. In this highly readable analysis of the discipline and profession of sociology, Berger discusses certain phenomena of human behavior, such as the way men construct their own biographies, from what is called the humanistic sociological perspective.

Bottomore, T. B. *Sociology, A Guide to Problems and Literature.* New York: Pantheon Books, 1962. An introduction to sociology in its broadest sense. A revised edition with emphasis on current subjects, recent studies, and controversies about changing social structure.

Doby, John T., ed. *An Introduction to Social Research.* New York: Appleton-Century-Crofts, 1967. A technical, though readable, account of the research methods used by contemporary sociologists.

Duverger, Maurice. *An Introduction to the Social Sciences.* New York: Frederick A. Praeger, 1964. A lucid exposition of the theoretical premises and technical procedures common to the sciences that take as their subject "man living in society."

Emmet, Dorothy, and Alasdair MacIntyre. *Sociological Theory and Philosophical Analysis.* New York: Macmillan, 1970. A collection of articles on the philosophy of sociology as it relates to other disciplines, including the natural sciences and philosophy.

Greer, Scott A. *The Logic of Social Inquiry.* Chicago: Aldine, 1969. This is a discussion of the basic assumptions and methods of sociological research by a working sociologist. Greer considers sociology as a symbol system, the problem of objectivity in sociology, and the place of sociology in the larger society.

Hammond, Philip E., ed. *Sociologists at Work: Essays on the Craft of Social Research.* New

York: Basic Books, 1964. Various sociologists tell how they conducted their research projects. An anecdotal and readable account of scientific methodology.

Hinkle, Roscoe C., and Gisela J. Hinkle. *The Development of Modern Sociology.* New York: Random House, 1954. The historical development of American sociology, its major assumptions, and its divisions into subareas, is traced in this short book.

Inkeles, Alex. *What Is Sociology?* Englewood Cliffs, N.J.: Prentice-Hall, 1964. A brief but comprehensive survey and summary of the history, approaches, and schools of sociological thought. This book also discusses the relationship of sociology to the other social sciences and notes many important studies and findings in the development of sociology.

Labovitz, Stanford, and Robert Hagedorn. *Introduction to Social Research.* New York: McGraw-Hill, 1971. A short but significant study of research methodology.

Madge, John H. *The Origins of Scientific Sociology.* New York: Free Press, 1962. Madge recounts the development of sociological methodology and theory; he gives a short history of sociology by devoting a chapter to each of several of the most famous empirical sociologists, their works, and their methods.

Mills, C. Wright. *The Sociological Imagination.* New York: Oxford University Press, 1959. This distinguished and controversial sociologist takes a critical look at sociology in this book and, in the process, defines some of the uses and rewards of the discipline.

Nisbet, Robert A. *The Sociological Tradition.* New York: Basic Books, 1966. Within the framework of certain key sociological concepts, such as community, authority, and status, Nisbet discusses ideas and theories that are at the core of the science of sociology, including the historical development of these ideas and theories. Especially interesting is a section on the effects of modernization upon sociological thought.

Selltiz, Claire, Marie Jahoda, Morton Deutsch, and Stuart W. Cook. *Research Methods in Social Relations.* New York: Holt, Rinehart, & Winston, 1959. A comprehensive survey of the use of empirical research by social scientists.

Wallis, W. Allen, and Harry V. Roberts. *Statistics: A New Approach.* New York: Free Press, 1956. An excellent explanation of the use of statistics with good coverage of such areas as how to read charts and tables.

Young, Pauline V. *Scientific Social Surveys and Research.* Englewood Cliffs, N.J.: Prentice-Hall, 1966. Young discusses collecting, classifying, and interpreting data in the social sciences.

I Elements of Social Life

2. Social Structure

*An outstanding feature of man's life is the degree
to which almost all his contacts with other men are
structured. This structuring is not always apparent.
When you see a friend in the evening and ask him
what he did that day, he will probably answer by
listing a string of activities that seem to him to be
the special events of that particular day—I got my
history paper back, I saw Mary Jane, I got a letter
from my parents, I bought a new record. In other
words, he tells you what set that day apart from the
others. Recurrent patterns of behavior are taken
so much for granted that people usually fail to
notice them, and your friend would not take the
trouble to tell you what he did that day that was
habitual. Our attention is caught by the unusual, the
surprising, the extraordinary.*

*But it is precisely the routine and usual events
of our lives that provide structure for human society.
From the sociological point of view the most
significant aspect of man's life is not the random
or the unique event, but the daily pattern. The
discipline of sociology is based on the assumption
that for the most part, human society consists of
constantly repeated or patterned acts that can be
described and predicted. It is the task of sociologists
to study the actions and attitudes of a given group
of people and to pick out the patterns that recur.
It is this analysis of social structure which gives us
a fuller understanding of the way man lives in society.*

1 THE MEANING AND IMPORTANCE OF SOCIAL STRUCTURE

Sociologists use the term *social structure* or *social organization* to describe the orderly or patterned way that people and groups of people relate to each other. To call such relationships structured or organized does not necessarily mean that they have been planned out knowingly or in advance, for this is often not the case. In fact, a first principle which the student of sociology must learn is that much of our social structure is the temporary outcome of daily minute adaptations and changes in the relationships between people. There are no social relationships in any society that, in theory at least, cannot be changed by the actions of the people who make up the society.

It might be more accurate to call social structure a process rather than a fixed thing or an end product. When we isolate a unit of social structure, we are looking at one moment in time, one point on a continuum of change. And yet, in spite of many changes and pressures toward change, society on the whole remains much the same from one year to the next. It is easiest to see the operation of this principle in some group with which you are familiar, for example a high school. Every year in the fall there is a different school enrollment as some students graduate and others take their places. And every day sees a slightly different group within the walls of the school — a new boy transfers in; someone drops out to take a job. Each week new policies are handed down from the superintendent's office; each year many educational changes may take

place. But no one would deny that there is a recognizable, relatively stable entity called George Washington High School with characteristics that remain the same over a long period of time. You can accurately say, "This is an educational institution and not a grocery store," or "The level of education here is higher than it is at Lincoln High," or "The relationship between students, teachers, and the principal always remains about the same." In other words, although the individuals that make up the school change every day, and though many policies and activities may continually change, the general nature of the school itself remains much the same and can therefore be analyzed or predicted.

This relatively enduring quality of the school is its social structure or social organization. The school is a stable group because it is organized. Each student and teacher knows in general how he is supposed to interact with the other members of the group: what the duties and obligations of students, teachers, administrators, and other personnel are. This year's school is much the same as last year's school because the group members are organized in the same way. Of course, not all schools are smoothly functioning places where everyone does just what he is supposed to do. This does not necessarily mean that the social organization of the school has broken down. A certain amount of variation from the rules is a built-in and expected part of every social structure. Such variation, and even conflict, can also be highly patterned and predictable. But it is quite possible for the social structure of a school to break down in the face of continued rule-breaking and conflict.

Continuing with our illustration of the school, we can also see the value of social organization. Imagine how it would be if, each morning, a group of individuals appeared at the high school building who had no orderly or patterned way to relate to each other, and therefore had to think of some way for everyone to work together so the younger members could get an education from the older members. It would be a long tedious process of trial and error, until they could finally determine who could teach which subjects, and who wanted to take those subjects, and how each subject should be taught. Then if a student was sick or a teacher decided to quit, and new people joined the group, the whole process would have to start all over again. It is clear that no one would ever manage to learn anything (except the necessity for social organization).

It is social structure that permits us to undertake most of the activities of everyday life. We do not have to think how we will treat our teachers, or what we will say to our sisters, or how we will be able to obtain the lamb chops we want for dinner. Most of the relationships that we have with other people have been turned into some kind of routine.

Because of the routine element of human relationships, individuals are spared the hundreds of little decisions which would have to be made before every act, and groups and societies can establish some degree of stability and continuity. But like most things in life, social structure has both its positive and its negative sides. It is quite possible to see social structure as a constraint on the individual, inhibiting his personal freedom. Sociologists sometimes portray social structure as akin to the strings on a puppet, which pull the individual around against his will. Yet, they also point out, it is the stability and support of social structure which gives man his greatest freedom; instead of having to use all his energies and ingenuity to transact his daily business, he can save them to write a sym-

"C'mon fellas, let's get organized."

The need for social organization is a popular subject for cartoons. *(The Ben Roth Agency, Inc.)*

phony or read a book or build a skyscraper. We shall have occasion to discuss both the positive and negative aspects of social structure many times throughout this book. The most important thing for the student of sociology to appreciate is that it is through a knowledge of social structure that we are able to understand and predict human behavior.

Much of the work sociologists have done has consisted of developing useful categories and definitions of social structure, enabling us to see the basic parts, and to uncover important distinctions and relationships among the parts. This is called classification and is the first step in any science. Indeed, the social sciences have not advanced nearly as far as the natural sciences in getting beyond the first and all-important stage of classification. In the next stages of development, the relationships among the classified parts are measured quantitatively and generalizations are developed about those relationships which seem to hold true in all societies.

This emphasis on classification as a first but major step to understanding society is reflected especially in the first several chapters of this book. In these chapters we will assemble a sociological "map" of society and culture, identifying the key features of social life, which are more fully discussed in the remainder of the book.

Sociologists have found that it is helpful to distinguish different levels of social structure or patterning. Generally, three levels are described—the social relationship level (between two persons), the group or organization level (structure and processes in organized groups), and the level of community or society (the social environment of groups and organizations). The study of social relationships is sometimes called *microsociology* (micro meaning "little"), whereas the study of communities and societies is referred to as *macrosociology* (macro meaning "large"). Groups and organizations fall somewhere between these two extremes. In the following topics, we will discuss each of these three levels of structure.

Some sociologists believe that the social relationships between individuals represents the basic unit of human social structure. In their view the group and the society are nothing more than clusters of relationships between individuals.[1] Most sociologists, however, feel that organized groups and societies also possess special properties which emerge as they organize. These group laws, actions, and patterns of organization are, in a sense, stamped on the minds of the individual members of the group, who view them as something external to themselves, to be taken account of, and to which they must mold their actions. For this reason, most sociologists think of a separate group level of "social reality" apart from the individual level of society.

The concept of social system is a useful way to express this social reality. A *social system* is a set of persons or groups who interact with one another; the set is conceived of as a social unit distinct from the particular persons who compose it. "Social system" can refer to any kind of social grouping, from a group of two friends to a large, complex society. It is widely used in sociology because it forces us to think of the way in which social pieces fit together into a whole and the basic similarities among all forms of social interaction. We can look at the social system of a high school and see how it compares with the social system of a business corporation; or we can compare a family with a football team. Each is a social unit in which people are pursuing a special set of goals, depending upon one another in various ways, and sharing a sense of common identity as a group.

1. This was especially true of the early American sociologists. See Roscoe C. Hinkle, Jr. and J. Gisela Hinkle, *The Development of Modern Sociology* (New York: Random House, 1954), chap. 1.

ERIC BERNE
Rituals and Pastimes

Introduction

Eric Berne, in his book Games People
Play, *has given us a shrewd analysis of
some of the behavior patterns expected in
relatively impersonal social interaction.
Here he discusses two patterns of interaction. One he calls the ritual; it applies to
the behavior of those who meet regularly but
don't know each other well—neighbors, for
example, or co-workers in the same large
company. The other pattern he calls the
pastime; it applies to relationships that have
to meet the demands of a longer period of
interaction, say five or ten minutes, but
still are not expected to lead to any intimacy.*

*Although Berne was trained as a psy-
chiatrist and worked as one until his death
in 1970, many of his insights are sociological
in nature.*

Rituals

Among the most instructive of informal
rituals are the American greeting rituals.
Although subject to considerable local
variations in details, the basic form remains
much the same, having been determined
by tradition.

1A: "Hi!" (or Hello or Good morning.)
1B: "Hi!" (or Hello or Good morning.)
2A: "Warm enough forya?" (or How
are you?)
2B: "Sure is. Looks like rain, though."
(or Fine, how are you?)
3A: "Well, take cara yourself." (or Okay.)
3B: "I'll be seeing you."
4A: "So long." (or Goodbye.)
4B: "So long." (or Goodbye.)

It is apparent that this exchange is not
intended to convey information. Indeed, if
there is any information, it is wisely withheld. It might take Mr. A fifteen minutes
to say how he is, and Mr. B, who is only
the most casual acquaintance, has no
intention of devoting that much time to
listening to him. This series of transactions is
quite adequately characterized by calling
it an "eight-stroke ritual." If A and B were
in a hurry, they might both be contented
with a two-stroke exchange, Hi—Hi. If they
were old-fashioned Oriental potentates, they
might go through a two-hundred stroke
ritual before settling down to business.

This ritual is based on careful intuitive
computations by both parties. At this stage
of their acquaintance they figure that they
owe each other exactly four strokes at each
meeting, and not oftener than once a day. If
they run into each other again shortly, say
within the next half hour, and have no new
business to transact, they will pass by
without any sign, or with only the slightest
nod of recognition, or at most with a very
perfunctory Hi-Hi. These computations
hold not only for short intervals but over
periods of several months. Let us now
consider Mr. C and Mr. D, who pass each
other about once a day, trade one stroke
each—Hi—Hi—and go their ways. Mr. C
goes on a month's vacation. The day after he
returns, he encounters Mr. D as usual. If
on this occasion Mr. D merely says "Hi!"
and no more, Mr. C will be offended. By his
calculations, Mr. D and he owe each other
about thirty strokes. These can be compressed into a few transactions, if those
transactions are emphatic enough. Mr. D's
side of the conversation properly runs
something like this (where each unit of
intensity or interest is equal to a stroke):

1D: "Hi!" (1 unit.)

2D: "Haven't seen you around lately."
(2 units.)

3D: "Oh, *have* you! Where did you go?"
(5 units.)

4D: *"Say, that's interesting.* How was
it?" (7 units.)

5D: "Well, you're sure looking fine."
(4 units.) "Did your family go along?"
(4 units.)

6D: "Well, glad to see you back."
(4 units.)

7D: "So long." (1 unit.)

This gives Mr. D a total of 28 units.
Both he and Mr. C know that he will make
up the missing units the following day,
so the account is now, for all practical
purposes, squared. Two days later they
will be back at their two-stroke exchange,
Hi–Hi. But now they will "know each
other better," i.e., each knows the other is
reliable in social interaction.

The inverse case is also worth considering.
Mr. E and Mr. F have set up a two-stroke
ritual, Hi–Hi. One day instead of passing on,
Mr. E stops and asks: "How are you?"
The conversation proceeds as follows:

1E: "Hi!"

1F: "Hi!"

2E: "How are you?"

2F: (Puzzled) "Fine. How are you?"

3E: "Everything's great. Warm enough
for you?"

3F: "Yeah." (Cautiously.) "Looks like
rain, though."

4E: "Nice to see you again."

4F: "Same here. Sorry, I've got to get to
the library before it closes. So long."

5E: "So long."

As Mr. F hurries away, he thinks to
himself, "What's come over him all of a
sudden? Is he selling insurance or something?" In terms of social interaction, he
is really asking, "All he owes me is one
stroke, why is he giving me five?"

An even simpler demonstration of the
business-like nature of these simple rituals

is the occasion when Mr. G says "Hi!" and
Mr. H passes on without replying. Mr. G's
reaction is "What's the matter with him?",
meaning, "I gave him a stroke and he
didn't give me one in return." If Mr. H
keeps this up and extends it to other
acquaintances, he is going to cause some
talk in his community.

Pastimes

Pastimes may be defined as a series of
semi-ritualistic, simple, complementary
transactions arranged around a single field
of material, whose primary object is to
structure an interval of time. Pastimes are
typically played at parties or during the
waiting period before a formal group
meeting begins; such waiting periods have
the same structure and dynamics as parties.
Pastimes may take the form described as
"chit-chat," or they may become more
serious, e.g. argumentative. A large cocktail
party often functions as a kind of gallery for
the exhibition of pastimes. In one corner
of the room a few people are playing
"PTA," another corner is the forum for
"Psychiatry," a third is the theater for "Ever
Been" or "What Became," the fourth is
engaged for "General Motors," and the
buffet is reserved for women who want to
play "Kitchen" or "Wardrobe." The
proceedings at such a gathering may be
almost identical, with a change of names
here and there, with the proceedings at a
dozen similar parties taking place simultaneously in the area. At another dozen in
a different social stratum, a different
assortment of pastimes is underway.

Pastimes may be classified in different
ways. The external determinants are sociological (sex, age, marital status, culture,
race, or economics). "General Motors"
(comparing cars) and "Who Won" (sports)
are both Man Talk. "Grocery," "Kitchen,"
and "Wardrobe" are all Lady Talk – or, as
practiced in the South Seas, Mary Talk.
"Making Out" is adolescent, while the

onset of middle age is marked by a shift to "Balance Sheet." Other species of this class, which are all variations of Small Talk are "How To" (go about doing something), an easy filler for short airplane trips; "How Much" (does it cost), a favorite in lower middle-class bars; "Ever Been" (to some nostalgic place), a middle-class game for "old hands" such as salesmen; "Do You Know" (so-and-so) for lonely ones; "What Became" (of good old Joe), often played by economic successes and failures; "Morning After" (what a hangover) and "Martini" (I know a better way), typical of a certain kind of ambitious young person.

Besides structuring time and providing mutually acceptable stroking for the parties concerned, pastimes serve the additional function of being social-selection processes. At the end of the party, each person will have certain players he would like to see more of, while others he will discard. The ones he selects are those who seem the most likely candidates for more complex relationships — that is, games. This sorting system, however well rationalized, is actually largely unconscious and intuitive.

Pastimes have a quite specific aspect of exclusiveness. For example, Man Talk and Lady Talk do not mix. People playing a hard hand of "Ever Been" will be annoyed by an intruder who wants to play "How Much" or "Morning After."

Pastimes form the basis for the selection of acquaintances, and may lead to friendship. A party of women who drop in at each other's houses every morning for coffee to play "Delinquent Husband" are likely to give a cool reception to a new neighbor who wants to play "Sunny Side Up." If they are saying how mean their husbands are, it is too disconcerting to have a newcomer declare that her husband is just marvelous, in fact perfect, and they will not keep her long. So at a cocktail party, if someone wants to move from one corner to another, he must either join in the pastime played in his new location or else successfully switch the whole proceeding into a new channel. A good hostess, of course, takes the situation in hand immediately and states the program: "We were just playing 'PTA.' What do you think?" Or: "Come now girls, you have been playing 'Wardrobe' long enough. Mr. J here is a writer/politician/surgeon, and I'm sure he'd like to play 'Look Ma No Hands.'"

Another important advantage obtained from pastimes is the confirmation of role. Thus in "PTA" one player may take the role of tough parent, another the role of righteous parent, a third the role of indulgent parent, and a fourth the role of helpful parent. All four experience and exhibit a parental role, but each presents himself differently. The role of each one is confirmed if it prevails — that is, if it meets with no antagonism, or is strengthened by any antagonism it meets, or is approved by certain types of people with stroking.

A pastime is not always easy to distinguish from an activity, and combinations frequently occur. Many commonplace pastimes, such as "General Motors," consist of what psychologists might call Multiple-Choice — Sentence-Completion exchanges.

A: "I like a Ford/Chevrolet/Plymouth better than a Ford/Chevrolet/Plymouth because . . ."

B: "Oh. Well, I'd rather have a Ford/Chevrolet/Plymouth than a Ford/Chevrolet/Plymouth because . . ."

It is apparent that there may actually be some useful information conveyed in such stereotypes.

Conclusion

Berne describes in detail the social patterns which guide our behavior in situations that seem casual. Not only do we expect to deal with certain topics in certain ways with the different people we meet, but we even expect a specific number of sentences to be uttered during our inter-

actions. As Berne points out, when a person does not talk for as long as we expect him to, we are insulted. If he offers more information than we expect, we are surprised.

An interesting thing about these expectations is that although they are very detailed and specific we are largely unaware that we have them.

2 SOCIAL RELATIONSHIPS AND SOCIAL ROLES

All social structure is created through *social interaction* between two or more people. The concept of social interaction is based on the observation that almost all human action is oriented toward other persons, designed to have meaning to them or to influence their state of mind and/or actions. A woman nodding to someone she meets on the street, an angry father scolding his child, and a secretary sharpening pencils for her boss in the morning, are all relatively patterned relationships with a significance both to the actor and to the other people involved—the passerby, the child, and the boss. In fact, these acts are expected by others, and the actor has reciprocal expectations about the way his actions will be received.

Social interaction occurs in a variety of ways, on a continuum that goes from the totally impersonal at one end to the greatest intimacy at the other. Interaction need not even include speech. Take for example the interaction of two strangers passing each other on the sidewalk. Typically they do not let their eyes meet. If by accident they happen to look at each other at the same time, each will shift his gaze quickly away. Both are well aware that to stare intently at the other

person would embarrass the other and be considered rude. That is a pattern of social interaction, even though it includes no words.

Adding words to the interaction makes it one degree more personal, but the interaction may still be as highly rigid and restricted. There are appropriate responses, different in each case, for a stranger you do not expect to see again, such as a fellow shopper in a department store; for strangers whom you know you will in the future see frequently, such as the other tenants in your apartment building; for those whom you know well professionally but not personally, such as your doctor; and for friends, teachers, lovers, bosses, and relatives. The abridgment by Eric Berne, in this chapter, explores some of the behavior patterns established for those who are acquaintances but not really friends, and the same sort of analysis can be applied to every kind of individual social interaction.

A comparison will show that in many ways the most rigid and restricting patterns of social interaction are those which are the most impersonal. There are only one or two socially approved ways to behave with an elevator man, whereas there are dozens of acceptable ways to behave with a parent.

Many social aggregates appear to have no social structure at all. People walking along a sidewalk in a city go about their business alone, in pairs, or in small clusters, without much concern for their fellow pedestrians. However, if one person stares at another too long, or steps into his path, the other person will feel frightened or insulted. Rather clear though minimal behavioral expectations do exist in most social aggregations. *(George W. Martin, DPI)*

The reason for this is that the interaction between an elevator operator and his passenger has little significance for either of the people involved. It occurs only infrequently in the case of the passenger, and the social bond which the interaction forms is a very weak one. On the other hand, the social bond between a parent and his child is extremely strong. The interaction extends over a long period of time; contact between the two people involved in the interaction is frequent; there is a high degree of intimacy and consequent potential for emotional gratification. The richness and depth of the interaction requires a much greater informality and spontaneity; hesitation or lack of openness would be resented, considered an insult. In place of rules and rituals to pattern their behavior is the mutual feeling of dependency and concern each feels for the other.

SOCIAL RELATIONSHIPS

In the course of a single day, each person who lives in modern Western society, and even in most primitive societies, interacts with many other people—perhaps as many as a hundred or more for a person who works in a busy office in some large city. Many of these social interactions are casual, one-time occurrences, or they are repeated so seldom that there is little continuity. Much social interaction, however, is continuing and of a more permanent nature. When a give-and-take interaction continues long enough for a relatively stable set of social expectations to develop, the interaction is called a *social relationship*. Society might aptly be described as a system of social relationships.

It is useful to think of social relationships in terms of the goals which are being sought by the individuals involved. We call a relationship *instrumental* if it is used as a means to some other end. The relationship between a customer and a clerk in a drugstore is instrumental; the customer's primary goal is to buy a bottle of aspirin that he needs to cure his headache, and the clerk's primary goal is to earn a living by selling the aspirin. The majority of daily relationships fall into this category of the instrumental. *Expressive* relationships are those which are valued for their own sake and have no goal beyond the pleasure each person takes in the relationship. Close friendships are usually expressive relationships; so are parent-child relationships, and those between lovers. Actually, most relationships combine both instrumental and expressive elements. As the customer is getting his change, he and the clerk may talk about baseball scores or an upcoming election; this adds a measure of expressiveness to their basically instrumental relationship. A friend may be asked to co-sign a loan or serve as a reference on a job application, which makes the relationship instrumental as well as expressive. Many sociologists contend that a growing proportion of relationships in modern society are primarily instrumental, creating a need for more relationships of an expressive type.

Five broad types of social relationships or social interaction seem to be universal and basic to mankind. They are: (1) cooperation, (2) conflict, (3) competition, (4) coercion, and (5) exchange.

Cooperation

Cooperation is the term used to describe the relationship in which people or groups act together in order to promote common interests or shared goals. In this way, they can achieve goals that might otherwise be difficult or impossible for each to achieve individually. In a broad sense, all of society and social life is based on cooperation. We band together in groups and societies to adapt to the environment and to meet environmental threats such as floods, famine, and pestilence; we work together to meet individual needs efficiently and to provide mutual protection from threats of other societies. Society would be inconceivable without a minimum of cooperative endeavor.

Sociologist Robert Nisbet has noted four main kinds of cooperation.[2] The oldest and most universal is *spontaneous* cooperation or mutual aid. It arises out of the needs and possibilities of a situation, as when two people cooperate on a homework assignment so they can both get better grades, or witnesses to an accident jointly give aid to the injured.

The cooperation which has held societies together throughout history may have originally arisen in a spontaneous manner, but as it was repeated it became age-old custom and tradition, passed on from generation to generation. The cooperation thus ingrained in a primitive tribe, a Chinese family, or a medieval village may be called *traditional* cooperation.

In modern societies, we rely less on traditional cooperation than on cooperation which is directed by some third party with a degree of authority, such as a boss who tells two co-workers to pool their efforts to accomplish a certain job, or a swimming instructor who tells his students to pair up when they go in the water. We also rely heavily on *contractual* cooperation, wherein the people or groups

2.   R. A. Nisbet, *The Social Bond* (New York: Alfred A. Knopf, 1970), pp. 66–69.

agree to cooperate in certain explicit ways, with the obligations of each clearly spelled out. This is the most common form of group cooperation, but it can be seen among individuals too—an example is a group of young mothers who take turns keeping each other's children so that each can have some free time for shopping and errands.

It should be stressed that people or groups do not need to be equals for cooperation to take place. It often happens that one group is larger, more powerful, richer, or better organized than the group with which it proposes to cooperate. When the need for cooperation is thus unequal, it is quite likely that the terms of the cooperative effort will reflect that inequality, with one group required to do more or collect a smaller reward.

We should also note that a relationship of cooperation may involve other types of social interaction as well. For example, all major airlines have cooperated in making reservations for customers on other airlines, and pooling certain airport equipment and facilities; this cooperation helps them all achieve their goal of making a profit. Yet they also compete with each other for customers and profits; thus cooperation is often combined with competition.

Conflict

Conflict has been defined as "the process of social interaction in which two or more persons struggle with one another for some commonly prized object or value."[3] Conflict is the opposite of cooperation. Defeat of an opponent is seen as essential for achieving the desired goal.

Conflicts arise because the benefits and rewards of a society are relatively limited. The interests of individuals pursuing these scarce resources clash as each tries to subdue the others as much as necessary to satisfy his own desires.

Conflict may take many forms. The sociologist Georg Simmel discussed four major types: wars between groups; feuds or factional strife within groups; litigation (a conflict which is handled legally and may be settled in the courts); and the conflict of impersonal ideals.[4] Conflicts over ideals, rather than over some desired material possession, have often been of the most merciless and destructive character.

Some philosophers and social thinkers have stated that conflict is a problem caused by faulty social organization and that under a perfect social system, conflict would not arise.[5] However, it seems hard to imagine a society where no two people would ever want the same thing and where nothing desirable was ever in short supply. As long as these conditions exist, then a certain measure of conflict is inevitable. A good social system is one that devises a means of handling conflict without injury to either party.

Because conflict has so often ended in unhappiness, destruction, violence, and even death, we naturally take a negative view of it. Several recent sociologists, following the lead of Georg Simmel, have emphasized that conflict has some positive aspects, and that even if society could somehow succeed in eliminating it, such a step might not be desirable.[6] Such a society would be lifeless, with little interest or dynamic quality. Conflict can serve as a force that integrates the people on each side of the conflict, bonding them firmly in a group; conflict may also lead to needed social change, for example by bringing groups into communication with one another, forcing them to face up to their problems.

---

3.   R. A. Nisbet, *The Social Bond*, p. 75.

4.   Georg Simmel, *Conflict and the Web of Group Affiliations,* trans. Kurt H. Wolff and Reinhard Bendix (New York: Free Press, 1955).

5.   Karl Marx and Friedrich Engels, *The Communist Manifesto* (Baltimore: Penguin Books, 1969).

6.   Lewis Coser, *The Functions of Social Conflict* (New York: Free Press, 1956).

TYPES OF SOCIAL INTERACTION

Type	Characteristics	Example
Cooperation	People or groups work or act together to promote common interests or shared goals.	Students working together on a home-work assignment.
Conflict	Two or more people struggle against each other trying to achieve a commonly prized object or value.	A legal dispute over right to a piece of property.
Coercion	One person or group forces its will upon another.	Colonists forcing natives to become slaves.
Exchange	One person acts toward another in a certain way in order to receive a reward or return for his behavior.	A secretary working for her boss; a husband bringing his wife a box of candy.
Competition	Individuals or groups struggle with each other to achieve the same goal, but their primary concern is directed toward achieving the goal, not toward each other.	National football teams competing for the national championship.

Competition

Competition may be thought of as a kind of cooperative conflict. In competition, individuals or groups struggle to reach the same goals, but their primary concern is directed toward the objects or goal being sought, rather than toward the competitors. As in conflict, one competitor will attain the goal, and one will be defeated, but the major focus of the process is not to defeat the competitor. Unlike cooperation, the actors seek the goal separately and in rivalry with one another.

To prevent competition from degenerating into conflict, it is necessary for the parties to agree ahead of time on the "rules of the game," and then to cooperate in sticking to these rules. This is true of competition in the marketplace, competition among students in a classroom, and competition between football teams. Competition is a widespread form of social interaction in stable, modern societies. It is central to the American system of individualistic capitalism.

Coercion

When one person or group forces its will on another, we call it *coercion*. To a large extent all forms of coercion ultimately rest on the threat of physical force or violence, and certainly that is one obvious means of coercing another person. But coercion is usually much more subtle than the open use or threat of violence. Love for a parent, respect for the flag, faith in God, and fear of loneliness can all be used as weapons of coercion too.

At first glance, coercion may not seem like a true relationship at all, because it appears so one-sided, as if the coercer does all the acting and the other person just sits there letting it happen. But in reality, the person being coerced does respond to and interact with the coercer; sometimes, of course, he is forced to. Indifference is one kind of response, apathy another, anger another. The response will have an effect on the coercer, who may be made to feel guilty, or self-satisfied, or afraid of some reprisal.

Like conflict, coercion is usually viewed as a negative kind of social relationship. We associate it with repellent practices such as slavery. However, coercion serves definite social functions, too. Although parents and educators may attempt to use other patterns of social interaction in their task of teaching children, the threat of coercion underlies the teaching of the rules of society, the instilling of a conception of what is right and what is wrong. Of course, coercion is more than a possibility in a majority of families. Putting a child who is getting out of hand in his room, or spanking the child who rode his tricycle onto the highway, are examples of commonly used coercions.

Exchange

When one person acts in a certain way toward another for the purpose of receiving a reward or return, we call it an *exchange relationship*. Most employer–employee relationships are of this type. The employee behaves in a certain way that accords with the wishes of the employer, and he is rewarded with a salary for his actions. However, exchange relationships go far beyond those which are based on money or goods as the reward. Many social exchange relationships are based on subjective emotional rewards. When one person behaves lovingly toward another, for example, he may do so for the purpose of receiving an emotional reward, such as gratitude or returned love. The work of sociologists such as George Homans[7] and Peter Blau[8] has established that exchange relationships based on gratitude are an extremely important component of social life. In many casual relationships, the trade of an action for gratitude or appreciation is the basic motivation. Making change for a stranger who wants to buy cigarettes from a machine, helping an elderly person across

the street, sending a little present to a co-worker when he is ill—underlying all these actions is the expectation that the other person will feel grateful for what you have done. The exchange relationship is also important in more intimate types of interaction. Obviously you do not love a person solely because you expect him to love you in return, but that expectation is a part of the relationship. If you never receive from the person you love any affection in exchange, or at least some measure of gratitude for the love you have offered, you will probably find that your feelings of love cannot survive the unfair exchange.

ROLE AND STATUS

Central to the analysis of organized social interaction are the concepts of role and status. Sociologists use the word *role* (adapted from the vocabulary of the theater) to denote the part, or pattern of behavior, which one is expected to play in social interaction. For every form of organized social interaction, there exists in the understanding of society what corresponds to a script, or model, which tells each person involved what is expected of him. To know one's role is to understand what behavior is expected or required in a particular situation.

The term role is used with two shades of meaning. The first meaning refers to the way an individual personality tends to react to a social situation and may be called an individual or interpersonal role. This is the meaning of the word role when we say, "She played an aggressive role when she dated John," or "He is always acting (playing the role of) the fool." Sociologists are generally more interested in another type of role, called a social role. A *social role* is a set of expectations and ways of behaving associated with a specific position in a social system. Such positions, called *social statuses,* include mother, teacher, doctor, president, tax collector. (The term "social status" is also used in the sense of a position ranked or value rated in a system of

7.   George C. Homans, *Social Behavior: Its Elementary Forms* (New York: Harcourt Brace Jovanovich, 1961).

8.   Peter M. Blau, *Exchange and Power in Social Life* (New York: John Wiley, 1964).

These men are involved in the cooperative venture of catching fish. The task requires carefully coordinated activity, and each person has a specifically defined role to perform. It is in everyone's interest to contribute, since together they can make a much larger catch than could any individual working alone. *(Photo by Jon Erikson)*

social stratification, but we will discuss this in chapter 7.) Sometimes the social role expectations are highly detailed, as in the case of many specialized work roles, and sometimes they are broad and elastic, as in the case of roles within the family.

Some social roles are so well-defined that even the dialogue has been filled in already. When the man at the newsstand says, "How are you?" as he hands you the evening paper, you know what you are expected to say. You don't give a detailed or literal answer, describing the exact state of your health, finances, or love life. You simply say "Fine," or "Too hot," or some other brief rejoinder; as Eric Berne points out, any other response will be puzzling to the one who asked the question.

But other roles leave more freedom for individual improvisation. When a husband calls his wife during his coffee break and asks how she is, she has a choice among a number of possible and acceptable responses, from the same noncommittal "Fine" she would give to the man at the newsstand to a blow-by-blow account of her morning with the children.

We must be careful here to distinguish between the way the role is written in society's script, and the way that an individual undertaking a particular role carries it out. For a number of reasons, ranging from imperfect understanding of the role to personal inadequacy, a person does not always do exactly what his role calls for. However, we still refer to him as playing a role, even if he does not play it correctly. To avoid confusion, some sociologists call the role as prescribed by society the ideal role, and the role as played by the individual the actual role. They may also be called the *prescribed role*[9] and the *role performance*.

It should be stressed that roles are not always as well-defined as they sound in our description. There is not always complete agreement throughout the society as to the definition of a role. Take, for example, the role of a movie star: some people maintain that the only obligation of the role is to provide entertainment; others say that the role also includes serving as a model of character or behavior for the star's fans, particularly his adolescent fans.

Then there are some roles which are in the process of being defined. For example, the role of a businesswoman in American society is still unclear, and few guidelines are provided for those who undertake to play it. The role will gradually be defined through the actions of those women who are currently performing it. In due time, the most successful of their improvisations will become a standard part of the script, and then newcomers to the role will better understand what is expected of them.

The principal importance of the role is to prescribe the way that one individual should behave toward another in the course of their interaction—doctor to patient, husband to wife, senator to constituent. It should be emphasized that the role not only regulates behavior, but also enables us to predict the actions of others and therefore to guide our own actions in an orderly way. The scope of the role is not limited to one relationship alone. A role also prescribes behavior and actions expected by other people not involved in the initial relationship. We can see this illustrated in the role of the teacher. When we

describe the role of a teacher we would first think of the way a teacher is expected to behave toward his students. But the role makes demands in other directions. A teacher is expected to have a certain kind of relationship with other members of the community as well. Perhaps he is expected to join a professional association, like the National Education Association; in many communities, he is expected to lead a highly moral private life at home and to be above suspicion; he may be expected to attend classes at a nearby college at night or over the summer, to demonstrate his willingness to improve his skills; he may be expected to volunteer his professional services to some community organization, such as a program set up to tutor disadvantaged children. None of these demands is directly related to the teacher–student relationship, and yet they are all a part of the role of teacher. This complex set of roles associated with a single status is called a *role set*.[10]

In the course of one day's social interaction, a person will play many different roles, and he must learn to balance the demands of his various roles. For example, in the evening a woman may be faced with two, or even more, opposing demands. In her role as wife, she should be available to listen sympathetically to an account of her husband's day at the office; but in her role as mother she should be fixing the children's dinner and supervising their homework. If she has undertaken other activities as well, and has work to do in her role as employee or a meeting to attend in her role as community worker, she may have real trouble in deciding her course of action. This is called *role conflict* or *role incompatibility*.[11] An example of role conflict is presented in the abridgment "The Hashers," accompanying this text.

In some cases, this kind of conflict between two courses of action can be built into a

9.   Theodore M. Newcomb, *Social Psychology* (New York: Dryden Holt, 1950).

10.   Robert K. Merton, *Social Theory and Social Structure* (New York: Free Press, 1954).

11.   See Jackson Toby, "Some Variables in Role Conflict Analysis," *Social Forces* 30 (1952), 323–327.

single role. A good example of this is in the role of military officer. To be successful, the officer must have the affection of his men, and their trust, for he is asking them to risk their lives at his word. But at the same time, the officer functions as an authority figure, to be obeyed instantly and without question. The first part of his role calls for a type of behavior that seems to the men kind, personally involved, and sympathetic; the second part of the role calls for behavior that appears stern and uncompromising. We may call this sort of opposing demand *role inconsistency* or *role strain.*[12]

12. William J. Goode, "A Theory of Role Strain," *American Sociological Review* 25 (August 1960): 483–496.

LOUIS A. ZURCHER, JR., DAVID A. SONNENSCHEIN, AND ERIC L. METZNER
The Hashers

From: "The Hasher: A Study of Role Conflict," by Louis A. Zurcher, Jr., David A. Sonnenschein and Eric L. Metzner, *Social Forces* 44 (University of North Carolina Press, June 1966), 505-514.

Introduction

This is a report of a study made by a social scientist, with the aid of two college students, of role conflict encountered by students who wait on tables in college dining halls. The particular situation studied was a sorority dining hall, but many of the observations made there would be true of other similar situations of role conflict. This study explains the way that the "hashers" (as the student kitchen workers are called) are expected to behave as they play their job role, and the way that they adjust to or accommodate these demands, which may conflict with their other roles, such as that of student.

The individual entering college for the first time has, through exposure to a popularized and dramatized stereotype, come to perceive the status of "college man" as incorporating the following characteristics and role expectations: (1) a young man who deserves a white-collar or "clean" occupation of more than average prestige, (2) a sophisticate, above average in intelligence, taste, and *savoir faire* — able to smoke a pipe with an air of casual indifference, (3) a "lover," a "man of the world" who dominates and manipulates the tender young coeds, (4) a "hail fellow well met" who can, at any time, spontaneously join in an impromptu frolicsome venture. These expectations are repeatedly reinforced in the informal academic setting.

Hashers at the subject university are male college undergraduate students who are employed as attendants in the kitchens of sororities and fraternities (in this paper, we will focus our attention on the unique social situation of the sorority hasher). In return for their work, hashers are given meals and, in some cases of additional responsibility, a few dollars a month. The job consists of setting tables; washing and drying dishes, silver, and utensils; cleaning up the kitchen; mopping floors; disposing of garbage; general handy work; and on occasion, carrying luggage for the girls. As it can be seen, the tasks are in general very similar to those of the "K.P." of military fame.

Even though it is part-time work, the job of hasher can be classified as a "service occupation." The hasher occupies the lowest level of the functional work hierarchy of the kitchen. At the top of the hierarchy is the house mother, then the cooks (in order of longevity), the head hasher, and finally, the hashers themselves (in order of longevity). This chain-of-command is rigidly enforced — a policy not unusual in an organized kitchen work setting.

The position of hasher in a sorority thus brings with it the behavioral expectations of (1) menial or "dirty" work, (2) low prestige, (3) a marked lack of sophistication, and (4) manifest subservience to and strict social distance from a group of college coeds.

It appears, therefore, that the individual who must enact both the role of college man and hasher experiences conflict, and it will be seen that this conflict manifests itself in the way they behave in the work situation, their attitudes toward and behavior with the girls for whom they work, and the attitudes of the girls toward and their behavior with the hashers. Furthermore, components within the informal organization of the work situation will be observed to provide the individual with group-structured defenses to the role conflict. These defenses become an integral part of the hasher role enactment and are learned along with the formal requirements of the job.

Results and discussion

It is immediately apparent to the observer that the hasher is not proud of his work and that he prefers not to be identified with the job.

The college student has, in general, a middle-class view of work — that is, work should enhance one's prestige, provide for the realization of one's talents, and be satisfying and desirable in itself. This view is in contrast to that of the lower class, which sees work as an unpleasant but necessary means of securing food and shelter, and as being neither interesting nor desirable in itself. To the members of the lower class who must pursue such "drudgery," the college student imputes low intelligence, irresponsibility, and generalized inferiority. The hasher then finds himself in the unique situation of having middle-class definitions and expectations of work, but performing tasks and conforming to expectations which clearly are representative of a lower-class job.

When in a position in which he must profess the nature of his employment, the hasher's admission is inevitably quickly followed by a qualifying statement: "It's a means to an end," "I'm just doing this until I find something more suitable," "It's the only job I could get with hours that won't interfere with my class schedule," and so on. The *temporary* nature of the job is stressed, and a point is made of demonstrating to the questioner that the hasher's primary role is that of student. The hasher's friends and acquaintances are often observed to ask him why he does such work, thus indicating a violation of their expectations of him as a college man. Sometimes a hasher will describe, with a leer, his job as an opportunity to "get near all those girls," and will gloss over the unpleasant realities of his task.

In the subject sorority house, there is a formal rule forbidding dating between the hashers and the sorority girls, and social intercourse within the house is maintained at as impersonal, employer-employee level as possible. Fraternization has been discouraged to the point where the girls and the hashers both feel uncomfortable if they have to interact on a level other than that called for by the job.

The no-dating rule in the subject sorority has been rigidly followed only for the last two years. The older hashers often speak of those "good olds days a couple of years ago" when the girls were "somehow much nicer." Pertinent here is the hasher's definition of the sorority member who is a "good kid." In every case interviewed, the hasher's description of this ideal sorority girl centered on the attribute of "naturalness" — that is, a tendency to "be herself" and not to "look down" on the hasher, thus not stressing his subservient role. A good house to work for is one in which you are "treated like a human being." Good kids and good houses then are those that treat the individual less like a hasher and more like a college man. Many of the hashers are upper classmen, yet they must take orders from and wait on freshmen girls. Any sorority member who minimizes this status threat is appreciated by the hasher as a "good kid."

The girls very often refer to the individual as "hasher," rather than by given name, and are quite free with orders and criticism. Any praise usually takes on a condescending tone–"nice hasher," "nice boy," and so on. The girl's view of the hasher in the subject sorority house is revealed by the fact that one of the initiation requirements for a pledge is that she sing a love song to a hasher while he sits on her lap. This is taken to be one of the initiation rites that "humbles the pledges." (Ironically, the hashers themselves use this as a kind of initiation rite for entrance into their informal work group. That is, the newest hasher is the one who is made available to the pledge for the love song, and after he has been so used, he is told by his fellow hashers that he now knows "what working in the sorority is really like.")

The hashers seem to get much satisfaction from "getting the girls' goats." The kitchen often resounds with gleefully shared exclamations like "Boy, did I get *her* mad!" and "I sure told *her* off!" Spilling of food while serving, ignoring an order, sharp answers to criticisms, and any other verbal aggression is rewarded with the plaudits of the other hashers – "That'll show them"; "That'll shape her up!" While in the kitchen the hashers will often deliberately make noises (loud talking, whistling, banging of pots and pans) with the intent of disturbing the girls. In the subject sorority, the hashers will save the food scraps from the preparation phase of the meal, and while

the girls are eating will overload the garbage disposal unit and convulse with laughter as the mechanism emits loud and excruciating gurgles, whines, and crunches. "It's hard to tell," reported one chuckling hasher, "which garbage disposals sound the worst – the ones out in the dining room, or the one in the kitchen."

Besides the deliberate casualness toward dropped food and the amused "what they don't know won't hurt them attitude," on numerous other occasions in the subject sorority minor assaults were made on foods to be served to the girls – e.g., a marble tossed into a gelatin and grape salad mold; a small amount of grass thrown in with cooking spinach ("for those cows"); each dinner roll "thrown around the bases" from one hasher to another before it was placed in the serving basket; a drop or two of blood from the cut finger of a hasher splashed into a pot of soup ("This ought to make those bloodsuckers happy!"); green food coloring added to the milk; salt shaker tops loosened so they would fall off in the girls' plates; etc. The actions themselves are, of course, less significant than the glee with which they are shared by the hashers who are "getting to the girls."

An extremely interesting phenomenon revealed by the participant observation (and confirmed in other than the subject sorority by interviews) is the nature of the derisive terms the hashers have for the girls. Almost always, the names have animal referents, and the animal is most often the pig–"Here they come, let's slop the troughs"; "Soueee" and "Oink-Oink" grumbled (on the kitchen side of the swinging door) as the hashers walk out of the kitchen to serve the food; "What do the pigs want now"; "Let's go clean out the feeding pens"; "Mush, you huskies!" The records contain a startling number of this kind of statement, as well as many other derogatory comments about the girls' manners, breeding, and femininity. It would appear that the hashers are projecting feelings of their own "low born" position upon the girls. It is almost as if they are saying, "See, we aren't so bad, look at those slobs out in the dining room!"

The physical appearance of the sorority girls is also called into question by the hashers. "They've all had their faces remodeled, and they still can't get dates." "A guy would have to be pretty hard up to take out one of these dogs." "They must have an 'ugly requirement' in order to get into this sorority." The hasher lets his peers know that even if he *could* date one of the girls in the sorority, he wouldn't.

Within the kitchen, escape mechanisms of various sorts are everywhere apparent. Horseplay is the order of the day, with episodic food throwing and water splashing bouts, word fads, running "in group" jokes, and general zaniness. Of particular interest are the sets of activities which the hashers in the subject sorority house referred to as "bits." A "bit" is a relatively organized session of play-acting, originally arising spontaneously, and having a central theme and roles for each of the hashers. For example, the "bit" for one work session staged the kitchen and dining room as a hell ship, with the hashers cast as the mutineers, the girls as "Powdered Pirates," and the cooks as "Ahab" and "Bly." Knives became "harpoons," the dinner meat became "salt horse," going out into the dining room was "walking the plank," one abundantly endowed sorority sister became the "treasure chest," and so on.

It would appear that the "bit" serves a number of functions for the hashers. It is, not unlike the therapeutic applications of psychodrama and role playing, an opportunity for a more or less legitimized expression of hostility. It serves also as a distraction from the repetitive drudgery and potential boredom of the hasher's work task, allowing him, in effect, to be more creative and expressive while on the job. Furthermore, the "bit," while affecting the

hasher's enactment of an interconnecting and interdependent set of fantasy roles, serves to tighten the cohesion of the informal work group. As one hasher said, not without price, "When we've got our own laughs going for us, this job is no sweat." Lastly, it would seem that the hasher welcomes the relatively clearly defined and uncomplicated roles of the "bit." Even if the play-acting roles are acknowledged fancy and are ephemeral, they are less ambiguous, less conflict-ridden, and less distasteful than his actual work role.

Other forms of symbolic withdrawal from the hasher work situation are also common. In the subject sorority house, the threats to quit, to leave the field, ran about 20 per week. Rarely did any hasher go through the entire week without stating his intention to quit next week. Each new work day brought with it a new challenge to "finish up faster than yesterday, and get the hell out of here."

In the kitchen, stories of the "I am a great lover" variety are daily bantered about by the hashers, expressed in a fashion that seems to insist "away from here, I really do manipulate and dominate the coeds." Many joking references and comic routines concerning homosexuality are observed, the hashers themselves using a falsetto voice or feigning homosexual characteristics. The homosexual routine does, in fact, at times represent itself with the elaborateness of a "bit." Such behavior is often seen in social environments where the masculine role is perceived by males to be threatened.

On those nights when the girls bring male guests to the sorority house, the hashers are especially belligerent. Venomously, the hashers comment about the dates the girls have—"wonder if she's paying him a flat fee, or by the hour." "God, she must have robbed a grave to get him!" On such occasions, the role conflict of the hasher is exacerbated, since he must wait on college *couples*. Some hashers flatly refuse to work at these times. Others will agree to work in the kitchen, but refuse to wait on table.

It appears that the degree of social distance between hashers and members is less a function of the size of the house than a function of its relative status on the campus. The "loser" sororities apparently have greater need to maintain class lines within their houses than do the "top" sororities. This relationship was difficult to assess and is cautiously presented, considering the techniques used in this study and the fact that the work setting of the hasher is affected by other variables — e.g., the managerial styles of the house mothers and the cooks. The significant point is that, in *all* the houses considered here, there was evidence of some degree of social distance between the hashers and the girls, of hasher role conflict, and of the hashers' need to abate that conflict.

Conclusion

Role conflict is a very uncomfortable position to be in. To reduce their discomfort the hashers had to take some kind of action. But they could not, or would not, drop either of their two roles. The alternative they found was to raise the status of hasher by trying to reduce the social distance between themselves and those whom they served. In a sense they were attempting to communicate that they were better than just a person who waited on tables.

This study illustrates what social structure is and how important it is. The demands and expectations discussed here are part of the social structure of the school and sorority house — they are "built into the situation." The hashers' role conflict would occur for whatever individuals filled the particular roles.

TOPIC

3 SOCIAL GROUPINGS

In the first part of this chapter, we have been concerned with the processes of interaction and the social roles through which human beings participate in social life. But the kind of interaction we have described usually takes place in social aggregates, or groupings — specific clusters of people who are to some degree organized and dependent upon one another. Social groupings range from relatively unstructured, casual, and rapidly changing systems of interaction to highly organized, formal, and enduring social entities. Sociologists are not in total agreement about how best to classify and discuss such groupings, but two basic ways of looking at them are commonly used. The first way is by degree of organization — to what extent the group is unorganized or organized. The second way is by the distinction between "unibonded," or single-purpose, specialized groups, and "multibonded" groups, or groups which include many purposes or activities. Both these types of classifications will be discussed below; but the first grouping type to consider, *social categories,* is not really a social group at all.

In the marketplace individuals come together for a single purpose: to buy and sell goods. Though the marketplace involves a great amount of competition, the participants also cooperate with one another by sticking to the "rules of the game." In preindustrial societies economic transactions may not involve money, but may be based on bartered exchange of needed goods—pots for produce, for example. *(Photo by Ken Heyman)*

CATEGORIES AND ORGANIZED GROUPS
Social categories

Individuals are often classified into various categories on the basis of a wide variety of characteristics: liberals and conservatives, left-handed and right-handed, high school graduates and college graduates, and so on. The individual members of such categories do not necessarily interact, form patterns of organization, or have anything in common beyond the one trait used to classify them. They are merely placed in such categories for the convenience of someone making a study or drawing some kind of comparison. They do not consist of a social group of interdependent persons in any meaningful sense. However, the fact of being thus classified together may awaken a feeling of shared interests or goals which can lead to the formation of a real, interactive social grouping. Recently, for example, various Women's Liberation groups have been formed by women who felt that their joint classification as "female" gave them shared experiences and viewpoints. In some cases, broad statistical categories are socially defined by others as having great consequences for the individuals who belong to them; such a category may become a meaningful group due to the special treatment given to its members by others. An example can be seen in racial categories. Historically, white Americans have treated all black Americans as if the fact of their race was the most important basis of grouping, more meaningful than any social characteristic. The result has been that many black Americans do form an interactive group, with a sense of group solidarity and loyalty.

Degree of organization

Social groupings vary widely in their degree of organization. A social group is highly organized when it has the following characteristics:[13]

1. A consistent and clear set of goals which the members are pursuing as a group.
2. A precise definition of the rights, duties, roles, and status of every member.
3. A clear indication of which relationships or forms of interaction are required from the members, which are prohibited, and which are recommended though not required.

An unorganized group does not have these characteristics. The whole set of relationships in such a group is vague, unstable, and without a consistent pattern. The group members do not have clear goals in mind; they do not know their position in the group—what is expected of them or what they can expect from others.

Relatively unorganized groupings include groupings with various degrees of structure. The least structured consists of activity for which Robin Williams has suggested the label *recurrent aggregative behavior.*[14] An example is the daily assembly of persons in buses, trains, and subways, or pedestrians walking along a sidewalk. Such situations are not completely unstructured. For example, there is a recognized way to distribute the seats on a bus—first come, first served, but feeble or handicapped persons, nuns, and pregnant women get special priority. However, it is not always so clear how we should act in an unstructured situation, and there may be a good deal of uncertainty and confusion. Have you ever watched two strangers on a narrow sidewalk silently try to work out a way to pass each other without colliding?

A more fluid kind of grouping which sometimes develops a greater amount of structure, but at the same time is still highly unorganized, is called *collective behavior.* It consists of such collected but relatively unorganized aggregations as crowds (masses at a public event, a gathering of persons on the street),

13. Adapted from P. A. Sorokin, *Society, Culture, and Personality* (New York: Cooper Square Publishers, 1962), chaps. 2 and 6.

14. Robin Williams, *American Society,* 3rd ed. (New York: Alfred A. Knopf, 1970), p. 506.

publics which momentarily surface around a political or social issue, mobs, and audiences. Each of these groupings is relatively spontaneous and temporary. More structured still are such groupings as *social movements* like the peace movement. We will discuss collective behavior and social movement in chapter 13.

Organized groups

In addition to the degree of organization, groups may vary in their size, duration of existence (temporary or permanent), complexity, methods of obtaining members, and so on. One of the most significant characteristics of a group is the scope of its interests, values, and goals. Those groups with a single major set of values and goals may be called *unibonded* (the term used by the famous Russian-American sociologist Pitirim A. Sorokin).[15] Historically, important groups have been organized around such single purposes or values as kinship; language; the state; occupational, economic, religious, or political values; and scientific, philosophical, educational, ethical, and other points of view. Organized, unibonded groups, or what may be called simply *organizations,* form the subject matter of chapter 5. Economic and governmental organizations are especially important in modern society, but we shall also examine in this book religious, educational, and other types of organizations as well.

There are, of course, thousands of small and temporary groups in every advanced society organized around almost every conceivable special interest. Most often these are relatively unimportant to the larger society, though they may be quite important to the individual members. Examples are temporary friendship cliques, discussion groups, and committees. Some sociologists use the term "group" to refer only to this type of small face-to-face, social group.

MULTIBONDED GROUPS

Multibonded or comprehensive groups, groups with more than one major set of goals and functions, have throughout history been the central and most important groups in a population. They include the family, clan, tribe, nation, caste, social estate (feudal), social class, and ethnic group.

Family groups

The family is the group most familiar to everyone and it generally constitutes a person's experience of group membership. Contrary to the opinion of some who regard the family as the simplest group, it is one of the most complex of the multibonded groups. A family may be defined as a group of people related to each other by blood and/or marriage or adoption, a group which typically performs the functions of providing for economic necessities, bearing and caring for children, educating the next generation, and teaching them about social interaction. No society has yet been discovered that did not have some kind of family group in its social organization, so it is a group basic to all mankind.

When we refer to the *nuclear family,* we mean the group composed of a husband, a wife, and their children. George Peter Murdock, in a careful study of 238 different societies, found that every one of these societies displayed some form of the nuclear family in its organization, although it was not always the primary unit of social organization, as it is in our society.[16]

The typical American family consists of a father, a mother, and two or three children. The father is usually the chief financial support, although in a growing number of cases mothers of school-age children are also taking jobs to add to the family income. The daily care of young children is the responsibility of the mother, who also takes care of the house they live in, provides meals and other

---

15. P. A. Sorokin, *Society, Culture, and Personality.*

16. George Peter Murdock, *Social Structure* (New York: Macmillan, 1949).

domestic duties (if the mother works, the father may share some of the responsibility in this area by shopping for groceries, doing the dishes, or caring for the children in the evening and on weekends). In our society, the school performs many of the educational functions, but the parents still have a major responsibility in that area, particularly with preschoolers, but also with school-age children. They help to motivate the children to do well in school, encourage their intellectual interests, and make decisions about special educational experiences, such as music, dance, camp, sports, and college.

In some cases the nuclear family is only one part of the basic family unit of organization. When one or more nuclear families live together with other relatives, such as aunts and uncles or grandparents, we call it an *extended family*. The extended family is not

MULTIBONDED GROUPS

Type	Characteristics	Example
Family	A group of persons related to each other by blood, marriage, or adoption which performs economic, sexual, educational and religious functions.	Has existed in all societies since prehistoric man.
Clan	A large kinship group whose members live in one geographical area and believe they are descended from a common ancestor. They have an enlarged family organization with one head or leader.	Scottish Highlands, e.g., the Campbells, the MacKenzies, the Stuarts.
Tribe	Several clans or kinship groups living together with a form of government which is separated from the family system.	American Indians, e.g., the Navaho, the Cree, the Ponca.
Caste	A closed hierarchical grouping in which a member's position, decided by birth, determines his social relationships, prestige, and place of residence.	India, e.g., the Brahmins, the Vaisyas.
Social Estate (or Social Order)	A group whose members share a common social rank, but whose structure is less rigid than a caste.	Europe in the Middle Ages, e.g., the estates of feudal lords.
Social Class	A group of people with similar social levels, especially in terms of money possessed or earned.	Western European Society, e.g., the capitalists and the proletarians.
Ethnic Group	A group distinguished from other groups in a society, especially a minority group in a larger society.	Italian-Americans, Jews, Irish, Negroes in the United States.

uncommon in our society. Often an elderly parent, or a younger sister or brother of one of the nuclear couple, joins the family unit for some period of time. The person thus added joins in the work of the family unit; a grandmother may baby-sit, help clean house, or contribute a certain sum of money to the household. The extended family is most likely to be characteristic of an agrarian society, where every extra pair of hands is a valuable asset in the struggle to make a living from the land. Extended families also appear frequently among the urban poor. In London's East End, New York's Harlem, Chicago's South Side, you will find many extended families because economic necessity forces several generations to live together.

Our marriage system is based on *monogamy;* one man is married to one woman. Marriages which involve more than one husband or one wife are called *polygamy.* The most common type is *polygyny,* in which one man has several wives; when the situation is reversed and one woman has several husbands, it is called *polyandry.* Murdock's study of 238 societies (which were mostly primitive) noted above found that 193 were characterized by polygyny, 43 by monogamy, and 2 by polyandry. Polygamy is not a widespread practice today, but we can see it in parts of Africa and in tribal societies in the Middle East, where it is permitted to the Moslem male to have four wives concurrently. The wives and all the children usually live together under one roof, sharing the domestic responsibilities.[17] Polygyny is often based on economic necessity; it helps to increase the number of births, or to compensate for a shortage of men, perhaps as a result of wars.

Clan and tribe

Both the clan and the tribe, which is a group of clans, consist of clusters of kinship groupings (groupings of people related in some way to one another) living in one geographical area. The members usually have the same race, language, and religion, and most cultural characteristics in common. The members of a *clan* believe they are descended from a common ancestor. The authority and government of the clan are an enlargement of the family pattern and have not yet evolved into a distinct state government.

A familiar example of clan organization is that of the Scottish Highlands, which had a true clan system until the eighteenth century, when the soldiers of King George I of England broke the power of the clans. Each of the Highland clans was headed by a laird, or leader, who had great authority over the lives of the members, including the power of life or death. The laird determined where the clan would live, how it would make its living, and who its friends and enemies would be. All property was held jointly by the clan, and administered for the common good by the laird. Although nuclear families existed, they, too, were subject to the laird's power, and there was an underlying understanding that children belonged to the clan rather than to their parents. It was quite common for the child of one family to be sent to another family to be brought up. Any clan member who needed food or money or protection could apply to the laird, whose duty it was to provide for the needs of the clansman. Similar clan organization is found in many other societies — among the natives of New Guinea, the Eskimos of the polar regions, in many African societies, and in the rural areas of India.

A clan is almost a closed group; that is, it does not permit the addition of many new members. How does a clan decide who belongs to it, who is kin? There is an obvious biological basis for kinship: the child of a clan member is also a member, as is the child of that child. But there are social definitions of kinship as well as biological ones. In some societies, the wife of a clan member, though

17. For an interesting study of polygamous family relationships, see Sylvia A. Matheson, *The Tigers of Baluchistan* (London: Cox and Wyman, 1967).

not a blood relative, is still considered to belong to the clan. Sometimes membership is extended through her to her own family. Or it may happen the other way around, with the husband being absorbed into the clan of the wife. A third possibility is that each spouse continues in his or her own clan, in which case there must be some established way of deciding the membership of the children.

A *tribe* consists of two or more clans, and due partly to its size, has a rudimentary form of government and authority distinct from the family and the kinship government of the clan. The tribal form of government later evolved into the modern nation-state. The tribe is more open to new members than the clan, because it is less dominated by blood kinship. Tribes have tended to take in new members through conquest or through a kind of merger with neighboring peoples. Because various groups may be included in a tribe, tribes often develop a much greater social diversity than clans.

Clans and tribes have dominated societies throughout most of world history. Today tribes continue in importance in many parts of Africa and Asia. Even many new nation-states consist mainly of loose conglomerations of tribal groups.

Social class, feudal estate, caste, and ethnic group

Social classes, feudal estates, and castes are related in that they are based on the similarities of power, wealth, and prestige of their members. They are closely related to the stratification or ranking system in a society, which will be discussed in chapter 7.

Castes, groups which in their pure form were until recently found in India, are the most rigid groupings known to man. The Indian system had four principal castes: the Brahmans, the caste of priests, scholars, and high government officials; the Kshatriyas, who were originally the soldier class, and in contemporary Indian society have become policemen and civil servants as well; the

Vaisyas, who are landed farmers, small merchants, and clerks in business and government; and the Sudras, who do the manual labor in the society. Originally, all others who did not belong to any of these groups were called pariahs or "untouchables." Within the last three decades the Indian government has outlawed caste discrimination and made discrimination against untouchables a punishable offense.

Each of the four main castes practiced widely variant social rites and rituals. Caste intermarriage was socially prohibited; even relatively impersonal social contact between castes was frowned upon. This prohibition gradually lost its force because of increasing exposure to Western customs and the growing industrialization of the country. Within each caste, there were numerous subcastes, often identified with one particular occupation, such as the practice of medicine, or banking, or doing other people's laundry. Or the subcastes could be identified with certain locations, such as a village entirely populated by that group.

A caste system may allow some degree of mobility from one group to another based on personal ability, but usually there are clearly defined limits to this privilege. For example, an Indian could, through marriage or on rare occasion through merit, effect a change in his subcaste. But his caste was fixed at birth and there was no action he could take that would change it.

Indian caste groups were multibonded in the sense that they were a strongly organized combination of religious, racial, occupational, language, territorial, and other elements. Since Indian caste groups emerged some four thousand years ago, they proved to be the most enduring and all-pervasive groups known to man. States, empires, and religions rose and withered away while caste groups remained unchanged. Though officially outlawed, caste attitudes continue to prevail, particularly in rural areas.

Social estates have been associated with

many periods of history, but we think of them most often in connection with medieval Europe (c. A.D. 1000–1500). The medieval feudal social system was basically divided into three segments — the nobility, the clergy, and the peasantry. They were separated from one another both by social attitudes and customs, and by legal rights and duties. The nobility were a military aristocracy; they governed the societies and defended them. The clergy were the religious and intellectual elite, but they also had many important administrative functions. The peasantry's main role was to supply labor services and support to the nobility and clergy.

The feudal estate system was based on land ownership and inheritance. Everyone lived directly or indirectly off the land; those who possessed land had power and freedom; all others were politically and economically dependent on them. Originally the feudal noble was a "vassal" who received a grant of land from a "lord" in return for personal and military services. This bond between lord and vassal, in which loyalty to the lord became a supreme virtue, was a powerful element binding together the society of the early Middle Ages.

Though social estates varied greatly among themselves and in different societies, they tended to be much more open to new members and less highly organized than castes. For example, new members of the peasantry were recruited not only by birth but through war, kidnapping, and purchase. The clergy estate was open to everyone. Most of the estates provided various ways in which membership could be ended. Thus the estates were much less inbred and much more heterogeneous than caste groupings. Also, the members of the different estates did not often live isolated in a certain circumscribed territory, but mingled together. In many ways, therefore, the feudal estates might be loosely described as diluted castes.

In Western societies, as feudal systems declined and towns and cities grew up, the social estates were replaced by strong social classes. These represented, in turn, a kind of diluted version of the social estate. *Social classes* were organized around economic and occupational similarities rather than around inherited land or inherited relationships to landholders. Examples of prominent social classes in Europe during the last three centuries are the industrial labor or proletarian class, the peasant-farmer class, the class of large landowners, and the capitalist and managerial classes. Each of these has had at times strong organizations and a powerful hold over its members.

Each of these kinds of powerful multi-bonded groups left behind a small reminder of its time in its influence on social interaction. Although our society is no longer organized primarily on the basis of kinship, there are still instances where the bond between relatives dominates the new kinds of social organization. The president of a corporation has been known to hire his nephew as Sales Manager. The feudal system of estates has vanished, but some executives and political figures still maintain a feudal network of personal assistants who are dependent on the leader's success. Many commentators have found similarities between the system of racial segregation in this country and the caste system of India. Social classes today are far weaker and less dominant than they were when Europe was developing urban and industrial societies, but they still play an important role in our lives, as we shall see in chapter 7.

The *ethnic group* is the subject of chapter 8. Sometimes it may exist more as a social category (persons who merely share certain characteristics), such as Americans of English descent, but it can also exist as a strong multi-bonded group combining a language, religion, and broad cultural heritage — as in the case of many Chinese and Japanese in this country. It might be said that any society, with its distinctive cultural heritage, constitutes an ethnic group. But we usually refer to a grouping as an ethnic group when it exists as a minority group in a society having a different cultural tradition.

Nation-state

The most powerful and dominant multi-bonded group in modern societies is the nation-state—a group which combines a powerful central state government with a common territory, usually a common language, and a strong sense of national identity. Most modern societies which we call "countries" are nation-states, but we should not assume that this is the only form of society. Societies in the past have been dominated by the family, by clans and tribes, by religious groups, and by caste, class, and social estate. The rise of nationalism and the modern nation-state will be discussed in chapter 15.

COMMUNITY AND SOCIETY

The terms community and society are among the most ambiguous in sociology. Sometimes, they are used interchangeably to refer simply to a group of people living together who share a common culture; often community refers to a small agglomeration of people, society to a larger one. It seems best to keep them as distinct concepts, but to bear in mind that neither refers to the specific kind of multibonded group we have been discussing. Rather, they should be thought of as very general concepts which loosely describe a population cluster or aggregation. Both consist of innumerable social relationships and unorganized, partly organized, and fully organized groups, both unibonded and multibonded; they represent the highest, most general level of social structure.

When the population cluster is relatively small, focused on individual residences and places of work, and based on daily patterns of interaction (such as daily trips to work, shopping, and school), the cluster may be called a *community*. Examples of communities are villages, towns, cities, suburbs, and metropolitan areas. The basic unit of the community is the family, and the community is the social setting for most everyday economic, political, recreational, religious, educational, and similar activities revolving around the family and residence unit.

In many historical societies, such as Greek city-states, or even in primitive tribes today, community and society were one and the same. In these settings there is no larger social entity above the local population cluster. Today, however, advanced technologies of communication and transportation have increased man's range, and the local community is usually but a small and by no means self-sufficient part of a larger population cluster known as a society. We shall discuss communities in detail in chapter 14.

Societies are the most inclusive, complex, and dominant type of social grouping. The word "society" used in this way should be distinguished from the word used in the very general sense to refer merely to the basic fact of human association, as in the phrase "the society of man"; it should also not be confused with the use of the word as in "high society"—the social life of wealthy, fashionable, or prominent persons. The major emphasis of sociological definitions, in distinguishing society from other groups, is on the notion of self-sufficiency. The society is that group, out of all the groups in existence at a particular time and place, which has the highest degree of self-sufficiency. Thus a person can live his entire life within a society without being dependent upon any other group to meet his basic needs. This is not true of a family, or a special purpose organization, or a weakened local community such as a residential suburb. It is also not completely true of the society called the United States, which, like all other modern nations, is becoming increasingly intertwined and interdependent with the rest of the world. Like local communities before them, independent societies are losing their self-sufficiency to a world network of interdependent societies.

Societies have been dominated by various multibonded groups throughout history, particularly the family, clan, or tribe, and presently the national political state. All types of societies, however, are distinctive in the following ways:[18]

1. Almost all social relationships occur within the boundaries of the society; those that do not—for example, relationships with foreign societies, are subject to strict control (citizenship, visas, passports, and immigration quotas).

2. The society establishes the social procedures and mechanisms by which all resources, economic and otherwise, are obtained and all needs are satisfied.

3. The final power and authority over the making of decisions, and the resolution of conflict, rests with society.

4. The society is usually the supreme organization to which its members give loyalty and which they are prepared to defend.

5. All the society's members share a common and unique culture and usually a common language.

18. Adapted from Marvin E. Olsen, *The Process of Social Organization* (New York: Holt, Rinehart & Winston, 1968), p. 96.

TOPIC

4 TYPES OF SOCIETIES

An important area of modern sociology is the study of large-scale social systems, or macrosociology. In order to make the comparative study of societies easier, macrosociologists have tried to construct methods of typing or categorizing societies. The interest in classifying societies is not a new or modern one; historians and philosophers were inventing classification schemes centuries before sociology was even a recognized area of study. The classical sociologists of the late nineteenth and early twentieth centuries invested a great deal of effort in developing master social types; these were often combined with a theory of social change, explaining how social life changed from one type to another.

Early classification systems were often flawed because they included strong value judgments of the society being classified. An example can be seen in the classification scheme suggested by the anthropologist Lewis Henry Morgan in the 1870s.[19] He divided all societies into three groups—savage, barbarian, and civilized. Essentially, "civilized" meant like modern Western society. Auguste Comte, the Frenchman who is often called the father of sociology, advanced a different scheme, based on the assumption that all societies passed through certain distinct stages of belief or ideology, evolving from the lower to the higher stages.[20] He distinguished the theological stage, from the dawn of civilization until about A.D. 1300, which was marked by an essentially religious orientation; the metaphysical stage, from A.D. 1300 to A.D. 1800,

19. Lewis Henry Morgan, *Ancient Society*, ed. L. A. White (1877; Cambridge, Mass.: Harvard University Press, Belknap, 1964).

20. Auguste Comte, *System of Positive Polity* (London: Longmans, Green & Co., 1877).

Hunting and gathering societies often have highly specialized economies based on one particular type of subsistence activity such as fishing or herding. In such societies there is relatively little occupational specialization: all men pursue the same activity. These societies are always small and organized mainly in terms of kinship. *(Summer Institute of Linguistics, Foto Jesco)*

which brought a shift to a more rational orientation to life; and the last stage, the positivistic or scientific stage, marked by a commitment to the pursuit of scientific knowledge.

All such classification schemes have obvious weaknesses, but they are valuable because they give us a viewpoint, a perspective, from which to consider the overall workings of a society. Here we will look at two classification schemes which view societies from very different perspectives. They are (1) classi-

fication according to the basic mode of subsistence, or the way basic necessities are provided, and (2) classification according to the basic patterns of social organization.

BASIC MODE OF SUBSISTENCE

The most important and basic of man's activities is providing for himself the necessities of food, clothing, and shelter. Several classification schemes have been developed based on the way that societies are organized to provide these necessities. The most thorough and detailed of these is the classification suggested recently by Gerhard Lenski which establishes eleven major types or subtypes of societies.[21] In Lenski's scheme, the oldest and simplest type is the *hunting and gathering society*. Such a society is characterized by a small and sparse population, a nomadic way of life, a very primitive technology, great emphasis on the ties of kinship, and a lack of occupational, economic, or institutional specialization. Isolated examples of this type of society still exist in the twentieth century, such as the Bushmen in the Kalahari desert of Africa and some Eskimo groups in North America, but anthropologists and sociologists predict they will be changed or destroyed by increasing contact with other, more technologically advanced societies.

With the discovery that plants such as wheat, rice, and other grasses could be cultivated and grown from seeds, the *horticultural society* was born. It probably originated near a fertile river valley in the Middle East about 9,000 years ago. The characteristics of a horticultural society are the cultivation of cereal grains for food, with hunting and gathering serving as supplementary means of obtaining food; the production of a variety of tools and household artifacts such as pots and dishes; the establishment of settled communities, sometimes numbering as many as 1,000 inhabitants; the growth of a small measure of trade in such items as salt, volcanic glass, and shells; and the creation of economic surpluses resulting in wealth for some members of the society.

Around 3000 B.C., the invention of the plow led to the *agrarian society*. This tool solved many of the problems of crop cultivation, such as the control of weeds and the maintenance of soil fertility. The margin of efficiency it provided created even greater crop surpluses

and eliminated the need for periodic moves to new fields. These factors led to certain social changes, such as the stratification of people into social estates based on landholding and the establishment of a small bureaucracy to control the expanding economy. The money economy was created, and important technological discoveries were made, such as gunpowder, clocks, windmills, and most important, the smelting of iron.

Lenski notes several other more specialized types of preindustrial societies, such as the fishing society, the herding society, and the maritime society, which specialized in international trade. All these preindustrial societies share many important organizational and cultural characteristics. A great change was introduced with the rise of the *industrial society*, which featured the growth of large and densely populated cities, the mechanization of nearly all forms of work, the establishment of bureaucratic patterns of social organization, the differentiation of social institutions, and the replacement of kinship ties with more impersonal relationships.

BASIC PATTERNS OF SOCIAL ORGANIZATION

Perhaps the most common classification of societies is that which divides them into two groups based on their patterns of social organization. In modern American sociology, these types are often called *communal* and *associational*.[22] However, this basic two-type distinction is a very old one, and the types have been given many other names. Confucius divided societies into two types, the "great similarity" and the "small tranquillity." Another very famous two-part typology is that of the classic German social theorist

21. Gerhard Lenski, *Human Societies* (New York: McGraw-Hill, 1970), chap. 6, pp. 118–142.

22. Ely Chinoy, *Sociological Perspective* (New York: Random House, 1968), p. 81.

23. Ferdinand Tönnies, *Community and Society* [*Gemeinschaft und Gesellschaft*], trans. and ed. C. P. Loomis (1887; English trans., New York: Harper & Row, Harper Torchbooks, 1963).

Ferdinand Tönnies (1855–1936), a German sociologist, studied basic patterns of social organization. From extensive research into the organization of many primitive and modern societies, he developed models for two major patterns of social organization: Gemeinschaft, characterized by close personal relations of the kind found in kinship or friendship groups; and Gesellschaft, characterized by commercialism and social interaction based on self-interest. These two models, which have greatly helped sociologists to analyze important differences between traditional and modern societies, were outlined and explained in Tönnies' book *Community and Society* (1887).

Ferdinand Tönnies.[23] He called one type Gemeinschaft (commune) and the other Gesellschaft (association). Emile Durkheim spoke of the mechanical and the organic society;[24] Robert Redfield called them folk and urban societies.[25] Each of these pairs refers to roughly the same set of social and cultural distinctions between the communal and associational types of society.

24.   Emile Durkheim, *The Division of Labor in Society,* trans. George Simpson (New York: Free Press, 1947).

25.   Robert Redfield, *The Folk Culture of Yucatan* (Chicago: University of Chicago Press, 1941).

A communal society is characterized by a number of factors.

1. There is a minimal amount of division of labor and specialization of roles. For example, there may be a distinction between the roles of males and females, old and young. But all the young males have approximately the same social role.
2. The family is the most important unit in the society, and is typically the basis of all social organization. There may be larger kinship groups, such as clans or tribes, but there is usually no other type of group membership.
3. Most social relationships are highly personal and tend to be long-lasting. Most daily transactions are heavily charged with emotional significance for the participants.
4. Behavior is for the most part regulated by custom and tradition. As a character in a story about life in a small Russian village puts it, "Every man knows what he expects of his neighbors, and what God expects from him."[26]

By simply reversing many of these characteristics, one arrives at a description of the associational society. In this kind of society, life loses much of its unity and cohesion. Division of labor by both men and social institutions leads to highly differentiated roles. Because of the limitations of these roles, many relationships are fragmented and most are impersonalized. The family group loses its importance because of the competition of all the other groups in society — occupational groups, religious groups, political groups, and clubs. Social relationships are less personal and also less emotional. Behavior is regulated by law rather than custom. Change is rapid.

Most sociologists agree that the historical trend since the Middle Ages has been away from the communal society and toward the associational society. Some hold that soci-

26.   Maurice Samuel, *The World of Sholom Aleichem* (New York: Alfred A. Knopf, 1943), p. 33.

ology arose because of the problems which this major shift created; scholars who noted the many new problems of the "modern age" felt the need for a more disciplined and scien-tific way of examining these problems and their causes.[27]

27. See Robert A. Nisbet, *The Sociological Tradition* (New York: Basic Books, 1966).

SUMMARY

For the most part, individuals and groups relate to each other in orderly and patterned ways that can be described and predicted. It is this *social structure* that establishes some degree of stability and continuity in our lives and enables us to handle our daily activities with efficiency, even while it imposes certain constraints on our behavior. Sociologists have distinguished various levels of social structure or patterning: the social relationship between two persons, the organization or group, and the community or society. Most sociologists believe that the group level has a "social reality" apart from its individual members. In studying and comparing social groupings they focus on the *social system,* group aspects that are distinct from the particular members.

All social structure is created through *social interaction,* ranging from rigid and restrictive impersonal patterns to spontaneous patterns which involve intimate forms of interaction. When interaction continues long enough for a relatively stable set of social expectations to develop, it is called a *social relationship.* Such relationships are *instrumental* if they are used as means to some other end. *Expressive relationships,* in contrast, are valued for their own sake and have no goal beyond the pleasure each person takes in the relationship. Most relationships combine both expressive and instrumental elements.

Sociologists have distinguished five types of social interaction that are basic to mankind: (1) *Cooperation* describes relationships in which people or groups act together to promote certain shared goals. Spontaneous cooperation or mutual aid may be repeated and become traditional cooperation. In mod-ern societies people often cooperate on a contractual basis, agreeing to cooperate in certain explicitly defined ways. (2) *Conflict* arises from competition for scarce resources and may lead to wars, feuds, litigation, or a clash of impersonal ideals. By uniting people on each opposing side, conflict can serve as an integrating force. It may also lead to needed social change. (3) *Competition* may be thought of as cooperative form of conflict in which individuals or groups focus on achieving a particular goal, rather than on defeating their competitors. (4) *Coercion* occurs when one person or group forces its will on another. (5) *Exchange* involves reciprocal returns or rewards, whether based on money or goods or on more subjective emotional rewards.

In every form of organized social interaction, individuals are expected to behave in particular ways: they are assigned a social *role* that corresponds to their specific position or social *status.* Role expectations may be highly detailed or they may leave considerable room for individual improvisation. Whether or not an individual's actual *role performance* corresponds to the ideal or *prescribed role* depends on his understanding of the expectations and on his ability or willingness to fulfill these requirements. In the course of a day a person will play many different roles and must balance the demands of his various roles. Such assignments not only regulate our behavior, but also enable us to predict the actions of others and, therefore, to guide our own actions in an orderly way. However, an individual may have difficulty in meeting social expectations if forced to play conflicting or *incompatible roles.* He may also be hampered by *role strain* if his role requires inconsistent behavior.

Social interaction usually takes place in aggregates or groupings that vary in the extent to which they are organized. These range from almost wholly unorganized social categories, to relatively unorganized recurring aggregates such as pedestrians or bus riders, to fluid collectives such as audiences, to slightly more structured groupings such as social movements, to highly organized groups with consistent and clearly defined goals and precisely defined behavioral expectations. Groups also vary in terms of their size, complexity, methods of obtaining members, and the scope of interests, values, and goals. *Unibonded* organizations, characterized by a single major set of values and goals, may be distinguished from *multibonded* or comprehensive groups with more than one major set of goals and functions. Multibonded groups include the family, both nuclear and extended; the clan, a closed group of kin living in one geographical area; the tribe, a group of clans; and social classes, feudal estates, and castes— all groups in which members share similar degrees of power, wealth, and prestige. Castes, which ascribe an individual's occupation and social status rather rigidly, are multibonded in that they are a strongly organized combination of religious, racial, occupational, territorial, and other elements. Feudal estates tend to be much less rigid and more heterogeneous than castes; social classes, organized around economic and occupational similarities, tend to be the most fluid of all. The most powerful and dominant multibonded group in modern societies is the nation-state—a group which combines a powerful central state government with a common territory, usually common language, and a strong sense of national identity.

At the highest and most general level of social structure, we find communities and societies, consisting of innumerable social relationships and distinct types of social groups. A *community* refers to a relatively small population cluster, focused on individual residences and places of work, and based on daily patterns of interaction. *Societies* are the most inclusive, complex, and dominant type of social grouping. While they may be variously dominated by distinct multibonded groups such as the family, clan, tribe, or nation-state, all societies are delineated by geographical boundaries; all have established procedures for allocation of social resources; all have the final power and authority over making decisions and resolving conflicts; they are usually the supreme organization that commands loyalty; and they are distinguished by a unique culture that is shared by all members.

Modern macrosociologists classify societies from two different perspectives: in terms of basic mode of subsistence, and in terms of basic patterns of social organization. In terms of subsistence patterns, societies range from small, nomadic *hunters and gatherers,* to *horticultural societies* that supplement their economies with cultivation of cereal grains, to sedentary and more densely populated *agrarian societies,* to *industrial* societies characterized by mechanization, bureaucratic patterns of social organization, institutional differentiation, and impersonal relationships. In terms of organizational patterns, societies may be distinguished as *communal* or *associational.* In communal societies there is minimal division of labor and specialization, relationships are based on kinship groups and are highly personal and durable, and behavior is regulated by tradition. Associational societies, characterized by the opposite features, have become the dominant form in the modern world.

GLOSSARY

Associational society   A society characterized by a division of labor, differentiated roles, imper-sonal relationships, little emphasis on family, and behavior regulated by laws. (page 71)

Caste   A closed social grouping based on heredity that determines its members' social relationships, prestige, and place of residence; was found principally in India. (page 66)

Clan   A large kinship group whose members inhabit one geographical area and believe they are descended from a common ancestor. (page 65)

Coercion   The relationship in which one person or group forces its will on another. (page 52)

Communal society   A society characterized by minimum division of labor, minimum specialization of roles, personal relationships, emphasis on family, and behavior regulated by custom. (page 71)

Community   1. A relatively small cluster of people centered around individual residences and places of work and based on daily patterns of interaction. 2. Any group of people who share common interests or traditions and who have a strong feeling of solidarity (or "sense of community"). (page 68)

Competition   The process of social interaction in which individuals or groups struggle with one another to attain the same goal; their primary concern is directed toward the object or goal which is being sought rather than toward each other. (page 52)

Conflict   The process of social interaction in which two or more persons struggle with one another for some commonly prized object or value. (page 51)

Cooperation   The relationship in which people or groups engage in joint action in order to promote common interests or shared goals. (page 50)

Ethnic group   Any group which is socially distinguished from other groups; usually a minority group in a large society. (page 67)

Exchange   A relationship in which one person acts in a certain way toward another in order to receive a reward or return. (page 53)

Expressive relationship   A social relationship which is valued for its own sake. (page 50)

Extended family   A family unit that consists of a nuclear family plus one or more relatives living together. (page 64)

Family group   The basic kinship unit; a group of people related to each other by blood, marriage, or adoption. (page 63)

Instrumental relationship   A social relationship which is merely a means to some other end. (page 50)

Macrosociology   The study of large-scale social systems and relations between these systems. (page 44)

Microsociology   The study of small-scale social systems and social relationships. (page 44)

Monogamy   Marriage in which there is only one mate at the same time. (page 65)

Multibonded group   A group organized around more than one major set of values and goals. (page 63)

Nation-state   A powerful multibonded group which combines a strong central government with a common territory, usually a common language, and a strong feeling of group identity. (page 68)

Nuclear family   A unit of family organization consisting of a couple and their children. (page 63)

Polyandry   A form of polygamy in which a wife has more than one husband at the same time. (page 65)

Polygamy   Marriage which involves more than one husband or one wife at the same time. (page 65)

Polygyny   Form of polygamy in which a husband has more than one wife at the same time. (page 65)

Role   1. A set of expectations and behaviors associated with a specific position in a social system (social role). 2. The way an individual personality tends to react to a social situation (individual role). (page 53)

Role, prescribed   A role as defined by cultural standards; the set of behaviors expected for all occupants of a status or position; an ideal role. (page 55)

Role conflict   Incompatibility between two or more roles that an individual performs in a given situation; also called role incompatibility. (page 55)

Role performance   A role as it is actually played by the occupant of a social position. (page 55)

Role set   A complex set of roles associated with a single status or position. (page 55)

Role strain   A feeling of conflict or stress caused by inconsistent demands of a single role; also called role inconsistency. (page 56)

Social categories   An aggregate of people who are not organized into a social group but who share certain socially important characteristics. (page 60)

Social class   A grouping of persons with similar status levels, especially in terms of money possessed or earned. (page 67)

Social estate   (or **social order**)   A social grouping whose members share a common social rank; less rigid and closed than a caste but more closed than a class. Usually associated with medieval European feudal society. (page 66)

Social interaction   The basic social process involving communication through language and gestures. Through the exchange of meanings individuals affect each other's behavior and mental states. (page 48)

Social organizations   Same as social structure.

Social relationship   A reciprocal (two-way) pattern of interaction between two or more persons that continues over a period of time so that a relatively stable set of social expectations develops. (page 50)

Social structure   The orderly or patterned way that people and groups relate to one another. (page 73)

Social system   A set of persons or groups who are interacting, are dependent on one another, and are somewhat integrated. The set is conceived of as a social unit distinct from the particular individuals who compose it. (page 44)

Society   1. The type of social grouping that includes the most functions and is most complex and dominant. It has the highest degree of self-sufficiency of all social systems.

2. A complex web of social relationships. (page 68)

Status   A position in a social system. (page 53)

Tribe   A social grouping which consists of two or more clans or other kinship groupings inhabiting a common territory and which has a form of government somewhat differentiated from the family system. (page 66)

Unibonded group   A group organized around a single major set of values and goals. (page 63)

SUGGESTED READINGS AND RELATED RESOURCES

I READINGS IN SOCIOLOGY

Biddle, Bruce J., and Edwin J. Thomas, eds. *Role Theory: Concepts and Research*. New York: John Wiley, 1966. This collection of fifty-one essays covers current thinking and research on role theory by sociologists and members of the other behavioral sciences.

Blau, Peter. *Exchange and Power in Social Life*. New York: John Wiley, 1964. Blau analyzes the interaction between political and economic institutions. His discussion of impersonal mechanisms of authority and informal communication patterns are of particular interest.

Bredemeier, Harry C., and Richard M. Stephenson. *The Analysis of Social Systems*. New York: Holt, Rinehart & Winston, 1962. Society as a social system is the focus of this book. It is an especially good example of the application of functionalism to the study of social structure.

Coser, Lewis. *The Functions of Social Conflict*. New York: Free Press, 1964. A book that was instrumental in reviving the concept of social conflict.

Demereth, N. J., and R. A. Peterson. *System, Change, and Conflict: A Reader in Contemporary Sociological Theory and the Debate Over Functionalism*. New York: Free Press, 1967. Some of America's foremost sociologists have contributed to this series of essays dealing with the analysis of social structure.

Durkheim, Emile. *The Division of Labor in Society*. Translated by George Simpson. New York: Free Press, 1964, especially chapters 2 and 3. This is a classic discussion of the changes in social structure brought about by increasing population and social density. It contains Durkheim's theory of the two types of society, which he called mechanical and organic.

————. *Suicide*. Translated by J. A. Spaulding and George Simpson. New York: Free Press, 1968. This study of the social factors that contribute to the incidence of suicide was one of the first sociological works to use statistics and contains the classic definition of "anomie."

Garfinkel, Harold. *Studies in Ethnomethodology*. Englewood Cliffs, N. J.: Prentice-Hall, 1967. This book is built around a case study of a person who underwent a sex-change operation; it discusses the ways in which she adapted to the expectations of those around her.

Greer, Scott A. *Social Organization.* New York: Random House, 1955. In this concise book, Greer discusses and analyzes the relationships among individuals in groups and societies.

Homans, George C. *Social Behavior: Its Elementary Forms.* Harper, 1961. The examination of interpersonal behavior, especially in small groups, is the subject of this book. It is a pioneering theoretical work.

Lipset, Seymour Martin. *The First New Nation.* New York: Basic Books, 1963. Lipset focuses on American social patterns; he describes them and traces their development through history.

Murdock, George Peter. *Social Structure.* New York: Macmillan, 1949. Murdock, a leading anthropologist, reported in this book his study of some 238 family and kinship systems. Of interest is the great variety of patterns family structures may take and the ways in which each type relates to other institutions.

Nisbet, Robert. *The Social Bond.* New York: Alfred A. Knopf, 1970. This recent work focuses on the nature of cohesion in society, or the social bond. Nisbet covers many specialized fields of sociology by explaining the elements of the social bond: interaction, groupings, authority, roles, status, norms, and social deviance.

Park, Robert E., and Ernest W. Burgess. *Introduction to the Science of Sociology.* Chicago: University of Chicago Press, 1924. The first American introductory sociology textbook, this work was perhaps the most influential of its kind in American sociology. It has just been reissued.

Parsons, Talcott. *The Social System.* New York: Free Press, 1964. Parsons, one of the most influential contemporary sociologists, presents in this work a theoretical and conceptual framework for the analysis of society as a social system.

Tönnies, Ferdinand. *Community and Society.* Translated by Charles A. Loomis. East Lansing, Mich.: Michigan State University Press, 1957. Originally published as *Gemeinschaft und Gesellschaft,* this work is one of the classic comparisons of two types of social structure: that which is dominated by personal or traditional relationships and that which is dominated by contractual relationships.

Weber, Max. *The Theory of Social and Economic Organization.* Translated by A. M. Henderson and Talcott Parsons. New York: Free Press, 1957. In this classic book, Weber presents his theory on how the meanings individuals give to objects, words, and actions affect their social behavior.

Williams, Robin M., Jr. *American Society: A Sociological Interpretation.* 2nd ed. New York: Alfred A. Knopf, 1960. Williams examines the structures and interrelationships of institutions in the United States. The book is especially useful in explaining American value patterns and sources of social cohesion.

Articles and Papers

Adler, Franz. "Toward a 'Simple' Mathematical Model of Society." *Sociological Inquiry* **37,** 2 (Spring 1967):211–216.

Bales, Robert F. "Task Roles and Social Roles in Problem-Solving Groups." In *Readings in Social Psychology,* Third Edition, edited by E. E. Maccoby, T. M. Newcomb, and E. L. Hartley, pp. 437–447. New York: Holt, Rinehart & Winston, 1958.

Cahnman, W. J., and A. Boskoff, eds. *Sociology and History: Theory and Research.* New York: Free Press, 1964.

Goode, William J. "A Theory of Role Strain." *American Sociological Review* **25** (August 1960): 483–496.

Homans, George C. "Social Behavior as Exchange." *American Journal of Sociology,* 1958, pp. 597–606.

Mack, Raymond W. "The Components of Social Conflict." *Social Problems* **12** (Spring 1965): 388–397.

Merton, R. K. "The Role-Set: Problems in Sociological Theory." *The British Journal of Sociology* **2** (June 1957):106–120.

Redfield, Robert, "The Folk Society." *American Journal of Sociology* **52** (1947):293–308.

Schneider, Louis. "Dialectia in Sociology," *American Sociological Review* **36** (1971).

Scott, Marvin. "On the Principle of Legitimacy for Sociological Activity." Essays in Sociological Explanation: On Neil J. Smelser. *Sociological Inquiry* **39,** 2 (Spring 1969):201–218.

Warriner, Charles K. "Groups Are Real." *American Sociological Review* **21** (October 1956): 549–554.

Whyte, William F. "The Social Structure of the Restaurant." *American Journal of Sociology* **54** (1949):302–310.

II RELATED RESOURCES

Nonfiction

Mauss, Marcel. *The Gift: Forms and Functions of Exchange in Archaic Societies*. New York: Norton, 1967. Mauss, a disciple of Durkheim, analyzes the functions of mass exchange between and within various societies.

Roth, Julius A. *Timetables*. Indianapolis: Bobbs-Merrill, 1963. Roth shows some of the ways in which people attempt to structure their careers within institutions. He finds that the relationships of individuals to institutions are often viewed in terms of the passage of time.

Fiction

Behan, Brendan. *Borstal Boy*. New York: Avon Books, 1961. An entertaining look at the patterning of interpersonal relationships in the British juvenile prison system by a well-known Irish writer who was once an inmate.

Kerouac, Jack. *On the Road*. New York: Viking, 1959. One of the fathers of the "beat generation" relates the story of a young man who is struggling to find and establish a role for himself.

Michener, James A. *Hawaii*. New York: Random House, 1959. A fictionalized history of the various ethnic groups of Hawaii. Contains many examples of the part played by the family in social organization.

Scott, Sir Walter. *Rob Roy*. Chicago: Belford, Clarke & Co., 1829. An account of the Scottish clan McGregor when it was ordered by the British government to disband. The novel contains good examples of conflict, cooperation, and coercion.

Solzhenitsyn, Aleksandr. *Cancer Ward*. Translated by Nicholas Bethell and David Burg. New York: Bantam Books, 1969. The characters in this story are cast in new and unfamiliar roles to which they must adjust when they become hospital patients. At the same time they are trying to adjust to a new social order after the Russian revolution.

3 Culture and Society

For the sociologist, the term "culture" has a meaning
very different from the one it generally conveys.
When someone refers to culture in ordinary conversation, the typical meaning is one particular kind of
life style, one that includes frequent attendance at
the theater and the opera, listening to classical music
instead of Andy Williams, and subscribing to The
Saturday Review and The Atlantic Monthly. However, to a sociologist, the word has a wider and more
abstract meaning. The culture of a society is its
beliefs, its knowledge, its language, its moral
principles, its various technical skills—in short,
its total "design for living." It is also the products,
the artifacts, which are produced in that society
by the application of skills and knowledge. We might
call culture man's social inheritance, as distinct
from his purely biological inheritance.

1 THE NATURE OF CULTURE

It is important to distinguish between the related concepts of culture and society. In some usages of the term "culture," there is no distinction—culture may be used broadly to mean all learned habits, the total way of life of a social group, or a group's social heritage; in this sense, culture includes society, the web of man's social relationships. This is the meaning of culture to most anthropologists; we will use it in this chapter especially when discussing anthropological viewpoints. In customary sociological usage, however, *culture* refers specifically to the values and ideas which give meaning to human social interaction but can be considered somewhat apart from such interaction. *Society,* on the other hand, is used to refer to human social interaction somewhat apart from underlying values and ideas. Thus to study a group's culture means to focus primarily on the underlying meaning and values of its relationships—some of which may be expressed by the material possessions or artifacts of the group. To study the society of a group is to look primarily at the patterns of organization and interaction built upon that cultural background. When, for example, a sociologist studies a business corporation in America, he begins with certain assumptions about the culture of which the group is a part. He assumes that it is based on the values of efficiency, practicality, material progress, equality, and scientific inquiry. This is the cultural background of the part of society he is studying. To a sociologist who is making a comparable study of ancient and modern cultures, those very values and attitudes would be the focus of his work,

for they serve to distinguish the culture of modern America from other cultures. In another culture the main underlying values might be loyalty, family tradition, or pleasing the gods.

Thus culture and society are actually two aspects of social life. They are different ways of looking at the same thing. Although the two concepts can never be wholly separated, and we often use the term *sociocultural* to express that fact, much work in the social sciences is based on the idea that they can be studied as somewhat separate aspects of human experience. *Culture* may be formally defined as the system of shared values and meanings of a group or society, including the embodiment of those values and meanings in material artifacts.

To the sociologist's ear, the term "uncultured," so often used by us to refer to people or groups of people who are unlike the members of our Western industrial society, is nonsensical. Every person is cultured because everyone must come into some contact with other humans, if only to survive, and he learns from them a culture. Even a hermit, though he may live under conditions of complete isolation, was once a part of a social network, and many of his attitudes (including, probably, his desire to be a hermit) are the results of the culture he learned while interacting with others.

The basic unit of culture is sometimes called a *culture trait*.[1] Obviously, there are

1. This term is used especially by anthropologists. See Edward Adamson Hoebel, *Anthropology,* 4th ed. (New York: McGraw-Hill, 1949), p. 499, and Ralph L. Beals and Harry Hoijer, *An Introduction to Anthropology,* 2d ed. (New York: Macmillan, 1965).

countless varieties of such learned cultural traits. Take one simple action like eating breakfast in the morning, and consider how many ways that alone can be done. You can eat the minute you wake up, or only after you have dressed and accomplished some household chores. You can eat alone, or with your family, or with a group of other people of your same sex or age, or with the whole community. You can eat rapidly, or slowly, in silence, or to the accompaniment of much conversation. You can sit at a table, or lie in bed, or squat on the ground, or carry your food with you as you walk to work. For this one action alone, we can imagine perhaps several hundred different ways of doing it. Then add in the other possible variations: the foods eaten, the ways the foods are prepared and served. Already we have more different possibilities concerning how to eat breakfast than we could count.

In spite of the almost innumerable possibilities, we find patterns which appear with great frequency, greatly narrowing the field of choice. It is very rare for breakfast to be eaten in a big crowd; people usually eat alone or in small family or kinship groups. It is rare for people to display a high degree of sociability at breakfast; long conver-

Behavioral traits may be classified as being due either to inherited or to learned causes. The imaginary case of Ergo Rauschlump illustrates this division.

HABITUAL BEHAVIOR

Inherited	Learned
Individual	
Ergo Rauschlump has three eyes	He has learned that wearing a black patch over one, a monocle in another and mascara on the third gets him invited to a lot of parties and a 4F draft status
Group	
Ergo belongs to a race which is characterized by an unusual metabolism which makes him more comfortable standing on his head; he does so frequently, which makes him very popular with his instructors	Fortunately, there are several other people in Springhope, Idaho (where he lives) with the same sort of metabolism; they have formed a yoga club
Universal	
Ergo is also human and, as such, has emotions which are mirrored on his face	Like everyone he laughs, smiles, frowns, grimaces, and scowls; he has learned, however, that wherever he goes, sharing is considered bad manners

sations are typically reserved for the evening meal. It is rare for breakfast to be a banquet of many courses; usually in the morning people resist being stuffed with rich food. If, on some morning, we see these usual habits being broken and people eating breakfast in a large group, talking and laughing, consuming rich and elaborately prepared foods, it is a clear sign that something extraordinary is happening. Human activities, then, are organized around a limited number of cultural patterns, the vast majority of which are known and documented.

An important question that scientists are still trying to answer is just how much of our behavior is learned and how much is inherited. What is the dividing line between culture and biology? One way to answer that question is to study and compare as many cultures as possible, and then to try to pinpoint certain traits that seem to appear in all cultures. Yet such universality still does not necessarily mean that the trait is biologically inherited. For example, all humans use fire and have a word for mother, but it is unlikely that either one of these is inherited—a baby is not born knowing what to call his mother; he has to be taught that. The adjacent table humorously shows how sociologists classify some habits as either learned or inherited, at several different levels of social complexity.

SYMBOLS IN CULTURE

Culture depends for its existence on man's ability to create and manipulate symbols. A *symbol* may be defined as a thing that stands for or suggests something else by reason of association.[2] All words and numbers are symbols; so are drawings, photographs, and any other attempt at representation. They are necessary for ease and convenience of communication, a sort of shorthand. When you want to let your friend know about the color of your new car, you simply tell him it is candy-apple red, instead of having to take him out to the garage to look at it for himself. Because we use symbols, we can transmit complex information rapidly. Because of symbols, we can both create and learn our culture.

Our use of symbols affects the way in which we look at the thing symbolized, which means that the symbols of a culture also serve to shape that culture. In studying this phenomenon sociologists have drawn on the work of semanticists,[3] scholars who have written about confusions that can arise, both intellectually and socially, when symbols are not understood as something separate from the things which they symbolize. The fact is that a symbol not only represents something but is also a way of predefining that reality, or of conveying a certain attitude toward the reality. A certain symbol may become so familiar to us that we no longer even notice it, or we distort the reality for which it stands.

For example, take the word "pig." On the simplest symbolic level, one step away from the concrete reality, pig stands for a domestic animal that walks on four feet, has a short curly tail, and makes a noise that we reproduce as "oink." As we go on to other levels of symbolization, other ideas are added to the picture of the pig. When you think of a pig, you may think of expressions like "dirty as a pigsty," "they live like pigs," "he made a big pig of himself"—all remarks that carry a weight of disapproval. Next you may think of Pigpen in the "Peanuts" comics, a boy that the older children deride for his unattractive scruffiness; or you may think of the stupid pig-

2. See Lyman Bryson et al., eds., *Symbols and Values: An Initial Study,* Thirteenth Symposium of the Conference on Science, Philosophy and Religion (New York: Cooper Square Publishers, 1964).

3. See Alfred Korzybski, *Science and Sanity: An Introduction to Non-Aristotelian Systems and General Semantics,* 4th ed. (Lakeville, Conn.: Institute of General Semantics, 1958); Stuart Chase, *Tyranny of Words* (New York: Harcourt Brace Jovanovich, 1938); and S. I. Hayakawa, in consultation with Leo Hamalian and Geoffrey Wagner, *Language in Thought and Action,* 2d ed. (New York: Harcourt Brace Jovanovich, 1964).

America, Land of Opportunity, where the world's tired, hungry, and poor could start afresh, seems to be choking on her own noxious air. By combining two incongruous but immediately intelligible symbols, the artist has dramatically conveyed a disturbing idea: the defilement of our land. We are jolted, by a simple picture, into an awareness of a new and not altogether comfortable national self-image. *(Photo by H. Armstrong Roberts)*

boy in *Ivanhoe*. Depending on your political orientation, pig may call to mind a picture of long-haired unwashed anarchists, or brutal policemen. All these ideas cluster around the single word "pig," and to some degree they are also symbolized by that word. Now consider what this additional symbolism does to one's view of the real thing, the pig itself. You go out for a ride in the country, and someone in the car says, "Oh look, there's a pig." You look at it, and what you see is a dirty and repulsive animal. You don't take the time to examine it as it really is; you judge the reality by the meaning that the symbol "pig," those three letters on a page, has for you.

SYMBOLS IN LANGUAGE

"Pig"

The dictionary will tell you that "pig" means the familiar animal in the upper left-hand corner. But the word may also symbolize various other images and ideas, depending on the context in which it is used.

Of course, in the case of the pig, the kind of attitude that we have toward it because of symbolization is not especially important, for pigs are not crucial to our culture. But what if we apply the same kind of analysis to the word "mother," or "truth," or "God," or "America"? Then we see clearly that the kinds of symbols a culture creates serve in their turn to shape the culture in other ways, some of them quite unexpected and often undesired. An example of this can be seen in modern-day Great Britain, where adjustment to current political reality is hampered by such symbolism. Everyone knows that today it is politically and economically impossible for Great Britain to

be the world power it once was, and that any assumption of this role could now cripple the nation. Yet the British have thought of their country in terms of great world power for so many generations — "the sun never sets on the British Empire" — that it is emotionally impossible for some of them to adjust to its loss immediately. Policies which are based on the complete acceptance of a secondary role tend to be unpopular, and political leaders who give up portions of the Empire and imperial rights risk losing power because of their actions, even though the public realizes that greater disaster for England is thus avoided. The symbol of Great Britain as world power may still carry as much weight as the current reality.

The whole question of the connection between language and culture is an area of investigation that is currently being given high priority by scholars and researchers in many different fields—anthropologists, sociologists, semanticists, and psychologists. The new discipline of linguistics focuses intensively on the connection between symbol and cultural meaning. Clyde Kluckhohn, discussing this connection, stated: "Every language is also a special way of looking at the world and interpreting experiences. Concealed in the structure of each different language are a whole set of unconscious assumptions about the world and life in it."[4]

Certain languages are especially constructed to convey certain ideas, which is why translation is always such an arduous task. The language of the Samoans is adapted to convey very precise information about fishing and boating in the Pacific; the language of the Eskimos makes many fine distinctions about the kinds of snow and ice; German is ideally suited for the discussion of philosophical concepts; and English is the language of technology. These differences are partly due to vocabulary; obviously an Eskimo language having nearly twenty separate words for the thing we call "snow" will be a more precise instrument for talking about snow.

This does not mean that language is a cultural prison. We can express ideas for which we have no single symbol. It does mean that the language exerts an influence in a certain direction, and may make it easier or harder to understand a given idea or concept.

Language is the most important of all our symbol systems, but a symbol need not be a word. It can be a sign, such as 卐. Or it can

be a picture. Or it can be a piece of clothing, a hair style, a gesture. In the adjacent abridgment Marshall McLuhan discusses the symbolic meaning that different kinds of clothing have for society, and the same sort of analysis can be applied to almost any medium of communication.

Although anyone can create or expand a symbol, there are people in every complex society who specialize in creating symbols or symbolic representations. They are the artists and intellectuals. The art and central ideas of a society are usually the best and clearest representation of its culture. As well as illustrating culture, art and ideas also influence its development. This is why governments, especially totalitarian ones, are always suspicious of, and seek to maintain control over, the artist and the intellectual. Though they are a small part of the population of any society, their manipulation of symbols can have important cultural significance.

COMPONENTS OF CULTURE

The major components of any culture may be divided, for purposes of study and analysis, into three categories.

(1) Cognitive aspects of culture. This refers to the ways the culture defines what exists, or the reality of the world. *Knowledge* is one of the cognitive components of culture; we use the term to refer to ideas and information which can be demonstrated to have empirical support, that is, objective and factual support. The most highly refined knowledge is that which comes from the physical sciences. As knowledge is less reliable, less capable of empirical demonstration, it shades off into *beliefs*—ideas or theories about the nature of the physical and social world. Beliefs also include ideas about supernatural reality, about God, spirits, afterlife, and similar "otherworldly" phenomena. A special kind of knowledge, which is directed toward practical applications in the physical and social world, is called *technology*. Tech-

4. Clyde Kluckhohn, *Mirror for Man* (1949; reprint ed., Greenwich, Conn.: Fawcett World Library, 1964), p. 124.

nology includes the methods and techniques used to build the Golden Gate Bridge; it also includes the methods the federal government uses to try to control economic problems such as inflation or unemployment.

(2) Normative aspects of culture. The normative system consists of values and specific rules of conduct (norms) with which man guides and regulates his behavior; it is man's ideas of the way things ought to be. The normative aspects of culture will be discussed in topic 2.

Some aspects of culture contain cognitive and normative ideas. This is true, for example, of *ideology*. An ideology is a system of beliefs about the social world which is strongly rooted in a set of values and interests. The leading ideologies of our time — democracy, capitalism, communism, socialism — represent large systems of ideas which are value systems, but systems adjusted to knowledge based on study and experience. Ideologies such as these indirectly dominate much of the human behavior of the modern world.

(3) Material aspects of culture. Machines, tools, books, clothing, and many other such things, make up the *material culture*. When an archeologist digs up the remains of an ancient city, it is the material aspects of the culture that he finds — a broken pot, a necklace carefully stored in a little wooden box, the foundations of a house. From these artifacts, he is able to reconstruct much of the non-material cognitive and normative aspects of the culture.

In a general sense all material artifacts express some symbolic cultural meaning, and the same artifact may have radically different societies. A colored piece of cloth which we know as the American flag is greatly honored and revered by most Americans; in some foreign countries and even within the United States it has been torn up and destroyed. In a remote primitive tribe it might be considered a pretty piece of material to be used for clothing. Our lives are greatly influenced by the material and man-made world, such as the "built-environment" of cities. The realm of material culture is created and can be changed by man, but it is equally useful to think of it as something which precedes each birth in our society and to which we must therefore adjust throughout our lives. In this respect it is the same as nonmaterial culture — man shapes it, but it also shapes man.

Societies vary greatly in terms of how rich their material cultures are in quantity and quality. This variation is sometimes expressed as levels of technological development, which suggest not only the quantity and quality of material artifacts but also the technological know-how required to produce such artifacts. In the last chapter we examined types of societies according to level of technological developments. While we are inclined to evaluate and label societies as ranging from "primitive" to "modern" or "advanced," it is important to point out that such labels do not imply *general* superiority or inferiority. Technological advancement is a great achievement of the human experience, but it does not necessarily lead to the attainment of general human happiness or moral or spiritual well-being.

MARSHALL McLUHAN
Clothing, Our Extended Skin

From *Understanding Media: The Extensions of Man* by Marshall McLuhan. Copyright © 1964 by Marshall McLuhan. Used with permission of McGraw-Hill Book Company.

Introduction

One of the most controversial figures in the social sciences is Marshall McLuhan. When his book Understanding Media: The Extensions of Man *appeared, it was widely read and just as widely debated. In the book he predicted, among other*

*things, that modern Western society would
become again a tribal society, that the
printed word would become outdated and
unused, and that an entire generation
of children brought up in the electronic age
would have a vastly altered consciousness.
McLuhan has both critics and supporters,
but even though not everyone agrees with
his ideas, he has unquestionably influenced
the contemporary discussion of culture.
The following excerpt deals with his interpretation of the cultural symbolism
expressed in clothing.*

Economists have estimated that an unclad
society eats 40 percent more than one in
Western attire. Clothing as an extension of
our skin helps to store and to channel energy,
so that if the Westerner needs less food,
he may also demand more sex. Yet neither
clothing nor sex can be understood as
separate isolated factors, and many sociologists have noted that sex can become a
compensation for crowded living. Privacy,
like individualism, is unknown in tribal
societies, a fact that Westerners need to
keep in mind when estimating the attrac-
tions of our way of life to nonliterate
peoples.

Clothing, as an extension of the skin,
can be seen both as a heat-control mechanism and as a means of defining the self
socially. In these respects, clothing and
housing are near twins, though clothing
is both nearer and elder, for housing
extends the inner heat-control mechanisms
of our organism, while clothing is a more
direct extension of the outer surface of the
body. Today Europeans have begun to dress
for the eye, American-style, just at the
moment when Americans have begun to
abandon their traditional visual style. The
media analyst knows why these opposite
styles suddenly transfer their locations.
The European, since the Second World War,
has begun to stress visual values; his
economy, not coincidentally, now supports
a large amount of uniform consumer goods.

Americans, on the other hand, have begun
to rebel against uniform consumer values
for the first time. In cars, in clothes, in
paperback books, in beards, babies, and
beehive hairdos, the American has declared
for stress on touch, on participation,
involvement, and sculptural values. America,
once the land of an abstractly visual
order, is profoundly "in touch" again
with European traditions of food and life
and art. What was an *avant-garde* program
for the 1920 expatriates is now the teen-
agers' norm.

The Europeans, however, underwent a
sort of consumer revolution at the end of
the eighteenth century. When industrialism
was a novelty, it became fashionable among
the upper classes to abandon rich, courtly
attire in favor of simpler materials. That
was the time when men first donned the
trousers of the common foot soldier
(or *pioneer,* the original French usage),
but it was done at that time as a kind of brash
gesture of social "integration." Up until
then, the feudal system had inclined the upper
classes to dress as they spoke, in a courtly
style quite removed from that of ordinary
people. Dress and speech were accorded
a degree of splendor and richness of texture
that universal literacy and mass production were eventually to eliminate
completely. The sewing machine, for
example, created the long straight
line in clothes, as much as the linotype
flattened the human vocal style.

A recent ad for C*E*I*R Computer
Services pictured a plain cotton dress and
the headline: "Why does Mrs. 'K' dress
that way?" — referring to the wife of
Nikita Khrushchev. Some of the copy of
this very ingenious ad continued: "It is an
icon. To its own underprivileged population and to the uncommitted of the
East and South, it says: 'We are thrif-ty,
simple, hon-est; peace-ful, home-y, go-od.'
To the free nations of the West it says
'We will bury you.' "

This is precisely the message that the

new simple clothing of our forefathers had for the feudal classes at the time of the French Revolution. Clothing was then a nonverbal manifesto of political upset.

Today in America there is a revolutionary attitude expressed as much in our attire as in our patios and small cars. For a decade or more, women's dress and hair styles have abandoned visual for iconic—or sculptural and tactual—stress. Like toreador pants and gaiter stockings, the beehive hairdo is also iconic and sensuously inclusive, rather than abstractly visual. In a word, the American woman for the first time presents herself as a person to be touched and handled, not just to be looked at. While the Russians are groping vaguely toward visual consumer values, North Americans are frolicking amidst newly discovered tactile, sculptural spaces in cars, clothes, and housing. For this reason, it is relatively easy for us now to recognize clothing as an extension of the skin. In the age of the bikini and of skin-diving, we begin to understand "the castle of our skin" as a space and world of its own. Gone are the thrills of striptease. Nudity could be naughty excitement only for a visual culture that had divorced itself from the audile-tactile values of less abstract societies. As late as 1930, four-letter words made visual on the printed page seemed portentous. Words that most people used every hour of the day became as frantic as nudity, when printed. Most "four-letter words" are heavy with tactile-involving stress. For this reason they seem earthy and vigorous to visual man. So it is with nudity. To backward cultures still embedded in the full gamut of sense-life, not yet abstracted by literacy and industrial visual order, nudity is merely pathetic. The Kinsey Report on the sex life of the male expressed bafflement that peasants and backward peoples did not relish marital or boudoir nudity. Khrushchev did not enjoy the can-can dance provided for his entertainment in Hollywood. Naturally not.

That sort of mime of sense involvement is meaningful only to long-literate societies. Backward peoples approach nudity, if at all, with the attitude we have come to expect from our painters and sculptors— the attitude made up of all the senses at once. To a person using the whole sensorium, nudity is the richest possible expression of structural form. But to the highly visual and lopsided sensibility of industrial societies, the sudden confrontation with tactile flesh is heady music, indeed.

There is a movement toward a new equilibrium today, as we become aware of the preference for coarse, heavy textures and sculptural shapes in dress. There is, also, the ritualistic exposure of the body indoors and out-of-doors. Psychologists have long taught us that much of our hearing takes place through the skin itself. After centuries of being fully clad and of being contained in uniform visual space, the electric age ushers us into a world in which we live and breathe and listen with the entire epidermis. Of course, there is much zest of novelty in this cult, and the eventual equilibrium among the senses will slough off a good deal of the new ritual, both in clothing and in housing. Meantime, in both new attire and new dwellings, our unified sensibility cavorts amidst a wide range of awareness of materials and colors which makes ours one of the greatest ages of music, poetry, painting, and architecture alike.

Conclusion

The clothing of a people is just as much a part of their culture as beliefs or artwork. McLuhan shows both how clothing affects the behavior of the members of a society and how the behavior or attitudes of those members affects their clothing. Thus, he gives a clear picture of the fact that culture and society are closely inter-related; each is to a large extent an expression of the other.

2 THE NORMATIVE SYSTEM

Human society would not be possible without rules of conduct, or standards of "proper" behavior. These rules, and the ways the rules are enforced, are referred to as the normative system. There are four important parts of a normative system. They are: the norms, from which the normative system takes its name; the values; the institutions; and the sanctions. Each of these four will be discussed in turn.

NORMS

The term *norm* is used by sociologists to mean any rule, or standard, which defines what people should or should not do, or think, or feel in any given social situation. Although individuals, families, or small groups have many private norms of their own, the most significant norms are those commonly held by a large segment of the society.

The word *norm,* and the adjective *normative,* should not be confused with the term *normal.* Normal means falling within the statistical average. It is not normal to be left-handed or to have red hair, but both these traits are acceptable according to the norms.

Norms may be viewed in several different ways. *Laws* are a formal and standardized expression of norms. It is possible for an action to be illegal (contrary to the laws) but to conform to certain informal social norms. An example of this is homosexuality. It is against the law in some states, but permitted, within limits, by some groups. One reason this particular act is not against some informal norms may be that it almost never results in a punishment that is socially visible. Only rarely does a homosexual face prosecution in court and a resultant criminal record. However, in another example, this

is not the case. Protests involving civil disobedience, such as the sit-ins in the South during the mid-sixties and the anti-war demonstrations of recent years, often do involve criminal prosecution, although they, too, are in accordance with norms held by a section of contemporary society.

Florian Znaniecki (1882–1958) specialized in the broad area of cultural order, and made important theoretical contributions to the study of social norms and social roles. Himself a Pole who emigrated to America at the outset of World War I, Znaniecki collaborated with an American colleague at the University of Chicago to write a classical empirical study on *The Polish Peasant in Europe and America* (1918–1920). Two other important works of his are *Cultural Sciences: Their Origin and Development* (1952) and *Social Relations and Social Roles* (1965). *(University of Chicago Press)*

William Graham Sumner (1840–1910) was one of the first important American sociologists. His greatest interest was in the influence of custom on social behavior; it was his belief that custom, or tradition, is the prime determinant of social action. His work was influenced by that of Herbert Spencer, whose political views he shared; he considered norms to be a "natural force," which governments should not interfere with or regulate in any way. His major work was *Folkways* (1906). *(Culver Pictures, Inc.)*

Norms may vary in their importance to society. Some norms can be broken without serious consequence. For example, in our society it is the norm for men to wear a suit and tie to the office. But if an accountant turns up one day in a turtleneck sweater and a suede vest, he will probably encounter nothing more than a lot of surprised looks, and possibly a hint from his boss that he should be back in a suit the next day. Norms like this one concerning office apparel, which are of little moral significance and easily tolerate some nonconformity, are often called *folkways* or social customs.[5]

5. William Graham Sumner, *Folkways* (1906; reprint ed., New York: Mentor Press, 1960).

Other norms are considered to be almost sacred laws, and transgressions bring serious consequences. When a man violates the norm against murder, it will not be excused or overlooked on the grounds that it only happened once or that he forgot he wasn't supposed to do it; he will be punished, whatever the circumstances surrounding his action. Norms like this, which a society sees as essential and which it enforces strictly, are called *mores*.

Norms are rules which a society believes should be obeyed by everyone, unless otherwise specified. Implicit in the concept of the norm, however, is the possibility that actual behavior might differ from the norm, for the norm is basically an ideal and not necessarily a reality. In fact, we might say that people *will* behave in ways different from the norms unless some kind of control or force is applied. It is the function of the normative system as a whole to provide that control, which is called the process of *social control*. (We will discuss social control more fully in chapter 12: Deviant Behavior and Social Control.)

VALUES

A *value* is an idea about what is good, or right, or wise, or beneficial. In other words, values are ideas by which men live. Because a value is more abstract than a norm, it is harder to define. Norms are more specific and relate to specific situations; values are the higher criteria by which norms are judged.

The sociologist studies norms by watching people's actions and then listening to the actors and to other members of the community comment on the observed behavior. But values refer not so much to what people do, or think, or feel, in a given situation, as to the broader principles that lie behind these specific actions. Of course, the sociologist may try to ask direct questions about values. He inquires of his subjects, "Why did you behave that way?" His problem is then to decide how to interpret the answer he gets. It is quite common to find that, because of ignorance, misunderstanding, lack of vocabulary, or deception, the reason given to him for some behavior is not the real one. Trying to separate truth from fiction, reason from rationalization, can be a difficult task.

Another way to set about identifying values in a society is to try to deduce them from the norms. Ruth Benedict did this in her study of Indians of the American West Coast.[6] She noted that tribal norms frequently demanded participation in frenzied orgiastic rituals, perhaps under the influence of drugs or a kind of hypnosis. From this observation, she deduced or concluded that emotionalism was a universal value in the society of these Indians. It is a logical hypothesis, but it is hard to determine how to prove it satisfactorily. Benedict tried to do it by questioning the Indians directly about their values, assuming she would receive responses that would agree with her theory. Instead, she got answers in direct conflict with her theory; the Indians claimed to value strict control of the emotions. This could be explained on the grounds that the Indians did not understand the question or the meaning of emotional control; in this case, the hypothesis could stand, but it is not proved. The conflict could also be explained by saying that the stated value was correct, and that the emotional behavior represented a temporary lapse from the ideal, admittedly a difficult one to achieve. In other words, deducing values from norms involves some guesswork or speculation.

This problem brings up the whole question of the relationship between values and norms. The question is confused by the fact that it is hard sometimes to tell the difference between the two; for instance, is freedom of the press a norm (a rule of conduct) or a value (a desirable principle)? On the subject of whether norms or values is the more basic concept, there are two theories. One school of thought gives great importance to the role of values in human behavior. Basic values, according to this theory, are implanted early in a person's life, and, once they are fixed, serve as a guide in all subsequent choices of behavior and attitude. Norms then evolve in the society because they are the logical outcome or specification of its values. Talcott Parsons sums up how values relate to an individual's personality:

There is reason to believe that, among the learned elements of personality in certain respects the stablest and most enduring are the major value-orientation patterns and there is much evidence that these are 'laid down' in childhood and are not on a large scale subject to drastic alteration during adult life. There is good reason to treat these patterns of value-orientation . . . as the core of what is sometimes called 'basic personality structure.'[7]

In our country, it is the norm for a businessman to set his prices on the basis of what he thinks he can get people to pay. According to the theory, this norm reflects a basic value first brought here by the early settlers of America, the value of personal economic freedom. Such a value logically led to the conclusion that government regulation of a private exchange was wrong, which led in turn to the norm regarding the setting of prices.

The opposing viewpoint gives much greater attention to the independent importance of norms.[8] As originally stated by William G. Sumner, this theory suggests that norms are simply habits developed over a period of years within a certain society. To justify the continuation of these habits, and per-

6. See Ruth Benedict, "Configurations of Culture in North America," *American Anthropologist* 34 (1932): 1–27.

7. Talcott Parsons, *The Social System* (New York: Free Press, 1951), p. 208.

8. William Graham Sumner, *Folkways*.

Clearly not everyone in a society adheres to the explicit norms of their culture. Moreover, if large segments of a society protest or refuse to comply with certain rules of conduct, the normative system may be changed. The early suffragettes, for example, succeeded in changing a law that denied women the right to vote. Today the women's liberation movement continues to protest norms that prescribe a subordinate role for women in our society. *(Bettmann Archive)*

haps also to conceal their ultimate irrationality, people in the society invent explanations of the reason things are done that way. In other words, values are a kind of afterthought—explanations by which the already ingrained norms of a society are claimed to be desirable. This viewpoint is summed up clearly by Judith Blake and Kingsley Davis, in a paper called "On Norms and Values":

It is the norms, not the values, that have the pressure of reality upon them. It is the norms that are enforced by sanctions, that are subject to the necessity of action and the agony of decision. It is therefore the norms that represent the cutting edge of social control. In this regard Sumner seems to have been more correct than some of his successors, for he emphasized the importance of the folkways and mores in understanding society rather than the vague slippery ideologies, rationalizations, and generalizations people use in justifying their observance or non-observance of norms.[9]

We can apply this theory to the same example of American ways of setting prices. Looked at in this light, one might say the American pricing system began as the result of the migration to a rich and unclaimed country. In practice, the most successful way to behave was to grab as much as you could. This became a habitual way of doing business, and the habit was later justified, both morally and socially, by inventing the value of personal economic freedom, which forbids regulation of an individual's business transactions.

Both points of view sound convincing to some degree, and it is hard to know how to choose between them, which is why the controversy has been going on for so long. As in many such theoretical controversies, there is probably some truth on both sides. There *are* some deep and basic values which can be traced in every known society. The sociologist Robin Williams has suggested that in American society today basic values include achievement and success, activity and work, efficiency and practicality, progress, material comfort, and equality.[10] On the other hand, these values do not develop out of the blue. They are developed, reinforced, and changed through day-to-day behavior regulated by norms. In this sense we can reasonably say that to some extent the norms precede them.

INSTITUTIONS

The most important norms in a society are those which are institutionalized. An *institu-*

tion may be defined as a formal and stable way of pursuing an activity that is important to the society. The family, for example, is an institution; it is the accepted way to pursue the important activities of sex, the rearing of children, and economic achievement. Other institutions help to regulate and pattern courtship, political use of power, and education of both young and old. Robin Williams says:

By defining problems and approved situations in certain ways, any particular institutional structure channelizes human experience along certain lines and ignores or prohibits other possibilities. It is a truism to say that the problems or evils of any society result partly from its most venerated institutions.[11]

The major institutions of any society thus provide the basic normative patterns of that society and culture. In this book, we will examine in detail the American institutions of the family, education, religion, and politics. Discussion of the institutions of law and economic activity are scattered in other chapters throughout the book. At the moment, our special concern with institutions is their connection with the normative system.

Institutions are essentially made up of norms, or social guidelines about what ought and ought not to be done in regard to important activities. Institutional norms are those which are accepted as obligatory by the total society. These norms are known to everyone in the social system; teaching them is an essential part of the education of the children of the society. These norms are also strongly enforced; their observance or non-observance is a highly emotional issue for most people. Some examples of institutionalized norms are those in the family which forbid adultery, regulate the care of dependent children, and require the man to provide economic support.

9. Judith Blake and Kingsley Davis, "On Norms and Values," in *Handbook of Modern Sociology,* ed. R. L. Faris (Chicago: Rand McNally, 1964), p. 461.

10. Robin M. Williams, Jr., *American Society: A Sociological Interpretation,* 2d ed. rev. (New York: Alfred A. Knopf, 1960), chap. 11.

11. Robin M. Williams, Jr., *American Society,* p. 38.

Institutional norms are the most meaningful and important norms of a culture, but it must be understood that there are other kinds of significant norms also. The institution is one end of the normative spectrum; at the other end is the purely personal norm of the single individual—for example, the shopper who decides she will never again buy a certain brand of detergent because it doesn't really get her laundry white. In between these two extremes are the wide variety of norms accepted by some groups—such as an office, a church congregation, a clan, a profession—and not by others. Some of these norms may have very little social significance; others may be a source of conflict because they are anti-institutional. For a complete understanding of any culture, it is desirable to know both the institutional and extra-institutional norms.

SANCTIONS

It is obvious that a society must have some way to enforce its norms, to make the individual behave according to the rules, even when it is difficult or unpleasant for him to do so. This is done through the pressure of *sanctions*. Sanctions can be either positive or negative. A positive sanction is some kind of reward offered to those who behave correctly; a negative sanction is a punishment for behaving improperly.

Sanctions may be applied officially or unofficially. An example of an official negative sanction is the jail sentence of three years imposed on a man who is caught robbing a grocery store. An official positive sanction is the promotion given an employee who has faithfully served the company's interests, or the $100 reward paid to a young boy who tells the F.B.I. the license number of the car he saw leaving the scene of a bank robbery. We call these sanctions "official" because each is applied by a member of a legally and formally organized authority.

There are also many cases where sanctions are applied unofficially; in fact, usually official sanctions are a last resort, and are used only after a variety of unofficial sanctions have been tried without apparent effect. Unofficial sanctions appear constantly in the course of daily social interaction. For example, on the day after the supervisor of an office typing pool publicly points out that Jane consistently types more letters than anyone else in the pool, the other members of the pool give only a cold greeting to Jane when she comes in and then "forget" to order coffee for her in the morning. The other typists see Jane's behavior as a threat to the group unity, since Jane's doing more work per hour will make the work output of the others look poor by comparison. By withdrawing their friendship, they apply a negative sanction to this infringement of group norms. To be reaccepted into the group, Jane will have to slow down and match her working speed to that already set by the group.

Sociological studies have pointed to a wide and highly imaginative variety of unofficial sanctions that occur in group interaction. Some examples of common negative sanctions that a group may impose upon one member whose behavior is not accepted were observed by a team investigating the relationships within a group of factory workers: maintaining a greater-than-normal distance, such as walking a longer route to avoid passing the desk of a worker being sanctioned; not laughing at that person's jokes; failure to express sympathy over problems or failures; and violation of normal rights of privacy. To express approval of someone's behavior, or positive sanctions, the members of a working group might say the person's name frequently, often addressing him by name before making any remark; obviously and dramatically display close physical contact, the classic example being the literal pat on the back; or adopt a suggestion the person makes about work procedure or policy.

Some sociologists feel that the effectiveness of all sanctions is based on the ultimate threat of physical violence, either personal or official, and that every other kind of sanction merely represents a gentle reminder that physical violence is possible. However, this view seems to overlook the fact that man is indeed a social animal, and that total withdrawal of approval and/or affection by other men does constitute a feared punishment, one no less frightening than violence, and possibly more traumatic in some cases.

CONFORMITY AND DEVIANCE

When a person behaves in accordance with the norms in a given situation, we say that he *conforms*. When he does not, we say he is *deviant*. The goal of social organization may be total conformity, but no society, no matter how harsh its methods of social control, ever succeeds in achieving that goal. There is always some degree of deviance.

There are several reasons for such deviance. One is simple ignorance. Because there are thousands of norms to be learned, it is obviously unlikely that everyone will learn every norm. Norms are learned informally, so that if the occasion for observing a norm never arises, it is quite possible that the norm may not be learned.

In some cases, a norm is held so unconsciously that it is never put into words. In such a case, the norm gains its definition when it is contrasted with deviance. The people in a group see one member doing something, and they all agree that it is wrong—but no one knew, or at least no one had ever said, that it was wrong until they saw him do it. This is especially true of norms held by informally organized small groups, such as a neighborhood coffee circle or a teen-age gang. Here we see one of the functions of deviance; it serves to define norms.

Deviance may also be due to poor or ineffective social control. In some cases the penalties or sanctions for deviance are

mild, and the potential rewards may outweigh the sanctions from an individual's point of view. Another cause of deviance is conflict of norms. An individual may belong to a group which holds some norm that contradicts or conflicts with an institutional norm. Sometimes even within a single group, norms conflict with each other. For example, we have one institutional norm which says "Thou shalt not kill," and another which says it is a citizen's duty to fight and kill other men during wartime; this creates a number of problems for those who must make rapid decisions about their conduct within the framework of such normative conflict.

The question which a group must face when it recognizes a deviant act is how that act, and the actor, should be regarded. Since the goal of the group, of society in general, is to restore the deviant to conforming behavior, the usual response is some sort of negative sanction, possibly many different kinds in an attempt to find one that succeeds. However, the application of negative sanctions is always a little dangerous. Most sanctions serve to isolate the individual in some way from the rest of the group and when an individual is isolated the group's social control over him is somewhat weakened. The end result may be that the deviant not only continues his initial nonconforming behavior but adopts other kinds as well. In short, he "drops out" of the normative system; if he drops out of the normative system of the society, he is beyond the reach of all but the most stringent social control, such as imprisonment.

In the past, most sociological studies of deviance viewed deviance as an individual or personal problem. A deviant was defined as a person who had somehow gone wrong; if only he would agree to behave properly, the "problem" would be solved. We now see that the situation is considerably more complex. Deviance is not necessarily an innate quality of some actions; deviance also lies in the eye of the beholder, and is a direct result of the way the beholder interprets the norms and the other person's behavior. In other words, when a person is labeled a deviant, it is the result of some interaction between that person and certain other members of society. Deviance may be as much a social quality as a personal one. The subject of deviance will be more fully explored in chapter 12.

ROBERT S. LYND
American Culture

From Robert S. Lynd, *Knowledge for What?* (Copyright 1939 © 1967 by Princeton University Press: Princeton Paperback 1970), pp. 59–62. Reprinted by permission of Princeton University Press.

Introduction

Robert S. Lynd, the author of the well-known Middletown *and* Middletown in Transition, *was a professor at Columbia University. Lynd points out in the following excerpt from* Knowledge for What? *the contradictory nature of our cultural values.*

As one begins to list the assumptions by which we Americans live, one runs at once into a large measure of contradiction and resulting ambivalence. This derives from the fact that these overlapping assumptions have developed in different eras and that they tend to be carried over uncritically into new situations or to be allowed to persist in long diminuendos into the changing future. Men's ideas, beliefs, and loyalties—their non-material culture—are frequently slower to be changed than are their material tools. And the greater the emotional need for them, the longer men tend to resist changes in these ideas and beliefs. These contradictions among assumptions derive also from the fact that the things the mass of human beings basically crave as human beings as they live along together are often overlaid by, and not infrequently distorted by, the cumulating emphases that a culture may take on under circumstances of rapid change or under various kinds of class control. In these cases the culture may carry along side by side both assertions: the one reflecting deep needs close to the heart's desire and the other heavily authorized by class or other authority.

Wherever, therefore, such dualism in assumptions clearly exists, both assumptions are set down together in the following listing. The juxtaposition of these pairs is not intended to imply that they carry equal weight in the culture. One member may be thrown into the scale as decisive in a given situation at one moment, and the other contrasting assumption may be invoked in the same or a different situation a few moments later. It is precisely in this matter of trying to live by contrasting rules of the game that one of the most characteristic aspects of our American culture is to be seen.

The following suggest some of these outstanding assumptions in American life:

1. The United States is the best and greatest nation on earth and will always remain so.
2. Individualism, "the survival of the fittest," is the law of nature and the secret of America's greatness; and restrictions on individual freedom are un-American and kill initiative.
   But: No man should live for himself alone; for people ought to be loyal and stand together and work for common purposes.
3. The thing that distinguishes man from the beasts is the fact that he is rational; and therefore man can be trusted, if let alone, to guide his conduct wisely.

But: Some people are brighter than others; and, as every practical politician and businessman knows, you can't afford simply to sit back and wait for people to make up their minds.

4. Democracy, as discovered and perfected by the American people, is the ultimate form of living together. All men are created free and equal, and the United States has made this fact a living reality.
But: You would never get anywhere, of course, if you constantly left things to popular vote. No business could be run that way, and of course no businessman would tolerate it.

5. Everyone should try to be successful.
But: The kind of person you are is more important than how successful you are.

6. The family is our basic institution and the sacred core of our national life.
But: Business is our most important institution, and, since national welfare depends upon it, other institutions must conform to its needs.

7. Religion and "the finer things of life" are our ultimate values and the things all of us are really working for.
But: A man owes it to himself and to his family to make as much money as he can.

8. Life would not be tolerable if we did not believe in progress and know that things are getting better. We should, therefore, welcome new things.
But: The old, tried fundamentals are best; and it is a mistake for busybodies to try to change things too fast or to upset the fundamentals.

9. Hard work and thrift are signs of character and the way to get ahead.
But: No shrewd person tries to get ahead nowadays by just working hard, and nobody gets rich nowadays by pinching nickels. It is important to know the right people. If you want to make money, you have to look and act like money. Anyway, you only live once.

10. Honesty is the best policy.

But: Business is business, and a businessman would be a fool if he didn't cover his hand.

11. America is a land of unlimited opportunity, and people get pretty much what's coming to them here in this country.
But: Of course, not everybody can be boss, and factories can't give jobs if there aren't jobs to give.

12. Capital and labor are partners.
But: It is bad policy to pay higher wages than you have to. If people don't like to work for you for what you offer them, they can go elsewhere.

13. Education is a fine thing.
But: It is the practical men who get things done.

14. Science is a fine thing in its place and our future depends upon it.
But: Science has no right to interfere with such things as business and our other fundamental institutions. The thing to do is to *use* science, but not let it upset things.

15. Children are a blessing.
But: You should not have more children than you can afford.

16. Women are the finest of God's creatures.
But: Women aren't very practical and are usually inferior to men in reasoning power and general ability.

17. Patriotism and public service are fine things.
But: Of course, a man has to look out for himself.

18. The American judicial system insures justice to every man, rich or poor.
But: A man is a fool not to hire the best lawyer he can afford.

19. Poverty is deplorable and should be abolished.
But: There never has been enough to go around, and the Bible tells us that "The poor you have always with you."

20. No man deserves to have what he hasn't worked for. It demoralizes him to do so.
But: You can't let people starve.

Conclusion
  Contradictory values are especially characteristic of, but by no means limited to, *large heterogeneous societies like the United States. They greatly complicate the analysis of culture in modern societies.*

TOPIC

3 ANALYZING CULTURES

All the social sciences focus on aspects of culture, but we do not call such work "the study of culture" unless it attempts to describe and analyze a culture as a unified whole. Describing and analyzing primitive cultures has been the main task of cultural anthropologists; the analysis of modern cultures has been carried out more often by sociologists. Although cultural anthropology and sociology have developed from different traditions, and to some extent from the work of different scholars, today they are quite similar. Many cultural anthropologists are studying modern as well as primitive societies, and sociologists are indebted to anthropology for many concepts and ways to approach the study of culture.

Studying a culture as a unified whole involves understanding the culture's major values and norms, seeing how these are reflected in social behavior, and perhaps analyzing the way in which the values and norms shape and are shaped by the material culture.

Years ago, before anthropology and sociology were established as fields of study, the description of foreign and primitive cultures was left to the traveler and the missionary, who recorded what they happened to observe in the course of their own activities. But these reports tended to be biased and incomplete. Then, in the last two decades

of the nineteenth century, more scientific methods began to be used. The first major figure in this work was the anthropologist Franz Boas (1858–1942).[12] Trained as a physical scientist, he applied the methods of science to his anthropological studies. He observed carefully, recorded everything he saw or heard, and asked questions to fill in the gaps. One characteristic in his work was that he regarded the people he studied in much the same way as one would look at a chemistry experiment. He was always the detached observer.

Bronislaw Malinowski (1884–1942) brought to the field a new influence, for he not only observed the cultures he studied but participated in them as well—a technique called participant observation. His studies of primitive island cultures in the South Pacific show a great depth of understanding and insight.[13] In the accompanying abridgment, Malinowski writes about his methods and principles of cultural study. Malinowski's standards of involvement are still commonly in force today. An anthropologist is expected to immerse himself in the culture he is studying for long periods

12. For a good account of Boas's life and work, see M. J. Herskovits, *Franz Boas: The Science of Man in the Making* (New York: Charles Scribner's Sons, 1953).

13. See Bronislaw Malinowski, *Argonauts of the Western Pacific* (New York: E. P. Dutton, 1922).

The culture of these New Guinea tribesmen may be "primitive" by our own standards, but studies by Malinowski and other anthropologists have shown that it is highly integrated and well adapted to its physical environment. *(Photo Researchers, Inc.)*

of time, perhaps two years; to be able to speak the language; and, as far as is possible, to join the community as a participant rather than only an observer.

It is not necessary to go off to an island or some obscure part of the globe to study a culture. The contemporary anthropologist, Elliot Liebow, author of *Tally's Corner*,[14] examined the culture of an inner city neighborhood in the black ghetto of Washington, D.C.

14. Elliot Liebow, *Tally's Corner: A Study of Negro Streetcorner Men* (Boston: Little, Brown, paper, 1967).

CULTURAL RELATIVITY AND ETHNOCENTRISM

We mentioned how the first descriptions of other cultures that came from travelers and missionaries tended to be biased. The men making the reports almost always judged the culture they were observing by the standards of their own culture. Those customs which were contrary to their own beliefs and values were labeled uncivilized or barbaric; those which fitted in with their own cultural viewpoint were accepted as modern, or civilized, or valuable. This tendency to evaluate other cultures in terms of our own, to consider ours right and that of others wrong, is called *ethnocentrism.*

Today the goal of the anthropologist and sociologist who studies other cultures is to avoid ethnocentrism. A first principle of all modern cultural studies is that every culture must be judged on its own terms, a principle known as *cultural relativity.* This principle holds that one cannot truly understand or evaluate cultural, social, and psychological facts meaningfully unless they are looked at in terms of the larger culture and society of which they are a part. What role do they play in that society, what needs do they serve, what values are associated with them? Of course, it is not possible to be totally free of all bias in favor of one's own culture, because everyone has both consciously and unconsciously accepted a whole set of norms and values which it is impossible to set aside completely when analyzing another culture. But it is nonetheless the ideal of the social scientist to be objective. We can see the rather painful conflict between rational objectivity of judgment and emotional commitment to one's own culture even in the work of such a detached scientist as Franz Boas. To a reader of his books, his essays, even his collected field observations, he sounds extremely objective. But his personal diaries and the letters he wrote to his family while he was in the field indicate the struggle he had with his own cultural inclinations to maintain this objective point of view. Telling of his work with the Indian tribes of the Canadian Northwest, particularly the Eskimos and the Bella Coola, he wrote:

In the meantime, screaming dirty children run about, sometimes a meal is eaten. Dogs and children force their way between the people; fires smoke so that one can hardly see.... In short, the whole thing is a test of patience. (Diary entry, Nov. 8, 1886)

Then I went to the Bella Coolas, who told me another idiotic story.... The fact that I obtain these stories is interesting, but the stories themselves are more horrible than some of the Eskimo stories. (Oct. 3)

I am very cross because my Tsimshian [an Indian tribe] deserted me.... From experience I should know that such things always happen, but it is easier said than done not to be angry about it. I told the good man, who by the way is very religious, that he was the greatest liar I had ever known and that I would tell his pastor about him. (Sept. 24)[15]

The problem of judging and relating to foreign cultures is not a problem for social scientists alone. Because of the various forces of socialization (discussed in the following chapter) every child grows up to believe that his own culture is "good" and "right." This outlook leads to an inevitable conclusion that people who do things differently are bad or wrong; so that when a member of one culture is exposed to another, unfamiliar culture, he sometimes becomes hostile, suspicious, or derogatory.

It is clear that ethnocentrism can serve a valuable function in a society, for if the members of the group believe that the norms and values of the culture in which they live are good, they will continue to subscribe to them. But ethnocentrism can also be a danger to the society, because it can lead to isolation of the society, inhibiting exchanges with other cultures that promote cultural growth and development. The successful society must therefore have some mechanism for overcoming excessive ethnocentrism and facilitating cultural exchange. Some primitive societies have made rituals of trade relationships with other groups which both procure needed items for the economy and foster cultural exchange. An example of such a tradition

15. Helene Boas Yampolsky, "Excerpts from the Letter Diary of Franz Boas on His First Trip to the Northwest Coast," *International Journal of American Linguistics* 24, no. 4 (October 1958).

is the once-a-year trip across the Sahara Desert undertaken by men of the Tuareg tribe to buy salt. They go in a great camel caravan, walking hundreds of miles each way, stopping at every oasis along their route. When they return with the salt, they sell it, which furnishes them with enough money or goods to live on until the next year's trip. Obviously there is an economic motive involved, but there is also a valuable cultural exchange carried on with all the tribes encountered during the trip. This exchange has kept the Tuareg, who live in extreme geographical isolation in the desert, in touch with technological progress and new ideas, so that they have been able to survive in the rapidly changing modern world.

In many societies, ethnocentrism is a serious problem because the nations of the modern world are very interdependent —people from many societies and cultures must interact with one another, and world survival may depend in part on a greater appreciation of the way others do things. Our society relies on education as the chief agent of combating the dangers of ethnocentrism. While still in grade school, children learn about people in other societies.

Yet even with so much preparation, and so much forewarning of differences between cultures, exposure to another culture often proves to be a disorienting experience. We use the term *culture shock* to describe the psychological distress caused when a person moves from his native or accustomed culture to a new one. Culture shock happens even to those who have had extensive preparation for the move, such as exchange professors, Peace Corpsmen, members of the diplomatic service, and even anthropologists. This is because cultural attitudes are woven into so many aspects of daily life, and are often so unconscious in character, that people don't recognize that they hold specific cultural attitudes—until some common expectation is not met or some barely realized rule of conduct is violated.

Bronislaw Malinowski (1884–1942) was chiefly responsible for changing anthropology from a speculative study into a true social science. Drawing on his knowledge of other fields, such as economics and psychology, he broadened the scope of his anthropological fieldwork until it became a careful analysis of a total culture. His viewpoint was a functional one; when he considered individual behavior or cultural institutions, he asked: "Does it work?" "Why?" "How?" In his subsequent teaching career, he helped to establish functionalism as the dominant approach of British social anthropology. Two of his most important works are *Argonauts of the Western Pacific* (1922) and *A Scientific Theory of Culture* (1944). *(Photo courtesy of Harcourt Brace Jovanovich, Inc.)*

FUNCTIONALISM

Functionalism is one of the most widely used approaches to the study of cultural traits. The functional technique is based on trying to find out how a cultural trait affects the rest of the culture or society. A trait which aids the society in meeting its needs or requirements is called a *functional trait,* and one which hinders a society in achieving its needs or requirements is called a *dysfunc-*

tional trait. For example, religion is said to be functional when it helps bind together members of a society; the army serves the function of protecting the country. A political machine is dysfunctional when it increases graft and corruption. Cultural traits can have both functional and dysfunctional aspects. The political machine can serve the function of providing immigrant groups with information about government and the special services they may need.

Let us consider the function of several American customs. It is the custom to give babies the same last name as their father. One reason is that it helps give the baby an additional identification; there may be many Johns in kindergarten, but only one John Turczynewycz. Moreover, this custom helps to emphasize the fact that the parents undertake the responsibility of caring for and rearing the child, that they regard him as theirs. It is a reminder of the kind of family organization we have, of the fact that the family constitutes an important social unit. The custom is in some ways arbitrary—the boy could be called John 149674, or as in some societies, John son of Harry—but it has a definite and understandable function.

The custom at weddings of having the bride stand on the groom's left is what is called a *cultural survival*—or a culture trait which has survived long after its original function has disappeared. The original reason for it was to keep the groom's right hand, his sword arm, free in case of any trouble from his enemies, the bride's family, or disgruntled suitors. Although the custom once served a function, today it is meaningless, since sword fights no longer break out at weddings, and outside of movies like *The Graduate*, brides are rarely abducted at the altar. On the other hand, there is no harm in the custom either. It can be classed as neutral, neither functional nor dysfunctional.

Functionalism points up the fact that a culture is not simply a random collection of traits, but a system where the different parts must fit together for proper functioning. Family life, economic procedures, laws, defense measures, and the various other cultural activities are closely intermeshed with one another; a change in one may effect changes in each of the others. This fitting together of cultural traits is known as *cultural integration*.

Lack of knowledge about the cultural integration of societies has been known to hinder our own society from dealing successfully with Third World nations. Where people raise large herds of unhealthy cattle, for instance, we have attempted to introduce selective breeding to upgrade the quality, failing to consider that in certain cultures a man's status is determined by the size of his herd and not its quality. The introduction of the new breeding methods threatens customs and values woven into the fabric of the entire society.

The function of an action or change can be classified as *manifest* and *latent*. Manifest functions are intended and recognized in advance; latent functions are neither intended nor recognized; they are consequences that are the unpredicted by-products of an action. In the example of the introduction of selective breeding given above, one latent consequence might be to reduce the status of certain chiefs, and thus alter the power structure of the society. Thus selective breeding could prove to be dysfunctional, if it produced a leadership vacuum and impaired the functioning of the group.

Functionalism is merely an approach or orientation toward studying social and cultural phenomena, and a very difficult one to carry out in practice. It requires extensive knowledge of the culture in question, and painstaking attention in analyzing the effects of a particular custom or trait in that culture. It was first developed by British anthropologists, but has had widespread popularity in American sociology over the last few decades. Its greatest value lies in directing attention to the meaning a part of culture has for the culture as a whole.

CULTURAL DIVERSITY

Each culture is adapted to meet a specific set of circumstances, both physical and social, and therefore each culture is different from all the others in the world; each is unique. We mentioned in the last chapter many different types of societies and cultures based on modes of subsistence, ranging from herding and food gathering to industry.

The physical circumstances influencing the development of a culture are those of climate, geography, population, and physiology (plant and animal life). Obviously, a group of people who live in the South Seas are not going to provide food for themselves by hunting seals and polar bears; they will have to eat the native fruit that grows there and learn to fish in lagoons or the open seas. A South Seas culture will be molded in certain ways by this necessary way of providing food. For example, the people are encouraged to lead a settled existence with fixed dwelling places, and magic or religious rites to ensure the safety of the fishermen will probably develop. Living in a warm and fertile climate may mean that less time has to be devoted to providing the essentials of survival—food and shelter—and that more time can be spent developing the artistic or ritual element of the culture.

Men have developed numerous relatively unique cultures, but the universality of basic human needs often results in similar cultural solutions. Some form of bread, for instance, is found in nearly every culture, although shape and size vary. *(Photo Researchers, Inc.)*

Yet these physical circumstances, important though they are, usually have less influence on the development of a culture than do the social circumstances of a society—particularly in complex societies. Social circumstances include the stage of technological development, the language, the prevailing ideologies, and the society's past history. These factors help determine *how* the South Seas group will organize itself to meet its needs, and whether the incantations over the departing fishing fleet will be uttered by a priest or a magician.

CULTURAL UNIVERSALS

So far we have stressed the differences in cultures, partly in order to overcome a natural ethnocentrism which assumes that "everyone" does things in generally the same way we do. But one can go too far in emphasizing cultural diversity. Comparisons of many cultures also indicate that there are fundamental similarities in social organization and cultural values. These similarities arise because every human group finds itself facing certain common problems and living within certain universal limitations.

We are all basically alike physically, and some sociologists believe that this accounts for many attitudes held in common. Man is an animal with bilateral symmetry; that is, he possesses his features in pairs—two eyes, two ears, two arms. Some sociologists believe that this explains the universal tendency toward dualistic ideology; Heaven and Hell, God and the Devil, good and bad, yin and yang, right and wrong. This is pure speculation, but certain features of social organization and culture do exist which are based on common biological characteristics. We all must eat and find shelter from the unfriendly elements. We all must take care of young and helpless children and deal with the problem of aging and ill parents. We all must adjust to the fundamental differences between the two sexes.

Every human community begins with these same circumstances.

Another cause of cultural similarities can be found in the dynamics of group life. If a group is going to be able to function at all, it must meet certain requirements. A group must have some form of organization, or the individuals will not be able to work efficiently together. Next, the group must possess some form of communication, so that everyone can find out what organizational decisions have been made. Leadership appears to be another essential element of group life; even if everyone participates in an equal degree, there must be some individual who undertakes the administrative tasks of the group. There must be some method of teaching the group organization to newcomers and children, and there must be some way to dramatize, or make concrete, the abstract quality of each individual's commitment to the group and its way of life. Thus each group must provide for such basic functions as penal sanctions, division of labor, and property rights in order to be able to stay together and continue to function.

The third kind of similarity can be classified as that caused by our shared environment. There are only a limited number of plants and animals that are edible and nutritious. There are only a limited number of methods of travel. We all get warmth and light from the same source, the sun. Only a certain shape of object, with a given degree of hardness, can be hurled through the air to kill an animal or another man. Only a small group of metals can be worked to make tools. Therefore, we find that many different cultures make stone or metal arrowheads of approximately the same size and shape. Every culture has turned to fire to provide an artificial source of heat and light at night. Every agricultural society has to provide water for its crops; every hunting society has to follow the wanderings of the animal it lives on. Nearly every society has created a form of bread. No group uses a square wheel, because it doesn't work.

So we see that every human group is faced with a certain number of identical problems and limitations, and for this reason we often see cross-cultural similarities that cannot be accounted for merely by an exchange of information and ideas. Yet it must always be remembered that these similar limitations and problems provide only the framework for the human society. Within this framework, each group works out its own, distinctively different solutions to the problems, thereby providing a high degree of cultural diversity.

SUBCULTURES

So far in this chapter we have been speaking of "a culture" as if it were a single set of norms and values accepted equally by every member of the society. In actual practice, that is never true. What we call the culture of a country or tribal group could more accurately be described as a sort of average of all the cultural behavior found within the group.

When a group of people within the culture formulate a way of behaving that includes some of the dominant features of this cultural average but also includes certain features not found elsewhere in the society, we call this a *subculture*. A subculture may spring up around some occupations, such as those in the medical or military fields. It may reflect a racial and ethnic difference, as does the subculture of black Americans. A subculture may be based on regionalism, as in the case of the southern states. It may be based on national origins; in our country, there are subcultures of various European countries, Puerto Rico, and China. Subcultures often develop in social classes and tend to set them even further apart, so that it becomes difficult to move from one to another.

Cultural traits constantly flow from one subculture to another, and into the cultural mainstream. An outstanding example of this is the influence on our culture of the subculture of black musicians. Their slang and their styles in dress have passed into other parts of the culture.

Each complex society has a variety of subcultures and an individual can function within more than one, sometimes passing through several stages as he grows older or his attitudes change. A subculture which is so different from the dominant pattern that it sharply challenges it is known as a *counterculture*.[16] Countercultures are typically found among the young. The hippie culture has strongly rejected traditional life-styles and created a set of norms which run counter to majority beliefs about work, patriotism, and material possessions. A counterculture reinforces its own rejection of another culture in many ways, and members who deviate from accepted ways are given support and encouragement by others in the subculture.

16. Theodore Roszak, *The Making of a Counter Culture* (New York: Doubleday, 1969).

BRONISLAW MALINOWSKI
The Ethnographer At Work

From *Argonauts of the Western Pacific* by Bronislaw Malinowski. Dutton Paperbacks edition, 1961. Used by permission of E. P. Dutton & Company.

Introduction

The anthropologist Bronislaw Malinowski gained great fame for his detailed study of the natives of the Trobriand Islands, in New Guinea. Argonauts of the Western Pacific, *the book from which this excerpt was taken, was his first book on the Islanders; it was published in 1922. Later works documented other aspects of life in the Trobriand Islands; they were* Crime and Custom in Savage Society, Sex and Repression in Savage Society, *and* The Sexual Life of Savages. *As an anthropological theorist, Malinowski has few followers today. But the brilliance and accuracy of his field work has never been surpassed, and it still offers an excellent model for the student to follow. This selection shows how Malinowski mixed science with imagination as he tried to record a culture; it also gives us a picture of a man who genuinely loves his work.*

Imagine yourself suddenly set down surrounded by all your gear, alone on a tropical beach close to a native village, while the launch or dinghy which has brought you sails away out of sight. Since you take up your abode in the compound of some neighboring white man, trader or missionary, you have nothing to do, but to start at once on your ethnographic work. Imagine further that you are a beginner, without previous experience, with nothing to guide you and no one to help you. For the white man is temporarily absent, or else unable or unwilling to waste any of his time on you. This exactly describes my initiation into field work on the south coast of New Guinea. I well remember the long visits I paid to the villages during the first weeks; the feeling of hopelessness and despair after many obstinate but futile attempts had entirely failed to bring me into real touch with the natives, or supply me with any material. I had periods of despondency, when I buried myself in the reading of novels, as a man might take to drink in a fit of tropical depression and boredom.

Imagine yourself, then, making your first entry into the village, alone or in company with your white guide. Some natives flock round you, especially if they smell tobacco. Others, the more dignified and elderly, remain seated where they are. Your white companion has his routine way of treating the natives, and he neither understands, nor is very much concerned with the manner in which you, as an ethnographer, will have to approach them. The first visit leaves you with a hopeful feeling that when you return alone, things will be easier. Such was my hope at least.

I came back duly, and soon gathered an audience around me. A few compliments in pidgin-English on both sides, some tobacco changing hands, induced an atmosphere of mutual amiability. I tried then to proceed to business. First, to begin with subjects which might arouse no suspicion, I started to "do" technology. A few natives were engaged in manufacturing some object or other. It was easy to look at it and obtain the names of the tools, and even some technical expressions about the proceedings, but there the matter ended. It must be borne in mind that pidgin-English is a very imperfect instrument for expressing one's ideas, and that before one gets a good training in framing questions and understanding answers one has the uncomfortable feeling that free communication with the natives will never be attained. I knew well that the best remedy for this was to collect concrete data, and accordingly I took a village census, wrote down genealogies, drew up plans and collected the terms of kinship. But all this remained dead material, which led no further into the understanding of real native mentality or behavior, since I could neither procure a good native interpretation of any of these items, nor get what could be called the hang of tribal life. As to obtaining their ideas about religion, and magic, their beliefs in sorcery and spirits, nothing was forthcoming except a few superficial items of folk-lore, mangled by being forced into pidgin-English.

It was not until I was alone in the district

that I began to make some headway and to find out where lay the secret of effective field-work. What is then this ethnographer's magic, by which he is able to evoke the real spirit of the natives, the true picture of tribal life? As usual, success can only be obtained by a patient and systematic application of a number of rules of common sense and well-known scientific principles, and not by the discovery of any marvellous short-cut leading to the desired results without effort or trouble. The principles of method can be grouped under three main headings. First of all, naturally, the student must possess real scientific aims, and know the values and criteria of modern ethnography. Secondly, he ought to put himself in good conditions of work, that is, in the main, to live without other white men, right among the natives. Finally, he has to apply a number of special methods of collecting and manipulating and fixing his evidence.

Proper conditions for ethnographic work

These, as said, consist mainly in cutting oneself off from the company of other white men, and remaining in as close contact with the natives as possible, which really can only be achieved by camping right in their villages. It is very nice to have a base in a white man's compound for the stores, and to know there is a refuge there in times of sickness and surfeit of native. But it must be far enough away not to become a permanent milieu in which you live and from which you emerge at fixed hours only to "do the village." It should not even be near enough to fly to at any moment for recreation. For the native is not the natural companion for a white man, and after you have been working with him for several hours, seeing how he does his gardens, or letting him tell you items of folk-lore, or discussing his customs, you will naturally hanker after the company of your own kind. But if you are alone in a village beyond the reach of this, you go for a solitary walk for an hour or so, return again and then quite naturally seek out the natives' society, this time as a relief from loneliness, just as you would any other companionship. And by this means of natural intercourse, you learn to know him, and you become familiar with his customs and beliefs far better than when he is a paid, and often bored, informant.

There is all the difference between a sporadic plunging into the company of natives, and being really in contact with them. What does this latter mean? On the ethnographer's side, it means that his life in the village, which at first is a strange, sometimes unpleasant, sometimes intensely interesting adventure, soon adopts quite a natural course very much in harmony with his surroundings.

Soon after I had established myself in Omarakana (Trobriand Islands), I began to take part, in a way, in the village life, to look forward to the important or festive events, to take personal interest in the gossip and the developments of the small village occurrences; to wake up every morning to a day, presenting itself to me more or less as it does to the native. I would get out from under my mosquito net, to find around me the village life beginning to stir, or the people well advanced in their working day according to the hour and also to the season, for they get up and begin their labors early or late, as work presses. As I went on my morning walk through the village, I could see intimate details of family life, of toilet, cooking, taking of meals; I could see the arrangements for the day's work, people starting on their errands, or groups of men and women busy at some manufacturing tasks. Quarrels, jokes, family scenes, events usually trivial, sometimes dramatic but always significant, formed the atmosphere of my daily life, as well as of theirs. It must be remembered that as the natives saw me constantly every day, they ceased to be alarmed or interested, or made self-conscious by my presence, and I ceased to be a disturbing element in the tribal life which I was to study, altering it by my very approach, as always happens with a newcomer to every savage community. In fact, as they knew that I would thrust my nose into everything, even where a well-mannered native would not dream of intruding, they finished by regarding me as part and parcel of their life, a necessary evil or nuisance, mitigated by donations of tobacco.

Later on in the day, whatever happened was within easy reach, and there was no possibility of its escaping my notice. Alarms about the sorcerer's approach in the evening, one or two big, really important quarrels and rifts within the community, cases of illness, attempted cures and deaths, magical rites which had to be performed, all these I had not to pursue, fearful of missing them, but they took place under my very eyes, at my own doorstep, so to speak. And it must be emphasized whenever anything dramatic or important occurs it is essential to investigate it at the very moment of happening, because the natives cannot but talk about it, are too excited to be reticent, and too interested to be mentally lazy in supplying details. Also, over and over again, I committed breaches of etiquette, which the natives, familiar enough with me, were not slow in pointing out. I had to learn how to behave, and to a certain extent, I acquired "the feeling" for native good and bad manners. With this, and with the capacity of enjoying their company and sharing some of their games and amusements, I began to feel that I was indeed in touch with the natives, and this is certainly the preliminary condition of being able to carry on successful field work.

Conclusion

At first, the task of analyzing another culture may not seem especially difficult. Yet Malinowski felt that you should be so immersed in the life of the culture under study that it becomes a full-time occupation, one in which you cut off for a time all contacts with your own culture. The total dedication necessary to fully understand another culture indicates how difficult the task is, and the high standards that a devoted scholar may sometimes set for himself.

SUMMARY

Culture and society are two related aspects of social life. Specifically, in studying a group's culture, we focus on the system of shared values and meanings; whereas in examining a society, we look primarily at the patterns of organization and interaction built upon that cultural background. A *culture trait* is the basic unit of a group's total design for living. Simple traits are organized in terms of a number of distinct and observable patterns that distinguish one culture from another.

Man's ability to create and learn a culture is based on his ability to communicate through symbols, notably language. The way in which we use symbols shapes our perception of reality and molds our attitudes toward the world around us. The vocabulary and structure of our language, for example, contain a set of unconscious assumptions, giving us a particular perspective that makes it easier to convey some ideas or concepts than others.

There are three major components of any culture: (1) cognitive aspects include our system of knowledge, ranging from our beliefs to our technology; (2) material aspects, the tools and artifacts used to manipulate and shape the environment, embody our cultural values and meanings; (3) normative aspects include the norms or rules that regulate behavior. More specifically, the normative system consists of (1) *norms,* or formal and informal codes of conduct, ranging from sacred laws or *mores* to more casual social customs or *folkways;* (2) values, or more enduring and abstract ideas, about what is good or right; (3) *institutions,* or the formal and stable ways of pursuing socially vital activities, such as rearing children or making a living; (4) *sanctions,* the rewards and punishments applied officially and unofficially to enforce conformity to norms and to control behavior that is socially defined as deviant.

In order to study a culture's major values and norms and to determine how these are reflected in social behavior, anthropologists and sociologists examine cultures as unified wholes through careful, in-depth observation and participation. Social scientists strive to avoid *ethnocentrism,* the tendency to evaluate other cultures in terms of their own. Scientific objectivity requires a high degree of *cultural relativity,* evaluation of each aspect of a culture in terms of the larger sociocultural context. While belief in the correctness of one's own cultural system helps to ensure social cohesion among the members of a society, ethnocentrism can also inhibit exchanges with other cultures and promote isolation or conflict as societies become increasingly interdependent. Exposure to another culture often causes *culture shock,* disorientation, or psychological distress.

A variety of approaches have been used in attempting to study cultural traits and their effect on the rest of the society. The functionalists focus on *functional* and *dysfunctional traits,* those which help or hinder a society in achieving its goals. Certain traits may be functional in some respects and dysfunctional in others. Other traits, which may appear to be meaningless, may actually be *cultural survivals,* traits that have lasted long after their original function has disappeared. Functionalism points up the fact that a culture is not simply a random collection of traits, but a system where the different parts must fit together for proper functioning. Any attempt to introduce changes into a society must consider the fact that cultures are *integrated* and that a change in one area may effect changes in other interrelated areas of the culture. In addition to its *manifest* or intended function, an action can also have unintended, unpredicted, or *latent* consequences.

Since each culture is adapted to meet a specific set of physical and social circumstances, each culture is unique. The environment, the stage of technological development, the language, the prevailing ideologies, and the society's past history all help to determine how a group will organize itself to meet its needs. Comparisons of many cultures, however, reveal fundamental similarities among them. Our physical similarities, our shared environment, certain requirements of group life (the need for organization, communication, leadership, and socialization) impose similar problems and limitations on all men. Within this common framework, each society devises its own distinctive solutions to the problems of human existence.

In actuality, many societies contain a number of *subcultures* in addition to the dominant system of values and behavior. Subcultures include some features of the cultural "average," but are distinguished by certain features not found elsewhere in the society. When a subculture is sharply different or opposed to the dominant pattern, sociologists speak of a *counterculture.* Every complex society has a variety of subcultures and an individual may participate in more than one, sometimes passing through several in the course of his life cycle.

GLOSSARY

Beliefs Ideas men hold about the natural or supernatural world which are not supported by objective or factual evidence. (page 87)

Conformity Behavior that is in accord with the norms of a social group or society. (page 97)

Counterculture A subculture that differs from and challenges the prevailing culture. (page 107)

Cultural integration The interwoven customs and values of a society. (page 104)

Cultural relativity The principle that a culture must be judged on its own terms and not in comparison to another culture. (page 102)

Cultural survival A culture trait that has survived after its original function has disappeared. (page 104)

Culture 1. The system of values and meanings shared by a group or society, including the embodiment of those values and meanings in material objects. 2. The way of life of a social group; the group's total man-made environment or social heritage. (page 82)

Culture trait The simplest significant unit of a culture. (page 82)

Deviance Behavior that does not conform to the norms of a social group or society. (page 97)

Dysfunction A function that has a negative effect. (page 103) (see *Function*)

Ethnocentrism The attitude that one's own culture or group is by nature superior, and the evaluation of another culture in terms of one's own culture. (page 102)

Folkways Social norms that are approved of and accepted by a society but not considered to be morally significant and not strictly enforced. (page 92)

Function The effect one unit of a culture or a society has on another unit or on the society as a whole. (page 103)

Functionalism An approach or orientation toward studying social and cultural phenomena. (page 103)

Ideology A system of beliefs about the social world which is strongly rooted in a specific set of values and interests. (page 88)

Institution A formal and stable way of carrying out an activity or function that is important to a society. (page 95)

Knowledge Ideas or information about the existing world which are supported by objective or factual evidence. (page 87)

Laws Standardized and formulated norms which regulate human conduct. (page 91)

Material culture All man-made physical objects. (page 88)

Mores Social norms that provide the moral standards of a group or society and which are strictly enforced. (page 92)

Norms, social A rule or standard which defines what people should or should not do, or think, or feel in any given social situation. (page 91)

Sanction A reward (positive sanction) or penalty (negative sanction) directed at a person or group to encourage or discourage certain types of behavior. (page 96)

Social control The process by which limits and checks are put upon the individual's behavior and people are motivated to conform to the norms of a group or society. (page 92)

Subculture The culture of a segment of society, such as a social group. (page 107)

Symbol A thing that stands for or suggests something else by reason of association. (page 84)

Technology Knowledge directed toward practical applications in the physical and social world. (page 87)

Value 1. An abstract and generalized conception of what is good, beneficial, desirable, and worthwhile.

2. A desired object or goal. (page 92)

SUGGESTED READINGS AND RELATED RESOURCES

I READINGS IN SOCIOLOGY AND ANTHROPOLOGY

Angell, Robert C. *Free Society and Moral Crisis*. Ann Arbor, Mich.: University of Michigan Press, 1958. From Angell's perspective, a society becomes well-integrated socially and culturally, and avoids moral crisis, when it has balanced interaction between norms, commonly held values, and prevailing conditions. He emphasizes the role of leaders and institutions in the adjustment of each of these elements to the other.

Benedict, Ruth. *Patterns of Culture*. Boston: Houghton Mifflin, 1961. Benedict uses examples from a variety of different cultures to show how each culture shapes personalities to produce useful members of that society.

Cahnman, W. J., and A. Boskoff, eds. *Sociology and History: Theory and Research*. New York: Free Press, 1964. This collection of essays describes and relates contributions which sociology and sociologists have made to the understanding of history.

Duncan, Hugh D. *Symbols and Social Theory*. New York: Oxford University Press, 1969. This book presents the work and contributions of a number of social theorists from widely divergent schools of thought.

Hall, Edward T. *The Silent Language*. New York: Doubleday, 1959. Hall shows that actions and behavior communicate with symbols as efficiently as words. He discusses the ways in which these symbols are invested with meaning.

Kluckhohn, Clyde. *Mirror for Man*. New York: Fawcett World Library, 1964. Kluckhohn demonstrates the value of the study of culture for explaining and predicting behavior. His work contains many explanations of ethnocentrism and culture shock.

Linton, Ralph. *The Tree of Culture*. New York: Alfred A. Knopf, 1955. In this posthumous study, the famous anthropologist traces the history of the development of culture throughout the world and presents a theory of cultural development and change.

Malinowski, Bronislaw. *The Dynamics of Cultural Change*. New Haven: Yale University Press, 1945. Culture is viewed by this early anthropologist as the vehicle that carries on social organization. He studied culture mainly from the point of view of its functions.

Mannheim, Karl. *Ideology and Utopia*. Translated by Louis Wirth and Edward Shils. New York: Harcourt Brace Jovanovich, 1936. This was the germinal work in the field of the sociology of knowledge. The book's focus is upon the nature of ideas and their impact upon society.

Redfield, Robert. *The Primitive World and Its Transformations*. Ithaca, N.Y.: Cornell University Press, 1953. Redfield's study is one of a series in which the effects of modernization upon primitive cultures is analyzed. Redfield sees the technological order becoming progressively more important than the moral order as societies move from isolated tribe to peasant society to civilization.

Shapiro. Harry L., ed. *Man, Culture, and Society*. New York: Oxford University Press, 1956. Specialists in physical, archaeological, and cultural anthropology contributed to this collection of essays and articles. It is a good source book on culture.

Sorokin, Pitirim. *Society, Culture and Personality*. New York: Harper, 1947. This distinguished sociologist presents a theory of the birth and development of ideas. He shows that culture is the product of ideas, that the various elements of culture are integrated through ideological systems.

Sumner, William Graham. *Folkways*. New York: Mentor, 1960. In this definitive work on customs, folkways, and mores, Sumner presents a theory of the emergence of norms and the normative order.

White, Leslie A. *The Science of Culture*. New York: Farrar, Straus & Giroux, 1949. White calls for a new science of "culturology" in this book, which emphasizes the importance of technology in cultural evolution.

Articles and Papers

Barnett, J. H. "Research Areas in the Sociology of Art." *Sociology and Social Research* **42**, 6 (July–August 1958):401–405.

Beel, George M., Charles L. Mulford, Gerald Klonglan, and J. Bohlen. "Goal Displacement and the Problem of Selecting Criterion Weights." *Proceedings of the Southwestern Sociological Association* **19** (1968):103–107.

Blake, Judith, and K. Davis. "On Norms and Values." In *Handbook of Modern Sociology*, edited by R. L. Faris. Chicago: Rand McNally, 1964.

Boswell, James. "Cultural Ethos of Primitive Tribes: Yir Yiront Kaingang and Auca." *Practical Anthropology* **15**, 4 (1968).

Gibbs, Jack P. "Sanctions." *Social Problems* **14**, 2 (Fall 1966): 147–159.

Hoult, Thomas F. "Functionalism: A Brief Clarification." *Sociological Inquiry* **33**, 1 (Winter 1963):31–33.

Jaeger, Gertrude, and Philip Selznick. "A Normative Theory of Culture." *American Sociological Review* **29** (October 1964):653–669.

Kluckhohn, Clyde. "The Study of Culture." In *The Policy Sciences,* edited by D. Lerner and

H. D. Lasswell. Stanford, Calif.: Stanford University Press, 1951.

Lipset, Seymour M. "The Value Patterns of a Democracy: A Case Study in Comparative Analysis." *American Sociological Review* **28** (August 1963):515–531.

Meggers, B. J. "Environmental Limitations in the Development of Culture." *American Anthropologist* **56** (1959):801–824.

Miner, Horace. "Body Ritual Among the Nicerema." *American Anthropologist* **58** (June 1956).

Ryan, Bryce. "The Resuscitation of Social Change." *Social Forces* **44**, 1 (September 1965): 1–7.

Sinha, Nirmal Chandra. "Asian Law and Usage in European Expression: Some Illustrations from Tibet." *Man in India* **46**, 1 (January–March 1966): 66–73.

Smith, Harold E. "Toward a Clarification of the Concept of Social Institution." *Sociology and Social Research* **48**, 2 (January 1964):197–206.

Yinger, Milton J. "Contraculture and Subculture." *American Sociological Review* **25** (October 1960):625–635.

II RELATED RESOURCES
Nonfiction

Bohannon, Paul. *Africa and Africans*. Garden City, N.Y.: The Natural History Press, 1964. A vivid description of the relationships of the colonial and native African cultures. A brief history of Africa is included along with a general statement of the elements that are distinctive to African art, religion, economics, and politics.

Hunter, Guy. *Modernizing Peasant Societies: A Comparative Study in Asia and Africa*. New York: Oxford University Press, 1969. Hunter discusses how the importation of institutions from technologically oriented countries to agriculturally undeveloped countries results in cultural upheaval.

Kenyatta, Jomo. *Facing Mount Kenya: The Tribal Life of the Kikuyu*. New York: Random House, Vintage, 1962. A rare document, this study of an agricultural East African tribe is written by a Kikuyu native who was educated in England. He, therefore, has a perspective on tribal life that a Western ethnographer could not achieve.

Lewis, Oscar. *The Children of Sanchez: Autobiography of a Mexican Family*. New York: Vintage Books, 1961. These autobiographies of a Mexico City family provide an interesting perspective on what it is like to live in another culture—in this case a culture of poverty.

Rosenberg, Bernard, and David M. White. *Mass Culture*. New York: Macmillan, 1957. A provocative examination of the contributions (for good or ill) of advertising, television, movies, and magazines to Western culture, and a conceptual formulation of the meaning of "mass culture."

Roszak, Theodore. *The Making of a Counter Culture*. New York: Doubleday, 1969. Roszak looks at the culture which young people are forming within, but in opposition to, the dominant American culture and examines the reasons for its formation.

Yablonsky, Lewis. *The Violent Gang*. Middlesex, England: Penguin Books, 1967. This is a good example of life in a subculture. It is a case study of a New York City gang whose major function is to fight with other gangs. Yablonsky, who includes transcripts of his conversations with members of the gang, offers a general theory of the behavior of such "near-groups."

Wolfe, Tom. *The Electric Kool-Aid Acid Test*. New York: Farrar, Straus & Giroux, 1968. Wolfe explores the cult-like quality of one hippie group in San Francisco, showing how the group totally absorbed its members through an elaborate system of beliefs.

Fiction

Baldwin, James. *Another Country*. New York: Dell, 1965. A story of misery and love in a deviant subculture, this novel tells of a young black musician trying to find a happy way of life in New York City.

Greene, Graham. *The Quiet American*. New York: Bantam Books, 1957. Greene writes of a young American diplomat who has recently graduated from Harvard and describes his first extracultural experience; he sharply portrays the diplomat's self-righteous and innocent response to the culture of French Indochina.

Kazantzakis, Nikos. *Zorba the Greek*. New York: Simon & Schuster, 1952. An educated Englishman, transplanted to rural Greece, is at first repelled by the culture, later attracted to it, and finally influenced by it. His experiences are instigated and guided by a Greek named Zorba.

Nordhoff, Charles, and James Norman Hall. *Pitcairn's Island*. New York: Pocket Books, 1962. This novel reconstructs the history of the *Bounty* mutineers. Cut off from their civilization, the mutineers attempt to create a new society on an unknown island by combining elements of British and Tahitian culture.

O'Faolain, Sean. *The Finest Stories of Sean O'Faolain*. New York: Bantam Books, 1965. A collection of vignettes, the book portrays the customs, mores, and morals of one nation — Ireland.

Steinbeck, John. *The Grapes of Wrath*. New York: Bantam Books, 1964. First published in 1939. This book describes the poverty and living conditions of the California migratory workers; the story shows how their degradation is a reflection of values of the dominant culture and its insensitivity to this subculture.

Films

The Birth of a Nation (Silent). David W. Griffith, 1915. This American film describes the Civil War period. Controversy has resulted from Griffith's use of black stereotypes and his sympathetic account of the beginning of the Klan. Griffith's justification, that he did not set out to create a biased film, may perhaps be traced to the socialization and ideas he received when growing up in the impoverished Southern home of a Confederate colonel and his wife.

Nanook of the North (Silent). Robert K. Flaherty, 1922. This film, based on Flaherty's own observations as an explorer in Northern Canada, was the first successful feature-length documentary about the Eskimo culture.

The Savage Innocents. Nicholas Ray, 1961. This drama portrays the culture shock sustained by a Western official and an Eskimo when they met.

Zorba the Greek. Michael Cacoyannis, 1964. Adapted from the novel by Nikos Kazantzakis.

4. Socialization

We may define socialization *as the process by which the culture of a group or society is instilled or internalized in the individual members of that group or society. This process is basically the same in every society no matter how different the cultures which are instilled. Socialization involves training people to accept a given culture, to develop personality and a sense of self, and to correctly play their own assigned roles in that culture. The process of socialization begins almost at birth and continues through life, for even in old age a person must still learn new roles, such as that of grandparent, "senior citizen," and retired businessman.*

We will begin this chapter with a discussion of the way the foundation for all social behavior is laid, with the development of the self. Although this topic deals with some of the concepts and theories of psychology, they will be viewed primarily from the social aspect. Topic 2 is devoted to socialization during childhood. The area of socialization after early childhood will be dealt with in topic 3. The final topic focuses on the way that the process of socialization affects personality and individuality.

1 THE PROCESS OF SOCIALIZATION

Certain features of man's biology make him a creature uniquely capable of socialization. One of these is his long period of childhood dependency; no animal remains a child for as much of its life as does man. His period of helplessness and dependence on the adult is much longer than that of any other member of the animal kingdom. This is actually an aid to socialization, as it strengthens the bond between the parent-teacher and the child-student and gives them the time to develop their relationship to a point of great efficiency.

Because man takes longer to mature, he has a longer learning period than any other animal. The biologist Desmond Morris has pointed this out in his book *The Naked Ape:*

He [man] not only became brainier at manipulating objects, but he also had a longer childhood during which he could learn from his parents and other adults. Infant monkeys and chimpanzees are playful, exploratory, and inventive, but this phase dies quickly. The naked ape's [man's] infancy was, in these respects, extended right through into his sexually adult life. There was plenty of time to imitate and learn the special techniques that had been devised by previous generations. His weaknesses as a physical and instinctive hunter could be more than compensated for by his intelligence and his imitative abilities. He could be taught by his parents as no animal had ever been taught before.[1]

1. Desmond Morris, *The Naked Ape* (New York: McGraw-Hill, 1967), p. 30.

In addition to his long period of childhood dependency, man has another characteristic that makes his socialization possible, and that is his ability to use language. Although other species have the vocal mechanisms needed, only man has the intellectual capacity to create and use extensive sets of symbols. Although social organization can be formed and directed with wordless communication, as it is among many other animal species, the complexity of human society is directly dependent on language to invent and sustain it. Verbal communication is the chief medium of socialization.

Finally, it should be noted that culture and socialization would not be necessary at all if man had strong *instincts,* that is, complex behavior patterns relatively fixed in biological nature. Instincts guide the social life of lower animals, and culture is not necessary. Birds, for example, accomplish many complicated social tasks, such as nesting and migration, by instinct rather than conscious intelligence. Man does possess biological drives, such as hunger, sex, sleep, and survival, but these drives are very general and undirected, and must be guided by a culture if they are to fit into human social circumstances.

BIOLOGICAL AND EMOTIONAL NEEDS OF INFANT AND CHILD

Socialization begins the first time a mother holds her baby; that is the beginning step in the long process of teaching the baby to recognize himself as an individual and his mother as another individual, and to con-

Socialization begins in the first few months of a baby's life. The human contact that a mother's fondling provides is crucial for the baby's development and even his survival. *(Lida Moser, DPI)*

struct a patterned kind of relationship with her. During the first few months of a baby's life, many of the socializing activities of the adults caring for the baby are directed toward satisfying biological or physical needs, for these seem the most pressing problems of the infant. Sometimes the very actions which are dictated by biology also serve to meet the baby's developing emotional needs; in fact, from the earliest moments of life biological and emotional needs are closely intertwined. In nursing the infant, or in holding the infant against her body while bottle feeding, a mother provides three necessities: warmth, which is especially important in the first few weeks of life; food, which the baby can't provide for himself at all; and human contact, both physical and emotional, a factor less tangible but no less significant for the baby's development, even for his survival. Infants

raised in orphanages with adequate health care but an absolute minimum of human contact, have been found to have much higher death rates than infants raised in orphanages that were similar but provided the infant with more human contact.[2]

Laboratory experiments with rhesus monkeys[3] showed that contact — both bodily contact and interaction with other monkeys — was a basic biological need. When the need was not met early in a monkey's life, it led

2. See John Bowlby, *Child Care and the Growth of Love* (Baltimore: Penguin Books, 1954).

3. Harry F. Harlow, "Love in Infant Monkeys," *Scientific American* 200 (June 1959):68–74; Harry F. Harlow and Margaret K. Harlow, "The Effect of Rearing Conditions on Behavior," *Bulletin of the Menninger Clinic* 26 (September 1962): 213–224; Harry F. Harlow and Margaret K. Harlow, "Social Deprivation in Monkeys," *Scientific American* 207 (November 1962):137–146.

to serious physical and emotional abnormal-
ities. Females grew up unable to perform as
mothers and often seriously mistreated their
offspring. The need for contact was so great
that when monkeys were placed in a cage
with two substitute mothers, one made only of
wire and the other covered by soft cloth,
the monkeys spent most of their time clinging
to the soft cloth mother. Even if they were
fed through the wire mother, they preferred
the soft cloth mother. If the cloth mother
was removed, the monkeys developed severe
behavior problems. The cloth mother seemed
to provide some of the comfort a real mother
would; but monkeys raised only with a cloth
mother still required contact with other
monkeys; even then, though apparently
normal, these "cloth-mothered" monkeys
in their own maturity were grossly defective
in mothering and many were unable to reproduce at all.

Psychologists believe that human babies
also have a basic biological need as well as
an emotional one to cling to a warm, shelter-
ing mother-figure, and to be stroked and
murmured at. Verbal communication is not
absolutely necessary, but some sort of mood
communication—smiles,   laughs,   gurgles,
coos, pats—is. The necessity for contact with
others continues even through adult life.

The baby's first idea of the "quality" of
life around him may come from the way in
which his biological needs are met. According to the theories of the psychiatrist Erik
Erikson, it is at this early stage of life that an
individual develops a basic pattern of feelings—ranging from trust to mistrust—about
the world around him. The infant whose needs
are met promptly and adequately, and with
positive emotional overtones, begins to view
the world as safe and comfortable, and its
inhabitants   as   trustworthy   and   helpful.
However, when the care is inadequate, inconsistent, or emotionally rejective, the child
may view his social environment as hostile
and untrustworthy, and approach each new
experience with feelings of fear and suspicion.

The biological and psychological aspects of the need
for physical contact have been clarified by Harlow's
experimental work with rhesus monkeys. Here an infant monkey is shown clinging to the soft cloth
mother substitute. He prefers this even though his
source of food is through the wire "mother." *(Photo
by Harry Harlow)*

If these feelings are reinforced in the later
periods of personality development they may
become a permanent part of the child's character as an adult.[4] (See the accompanying
abridgment for a summary of Erikson's views
on socialization and the self.)

Psychological evidence, such as that col-

4. Erik Erikson, *Childhood and Society* (New York:
W. W. Norton, 1950), chap. 7.

lected by John Bowlby,[5] indicates that a child who is deprived of loving care will grow up unable to offer love to others or cope with it when it is offered; in addition, he will probably show a wide variety of other severe emotional problems.

By the time he is about three months old, a baby can recognize specific human faces; he knows his own parents. If he is to develop into an emotionally healthy adult, the baby at this stage must begin to send and receive stronger communications of emotion. At first these communications will be made nonverbally—for example, by body movements, facial expression, and nonverbal vocalization. Gradually, sometime in the second year of the baby's life, language takes on more importance. From this point on, a major part of the process of socialization involves developing the child's use of language and encouraging language as a replacement for emotional expression unacceptable to the culture.

It is important to remember that the emotional relationship between parent and child must flow in both directions if the process is to be truly socializing. The baby must also be allowed, and later encouraged, to express his own emotions to his parents. At the early stage of development that we are discussing, three basic emotions are assumed to be felt by the baby. One is an affectionate response to the love expressed by the parents. Second is a feeling of anxiety, which seems to be an inevitable result of man's lengthy childhood dependence. At first, he fears only that his protectors may fail to meet his needs; later in life, as he becomes increasingly socialized, he begins to fear also that he himself will fail. Man pays for his advanced powers of reasoning and his orderly society with anxiety, and every individual must learn to come to terms with it. The third emotion

noticeable in children is the anger felt when facing such things as deprivation, frustration, or neglect. At first a child will express this feeling very openly, but in most cultures, including ours, he will eventually be taught to restrain his anger. This is because anger is a potential source of social disruption, and thus a danger to social life, which depends so greatly on mutual cooperation.

THE SELF AS A SOCIAL PRODUCT

In the course of the interaction between child and parents that is designed to meet the basic biological and emotional needs outlined above, another process is taking place. The child is learning to define himself as a person, in the social sense of the word. He is developing a personality, a most important aspect of which is his sense of *self*—his awareness and feeling about his own personal and social identity.

In fact, the sense of self can *only* come about as a result of social interaction. A newborn infant does not differentiate himself from his mother. Gradually in the next few months he begins to see his mother as one person and himself as another. Then he may vaguely sense her as a protector and himself as a dependent. He goes on to feel himself as loved and her as loving. As interactions with his mother become more complex, they also become more definitive. He learns that he is small and she is large, that she is a female and he is a male, that she is the teacher and he is the pupil, and that she is a mother and he is a son. A child who is reared in circumstances of near isolation is gravely handicapped both emotionally and socially, for he never has the opportunity to see himself reflected in the eyes of others, or to sense, through social interaction, his own identity.

The influential American sociologist Charles Horton Cooley referred to this reflection in the eyes of others as the "looking glass self." He suggested that it has three main components: our perception of how behavior appears to others; our perception

5. John Bowlby, "Grief and Mourning in Infancy and Early Childhood," in *The Psychoanalytic Study of the Child,* vol. 15 (New York: International University Press, 1960).

George Herbert Mead (1863–1931) was a pioneer in the field of social psychology. His main concern was the relationship between man's personality and the society in which he lives. Earlier sociologists had stressed the mechanisms by which men formed societies: Mead concentrated on the ways in which society forms man. Mead never wrote a book, but his students at the University of Chicago, realizing the value of his ideas, made stenographic transcripts of his lectures and had them published in a series of books. The most famous of these is *Mind, Self, and Society* (1934). *(University of Chicago Press)*

of their judgment of this behavior; and our feelings about those judgments.[6] In brief summary, if we think that others approve of the things we do, we too approve of them. Through many encounters with the judgments of others the self is formed, as a social product. The most important of these social encounters are, according to Cooley, those taking place in primary groups (which are discussed in the next chapter).

The need for social interaction to define the self continues through life. We learn new roles and gradually alter our self-image by using the information we receive from in-

teraction with others, a process which is similar to what the computer experts call "feedback."

It is also true that people who lead relatively isolated lives, such as elderly people in poor health or even some suburban housewives who are separated from adult companionship, begin to feel a loss of identity through lack of interaction or feedback, and experience psychological stress. Prolonged solitude is prescribed to help achieve loss of identity in the mystical religions, which stress the goal of losing self-awareness, or submerging one's selfishness, for the purpose of greater awareness of God or a higher reality. The monk living in a hermit's cave, or the holy man dwelling alone on the mountain, does indeed "lose himself," for lack of social contact blurs his self-identity.

MEAD AND SYMBOLIC INTERACTIONISM

George Herbert Mead was one of the most important theorists regarding the process of socialization and the way that social interaction helps to develop a sense of self. Mead, whose work was based in part on the earlier contributions of Cooley, was the chief architect of the important school of thought in social psychology known as *symbolic interactionism*.[7] Mead divided the self into two parts, the "I" and the "me." The "I" represents the spontaneous, unique, and natural characteristics of each individual, for example, the unfettered motivations and drives found in every normal infant and child. The "me" represents the specifically social components of the self—the internalized demands of society and the individual's awareness of these demands. The "I" develops first; the "me" takes much longer, because one must first learn what the expectations and rules of his society are. The "me" usually acts as a

6. Charles Cooley, *Human Nature and the Social Order* (New York: Schocken Books, 1964).

7. George Herbert Mead, *Mind, Self and Society,* ed. Charles W. Morris (Chicago: University of Chicago Press, 1934).

sort of censor of the "I"; it is based initially on the demands and expectations of the parents and later on the demands and expectations of the larger society. Mead suggests that the development of self involves a continuing conversation between the "me" and the "I," which Mead called *minding*.

George Mead also pointed out that there is a difference between the social demands and expectations made by those with whom you have a close personal relationship and whose judgments are important to you, and the impersonal demands made by society. The first sort of demand he called demands of *significant others;* an example of this would be the demands that parents make on a child. The other type is the demand of *generalized others*. A child learns to respond first to the demands of significant others; response to generalized others comes at a later stage of development.

According to Mead, the self develops in three distinct stages. First is the *imitative* stage, when the child copies what he sees his parents doing. A girl will play on the floor with pots and pans while her mother is cooking; a boy will play with tools while his father is fixing things around the house. At this stage of development the child has no real conception of himself as a separate social being.

In the second stage, which Mead called the *play* stage, the child plays more creatively at adopting social roles. He pretends to be his mother or his father; he pretends to be the milkman or kindergarten teacher. It is at this stage that children begin to see themselves as social objects, *"me* do this," *"I* do that," *"Jane* change dolly." The "me" begins to develop during this stage, but the child does not yet see role playing as an obligation or a social necessity—the child merely plays at the social roles of life.

The third stage of the child's self-development comes when the child is able to take (rather than play) a role in a social situation with a real awareness of his importance to the

Sigmund Freud (1856–1939) developed the technique of psychoanalysis as a tool to help treat patients with emotional and mental problems. After years of practicing psychiatry, he incorporated the discoveries he had made regarding the human mind into a broad theory of human emotional development. He was the dominant influence on psychological thought for more than a generation, and left behind him more than twenty-four volumes of his work. Although most sociologists considered unsuccessful his efforts to apply his theories of psychodynamics to problems of culture and social development, his works did much to shape the developing fields of psychiatry and social psychology. The best sources for an understanding of Freud's theories are: *The Interpretation of Dreams* (1900); *The Psychopathology of Everyday Life* (1904); *A General Introduction to Psychoanalysis* (1917); and *Outline of Psychoanalysis* (1940). *(Culver Pictures, Inc.)*

group and the group's importance to him. George Mead used the metaphor of a game to describe this stage, referring to the complex behavior that is required to participate in organized games. In baseball, for example, one does not act out a highly specific individual role. The player must continually adjust his behavior to the needs of the team as a whole and to the specific situations that arise in the game. Above all he must follow an impersonal set of demands and expectations—

the rules of the game. It is at this point that Mead would say the boy is responding to a generalized other—the organized community or group that gives to the child his unity of self. Gradually, the child learns to take on the point of view not only of his parents, his friends, and his teammates, but of organized society as a whole.

SIGMUND FREUD

Sigmund Freud was the founder of psychoanalysis and the most important scholar of human behavior in this century. While Charles Cooley and George Mead emphasized the self as a social product and the importance of language and symbolic communication, Freud stressed the biological basis and emotional forces of the socialization process.[8]

Freud thought of the personality as divided into three segments: the "id," the "ego," and the "superego." The superego roughly corresponds to Mead's "me"—the internalization of socially learned "shoulds" and "oughts," the censor and social control mechanism of the personality. The id is a great reservoir of unconscious biological and psychological drives, especially sexual drives. The emphasis Freud put on the id

8. A good introduction to Freud's thought is Calvin S. Hall, *A Primer of Freudian Psychology* (New York: New American Library, 1954).

was a hallmark of his theory. Freud's theory, especially as it developed in his later years, held that the ego acted as a mediator between the demands made by the superego and the domination of the individual by the id. He theorized that these three elements must be balanced at the various stages of human development if normal, healthy functioning was to be achieved.

Many sociologists today feel that Freud overemphasized the biological factors which determine personality, and gave insufficient consideration to social factors. But Freud did give great importance to the child's social experiences within his family. In fact, some scholars believe that, in addition to his theories of the unconscious, his most lasting contribution was his analysis of the importance of the childhood experience.

Many scholars have built on Freud's work and made further significant theoretical contributions, usually pointing out more clearly the importance of social and cultural factors to the dynamics of human behavior. Alfred Adler, Carl Jung, Karen Horney, and Erich Fromm are well-known examples. Erik Erikson, whose theory of the eight steps of man's development is presented in the abridgment already mentioned, is an important contemporary psychological theorist who "stands on the shoulders" of Freud.

DAVID ELKIND
Erik Erikson's Eight Ages of Man

Abridged from "Erik Erikson's Eight Ages of Man," *The New York Times Magazine,* © April 5, 1970 by The New York Times Company. Reprinted by permission.

Introduction

In this article, David Elkind, himself a professor of psychology and psychiatry, examines and explains the contributions

Erik Erikson has made toward the understanding of self-development. Erikson has built on Freud's psychological insights by combining them with information about the social development of the self, showing how at each stage of life a person must establish certain new orientations toward the social world he lives in, as well as toward the growth of his inner self. Erikson has identified eight stages of development, from birth to old age; these are described here in sequence. Each stage opens up a new dimension of social interaction, and new possibilities for relationships with the self and the social environment.

Trust vs. mistrust

The first stage corresponds to the oral stage in classical psychoanalytic theory and usually extends through the first year of life. In Erikson's view, the new dimension of social interaction that emerges during this period involves basic *trust* at the one extreme, and *mistrust* at the other. The degree to which the child comes to trust the world, other people and himself depends to a considerable extent upon the quality of the care that he receives. The infant whose needs are met when they arise, whose discomforts are quickly removed, who is cuddled, fondled, played with and talked to, develops a sense of the world as a safe place to be and of people as helpful and dependable. When, however, the care is inconsistent, inadequate and rejecting, it fosters a basic mistrust, an attitude of fear and suspicion on the part of the infant toward the world in general and people in particular that will carry through to later stages of development.

It should be said at this point that the problem of basic trust-versus-mistrust (as is true for all the later dimensions) is not resolved once and for all during the first year of life; it arises again at each successive stage of development. There is both hope and danger in this. The child who enters school with a sense of mistrust may come to trust a particular teacher who has taken the trouble to make herself trustworthy; with this second chance, he overcomes his early mistrust. On the other hand, the child who comes through infancy with a vital sense of trust can still have his sense of mistrust activated at a later stage if, say, his parents are divorced and separated under acrimonious circumstances.

Autonomy vs. doubt

Stage Two spans the second and third years of life, the period which Freudian theory calls the anal stage. Erikson sees here the emergence of *autonomy*. This autonomy dimension builds upon the child's new motor and mental abilities. At this stage the child can not only walk but also climb, open and close, drop, push and pull, hold and let go. The child takes pride in these new accomplishments and wants to do everything himself, whether it be pulling the wrapper off a piece of candy, selecting the vitamin out of the bottle or flushing the toilet. If parents recognize the young child's need to do what he is capable of doing at his own pace and in his own time, then he develops a sense that he is able to control his muscles, his impulses, himself and, not insignificantly, his environment—the sense of autonomy.

When, however, his caretakers are impatient and do for him what he is capable of doing himself, they reinforce a sense of shame and doubt. To be sure, every parent has rushed a child at times and children are hardy enough to endure such lapses. It is only when caretaking is consistently overprotective and criticism of "accidents" (whether these be wetting, soiling, spilling, or breaking things) is harsh and unthinking that the child develops an excessive sense of shame with respect to other people and an excessive sense of doubt about his own abilities to control his world and himself.

If the child leaves this stage with less autonomy than shame or doubt, he will be handicapped in his attempts to achieve autonomy in adolescence and adulthood. Contrariwise, the child who moves through this stage with his sense of autonomy buoyantly outbalancing his feelings of shame and doubt is well prepared to be autonomous at later phases in the life cycle. Again, however, the balance of autonomy to shame and doubt set up during this period can be changed in either positive or negative directions by later events.

Initiative vs. guilt

In this stage (the phallic stage of classical psychoanalysis) the child, age 4 to 5, is pretty much master of his body and can ride a tricycle, run, cut and hit. He can thus initiate motor activities of various sorts on his own and no longer merely responds to or imitates the actions of other children. The same holds true for his language and fantasy activities. Accordingly, Erikson argues that the social dimension that appears at this stage has *initiative* at one of its poles and *guilt* at the other.

Whether the child will leave this stage with his sense of initiative far outbalancing his sense of guilt depends to a considerable extent upon how parents respond to his self-initiated activities. Children who are given much freedom and opportunity to imitate motor play such as running, bike riding, sliding, skating, tussling and wrestling have their sense of initiative reinforced. Initiative is also reinforced when parents answer their children's questions (intellectual initiative) and do not deride or inhibit fantasy or play activity. On the other hand, if the child is made to feel that his motor activity is bad, that his questions are a nuisance and that his play is silly and stupid, then he may develop a sense of guilt over self-initiated activities in general that will persist through later life stages.

Industry vs. inferiority

Stage Four is the age period from 6 to 11, the elementary school years (described by classical psychoanalysis as the *latency phase*). It is a time during which the child's love for the parent of the opposite sex and rivalry with the same sexed parent (elements in the so-called family romance) are quiescent. It is also a period during which the child becomes capable of deductive reasoning, and of playing and learning by rules. It is not until this period, for example, that children can really play marbles, checkers and other "take turn" games that require obedience to rules. Erikson argues that the psychosocial dimension that emerges during this period has a *sense of industry* at one extreme and a *sense of inferiority* at the other.

The term industry nicely captures a dominant theme of this period during which the concern with how things are made, how they work and what they do predominates. It is the Robinson Crusoe age in the sense that the enthusiasm and minute detail with which Crusoe describes his activities appeals to the child's own budding sense of industry. When children are encouraged in their efforts to make, do, or build practical things (whether it be to construct creepy crawlers, tree houses, or airplane models—or to cook, bake or sew), are allowed to finish their products, and are praised and rewarded for the results, then the sense of industry is enhanced. But parents who see their children's efforts at making and doing as "mischief," and as simply "making a mess," help to encourage in children a sense of inferiority.

During these elementary-school years, however, the child's world includes more than the home. Now social institutions other than the family come to play a central role in the developmental crisis of the individual.

Identity vs. role confusion

When the child moves into adolescence (Stage Five—roughly the ages 12–18), he encounters, according to traditional psychoanalytic theory, a reawakening of the family-romance problem of early childhood [love for the parent of the opposite sex]. His means of resolving the problem is to seek and find a romantic partner of his own generation. While Erikson does not deny this aspect of adolescence, he points out that there are other problems as well. The adolescent matures mentally as well as physiologically and, in addition to the new feelings, sensations and desires he experiences as a result of changes in his body, he develops a multitude of new ways of looking at and thinking about the world. Among other things, those in adolescence can now think about other people's thinking and wonder about what other people think of them. They can also conceive of ideal families, religions and societies which they then compare with the imperfect families, religions and societies of their own experience. Finally, adolescents become capable of constructing theories and philosophies designed to bring all the varied and conflicting aspects of society into a working, harmonious and peaceful whole. The adolescent, in a word, is an impatient idealist who believes that it is as easy to realize an ideal as it is to imagine it.

Erikson believes that the new interpersonal dimension which emerges during this period has to do with a sense of *ego identity* at the positive end and a sense of *role confusion* at the negative end. That is to say, given the adolescent's newfound integrative abilities, his task is to bring together all of the things he has learned about himself as a son, student, athlete, friend, scout, newspaper boy, and so on, and integrate these different images of himself into a whole that makes sense and that shows continuity with the past while preparing for the future. To the extent that the young person succeeds in this endeavor, he arrives at a sense of psychosocial identity, a sense of who he is, where he has been and where he is going.

In contrast to the earlier stages, where parents play a more or less direct role in the determination of the result of the developmental crises, the influence of parents during this stage is much more indirect. If the young person reaches adolescence with, thanks to his parents, a vital sense of trust, autonomy, initiative and industry, then his chances of arriving at a meaningful sense of ego identity are much enhanced.

The reverse, of course, holds true for the young person who enters adolescence with considerable mistrust, shame, doubt, guilt and inferiority. Preparation for a successful adolescence, and the attainment of an integrated psychosocial identity must, therefore, begin in the cradle.

Over and above what the individual brings with him from his childhood, the attainment of a sense of personal identity depends upon the social milieu in which he or she grows up. For example, in a society where women are to some extent second-class citizens, it may be harder for females to arrive at a sense of psychosocial identity. Likewise at times such as the present, when rapid social and technological change breaks down many traditional values, it may be more difficult for young people to find continuity between what they learned and experienced as children and what they learn and experience as adolescents. At such times young people often seek causes that give their lives meaning and direction. The activism of the current generation of young people may well stem, in part at least, from this search.

Intimacy vs. isolation

Stage Six in the life cycle is young adulthood; roughly the period of courtship and early family life that extends from late adolescence till early middle age. For this stage, and the stages described hereafter, classical psychoanalysis has nothing new or major to say. For Erikson however, the previous attainment of a sense of personal identity and the engagement in productive work that marks this period gives rise to a new interpersonal dimension of *intimacy* at the one extreme and *isolation* at the other.

When Erikson speaks of intimacy he means much more than love-making alone; he means the ability to share with and care about another person without fear of losing oneself in the process. In the case of intimacy, as in the case of identity, success or failure no longer depends directly upon the parents but only indirectly as they have contributed to the individual's success or failure at the earlier stages. Here, too, as in the case of identity, social conditions may help or hinder the establishment of a sense of intimacy. Likewise, intimacy need not involve sexuality; it includes the relationship between friends. Soldiers who have served together under the most dangerous circumstances often develop a sense of commitment to one another that exemplifies intimacy in its broadest sense. If a sense of intimacy is not established with friends or a marriage partner, the result, in Erikson's view, is a sense of isolation—of being alone without anyone to share with or care for.

Generativity vs. self-absorption

This stage—middle age—brings with it what Erikson speaks of as either *generativity* or *self-absorption,* and stagnation. What Erikson means by generativity is that the person begins to be concerned with others beyond his immediate family, with future generations and the nature of the society and world in which those generations will live. Generativity does not reside only in parents; it can be found in any individual who actively concerns himself with the welfare of young people and with making the world a better place for them to live and to work.

Those who fail to establish a sense of generativity fall into a state of self-absorption in which their personal needs and comforts are of predominant concern. A fictional case of self-absorption is Dickens' Scrooge in "A Christmas Carol." In his one-sided concern with money and in his disregard for the interests and welfare of his young employee, Bob Cratchit, Scrooge exemplifies the self-absorbed, embittered (the two often go together) old man. Dickens also illustrated,

however, what Erikson points out: namely, that unhappy solutions to life's crises are not irreversible. Scrooge, at the end of the tale, manifested both a sense of generativity and of intimacy which he had not experienced before.

Integrity vs. despair

Stage Eight in the Eriksonian scheme corresponds roughly to the period when the individual's major efforts are nearing completion and when there is time for reflection—and for the enjoyment of grandchildren, if any. The psychosocial dimension that comes into prominence now has *integrity* on one hand and *despair* on the other.

The sense of integrity arises from the individual's ability to look back on his life with satisfaction. At the other extreme is the individual who looks back upon his life as a series of missed opportunities and missed directions; now in the twilight years he realizes that it is too late to start again. For such a person the inevitable result is a sense of despair at what might have been.

Conclusion

In important ways, Erikson's theory is really an extension of Freud's work. To Freud the personality was almost completely shaped in early childhood, with any basic change after that time being extremely difficult to initiate and complete. Erikson feels that basic personality changes can occur at any point of life. Erikson also believes that the personality is continually being shaped at different stages of life by important "decisions" an individual makes about alternative ways to orient himself to the world. These decisions are influenced by a wide range of social conditions. To Freud the parents were the prime influence on the personality development of the child. Erikson extends the influencing factors to peers, acquaintances, spouses, and others.

2 SOCIALIZATION IN CHILDHOOD

When established values and attitudes appear seriously threatened, as they are from time to time in any changing society, attention focuses on the family, where children receive their early socialization. It is the parent who teaches the child social values, self-control, and role behavior, each essential to the stability of the society.

Thus, in the sixties and early seventies, in reaction to what was termed the "youth revolution"—essentially a middle-class phenomenon—the mass media commonly blamed "permissive" parents for a decline in moral values, a growing defiance of authority, and the adoption of innovative life styles. They spoke of the "Spock generation." Dr. Benjamin Spock vigorously denied that his handbook of infant and child care, a best-seller since the mid-forties, had in any way advocated permissive child rearing. But his denials were generally overlooked, especially when he became quite open in defying the government in the matter of the Vietnam war.

The processes and factors which account for the "youth revolution" are not at all clear (other commonly cited "causes" are the Vietnam war, the situation in the universities, and racial tensions); but something seemed to have happened in the socialization of middle-class American children that was reflected in their behavior as adolescents and interacted with the dynamics of the culture. To better understand this interaction, let us examine some of the patterns of childhood socialization.

THE GOALS OF SOCIALIZATION IN CHILDHOOD

Living in society demands a high degree of self-control. The process of teaching the child self-control begins in a formal way when the parents institute toilet training. This is usually his first major introduction to society's demands for self-control; the way he views and responds to demands for other kinds of self-control may be significantly colored by how he fares in this important experience.

Demands for self-control later progress from physical demands, as in toilet training, to emotional ones, such as the curbing of angry responses to a parent or sibling. Other demands for self-control come when the child is asked to put off an immediate pleasure for a future one, or to change some action or behavior to make it more socially acceptable. These are all hard lessons for a child to learn.

To assist the child in his efforts at self-control, values are usually taught at the same time. A child who resents being asked to share his toys with his sister is helped to acquire the self-control necessary for such an action when his parents teach him the value of cooperation. They explain that his sister will then share her toys with him; they also make it clear that this cooperation is helpful to him and approved of by others. Later, his parents will urge him not to play after school until he has first done his homework, and at the same time will teach him the value of "getting ahead," or worldly success.

There is strong reason, according to many investigators in this area, to believe that an individual's basic values are formed by the age of six. The evidence from many fields of study clearly indicates that the family is by far the most important agency of teaching in the area of values.

The third important goal of childhood socialization is the learning of role behavior through family interaction. Shortly after the child begins to develop a self-image by contrasting himself with others in the family, he also learns that certain behavior is appropriate to his own image, while different behavior may be called for in other family members. For example, a boy may see that he is allowed to cry, but his father does not allow himself to cry. He notices that his mother spends many hours taking care of him and his needs; his father spends fewer hours but still performs some of the same tasks; his sister never does more than play with him. Little by little, he learns not only the kind of behavior he must display in his roles as child, son, brother, but also the expected reciprocal behavior of the people with whom he interacts in the course of his role playing—what might be called the supporting cast of characters.

Some of the roles the child learns in this way will soon be outgrown and forgotten. For instance, he will substitute for his role as toddler-at-home the role of schoolchild, much of which he will learn outside the family, at school, and from his friends. But some role behavior learned in the first few years of life in the family sticks for a much longer time. A prime example is that of role differentiations along sex lines, for the outlines of these roles are learned very early. The child is taught, either by word or example, that men go out to work and women stay at home to take care of the house and the children, or that men are stern and demanding and women are submissive and yielding, or that men have short hair and women have

long hair. All through life, these characteristics will be part of his concepts of the male and female roles, and it will be very difficult for him to change them permanently. The basic types of male-female, and also husband-wife, behavior linger for years, sometimes causing the individuals difficulty in adapting to changed conditions, especially in times of rapid or widespread social change like today. An increasing number of women, for example, now work outside the home and are being educationally prepared for careers.

Some married women have noted a peculiar phenomenon of male behavior caused by the early learning of sex roles. When a man is dating, he may encourage and admire miniskirts, see-through blouses, a successful career, aggressive sexuality, and economic independence in the woman he loves. But if he marries her, things often change abruptly, and all such behavior suddenly meets with disapproval. One reason for this confusing and contradictory behavior is that the man's concept of the role behavior of a girlfriend was learned from his peers in late childhood and adolescence, whereas his concept of correct wifely role behavior was learned from his parents perhaps twenty years earlier, and therefore reflects what is essentially a different subculture.

REWARDS AND PUNISHMENTS

The principal problem in the socialization of children is motivating them to learn the culturally patterned behavior taught by their parents. The process is undertaken before they are either old enough or experienced enough to be aware of its necessity or its value to them, and therefore they must be given some substitute reason to cooperate, if the parents are to succeed in their task.

We may think of these motivations or reasons as divided into two main types—punishments and rewards. Parents always use both, depending on the specific circumstances, but sociologists have discerned broad patterns of socialization methods that correspond to each of these types of motivation. When the process of socialization depends mainly on the use of punishment to motivate the child, emphasizing obedience, it is called *negative* or *repressive socialization.* When reward provides the chief motivation, and the socialization emphasizes the participation of the child, it is called *positive,* or sometimes *participatory, socialization.*

There are wide variations in methods of socialization among different cultures and different segments of the same society. In our society, sociologists have observed a strong tendency for socialization methods to vary according to social class distinctions. (A full discussion of social class will be presented in chapter 7: Social Stratification.) In a pioneering study done at the University of Chicago in the 1940s, it was hypothesized that lower-class parents were more likely to choose repressive socialization, while middle-class parents tended to use participatory socialization.[9] The study concluded that there was less physical punishment, more emphasis on individual achievement, and earlier training in responsibility and independence among middle-class families. A later study at Harvard confirmed these class distinctions, concluding: "Upper-lower-class parents employ physical punishment, ridicule, and deprivation of privileges more commonly than do upper-middle-class parents. It appears likely that the upper-middle-class parents use reasoning and praise more often."[10] Another study, by Miller and Swanson at the University of Michigan, found that the lower-class mother was more inclined to use physical punishment and

A sense of personal identity is acquired partly through the goals or aspirations instilled during socialization. A child's self-image will reflect the way his parents perceive and expect him to be. Their ambitions and expectations for the child are in turn influenced by their own psychological needs, their values, and social position. In our society, many little girls aspire to be teachers, nurses, secretaries, and mothers— all occupations traditionally regarded as more appropriate and rewarding for females than for males. *(Photo by Jon Erikson)*

9. Martha Ericson, "Child Rearing and Social Status," *American Journal of Sociology* 52 (1946):190–192.

10. Eleanor E. Maccoby and Patricia K. Gibbs, "Methods of Child Rearing in Two Social Classes," in *Readings in Child Development,* ed. William E. Martin and Celia Burns Stendler (New York: Harcourt Brace Jovanovich, 1954).

more likely to make arbitrary demands for obedience rather than reasoned requests for cooperation.[11]

A major reason for this class difference in method of socialization is an economic one. Lower-class families tend to have a larger family size, smaller income, more crowded living conditions, and greater scarcity of material possessions. Therefore it becomes necessary for the child to "stay out of the way," and "not get into any trouble." If a curious child breaks or damages a household possession, it is difficult to replace it. The result is that for poor families, the definition of a good child is likely to be a child that literally does nothing. Middle-class parents have the economic margin—the time, space, and material wealth—to be able to encourage activism and participation in their children.

Another reason for different socialization methods is that the occupations held by lower-class persons require complete conformity and obedience—for example, a job on an assembly line in a factory. It is important that the worker show up for work regularly and "do his job," not that he be independent, active, and creative. The traits of "sticking to the rules" and "following orders" are therefore given great importance in lower-class families, and rather rigidly enforced through the use of physical punishment.

There are strong indications that the choice of socialization method may affect not only social behavior but also intellectual development. Other studies have shown that there is also a significant class difference in the ability of children to conceptualize, with the middle-class child having a higher ability than the lower-class child. In addition, the middle-class child is likely to be socialized to a particular set of values that includes hard work to get ahead and achieve worldly success. These factors directly affect performance in school and through that, ability to earn a living. Through socialization, the class stratification of our society perpetuates itself; the children of the poor are very likely to grow up poor themselves.

Some educators and psychologists have suggested that an overemphasis in socialization on either reward or punishment can be harmful to the development of the child. In the accompanying abridgment, one of these men, A. S. Neill, claims to substitute "freedom." In place of punishment and reward, he submits that the child thrives when he is allowed to make his own social adaptations as he becomes rationally aware of their necessity.

CHILD REARING IN TWO MODERN CULTURES

In the debate over child-rearing practices it is interesting to look at the socialization patterns of other modern cultures in comparison with our own. In the last several decades considerable attention has been focused on the differences in child rearing between the United States and the Soviet Union. Much childhood socialization in Russia is carried out in the baby and child care centers of the collectives. Ordinarily toilet trained by 18 months, the children of the collectives are taught from early childhood to be self-reliant. Obedience and work-sharing values are strongly emphasized. These values are impressed on the young in their everyday encounters with peers and adults. In schools, the rules of discipline are enforced by other children according to established procedures; the Russian child is taught that it is his duty to report the misbehavior of other children. On the street, adults will reprimand the children of a friend or even someone not known to them—a practice which is exceedingly rare in the United States.

Yet the communal setting, discipline, and close supervision are always tempered with warmth and love, according to one observer,

11. Daniel R. Miller and Guy E. Swanson, *Inner Conflict and Defense* (New York: Holt, 1960, Schocken Books, 1966).

social psychologist Urie Bronfenbrenner.[12] He found in a major analysis of child rearing in the two cultures, reported in *Two Worlds of Childhood,* that Russian babies get more physical fondling and contact than American babies, and Russian mothers tend to be somewhat more solicitous with their children, though never permissive.

By contrast, Bronfenbrenner finds that Americans appear neglectful of their children. He notes that American youngsters are left to spend more time with other children without adult planning, supervision, or control. As a consequence, he believes that parents are abdicating their authority to chil-

12. Urie Bronfenbrenner, *Two Worlds of Childhood: U.S. and U.S.S.R.* (New York: Russell Sage Foundation, 1970).

dren's peer groups. As another indication of parental indifference, American children spend a vast amount of time watching television, far more than in any other society.

The most striking difference in the "product" of these two contrasting socialization structures is that the Soviet Union is much more successful in developing a child who conforms to adult standards of proper conduct. Soviet children and youth are, on the whole, much less anti-adult, aggressive, rebellious, and delinquent than their American counterparts. Bronfenbrenner also determined that England, which has a socialization structure most like ours among the nations of the world, also equals us in the large amount of behavior problems, juvenile delinquency, and youthful violence.

A. S. NEILL
Rewards and Punishment

From *Summerhill: A Radical Approach to Child Rearing* by A. S. Neill, copyright 1960, Hart Publishing Company, New York.

Introduction

A. S. Neill is an educator with an unusual theory that is not so much educational (in the sense in which we generally use the term, to refer to the activities of a school) as it is developmental—it applies to the entire upbringing and socialization of the child. He proposes that all children ought to be self-regulatory; that is, that they should be left to decide for themselves what to study, how to respond to people, and whether to follow family customs or not. His thesis is that man is a social animal who will inevitably work out his own form of socialization, which will be all the more effective for being chosen voluntarily rather than pressed on him by his parents or teachers. Neill started a school in his native England on these principles, and schools following his model have been started in many other places around the world. In 1960, he published an account of his theories and his experience at the school in a book entitled Summerhill, *the name of the school. In the chapter from which this reading was taken, he discusses the shortcomings of the usual parental methods of socialization by reward and punishment.*

The danger in rewarding a child is not as extreme as that of punishing him, but the undermining of the child's morale through the giving of rewards is more subtle. Rewards are superfluous and negative. To offer a prize for doing a deed is tantamount to declaring that the deed is not worth doing for its own sake.

Giving rewards has a bad psychological effect on children because it arouses jealousies. A boy's dislike of a younger brother often dates from the mother's remark, "Your little brother can do it better than you can." To the child, the mother's remark is a reward given to brother for being better than he is.

When we consider a child's natural interest in things, we begin to realize the dangers of both rewards and punishment. Rewards and punishment tend to pressure a child into interest. But true interest is the life force of the whole personality, and such interest is completely spontaneous. It is possible to compel attention, for attention is an act of consciousness. It is possible to be attentive to an outline on the blackboard and at the same time to be interested in pirates. Though one can compel attention, one cannot compel interest. No man can force me to be interested in, say, collecting stamps; nor can I compel myself to be interested in stamps. Yet both rewards and punishment attempt to compel interest.

I have a large garden. A group of little boys and girls would be of great assistance during weeding time. To order them to help me with my work is quite possible. But these children of eight, nine, and ten years of age have formed no opinion of their own on the necessity of weeding. They are not interested in weeding.

I once approached a group of small boys. "Anyone want to help me do some weeding?" I asked. They all refused. I ask why. The answers came: "Too dull!" "Let them grow." "Too busy with this crossword puzzle." "Hate gardening."

I, too, find weeding dull. I, too, like to tackle a crossword puzzle. To be quite fair to those youngsters, of what concern is the weeding to them? It is *my* garden. *I* get the pride in seeing the peas come through the soil. *I* save money on vegetable bills. In short, the garden touches my self-interest. I cannot compel an interest in the children, when the interest does not originate in them. The only possible way would be for me to hire the children at so much an hour. Then, they and I would be on the same basis: I would be interested in my garden, and they would be interested in making some extra money.

A reward should, for the most part, be subjective: self-satisfaction in the work accomplished. One thinks of the ungratifying jobs of the world: digging coal, fitting nut No. 50 to bolt No. 51, digging drains, adding figures. The world is full of jobs that hold no intrinsic interest or pleasure. We seem to be adapting our schools to this dullness in life. By compelling our students' attention to subjects which hold no interest for them, we, in effect, condition them for jobs they will not enjoy.

If Mary learns to read or count, it should be because of her interest in these subjects — not because of the new bicycle she will get for excellence in study or because Mother will be pleased.

One mother told her son that if he stopped sucking his thumb, she would give him a radio. What an unfair conflict to give any child! Thumbsucking is an unconscious act, beyond the control of will. The child may make a brave, conscious effort to stop the habit. But like the compulsive masturbator, he will fail again and again, and thereby acquire a mounting load of guilt and misery.

Parental fear of the future is dangerous when such fear expresses itself in suggestions that approach bribery: "When you learn to read, darling, Daddy will buy you a scooter." That way leads to ready acceptance of our greedy profit-seeking civilization. I am glad to say that I have seen more than one child prefer illiteracy to a shiny new bicycle.

A variant of this form of bribery is the declaration that seeks to touch off the child's emotions: "Mommy will be very unhappy if you are always at the bottom of the class." Both methods of bribery bypass the child's genuine interests.

Punishment can never be dealt out with justice, for no man can be just. Justice implies complete understanding. We cannot be just because we do not understand ourselves, and do not recognize our own repressed strivings. This is tragically unfair to the children. An adult can never educate beyond his own complexes. If we ourselves are bound by repressed fears, we cannot make our children free. All we do is bestow upon our children our own complexes.

If we try to understand ourselves, we find it difficult to punish a child on whom we are venting the anger that belongs to something else. Years ago, in the old days, I whacked boys again and again because I was worried—the inspector was coming, or I had had a quarrel with a friend. Or any other old excuse would serve me in place of self-understanding, of knowing what I was really angry about. Today, I know from experience that punishment is unnecessary. I never punish a child, never have any temptation to punish a child.

Punishment is always an act of hate. In the act of punishing, the teacher or parent is hating the child—and the child realizes it. The apparent remorse or tender love that a spanked child shows toward his parent is not real love. What the spanked child really feels is hatred which he must disguise in order not to feel guilty. For the spanking has driven the child into fantasy: *I wish my father would drop dead.* The fantasy immediately brings guilt—*I wanted my father to die! What a sinner I am.* And the remorse drives the child to the father's knee in seeming tenderness. But underneath, the hatred is already there—and to stay.

What is worse, punishment always forms a vicious circle. Spanking is vented hatred, and each spanking is bound to arouse more and more hatred in the child. Then as his increased hatred is expressed in still worse behavior, more spankings are applied. And these second-round spankings reap added dividends of hatred in the child. The result is a bad-mannered, sulky, destructive little hater, so inured to punishment that he sins in order to trigger some sort of emotional response from his parents. For even a hateful emotional response will do when there is no love emotion. And so the child is beaten—and he repents. But the next morning he begins the same old cycle again.

So far as I have observed, the self-regulated child does not need any punishment and he does not go through this hate cycle. He is never punished and he does not need to behave badly. He has no use for lying and for breaking things. His body has never been called filthy or wicked. He has not needed to rebel against authority or to fear his parents. Tantrums he will usually have, but they will be short-lived and not tend toward neurosis.

True, there is difficulty in deciding what is and what is not punishment. One day, a boy borrowed my best saw. The next day I found it lying in the rain. I told him that I should not lend him that saw again. That was not punishment, for punishment always involves the idea of morality. Leaving the saw out in the rain was bad for the saw, but the act was not an immoral one. It is important for a child to learn that one cannot borrow someone else's tools and spoil them, or damage someone else's property or someone else's person. For to let a child have his own way, or do what he wants to *at another's expense,* is bad for the child. It creates a spoiled child, and the spoiled child is a bad citizen.

Punishment in most homes is punishment for disobedience. In schools, too, disobedience and insolence are looked upon as bad crimes. When I was a young teacher and in the habit of spanking children, as most teachers in Britain were allowed to do, I always was most angry at the boy who had disobeyed me. My little dignity was wounded. I was the tin god of the classroom, just as Daddy is the tin god of the home. To punish for disobedience is to identify oneself with the omnipotent Almighty: *Thou shalt have no other Gods.*

Solomon with his rod theory has done more harm than his proverbs have done good. No man with any power of introspection could beat a child, or could even have the wish to beat a child.

Punishment has nothing to do with hot temper. Punishment is cold and judicial. Punishment is highly moral. Punishment avows that it is wholly for the culprit's good. (In the case of capital punishment, it is for society's good.) Punishment is an act in which man identifies himself with God and sits in moral judgment.

Many parents live up to the idea that since God rewards and punishes, they too should reward and punish their children. These parents honestly try to be just, and they often convince themselves that they are punishing the child for his own good. *This hurts me more than it hurts you* is not so much a lie as it is a pious self-deception.

One must remember that religion and morality make punishment a quasi-attractive institution. For punishment salves the conscience. "I have paid the price!" says the sinner.

At question time in my lectures, an old-timer often stands up and says, "My father used his slipper on me, and I don't regret it, sir! I would not have been what I am today if I had not been beaten." I never have the temerity to ask, "By the way, what exactly *are* you today?"

To say that punishment does not *always* cause psychic damage is to evade the issue, for we do not know what reaction the punishment will cause in the individual in later years. Many an exhibitionist, arrested for indecent exposure, is the victim of early punishment for childish sexual habits.

If punishment were ever successful, there might be some argument in its favor. True, it can inhibit through fear, as any ex-soldier can tell you. If a parent is content with a child who has had his spirit completely broken by fear, then, for such a parent, punishment succeeds.

What proportion of chastised children remain broken in spirit and castrated for life, and what proportion rebel and become even more anti-social, no one can say. In fifty years of teaching in schools, I have never heard a parent say, "I have beaten my child and now he is a good boy." On the contrary, scores of times, I have heard the mournful story, "I have beaten him, reasoned with him, helped him in every way, and he has grown worse and worse."

The punished child does grow worse and worse. What's more, he grows into a punishing father or a punishing mother, and the cycle of hate goes on through the years.

The punishment that takes the form of a lecture is even more dangerous than a whipping. How awful those lectures can be! "But didn't you *know* you were doing wrong?" A sobbing nod. "Say you are sorry for doing it."

As a training for humbugs and hypocrites, the lecture form of punishment has no rival. Worse still is praying for the erring soul of the child in his presence. That is unpardonable, for such an act is bound to arouse a deep feeling of guilt in the child.

Another type of punishment—noncorporal but just as injurious to a child's development—is nagging. How many times have I heard a mother nag her ten-year-old daughter all day long: *Don't go in the sun, darling . . . Dearest, please keep away from that railing . . . No, love, you can't go into the swimming pool today; you will catch your death of cold!* The nagging is certainly not a love token: it is the token of the mother's fear that covers unconscious hate.

I wish that the advocates of punishment could all see and digest the delightful French film telling the life story of a crook. When the crook was a boy, he was punished for some misdeed by being forbidden to partake of the Sunday evening meal of poisoned mushrooms. Afterward, as he watched all the family coffins being carried out, he decided that it didn't pay to be good. An immoral story with a moral, which many a punishing parent cannot see.

Conclusion

When Neill states that "true interest is the life force of the whole personality, and such interest is completely spontaneous" he lays the foundation for his entire argument. But is his hypothesis correct? Are interests "completely spontaneous"? Most sociologists would argue

that they are not. Interests are obtained in large part from the meanings and values of culture which are instilled in the individual through socialization. Thus socialization must precede interests. The question also remains, if reward and punishment are the main methods of socialization, does Neill offer any reasonable substitutes? Are there any "disguised" rewards and punishments in his environment? What about the role of the peer group where parental or adult guidance is weak?

TOPIC 3 SOCIALIZATION AFTER CHILDHOOD

Until a child is about six years old the chief agent of his socialization in our society is the family. Thereafter the burden of socialization gradually shifts onto other social units, and by the time he reaches adulthood, the family no longer plays a major role as socializer of the individual. This does not mean, however, that the socialization of a person ends at childhood, as we shall see.

THE SCHOOL'S ROLE IN SOCIALIZATION

The first agency outside the family which assumes some responsibility for socializing children is normally the school. The school and the institution of education will be discussed in more detail in chapter 9. For the moment, we are concerned only with the way it affects the individual's progress toward social adjustment.

The aspect of socialization in which the school is most expert and to which it is

most obviously adapted, is the teaching of skills and attitudes which children will need to become integrated into the larger society. At school, they learn the technical and intellectual heritage of their culture, so that each new generation will be able to benefit from previous experience and discoveries made over many years of trial and error. In a society as complex and technologically advanced as ours, the transmission of this part of the culture is a most important and lengthy undertaking, which is why the institution of education is so integral a part of our lives for fifteen or twenty years. In some societies, ones that have less specialized knowledge to impart, schooling is a very brief episode in a child's life.

There are other kinds of socialization which also occur at school. For instance, children learn new role behavior, oriented more toward the wider society than that

At school, children are taught not only necessary educational skills, but also a set of attitudes toward their society. Here we see children being taught the value of patriotism, as they pledge allegiance to the flag. *(Photo by Ken Heyman)*

which they have already learned at home. The teacher tells them what is expected of them as students, as members of a highly organized group, and as citizens of their country and their society. The class may study "citizenship," and have the rules of society thus formally taught them. Informally, the teacher will comment on the daily behavior of the students, praising acceptable behavior and censuring the unacceptable. In fact, in many schools, each child is actually graded on his report card for his progress in social adjustment, under categories such as "obeys rules and regulations," "shows self-control," "gets along with others," or "follows directions."

A third aspect of socialization conducted by schools is individual adjustment to impersonal rules and authority. The child has already learned from his parents that he must obey them, and he also knows from experience that his parents have authority over him. But the nature of the relationship between parent and child is personal and emotional. The child obeys his parents because he loves them, and because he is dependent on them and their goodwill in a way that he can easily recognize. At school, children learn to obey "the rules" rather than only an individual. It is the school which commands his respect and obedience; his personal relationship with his teacher is just a part of his relationship to the impersonal organization.

◀ PEER GROUPS

When a child starts school, he is at the same time exposed to another agency of socialization, the *peer group*. This is the term used to denote a grouping of individuals of the same general age and with approximately the same social position. It should be pointed out that members of the same peer group are not necessarily friends. For example, all the children in a given second grade class constitute a peer group, but they are by no means all friends with each other.

In childhood, peer groups are formed largely by accident of association, but later in life more choice is exercised. At seven, one's peer groups are the class at school, subgroups of that class, and the other children of the same age who live in the neighborhood. At thirty-seven, one chooses a peer group more on the basis of congeniality due to such things as common interests and activities, and similar income, or occupation, or social position; age limitation becomes more flexible, so that, for example, people between the ages of 30 and 45 might qualify as members of a 37-year-old's peer group.

The peer group exercises more and more influence over the process of socialization with every year of childhood. Since the child in our society is dependent for a prolonged period of time, peer groups are very important in helping both the child and the parents to end the period of dependence. The adolescent is helped to find and work out a place in a society of equals unlike his place in the family, where he will always be subordinate.

Some sociologists have suggested that in modern Western societies the peer group has become an extremely important socializing agent; one of the leading proponents of this theory is David Riesman, in his book *The Lonely Crowd*.[13] Riesman concluded that for many people the approval of a peer group was the most important motivating factor in social behavior. Since his study, carried out twenty years ago, this trend does not seem to have diminished. There is evidence that late adolescent and young adult peer groups have an even more dominant role than in previous years, often in opposition to the norms and values of the society in general. Some encourage, for example, the use of marijuana, the rejection of a financial yardstick for measuring success, and premarital sexual relationships, all of

13. David Riesman et al., *The Lonely Crowd* (New Haven: Yale University Press, 1950), pp. 19–24.

During adolescence, the peer group becomes a major influence on social behavior. Studies have shown that the informal networks, established and maintained in high schools by the students themselves, frequently counteract attempts of the formal or official school structure to transmit community approved values. Cliques, gangs, and clubs often provide alternative routes for gaining social approval and support. The hippy counter-culture that developed in the 1960s rejected a broad range of traditional social demands, living arrangements, and indicators of success, and developed new norms of its own. *(Photo by Ken Heyman)*

which are at odds with the norms which prevail in society at large. But the peer group members who espouse these actions are not expressing a freedom from social control, or a rejection of social order, even though they use rhetoric which implies such freedom and rejection. In truth, they are committed to the peer group which sponsors their actions, and they are highly dependent on it for support and approval—even more so because they have cut themselves off from many other sources of social support. They show basically the same orientation toward the peer group as do their parents; the only difference is in the behavior and values which the peer groups dictate. During adolescence, the peer group is undoubtedly the major agent of socialization and its opinion often becomes more important to the individual adolescent than that of the family, the school, or the society at large.

ADULT SOCIALIZATION

By the time one reaches adulthood, much of the process of socialization is completed. The individual possesses an image of the self, both real and ideal; a commitment to the common norms and values of the society; the ability to exercise self-control;

and the willingness to subordinate some personal desires to the impersonal rules of society. The adult has also learned the basic skills of living in his society. But he still has many new roles to learn and all the suitable role behavior to accompany them.

The most common and important of these new roles relate to acquiring independence from parents, marriage and having children of one's own, assisting elderly parents, and finally becoming elderly and dependent oneself. Each of these life stages calls for a continuing process of socialization, and the learning of new social roles. For the worker we can add the change of job, rise or decline in status, and eventual retirement. A growing number must face divorce, remarriage, and widowhood. Most American families must sometime face the temporary dislocation of a change of neighborhood or community.

Adult socialization differs from that of childhood in several ways: the adult is more likely to understand the reasons for his new undertaking; in some respects he is more highly motivated and a number of new roles are voluntarily chosen by him. Another major factor of adult socialization in modern societies is the redefinition of roles. An individual may become engaged in a new socialization process not due to a new role, but because the present role changes its content. The best example is the emerging redefinition of the role of wife. At one time wives were to care for their homes and families, help their husbands find peace and contentment, and have few responsibilities outside the home. This traditional definition is now being called into question, and there is every indication that we are witnessing a major restructuring of the wifely role. This will be discussed more fully in chapter 6, The Family.

RESOCIALIZATION

There are certain circumstances in which a more drastic change in adult behavior and attitudes is attempted. *Resocialization* is a process involving a radical change, in both role behavior and values, to a new way of life which is inconsistent or incompatible with the former one. A radical change in values is a factor not commonly found in continuing adult socialization to new social demands. An extreme case of resocialization is the "brainwashing" sometimes applied to prisoners in times of war and revolution. This is specifically a restructuring of political ideology, but it also involves a complete change of role definitions. Relatively few people undergo this form of resocialization and its long-term effectiveness is not clear, but it represents a frightening application of what is known about socialization.

A much more common and moderate kind of resocialization is that used in the military as it trains civilians to be soldiers. The underlying aim of basic training is to erase the civilian self-image that an individual has developed, and replace it with a military one. The process begins with the physical removal of the recruit from his former life. He is confined to the army base; he must give up his individualistic clothes that serve as a means of self-identification; he must also submit to the uniform hair style. Names are used as little as possible. Instead the recruits are addressed as "soldier" or by their rank. Under this pressure, the self-image gradually changes. At the same time, the recruits are indoctrinated into the role behavior expected of them: the salutes to officers, the concern for a neat and orderly appearance, the following of orders without question—all these traits identify the role of soldier.

Army training also seeks to weaken certain civilian norms and values and in some cases to replace them with new ones. The value of self-determination must be discouraged, for example, and in its place is substituted the value of submission to authority. The value of individual achievement is replaced by one of group cooperation. This substitution of new and satisfying values is a crucial part of the process of resocialization; the old norms and values cannot be given up until there is something equally useful to take their place.

Statistics show that the army is a very efficient resocializer. Since World War II it processed hundreds of thousands of men who had little or no commitment to the army's social patterns, who were there only because the draft forced them to be. They came from many different backgrounds. And yet after the intensive period of resocialization in basic training, nearly all these men conformed, at least outwardly, to the norms and values of the army.

There are other examples of resocialization in our society. All those who have pow-

erful religious or ideological conversions have undergone some kind of resocialization; to become a Catholic, an Adventist, or a Marxist, one must acquire a new ideal self-image, a reinterpretation of society, and many other new norms and values. Peter Berger has pointed out that psychoanalysis is essentially a kind of resocialization, in which the analyst tries to alter both the real and the ideal self-image of the patient, as well as introduce many new patterns of behavior and interpretations of roles.[14] There is some uncertainty about the long-range effects of all these forms of adult resocialization, and there are many cases in which the individual slowly returns to older norms and values.

14. Peter Berger, *Invitation to Sociology: A Humanistic Perspective* (New York: Doubleday, 1963), p. 62.

CHARLES C. MOSKOS, JR.
Why Men Fight

"Why Men Fight" by Charles C. Moskos, Jr. Published by permission of Transaction, Inc. from trans*action* 7, November 1969. © 1969 by Transaction, Inc.

Introduction

This paper is the result of two trips Moskos made to the combat zone in South Vietnam, during which time he accompanied members of a rifle squad as they went through their daily tasks; later he had formal interviews with most of the men. Moskos says: "The attitudes expressed by the formally interviewed soldiers constantly reappeared in conversations I had with numerous other combat soldiers.... I was struck by the common reactions of soldiers to the combat experience and their participation in the war."

The purpose of Moskos's inquiry was to find out what made these men fight. His findings differ somewhat from the explana-

*tion that grew out of sociological study of World War II combat units—that the main combat motivation came from primary groups. Moskos believes that the prime motivation that makes soldiers fight is the depth of the soldiers' socialization to American society. In this excerpted part of the article, which originally appeared in trans*action *magazine, he explains the reasons for his conclusion.*

I propose that primary groups maintain the soldier in his combat role when he has an underlying commitment to the worth of the larger social system for which he is fighting. This commitment need not be formally articulated, nor even perhaps consciously recognized. But the soldier must at some level accept, if not the specific purposes of the war, then at least the broader [moral virtue] of the society of which he is a member. Although American combat soldiers are extremely reluctant to voice patriotic rhetoric, this should not obscure the existence of more latent beliefs in the legitimacy, and even superiority, of the American way of life.

Quite consistently, the American combat soldier displays a profound skepticism of political and ideological appeals. Anti-ideology itself is a recurrent and integral part of the soldier's belief system. They dismiss patriotic slogans or exhortations to defend democracy with, "What a crock," "Be serious, man," or "Who's kidding who?" In particular they have little belief that they are protecting an outpost of democracy in South Vietnam. As one soldier put it, "Maybe we're supposed to be here and maybe not. But you don't have time to think about things like that. You worry about getting zapped and dry socks tomorrow. The other stuff is a joke."

In this same vein, when the soldier responds to the question of why he is in Vietnam, his answers are couched in a quite individualistic frame of reference. He sees little connection between his presence in Vietnam and the national policies that brought him there. Twenty-seven of the thirty-four combat soldiers I interviewed defined their presence in the war in terms of personal misfortune. Typical responses were: "My outfit was sent over here and me with it," "My tough luck in getting drafted," "I happened to be at the wrong place at the wrong time," "I was fool enough to join this man's army," and "My own stupidity for listening to the recruiting sergeant." Only five soldiers mentioned broader policy implications—to stop Communist aggression.

Because of the combat soldier's overwhelming propensity to see the war in private and personal terms, I had to ask them specifically what they thought the United States was doing in Vietnam. When the question was phrased in this manner, the soldiers most often said they were in Vietnam "to stop Communism." This was about the only ideological slogan these

American combat soldiers could be brought to utter; nineteen of the thirty-four interviewed soldiers saw stopping Communism as the purpose of the war. But when they expressed this view it was almost always in terms of defending the United States, not the "Free World" in general and certainly not South Vietnam. They said: "The only way we'll keep them out of the States is to kill them here," "Let's get it over now, before they're too strong to stop," "They have to be stopped somewhere," "Better to zap this country than let them do the same to us."

Fifteen of the soldiers gave responses other than stopping Communism. Three gave frankly cynical explanations of the war by stating that domestic prosperity in the United States depended on a war economy. Two soldiers held that the American intervention was a serious mistake initially; but that it was now too late to back out because of America's reputation. One man even gave [an ecological] interpretation, arguing that war was needed to limit population growth. Nine of the soldiers could give no reason for the war even after extensive discussion. Within this group one heard responses such as: "I only wish I knew," "Maybe Johnson knows, but I sure don't," and "I've been wondering about that ever since I got here."

I asked each of the nineteen soldiers who mentioned stopping Communism as the purpose of the war what was so bad about Communism that it must be stopped at the risk of his own life. The first reaction to such a question was usually perplexity or rueful shrugging. After thinking about it, and with some prodding, twelve of the men expressed their distaste for Communism by stressing its authoritarian aspects in social relations. They saw Communism as a system of excessive social regimentation which allows the individual no autonomy in the pursuit of his own happiness. Typical descriptions of

Communism were: "That's when you can't do what you want to do," "Somebody's always telling you what to do," or "You're told where you work, what you eat, and when you shit." As one man wryly put it, "Communism is something like the army."

I should stress again that the soldiers managed to offer reasons for the war or descriptions of Communism only after extended discussion and questioning. When left to themselves, they rarely discussed the goals of America's military intervention in Vietnam, the nature of Communist systems, or other political issues.

Americanism

To say that the American soldier is not overtly ideological is not to deny the existence of values that do contribute to his motivation in combat. Despite the soldier's lack of ideological concern and his pronounced embarrassment in the face of political rhetoric, he nevertheless displays an elemental American nationalism in the belief that the United States is the best country in the world. Even though he hates being in the war, the combat soldier typically believes—with a kind of joyless patriotism—that he is fighting for his American homeland. When the soldier does articulate the purposes of the war, the view is expressed that if Communist aggression is not stopped in Southeast Asia, it will only be a matter of time before the United States itself is in jeopardy.

The soldier definitely does *not* see himself fighting for South Vietnam. Quite the contrary, he thinks South Vietnam is a worthless country, and its people contemptible. The low regard in which the Vietnamese—"slopes" or "gooks"—are held is constantly present in the derogatory comments on the avarice of those who pander to G.I.'s, the treachery of all Vietnamese, and the numbers of Vietnamese young men in the cities who are not in the armed forces. Anti-Vietnamese sentiment is most glaringly apparent in the hostility toward the ARVN (Army of the Republic of Vietnam, pronounced Arvin) who are their supposed military allies. Disparaging remarks about "Arvin's" fighting qualities are [common and typical].

A variety of factors underlie the soldier's fundamental pro-Americanism, not the least of them being his immediate reliance on fellow Americans for mutual support in a country where virtually all [native] people are seen as actual or potential threats to his physical safety. He also has deep concern for his family and loved ones back home. These considerations, however, are true of any army fighting in a foreign land. It is on another level, then, that I tried to uncover those aspects of American society that were most relevant and important to the combat soldier.

To obtain such a general picture of the soldier's conception of his homeland, I asked the following question, "Tell me in your own words, what makes America different from other countries?" The overriding feature in the soldier's perception of America is the creature comforts that American life can offer. Twenty-two of the soldiers described the United States by its high-paying jobs, automobiles, consumer goods and leisure activities. No other description of America came close to being mentioned as often as the high—and apparently uniquely American—material standard of living. Thus, only four of the soldiers emphasized America's democratic political institutions; three mentioned religious and spiritual values; two spoke of the general characteristics of the American people; and one said America was where the individual advanced on his own worth; another talked of America's natural and physical beauties; and one black soldier described America as racist. Put in another way, it is the materialistic—and I do not use the word [to belittle]—aspects of life in America that are most relevant to combat soldiers.

The big PX

The soldier's belief in the superiority of the American way of life is further reinforced by the contrast with the Vietnamese standard of living. The combat soldier cannot help making [hateful] comparisons between the life he led in the United States—even if he is working class—and what he sees in Vietnam. Although it is more pronounced in the Orient, it must be remembered that Americans abroad—whether military or civilian—usually find themselves in locales that compare unfavorably with the material affluence of the United States. Indeed, should American soldiers ever be stationed in a country with a markedly higher standard of living than that of the United States, I believe they would be severely shaken in their belief in the merits of American society.

Moreover, the fighting soldier, by the very fact of being in combat, leads an existence that is not only more dangerous than civilian life, but more primitive and physically harsh. The soldier's somewhat romanticized view of life back home is buttressed by his direct observation of the Vietnamese scene, but also by his own immediate lower standard of living. It has often been noted that front-line soldiers bitterly contrast their plight with the physical amenities enjoyed by their fellow-countrymen, both rear-echelon soldiers as well as civilians back home. While this is superficially true, the attitudes of American combat soldiers toward their [fellow Americans] are actually somewhat more ambivalent. For at the same time the soldier is begrudging the civilian his physical comforts, it is these very comforts for which he fights. Similarly, they envy rather than disapprove of those rear-echelon personnel who engage in sub-rosa profiteering.

The materialistic ethic is reflected in another characteristic of American servicemen. Even among front-line combat soldiers, one sees an extraordinary amount of valuable paraphernalia. Transistor radios are practically universal. Cameras and other photographic accessories are widely evident and used. Even the traditional letter-writing home is becoming displaced by tape recordings. It seems more than coincidental that American soldiers commonly refer to the United States as "The Land of the Big PX."

Another factor that plays a part in combat motivation is the notion of masculinity and physical toughness that pervades the soldier's outlook toward welfare. Being a combat soldier is a man's job. Front-line soldiers often cast [damaging remarks] on the virility of rear-echelon personnel. A soldier who has not experienced combat is called a "cherry" (i.e., virgin). Likewise, paratroopers express disdain for "legs," as non-airborne soldiers are called. This he-man attitude is also found in the countless joking references to the movie roles of John Wayne and Lee Marvin. These definitions of masculinity are, of course, general in America and the military organization seeks to capitalize on them with such perennial recruiting slogans as "The Marine Corps Builds Men" and "Join the Army and Be a Man."

Needless to say, however, the exaggerated masculine ethic is much less evident among soldiers after their units have been bloodied. As the realities of combat are faced, more prosaic definitions of manly honor emerge. (Also, there is more frequent expression of the male role in manifestly sexual rather than combative terms, for example, the repeatedly heard "I'm a lover not a fighter.") That is, notions of masculinity serve to create initial motivation to enter combat, but recede once the life-and-death facts of warfare are confronted. Moreover, once the unit is tempered by combat, definitions of manly honor are not seen to encompass individual heroics. Quite the opposite, the very word "hero" is used to describe negatively any soldier who recklessly jeopardizes the unit's welfare. Men try to avoid going out on patrols with individuals who are overly anxious to make contact with the enemy. Much like the slacker at the other end of the spectrum, the "hero" is also seen as one who endangers the safety of others. As is the case with virtually all combat behavior, the ultimate standard rests on keeping alive.

Conclusion

The immense influence of the socialization process on the individual is perhaps nowhere seen as clearly as in wartime. Men on both sides are risking their lives in part because of "an underlying commitment to the worth of the larger social system" of which they are a part. The feeling that their society is so worthy stems almost entirely from socialization, not from comparative evaluation or rational choice.

TOPIC

4 SOCIALIZATION AND THE INDIVIDUAL

In the last two topics we have examined socialization primarily from the point of view of society. In this topic we shall look at socialization from the viewpoint of the individual, discussing particularly the relation of culture and socialization to the individual personality.

THE SOCIOCULTURAL SHAPING OF PERSONALITY

Personality is an organized system of behavior, attitudes, beliefs, and values characteristic of a person. It is probably a natural human trait for each person to value himself as a unique addition to the world; in our Western societies, this trait is magnified by our extreme emphasis on individuality. The trait is expressed in the common view of personality—that it is strictly a *personal* phenomenon. However, sociologists and social psychologists do not view personality as a form of uniquely personal self-

expression. They are interested in those aspects of personality which are not personal but social—formed under the influence of the process of socialization and through the medium of social or symbolic interaction. One's personality is not a random or unique occurrence; it is very much the product of the social and cultural forces around it.

An example of this can be seen in what is called "national character." We say that Frenchmen and other Latins are very expressive in their personal relationships, while Englishmen and Swedes are rather unemotional; and that Americans are very achievement-oriented while persons in many Third World countries emphasize different motivations. Although these generalizations are to some extent stereotypes, there is reason to believe that there are psychological as well as cultural differences among nations, despite the great variation within each nation. When we see many people behaving in ways that appear to be similar, it suggests that their behavior is not wholly a matter of personal choice. The emotional differences among the French, English, and Swedes are developed through childhood socialization; each society rewards and punishes slightly different forms of emotional display. Similarly the achievement motivations of American children, when compared to their Third World counterparts, are more heavily rewarded and reinforced.

Think of the things that are commonly described as personality traits. In what terms would you describe your own personality—cheerful, competitive, shy, hot-tempered, eager to get ahead in the world, cooperative? All these traits, that seem to be so much a part of your own unique individuality, are in fact to some extent culturally patterned. They are more common in some cultures, and some segments of a given culture, than in others; they derive in part from different patterns and content of socialization. Even characteristics such as the level of intelligence or stupidity may be due in part to socialization. Studies have shown a relationship between methods of socialization and intellectual development. For example, in homes typical of the American middle class, the display of curiosity and conceptualization is encouraged and praised, whereas in lower-class homes, such behavior is seen as a threat to the obedience and passivity most valued in children. This difference in parental attitude and the attendant differences in socialization, plus a difference in opportunity for educational experience and availability of educational materials, result in a marked contrast in the ability of children to learn by the time they reach junior high school: the lower-class child may be a "slow learner" and the middle-class child may be a "high achiever." Many other examples of the way in which individual personalities are shaped by social and cultural factors will be discussed throughout this book.

BIOLOGICAL DETERMINATION OF PERSONALITY AND SOCIAL ROLES

It is probable that some important personality traits and social behavior are not learned but are genetically transmitted; this has long been an area of great interest and study. Much of this interest has focused on the behavior and personality traits which are associated with sex roles; one would suppose that these roles would tend to be more biologically determined than other roles. There is still a great deal of uncertainty about the degree to which sex roles may be biologically rather than socially determined. For instance, many would maintain that caring for children is a biologically determined feminine trait, and that therefore women will always be more adapted to it than men. Or to take another example, in a recent book entitled *Men in Groups*,[15] Lionel Tiger suggests that the tendency of men to gather in groups that do not admit females, such as golf clubs and men's bars, has a biological basis dating back to the anthropoid hunting groups; he maintains that this biological need of males is so strong that we must continually devise suitable outlets for it. War, he contends, might be an example of an unsuitable outlet for this basic drive or need.

The classic denial that sex roles are biologically determined is contained in the famous studies by Margaret Mead of three primitive tribes in New Guinea. In *Sex and Temperament in Three Primitive Societies* (1935)[16] Margaret Mead reported that in the Arapesh tribe both men and women were, ideally, gentle, unaggressive, and responsive—a temperament which in our society is usually associated only with women. In the Mundugumor tribe she found that men and women were both quite aggressive, even violent—a temperament we normally associ-

15. Lionel Tiger, *Men in Groups* (New York: Random House, 1969).

16. Margaret Mead, *Sex and Temperament in Three Primitive Societies* (Magnolia, Mass.: Peter Smith, 1935).

ate only with men. In the Tchambuli tribe the sex roles were very different for men and women, but the temperaments associated with the sexes were the opposites of the roles in our Western society: the men were passive and subordinate; the women were dominant and aggressive.

For a long time some social theorists have held that aggression is a specifically male trait, linked to early man's need for efficient hunting and defense of his territory. This view runs counter to Margaret Mead's findings. The view has also been partially refuted by studies which show that aggression is a type of social behavior that may be taught to people.

No study that has followed Mead's has been able to provide evidence nearly as convincing as hers. Some personality and role differences between men and women do seem to be so universal that they cannot be completely explained as cultural phenomena. In almost all societies the care of children is assigned to women; military combat, and fishing and hunting are assigned to men. Men are almost universally the more aggressive and dominant sex. This is probably due to man's greater muscular strength, which gives him inherent physical power over women. Similarly, a woman's biological ability to bear children dictates a more shelter-bound existence, at least during certain periods of her life. In primitive societies this is imperative during the first few years of each child's life because women must breast-feed their children.

Human personalities are shaped by certain fundamental biological needs such as hunger, sex, and thirst, as well as by the biological conditions of birth, maturation, and death. Various scientific investigations have shown, however, that the inherited, or biologically determined, human needs and drives are capable of being molded in a great variety of ways by diverse cultures. The relative importance of biological and sociocultural factors in personality development

is an intriguing issue, but one which may never be fully resolved. With the present division of the sciences, the work of sociologists tends naturally to emphasize the sociocultural.

It is important to distinguish between the role of biological factors in the determination of such broad social patterns as "national character" and structured social roles, and the much greater biological influence on the physical and emotional traits of individuals. Each individual is born with certain genetic, or biological traits which help shape his personality and social behavior. There is much evidence to indicate that just as people are born with genes that make them tall or short, they are born with distinct personality traits. For example, some people are born more introverted, occupied with their own thoughts and inner experiences; others are more extroverted and direct more of their energy toward others. There probably is also an inborn difference between active and passive people.

ROLES AND PERSONALITY

The social nature of personality can be illustrated quite clearly in social roles. A common experience is for a person sometimes to find himself in a situation where he feels like a bumbling idiot, unable to think of the right thing to say or do, and feeling that everyone around him thinks even worse of him than he does of himself at that moment. Luckily, the reverse also sometimes happens, on those wonderful days when one finds oneself being far more witty, charming, and intelligent than usual.

How does one account for these sudden apparent changes of an entire personality? The answer could lie in the nature of social role behavior. What may have happened to the person who feels like a bumbling idiot is that due perhaps to some initial error or awkwardness, he has suddenly been cast in the role of buffoon of the group; when he feels witty and charming he may have taken on the more pleasing role of "life of the party." Once cast in the role, a person actually begins to assume the attributes that the group has given to that part, and it is interesting to note that this holds true even in cases where the role is a "bad" one; the person playing the buffoon will actually take on many characteristics of stupidity which he had previously never possessed.

Of course, role demands are usually not so extreme as the examples we have just mentioned. Many adults do notice that they behave somewhat differently with their parents (where they play the role of a grown-up child) than they do with their child (where they play the role of a parent). But in general they recognize a degree of consistency in their behavior. Several factors help keep these traits relatively stable.

There is in the human personality what is called a strain to be consistent. When a person finds himself in a role that calls for behavior traits which conflict with his usual set, he is uncomfortable and feels a sense of stress. He may try to resolve the conflict by modifying the role, so that his accustomed behavior will suit its demands. He may try to get out of the role. Or, he may perform the role in a perfunctory manner, dropping most of the secondary attributes; this is rather like wearing a sign that says, "I'm only doing this because I have to, I don't really believe in it." Sociologists call this kind of solution *role distance*. A drastic solution, if for some reason none of the above is permissible, is to drop the old behavior and try to reintegrate the personality around the behavior demands of the new role. Another extreme measure is to try to compartmentalize oneself, saying, "I am this kind of a person here but that kind of a person there." This comes dangerously close to mental disorder and personality breakdown.

However, it is only rarely that new roles create such severe problems. In most cases, the individual simply adds or subtracts some personality trait to adapt to a new role, or rearranges the emphasis on the traits he has. For example, when a medical student becomes a doctor, he usually exhibits characteristics like a reassuring bedside manner and an authoritative manner of speech. This is not because such traits come as some magic bonus along with his M.D., but because playing the role of the doctor calls for the development of these secondary role characteristics—others *expect* him to display these characteristics, and they are therefore necessary to the successful carrying out of the doctor role.

MAN IN SOCIETY

Because the individual is largely a social product, and we can explain much of his behavior by understanding his sociocultural milieu, we should be careful not to conclude that man is, therefore, only a kind of puppet manipulated by society. Man may be the product of society, but society is the invention of man; society is in man, but man is also in society.

This problem of the relationship between the individual and society is as much a problem for philosophers and theologians as for social scientists. Indeed, it is a question which has occupied the thoughts of great men throughout history. Although the philosophic assumptions of social scientists vary somewhat, most tend to see man as an active being who, while he acts in many standardized ways, has the capacity to create and change social structure.[17]

What is the social scientist able to tell us specifically about this age-old problem? First, all forms of socialization, even those which take place in early infancy, require the cooperation of the individual. Outside of a few very abnormal situations, such as a concentration camp, it is impossible to socialize an unwilling subject, because so-

17. See Dennis H. Wrong, "The Oversocialized Conception of Man in Modern Sociology," *American Sociological Review* 26, no. 2 (April 1961).

Socialization does not end with childhood. As adults, individuals assume new roles and undergo new experiences that may change their attitudes, values, and self-conceptions. As leaders of social protest movements, many priests and nuns have challenged and redefined their traditional roles as defenders of the *status quo*. *(Bruce Davidson, Magnum)*

cialization is not something a person can soak up as a sponge does water; he must participate, act, and take part in the process if it is to succeed. Each person has some power to reject the teachings of society. A person accepts socialization because he sees that it is to his advantage to do so. But each person exercises some degree of selection over his socialization, and when he feels that he is being asked to learn or do something which will bring him no advantage, he may very well reject the request.

As one grows older, one's powers of selectivity increase. We all know someone who has made dramatic changes in his life which run counter to the dominant social patterns. The man who throws over a busi-

ness career to become a minister, the woman who establishes a new career at middle age, the college dean who gives up a position in a northern university to teach in a small, black college in the South—these are examples of people who have rejected the script that society has provided, who have refused to play the roles they were assigned, and who have decided to try to find other patterns of behavior that seemed to have more personal relevance. Less dramatic examples occur daily, as people constantly adopt roles and rules to meet their own circumstances.

Another way in which it is possible to assert individuality within the limits of the social organization is by using the social system for personal advantage. Inmates of an institution, such as a prison or an asylum, are expert at this. So are executives of large bureaucracies, who know how to use the power of their institutions to gain personal ends. The books of Stephen Potter, or the system he called "One-upmanship,"[18] are a humorous explanation of a perfectly serious situation, using social rules and norms as a kind of weapon for personal advantage. For example, Potter suggests that extreme politeness, the punctilious performance of every social duty, can disconcert others so that they are open to manipulation.

There are times when no amount of evasion of institutional expectations and social duty, no amount of manipulation of social role, can reconcile the individual to the social demands made on him. He still has one alternative, and that is to change society.

No matter how complex a society may seem, and no matter how many systems there are for ensuring conformity, it is still true that society is man-made, and therefore, can also be changed by man. Sometimes society is changed by the actions of a single exceptional individual—a Napoleon or an Alexander the Great who introduces, and enforces, great social change. But more often change comes about through the continuing pressure of nameless individuals. A single act of nonconformity is a deviation; but when the act is repeated over and over, it can be a social revolution. When one black refused to sit in the back of the bus, he was thrown in jail or fined; when thousands refused, the laws were changed. Through his individual actions, through his effect on the molding of opinion in his peer group, and other groups of which he is a member, a single person can be a force of change.

SUMMARY

Socialization, the process by which the culture of a group or society is instilled or internalized in its members, begins at birth and continues throughout the life of every individual. Man's long period of biological dependency and his ability to use language make socialization possible, while his lack of strong instinctual mechanisms make an extended period of social learning essential.

During the first few months of a baby's life, socializing activities are directed toward satisfying the infant's biological and emotional needs for warmth, food, and human contact. The kind of care he receives will strongly influence his life-long perceptions, attitudes, and feelings about the world around him. During the early stages of

18. Stephen Potter, *The First Lifemanship Guide* (New York: McGraw-Hill, 1965).

life infants seem to express three basic emotions: affection, dependence anxiety, and anger in response to frustration or neglect.

As a result of social interaction in the family, the child begins to develop a sense of self, or what Charles Horton Cooley has referred to as a "looking glass self," consisting of (1) perception of how behavior appears to others, (2) perception of their judgments of this behavior, and (3) feelings about those judgments. Throughout life we continue to define ourselves through social interaction.

According to the theory of George Herbert Mead, whose work is a major source for a school of thought called *symbolic interactionism,* the self consists of two parts: the "I" or the unique, spontaneous, and inherent characteristics of each individual; and the "me" or the gradually developed social component which acts as a censor of the "I." The "me" is based initially on the demands of *significant others* (individuals with whom the child has an important and close relationship), and later on impersonal demands made by *generalized others* (the larger society). The development of a sense of self involves a continuing conversation between the "me" and the "I." Mead has distinguished three stages in this process: (1) the *imitative stage,* when the child simply copies his parents' activities; (2) the *play stage,* when the child pretends to be other people or creatively adopts certain social roles; (3) a *role-taking stage,* when the child actually takes a serious role in a social situation with a real awareness of his importance to the group and vice versa.

Sigmund Freud focused on the biological and emotional, rather than the social forces, in the socialization process. He conceived of personality in terms of three segments: (1) the "id," the reservoir of unconscious biological and physiological drives; (2) the "ego" or mediator between the internalized demands of society and the id; and (3) the "superego," the censor and social control mechanism of the personality.

There are three major goals of childhood socialization from the point of view of society: to instill self-control, basic social values, and appropriate role behavior. While an individual's basic values are probably formed by the age of six and are relatively enduring, some of the roles learned in childhood will be outgrown. Others, such as sex-differentiated behavior, are fairly permanent.

Parents use both rewards and punishments in motivating their children to learn appropriate behavior patterns. There are wide variations in socialization methods, that reflect differences in economic circumstances, and cultural values. Two patterns which vary by social class in the United States are *negative* or *repressive socialization,* emphasizing obedience and relying on punishment, and *positive* or *participatory socialization,* based on reasoning and reward. These different socialization methods

may have long-run effects in such areas as intellectual achievement and school performance. A noteworthy difference in socialization patterns among cultures is illustrated by the discipline and collectivist orientation of child rearing in the Soviet Union compared with the more permissive and individualistic orientation in the United States.

After a child enters school, the family's role as an agent of socialization gradually decreases. In a complex technological society such as ours, the school has become increasingly important in transmitting specialized knowledge and skills, in instilling new role behavior necessary for social adjustment, and in teaching obedience to impersonal rules and authority.

At school the child becomes heavily influenced by the peer group, composed of individuals of the same general age and social position. As the individual matures, the peer group assumes greater importance in his life and helps to end the period of dependence on the family. Some sociologists maintain that in modern Western society peer group approval has become the most important motivating factor in social development, particularly during adolescence. Membership in this group does not free the individual from social control but provides an alternative means for social support and substitutes another set of values and norms, sometimes counter to those of the larger society.

Even as adults, people continue to learn new roles as they change occupations or residence, marry and remarry, and grow old. Sometimes more radical changes, such as joining the army, require an individual to become *resocialized,* to adopt new values and role behavior that are inconsistent or incompatible with former patterns, and to acquire a new self-image.

One's *personality*—the organized system of behavior, attitudes, beliefs, and values characteristic of a person—is shaped by the social and cultural forces around it. National character studies have indicated that some aspects of personality are common to a specific culture. While human personalities are based on certain fundamental biological needs such as hunger, sex, and thirst, the way in which these needs are met can take many culturally molded forms.

Personality is also shaped by the roles an individual must play. When role demands are contradictory or call for behavior that is felt to be alien or inconsistent, the individual may try to modify or avoid the role, perform his part in a perfunctory way (i.e., develop *role distance*), completely drop old behavior patterns, or compartmentalize his personality. Since socialization requires the cooperation and participation of the individual, everyone has some power to reject, modify, or accept social demands.

GLOSSARY

Generalized other A generalized conception an individual has of the expectations and attitudes of a group or society; this conception is incorporated into his personality and helps to determine his behavior. (page 123)

Instinct Complex behavior patterns which are biologically inherited and typical of all animals in a given species. (page 118)

Minding A hypothetical communication between the "I" and the "me" in the social psychological theory of George Herbert Mead. (page 123)

Participatory (positive) socialization A method of socialization which emphasizes the participation of the child and the use of rewards and positive sanctions. (page 131)

Peer group A grouping of individuals of the same general age and having approximately the same social position. (page 139)

Personality An organized system of behavior, attitudes, beliefs, and values characteristic of a person. (page 146)

Repressive (negative) socialization A method of socialization which emphasizes obedience and the use of punishment and other negative sanctions. (page 131)

Resocialization A process involving a radical change, in both role behavior and values, to a new way of life which is inconsistent or incompatible with the former one. (page 141)

Role distance The maintenance of psychological distance between an individual's personality and his role. (page 149)

Self That aspect of an individual's personality which consists of his awareness and feelings about his own personal and social identity. (page 121)

Significant others Those people who have the greatest influence on an individual's evaluation of himself and on his acceptance or rejection of social norms. (page 123)

Socialization The process by which the culture of a group or society is taught to, and instilled or internalized in, the individuals who live in that group or society. (page 117)

Symbolic interactionism A social psychological theory that stresses the importance of communication through language and gestures in the formation and maintenance of personality and social relationships. (page 122)

SUGGESTED READINGS AND RELATED RESOURCES

I READINGS IN SOCIOLOGY AND SOCIAL PSYCHOLOGY

Brim, Orville, and Stanton Wheeler. *Socialization after Childhood*. New York: John Wiley (Paper), 1966. These two essays by Brim and Wheeler provide a perspective on the major problems encountered in the study of socialization; they focus upon one of the most important situations in which adult socialization occurs—the large-scale bureaucratic organization.

Cooley, Charles H. *Human Nature and the Social Order*. New York: Schocken Books (Paper), 1962. First published in 1902, this book presents Cooley's interpretation of the social and cultural factors which influence development of the "self."

Eisenstadt, S. N. *From Generation to Generation*. New York: Free Press (Paper), 1956. Eisenstadt analyzes forms of socialization in different age groups, particularly socialization in adolescent peer groups.

Elkin, Frederick. *The Child and Society*. New York: Random House, 1960. This description of the impact of society upon the socialization of children and the formation of personality is based on role theory.

Erikson, Erik. *Childhood and Society*. Rev. ed. New York: W. W. Norton, 1964. Erikson writes about the roots of ego and personality development—socialization in childhood.

Goffman, Erving. *Asylums: Essays on the Situation of Mental Patients and Other Inmates*. New York: Doubleday, Anchor (Paper), 1961. This is a study of the effects of total institutionalization on inmates' previous social relationships; the process of resocialization within the closed institution; and the means by which the inmate learns to "play the system."

————. *Stigma: Notes on the Management of Spoiled Identity*. Englewood Cliffs, N.J.: Prentice-Hall (Paper), 1963. This study focuses on situations in which individuals are unable to conform to standards which society calls normal.

Lipset, S. M., and L. Lowenthal. *Culture and Social Character*. New York: Free Press, 1961. This collection of essays reviews, criticizes, and appraises the concepts developed in *The Lonely Crowd* by David Riesman. (See below.)

Miller, Daniel, and Guy Swanson. *The Changing American Parent*. New York: John Wiley, 1958. This empirical study points out the differences in the means and the normative content of socialization among American social classes.

Parsons, Talcott. *Social Structure and Personality*. New York: Free Press, 1965. Using a refined Freudian theory of personality development, Parsons traces the psychological stages of the life cycle; within this theoretical framework, he discusses the relationships among social structure, American values, and the concepts of health and illness.

Riesman, David, et al. *The Lonely Crowd*. New Haven: Yale University Press, 1961. In this discussion of the effects of modern culture upon personality, Riesman makes the now-famous distinction between the "inner-directed" and "other-directed" man.

Sears, R., E. Maccoby, and H. Levine. *Patterns of Child Rearing*. New York: Harper & Row, 1957. This study is based on data collected from 379 American mothers on how they rear their children; it points out differences and similarities of patterns of socialization.

Shibutoni, Tamotsu. *Society and Personality*. Englewood Cliffs, N.J.: Prentice-Hall, 1961. Shibutoni analyzes the relationship between social interaction and the development of a self-concept; he bases his analysis on the concept of "perception"—how society and the individual perceive one another.

Spiro, Melford. *Children of the Kibbutz*. New York: Schocken Books (Paper), 1965. Spiro studies the socialization and personality development of children who are being raised in the communal life of an Israeli kibbutz.

Strauss, Anselm, ed. *George Herbert Mead: On Social Psychology*. Chicago: University of Chicago Press (Paper), 1965. In this collection of Mead's lectures and papers, which includes "Mind, Self and Society," he lays the foundation for a theory that an individual's concept of self and his social behavior result from his perception of how others feel and act toward him.

Articles and Papers

Becker, Howard S., and Anselm L. Strauss. "Careers, Personality and Adult Socialization." *American Journal of Sociology* (1956):253–263.

Becker, Howard S., and Blanche Geer. "The Fate of Idealism in Medical School." *American Sociological Review* **23** (1958):50–56.

Blumer, Herbert. "Society as Symbolic Interaction." In *Symbolic Interaction,* edited by J. G. Manis and B. N. Meltzer, pp. 139–148. Boston: Allyn and Bacon, 1967.

Breen, Leonard Z. "Some Problems in the Field of Aging." *Sociology and Social Research* **41**, 6 (July 1957):412–416.

Dyer, Jack L. "A Summer Work-Study Program in Mental Health." *Proceedings of the Southwest Sociological Association* **16** (1966):19–23.

Harmsworth, Harry C. "Family Structure on the Fort Hall Indian Reservation." *Family Life Coordinator* **14**, 1 (January 1965):7–9.

Hodges, Daniel L. "The Self and Cognitive Balance: Improvements in Balance Theory's Predictive Power." *Pacific Sociological Review* **9**, 1 (Spring 1966):22–34.

Inkeles, Alex. "Personality and Social Structure." In *Sociology Today,* edited by R. K. Merton et al. New York: Harper and Row, Harper Torchbooks, 1965.

Ogburn, W. F. "The Wolf Boy of Agra." *American Journal of Sociology* **64** (March 1959):449–454.

Schaffler, T. R. "A Formula for the Process of Socialization." *Journal of Educational Sociology* **27**, 2 (October 1953):60–67.

Spiro, Melford. "Is the Family Universal?" *American Anthropologist* **56** (October 1954):839–846.

Swanson, Guy E. "Mead and Freud: Their Relevance for Social Psychology." *Sociometry* **24** (December 1961):319–339.

Wrong, Dennis H. "The Oversocialized Conception of Man in Modern Sociology." *American Sociological Review* **26**, 2 (April 1961).

II   RELATED RESOURCES
Nonfiction

Bowlby, John. *Child Care and the Growth of Love*. Middlesex, England: Penguin, 1957. This concise presentation of how maternal deprivation affects the emotional growth of a child and his behavior as an adult, was prepared for a United Nations Commission. The book discusses ways to prevent maternal deprivation.

Brown, Roger. *Social Psychology*. New York: Free Press, 1965. Brown introduces the major social psychological schools of thought and discusses the relationship of psychology to social structure.

Freud, Sigmund. *Civilization and Its Discontents*. New York: W. W. Norton (Paper), 1962. In this book Freud presents his views on the continuing conflict between an individual's desire for freedom and the demands made on him by society.

Fromm, Erich. *Escape from Freedom*. New York: Avon (Paper), 1965. From Fromm's point of view modern governments that control the individual, both democratic and totalitarian, are overwhelming man's individuality. Fromm writes about modern man's lack of awareness of social reality, and the resulting dehumanization of his life.

Hunt, Robert. *Personalities and Cultures*. Garden City, N.Y.: Natural History Press (Paper), 1967. Hunt's book discusses Freud's psychoanalytic theory of personality and defines the personality's role in forming culture.

Jay, David. *Growing Up Black*. New York: Pocket Books (Paper), 1968. The essays which appear in this book were written by black adults about their childhoods in America.

Redl, Fritz, and David Wineman. *Controls from Within: Techniques for the Treatment of the Aggressive Child*. New York: Free Press (Paper), 1965. In this book, Redl and Wineman discuss how a child's environment and play activities can be controlled so that they contribute to his development and personality growth.

Wickes, Frances. *The Inner World of Childhood*. New York: Signet Books (Paper), 1968. The crucial relationship between parent and child is examined in this book; it emphasizes the influence this relationship exerts on the child's relationship outside the family.

Fiction

Cummings, E. E. *The Enormous Room*. New York: Random House, Modern Library, 1949. This story relates the experiences of an American in a French prison during World War I. The changes in values and attitudes that he undergoes are good examples of resocialization.

Golding, William. *Lord of the Flies*. New York: G. P. Putnam's Sons, 1959. A group of young English schoolboys are stranded on an uninhabited island, where they regress to savagery. The novel presents some interesting projections of what may result when a child's socialization is suddenly interrupted.

Heller, Joseph. *Catch 22*. New York: Dell (Paper), 1969. A humorous novel about World War II that points out how the army tries to resocialize soldiers, with varying degrees of success.

Markandaya, Kamala. *Nectar in a Sieve*. New York: Avon (Paper), 1954. This is a story of a simple woman of India, her husband and children, and their struggle to survive against nature, changing times, and poverty.

Wolfe, Thomas. *You Can't Go Home Again.* New York: Dell (Paper), 1960. Wolfe's autobiographical account of a young man's realization that his early friends have changed (so that his relationships with them can never be the same) is an illustration of socialization as an ongoing process.

Wright, Richard. *Black Boy.* New York: Harper & Row, 1969. An absorbing tale of a black child's dawning awareness of racial differences and discrimination. As he grows older he is socialized to the traditional attitudes and mechanisms his subculture has developed for dealing with racism.

Films

The Big House. George Hill, 1930. Although this film has a romantic ending, it is a remarkable portrayal of prison life. It points out the conflict between a prison's social function and the actual negative resocialization of the inmates. It also shows how the inmates learn to "play the system" in order to survive within the prison's social system.

Cool Hand Luke. Stuart Rosenberg, 1967. This movie, set in a Georgia prison, gives a taste of what it is like to be in prison and working on a chain gang, but the film is primarily concerned with some men's refusal to be resocialized and to conform.

The Cool World. Shirley Clarke, 1964. In this quasi-documentary film Miss Clarke deals with the values and norms of a group of juvenile delinquents in Harlem. In order for "Duke," a fifteen-year-old boy, to attain his sense of manhood and identity he must go through the only channel available to him—what the dominant culture would call the "anti-social" channel.

The Last Picture Show. Peter Bogdanovich, 1971. The decline of an era, the watershed of a life-style seen through the eyes of teen-age boys in a small town in Texas. The boys have little to guide them in their socialization process.

Summer of '42. Robert Mulligan, 1971. This film offers a humorous and poignant description of the socialization of teen-agers and the impact of their peers on the process.

5. Primary Groups and Organizations

Man comes into the world as a full-fledged member of a group—the family—and in the natural course of events continues to acquire membership in an ever-widening range of groups as he attends schools, meets his religious and social needs, and works at a job. These memberships enable him to fulfill his roles, whether imposed by his own needs or by his place in society. His need to relate to many different groups is a basic one that appears to be particularly strong in Americans, as de Tocqueville noted a century and a half ago. Since then, the phenomenal growth of American organizations in number, size, and variety—from the highly structured and usually long-enduring organizations of big business and labor to the less structured and often short-lived hobby and singles clubs—has reflected the requirements of a highly dynamic and changing society.

Two kinds of organized social groupings have commanded the bulk of sociological attention over the years. First are primary groups, which are characterized by the type of relationships of which they are composed; second are the organized uni-bonded groups which are usually called simply organizations—both by the sociologist and the layman. Sociologists in recent years have been interested especially in large, complex organizations, which have become so powerful in modern societies.

(Photo by Ken Heyman)

1 PRIMARY GROUPS

Primary groups have been the basic building blocks of human societies throughout world history. They are groups characterized by *primary relationships,* that is, social relationships which are intimate and personal and involve many facets of our personalities. Primary relationships are always found in primary groups, but they also may be found between individuals in almost every kind of organization and setting in society.

Groups which are characterized by primary relationships tend to be small, thus providing the opportunity for face-to-face interaction. They are relatively durable, with the same people interacting over extended periods in such a way that the group can persist even in the face of various kinds of stress. The members come to have a strong sense of group identity—a "we" feeling. Such groups usually undertake activities directed toward a wide variety of goals, rather than limiting themselves to only one special purpose. The best examples of primary groups are: the family, in every respect the most important of the primary groups (discussed in chapter 6); youthful peer groups, such as children's play groups and boys' gangs; some neighborhood circles and adult social clubs; and informal groups within complex organizations, such as soldiers' buddy groups and factory cliques.

The meaning of the term "primary" has changed somewhat over the years. It was coined by Charles H. Cooley in the early part of this century to refer to such groups as the family and the children's play group, which are primary in the sense that they come first chronologically in the process of so-

cialization.[1] In addition, Cooley regarded them as the groups of primary importance in shaping the human personality. He called them the "nursery of human nature." Since Cooley's day, the term has come to be applied to all groups, including those of significance only in adult life, in which the relationships are similar to those in the family. Examples are fraternities and sororities and even small political groups, whose members have strong feelings of "brotherhood" and solidarity.

The term *secondary relationship* was not used by Charles Cooley, but has since become a common term in the vocabulary of sociology. It means a relationship which is specialized, formal, or standardized by normative codes, and lacking in emotional content. It does not involve an individual's whole personality. Examples are the relationship between clerk and customer, doctor and patient, employer and employee. Most of a person's relationships in contemporary society seem to be of this nature.

The study of primary groups has had a special significance in sociology because of the important functions which primary groups have in society.[2] Not only is the primary group essential in shaping the human personality and providing the setting for fuller individual development, but it also is a basic unit of social control and social

1. Charles H. Cooley, *Social Organizations* (New York: Charles Scribner's Sons, 1909), part 1.

2. See Edward Shils, "The Study of the Primary Group," in *The Policy Sciences,* ed. Daniel Lerner and Harold D. Lasswell (Stanford, Calif.: Stanford University Press, 1951), chap. 3.

cohesion. Many scholars and social critics feel that the strength and vitality of a society rests on the strength and vitality of its primary groups.[3] Studies of complex formal organizations indicate that the same thing may hold true for such organizations—the efficiency of an organization is as dependent upon its informal network of personal relationships and groups as on its formal structure.[4]

THE PRIMARY RELATIONSHIP

The primary relationship has five basic characteristics:

(1) It includes a variety of roles and interests of each individual in the relationship. For example, there is a teacher role and a child role, but if the relationship between the two never goes beyond the limits of this pair of roles, then it is not a primary relationship. In a primary relationship, a teacher and student may also be co-workers, for example when they are engaged together on a research project; they may be friends, and meet after work for social purposes; sometimes they may even be rivals, competing for the attention or praise of others. In technical sociological terms a primary relationship is general and diffuse rather than specialized and segmented.

(2) The primary relationship involves the whole personality. This is because it includes a wide variety of roles and interests. For example, within a work primary group, the members know each other as workers, but their knowledge does not stop there. Through meetings outside the office, and conversation during office hours, they get to know each other as fathers, husbands, suitors. They each know something of the way the others handle their finances, fill in their leisure time, and relate to their children. They have opportunities to observe each other in a number of different roles and situations, and they may come to value each other as much for the performance of some other role, in which they are not centrally involved, as they do for the working or friendship roles which they share. This differs markedly from relationships in other groups—for example, the students in large university lecture courses—who see each other only in the particular working role that accounts for their being temporarily together.

(3) The primary relationship involves free and extensive communication. Individuals engaged in a primary relationship ordinarily feel that they can and should communicate extensively and with relative freedom. One neither expects, nor wishes, the butcher to explain why he feels so depressed on a particular morning, but it is felt that a husband ought to communicate such an explanation. In the butcher, silence is a courtesy, but in the husband, it is a withdrawal or an evasion, and therefore becomes a source of concern. The free communication of feelings and attitudes in a primary relationship supplements each person's observation of the other's behavior in ways that help reveal the total personality. It makes possible a deeper form of relationship.

(4) The primary relationship is personal and emotion-laden, because it is a wide-ranging relationship between many facets of each person's personality. Nevertheless, it is not always a strongly affectionate relationship. All relationships involve a certain amount of stress; the primary relationship can be highly stressful because of its emotion-laden character.

In a primary *group* there may well be members who dislike, even detest, some of the

3.   For example, Erich Fromm, *The Sane Society* (New York: Holt, Rinehart & Winston, 1965) and Lewis Mumford, *The Transformation of Man* (New York: Collier Books, 1962).

4.   The classic statement of this was Elton Mayo, *The Human Problems of Industrial Civilization* (New York: Macmillan, 1933). Also see Rensis Likert, *New Patterns of Management* (New York: McGraw-Hill, 1961).

CHARACTERISTICS OF PRIMARY AND SECONDARY RELATIONSHIPS

Primary Relationship	Secondary Relationship
1. **Includes a variety of roles and interests of each of the participants. It is general and diffuse in character.**	1. Usually includes only one role and interest of each participant. It is specialized in character.
2. **Involves the total personality of each participant.**	2. Involves only those aspects of the personalities of the participants that are specifically relevant to the situation.
3. **Communication is free and extensive.**	3. Communication is limited to the specific subject of the relationship.
4. **Is personal and emotion laden.**	4. Is relatively impersonal and unemotional.
5. **Is not easily transferable to another person.**	5. Is transferable to others; that is, the participants are interchangeable.

Primary relationships, such as those between friends, mother and child, or husband and wife, are usually sources of emotional expression and gratification. Secondary relationships are more efficient for transacting business and are characteristic of modern urban-industrial society.

other members. In other words, not all relations in a primary group are purely primary, but the members stay in the group, and the group continues to function. In a family group, the reasons for this are fairly obvious, but the same thing can be observed in working or social primary groups. The members who do not like each other maintain their primary relationship because they are getting some personal satisfaction from the group other than affection. It might be respect, or emotional support, or status, or economic benefit. This satisfaction or benefit outweighs the lack of affection or personal affinity and makes the continuance of the relationship desirable to all parties.

(5) The primary relationship is not easily transferable, because it involves a special response to the unique attributes of another individual. If you are at a store buying a television set and you don't like the way the

salesman behaves, you can simply take your business to another salesman—that is, transfer the relationship to another person who plays the role of salesman. However, in the case of a close relationship with a boyfriend or girlfriend, the feelings involved cannot quickly or easily be transferred to another individual.

FUNCTIONS OF THE PRIMARY RELATIONSHIP FOR THE INDIVIDUAL

One of the chief values of a primary relationship is that it gives each individual a chance to develop, to display, and to gain recognition of a larger part of his total personality than is offered by other relationships. A primary relationship helps the individual form a deeper self-image, one that goes beyond the demands of whatever role or roles he is currently playing. Although the self-image formed by any one primary relationship (particularly in the family) may change under the influence of later evaluations or new attachments, elements of that self-image may persist far beyond the life of the relationship.

There are many other functions, all of which help to sustain and support the individual. Primary relationships serve as teachers and interpreters of societal values and norms, that is, they are agents of socialization, as discussed in the last chapter. The primary relationship and the primary group are in fact the most important channels through which the individual learns the major beliefs and expectations of society, and the patterns of behavior necessary for successful adaptation to that society.

Since the primary relationship implies an acceptance of the whole individual, it is a source of security during conflicts with other individuals or groups, and even with society in general—the law, public opinion, or conditions of inequality. A primary relationship gives one the feeling of having "someone on my side," which is a valuable kind of emotional support.

The importance of the primary relationship is shown by situations in which primary ties are suddenly severed. The child who loses a parent through death or divorce, the adolescent with a broken love affair, the mother who loses a spouse, the very old person who has been unable to replace the primary relationships ended by death—all these people are in situations where primary ties have been weakened or snapped, and they suffer stress because of it.

THE PRIMARY GROUP IN MODERN SOCIETY

The primary group has always been the basic unit of social organization. In the earliest human societies, it was probably the only kind of group that existed. The primitive society was tightly bound together into a unity of primary relations by ties of blood and tradition. Sociologist Edward Shils calls

this oldest kind of group the *primordial primary group*.[5] Membership in it was involuntary.

In modern society, primary groups are more voluntary in nature. Except in the case of the family into which one is born, primary groups tend to be based on a voluntary choice of family, friends, and work associates.

Contemporary primary groups may also be organized around a number of different

5. Edward Shils, "Primordial, Personal, Sacred and Civil Ties," *British Journal of Sociology* 8 (1957): 130–145.

Children's play groups are a universal form of primary group and together with the family have been called the "nursery of human nature." Play groups provide a setting where children develop a self-image through reflection in the eyes of others. This reflection is not always of a positive nature, as these children may be indicating. *(Photo by Ken Heyman)*

Peer groups serve as an important source of emotional support and solidarity, particularly when the family is fragmented by social pressures. Sometimes they assume the form of a kinship unit, with members regarding themselves as "brothers." Youthful peer groups form most commonly around play activities. *(Photo by Ken Heyman)*

beliefs and ideologies—called by Shils *ideological primary groups*. Religious belief often forms the basis of a primary group's common bond. Religious organizations have continued to provide a local setting for primary relationships to a relatively high degree in this country. The newer, cult-like religions—the storefront churches in the big cities of the northeast, the little chapels and tabernacles to be found in the cities of the west coast—serve this purpose, and it is interesting to note that these are the churches that are growing fastest today. The newer churches in the suburbs also generate many

informal primary relationships and groups among their members.

Social and political ideologies may also serve as the bond which holds together a primary group. The members are drawn together by their common beliefs, but they may derive more than political or social support from the group; it may become an important source of primary relationships.[6]

To a great extent, primary groups today have been overshadowed by the larger and

6. Jack Newfield, *A Prophetic Minority* (New York: New American Library, 1966), especially chap. 2.

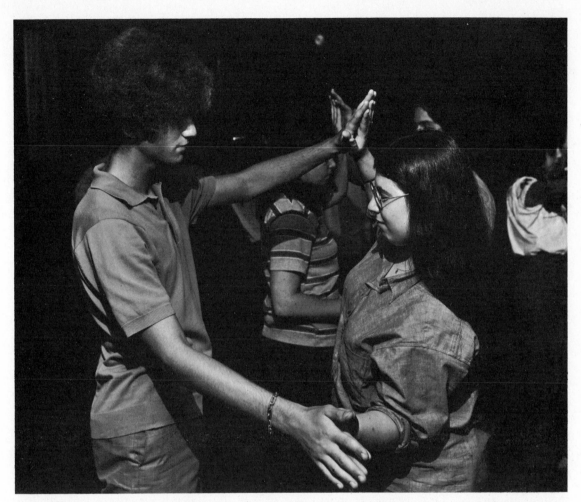

The proliferation of encounter groups in our society reflects the widespread search for more rewarding primary relationships, indicating that individuals are failing to find sufficient satisfaction in the traditional primary groups. An increasing number of people, particularly in the middle class, are expressing a need to find a setting where they can "be themselves," can break through carefully prescribed role expectations of secondary relationships, and can make fuller contact with others, including physical contact. *(Hugh Rogers, Monkmeyer)*

more impersonal "secondary" groups, such as complex formal organizations to be discussed in the next three topics. Where once children were taught at home by their mother, they now go to public school with hundreds of other children, in an organizational setting. Work used to be performed by the members of the family together, as it still is among the 5 percent of Americans who live on farms today, but for most people work is now performed in an impersonal setting, and many co-workers are just strangers with familiar names. Even government was once personal, in the days when the village headman (or in more recent small-town America, the town mayor) was a personal acquaintance or a relative of everyone who lived there. Today, most Americans live in large urban areas and have never actually met their mayor, governor, or president.

Most sociologists agree that there has been a decrease in the proportion of our total daily social relationships that may be classified as primary. This may be due partially, however, to the fact that we have many more relationships each day, so that the actual number of primary relationships has not decreased as much as it may seem. More debatable is the question of whether there has also been a corresponding decrease in the *quality* of such primary relationships. One reason which is often suggested to account for such a decrease is that the proportionately few primary relationships which do remain are subject to great strain. As we shall discuss in chapter 6, for example, the family relationships of husband and wife or parent and child are subject to great strain in modern society because they have to bear the burdens which were once shared by relatives and by the local neighborhood and community. Divorce and family breakdown, of course, may deny individuals even these primary relationships.

On the other hand, some sociologists feel any decline in the quality of primary relationships may be offset by the fact that more of our primary relationships are voluntary. Our increased freedom from ties to family, neighborhood, and other traditional groups enables us to truly choose our friends. These friendships may be more meaningful to us than many relationships that we are thrust into by birth and which are perhaps more shallow in nature. This argument applies most forcefully to adults who are highly mobile and have many economic and social opportunities to choose friends voluntarily.

Of greatest concern to social scientists is the possibility that the network of primary relationships that surrounds the growing child has declined in quality. The child does not have much mobility or choice; he is completely dependent on the social environment into which he is born. Any decline in the childhood environment, therefore, would likely have serious and long-lasting consequences. Some feel, however, that the social environment of the child has in fact improved over the years because of better education and child-rearing practices, improvements based on increased knowledge of psychology and family development.

It is difficult to know what effect a decline in both quantity and quality of primary relationships might have on individuals in our society. Some sociologists and psychologists link it with the growing rate of mental illness, of social dropouts, and of retreat into the indifference of alcohol, drugs, and social apathy, but the relationship has not yet been fully demonstrated. We can say with certainty, however, that modern society has produced a large number of people who are searching for some kind of meaningful group membership or relationship. This is especially noticeable in young people and their devotion to their peer groups. It can be seen in the movement toward the founding of communes, which may be interpreted as an attempt to reconstruct the conditions of the primordial primary group. It can even be seen in the concern for greater participation in and local control of large institutions and bureaucracies, such as governments, schools, universities, and hospitals. The search for a deeper and more meaningful way of living, for the development of more "primary qualities" in life, seems an important characteristic of our times.

ELLIOT LIEBOW
Friends and Networks on the Corner

Introduction

This abridgment comes from a chapter of Elliot Liebow's book, Tally's Corner. *The book is based on an intensive study of a group of black men who customarily gathered on a street corner in inner-city Washington, D.C. Liebow studies the relationships of the men with one another and with other members of the community — with parents, wives, children, girl friends, employers, brothers, and friends. This chapter focuses on the primary relationships established between the various men who spent time on the corner. Liebow observes that these relationships were of great importance to each person involved, but that they were often unsuccessful relationships, partly because of the burden they had to carry in providing too many different kinds of support and gratification.*

More than most social worlds, perhaps, the streetcorner world takes its shape and color from the structure and character of the face-to-face relationships of the people who live in it. Unlike other areas in our society, where a large portion of the individual's energies, concerns, and time are invested in self-improvement, career and job development, family and community activities, religious and cultural pursuits, or even in broad, impersonal social and political issues, these resources in the streetcorner world are almost entirely given over to the construction and maintenance of personal relationships.

On the streetcorner, each man has his own network of these personal relationships.

In toward the center are those persons he knows and likes best, those with whom he is "up tight": his "walking buddies," "good" or "best" friends, girl friends, and sometimes real or putative kinsmen. These are the people with whom he is in more or less daily, face-to-face contact, and whom he turns to for emergency aid, comfort or support in time of need or crisis. He gives them and receives from them goods and services in the name of friendship, ostensibly keeping no reckoning. Routinely, he seeks them out and is sought out by them. They serve his need to be

with others of his kind, and to be recognized as a discrete, distinctive personality, and he, in turn, serves them the same way. They are both his audience and his fellow actors.

So important a part of daily life are these relationships that it seems like no life at all without them. Old Mr. Jenkins climbed out of his sickbed to take up a seat on the Coca-Cola case at the Carryout for a couple of hours. "I can't stay home and play dead," he explained, "I got to get out and see my friends."

In general, close friendships tend to develop out of associations with those who are already in one's network of personal relationships: relatives, men and women who live in the area and spend much of their time on the street or in public places, and co-workers. The result is that the streetcorner man, perhaps more than others in our society, tends to use the same individuals over and over again: he may make a friend, neighbor and co-worker of his kinsman, or a friend, co-worker and kinsman of his neighbor.

One of the most striking aspects of these overlapping relationships is the use of kinship as a model for the friend relationship. Most of the men and women on the streetcorner are unrelated to one another and only a few have kinsmen in the immediate area. Nevertheless, kinship ties are frequently manufactured to explain, account for, or even to validate friend relationships. In this manner, one could move from friendship to kinship in either direction.

The most common form of the pseudo-kin relationship between two men is known as "going for brothers." This means, simply, that two men agree to present themselves as brothers to the outside world and to deal with one another on the same basis. Going for brothers appears as a special case of friendship in which the usual claims, obligations, expectations, and loyalties of the friend relationship are publicly declared to be at their maximum.

Sea Cat and Arthur went for brothers. Sea Cat's room was Arthur's home so far as he had one anywhere. It was there that he kept his few clothes and other belongings, and it was on Sea Cat's dresser that he placed the pictures of his girl friends (sent "with love" or "love and kisses"). Sea Cat and Arthur wore one another's clothes and, whenever possible or practical, were in one another's company. Even when not together, each usually had a good idea of where the other was or had been or when he would return. Generally, they seemed to prefer going with women who were themselves friends; for a period of a month or so, they went out with two sisters.

Sea Cat worked regularly; Arthur only sporadically or for long periods not at all. His own credit of little value, Arthur sometimes tried to borrow money from the men on the corner, saying that the lender could look to his "brother" for payment. And when Sea Cat found a "good thing" in Gloria, who set him up with a car and his own apartment, Arthur shared in his friend's good fortune. On the streetcorner or in Sea Cat's room, they laughed and horsed around together, obviously enjoying one another's company. They cursed each other and called each other names in mock anger or battle, taking the liberties that were reserved for and tolerated in close friends alone.

A few of the men on the corner knew that Sea Cat and Arthur were, in fact, unrelated. A few knew they were not brothers but thought they were probably related in some way. Others took their claim to kinship at face value. Even those who knew they were merely going for brothers, however, accepted this as evidence of the special character of their friend relationship. In general, only those who are among the most important in one's personal network can distinguish between real and pseudo-kin relationships, partly because the question as to whether two men are really brothers or are simply going

for brothers is not especially relevant. The important thing for people to know in their interaction with the two men is that they say they are brothers, not whether they are or not.

Most friendships are born in relationships or situations in which individuals confront one another day by day and face to face. These friendships are nurtured and supported by an exchange of money, goods, services and emotional support. Small loans, ranging from a few pennies up to two or three dollars, are constantly being asked for and extended. Leroy watches Malvina's children while she goes out to have a few drinks with a friend. Tonk and Stanton help Budder move the old refrigerator he just bought into his apartment. Leroy borrows a bottle of milk for the baby from Richard and Shirley. Sara gives Earl three dollars to get his clothes out of the cleaners. Sea Cat and Stoopy find Sweets knocked unconscious on the sidewalk, carry him home and put him to bed. Tonk and Richard go down to the police station to put up five dollars toward Tally's collateral.

In ways such as these, each person plays an important part in helping and being helped by those in his personal network. Since much of the cooperation between friends centers around the basic prerequisites of daily living, friends are of special importance to one's sense of physical and emotional security. The more friends one has or believes himself to have, and the deeper he holds these friendships to be, the greater his self-esteem and the greater the esteem for himself he thinks he sees in the eyes of others.

The pursuit of security and self-esteem push him to romanticize his perception of his friends and friendships. He wants to see acquaintances as friends, and not only as friends but as friends with whom he is "up tight," "walking buddies," "best friends," or even brothers. He prefers to see the movement of money, goods, services and emotional support between friends as flowing freely out of loyalty and generosity and according to need rather than as a mutual exchange resting securely on a quid pro quo basis. He wants to believe that his friendships reach back into the distant past and have an unlimited future; that he knows and is known by his friends intimately, that they can trust one another implicitly, and that their loyalties to one another are almost unbounded.

Friendship is at its romantic, flamboyant best when things are going well for the persons involved. But friendship does not often stand up well to the stress of crisis or conflict of interest, when demands tend to be heaviest and most insistent. Everyone knows this. Extravagant pledges of aid and comfort between friends are, at one level, made and received in good faith. But [at] another level, fully aware of his friends' limited resources and the demands of their self-interest, each person is ultimately prepared to look to himself alone.

The recognition that, at bottom, friendship is not a bigger-than-life relationship is sometimes expressed as a repudiation of all would-be friends . . . or as a cynical denial that friendship as a system of mutual aid and support exists at all. When Tally threatened to withdraw his friendship from Richard, Richard dismissed this as no real loss. "Richard's the only one who ever looked out for Richard," he said.

Attitudes toward friends and friendships are thus always shifting, frequently ambivalent, and sometimes contradictory. One moment, friendship is an almost sacred covenant; the next, it is the locus of cynical exploitation: "Friends are [good only] for money."

The overall picture is one of a broad web of interlocking, overlapping networks in which the incumbents are constantly — however irregularly — shifting and changing positions relative to one another. This fluidity and change which characterizes personal relationships is reflected in neighbor and kin relationships, in family, household, indeed in the whole social structure of the streetcorner world which rests to so large an extent precisely on the primary, face-to-face relationships of the personal network.

Conclusion

One of the main functions of primary relationships is to give security to its members. To the people who go to the streetcorner, security appears to be a prime objective. This is one reason the kinship model is used as a basis for some of the friendships. A brother relationship is one that is enduring; two "brothers" will always be "related" to one another.

Primary relationships with peers are important to young people in all segments of society. In this segment of society, they often are the only personally rewarding kind of relationship that a young person has.

TOPIC

2 THE NATURE AND TYPES OF ORGANIZATIONS

Within human societies, individuals characteristically form into groups to accomplish special purposes. These special-purpose groups are called organizations. According to anthropologists, organizations for hunting were already present in the societies of man's ape-like ancestors. Ancient civilizations had large and powerful organizations to carry out religious, political, and military functions—the Egyptian pyramids could not have been built without the aid of complex organization, and the accomplishment of medieval society sprang from the large, complex organization of the Catholic church. Modern, urban-industrial society has produced a profusion of large-scale, complex organizations that extend into all areas of everyday life, to a greater degree than any society known in past ages. This emphasis on organizations has primarily been due to the high value placed on rationality and efficiency in modern times, for it is in the achievement of these values that organizations excel. Organizations come in a bewildering variety, ranging from a six-member club of girls in the fourth grade to the federal government with its millions of employees. The first task for the social scientist is to define the various organizations, establish a terminology that can be used to discuss them, and categorize the major types to be found in our society.

The term "organization" is not the only term sociologists use to refer to this type of social grouping, but it is the only term we will use in this text. We will use the term "association," but only to refer to the voluntary association, a specific type of organization discussed later in this topic.

DEFINITION AND CLASSIFICATION OF ORGANIZATIONS

What is an organization, and how does it differ from other social groups? An *organization* may be defined as a social group that has been deliberately and consciously constructed in order to seek certain specific goals.[7] All groups strive to accomplish certain aims, but in many groups the aims are

7. This definition, and the characteristics which follow, are adapted from Amitai Etzioni, *Modern Organizations* (Englewood Cliffs, N.J.: Prentice-Hall, 1964), p. 3.

very general and unstated. In some cases each individual in a group may have separate goals. In an organization, however, the goals are clearly stated and well understood. Besides having clearly stated and specific goals, an organization has the following basic characteristics:

1. There is a division of labor and power which is designed to make the group a more efficient agent for achieving the organization's goals.
2. There is a concentration of power in the hands of leaders or executives who use that power to control the activities of the organization and direct them toward organization goals.
3. The membership is routinely changed rather than fixed. New members may be added when necessary, and old ones who prove unsatisfactory may be removed.

Some examples of organizations are clubs, schools, churches, hospitals, prisons, business corporations, and government agencies. Many important groups do not fit under this definition. A family would not be called an organization, because its members are not routinely replaceable and it does not have specific goals. The group of people who wait for the bus every morning at the same corner are not an organization because they have no division of labor or centers of power. An ethnic group, such as Italian-Americans, is not an organization; but a group like the Sons of Italy, composed entirely of members of Italian ethnicity for the purpose of improving the public image of the Italian-American, is clearly an organization. A group of friends, even when they have a highly patterned set of relationships, as did the men who gathered at Tally's Corner, are usually not an organization because they lack defined goals.

It is important here to distinguish between organizations and the primary groups which we discussed in the last topic. Firm lines cannot always be drawn: some primary groups are quite highly organized and some organizations have many of the qualities of primary groups. The most important difference between the two kinds of groups lies in the relationships of the individual members to one another. In a primary group, they are interested in each other as total persons, but in an organization, they need know each other only in one or more specialized roles. Of course it is quite possible and often necessary for primary relationships to develop within an organization, and this often happens with co-workers in an office. But primary relationships are not the basis for the functioning of an organization, as they are for the primary group. Another important distinguishing factor is that of purpose. The organization deliberately focuses on a specific goal; a primary group has more general goals. In both cases, the group may either be expressive (that is, for the purpose of emotional gratification) or instrumental (that is, for the purpose of accomplishing a task), but the primary group is in most instances expressive, while the organization is more likely to be instrumental. Generally speaking, an organization is larger than a primary group. A primary group must be small enough to allow the continual face-to-face contact of all the members; but a complex organization may have thousands of members who are unacquainted even with each other's names and faces.

There are many different kinds of organizations, and sociologists have devoted a great deal of attention to devising scientifically useful classification schemes. The simplest way to distinguish between organizations is according to the types of relationships between members within each organization. In a *formal organization* the relationships are defined by a specific and formally stated set of rules and regulations, such as the rules of conduct in the Marine Corps. In an *informal organization* the members interact in a more personal way that develops spontaneously—for example, as in a hobby club.

Two other factors often used to classify organizations are size and complexity.

One system for classifying organizations was devised by Peter Blau and Richard Scott; the system is based on an examination of the individuals or group who benefit most from the goals of the organization.[8] Four categories are used: (1) mutual benefit associations, such as a veterans' group, in which the benefit is mainly to the membership; (2) business concerns, such as Minnesota Mining and Manufacturing, in which the benefit is mainly to the owners; (3) service organizations, such as the Red Cross or a public high school, in which the benefits are mainly to users or clients; and (4) commonweal organizations, such as the Defense Department, in which the benefit is to the entire society or the public at large.

Another important system of classification has been suggested by Amitai Etzioni, who proposes three types based not on goals but on the way the organization obtains its members' cooperation or compliance with goals and regulations.[9] He calls the first type coercive, wherein some kind of force is used; examples are prisons, or prisoner-of-war camps. The second type includes organizations with which people comply for utilitarian or practical purposes; this is the case with most businesses and with a peacetime army. The third type is one in which members cooperate because they share the norms of the organization; this can be seen in religious organizations, schools, and most voluntary associations.

FORMAL AND INFORMAL STRUCTURE

As we noted above, one way of distinguishing between organizations is according to the type of relationships among the members, ranging from formal to informal. Al-

8. Peter M. Blau and W. Richard Scott, *Formal Organizations: A Comparative Approach* (San Francisco: Chandler, 1962), pp. 42–45.

9. Amitai Etzioni, *A Comparative Analysis of Complex Organizations* (New York: Free Press, 1961), pp. 66–67.

Religious orders, such as the one to which these nuns belong, are formal organizations with many of the accompanying characteristics. For example, the members wear specified, identifying clothes; the group conforms to a prescribed pattern of behavior; and authority is distributed through a clearly defined hierarchy. *(Grey Villet)*

though we often say that a certain group is or is not a formal organization, it is more useful to think of all organizations as having both formal and informal structure, but in varying degrees. When formal patterns predominate we may label the organization *formal;* when informal patterns predominate we label the organization *informal.*

Formal structure

What is called the *formal structure* of an organization is the explicit and formally stated set of rules and regulations that define the activities of the members. The mechanisms of formal structure include charts, constitutions, by-laws, chains of command, and time schedules for meeting goals. Usually

these things are written down, but that need not always be true. A small group—say a club of little girls—may be formally organized in the sense of having officers, a goal, and a method of conducting meetings which is agreed upon but not written down; since it is so small and simple, the members can keep the organizational structure in their heads.

In a formally structured organization, each member is assigned some share of the task which the group hopes to accomplish. At the same time, his relationship with other members assigned other parts of the task is defined. That is, the amount of authority which each has over the others and the expected patterns of communication and coordination between members are spelled out. Who will make decisions, and where, when, and by what method, are also established, along with some method of choosing group leaders. Generally, it is also necessary to provide some formal means of discipline—explicit sanctions, both positive and negative, which representatives of the organization can bring to bear on individual members—to ensure that members keep to the established structure. Positive sanctions, such as promotions and raises, titles and plush offices, election to office, and all the "fringe benefits" (such as expense accounts, cars, and invitations to social events) are used to motivate or reward individual members who correctly carry out the assigned task. Negative sanctions, such as being demoted, or fired, or passed over for promotion or office, are imposed on those members who do not keep to the rules. It is common for a large and complex organization to institute some formal means of measuring the performance of its members in carrying out their assigned tasks. The salary review, the periodic "fitness report," and the annual evaluation by a superior, are such measurements.

The use of formal structure often improves efficiency and therefore goal achievement. However, the formality of an organization sometimes stifles creativity and initiative in its members (observation of this phenomenon has made many sociologists critical of bureaucracy) and this interferes with the efficient achievement of goals. Sometimes the rigidity of a formal organization prevents needed adaptations to changing social or economic conditions; this can be seen in the history of many failed businesses. For example, most buggy makers went bankrupt in the early decades of the twentieth century. Their rigid organizational structure prevented their adaptation to the advent of the automobile. In recent years the tobacco companies have exhibited a more flexible structure. As cancer research threatens to diminish the sale of cigarettes, the tobacco companies have diversified into other industrial areas.

The most significant way the formal organization of a group can hinder goal achievement is when maintaining and perpetuating the organization becomes more important than the formally stated goals. Members spend their time and efforts to preserve the organization or maintain or achieve positions in the hierarchy, rather than to achieve the goals of the organization. Philip Selznick noted this tendency in his study of the Tennessee Valley Authority.[10] In the face of community pressure many employees attempted to retain the existing structure of the organization rather than try to achieve the organization's stated goals. In *The Peter Principle* (see excerpt), Laurence Peter describes how some organizational members attach greater priority to attaining a high position in the hierarchy than to helping the organization achieve its goals.[11]

In the same way, goals may be altered to fit into the evolving structure of a formal organization. An example can be seen in the labor union. Originally, its goal was the limited one of forcing employers to negotiate with workers on issues of wages and working conditions. As unions grew, and became themselves bureaucratized, their goals changed to reflect their new structure. They now aspire to play an important role in the planning of industrial development and in the workings of the political process.

Informal structure

What is called *informal structure* pertains to personal relationships in an organization which develop spontaneously as members interact. All organizations have some informal relationships. They are needed to supplement the formal structure. The formally defined rules and regulations do not cover

10. Philip Selznick, *TVA and the Grass Roots* (Berkeley: University of California Press, 1949).

11. Laurence J. Peter, *The Peter Principle* (New York: William Morrow, 1969).

THE PETER PRINCIPLE

"IN A HIERARCHY EVERY EMPLOYEE TENDS TO RISE TO HIS LEVEL OF INCOMPETENCE"

The competence of an employee is determined not by outsiders but by his superior in the hierarchy. If the superior is still at a level of competence, he may evaluate his subordinates in terms of the performance of useful work — for example, the application of medical services or information, the production of sausages or table legs, or the achievement of whatever are the stated aims of the hierarchy. That is to say, he evaluates output.

But if the superior has reached his level of incompetence, he will probably rate his subordinates in terms of institutional values: he will see competence as the behavior that supports the rules, rituals, and forms of the status quo. Promptness, neatness, courtesy to superiors, attention to internal paperwork, will be highly regarded. In short, such an official evaluates input.

"Rockman is *dependable.*"

"Lubrik contributes to the *smooth running* of the office."

"Rutter is *methodical.*"

"Miss Trudgen is a *steady, consistent* worker."

"Mrs. Friendly *co-operates* well with colleagues."

In such cases, internal consistency is valued more than efficient service. This is an inversion of the means-end relationships.

From *The Peter Principle: Why Things Always Go Wrong* by Dr. Laurence J. Peter and Raymond Hull. Reprinted by permission of William Morrow and Company, Inc. Copyright © 1969 by William Morrow and Company, Inc.

---

all the problems that an organization must deal with, and may in some cases even be less efficient than informal rules. For example, when the air traffic controllers were negotiating for higher wages in 1970, they used the strategy of obeying all the rules to create a work slowdown. They did not employ the many informal rules that are used when the airports function normally — they proved that "going by the book" entirely is often quite inefficient.

Informal structure helps a group take into account, and adapt to, changing circumstances which might otherwise destroy the formal structure and the organization as a whole. Often the formal rules cannot change fast enough to cope with immediate needs and problems. For example, Albert K. Cohen describes the situation of a chemical mortar battalion in the Philippines at the end of World War II.[12] On the day the Japanese surrendered, the battalion commander realized that the morale of the unit, which had been

12. Albert K. Cohen, *Deviance and Control* (Englewood Cliffs, N.J.: Prentice-Hall, 1966), pp. 78–79.

high due to the importance of its task, might suffer because that task was now completed. He knew that it might be months before the men received orders to return home and that until that time came they must be kept occupied or morale would collapse. The commander therefore decided to give the men a variety of educational courses. But he required such equipment as books and blackboards, and it might take months to obtain them through normal channels. He turned to informal channels, managed to secure the material quickly, and was able to maintain a high morale.

Informal structure also helps balance the demands of the work role with the total personalities of those performing the roles. The role of any employee involves only a part of his personality. Informal structure can take into account some of his more personal traits — personal affinities and dislikes, abilities and talents, feelings about the role and amount of role distance, value orientations — and thus provide opportunities for individual satisfaction.

Other values of informal structure are that it can take into account personal preferences and attitudes which otherwise might be a source of tension and eventual disorganization, and that it can make the organization more appealing to a diverse membership — in short, that it lends a "human" touch to the impersonality of the formal rules and regulations. An example of a group in which informal organization plays a major part can be seen in the accompanying abridgment about flying saucer clubs.

BUREAUCRACY

The extreme type of formal organization structure, which organizations approach to varying degrees, is called *bureaucracy*. The term "bureaucracy" as it is popularly used has a number of unfavorable associations. The image evoked by the word "bureaucrat" is that of a narrow-minded individual so bogged down and tied up by red tape that he has lost sight of his original function. To the sociologist, however, a bureaucracy is simply a type of organizational structure, with its own strengths and weaknesses. Robert Merton has defined a bureaucracy as "a formal, rationally organized social structure [with] clearly defined patterns of activity in which, ideally, every series of actions is functionally related to the purposes of the organization."[13]

A classic study of bureaucracy was made by Max Weber in the early twentieth century.[14] His description of the bureaucratic form of organization is still widely used today. Weber said that a bureaucracy had the following identifiable characteristics:

1. Division of the staff and the workload into smaller units called offices or bureaus. The responsibility of each bureau is care-

13. Robert K. Merton, *Social Theory and Social Structure* (New York: Free Press, 1956), p. 195.

14. Max Weber, *From Max Weber: Essays in Sociology,* ed. and trans. H. H. Gerth and C. Wright Mills (New York: Oxford University Press, 1946, paper edition, 1958), chap. 8.

Max Weber (1864–1920) is often considered the greatest single influence on modern sociology. A scholar of law, history, and economics (as well as sociology), he wrote extensively in many different areas. But his dominant concern was to trace the features that characterize a capitalistic society — its religion, economy, bureaucratic organization, and legal foundation. Weber's best-known and most controversial work was *The Protestant Ethic and the Spirit of Capitalism* (1904–1905), but of even greater importance were the classic analyses of bureaucracy, authority, and social stratification contained in his four-volume *Economy and Society* (1922). *(Brown Bros.)*

fully described, and the jobs of the officials who work in it are also completely planned out in advance.

2. Clear-cut lines of authority and responsibility. Employees are organized in a hierarchy, with each official responsible to a superior on the next level. This helps to coordinate activities into one broad policy or goal-seeking effort.

3. Employment of personnel based on their technical or professional qualifications. In a bureaucracy, it is common for each job to have a specific list of needed qualifications — a certain educational level, so many years of experience, and so on. A

man is hired on the basis of how closely his personal qualifications meet the job requirements.

4. Rules and regulations governing the way officials are to perform their jobs. A person is expected to assume an exact degree of responsibility, no more and no less. The authority of employees to issue orders and commands is strictly limited by sets of rules, which cannot be changed to suit individual abilities or inclinations.

5. The establishment of a bureaucratic career, with specific lines of promotion or advancement, and rewards in the form of tenure and seniority for years of service.

The strength of bureaucratic structure is its efficiency. By making a position not dependent upon a particular person and his unique personality many potential problems are neutralized, such as personal antagonisms that interfere with job performance. This is often called separating the office from the officeholder. Bureaucratic structure also provides continuity. People are loyal to the total organization rather than to an individual person; they become accustomed to the idea that the same job will be performed by changing faces. Officials who are hired because they have the needed abilities for a job are likely to perform much better than those who are hired because they are the boss's nephew, or come from the same town as the owner. The system by which each official's work is reviewed by someone higher up in the hierarchy is a safeguard against incompetence. The reason for the rapid spread of bureaucratic structure in this century is its well-demonstrated efficiency and effectiveness. Although people may need to learn new skills, new values, and new social attitudes to adapt to a bureaucracy, modern societies struggle to make these difficult changes for the gains in efficiency that the new organizational pattern offers them.

However, bureaucracy is not a perfect form of organizational structure. Some of the very factors which produce its efficiency may

at the same time lead to certain problems; it is these problems which loom so large in the popular imagination. Bureaucracies have a tendency to become too rigid; as we noted above, highly formal structures may stifle innovation and creativity. Bureaucracies produce an overcautious attitude in their employees, coupled with a strong desire not to disturb the status quo. The impersonality which makes the organization efficient also makes it a problem in human terms. Bureaucracies which are engaged in public service have a tendency to treat the people they are supposed to be serving in the same impersonal manner in which they treat their internal organization; this attitude interferes with the accomplishment of their service goal. Impersonality is difficult for the employees to deal with in their own jobs too; people like to believe that they are personally valuable. Many of these problems, especially the human consequences of impersonality, are among the central issues of modern society.

VOLUNTARY ASSOCIATIONS

Voluntary associations are very difficult to define precisely, but their importance in the United States has been commented on by social historians and investigated by sociologists. They are groups organized by individuals to pursue some common interest; formal control over the members of such a group is minimal. Voluntary associations are generally "spare-time" organizations whose members are usually unpaid volunteers. Examples of voluntary associations are the Girl Scouts, hobby clubs, PTAs, the League of Women Voters, some professional associations, amateur sports teams, political interest groups, and service organizations such as Rotary and Kiwanis.

Sociologists have been especially interested in the function of voluntary associations in society. It is clear that they provide a means by which individuals can accomplish social goals impossible for them

ASSOCIATIONS AND SOCIETIES IN THE UNITED STATES

Organization title	No. of members
National Council of Churches of Christ in the U.S.A.	42,000,000
American National Red Cross	36,000,000
American Automobile Association	14,000,000
A. F. of L.-C. I. O.	13,600,000
Group Health Association of America	8,000,000
Y.M.C.A.	7,500,000
Boy Scouts of America	6,000,000
National 4-H Club Foundation	4,382,000
Girl Scouts of America	3,920,000
Country Women's Council, U.S.A.	3,000,000
Order of the Eastern Star	3,000,000
American Legion	2,700,000
American Association of Retired Persons	2,700,000
American Farm Bureau Federation	1,900,000
Veterans of Foreign Wars of the U.S.	1,700,000
Benevolent and Protective Order of Elks	1,500,000
Independent Order of Odd Fellows	1,200,000
Knights of Columbus	1,150,000
Loyal Order of Moose	1,100,000
National Education Association	1,100,000
National Rifle Association of America	1,100,000
Young Democratic Clubs of America	1,000,000
Lions International	967,000
American Legion Auxiliary	922,000
Imperial Council of the Ancient Arabic Order of Nobles of the Mystic Shrine	878,000
Fraternal Order of Eagles	850,000
Camp Fire Girls	700,000
National Grange	600,000
Young Republican National Federation	600,000
Supreme Council 330, Ancient Accepted Scottish Rite of Freemasonry, Southern Jurisdiction	570,000
B'nai B'rith	500,000
National Association for the Advancement of Colored People	361,000

Compiled from figures given in *Official Associated Press Almanac 1973,* (New York: Almanac Publishing Co., 1972), p. 493.

Organizational pluralism is characteristic of the United States. Voluntary associations such as these have large and active memberships, and exert a great influence on American life.

to reach alone. This is particularly true in the field of political action. A large and well-organized voluntary association can have great influence on the actions of the government and the policies of the state. An example can be seen in the National Rifle Association of America, which mobilized to express and protect the interests of hunters and sportsmen at a time when the passage of strict gun control laws seemed almost inevitable. The American concept of democracy relies heavily on the continuing existence of many voluntary associations, which provide channels for the expression of opinion and the initiation of action in the political sphere, and which help to mediate between the individual and the centralized governmental and economic units of our society. (In chapter 15, we will discuss more completely the political significance of voluntary associations.)

Other functions have been pointed out as well. The voluntary association provides a way for individuals to cultivate and participate in a number of individual activities and interests. Sports clubs are a perfect illustration. A bowling club may build lanes for its members, where they can play whenever they want to; it may offer lessons to help members improve their game, or teach its fundamentals to the children or wives of members; it organizes tournaments and matches, so that good players can have the opportunity to compete; it may sponsor a professional tournament to draw the top players in the country to that area, so members can watch experts in action. The same holds true for camera clubs, wine-tasting societies, and other voluntary groups.

Voluntary associations often serve as an arena for social experimentation. A local women's club tries out a program to provide day-care centers for the children of working mothers, or hot breakfasts for children in a slum-area school. If the program is successful, it may become the obligation of the city government to continue and expand it; if it fails, it can easily be discarded. We have noted that it is not easy for large bureaucracies to be truly innovative or experimental; thus this role often falls to other groups, such as voluntary associations. An example of how this works might be drawn from the field of the theater. Hundreds of experimental plays—plays with no dialogue, with nude actors, with lines sung instead of spoken—are performed each year by little theater groups, composed of actors and others who are deeply interested in innovative theater. Most are unsuccessful and are never heard of again. Successful ideas or techniques find their way into commercial theaters, where production costs are too high to risk very much experimentation. The musical "Hair" was first performed by a voluntary association in a temporarily empty store; it eventually became a highly successful Broadway show, backed by a large corporation earning millions of dollars.

A fourth function of voluntary associations is that they provide a way to participate in and become involved in community activities. Anyone who cares to may join and be active in a large number of such groups. Membership teaches necessary social skills and creates a sense of commitment to society. Studies show that the individuals who are the most thoroughly integrated into the community are those who also tend to join voluntary associations—people with good educations, families, and better than average social status. There is evidence that this kind of widespread social participation is learned in childhood (joining the Boy Scouts, for example).

Voluntary associations may also be dysfunctional for society. Critics hold that voluntary associations often prevent the government from assuming responsibility which it should bear in such areas as health, welfare, and recreation. This criticism is especially telling because it appears that those who could most benefit from the opportunities provided by voluntary organizations, those who are socially marginal, are least likely to join them.[15] This is partly due to the fact that many voluntary organizations are exclusive and sometimes discriminatory, expensive to join, and dominated by middle-class leadership. Further, the high value placed on "volunteerism" in American life is often used as a reason to oppose government efforts on behalf of those outside of the voluntary organizational network. Another line of criticism holds that many vol-

15. Floyd Dotson, "Patterns of Voluntary Association among Urban Working-class Families," *American Sociological Review* 21 (February 1956):13–38.

A joining of mutual interests and a shared commitment to a social ideology are the basis for many of the voluntary associations in our society. The Rotary Club is a particularly well-established American organization with a large national membership. Drawn primarily from the ranks of successful businessmen, the Rotary is committed to community service and the ethic of civic responsibility. Like many ideologically based organizations, Rotarian solidarity is reinforced by certain rituals and by symbols such as the motto "Above Self." *(Charles Harbutt, Magnum)*

untary associations are shallow and insignificant and that the great amount of time devoted to them could better be spent elsewhere—in family life, giving help to those in need, or helping to end pollution.

Whatever its benefits and drawbacks, the voluntary association is a strongly marked feature of American life. This type of organization is almost nonexistent in primitive societies, and is not a widespread phenomenon in most other modern societies. The variety of voluntary associations and their enthusiastic membership has been an important and to some extent unique characteristic of the American scene almost since the beginnings of the nation.

H. TAYLOR BUCKNER
The Flying Saucerians

Abridged from H. Taylor Buckner's "The Flying Saucerians: An Open Door Cult," printed in *Sociology and Everyday Life,* ed. Marcello Truzzi (Englewood Cliffs, N. J.: Prentice-Hall, 1968), pp. 226–230.

Introduction

This abridgment details an organization of the most informal type, the antithesis of a bureaucracy. Professor Buckner has investigated groups of persons interested in flying saucers. Obviously the potential membership of such a voluntary association is extremely limited, so that maintaining a group large enough to survive is a real challenge. Buckner found that the groups meet the challenge by adopting a very loose and informal organization which permits the coexistence of greatly differing views.

The flying saucer movement started as just another distinct occult philosophy but it gradually changed and is now an open door cult. How did this come about?

The most important single fact about the flying saucer clubs I have had contact with is that they were organized by people who were functioning within the occult social world. One particular club which I have followed for several years and whose records I have been able to examine is perhaps typical in this regard. Its organizer was a late-middle-aged lady whose formal education had ended with the fourth grade. She uses the title "Reverend" which she was given by a man who claims the title himself, and who has been taken to task by the State of California for dispensing titles for a fee. She was familiar with all of the major occult philosophies. When she decided that this new field of flying saucers was of more than passing interest, she decided to start a club. Apparently this was entirely on her own as no other organizations of any size existed then. She rented a small hall for the first meeting, and immediately ran into difficulty. The owner objected to having "Flying Saucer" on his bulletin board. The name was changed to "Space-Craft Club" to satisfy this difficulty. Having a hall she then mailed out postcards to her "friends." Her friends, of course, were people she knew from her contacts in the world of occult seekers. To this first meeting of a new club in February 1956 from a single mailing of postcards came thirty-five people. The first three meetings consisted of quite straightforward flying saucer information. The fourth meeting was on "Space People in the Bible."

What is the flying saucer story? The flying saucer clubs were organized around a fairly simple idea. In brief it is that intelligent beings from other planets, disturbed by mankind's development of atomic energy, have appeared above earth in flying saucers with the intent of saving man from himself. In its original formulation, which was the formulation current when most clubs were formed, the flying saucer is a material object which operates on magnetic energy and is free of the laws of acceleration and inertia. They also "vibrate" in some way so that they can disappear. The pilots bring a new message to the men of earth which is roughly "do unto others as you would have them do unto you." Even space people seem to have a norm of reciprocity.

Even given all of its ramifications and variations this is not a very complex revelation, and the occult seekers who joined the club were probably soon able to look elsewhere for new revelations. The response of the club was to tie flying saucers up with occultism of various types. Thus flying saucers were supposed to be the way of travel between Atlantis and Venus and between Mu and Venus. Also flying saucers are supposed to travel between various astral levels. When beliefs like this become diffused throughout a social world it becomes very difficult to determine what is distinctively a property of flying saucers. The flying saucer thus becomes a Rorschach blot. Anyone with any occult line to sell can hook it up to flying saucers in some way to have it accepted by the flying saucer club. For several years this took place. Then, around 1960, a strange thing began to happen. The audience in the flying saucer clubs began to lose interest in flying saucers. A common remark was "we know all about that!" Which implies that they were no longer interested in hearing about it. In the terms used by members, "we have advanced" from those elementary insights to more complex insights. Thus various occult lines were presented from the flying saucer platform in a nonexclusive fashion with no particular emphasis on one line or another.

Through this process of the gradual elimination of interest in flying saucers, the flying saucer clubs have become a permanently constituted audience. In many ways it is a selective audience, but it is an audience which is willing to listen to just about anything occult.

The personal characteristics of the audience are of particular significance because they related to the survival of the flying saucer organization. The observations I have made could be presented in statistical form, but I feel that this would only obscure the fact that most of them are based on judgments and on talking with limited numbers of people in something less than a cross-sectional survey design.

First of all, the members are old. The average age is probably around 65 and there are very few people under 50. Most of the members are women. The ordinary meeting, then, will have an audience which is at least 80 percent composed of women over 50 years old. Secondly, most of the members seem to be widowed or single. There are very few couples who attend. Third, the socioeconomic status of the members seems to hover around the upper-working-class and lower-middle-class line.

Fourth, the formal education level of most members is quite low. This has a consequence in that although they spend all their time learning, and consider themselves "students," they do not learn things in an ordered and disciplined way, but build up chunks of disconnected knowledge which they cannot bring to bear on a problem and which they cannot systematize. Fifth, the physical health of the audience appears to be bad, even worse than would be accounted for by the high average age. Many members are deaf, many have very poor vision, many walk with the aid of sticks, and many more display obvious physical handicaps of other types. Sixth, the audience, as a group, has a norm of "anything goes" in several areas. No behavior and no ideas, except those in bad taste, are considered illegitimate. All human defects are treated with kindness even to the extent of disrupting a meeting so that a late-arriving person with hearing difficulties can be given a front row seat.

The flying saucer clubs as organizations have difficulties. Having few members who are explicitly interested in flying saucers is one thing, but having an audience that on one level is willing to learn about anything occult but that would gradually drift away if only one line were emphasized, and on another level having an audience that will drift away if they don't feel they are being benefited, is quite another. It poses problems for the person who must choose the speakers; they must always have something "new" to say and it must be helpful.

The strain toward variety is clear. But unrestrained variety is chaotic and would lead to a small average attendance, as any single line may attract a fairly specific audience. A decision must be made whether or not to present a line and the decision is made in large part on the basis of whether it will attract an audience. Some things can pe presented in a convention, where people will sit still for them, but could not be presented in a meeting, where no one would come. The founding of the Universal Party, the saucerians' political party, drew exactly 11 people, 6 of whom had set it up, 4 members of the "audience," and me. Attendance like that doesn't pay the rent.

The characteristics of the audience affect what they want to hear. Time after time, the "good" speakers are the healers. Anything which has to do with physical disease will draw a good sized audience. The healers are usually con-men of some talent, and they use the flying saucer club platform to make their pitch for expensive treatments or therapy. Thus, given limited amounts of money, healing speakers are a self limiting group. Flying saucer clubs will never become exclusively devoted to healing speakers, but they will continue to drift toward an exclusive interest in the magic healing of problems, social, economic, political, physical, and mental, of the aged. And this drift will continue without anyone making a conscious organizational decision to do so. (No one ever seems to make conscious organizational decisions in flying saucer clubs. Things just come up and happen.)

The process of organizational survival could almost be described as a stochastic process, whereby speakers are chosen more or less at random, and the effect of the speaker observed, and taken into account in the selection of other speakers. This process is limited by the available speakers, by the open door policy, and by the overall goals of the organization, but it works. The flying saucer clubs have maintained themselves in the face of the loss of interest in flying saucers by choosing a goal so general—building a better world—that it can legitimate anything. Then drifting with the interests of the audience the organizations manage to survive. They are not prospering however; it takes more than drift to build.

Conclusion

Most organizations put the achievement of their goals before the personal feelings of their members. Of course, they do not ignore the feelings of their members; they try to be sensitive to them, but goal achievement still comes first. In the flying saucer clubs the main goal of the organization was to get more members and keep the ones they had. Satisfying the members, therefore, was always the first order of business. Even the founding idea of the flying saucer clubs was virtually abandoned to continue the existence of the organization.

TOPIC

3 THE ACHIEVEMENT OF ORGANIZATIONAL GOALS

Every organization, whatever its type or special purpose, has to coordinate the behavior of its members in order to achieve its organizational goals. Members must know what to expect from each other, activities must be combined in efficient ways, and the group behavior must be somewhat stable. Every organization has certain character-

leadership does this

istics and processes by which it obtains this coordination. In this topic we shall discuss the processes of control and participation, leadership, communication, organizational identity, and socialization.

CONTROL AND PARTICIPATION

Control over the actions of individual members and the participation of members in the organization's activities and policy making varies greatly. Generally, if there is a high level of organizational control, there is also a low level of membership participation. Sociologists have identified two main types of control and participation patterns within organizations—*authoritarian* and *democratic*.

In an authoritarian pattern broad control is exerted over the organization's members. This control may even extend to the behavior of members toward nonmembers in the larger society. The authoritarian group often tells its members how to dress, what friends or associates to select, even what pleasures to seek. Organizations with many involuntary members, such as the army, are typically authoritarian. Groups which force their members extralegally (without legal support) to remain in the organizations are also usually authoritarian. The Ku Klux Klan and the Mafia are illustrations of such groups. But authoritarian patterns are not limited to involuntary and extralegal organizations; big businesses, for example, move executives from one branch office to another without necessarily taking into consideration the employee's wishes.

An authoritarian organization usually has a hierarchical structure (positions ranked from top to bottom), and decision and policy making lie chiefly in the hands of the officials near the top of the hierarchy. In some cases, these men may exercise their powers virtually unchecked and even unchallenged, with truly dictatorial powers. In other instances, they may be popularly elected or responsible to an elected official. However, responsibility to an electorate does not always make an author-

itarian group responsive to the demands of that electorate. The typical authoritarian organization offers its members little chance to direct or influence group policies and actions. Usually, it also gives them little to do beyond their share of the group labor.

In the democratic pattern of control and participation, members are expected to participate in a variety of group activities. They help to direct the group by means of votes and elective officeholding. Their opinions are frequently solicited by the leaders named to make decisions. A democratic organization will rarely try to adopt rules and regulations to completely control the behavior of members; it will often be reluctant to regulate the behavior of members even when they are participating in group activities.

Our society highly values democracy and full individual participation in most affairs, and we expect to participate in the decision-making process of organizations to which we belong. Our expectation usually produces high group morale in those organizations which do stress democratic participation. The high morale shows up in loyalty on the part of the members, and in a high degree of organizational cohesion. The great involvement of members may be offset, however, by some of the drawbacks of the democratic pattern. Authoritarian structures excel at the smooth coordination of activities because members follow a unified leadership. In a democratic structure, where there is less control over members' behavior, coordination is more difficult. For this reason, among others, goal achievement may be less efficient in democratic organization. This is the price to be paid for a greater attention to the immediate needs and desires of the individual members.

We have spoken of these two different categories of organizational control as opposites, but they may very well coexist in a single organization, just as formal and informal structures do. In fact, democratic participation commonly exists in most organizations as a counterbalance to control. Within a large bureaucracy, some relationships may be governed by strongly authoritarian regulations, whereas others may have a great deal of democratic leeway. Take as an illustration the structure of General Motors. For the factory workers at the bottom, the structure is relatively democratic. There is little attempt to regulate their behavior on the job, except for obviously necessary safety rules, and no attempt whatsoever to exert control outside working hours. The production quotas are fixed democratically, and the supervisors of the work are often elected or chosen because of their popularity with the workers. But the organization presents a different face to members of its executive and administrative staffs. There are more regulations, and the company's control over promotion may dictate appearance, friendships, and style of home life as the members attempt to assume life styles acceptable to the management. Promotion is decided entirely from above, with no participation by those directly concerned. For these men, General Motors is a relatively authoritarian organization. At the very top, on the board of directors, things once more become democratic. Policies are determined by majority votes, and decisions about important matters may be reached by informal consensus.

In discussing this subject we should be careful to distinguish between the structure of the organization and the behavior of the individual. The president of the college dramatics club may behave in an authoritarian way, making all decisions single-handedly as to what plays should be performed and who should be cast in them, snapping orders at the other officials and at the members, and making unreasonable demands on members' time and capabilities. But the club itself is organized in a democratic way and the president is elected to his position. Sometimes we see the reverse situation, as, for example, in the case of a

prison warden who has the inmates vote on regulations governing leisure time activities or kitchen menus; here the individual is behaving democratically in an authoritarian structure. A gross imbalance between behavior and structure is a source of social stress that calls for correction. It may take the form of some change in the structure (regulations concerning prison administration are changed to make it a more democratic organization) but the more usual result is the departure of the individual (the warden is fired and the president is voted out). Although behavior and structure are separate factors, they must correspond to some extent.

LEADERSHIP

No organization can function effectively without some kind of leadership. Even in groups totally committed to the ideal of participational democracy and opposed to the idea of elite leaders, leadership is necessary and group leaders emerge. A leader plays several important roles. He acts as a decision maker; as an administrator, ensuring that the group's policies are carried out and the group's activities coordinated; and as a monitor, continually reviewing the group's performance to determine if changes in the group may be necessary. He also represents the group to the outside world. An example of these roles can be seen in the last abridgment. It was the leaders of the flying saucer clubs who observed the reaction of club members to the various speakers and subjects; it was the leaders' processing of group feedback that gave the group its goal of building a better world. In the same way, leaders are alert to the development of group norms and values and often serve to articulate them for the group.

In certain cases, it is the presence and personality of the leader that evokes the loyalty of the organization's members. In such groups, the organization itself is typically secondary to the leader; if he leaves, the

The personal charisma and energy of one man, Cesar Chavez, have been major factors in the organization of the California farm workers. Chavez built a union from the ground up that has become powerful enough to confront and win recognition from established economic interest groups and political leaders. Recently, he has developed a national following that draws on workers and members from many segments of our society. *(UPI)*

organization will break up. This "charismatic" type of leadership can be extremely effective, but it leaves the organization in obvious danger if it loses its leader.

Many social scientists have been interested in the process by which leaders develop within organizations and are recognized as legitimate. The average person thinks of leadership as an inborn personal quality; either you have it or you don't. We even speak of the "born leader," implying that certain people are somehow genetically selected to take charge of others. In reality, leadership is a quality not only of a person but also of a situation; it is not only a personal attribute, but also a relational one. "Leader" is a role that one plays, and sometimes there are very few requirements for the part. It is not easy to demonstrate empirically that a leader needs any more intelligence or special training than any other group member; his seeming superiority may be the result of his role as leader. By play-

ing his role, he may very well come to know more about the group's activities and goals, and understand them better, than anyone else in the group—but he need not start out that way.

Studies of the way leaders are chosen also indicate that leadership is sometimes largely situational. A significant study on this topic was done in World War II, on new draftees.[16] As each group arrived, superior officers simply designated some man in the group as temporary leader; his only qualification was being first in line. It was discovered that in the majority of cases, these same men were later chosen group leaders by the men themselves, and that the men felt these leaders were "well qualified" for the position. In other words, assuming a leadership role sometimes qualifies one to be a leader. Other studies show that leaders are sometimes

16. R. L. French, "Sociometric Analysis of Individual Adjustment among Naval Recruits," *Journal of Abnormal Psychology* 46 (1951):64–69.

chosen by accident of circumstance—they start the group, or they have access to some facility or information the group needs, or they seem the most available and/or willing member. This is particularly true in voluntary associations.

Many sociological studies have been done on the recruitment of leaders. A number of studies found that in complex organizations, the very top level of executives or leaders is usually drawn drom a small, self-perpetuating group—a group which any outsider finds difficult to penetrate. This group is called an oligarchy. The most famous study of oligarchies was done by Robert Michels; it is discussed in his book *Political Parties*.[17] Michels put forth the "iron law of oligarchy" which holds that power in an organization tends to flow to a few people at the top of the organization's hierarchy. Members lower in the hierarchy will be very submissive because the leaders are so powerful. When the leaders are replaced, they will be replaced by people much like the old leaders; thus the leadership is self-perpetuating. Michels concluded that the rise of oligarchies is probably inevitable in most kinds of organization (including the organization of the American government, even though it is based on representational democracy and not formally classified as an oligarchy).

COMMUNICATION

As we have stated above, the key feature of any organization is that it is formed to achieve specific goals, and if the goal is to be reached, all the members must work together. But labor in an organization is divided; there are workers in many different kinds of jobs requiring different levels of skill, training, and intelligence. To get this diverse group of individuals to work together cooperatively is not easy—it requires a great deal of communication between the vari-

17. Robert Michels, *Political Parties: A Sociological Study of the Oligarchical Tendencies of Modern Democracy* (New York: Free Press, paper, 1966).

ous members and positions of the organization.

Patterns of communication will be determined both by the formal and the informal structure of the organization. The formal structure tells the members the directions in which communication should flow. Formal channels of communication are usually arranged according to the hierarchical relations between members and are meant to determine the flow of authority as well as of information. An organization chart like the one reproduced here assists communication by making it clear where each employee should go to obtain either facts or orders. The use of formal communication channels can be encouraged by making them explicit in this way.

However, the formal channels of communication will inevitably be supplemented by informal patterns; sometimes they are actually supplanted by them and much of the business of the organization is carried on through informal channels. Informal communications often focus on shortcuts for getting work done. When the formal rules of the organization interfere with the most efficient operation of the organization, workers will informally communicate on how best to handle certain problems that the rules do not cover.

Examples of informal channels of communication, by which information is transmitted to people other than those indicated on the formal chart, are:

1. Through primary relationships among group members. Ms. Jones in Accounting is dating Mr. Adams in Sales, and they discuss the business concerns of their day over dinner.
2. Through eavesdropping, either accidental or otherwise. The secretary to the Vice-President overhears the plans for next year's sales campaign, and mentions it to another secretary, who passes it on to her boss.
3. Through personal preference based on work capability. An employee takes a

CORPORATION ORGANIZATION CHART
(adapted and abridged from the Chrysler Corporation Organization Chart)

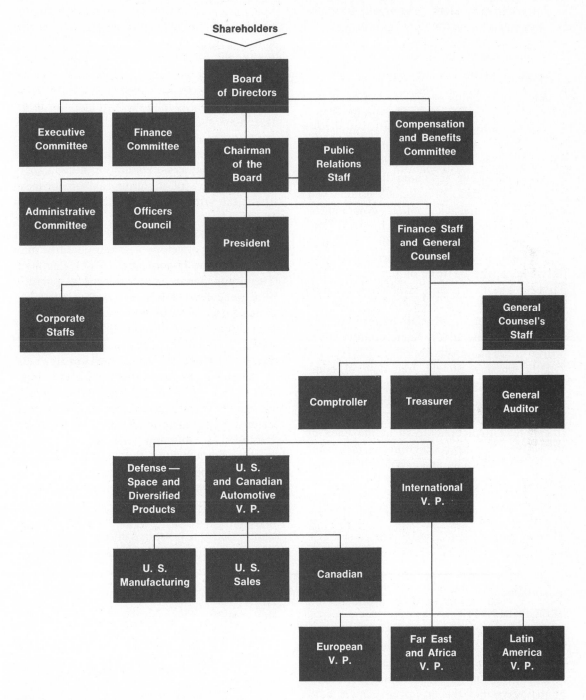

This diagram is a typical organization chart which sets forth formal chains of command within a complex modern corporation.

problem to the second Vice-President because he doubts the capability of the first Vice-President, the man formally designated to deal with the problem.

4. Through personal affinity based on joint membership in some other organization or social grouping.

This last is quite common. Although the relationship of those particular group members falls short of a primary relationship, the members prefer to communicate informally among themselves. Several studies, for example, have indicated that members of minority, ethnic, or religious groups will form an informal channel of communication, as a way of helping each other. The black employees in the home office of a large corporation may form an information pool; the same might be true of the Jewish employees. The two members of the sales staff who attended college at Ohio State may form an informal communication pattern, or the ones who belong to the same country club, or live in the same suburb.

Although a relatively free flow of communication generally leads to greater organizational efficiency, an unregulated flow of communication has a number of drawbacks. It can lead to a breakdown in the lines of authority or a distraction from the important business to be done, and privileged information necessary to the success of the organization may fall into the wrong hands. That is why most organizations try to provide certain channels of communication and discourage many of the unofficial paths (some companies, for example, prohibit dating between employees), in the hope of striking a functional balance.

GROUP IDENTITY

Every organization seeks to establish some kind of group identity strongly valued by the members to help in maintaining the group as a cohesive unit. Group identity is the total of the ways that the group is defined, both by members and nonmembers. The identity of

any group organization is largely dependent on the goals and normative system of the group, and the character of its membership. An organization can determine goals, and norms and values, for itself upon establishment (although, of course, they may change during the life of the organization). But an organization cannot entirely prefabricate an identity. Identity evolves through the interaction of members with each other, as they try to understand what membership means to them, and also through members' interactions with nonmembers. The more nonmembers treat members of the group as somehow set apart, the stronger will be the sense of group identity.

A good example of one way in which an organization develops a strong identity may be seen in the history of the Black Panthers. The group began as an informal association of a very few young men with similar life experiences and outlooks. Originally the organization was subordinate to the personalities of the founders, especially Bobby Seale and Huey Newton. However, the way in which the Panthers publicly defined their goals—the establishment of total equality for blacks and the use of force as a means of defense—caused nonmembers to define Black Panthers as "different." Extensive coverage in the news media of the activities of a few of the members, such as Seale, Newton, and Eldridge Cleaver, helped build up a mystique around membership in the group, and the members reacted to the definition and incorporated this mystique into their own sense of group identity. They became a strong organization, able not only to overcome the loss of most of their initial leaders who were jailed, killed, or exiled, but even to grow in strength. Their strong identity was not only a calculated move by the group or its leaders, but was also an inevitable outcome of interaction between members and nonmembers.

Identity is bolstered by certain symbolic means. These may include an organization

FORMAL AND INFORMAL CHANNELS OF COMMUNICATION IN A CORPORATION

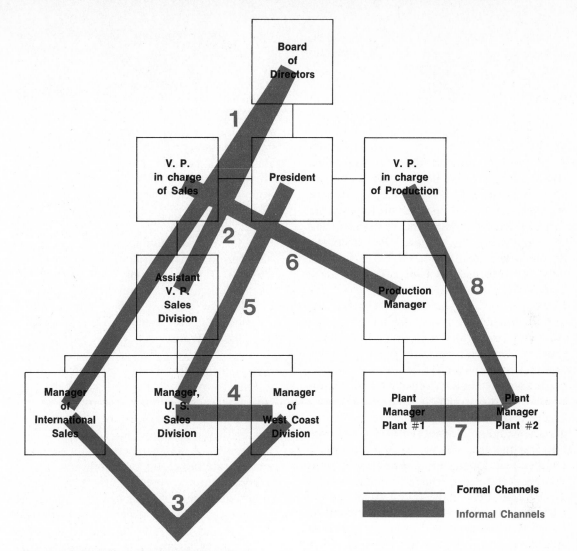

_____ Formal Channels

▬▬▬▬▬ Informal Channels

Key to Informal Channels of Communication

1. One of the members of the board of directors is a frequent traveler and often visits the Manager of the International Sales Division at his villa in Rome.
2. The Assistant Vice-President of the Sales Division is the nephew of a board member.
3. The Manager of International Sales frequently telephones the West Coast Sales Manager because he doesn't particularly like the Manager of the U. S. Sales Division and it is inefficient to channel all his communications through the Assistant Vice-President.
4. The Manager of the West Coast Sales Division likes both of the other sales division managers but is envious of the Assistant Vice-President.
5. The Manager of the U. S. Sales Division is a frequent golf partner of the president.
6. The Vice-President in charge of Sales often needs information about the supply of certain models. The president is too busy to be bothered with such details, and the Vice-President in charge of Production doesn't have the information he needs, so he calls the Production Manager.
7. The two plant managers frequently call each other because it is more efficient than communicating through the Production Manager.
8. The Plant Manager of Plant #2 is married to the daughter of the Vice-President in charge of Production.

insignia, uniforms, flags, passwords, hand-shakes, gestures, dress that amounts to costume, and ways of ornamenting one's person. Still using our illustration of the Black Panthers, we can see several identity symbols. They have an insignia, the crouching black panther. They often wear a sort of uniform—black pants, black leather jacket, black beret, black sunglasses. They also originated other symbols which were appropriated by the black power movement in general and cease to serve to identify the user as a Panther; examples are the clenched fist salutes and the slogan, "Power to the People." The Panthers have had to replace these identity symbols with new ones more specific to the group.

An organization can also achieve its identity through its leader, for he may come to symbolize the whole group to both members and nonmembers. Norman Thomas was such a leader for the Socialist Party.

All these symbols of organizational identification become valuable to the members. Members have a natural tendency to imbue the group and its identity with value, because they see the group as an extension of themselves. The longer an organization is in existence, the more value it accumulates for the members who have invested their time, energy, and emotions in it. This is a strong force for cohesion; unfortunately, it may also be a strong force against change of any kind, including necessary adaptations to new conditions.

SOCIALIZATION TO THE GROUP

One of the most vital processes of any organization is the socialization of new members. Through socialization the new members learn how to carry out their assigned duties and internalize the group values and norms that will support their activities. During the socialization process the new member gradually identifies with the organization, distinguishes between members and nonmembers, and accepts membership in the

organization as important. This is an example of continuing adult socialization, which we discussed in chapter 4.

Socialization may consist of a formally organized course of study: the army has its basic training, a university has orientation week, and the Catholic church has its catechism classes. Sometimes the ceremonial rituals that confirm membership serve to stress the individual's dedication to the group and its values, as when one must swear an oath or sign a pledge. Often there is no formal mechanism for socialization before or at the time of joining, and the socialization process is incorporated into certain group activities. Group meetings can often serve this function. Newsletters and bulletins, periodic conventions, and commemorative occasions, such as Founder's Day or National Girl Scout Week, also serve socialization purposes. A great deal of socialization is done informally, in the daily interactions of the group members. Old members may explicitly teach new ones "the ropes," meaning the normative system of the organization, or they may simply tell anecdotes about the group and its members which serve to demonstrate the group viewpoint.

Organizations commonly use a number of important types of socialization. Much of the socialization to general organizational life is conducted by the socializing agencies of the larger society, especially by schools and colleges. The organization conducts the more specific *training*, which teaches specialized skills and the organization's values and norms.

A program of *apprenticeship* is another type of socialization. It is similar to training, but less formal; the instructor is a member of the organization who serves as a model to be copied. Apprenticeship may range from a few days of following someone around as he performs his tasks to a program of several years' duration. In large corporations, for example, the president of a company customarily picks his successor several years in advance and begins to apprentice him to the job.

Erving Goffman has mentioned another, very different type of organizational socialization, which he has termed "mortification."[18] "Mortification" refers to systematic attempts to destroy old concepts of the self and patterns of activity by means of humiliation, contests of will, and debasement. Goffman observed this in the mental hospital he studied; it is also prevalent in many other coercive organizations, such as prisons, concentration camps, and to a certain extent, the army.

Another type of socialization to organizational goals is the sudden experience we call *conversion*. In conversion, one experience or a set of experiences produces a sudden change in values, and then in behavior. We think of this process mainly in terms of religious groups; however, it occurs in many other areas of life as well. For example, a youngster watching a series of plays can become suddenly "stagestruck," and wish to dedicate the rest of his life to the theater.

Organizations of all types rely on the mechanism of *anticipatory socialization*. When a person wants to belong to the organization or to a certain part of it (the executive group, for instance), he observes the way members behave, dress, talk, and work, and he tries to model himself after that pattern. By the time he is allowed to join the group, he is already well socialized to it.

THE ORGANIZATION AND THE NEEDS OF INDIVIDUALS

As a member of an organization, a person is playing only one of his many roles. At times, the demands of his organizational role may oppose the demands of his other roles, presenting him with the problem of role conflict. For example, an executive of a large company may be required to spend a week in a distant city, training employees

18. Erving Goffman, *Asylums* (New York: Doubleday, Anchor, 1961), chap. 1.

of a branch office. This trip may be a necessary part of his organizational role, but it may conflict with his role of husband and father. Each organization tries to instill in its members the feeling that the demands of their organizational roles should supersede all other role demands, but this does not necessarily lessen the role conflict of individuals.

It is important to remember also that each employee of an organization is not just a role player, but a personality with individual needs, desires, and fears. Not all personalities are able to cope successfully with the many demands of an organization, such as giving or taking orders, working closely in a teamwork situation, putting aside immediate personal goals for long-term goals of the organization, and so on. Many of the difficulties of running an organization stem from the problems of fitting various personalities into organizational positions and ensuring that they will perform their roles well.

A person joins a voluntary association because he feels it will be of some value to him. He gives his cooperation to a business organization for the same reason. Membership must in some way further his own goals. These goals need not be the same as the organization's—they may be supplementary or complementary—but they must not be in serious conflict if the organization is to survive. For example, women who join the Colonial Dames may do so with the goal of improving their own social status by this publicly recognized identification with the top level of the American ethnic hierarchy, the Anglo-Saxons (to be a member you must prove descent from an early English settler of the colonies). However, the stated goal of the organization itself has nothing to do with status. The group has formulated its goal as the preservation of landmarks and monuments of American colonial history; their projects include the restoration of the old church of the first colony at Jamestown, Virginia, and the refurnishing and opening to the public of a number of houses in the colonial style. Although the organizational goal may not be at all the same as the personal goals which lead individual members to join the group, the organization is nevertheless successful, because the group goal permits fulfillment of individual goals. The work of the group demonstrates to the community the value of the Anglo-Saxon heritage of America and thus reinforces the members' claim to status.

Now let us suppose that the group, keeping its same members (and requirements for membership), changed its goals—let's say the Colonial Dames decided to correct historical injustice by compensating American Indian tribes for the land which early settlers stole from them. This goal would in effect be pointing out the shortcomings

(stealing land) of those Anglo-Saxon ancestors and thereby devaluing those ancestors as status symbols. The group goal would be in opposition to individual goals. Members would soon begin leaving the organization because it no longer served their needs; they might start some kind of country club with membership based on some obvious status consideration as a substitute.

Sometimes it is possible for an individual to make an organization serve his needs even when the organization's explicit goals run counter to his own. We call this "working the system," and it can be seen in the army, in prisons, and in large bureaucratic organizations. Usually this procedure is known to officials and tolerated by them because it reconciles what would otherwise be a source of serious conflict.

TOPIC 4

ORGANIZATIONAL DEVELOPMENT AND CHANGE

Organizations, like people, cannot long remain static. They must grow, change, and adapt to the changing conditions of the world around them. We will first look at one of the most significant types of organizational change, that which we refer to as institutionalization, and then consider some factors or organizational change which lie outside the organization. We will close with some observations on the way modern organizations in turn introduce social change.

INSTITUTIONALIZATION

When an organization is successful in its bid for members, manages to evoke their

loyalty, is efficient in achieving its goals, and is accepted by the larger community, it usually settles into a stable, orderly system with a relatively unchanging set of goals and values. In short, it becomes institutionalized.

Institutionalization is a natural evolutionary process that is part of organized social life. When first established, an organization is free to experiment a great deal: its goals are flexible, it can choose from many alternative ways to pursue its goals, and the relationships between its members tend to be informal and adaptable. But as an organization operates and grows, its structure is gradually dominated by institutionalized forms. First, a set way of carrying out the group's activities becomes established—this is sometimes referred to as SOP, Standard Operating Procedure. This set procedure, of course, limits the freedom of the organization to choose alternative actions. Second, as the organization establishes set procedures, it requires more formal relationships, which are stable and predictable, among its members. Informal relations become a smaller part of the total web of relationships. Third, the overall structure and the goals become increasingly rigid. As the informal relationships become less important, new paths of communication and new structures within the organization become more difficult to establish.

An institution may eventually make so great an investment in its structure and pursuit of goals that it cannot change to new goals, except with great difficulty. Maintaining the status quo becomes more important than exploring new ideas and changing; indeed maintaining the organization can become just as important as pursuing the original goals. Some organizations, especially those that are large and complex, may evolve into the extreme, bureaucratic form of structure, but that is not an inevitable outcome of institutionalization.

John Kenneth Galbraith has pointed out some important differences between young business organizations and their older and more institutionalized counterparts.[19] The young and small business, in what he calls the entrepreneurial stage, is concerned almost exclusively with making money, and that is the standard for all decision making within the organization. The institutionalized corporation, or the mature company in Galbraith's terminology, is willing to spend money and time on things not connected with this goal, such as bolstering the com-

pany's public image, and developing unprofitable products to give status to a particular branch or executive of the company.

Although institutionalization may make an organization too rigid, for the most part it is a beneficial process. As relationships become more orderly and predictable, coordination among members and continuity of the organization are improved. As knowledge and experience about how to function best are accumulated, the necessity for inefficient trial and error is minimized.

SOME EXTERNAL SOURCES OF CHANGE

Institutionalization is just one of the ways in which an organization can change. Some of the important sources of change which lie outside an organization are (1) new members; (2) competing organizations; and (3) people or groups served by the organization.

Change is likely to occur if new members who are accepted into an organization are quite different from the present members. We can see an example of this in the Student Non-Violent Coordinating Committee (SNCC). As is suggested by its name, the organization originally had a membership that was committed to nonviolent resistance as a means of changing the status of American blacks. Then a number of young people with more militant attitudes joined, and the organization began to change; the change was accelerated by the departure of many of the old members, who were uncomfortable with the rhetoric and actions of the new ones. Eventually the group dropped "Non-Violent" from its name, and assumed a position in the society totally different from the one it had earlier.

Sometimes just one new member can alter the course of an organization, especially if the new member is in a position of leadership. When Robert Townsend became the President of Avis Rent-A-Car, he radically changed the character of the organization. He placed new personnel in important positions, created new positions and phased out

19. John Kenneth Galbraith, *The New Industrial State* (Boston: Houghton Mifflin, 1967).

others, began a new advertising campaign to change the company's public image, and substantially increased the sales profits.

An organization can, of course, exert a good deal of influence on the selection of members, but it cannot completely control who joins the organization, or what influence the new members have. The United States Army, which carefully screens potential new recruits, has taken in many people who are disruptive to the system. Some of these soldiers did in fact call for, and help generate, a reexamination of the army way of life.

Many organizations compete with other organizations for the attention of the publics they serve. Competing organizations may have powerful influences over one another; when one organization is somewhat less successful than the other—for example, if one business earns smaller profits—basic changes in the less successful organization may be necessary to improve its position. An organization which out-competes its competitor will, of course, attempt few (if any) organizational changes; it will only want to maintain its superior position.

Sometimes the very efforts the organization makes to achieve its goals lead to change in the organization, or perhaps to change in the goals; this is particularly true of service organizations. An example may be seen in a city Consumer Affairs Department. Its goal is to protect city residents from fraud, deceit, and abuse by merchants and manufacturers. Since it has only limited powers

The giant corporation has become a fixed feature of modern America. Specialization, conformity, and impersonality are the characteristics that have ensured its efficiency and success, and are also the earmarks of discontent in the twentieth century. Among those who feel a sense of alienation, increasingly the question is being asked, "Does economic well-being depend on the elimination of more personal and communal forms of organization?" *(UPI)*

in most cases, it must often achieve its goal by negotiating with the merchants or manufacturers in question. In order to obtain necessary cooperation, the organization may take certain steps to alter its mode of operation, such as appointing a manufacturer to a high position in the group or agreeing not to prosecute for certain offenses, steps which may result in other significant changes in the organization.

Other major external sources of change are the development of new technology, the opening up of new markets or sources of supply, and changing interests, attitudes, and values in the population as a whole. If the people an organization serves change their requirements or demands, the organization must change to accommodate them.

THE ORGANIZATIONAL REVOLUTION

For thousands of years man was surrounded by, and worked for, small and simple organizations. Within the last several centuries, however, large and complex organizations have become permanent and dominant fixtures of every modern, urban-industrial society. The major activities of modern society — business, education, religion, government, politics — all require large organizations for effective and efficient functioning. This trend toward large organizations is sometimes called the organizational revolution.

For every society, the organizational revolution involves a loss as well as a gain; no matter how much we desire the benefits of efficient modern organizations, we are usually sorry to lose the more personal and communal way of living that was part of the older society. Many social critics[20] regard this as a truly great loss for man, but acceptance of this loss seems to be a necessary condition of modernization; refusal to give up the more personal and communal forms of organization is doubtless one reason so

many nations have been slow to achieve modernization.

It is not only the structure of our society that is changed by the organizational revolution. Our culture is changed as well, although many of the cultural values and attitudes which this revolution requires — hard work, achievement, thrift, worldly success, and saving (and all forms of "deferred gratification") — have been part of our Western tradition for a long time. The cultural change is much greater in a society with conflicting values. In Saudi Arabia, for instance, a country still largely untouched by modern organizations, achievement is often viewed as a gift of Allah (God) rather than a personal merit; saving is a sign of selfishness and lack of confidence in Allah. The organizational revolution, when it comes, will bring a profound change to the entire culture.

The complexity of modern society has created new problems for individuals in adapting to society and developing personalities. These problems have been widely discussed in well-known books such as *The Organization Man,* by William H. Whyte, Jr.[21] and *The Lonely Crowd* by David Riesman.[22] Modern Americans are faced with the need to cope with the frustration, isolation, and impersonality that organizations bring to a society. They are forced to shuttle back and forth among many different social units and social roles. Both Whyte and Riesman suggest that modern man has been reasonably successful in balancing the demands of the organization against his private feelings and desires, though this is a continuing source of conflict. They also note that conformity and compatibility, values which help make organizations efficient, seem to have become more characteristic of American social life outside the organization, in the larger society.

20.   For example, Lewis Mumford, *The Transformation of Man* (New York: Collier Books, 1962).

21.   William H. Whyte, Jr., *The Organization Man* (New York: Simon & Schuster, 1956).

22.   David Riesman et al., *The Lonely Crowd: A Study of the Changing American Character* (New Haven: Yale University Press, 1950).

C. NORTHCOTE PARKINSON
The Rising Pyramid

Introduction

Parkinson is a rare combination of humorist and astute social analyst. When we finish laughing over what he has said, we begin to see the truth behind it. In this excerpt, Parkinson turns his attention to the way bureaucracies may virtually manufacture work which often has no connection with true productivity, and thus cause their staffs to increase rapidly. The element of exaggeration in Parkinson's writing adds to the humor but does not unreasonably distort the basic truth involved. This selection begins with a statement of Parkinson's Law.

Work expands so as to fill the time available for its completion. General recognition of this fact is shown in the proverbial phrase "It is the busiest man who has time to spare." Thus, an elderly lady of leisure can spend the entire day in writing and dispatching a post card to her niece at Bognor Regis. An hour will be spent in finding the post card, another in hunting for spectacles, half an hour in a search for the address, an hour and a quarter in composition, and twenty minutes in deciding whether or not to take an umbrella when going to the mailbox in the next street. The total effort that would occupy a busy man for three minutes all told may in this fashion leave another person prostrate after a day of doubt, anxiety, and toil.

Granted that work (and especially paper work) is thus elastic in its demands on time, it is manifest that there need be little or no relationship between the work to be done and the size of the staff to which it may be assigned. A lack of real activity does not, of necessity, result in leisure. A lack of occupation is not necessarily revealed by a manifest idleness. The thing to be done swells in importance and complexity in a direct ratio with the time to be spent. This fact is widely recognized, but less attention has been paid to its wider implications, more especially in the field of public administration. Politicians and taxpayers have assumed (with occasional phases of doubt) that a rising total in the number of civil servants must reflect a growing volume of work to be done. Cynics, in questioning this belief, have imagined that the multiplication of officials must have left some of them idle or all of them able to work for shorter hours. But this is a matter in which faith and doubt seem equally misplaced. The fact is that the number of the officials and the quantity of the work are not related to each other at all. The rise in the total of those employed is governed by Parkinson's Law and would be much the same whether the volume of the work were to increase, diminish, or even disappear. The importance of Parkinson's Law lies in the fact that it is a law of growth based upon an analysis of the factors by which that growth is controlled.

The validity of this recently discovered law must rest mainly on statistical proofs, which will follow. Of more interest to the general reader is the explanation of the factors underlying the general tendency to which this law gives definition. Omitting technicalities (which are numerous) we may distinguish at the outset two motive forces. They can be represented for the present purpose by two almost axiomatic statements, thus: (1) "An official wants to multiply subordinates, not rivals" and (2) "Officials make work for each other."

To comprehend Factor 1, we must picture a civil servant, called A, who finds himself overworked. Whether this overwork is real or imaginary is immaterial, but we should observe, in passing, that A's sensation (or illusion) might easily result from his own decreasing energy: a normal symptom of middle age. For this real or imagined overwork there are, broadly speaking, three possible remedies. He may resign; he may ask to halve the work with a colleague called B; he may demand the assistance of two subordinates, to be called C and D. There is probably no instance in history, however, of A choosing any but the third alternative. By resignation he would lose his pension rights. By having B appointed, on his own level in the hierarchy, he would merely bring in a rival for promotion to W's vacancy when W (at long last) retires. So A would rather have C and D, junior men, below him. They will add to his consequence and, by dividing the work into two categories, as between C and D, he will have the merit of being the only man who comprehends them both. It is essential to realize at this point that C and D are, as it were, inseparable. To appoint C alone would have been impossible. Why? Because C, if by himself, would divide the work with A and so assume almost the equal status that has been refused in the first instance to B; a status the more emphasized if C is A's only possible successor. Subordinates must thus number two or more, each being thus kept in order by fear of the other's promotion. When C complains in turn of being overworked (as he certainly will) A will, with the concurrence of C, advise the appointment of two assistants to help C. But he can then avert internal friction only by advising the appointment of two more assistants to help D, whose position is much the same. With this recruitment of E, F, G, and H the promotion of A is now practically certain.

Seven officials are now doing what one did before. This is where Factor 2 comes into operation. For these seven make so much work for each other that all are fully occupied and A is actually working harder than ever. An incoming document may well come before each of them in turn. Official E decides that it falls within the province of F, who places a draft reply before C, who amends it drastically before consulting D, who asks G to deal with it. But G goes on leave at this point, handing the file over to H, who drafts a minute that is signed by D and returned to C, who revises his draft accordingly and lays the new version before A.

What does A do? He would have every excuse for signing the thing unread, for he has many other matters on his mind. Knowing now that he is to succeed W next year, he has to decide whether C or D should succeed to his own office. He had to agree to G's going on leave even if not yet strictly entitled to it. He is worried whether H should not have gone instead, for reasons of health. He has looked pale recently — partly but not solely because of his domestic troubles. Then there is the business of F's special increment of salary for the period of the conference and E's application for the transfer to the Ministry of Pensions. A has heard that D is in love with a married typist and that G and F are no longer on speaking terms — no one seems to know why. So A might be tempted to sign C's draft and have done with it. But A is a conscientious man. Beset as he is with problems created by his colleagues for themselves and for him — created by the mere fact of these officials' existence — he is not the man to shirk his duty. He reads through the draft with care, deletes the fussy paragraphs added by C and H, and restores the thing back to the form preferred in the first instance by the able (if quarrelsome) F. He corrects the English — none of these young men can write grammatically — and finally produces the same reply he would have written if officials C to H had never been born. Far more people have taken far longer to produce the same result. No one has been idle. All have done their best. And it is late in the evening before A finally quits his office and begins the return journey to Ealing. The last of the office lights are being turned off in the gathering dusk that marks the end of another day's administrative toil. Among the last to leave, A reflects with bowed shoulders and a wry smile that late hours, like gray hairs, are among the penalties of success.

Conclusion

Bureaucracies are among the most praised and most condemned groupings known to man. They are praised for being the most efficient social structure ever devised; at the same time they are condemned for generating so much red tape that they cannot accomplish anything efficiently except the irritation of all those who come into contact with them. Parkinson gives one view of bureaucracy. From what you've read in this chapter, and from your own contacts with bureaucracies, what is your evaluation of Parkinson's Law? Is it an inevitable fact, or is it something that can happen, but does not happen very often? Has your college administration fallen prey to Parkinson's Law?

SUMMARY

The small, durable, and highly personal units known as *primary groups* are the oldest and most basic form of social grouping. They continue to have important social functions in shaping the human personality, in providing a setting for individual growth and development, and in helping to maintain social control and cohesion. Primary groups are characterized by *primary relationships,* that is, social relationships that involve many facets of our personalities, a variety of our roles and interests, and free and extensive communication, and that are personal, emotion-laden, and not easily transferable. They stand in contrast to *secondary relationships*—the majority of our social relationships in modern societies—which are specialized, standardized, and lacking in emotional content.

It is within the primary group that we first develop a sense of self and learn the norms and values essential to participation in society. Such groups also provide the individual with essential emotional support and security. Primary groups in modern industrial society are being overshadowed by larger and more impersonal secondary groups, and primary relationships have been placed under tremendous strain in trying to meet the emotional needs of individuals.

Individuals also belong to *organizations,* which can be defined as special-purpose "secondary" groups deliberately constructed to seek certain clearly defined goals. Division of labor, concentration of power, and a fluid membership contribute to the rationality and efficiency that distinguish organizations from other types of social groups. In contrast to primary groups, the members of an organization interact in terms of specialized roles.

Organizations can be classified on the basis of whom they benefit: the members, owners, clients, or the public at large. Alternatively, organizations can be distinguished in terms of the method of obtaining compliance and cooperation. The formal structure of an organization includes explicitly stated regulations that define the activities of members in terms of specialized tasks. Although this structure is ideally designed to improve efficiency, organizational goals may be blocked if the formal structure becomes overly rigid and more concerned with perpetuation of the organization than with accomplishing the stated objectives. The informal structure, which develops spontaneously as members of the organization interact, serves to supplement the formal structure, to adapt it to changing circumstances, and to balance the demands of the members' work roles and personality needs. Formal organizational structure and control is most highly developed in *bureaucracies,* and is minimally apparent in *voluntary associations* that are developed by individuals to pursue some "spare-time" social or political objective or recreational activity. As arenas for social experimentation and social participation, they are an important and rather unique feature of American life.

Organizations may be coordinated through authoritarian control based on hierarchical structure and arbitrary policy making, through democratic participatory methods, or through some combination of the two. In both types of structure, recognized leaders emerge or are recruited to act as decision makers, administrators, and spokesmen. These leaders may be popularly recognized and chosen because of outstanding personal qualities or charisma, they may be selected by accident of circumstance, or they may be drawn from a small, self-perpetuating group, an oligarchy.

Regardless of the formal control structure or pattern of leadership, every organization depends on formal and informal communication networks to ensure cooperation among its members. Cohesion must also be maintained through a symbolically bolstered group identity that reflects group norms and goals. Finally, continued and successful organizational operation depends on socializing group members: teaching them to carry out assigned functions and to internalize group values and norms. Despite efforts to instill in each member a commitment to his organizational role, however, an individual may experience conflict between these demands and his other roles and personal needs.

As organizations grow and mature, they become more orderly and predictable and less flexible or changeable: they become institutionalized. Every organization must grow and adapt to changing circumstances. Changes may develop in response to new leaders or personnel, to pressure from competing organizations, to the demands of the clientele, or to technological innovations. Every modern industrial society has experienced an organizational revolution: a transformation from a society characterized by simple and personal groups to one dominated by large and impersonal organizations. This revolution may have modified our culture by promoting conformity and compatibility and at the same time it has generated problems of frustration, isolation, and impersonality for the individual.

GLOSSARY

Anticipatory socialization The learning of the beliefs, values, and norms of a role or group as preparation for taking on the role or joining the group. (page 191)

Apprenticeship A type of socialization in which a new member of an organization observes and copies the role of an established member. (page 190)

Authoritarian structure An organizational structure in which the leadership exerts broad control over the members. (page 183)

Bureaucracy A large-scale type of organization in which various functions are separated and carried out by special highly trained individuals, departments, or bureaus; which is organized by formal rules; and which is coordinated and controlled by a hierarchical chain of command. (page 175)

Conversion A sudden change in values and then behavior, caused by one experience or set of experiences. (page 191)

Democratic structure An organizational structure in which the members participate in decision making. (page 183)

Formal organization An organization in which formal structures predominate. (page 171)

Formal structure An organizational structure which consists of a specific and formally stated set of rules and regulations that define the activities of the members. (page 172)

Informal organization An organization in which informal structures predominate. (page 171)

Informal structure An organizational structure consisting of personal relationships which develop spontaneously as members interact. (page 173)

Organization A social group that has been deliberately and consciously constructed in order to seek certain specific goals. (page 170)

Primary group A group, usually relatively small, durable, and unspecialized, in which primary relationships predominate. The members of a primary group have a strong sense of group identity. (page 160)

Primary relationship A personal, emotion-laden, and not easily transferable relationship which includes a variety of roles and interests of each individual. It involves free and extensive communication and the interaction of whole personalities. (page 160)

Primordial primary group A primitive group, such as a peasant village or folk community, which is united by common biological, cultural, and neighborhood ties, and in which membership is not voluntary. (page 163)

Secondary relationship A relationship which is specialized, relatively unemotional and impersonal, and involving a limited aspect of one's personality. The participants in a secondary relationship are usually quite interchangeable. (page 160)

Training A type of socialization to an organization which teaches specialized skills and the organization's values and norms. (page 190)

Voluntary association An organization which is freely organized by individuals for the pursuit of some common interest; usually members are unpaid volunteers and there are few formal control mechanisms. (page 176)

SUGGESTED READINGS AND RELATED RESOURCES

I READINGS IN SOCIOLOGY

Blau, Peter M. *The Dynamics of Bureaucracy*. 2d ed. Chicago: University of Chicago Press, 1963. In contrast to prevailing opinions, Blau attempts to show that administrative structures are not static; he writes about the internal tensions and cohesions which make change possible in a bureaucracy.

Caplow, Theodore. *Principles of Organization*. New York: Harcourt Brace Jovanovich, 1964. As an introductory study of the nature of complex organizations and conflicts within them, this book will fill the needs of most undergraduates for a basic resource. Chapter 5, "Making the Organizational Man," is particularly interesting and useful.

Cooley, Charles Horton. *Social Organization*. New York: Schocken Books (Paper), 1962. First published in 1909. The original definition of a primary group is contained in this book, with an analysis of its structure and relationship to social organization.

Downs, Anthony. *Inside Bureaucracy*. Boston: Little, Brown, 1967. Presenting a positive approach to bureaucracies, this study provides the introductory student with a basic description of the nature, functions, and problems of a bureaucratic organization.

Etzioni, Amitai. *Modern Organizations*. Englewood Cliffs, N.J.: Prentice-Hall, 1964. Within this concise and thorough analysis, Etzioni develops a clear definition of complex organizations. He also includes a discussion about various theories of complex and modern organizations and their relationship to society.

Gans, Herbert. *The Urban Villagers*. New York: Free Press (Paper), 1965. Herbert Gans made a study of the life style of working-class Italians in the West End of Boston. He portrays the importance of primary relationships in their lives, with particular emphasis on the importance of peer groups.

Gerth, H. H., and C. Wright Mills. *From Max Weber*. New York: Oxford University Press

(Paper), 1967. The well-written introductory section by Gerth and Mills, "Bureaucracy and Charisma: A Philosophy of History," is especially helpful in understanding Weber's thoughts on bureaucracy and leadership within a group. Other pertinent chapters from Weber's own writing are: 8, "Bureaucracy"; 9, "The Sociology of Charismatic Authority"; and 10, "The Meaning of Discipline."

Gouldner, Alvin. *Patterns of Industrial Bureaucracy*. New York: Free Press, 1954. In this study Gouldner describes the organization of a factory, using Max Weber's theory of bureaucracy as a guide. He also includes an appendix on "Field Work Procedures—The Social Organization of a Student Research Team," which provides the introductory student with a behind-the-scenes look at the procedures involved in gathering research data.

Hage, J., and M. Aiken. *Social Change in Complex Organizations*. New York: Random House, 1969. Hage and Aiken have put together a well-balanced selection of sociological writings on the problems of organizational change.

Homans, George. *The Human Group*. New York: Harcourt Brace Jovanovich, 1950. In this summary and discussion of theories and research on social groups, Homans emphasizes the influence of feedback from the group upon the group leader. He also hypothesizes that the group goal is the key factor in group cohesion and that a high degree of cohesion gives a group social power greater than the sum of the individual power of its members.

Hopkins, Terence K. *The Exercise of Influence in Small Groups*. Totowa, N.J.: Bedminster Press, 1964. In this readable study, Hopkins discusses many aspects of group dynamics, such as how group leaders arise, how opinion changes among members, and how the stability or instability of the group fluctuates.

Litterer, Joseph. *Organizations: Structure and Behavior*. New York: John Wiley, 1963. This study describes what happens within large formal and informal organizations, and what the individual must do to adjust to and be integrated into them.

Lucas, Rex. *Men in Crisis*. New York: Basic Books, 1969. This study of a Canadian mine disaster and the week-long struggle for survival of two small groups trapped in it, has added greatly to the understanding of small-group behavior in extreme situations.

Olmsted, Michael S. *The Small Group*. New York: Random House, 1959. Unlike most works in small-group research, this review places special emphasis upon research among both primary and secondary groups.

Presthus, Robert. *The Organizational Society*. New York: Random House, Vintage Books, 1962. This study discusses especially the conflicts which arise between large-scale organizational goals and individual growth and creativity.

Selznick, Philip. *TVA and the Grass Roots: A Study in the Sociology of Formal Organization*. Berkeley, Calif.: University of California Press, 1949. Selznick's study provides the reader with a concrete example of a large organization which, although established to help the community in specific ways, grew into a bureaucracy whose purpose was partly the preservation of itself.

Whyte, William. *The Organization Man*. New York: Doubleday, Anchor (Paper), 1957. In this important description of American life as it is affected by large organizations, Whyte discusses the meaning of this life for the individual and the institutions he serves.

Wilensky, Harold. *Organizational Intelligence*. New York: Basic Books, 1967. Wilensky discusses the relation of experts and intellectuals to men in power, a subject especially relevant to contemporary America.

Articles and Papers

Anderson, Theodore R., and Seymour Warkov. "Organizational Size and Functional Complexity: A Study of Administration in Hospitals." *"American Sociological Review* **26** (February 1961): 23–28.

Blau, Peter M. "Cooperation and Competition in a Bureaucracy." *American Journal of Sociology* **59** (1954):530–535.

Brown, Robert Gay, Raymond V. Bowers, and Clifton D. Bryant. "Technological Change and the Organization Man: Preliminary Conceptualization of a Research Project." *Sociological Inquiry* **32**, 1 (Winter 1962):117–127.

Etzioni, Amitai. "Two Approaches to Organizational Analysis: A Critique and a Suggestion." *Administrative Science Quarterly* **5** (September 1960):257–278.

Faris, Ellsworth. "The Primary Group: Essence and Accident." *American Journal of Sociology* **38** (July 1932):41–50.

Gouldner, Alvin. "Red Tape as a Social Problem." In *Reader in Bureaucracy,* edited by Robert Merton et al., pp. 410–418. New York: Free Press, 1952.

Howton, F. William. "Work Assignment and Interpersonal Relations in a Research Organization: Some Participant Observations." *Administrative Science Quarterly* **7**, 4 (March 1963):502–520.

Rosengren, William R. "Communication, Organization, and Conduct in the 'Therapeutic Milieu.' " *Administrative Science Quarterly* **9**, 1 (June 1964):70–90.

Shils, Edward. "Primordial, Personal, Sacred and Civil Ties." *British Journal of Sociology* **8** (1957):130–145.

————. "The Study of the Primary Group." In *The Policy Sciences,* edited by D. Lerner and H. D. Lasswell. Stanford, Calif.: Stanford University Press, 1951.

Sills, David L. "Voluntary Associations: Sociological Aspects." In *International Encyclopedia of the Social Sciences,* edited by David L. Sills, vol. 16, pp. 362–379. New York: Free Press, 1968.

Simpson, Richard L., and W. H. Gulley. "Goals, Environmental Pressures, and Organizational Characteristics." *American Sociological Review* **27**, 3 (June 1962).

Stewart, Robert L., and Glenn M. Vernon. "Four Correlates of Empathy in the Dating Situation." *Sociology and Social Research* **43**, 4 (March–April 1959):279–285.

Udy, Stanley H., Jr. "Administrative Rationality, Social Setting and Organizational Development." *American Journal of Sociology* **68**, 3 (November 1962).

Wright, Charles R., and Herbert H. Hyman. "Voluntary Association Memberships of American Adults." *American Sociological Review* **23** (1958):284–294.

II RELATED RESOURCES
Nonfiction

Buber, Martin. *Between Man and Man.* 1947. Reprint. New York: Macmillan (Paper), 1965. Buber writes about a type of face-to-face relationship to which a man is able to bring his genuine self, and in which he can "experience the other side" of the relationship. In this book, Buber applies this concept to critical problems faced by modern man.

Fromm, Erich. *The Art of Loving.* New York: Harper & Row, 1956. Fromm defines love in philosophical and psychological terms and gives evidence for viewing it as a key factor in the integration and cohesion of societies. From a psychological perspective based on human needs, he elaborates a typology of love and demonstrates its usefulness in the analysis of interaction.

Goodman, Paul. *People or Personnel.* New York: Random House, Vintage Books (Paper), 1969. Especially relevant to the present chapter are Goodman's chapters on "The Sentiment of Powerlessness in American History"; "Personnel and Persons"; and Appendix VIII, "An Example of Spontaneous Administration."

————. *Like a Conquered Province.* New York: Random House, Vintage Books (Paper), 1969. The chapters which are pertinent to a discussion of organizations are those on "Morality of Scientific Technology"; "The Psychology of Being Powerless"; and Appendix 3, "Education Industries."

Mayer, Martin. *Madison Avenue, U.S.A.* New York: Pocket Cardinal (Paper), 1967. An interesting study of the internal structure of the advertising business—agencies, clients, and the personalities that control America's buying habits.

Montagu, M. F. Ashley. *The Direction of Human Development.* New York: Harper and Brothers, 1955. Montagu traces the social and psychological development of the child from the prenatal period. He points out that the social development of all men hinges upon socialization of individuals by primary groups.

Peter, Laurence, and Raymond Hull. *The Peter Principle,* New York: Bantam Books (Paper), 1970. Dr. Peter's "principle" is an analysis of organizational hierarchy based on levels of incompetence: "In a hierarchy, every employee tends to rise to his level of incompetence." He provides the reader with examples of his principle and suggestions for avoiding incompetence in oneself and recognizing it in others.

Townsend, Robert. *Up the Organization.* New York: Alfred A. Knopf, 1970. Townsend offers advice for coping with stringent organizational regulations as well as suggestions for constructive alternatives.

Fiction

Calmer, Ned. *The Anchorman*. New York: Doubleday, 1970. This novel revolves around Lloyd Gardner, a new major network anchorman, who struggles with the conflict between business values and news reporting, and the temptation to "sell out" to the system.

Compton, D. G. *Steel Crocodile*. New York: Ace Books, 1969. This absorbing book describes what life could be like before the end of this century in a computer-dominated world.

Fox, Paula. *Desperate Characters*. New York: Harcourt Brace Jovanovich, 1970. In her story Paula Fox portrays some of the contemporary problems in primary and secondary relationships; she focuses on a loveless, middle-aged marriage, a white liberal's guilt about blacks, and the generation gap.

McCarthy, Mary. *The Group*. New York: Signet Books (Paper), 1963. Mary McCarthy's novel recounts the intimate lives of eight Vassar graduates, and brings out the social forces and personality traits that lead the women of this group into various postgraduate ways of life.

Page, Martin. *The Yam Factor, and Other Insights into the Lives and Customs of the Executive Tribes of America*. Garden City, N. Y. Doubleday, 1972. A tongue-in-cheek comparison of American corporate and primitive tribal behavior; the author notes similarities in organization and function.

Sartre, Jean-Paul. *No Exit*. New York: Alfred A. Knopf, 1963. A one-act play that depicts a small group of people who must forever remain confined to a single room.

Snow, C. P. *The Affair*. New York: Charles Scribner's Sons, 1960. A thirteen-man faculty of a small English boys' school is thrown into turmoil when one of the faculty is accused of publishing fraudulent research. The story portrays the rigid structure of an academic organization.

_____. *The Masters*. New York: Charles Scribner's Sons, 1960. Same school, same faculty. This time the old headmaster is dying, and the rest of the faculty must choose a replacement for him.

Films

Dr. Strangelove. Stanley Kubrick, 1963. This film is a farce about what might happen if the military bureaucracy and scientific technology were allowed to have complete control of our defense system—and therefore control of the world's future.

Shame. Ingmar Bergman, 1968. This compelling film portrays a war machine's demoralizing effect on those who work within its structure or who are accidentally caught in it as middlemen.

II Social Patterns and Social Institutions

6. The Family

The family is the most universal social institution.
In one form or another, it has been found throughout
human history and in every known society. All other
social institutions, such as religion, government,
and education, originally were formed and developed
within family systems, later breaking off into their
own separate spheres. The family has also been the
dominant social tie of most individuals in all ages.
It is because the family is the most universal
and "primal" institution that we have chosen it to
lead off our discussion in Part II.

A family group *may be defined as a relatively
permanent group of two or more people who are
related by blood, marriage, or adoption, live together,
and cooperate economically. The overwhelming
majority of people belong during their lifetimes to
two basic family groups: the one they grew up in
(called the* family of orientation) *and the one they
form themselves as adults (called the* family
of procreation).

In this chapter we will begin by examining the
major functions of the family in modern societies.
Topic 2 focuses on the organization of the family
and variations in family patterns. Mate selection,
marriage, divorce, and widowhood in the United
States are the subject of topic 3. In topic 4 we look
at changes in the family and consider alternatives
to the traditional family.

1 THE FUNCTIONS OF THE FAMILY

In small, primitive societies, the family provides for most of its members' needs. The entire family cooperates to make tools, build shelters, and to hunt, gather, or grow food. Parents and elders are responsible for teaching children the skills they will need as adults, as well as for instilling in them a sense of right and wrong. Usually religious practices are woven into the pattern of daily family life. Authority is vested in the head of the family, who allocates responsibility and goods and settles disputes. There is no need for formal political structures or for laws in such societies. The family is largely self-sufficient.

In modern, complex societies, which require economic specialization and mobility, the family has fewer functions. Schools and teachers are largely responsible for formal education, churches and priests for religion, government and police for social control. Nevertheless, the family continues to be an essential part of society, and the overwhelming majority of modern families can be classified as multibonded groups (comprehensive groups with more than one major function).

Socialization is one important continuing function of the family. Sociologists agree that socialization begins at home: it is here the child learns who he is, what he can and should expect in life, and how to behave toward others in his society. For most people, the family also functions to provide the first and most important experience of belonging to a primary group. Although the composition of the family changes with birth and death, marriage and divorce, family relationships are the chief source of affection and companionship for most people throughout their lives. In addition, the family is the basis for regulat-

ing sexual behavior and reproduction; norms governing incest, adultery, and legitimacy are tied to family structure. These major family functions will be emphasized in this topic. However, we should not overlook subsidiary functions: economic support, the granting of social status, protection and security, transmission of material goods through the generations, and mediation between the individual and the larger culture.

SOCIALIZATION

There are a number of ways in which the family is especially well suited to the task of socialization. First, it is a small group, in which all the members can have constant face-to-face contact with each other; this means that the child's progress can be closely observed and individual adjustments made as necessary. A second factor is that parents are well motivated for this task; the child is *their* child, and represents a biological and social extension of themselves. They have an emotional tie to the child. Many studies have indicated that the most meaningful and effective kind of social interaction for the purpose of socialization is that with great emotional content, rather than interaction confined solely to the intellectual level. To these two factors must be added one of practicality. As long as the family system endures in any society, the parents will play the main role in socializing children because parents are the ones with whom children spend most of their time during the years when the socialization process takes place.

Although there are many reasons why the family is, and probably always has been, the prime socializing agent in all societies, it is not

In Western society, the nuclear family plays a full and nearly exclusive role in early socialization. Parents, the dominant forces in an infant's life, offer him affection and support, but are also a source of tension and frustration. Within this emotionally charged network, the young child must learn to satisfy his biological and emotional needs and develop a sense of self. While relations between husband and wife, parents and children, and among siblings are based on expectations of intimacy, affection, and trust, the reality may fall far short of the ideal. But there are few alternatives to the family as a source of emotional gratification. *(Hella Hammid, Rapho-Guillumette)*

always a very effective or efficient socializer. Parents sometimes have scant understanding of the process they are undertaking; their goals may be fuzzy and unspecific. Essentially they reproduce what they are able to remember of their own upbringing, adding to it ideas they acquire from other people often similarly uninformed.

Societies that are consciously trying to change, or to accomplish new social goals as rapidly as possible, have experimented with other agencies of socialization that seemed at the outset to be more efficient. In the early years of the Communist regime in the Soviet Union, government officials tried to minimize the importance of the family for political reasons, but the attempt was a failure. Today, the Soviet Union has one of the strongest family systems among the industrially advanced countries. In Communist China, young children are sent to day-care centers, where much of their socialization takes place in peer groups under the guidance of an instructor. The outcome of this effort is as yet unknown;

yet here, too, the family seems to have remained strong.

The most fully investigated experiment with replacing the family as a basic socializing agent exists in modern Israel, where children in the kibbutzim (collective agricultural settlements) live apart from their parents; their socialization is primarily in the hands of specially trained personnel. Several studies indicate that this has been quite successful in imparting the values and attitudes of the new Israeli society.[1] However, the kibbutzim are unique because they are small, strongly integrated around common values, and in a constant state of emergency. It has been noted that the kibbutzim represent a kind of extended family and that the parents have more uninterrupted time with their children each day (two or three hours) than the average American parents. Further, recent evidence indicates that the family is gaining strength on the kibbutzim—a growing number of kibbutz children are living with their parents.

In other societies, experiments with socialization outside the family unit have given rise to serious problems. Such experiments have sometimes been successful for limited periods of time in socializing the child to a special culture and circumstance, but in the long run they have usually failed. Allocating socialization to other agencies or institutions may involve breaking up the family and kinship system, a step which so far has been unacceptable to most cultures. The family unit is deeply ingrained, dating back to our prehuman anthropoid ancestors. The complexities and subtleties that the family unit brings to socialization are difficult to duplicate in a communal or institutional setting.

AFFECTION AND COMPANIONSHIP

Human warmth and affection are as important to the infant and child as food and shelter.

1. Melford E. Spiro, *Children of the Kibbutz* (Cambridge, Mass.: Harvard University Press, 1958). Bruno Bettelheim, "Does Communal Education Work: The Case of the Kibbutz," *Commentary* 33 (February 1962), 117–125.

Lack of "mothering" may stunt a child's physical, intellectual, and emotional growth as well as his social development. René Spitz showed this to be the case in a study conducted during the late 1940s. Spitz studied two groups of children who had been institutionalized at an early age. Both groups received perfectly adequate physical care: they lived in clean, light nurseries and were fed, washed, and turned regularly. However, in one of the institutions the attendants were responsible for large numbers of children and did not have time to handle and play with the infants. A high proportion of these children died of marasmus, a gradual wasting away. Others grew up severely retarded and emotionally disturbed. In the second institution, the attendants did have time to "mother" the children. Here premature death, retardation, and emotional disturbances were the exception, not the rule. It is a function of the family to provide this needed love and attention.

The family performs a similar function for adults, who may not die for lack of love, but need a great amount of affection and companionship nonetheless. In the past, most people spent their entire life in the community where they were born and raised, and many continued to live with their parents and brothers and sisters after they were married and having children of their own. In the "primary community," where everybody knew everybody else, and in the extended family, opportunities for friendly talk and for support in times of trouble were numerous. In modern societies, these opportunities are often not available. Parents and children live by themselves, visiting other relatives only occasionally. The family moves when the father receives an offer for a better job in another city or when they can afford a house in a better neighborhood; relationships with outsiders tend to be transitory. Isolation and mobility force family members to depend heavily on one another for affection and companionship.

Because the family is one of the few ongoing sources of intimacy in modern societies, people continue to marry, even though a sexually active single life has become possible for both men and women. And when an individual's emotional needs are *not* met within the family circle, the family is more likely to break apart than it was in the past. Outside agencies can provide many of the other services once performed by the family, but if affection and companionship are missing, there is often little to hold the modern family together. This is one factor which accounts for the high divorce rate in modern societies.

SEXUAL REGULATION

No society has ever advocated total promiscuity, as far as we know, but norms governing sexual behavior do vary widely from society to society. For example, many cultures permit adolescents to engage in sexual activity before marriage; some even encourage sexual experimentation as a way of preparing young people for marriage and determining if a young girl is fertile. Traditionally, Eskimos offered their wives to honored guests as a gesture of hospitality. But no society leaves sexual matters entirely to the individual.

There are obvious reasons for the norms governing sexual behavior: pregnancy and reproduction. Contraceptives and abortion are by no means twentieth-century inventions, but only recently have reliable birth control devices and safe abortions become widely available. In the past, conception was an ever-present possibility. Once a baby is born, someone has to provide him with food, shelter, warmth, and affection. During the child's first years, it is difficult for his mother to care both for herself and for him. In our society and most others, the role of provider falls mainly to the baby's father. But who is the father? Sexual regulations, institutionalized in marriage and families, limit the choice of sexual partners, thus enabling society to assign responsibility for children. This is their primary function.

Sexual norms in America can be traced back to the Old Testament, which placed severe restrictions on sex outside of marriage,

particularly adultery. The early Christians built on this tradition. In the fifth century, St. Augustine equated sex with animal lust and argued that sex for any purpose save procreation was sinful. In the late fifteenth century the courts of England began to take responsibility for prosecuting people who had committed various "immoral acts," labeling these acts crimes. The Puritans carried this tradition to America, where in the early days people who engaged in intercourse outside of marriage were fined, whipped publicly, and sometimes forced to marry. In fact, adultery was punishable by death in Massachusetts until 1649. Many of these old laws have been dropped, but most states still consider adultery, homosexual acts, and sexual relations with a girl who is under age (statutory rape) crimes. Thus, norms regulating sexual behavior in this country are tied to religious beliefs and enforced by law.

When Dr. Alfred Kinsey published the results of his survey of over 12,000 Americans in *Sexual Behavior in the Human Male* (1948) and *Sexual Behavior in the Human Female* (1953), many Americans were shocked. Kinsey found that although 90 percent of all acts of sexual intercourse in this country take place within marriage, half of the women and two-thirds of the men he interviewed had engaged in sex before marriage, and 26 percent of married women and 50 percent of married men had participated in extramarital affairs. Given the widespread belief in the ideals of premarital virginity and postmarital fidelity, these data were surprising.

Recent studies indicate that the percentage of young people having sex before marriage and the percentage of married people having affairs have risen only slightly over the years, despite much talk of a sexual revolution. However, there is some evidence that *attitudes* about sex have changed more markedly.[2] Many people have begun to see sex as a legitimate way of expressing emotional attachment,

2.   Robert R. Bell. *Premarital Sex in a Changing Society* (Englewood Cliffs, N.J.: Prentice-Hall, 1966).

with or without marriage. Some consider sex a primary source of play and entertainment. And some argue that any sexual behavior is acceptable, as long as both partners are willing and neither is harmed by the experience.

What effect these emerging values will have on the American family remains to be seen. It is possible that if all prohibitions against extramarital sex are removed, people will no longer feel a need to get married, or to remain with their mate if they do marry. The family system could fall apart, with very serious consequences for the performance of socialization and companionship functions. On the other hand, it has been argued that a certain amount of premarital and extramarital experimentation could reduce the pressures that exist within a life-long exclusive relationship.

TOPIC 2 PATTERNS OF FAMILY ORGANIZATION

The basic family unit described in the preceding section—an independent husband and wife live in a separate house, maintain an exclusive sexual relationship, and take primary responsibility for rearing their children and providing each other with affection and companionship—is the generally accepted pattern in American society. But it is of course not the only family type to be found in this country. Many Americans live with their parents and other relatives, especially an aging parent or unmarried brother or sister. And one-parent families are not uncommon. In addition, there is room for considerable variation *within* the "ideal" American family, especially with regard to patterns of family authority and interaction with the community. This topic examines these variations, with particular emphasis on the relationship between social conditions and family organization.

KINSHIP AND FAMILY

Sociologists and anthropologists distinguish between *kin* and *family*. Kin are people who are related by common ancestry or origins. Most often kin are blood relatives—parents, brothers and sisters, aunts and uncles, grandparents, great aunts and uncles, first, second, and third cousins—in short, all the people with whom an individual has biological ties. This group may come together for Thanksgiving or Christmas, for marriages and funerals, or never at all.

Kin do not function as a group in an ongoing manner, as parents and children do, but they do recognize certain ties to one another. Recently, many young blacks have begun to call one another "Brother" and many feminists to call one another "Sister." In so doing, they are making use of the idea that kin have a closer relationship than nonkin; that brother- and sisterhood imply certain rights and obligations between individuals. We might hesitate to ask a friend for a loan, but not to ask a brother; we invite a cousin we have just met for the first time to dinner that night, but not a stranger we have just met. This is the primary function of kinship: to establish an affinity between people, and with this certain rights and obligations.

The family is a group of kin who live together and function as an ongoing cooperative unit for economic and other purposes. In America, the family is a small group, usually parents and their children. In many societies, however, the family includes other relatives and several generations. For example, a group of brothers and their wives, their sons, and their sons' wives and children may live together or near one another, combining efforts to raise food, maintain the home, and raise the children. If they function as a single unit, sociologists consider them a family. If, however, they simply live next door to one another and do not pool their resources, they would be considered separate families.

Societies differ widely in their cultural definitions of kin and family. In some, the *consanguine family*, or biological relatives, are considered most important; in others, it is the *conjugal family*, or relatives by marriage. (A person's parents, parents' relations, and brothers and sisters, are consanguine relatives; his spouse and in-laws are conjugal relatives.) Among the Pueblo Indians, for example, consanguine relatives are most significant and marriage and divorce are treated quite casually. When a couple marries, the man moves to his wife's household; if they find they are incompatible and divorce, he moves back to his mother's household with little fuss. But even while they are married, he rejoins his consanguine family for ceremonies and whenever they need help with a harvest. They are his true family. In other societies, young men and women traditionally marry someone who lives in another village. Once married they move to the spouse's household and become part of his or her family. All ties with the consanguine family are broken. If the two families were to feud, the person would be expected to side with his conjugal family.

In America, most people recognize both consanguine and conjugal relatives as family,

a fact which often leads to conflict, as a man tries to balance his praise for his mother's and wife's cooking, and a woman tries to reconcile obligations to her parents and husband. However, we usually limit the definition of conjugal kin to a spouse's parents, brothers and sisters, and their children. (We do not say "I saw my cousin-in-law" but "I saw my husband's cousin.") In part this is because Americans tend to focus on immediate kin, first in the family of orientation, later in the family of procreation.

NUCLEAR AND EXTENDED FAMILIES

While the characteristic family type in America is the *nuclear family*—a husband, wife, and their children living apart from other relatives—certain variations on this pattern occur frequently. Death and divorce leave many families with only one parent for a time; an elderly parent of the husband or wife may join the household; economic pressure may force a married child to bring his spouse to live with his family of orientation. In other cases, the brother or sister of one of the parents may join the family; a widowed man with children may ask his unmarried sister to live with them and help care for the children.

The "intact" nuclear family is most typical of middle-class America. One-parent nuclear families are more common among the poor than in the middle class for a number of reasons, some of which emerge clearly from demographic statistics. Rates of illegitimate births, maternal mortality during childbirth, and separation and divorce are higher among the poor.[3] Other reasons, harder to measure, are widespread unemployment among unskilled workers and the inadvertent pressures of the welfare system. In many states, a family with an unemployed father cannot receive assistance if the father is present in the household. Sometimes a father will leave home so that his wife can go on welfare to support the

3.   Lee Rainwater, *And the Poor Get Children* (Chicago: Quadrangle Press, 1960).

Although the nuclear family exists universally in some recognizable form, in many cultures it is embedded in an extended family system. Several generations may live together under one roof or in a family compound, forming a residential and economic unit. This arrangement, once very common when the United States was an agriculturally based nation, is rapidly disappearing under today's fluid and highly mobile social arrangements. *(Nina Leen, Life)*

children. Even if he managed to find employment as an unskilled laborer and worked full time all year long for the federal minimum wage, his salary would be below the official poverty level for a family of four. Thus, poverty imposes strong pressures toward family dissolution. Further analysis of this situation, and a discussion of its implications for the society at large, appears in chapter 7: Social Stratification.

At the same time, we find ties to the *extended family* stronger in lower-class families, while middle-class families tend to form a more self-contained and "isolated" nuclear family unit. Many of the causes of this class difference in family organization can be traced to economic conditions. Middle-class families with higher incomes (often with some additional financial assistance from parents) can afford to hire someone to baby-sit for their children, to help them move their furniture to a new house, or to care for sick members of the group. They can afford to borrow money from the bank when they need it in an emergency, to buy their own car for family errands, and to go to an employment agency for a new job when they need one. For poorer families, the purchase of these services is a luxury they cannot afford. The family must manage to perform these services through the cooperation or mutual aid of family members and relatives. A sister will babysit, a grandmother will come to care for a sick spouse, a brother will lend 50 dollars until the next payday or ask his friends if they know of any jobs that are open, a cousin will drive the children to their dental appointment across town, and all the able-bodied men in the family will lend a hand on moving day. It is only because of this network of mutual assistance that families with low incomes are able to provide for the needs of their members and meet most emergencies. Obviously, the more family members a person has to call on for such help, the more likely it is that he will find someone who is in a position to give the help he needs. So large families, and strong family ties, are a definite advantage in this respect.

We may extend the application of this difference between lower- and middle-class families to other societies and say that the more difficult living conditions are in a society, the more the family group will be extended to include more members than just the nuclear family.[4] In primitive societies where existence is marginal (such as many of the societies of New Guinea, the Australian bush country, and the coastal islands of South America), we find that the family group is often spread to include an entire tribe or village. Even in

fairly recent history in the United States, during frontier times, family groups were much more extended than they are today.

In the last several centuries, there has been a steady though uneven trend toward the nuclear family as the principal form of family organization in modern, complex societies.[5] The primary cause of this change from the older form of the extended family to the nuclear family has been industrialization. There are at least three reasons industrialization has led to such a change. The first is that industrialization makes the family more mobile.[6] It is no longer tied to a specific piece of land to make its living, but moves to where jobs are available. Mobility thus weakens kinship ties in the extended family.

Industrialization also has hastened the emancipation of women by making it possible for them to hold jobs outside the home. (The industrial system has come to depend greatly on the services of women; more than one-third of the work force today is female.[7]) This emancipation has reduced the importance of some of the basic functions of the extended family, for example, the domestic training of the female children and the creation of a niche for the unmarried, widowed, or divorced woman. Similarly, it has made the nuclear family, with its more limited set of responsibilities, far more necessary.

Perhaps most important of all the factors leading to the decline of the extended family is the change in the underlying economic dynamics of societies. In an agrarian society, each member of the family does economically productive work. Children and old people do less than able-bodied adults, but they each make a contribution to the economic welfare of the family unit. In such a case, the extended family offers an economic advantage. Things

4.   Meyer F. Nimkoff and Russell Middleton, "Types of Family and Types of Economy," *American Journal of Sociology* 66 (1960), 215–225.

5.   William J. Goode, *World Revolution and Family Patterns* (New York: Free Press, 1963), pp. 366–380.

6.   Clark Kerr, J. T. Dunlop et al., *Industrialism and Industrial Man* (Cambridge, Mass.: Harvard University Press, 1960), p. 35.

7.   National Industrial Conference Board, *The Economic Almanac, 1967–68* (New York: Macmillan, 1967), p. 29.

The contemporary middle-class nuclear family has become a closed and relatively isolated group that tends to turn inward and requires high levels of commitment and cooperation. Members rely heavily on each other for help, sociability, and emotional support and may draw sharp distinctions between the family ingroup and the larger community. The pattern of mutual dependence is increased when social relationships in the outside world are impermanent and largely impersonal. *(DPI)*

are quite different in an industrial society. The very young, the very old, and the physically weak are unemployable. They produce little for the family unit, yet they consume at the same rate as a producer. The result is that an extended family unit, with aged parents or other dependent relatives, is a burden rather than an advantage.

The change from the extended family to the nuclear family has brought with it greater freedom for the individual. In the extended family, individual needs and conjugal ties are generally subordinated to the needs of the larger group. Privacy is difficult to obtain. But there are drawbacks to the nuclear family too. While the individual is freed from a broad network of responsibility and obligations, others are no longer obligated or responsible to him. The total effect may be one of human social isolation. There is frequently a loss of emo-

tional and economic support because the family is now such a small unit. Each person has fewer people to turn to for gratification, affection, companionship, or assistance. The narrowing of opportunity for intimate contact in turn puts a great strain on the relationships of the individuals in the unit, because they have to bear such a large burden. As the scope of family activities and relationships narrows, the emotional significance of the remaining bonds are increased.

ALLOCATION OF AUTHORITY

Traditional, extended families are usually *patriarchal*. The oldest man dominates, sometimes wielding authority in extremely arbitrary ways. The patriarch has the final word in all decisions regarding family members, from whether the family should invest in new equipment for the family farm or store to such personal decisions as whom a daughter should marry. Women may run the kitchen and rule the nursery in a patriarchal family, but a mother's ultimate weapon is the threat, "I'll tell your father." A son or son-in-law may know more about modern agriculture than the father, but overt display of this knowledge might lead to recrimination. In such families, adult sons, sons-in-law, women, and children are all subject to the patriarch's authority. His word is law.

Although the degree of subordination to the husband-father varies from culture to culture, and women often exercise a good deal of covert power, particularly over children, *matriarchal* families, in which authority is allocated to the oldest woman in the family, are rare. Women may dominate the family when men are absent for long periods of time, as is true in Scandinavian fishing villages or when a society is at war. Economic hardship may also create female-headed households, as when men leave the family they cannot support. Approximately 47 percent of black and 38 percent of white American families with incomes under $3000 a year are headed by women.[8] But so far as we know, matriarchal families are exceptional. Most often, women rule the family by default.

However, a new pattern seems to be emerging in American and other modern societies: the *egalitarian* family. Egalitarianism within the family seems to be tied to industrialization. One of the first effects of the move from an agrarian to an industrialized society is that men are away from the family for long hours of the workday, which in many countries is still six days a week. But this does not mean that women inherit the authority men leave behind. Because industrialized societies require skilled, educated workers, the need for education grows with technology, and author-

ity over children is increasingly given to schools and teachers. Often parents cannot teach children what they need to know: the math they learned in school, for example, is quite outdated. In general, parental authority over children declines. With some of the responsibility for children taken off her hands, a mother has more freedom to take work outside the home, to participate in community affairs, and so on. In response to these changes, husbands and wives have begun to share family authority and in some cases to extend the right to participate in decision-making to their children. They have also begun to share some housekeeping and child-rearing responsibilities which traditionally have been reserved for women. To be sure, in most cases the husband's occupation still determines where and how the family will live. (Only very rarely does a family move because the mother has been offered a job in another city.) But the trend in modern nuclear families is toward egalitarianism.

DESCENT AND RESIDENCE

No matter how questions about family composition and authority structure are resolved, every culture must provide answers to three other problems that concern the family: Where shall the new family of procreation live? To what kin group do children belong? Who shall inherit whatever is left over from the previous generation? Different answers to these questions have led to additional variations in family organization throughout the world.

Patterns of marital residence—where a young couple lives after marriage—vary from society to society. In *patrilocal* societies, sons are expected to bring their brides to their parents' house or to live nearby, while daughters are expected to move to their husband's household. In *matrilocal* societies, the reverse is customary: daughters remain in their parents' household and sons move in with their wives and in-laws. Although some American families follow the matrilocal and patrilocal

8.   Robert F. Winch and Rae Lee Blumberg, "Societal Complexity and Familial Organization," in Arlene and Jerome Skolnick, *Family in Transition: Rethinking Marriage, Sexuality, Child Rearing, and Family Organization* (Boston: Little, Brown, 1971), p. 142.

patterns, particularly first and second generation immigrants, most newly married couples set up a separate residence independent of either spouse's parents, what sociologists and anthropologists call *neolocal.* Neolocal residence gives the family mobility, privacy, and room for individualism, but it also tends to isolate the family, as noted earlier.

Patterns of descent are usually, but not always, related to residence patterns. In patrilocal societies, descent is most often *patrilineal,* that is, children — both males and females — belong to the kin group of their father. In matrilocal societies, descent is usually *matrilineal;* children are affiliated with their mother's kin group. And societies practicing neolocal residence typically have a *bilateral* system of descent; children usually feel that they are equally related to both their mother's and father's side of the family.

Closely related to the question of descent is that of inheritance. In patrilineal societies, inheritance is most often passed on from father to son; a son acquires his father's social rights and obligations as well as his land and possessions. In matrilineal societies, inheritance frequently passes among the male members of the matrilineal kin group; in other words inheritance passes from a brother to his sister's son. Finally, in bilateral societies, such as our own, a child inherits from both his mother and his father, and he passes this inheritance on to his own sons and daughters.

INTERACTION WITH THE COMMUNITY

In small, primitive societies, a single family or kin group may comprise a third or half of the entire community. Familial rights and obligations cover nearly all social interaction. Children learn at an early age how they are related to each member of the community and how they should act toward them. In modern societies, children and adults usually spend far more time outside the family with non-kin than with kin. Nevertheless, the family continues to mediate or regulate interaction between family members and the outside world.

In analyzing patterns of interaction with the community, sociologists have noted an important distinction between open and closed families.[9]

The *open family* is one that encourages interaction with people outside the family group. Children are urged to "make friends" with other children, to bring them home to play and to visit their houses. The adults have a number of non-kin friends, and participate in numerous activities outside the home. Typically, members of an open family turn to others for emotional gratification and support. The husband may discuss business problems with co-workers as well as his wife; the wife will share her triumphs and worries as a mother with friends; children play as often with friends as with their brothers and sisters. This does not mean the open family is weak. In fact, there is reason to believe it is stronger than the closed one. Because members of an open family have more outside sources of satisfaction, the family group is subject to fewer strains.

In the *closed family,* the emotional burden falls almost entirely on family members. The closed family characteristically views outsiders with either suspicion or distrust. If on some occasions, an outsider does gain the confidence of a family member, and the family member begins to turn to the outsider, the family will exhibit signs of jealousy and resentment, and will use its influence to discourage the friendship. Within the closed family, members rely on each other for love, affection, emotional support and approval, companionship, help, advice, and assistance.

There are several dangers in prolonged adherence to the closed family pattern. One is that the emotional burdens of the relationship may become too heavy, with the result that the family disintegrates in a burst of quarrels and fights. Another is that a closed structure may leave the family members so dependent on the family unit that they are

9.   Elizabeth Bott, *Family and Social Network* (London: Travistock, 1957).

unable to cope with the outside world. On the other hand, the closed family can perhaps better withstand the strains of social and geographical mobility that characterize industrialized society. In addition, the degree of intimacy that develops in such families can bring much emotional satisfaction.

Social and geographic mobility in our own society tend to favor the development of the closed or isolated family; because society is so fluid, it is difficult for a person to develop the network of extrafamilial relationships that characterize the open family pattern. In many families, there is a kind of alternation between the two patterns. During a period of stability, a family puts down roots in a community and begins to open itself up to outsiders. Then a move is necessary, and the family becomes closed again, until it is secure in its new environment.[10]

ETHNIC AND CLASS DIFFERENCES IN FAMILY STRUCTURE

Sociologists have long noticed that patterns of interaction with the community, descent and residence, allocation of authority, and so on vary from group to group in the United States. Given the ethnic heterogeneity of the American people, a leading question has always been to what degree are these differences in family life-style related to ethnic background. Do Italian-Americans maintain close ties with their extended families because kin groups were strong in Italy? Does the heritage of slavery, where marriage was forbidden and families deliberately broken apart, explain the relatively high proportion of female-headed households among contemporary blacks? Herbert Gans's study of an Italian working-class neighborhood in Boston, *The Urban Villagers,* was designed in part to seek answers to these kinds of questions.[11]

10. Bernard Farber, *Family: Organization and Interaction* (San Francisco: Chandler Publishing, 1964), p. 321.

11. Herbert J. Gans, *The Urban Villagers* (New York: Free Press, 1962), chapter 11.

Comparing his findings to other studies, Gans concluded that the lower and working classes are much the same the world over; differences in family organization seem more the result of social class differences than ethnic background.

Life for the very poor or lower-class family is totally unpredictable. Only rarely is the lower-class man able to provide adequate financial support. As a result, his position in the family is marginal. A woman and her children are the primary family group in the lower class.

Unlike the very poor, working-class or blue-collar men (semi-skilled and skilled workers) are able to support a family, and they tend to see their jobs primarily as a means to hold the family together, but they are not always economically secure. They tend to distrust outsiders and to depend on the extended family for emotional gratification and support in time of trouble. In contrast to the working and lower classes, middle-class families (where the father is typically in a clerical, sales, business, or professional position) are more open. They tend to believe society is on their side. In their concern for achievement and upward mobility, the middle-class family focuses on helping the father, whose job determines their higher social position and life style, and on obtaining the best possible education for the children, who are expected to move up the social ladder.

The upper-middle-class family (where the father is typically in a prestige profession or high corporate position) is both more introspective and more socially active than any of the others. Financially secure, professionals usually see their jobs as a route to personal development and as a way of contributing to society. In the upper-middle-class family, the emphasis is on individualism and personal satisfaction (rather than achievement) for the husband, wife, and for the children.

In summary, the lower-class family tends toward matriarchy by default; the working-class family is often a closed, extended family, where members rely on consanguine relatives; the middle-class family is an open, conjugal unit, relatively isolated from other relatives and geared toward mobility; and the upper- middle-class family tends to be individualistic and egalitarian. The subject of social class, and its many other social consequences, is the focus of the following chapter.

ROBERT O. BLOOD, JR.
Marriage Patterns in Japan and America

Abridged with permission of The Macmillan Company from *Love Match and Arranged Marriage* by Robert O. Blood, Jr. Copyright © 1967 by Robert O. Blood, Jr.

Introduction

This article is based on a study that compared family structure and processes in Detroit and Tokyo. The Detroit and Tokyo couples studied were drawn from the middle class of each country. The Tokyo couples were all love-matched—their marriages were based on love, rather than the traditional arrangement between two families—which makes them representative of more modern, "vanguard" Japanese families.

The Japanese family conforms to the same general patterns as the American; it is monogamous, and the authority and family descent rest with the father. This basic similarity makes the differences between them all the more interesting—for example, the discovery that Japanese women were less reserved in confiding their worries and problems to their husbands than the American women were. Here we have abridged Blood's descriptions of some of the ways in which Japanese and American marriages differ in their internal workings.

The division of labor

[Because of the] "servant wife" concept [used] in discussing traditional Japanese marriages, we should expect Tokyo wives to do more housework than Detroit wives.

Take for example the question of food shopping. Most Detroit wives shop once a week at a supermarket many blocks from home. Buying in large quantities, they can hardly carry the heavy bags home. In some cases, a wheeled basket solves the problem. More often, the wheeled vehicle is the family car. Since the husband usually drives to work and few families have more than one car, the shopping must be done when the husband is home. This increases the possibility of doing it jointly, because men do most of the driving.

In Japan, by contrast, the first supermarket in the entire country opened in Yokohama in 1959. Even though Tokyo department stores have large food departments, few housewives depend on them for ordinary supplies. Instead, neighborhood food shops (butcher shop, fish market, fruit store, and so forth) within easy walking distance of home are the main source of everyday shopping. The term *everyday* is literally correct because tiny Japanese kitchens lack storage facilities for keeping food fresh from day to day. Most housewives shop at least once a day for small quantities of food.

Department stores are more frequently used for special occasions. Hence, we thought husbands might stop on their way home from work to buy some special delicacy to suit their own taste. However, Japanese husbands do less specialty shopping than American husbands do of general food shopping.

The husband's clothes are another case in point. Although we unfortunately have no parallel question from Detroit, it seems doubtful that American wives so consistently buy his ordinary clothes (such as underwear and handkerchiefs). In Tokyo, 55 percent of the wives carry this responsibility exclusively, contrasted with only 2 percent of the husbands. Even more strange to Americans is the task of picking up after the husband undresses. The American norm is clearly self-reliance and any man who leaves his clothes strewn around is sure to be labelled "messy." But the traditional Japanese norm is for the wife to be valet. Even in our vanguard sample, wives typically do all the picking up (41 percent of the wives— twice the proportion of self-reliant men). To be sure, the lack of closets in most Japanese homes would cause many an American husband to call for help in folding up his clothes so they could be laid away successfully in a dresser drawer. Nevertheless, the dominant note in the Japanese pattern seems to be not technical competence so much as personal service: "The servant wife at your service, sir!"

Only where sheer biological factors are involved do the two groups behave the same. Carrying heavy objects in Tokyo and mowing Detroit lawns are done primarily by the sex with the sturdier physique and the larger muscles. This efficient arrangement has not always existed in Japan. In the feudal era, patriarchal prestige led servant wives to assume staggering burdens despite biological weakness. Even today, peasant wives labor in rice paddies alongside their husbands, and poverty-stricken urban women labor on road construction. For the middle-class, however, chivalry has arrived and freed women from burdens they used to bear.

With some exceptions, then, the division of labor in Tokyo is skewed in the wife's direction. This is not entirely a matter of ideological differences between the two countries. It is partly a functional adaptation to different stages of economic development. Japan's standard of living may be sky-rocketing but it still has a long way to soar to catch up with America's. So Japanese husbands labor longer hours away from home. (The standard work week for Detroit husbands is 40 hours, for Tokyo husbands, 50.) Japanese men are thus less available for domestic tasks. In this sense, servant wives are balanced by hardworking husbands in the total division of labor (*outside* as well as *inside* the home).

Feminine drudgery is compounded by inadequate household equipment. Old-fashioned kitchens were tiny, gloomy, and inefficient. In urban apartments they might be just an alcove off the living room or double as an entry way. The stove was hardly more than a hot plate (electric burner or gas jet). The sink usually had only one tap—for cold water. Even new refrigerators hold only one day's food supply, just like the traditional ice box (so small the iceman rides a bicycle). The inconvenience of shopping in decentralized specialty shops has already been mentioned. Add the lack of ready-to-serve foods and it can be seen why Japanese husbands would hesitate to invade the kitchen even if they had the time.

Technological change is whirling through Japan. Electric rice-cookers, portable washing machines, tiny vacuum cleaners, and other adaptations to the Japanese scene are selling like proverbial hotcakes. Economic development will slash the housewife's working hours in Japan as it has in the U.S.A. In the meantime, many a Japanese housewife has stubborn facts to contend with as well as a stubborn husband.

Companionship

From the sharp, rigid division of labor in Japan we would expect less companionship between husbands and wives in leisure-time activities. Segregation of the sexes in task areas removes a potential foundation for integration of the sexes in nontask areas.

More concretely, the economic under-development that shapes the Japanese division of labor also impedes recreational companionship by reducing available leisure. So much energy must be devoted to achieving a higher standard of living that little is left for anything else. Nor are material resources available. There is too little money for purchasing spectator entertainment, recreational equipment, or transportation to recreation sites.

We should expect this to affect most heavily those activities that require the most resources. Verbal communication between husband and wife should be impaired least, but activities that require facilities for entertaining, cost money for traveling, or consume many hours should be appreciably reduced in Japan.

External sociability

Contact with persons outside the household may occur either in the home or elsewhere, but is *external* in the sense of involving other persons.

In the United States, contact often occurs within the home. So important is entertaining guests that Blood and Wolfe (1960) designate a major role of the middle-class housewife as "hostess-companion." The living room in winter and patio in summer provide space for home-cooked meals, light refreshments, or cocktails for countless guests.

Japanese entertaining is throttled by limited space and equipment. The per capita square footage of indoor and outdoor space is substantially less in crowded Tokyo than in sprawling Detroit. Kitchens that are inefficient for family purposes hardly lend themselves to serving guests. Hence, what little entertaining is done at home is apt to be catered (sent in ready made from neighborhood food shops) at a fancy price. Or if meager accommodations are unworthy of an honorable guest, he will be entertained in a private room in a restaurant, thus incurring costs not only for food but for facilities at a budget-taxing price.

Given inadequate facilities and funds, entertaining is restricted chiefly to social obligations. Because a sense of duty is strong in Japanese culture, care is taken not to impose an obligation on others to reciprocate with entertainment they could not afford. This sensitivity further inhibits handing out invitations broadcast in light-hearted American fashion. To be sure, Emily Post encourages social reciprocity too, but the obligation to return favors is taken less seriously and frequently discharged wholesale in massive cocktail parties or barbecues.

The greater importance of external sociability in American marriages is intensified by contact with nonrelatives. Fumi Takano contrasted this aspect of family life in Japan and the United States after studying at Radcliffe in 1953–54:

> In America, a man and his wife form one social unit. That is, at nearly all social functions a man is accompanied by his wife, or rather, a woman is accompanied by her husband. But in Japan, on most social occasions, men alone are invited. I heard the other day of the case of a Fulbright professor, and his wife, who invited the faculty, and their wives, of the [Japanese] college they were assigned to, and found to their great surprise that most of the wives had never met each other. That was not at all an exceptional case. Japanese women seldom attend social functions. Men go visiting their friends by themselves, they go to parties by themselves, they go to movies by themselves or with their friends. And most Japanese women would never think of going out with their husbands, leaving their children at home.

Vogel (1963) describes the paralyzing impact of uncertainty on how to behave in the strange and unfamiliar role of couple-to-couple sociability that makes the first venture of pioneers less than pure enjoyment:

> When talking with us, many [Japanese women] expressed envy of American wives who go out with husbands, and many were curious as to what it would be like. Several went so far as to try it for the first time during our stay, but reported that they were too tense to enjoy themselves. When out with husbands and their friends, they have to be so careful to behave properly that it is

difficult to go beyond polite pleasantries. Moreover, they must be so retiring that they generally prefer the more relaxed times with their lady friends. One wife, upon hearing about a husband and wife going on a trip for a few days, responded, "How nice," but after a moment's reflection added, "but what would they talk about for so long?"

External sociability is so rare that it contributes little to husband-wife companionship in Tokyo. This does not mean that there is no companionship of any kind, but that it assumes forms which cost less time, money, and—we should now add—social involvement. External sociability is not the crucial form of companionship in any case. If we defined companionship as the couple's enjoyment of each other's presence in joint activity, that presence is most complete when others are excluded.

Our median Tokyo couple go out together just for a good time twice a month after marriage. This dating companionship is the essence of marital companionship. It most directly reproduces premarital dating which is the essence of courtship.

Against the backdrop of Japanese history, this regular married dating stands forth in bold relief. Traditionally, entertainment was designed for men only and supplied by professional women while wives stayed home to defend paper and bamboo houses from theft and fire. The latter could come either from within (should an earthquake occur) or from without (as urban homes were huddled together). Only recently have pioneering builders freed wives from housesitting by using fireproof concrete construction and providing keys for locking doors from the outside.

When wives no longer have to guard their homes, they are free to go out with their husbands. The fact that they actually do so as often as twice a month suggests considerable motivation in both partners. Dating has captured the imagination of the younger generation. Its near ubiquity before marriage is extended even further after marriage

(only 2 percent of our couples never go out together). In this crucial form of companionship, Japanese marriages strikingly resemble American marriages.

Internal communication

Tokyo husbands inform their wives of the day's events on returning from work almost as often as Detroit husbands. The norm for Detroit is daily reports whereas the mode in Tokyo is almost daily. We know for sure that American husbands are normally more informative than Japanese men. This difference may even be underestimated because a slight difference in question wording tends to restrict the American reference to work-related events.

What are the possible reasons for less informative companionship in Japan? We have already mentioned the interference created by a sharper division of labor and less leisure. These factors are intensified by voluntary segregation of what little leisure time there is. In a fashion reminiscent of working-class Americans, Tokyo salary-men linger after work with their company friends and give them some of the informative messages that might otherwise go to wives.

A Japanese weekly magazine blames the wife's traditional seclusion for the husband's failure to find her a stimulating audience:

> In Japan the wife is nailed into the home and has few topics in common with her husband. This is the primary reason why her idol and master returns [from work] so slowly (cited from the Shukan Asahi of February 23, 1961, in Plath, 1964).

Some Japanese men feel it is unmanly to communicate with their wives. One businessman's reticence was described to me by his wife:

> My husband is a typical Japanese. He's never been abroad and was the eldest son, so his whole family respected him and he feels everyone should do things for him. He is thoughtful of others but doesn't express it very much. He doesn't say much, has to be asked what he is thinking. He's

supposed to be home from work at 6:30 but because he has to wine and dine his customers he usually gets home about midnight. He always wants me to have a meal ready for him when he gets home. When we were first married, he never called to say when he would be home because he held that a man shouldn't have to think about his wife, especially in front of other men. But he has been watching other men in the office call their wives to avoid trouble, and now he calls to say he will be late, as a help in preparing his meal.

"... especially in front of other men"—social pressure even reduces communication of useful messages.

Some Japanese couples feel that they are so intimate that they don't need to communicate overtly. Since the partner knows he is loved, there is no need to say so.

Could Japanese men have less to report than American? Perhaps their less mobile occupational system (the fact that men rarely change companies and that promotions depend on seniority) produces less exciting news to share. By contrast, Americans change not only jobs but fields in the course of fluid careers. Particularly the young men in our Detroit subsample are still on the make, still mobility oriented, still hoping they'll outstrip their fellows. Men striving for high stakes understandably bubble over with good news or bad news for wives dependent on the outcome. (Blood and Wolfe find that wives don't begin losing hope of further mobility for their husbands until after age 40.)

We should not exaggerate the difference, however. Obviously these Japanese men have come a long way from the conventional aloofness and mystery of haughty males who did not deign to reveal their "private" lives to servant wives. Westernization and modernization have obviously transformed these men as well as their wives. A new emphasis on love and understanding in Tokyo marriages has revolutionized the old relationship between the sexes, replacing

it with a degree of reciprocity that is within sight of absolute symmetry and even closer to catching up with American informative companionship.

Emotional therapy

We hypothesized that American wives would be more verbal than Japanese wives, but they turn out to be strikingly less so. Only half as many "always" tell their troubles and twice as many "never" do. Detroit wives are selective but Tokyo couples seldom are. The wives tell their troubles unusually freely, while a significant minority of the men are stoics.

Our main problem, though, is the Japanese wives' heavy dependence in time of trouble. One clue is their great emphasis on the importance of understanding in marriage. Whereas Detroit women glorify companionship (which means having "good" times together), Tokyo women bypass that concept to emphasize love and understanding.

So far, so good, but we haven't explained very much when we say that Japanese couples tell their troubles because they believe it is important to tell one's troubles! Why do they believe it is important in the first place? One reason may be that Japanese take their troubles more seriously than Americans. This is a sweeping statement, to be sure, but it is one of my indelible impressions of Japan.

From several perspectives, Japanese wives win first prize for emotional openness. After all our comments about emotional reserve this sounds inconsistent. Then we referred to reserve with strangers. Now the openness is with a legitimate audience—the marriage partner. In fact, public reserve probably increases the need for private openness.

But husbands and wives are not equally open. Communicating troubles is another aspect of feminine expressiveness—of words, of emotions. Not only verbal facility but emotional liability are feminine predispositions. Whatever the reasons, this is an era in which Japanese men and women do not behave the same. Our guess is that American men, too, are less emotionally expressive than their wives. (How husbands in the two countries compare remains to be discovered.)

With twice as many wives as husbands always telling their troubles, Japanese marriages are conspicuously asymmetrical. Another way of saying this is that Japanese wives are more emotionally dependent on their husbands than vice versa. Feminine dependence may reflect residual patriarchalism. When men are older, better educated, and more worldly wise, we should expect them to offer shoulders to cry on. Perhaps the selectivity practiced by American wives requires more emancipation and more structural equality than Japanese wives have yet achieved. If so, feminine emotional dependence may decline in Japan as Westernization continues.

Summary

What then is the overall shape of marriage in Japan and the United States? At least as far as these samples are concerned, the Japanese shape is narrow and constricted. It rests on a narrow population base — two parents and two children — and has less involvement with the outside world of kin and especially nonkin.

Husband and wife are more sharply separated from each other in their working hours, because external work is more time-consuming and housework is more segregated. But in what little leisure they have, Japanese couples achieve a good deal of intimacy via marital dating, internal communication, and a heavier-than-American emotional reliance in time of crisis. The power structure of their marriages seems just as equalitarian as ours. However, elements of asymmetry in their marriages (and perhaps to a lesser extent in ours) reflect differential sex roles. Wives are more verbally expressive and more emotionally expressive in Japan than in America. There is probably more pervasive equalitarianism and reciprocity in America's companionable marriages than in Tokyo's love matches and romantic arranged marriages.

Conclusion

This article indicates how the internal workings of a family group are greatly shaped by the surrounding culture. The Japanese family system, although quite similar in its basic organization, differs from ours because it is molded by cultural traits carried over from preindustrial Japan, by the stage of Japan's economic development, and by the physical conditions in local neighborhoods. One could hypothesize that as social conditions in Japan become more like those in the United States, the dynamics of the Japanese family system will also become more like ours, but some differences will probably always remain because of different cultural traditions.

TOPIC

3 MATE SELECTION, MARRIAGE, AND DIVORCE

In extended families, a son or daughter's choice of a marriage partner affects the entire family. An arrogant daughter-in-law, a lazy son-in-law, or a spouse who wants to lure the son or daughter away from the extended family are seen as distinct threats to family stability. In such families, the head of the household plays an active role in mate selection, sometimes dictating whom his children will marry. The same is true in small, primitive societies, where marriages play an important role in determining a family's standing in the community. Here marriage is often seen as a way of creating alliances between kin groups: mate selection is too important a decision to be left to individuals.

Americans often find the thought of arranged marriages distasteful. Such marriages are not in keeping with the importance we place on romantic love, nor are they particularly appropriate for our pattern of family organization, with its strong emphasis on the nuclear family. In societies that practice arranged marriages, however, couples have large families to whom they can turn for affection and support. If a spouse is not "perfect," it does not matter quite as much as it does in the isolated, nuclear family. The conjugal relationship is but one of many close, personal relationships. Mate selection, marriage, and divorce are not primarily personal affairs.

Because one of the primary functions of marriage in modern societies such as our own is to provide individuals with companionship and intimacy—perhaps the only intimate relationship they will know—we place a great deal of emphasis on personal choice. Since married couples in the United States generally set up their own households apart from kin, a person's choice of a marriage partner may not directly affect anyone but the couple and their children on a day-to-day basis. Romantic love has become the idealized basis of marriage in Western societies; and family alliances are seldom important.

CHOOSING A MARRIAGE PARTNER

All cultures place some restrictions on marriage partners, and America is no exception. Incest taboos, usually covering the nuclear family but sometimes extended to include other relatives, are universal. In this country sexual relations and marriage between parents and children, and brothers and sisters are strictly forbidden. (In fact, the only officially sanctioned exceptions to this rule known in history are the royal families of Egypt and Hawaii, where brothers and sisters married.) A few states also outlaw marriages between first cousins; some societies have prohibited marriage between relatives up to sixth cousins. Many reasons have been suggested to account for the universality of the incest taboo. A common sociological explanation is that it prevents potentially disruptive conflict within the kinship group.

Some cultures have norms prescribing *endogamy:* a person must marry within his own group. This is true among Orthodox Jews, who traditionally mourn the death of a child who marries a non-Jew. Endogamy was also enforced in the South where, until the late sixties, interracial marriage was illegal in fourteen states. Other cultures prescribe *exogamy:* a person must marry outside the group of which he is a member. This is often the case in small societies where nearly everyone in the immediate community is related by blood or marriage.

In America today, only incestuous marriages are formally prohibited. Officially, whites are free to marry blacks, Jews to marry Protestants, socialites to marry janitors, and so on. But in practice, most Americans marry people with the same social, racial, ethnic, and religious background—a pattern called *homogamy* (like marrying like). There are numerous reasons for this pattern. Some American subcultures actively discourage exogamy. Generally it is difficult for a Catholic to marry a non-Catholic in church unless the spouse promises to raise the children in the Catholic faith. Some rabbis make the same demand of a non-Jew who is marrying a Jew before they will perform the marriage ceremony. Parental pressure and perhaps the threat of disinheritance may prevent a debutante from marrying someone beneath her in social status. Social disapproval of interracial marriage—among blacks and whites—lessens the chances of their marrying. Added to this is the fact that Americans rarely socialize with people from

Whereas in many societies a marriage may serve to establish or to cement a bond between two extended families or clans, in modern Western society marriage is essentially a partnership involving only two people. Although we idealize freedom of choice and the notion of romantic love, studies have shown that Americans in fact tend to marry people within their own racial, class, and age group. It is not simply coincidental that we so frequently marry the girl or boy down the block. Our choices are often limited by practical and social considerations that may be unrecognized, but are nonetheless real. (Photo by Ken Heyman)

radically different backgrounds. Neighborhoods tend to be racially, ethnically, religiously, and economically homogeneous; so do neighborhood schools. The overwhelming majority of college students are middle class. On the job, people usually work with people of similar educational backgrounds. Opportunities for meeting people with very different backgrounds in a social setting are limited. Despite the melting pot ideal, the poor and the rich, blacks and whites, Italian- and Polish-Americans, Catholics and Jews do not mix very often.

As a result of these informal pressures and social habits, most American marriages are homogamous. Estimates of black-white marriages indicate that only 1 of every 1,200 marriages is interracial (a total of some 2,000 interracial marriages a year). In most of these marriages, the husband is black and above his wife in social standing.[12] According to a 1962 study, 93 percent of Jews marry Jews, 91 percent of Catholics marry Catholics, and 78 percent of Protestants marry Protestants.[13] Interclass marriages are more common than either interracial or interfaith marriages. A study of 396 representative couples revealed that 55 percent of the marriages were between people of the same class, 40 percent between people one class apart, and only 5 percent between people more than one class apart. In 64 percent of interclass marriages, the husband's social standing was above his wife's.[14] Finally, people usually marry within their own age group. In 1970, the median age difference between spouses in this country was 2.4 years.[15]

LOVE AND MARRIAGE

These statistics do not erase the fact that most Americans believe in love. We talk about it, sing about it, write novels, plays, and poems

12.   Paul H. Jacobson, *American Marriage and Divorce* (New York: Rinehart, 1959).

13.   Robert O. Blood, *Marriage* (New York: Free Press, 1962), p. 69.

14.   Julius Roth and Robert F. Peck, "Social Class and Social Mobility Factors Related to Marital Adjustment," *American Sociological Review,* 16 (1951), p. 481.

15.   *Statistical Abstracts of the United States* (Washington, D.C.: U.S.G.P.O., 1971), p. 60.

about it. Most of us consider that a prerequisite for marriage is the sentiment which is a mixture of sexual attraction, feelings of excitement and even ecstasy, and idealization of the loved one. Many consider a loss of this kind of love an adequate cause for divorce. The entire complex of norms surrounding marriage —from sexual fidelity to neolocal residence— is tied to the idea of romantic love. What effect does this have on marriage?

We have very little data in this area, but it is probable that romantic love by itself is not the best basis for a lasting marriage. Many people meet, fall madly in love, and marry in one sweep of emotion. They expect the excitement of new love—of what one family relations expert has called "romantic infatuation"[16]—to survive years of domestic routine, and feel cheated when they or their spouse no longer tremble and sigh in anticipation of making love. The idea that this kind of excitement *should* last forever puts a strain on both partners. Disappointment may lead to bitterness within the marriage, adventures outside the marriage, and perhaps to divorce.

On the other hand, when two people live alone together for most of their adult lives— sharing intimacy only with their children— their happiness depends on a high degree of reciprocity. To satisfy each other emotionally, they must continue to recognize each other's needs and desires, share experiences, value one another, and so on. According to Nelson Foote, reciprocity and social equality are the essence of conjugal love, which he describes as "that relationship between one person and another which is most conducive to the optimal development of both."[17]

This kind of reciprocity is highly related both to the personal maturity of each marriage partner and to the similarity or at least compatibility of their basic values and beliefs. Mate selection in terms of these factors is by no means an automatic outcome of physical attraction and romantic infatuation. Sociologists have been especially interested in the factor of value and belief similarity, which is associated with common group and subcultural ties. There are strong indications that this may be the dominant social factor in accounting for marital stability.[18]

MARRIAGE

Our own marriage system is based on *monogamy;* one man is married to one woman.[19] Approximately 2,179,000 Americans got married in 1970, three out of four for the first time. The mean age at first marriage for men was 23.1 years, for women 20.9 years in 1971. These average ages rank about the lowest among the Western nations, though they are rising slightly at the present time. In 1966, only 6.5 percent of men and 5.7 percent of women between the ages of 45 and 54 had never been married. Husbands and wives, living together, headed 90 percent of the 50 million families in America in 1967, and 56 percent of these families included children under the age of 18. The data thus suggest that the majority of Americans marry and spend most of their lives in families; indeed a higher percentage of persons get married in the United States than in any other modern society.

One of the most interesting questions is how adequately are these marriages fulfilling the important functions of the family discussed in the first topic. One of these functions, socialization, was discussed in chapter 4. Here we shall briefly discuss the affection-companionship function. A major indication of failure in this area is of course the rate of divorce and marital breakdown. Accurate data about the "emotional quality" of continuing marriages

16.   Paul Popenoe, *Marriage Is What You Make It* (New York: Abbey, 1970).

17.   Nelson Foote, "Love," *Psychiatry,* vol. 16 (1953), p. 247.

18.   Carle C. Zimmerman and Lucius F. Cervantes, *Successful American Families* (New York: Pageant Press, 1960).

19.   For an interesting study of polygamous family relationships, see Sylvia A. Matheson, *The Tigers of Baluchistan* (London: Cox and Wyman, 1967).

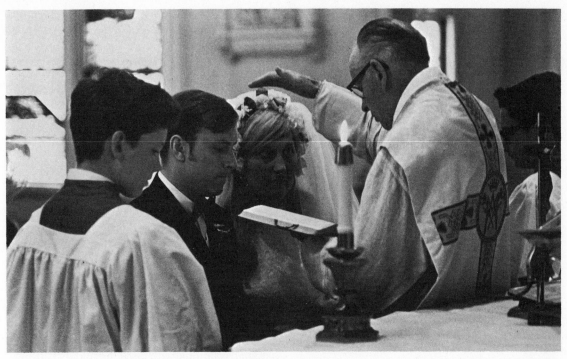

The phrase, "Till death do us part" no longer aptly describes the course of an increasing number of American marriages. Traditionally, we have regarded our marriage system as monogamous. However, some social scientists believe that the term "serial monogamy" is more appropriate. Many people marry and divorce repeatedly, so that in the course of a lifetime an individual may have many marriage partners, but always one at a time. *(Photo by Jon Erikson)*

are very difficult to obtain; however, two recent studies suggest that, at the very least, there may be a gap between the ideal and reality.

In an intensive study of relationships in 58 working-class marriages, Mirra Komarovsky suggests that working-class couples expect relatively little from each other.[20] Husbands and wives tend to lead separate lives, the husband spending time with his cronies, the wife with female relatives and friends. Sex roles are clearly defined. Both partners believe that women are not interested in sports, cars, and the like, and that men have a right to be insulated from children and trivial "women's talk." Although 37 percent of the wives Komarovsky interviewed wished their husbands would talk to them more, an equal per-

centage were content with minimal communication. In general, these couples did not seem to consider closeness and companionship essential or even appropriate. About one-third of the sample described their marriages as happy, one-third as moderately happy, and one-third as unhappy. So long as the family stayed together and kept above water financially, the couples were more or less content. Most saw marriage as a utilitarian relationship.

In another study, John Cuber and Peggy Haroff interviewed 437 married, upper-class Americans.[21] They were able to identify five types of marital relationships. "Conflict-habituated" couples thrive on tension and hostility, devoting much of their time together to controlled battles. "Devitalized" couples have

20. Mirra Komarovsky, *Blue-Collar Marriage* (New York: Random House, 1964).

21. John Cuber and Peggy Haroff, *The Significant Americans: A Study of Sexual Behavior among the Affluent* (New York: Appleton-Century-Crofts, 1965).

drifted away from each other over the years, and tend to believe that detachment and apathy are inevitable in a long-term marriage. "Passive-congenial" relationships exist between couples who never expected very much from each other and feel content with a low level of intimacy. The term "vital" describes marriages where the couple are actively involved with one another, emotionally, socially, and in some cases professionally. The "total" marriage, type five, is one in which husband and wife seem to have no existence independent of each other.

It is very risky to generalize from either of these studies about the married population in the United States as a whole. Clearly, however, the emotional bonds of marriage take many different forms in keeping with the widely varying personality types and social situations of the marriage partners. Though the positive emotional quality of many marriages falls short of the ideal, there is reason to believe that historically it has never been very high; in fact it may have increased over the years. In any case, Americans continue to marry at a very high rate and there is a great deal of evidence that, for men at least, those who do are physically and emotionally better off than those who do not. Married men, compared to those who remain or become single, show lower rates of mental illness, physical ill health, suicide, alcoholism, and they also tend to live longer.

In recent years, sociologists have also investigated the extent to which American marriages have succeeded in fulfilling the third primary function of the family—sexual satisfaction and regulation. Surprisingly perhaps, Cuber and Haroff found that sexual satisfaction was relatively unimportant to the people they interviewed. They wrote,

. . . this pervasive accent on sex [in movies, popular music and so on] seems not to have much shaped the habits and tastes of the significant Americans. . . . Many remain clearly ascetic where sex is concerned. Others are simply asexual. For still others, sex is over-laid with such strong hostility that an anti-sexual orientation is clear. In sum we found substantial numbers of men and women who in their present circumstances couldn't care less about anything than they do about sex.[22]

Nevertheless, Cuber and Haroff found that some infidelity occurred in all but the "total" marriages. Another researcher, Robert Bell, suggests various reasons why people wander from the marriage bed: the need for variety; retaliation for a wandering spouse; general rebellion; a search for emotional gratification; an attempt to forestall declining physical powers; and enjoyment.[23]

The double standard is much stronger in the working class than in either the middle or lower class. This standard works within the marriage as well as without. Komarovsky found that 15 percent of the wives she interviewed engaged in sex because they felt it was their duty. Only 30 percent reported good sexual relations with their husbands, 40 percent were merely satisfied, and 30 percent were unhappy with their sex lives. Other researchers—including Kinsey—have suggested that sexual happiness varies with social class and education, particularly for women: college-educated women are more likely to enjoy sexual relations than lower-class women.

MARITAL DISSOLUTION

Approximately one in every four marriages in this country ends in divorce, the highest rate in any major nation. In addition, the number of marriages broken by separation and full or partial desertion probably equals the number dissolved by divorce. Thus it safely can be said that family breakup in the United States is a very common phenomenon. One fact which has been most alarming to many family relations experts is the great increase in the number of divorce actions which involve families with dependent children. About one-

22.   John Cuber and Peggy Haroff, pp. 171–72.
23.   Robert Bell, *Premarital Sex in a Changing Society* (Englewood Cliffs, N.J.: Prentice-Hall, 1966).

third of divorces involved children in 1923; by 1963 the figure had climbed to two-thirds.[24]

Most divorced persons remarry quickly; however, their chances for success in second and subsequent marriages are not as high as in first marriages. This pattern of marriage, divorce, and remarriage, which often happens several times in the course of a person's life, has led some sociologists to characterize our marriage system as "sequential polygamy." Jessie Bernard has said that "probably more persons practice plural marriage in our society today than in societies that are avowedly polygamous."[25]

The general sociological dimensions of divorcing persons are fairly well established. Young couples who married in their teens are most likely to get a divorce, usually after a rather short period of married life; and divorce rates are higher in the lower and working classes than in the middle and upper classes. It is often difficult to determine why a particular marriage has failed, however. Adultery, desertion, cruelty, non-support, alcoholism, and insanity are the only legal grounds for divorce in many states, although state laws are presently in the process of changing. In many cases, real and legal grounds for divorce differ. The real reasons more often include personality conflicts, economic hardships, conflicts over child rearing, religious differences, troubles with "in-laws," and sexual incompatibility.

On a broader level, the high divorce rate is almost certainly related to features of instability in American society. Some of these features, such as the "isolation" of the nuclear family, have been discussed previously in this chapter. Others include the very high rate of residential mobility (the movement of persons from one home to another which uproots their neighborhood life), the redefinition of family roles (discussed in the next topic), and ethnic heterogeneity (persons with conflicting values and different backgrounds who marry).

An important point about our high divorce rate which is often overlooked is that in most other modern societies the family receives a much larger amount of governmental support than in the United States. Most of the advanced European nations support the family with a wide range of social and welfare services, including family allowances (extra money given to families with dependent children), preferential treatment in housing, child-care programs for the children of working mothers, and free childhood dental and health care. These help to ease some of the major strains which underlie family breakdown, especially in the areas of economic support and child care. In the United States the family is regarded as a part of one's private sphere, and, therefore, not a very suitable focus for governmental action and public concern. Yet at the same time the country continues to expect a great deal from the family. As Robin Williams puts it, "high expectations are imposed on a relatively vulnerable structure."[26]

The fact that divorce is permitted in modern America much more freely than in former times probably also contributes to the high divorce rate. It is even reasonable to suggest that as divorce becomes more common, marital breakup occurs at a lower level of internal strain than previously.

WIDOWHOOD

Marriages also end when one of the partners dies. There are approximately 11 million widows and widowers in this country. Most of these (80 percent) are women because women usually marry men a few years older than themselves, and women tend to live longer than men. In addition, widows do not remarry as often as widowers do. The position of widows in this country is far from enviable. Most have depended on their husbands for

24. *Divorce Statistics Analysis, United States, 1963. Public Health Service Publication No. 1000*, Series 21, No. 13, pp. 6–39.

25. Jessie Bernard, *Remarriage: A Study of Marriage* (New York: Drydan Press, 1956), p. 46.

26. Robin Williams, *American Society* (New York: Alfred A. Knopf, 1970), p. 96.

financial support and are therefore unprepared to enter the job market. With inflation and the rising cost of living, pensions, social security, and life insurance policies are often inadequate. While some widows move in with a married son or daughter, many others lead exceedingly lonely lives, cut off from friends (who prefer to socialize with other couples) and family, and they are reduced to a lower standard of living than that to which they had become accustomed. Widows make up a high percentage of those who are classified as poor.

TOPIC

4 THE CHANGING AMERICAN FAMILY

Most of us grew up in isolated, nuclear families. We spent much of our childhood in school and with peers. Friends changed as we moved from one neighborhood or city to another, and from elementary to junior and senior high school and college. Our mothers may have consulted Dr. Spock for child-rearing advice, as often as their own mothers. We visited relatives only occasionally. We learned that we were expected to move on, to leave home and get a better job than our parents had.

Because it is the only pattern of family organization we know, most of us take this emphasis on the nuclear family for granted. But the nuclear family is a relatively recent "invention," one that has solved some problems and created others. The isolated conjugal family allows individuals a great deal of freedom and mobility, but it also limits their opportunities for emotional support and gratification. Dissatisfaction with this family type, as expressed in divorce rates and in experiments in communes, seems to be growing. Where is the American family headed? This topic examines demographic pressures for change, some of the changes in family roles that are already taking place, and alternatives to the family that are being considered.

DEMOGRAPHIC CHANGES

A great many changes in the family stem from underlying population or demographic trends that are characteristic of all modern societies. As late as 1920, the average American lived from 54 to 55 years. Today the average man lives to be 67, the average woman, to 74. With mandatory retirement at 65 in most industries, people are often left idle for the last 10 or so years of their life. This means that persons should plan for and families must adapt to a significant section of life in which occupational pursuits are not primary; these declining years are often dominated by poverty and ill health.

In addition, child rearing is no longer a lifetime career. At the turn of the century, the average American woman married at 22, had her first child at 23, and her last at 32. Today the average woman marries at 20, has her first child at 22, and her last at 26. By law, these children must go to school, which means that at the age of 31 or 32, the average woman has some free time during the day; and by the age of 43, when her last child will have left home, her active child-rearing days are over. Thus demographic and social changes have shortened the childbearing and child-rearing phases

AMERICAN FAMILY CHARACTERISTICS: 1971

	Families	Percent
Number of Families Investigated	51,948,000	100.0
White	46,535,000	89.6
Nonwhite	5,413,000	10.4
Characteristic		
Family size:		
2 persons	18,282,000	35.2
3 persons	10,724,000	20.6
4 persons	9,899,000	19.1
5 persons	6,528,000	12.6
6 persons	3,381,000	6.5
7 persons or more	3,133,000	6.0
Children under 18 years of age		
(not including adopted children)		
No children	23,161,000	44.6
1 child	9,163,000	18.5
2 children	8,915,000	17.2
3 children	5,380,000	10.4
4 children or more	4,878,000	9.4
Residence:		
Nonfarm	49,600,000	95.5
Farm	2,347,000	4.5
Age of family head:		
Under 25 years	3,745,000	7.2
25-34 years	10,649,000	20.5
35-44 years	10,840,000	20.9
45-54 years	11,065,000	21.3
55-64 years	8,473,000	16.3
65 years or older	7,175,000	13.8
Marital status of family head:		
Married	45,222,000	87.1
Separated	1,263,000	2.4
Widowed	2,757,000	5.3
Divorced	1,584,000	3.0
Single	1,119,000	2.2

SOURCE: U.S. Bureau of Census. Published In *Official Associated Press Almanac 1973,* (New York: Almanac Publishing Co., 1972), p. 438.

of the family life cycle,[27] lengthened the "empty nest" period (after children leave home), and increased the chances of prolonged widowhood. These changes have caused many women to become increasingly independent, and to combine a lifetime occupational pursuit with child rearing.

27.   The family life cycle may be divided into six stages: marriage to birth of first child; childbearing; child rearing; first to last child married; the "empty nest"; and widowhood.

CHANGING FAMILY ROLES

As the Women's Liberation Movement has dramatized, society has only begun to adjust to these changes. Over 45 percent of the work force between the ages of 35 and 44 is now female.[28] However, American women's occupational status remains low. Fewer women attain managerial and professional positions than men, and when they do, they often earn less than men for equal work. One reason is that most women must interrupt their work careers to bear and raise children. On a subtler level, both men and women are taught to see a woman's future in the terms of motherhood and to label competitiveness "masculine."

Some changes have been made. Birth control devices are now widely available, and many laws against abortion have been repealed. Day-care centers have opened around the country to assist the working mother, though they are still in very short supply and often provide inadequate care. Women's Movement groups are working for an Equal Rights Amendment to the Constitution, and for a law guaranteeing pregnancy-leave pay. And many couples, especially in the upper-middle class, have begun to share household chores and responsibility for children.

Sociologist Jessie Bernard suggests this may be just the beginning. Referring to the radical feminists, who reject marriage, the mother-sex object feminine role, and even the need for sex, she writes:

They are preparing us for a world in which reproduction is going to be only a very minor part of a woman's life, a world in which men and women are going to have to relate to one another in ways quite removed from reproduction, both in marriage and outside it. . . . I see them as helping us to catch up with revolutions that have already occurred or are in process, with revolutions which the technologists have precipitated and which we must come to terms with.[29]

28.   *Statistical Abstracts of the United States* (Washington, D.C.: U.S.G.P.O., 1971), Table 333.

29.   Jessie Bernard, "Women, Marriage and the Future," *The Futurist* (April 1970), p. 42.

One of the most important aspects of this family role redefinition is the effect it may have on the family's function in the socialization of children. We are just beginning to investigate the child-rearing problems which may be created when the mother directs much of her energy and activity outside the home during the child-rearing phases of the family life cycles. Evidence is growing that adults in America spend less time and energy in raising their children than adults in other advanced societies.[30] Further, as we have noted, the United States ranks very low in public services to the family, such as day care, public recreation, health, out-of-school educational opportunities, and homemaking services. A decline in maternal care for children, without compensation from increased paternal assistance or outside services, could have serious long-run consequences. This is why many persons, including many women in the women's liberation movement, are striving to obtain a more important role for the father in child rearing, and more community services directed toward child care and development.

ALTERNATIVES TO THE NUCLEAR FAMILY

There is of course the alternative of bachelorhood. If sexual norms are relaxed to the point where neither single males nor females must face periods of involuntary celibacy, more people may decide they prefer not to get married at all. Childless marriages and cohabitation without marriage are other alternatives for individuals who want to pursue careers full-time, but dislike returning to an empty apartment at night. If chosen by a large enough number of persons, these alternatives in the long run threaten the reproductive capacity of the society, although that is not a problem at present.

One of the most controversial alternatives to the nuclear family is the commune. Accord-

30.   See Urie Bronfenbrenner and John C. Coudry, *Two Worlds of Childhood: U.S. & U.S.S.R.* (New York: Russell Sage, 1970).

In an effort to find an enduring alternative to the isolated nuclear family and more satisfying primary relationships, some young people are experimenting with a communal life style. The focus is on group interaction, intimacy, and communication. Commune members are often thought of as brothers and sisters, and the commune as an extended family. Typically, these groups are made up of young people who identify with the counter-culture movement and who are drawn from the middle and upper classes. (Dennis Stock, Magnum)

ing to recent estimates there are some 1,000 functioning rural and urban communes in America today. Many groups of young people have "returned to the land," setting up farming communes where they hope to lead a simple, noncompetitive life. In cities, communes have been started by people who share a common interest: in politics, religion, art, and so on. Elsewhere two or more couples have moved together, sharing a house and responsibility for cooking, cleaning, and caring for children. In essence, communes are an attempt to escape the isolation and possessiveness of the nuclear family; an attempt to recreate the extended family without the binding, formal ties of marriage and kinship.

Whether communes are simply experimen-tation of the "radical fringe" or a workable alternative for the future remains to be seen. As we discussed in topic 1, they have not proved very successful in accomplishing the socialization function. Indeed, a high percentage of communes do not have children as members; some do not even allow them.

Communes have been more successful in providing a refuge for young adults at pre-family stages of the life cycle, which for a growing number of young people now lasts into the late 20's and early 30's. The rate of breakup of communes, however, is probably higher than that of nuclear families at the present time. It is often said that one major weakness of the nuclear family is that it is very difficult to adjust to just one person all your life. In the commune, an individual must intimately adjust on a day-to-day basis to six, eight, or more persons. In this age of the individualized personality, when "doing your own thing" is a commonly verbalized norm, primary relationships with this many people in one household can be highly stressful. This helps to account for the high membership turnover in communes.

In conclusion, the family as an institution is in a state of some disarray in contemporary American society. But at the same time there is a growing awareness that the functions it serves are among the most important to further human development. The nuclear family, in spite of its historically curtailed functions, continues as probably the single most important institution in the life of any individual, shaping his personality, values, and life chances.

The American Family: Future Uncertain

"The American Family: Future Uncertain," (*Time* December 28, 1970), pp. 34–39. Reprinted by permission of Time Magazine. © 1970 Time Inc.

Introduction

According to many experts the family as an institution is in trouble. Increased mobility, the changing role of women, and the counterculture of the young are some of the factors threatening the traditional family. The following article resulted from a 1970 White House Conference on Children.

"America's families are in trouble — trouble so deep and pervasive as to threaten the future of our nation," declared a major report to last week's White House Conference on Children. "Can the family survive?" asks Anthropologist Margaret Mead rhetorically. "Students in rebellion, the young people living in communes, unmarried couples living together call into question the very meaning and structure of the stable family unit as our society has known it." The family, says California Psychologist Richard Farson, "is now often without function. It is no longer necessarily the basic unit in our society."

The data of doom — many familiar, some still startling — consistently seem to support this concern. One in every four U.S. marriages eventually ends in divorce. The rate is rising dramatically for marriages made in the past several years, and in some densely-populated West Coast communities is running as high as 70%. The birth rate has declined from 30.1 births per thousand in 1910 to 17.7 in 1969, and while this is a healthy development in many respects, it implies considerable change in family life and values. Each year, an estimated half-million teen-agers run away from home.

The crisis in the family has implications that extend far beyond the walls of the home. "No society has ever survived after its family life deteriorated," warns Dr. Paul Popenoe, founder of the American Institute of Family Relations. Harvard Professor Emeritus Carle Zimmerman has stated the most pessimistic view: "The extinction of faith in the familistic system is identical with the movements in Greece during the century following the Peloponnesian Wars, and in Rome from about A.D. 150. In each case the change in the faith and belief in family systems was associated with rapid adoption of negative reproduction rates and with enormous crises in the very civilizations themselves."

It is not necessary to share this apocalyptic decline-and-fall theory to recognize many interrelated dangers to both society and family. Each of the nation's forces of change and conflict meet within the family. The "counterculture" of the young, the effects of the war, economic stresses and the decay of the cities—all crowd in on the narrow and embattled institution. The question, of course, is not whether the family will "survive," for that is like asking whether man or biology or society will survive. The question is whether it can survive successfully in its present form. All the evidence shows that in order to do so, it needs help.

Precisely that was uppermost in the minds of 4,000 delegates from across the nation who met in Washington last week for the once-in-a-decade Conference on Children. Among the proposals they urged on President Nixon were the establishment of a National Institute for the Family; universal day-care, health and early learning services in which parents would play a major role; the creation of a Cabinet-level Department of Family and Children; and an independent Office of Child Advocacy. There was also a lavish list of demands—though more modest than the one ten years ago—covering everything from prevention of child injuries to reforming the judiciary system.

Weakened supports

Yet if the demands made on the Government in behalf of the family were too vast, this was in a sense only an understandable reaction against the fact that too many vast demands are made on the family these days. Throughout most of Western history, until the 20th century, society as a whole strongly supported the family institution. It was the family's duty to instruct children in moral values, but it derived those values from church, from philosophers, from social traditions. Now most of these supports are weakened, or gone. Yet politicians and other prophets often blame the family for decline in morals and morale—as if the family could be

separated from society. The forces that are weakening the U.S. family structure are at the very heart of the changes that are taking place in American civilization. Some of the most significant:

Mobility

The mass exodus from rural to metropolitan areas, the increasingly common and frequent corporate transfer, the convenience of the automobile and the highway system built to accommodate it—all have contributed to a basic change in the character of the family. In the less complicated, less urbanized days, the average U.S. family was an "extended" or "kinship" family. This meant simply that the parents and their children were surrounded by relatives: in-laws, brothers, sisters, aunts, uncles, grandparents, cousins. If the relatives did not live within the same household, they were next door or down the block or on the next farm. But as Americans became more mobile, the kinfolk have been gradually left behind. As a result, the typical family has evolved into an isolated "nuclear" family. It consists simply of a father, a mother and their children, and is usually located miles away from the home of the nearest relative.

Says Dr. John Platt, associate director of the University of Michigan's Mental Health Research Institute: "All sorts of roles now have to be played by the husband and wife, whereas in the older, extended family they had all sorts of help—psychological support, financial advice, and so on. The pressures of these multiple roles are partially responsible for the high rates of divorce, alcoholism, tranquilizers, etc."

Women's changing role

"Put very simply," says Cornell Political Sociologist Andrew Hacker, "the major change in the family in recent years, and the problems of the future, are both summed up in one word: women. In the past and until very recently, wives were simply supplementary to their husbands, and not expected to be full human beings. Today, women are involved in much greater expectations and frustrations. For one thing, 40% of U.S. women are now employed. When a woman is working, she tends to have a new perception of herself. I see this most egregiously in those women who go to liberal arts colleges, because there the professor takes them seriously, and this gives them big ideas. The unhappiest wives are the liberal arts graduates. The trouble comes from the fact that the institution we call marriage can't hold two full human beings—it was only designed for one and a half."

It is not only woman's aspirations that have changed, Hacker adds, but society's support of her as a wife. "In the past, the role of wife and mother was reinforced by the church and the community. The whole complex descended on women and said, 'This is what you are; this is where you will be.' Now marriage has to be on its own, because the reinforcements are no longer there. So women are listening to all the subversive messages."

One Women's Lib theoretician, Margaret Benston, has made an economic analysis that places the blame for the "exploitation" of women directly on the family. Since women's work in the home is not paid for, she reasons, it is considered valueless by society. Moreover, at present, equal opportunity of employment simply means that a woman has two jobs: one at work and one at home. All work must therefore be taken out of the home and paid for like any other product; only such innovations as communal kitchens and universal child-care centers will "set women free," she says.

Apotheosis of childhood

In the Middle Ages, children were considered miniature adults, according to French Sociologist Philippe Aries. At about the age of seven, they were sent to other homes to serve as apprentices and often as servants. Thus they grew up in huge households, with no dependence on their parents. In contrast, the child of today, as the center of the tiny nuclear family, has become its *raison d'être* and is therefore kept psychologically, financially and emotionally bound to it.

Without realizing it, many American mothers, under the aegis of benevolent permissiveness and the pressure of civic obligations, actually neglect their children. Others, imbued by Dr. Spock with the notion that every child has a unique potential and that it is her mission to create a near-perfect being, become the child's shadow, with equally damaging results, according to Brandeis Sociologist Philip Slater. The child soon recognizes that he is the center of an extraordinary effort and that his happiness is a matter of great stakes. He will seldom turn out exactly as planned, and when family dissension ensues, the mother will resent her "sacrifices." Moreover, though she may have brought up her child to be "more cultured, less moneygrubbing, more spontaneous and creative" than she herself was brought up to be, she is nevertheless upset when he then refuses to remain on the same treadmill as his parents.

That refusal takes place in adolescence, which like childhood is a modern development. Thus the family has had no long historical experience in dealing with the new rebelliousness. Unlike youths of the pre-industrial age, who simply entered some form of apprenticeship for the adult world at the age of puberty, millions of teenagers now remain outside the labor force to go to college. It is this fact that has made possible the existence of today's separate youth culture, by which parents feel surrounded and threatened in their sense of authority. "A stage of life that barely existed a century ago is now universally accepted as an inherent part of the human condition," says Yale Psychiatrist Kenneth Keniston. Keniston, in fact, now postulates still another new stage of life, that between adolescence and adulthood: he calls it "youth." The youth of the technetronic or post-industrial age often remain out of the work force until their late 20s. "They are still questioning family tradition, family destiny, family fate, family culture and family curse." Naturally, their very existence unsettles the families from which they sprang, and delays the development of the new life-styles that they will eventually adopt.

Limited usefulness

According to Sociologist Reuben Hill, among others, the family has traditionally performed seven functions: reproduction, protection and care of children, economic production of family goods and services, socialization of children, education of children, recreation, and affection giving. But during the past century, he says, the economic, educational, recreational and socializing functions have been lost in varying degrees to industry, schools and government.

In three areas of traditional family life there has been little erosion: reproduction, child care, affection. As a matter of fact, many experts believe that the affectional function is the only one left that justifies the continued support of the family as a social institution. As "community contacts" become more "formal and segmental," says Hill, people turn increasingly to the family "as the source of affectional security that we all crave."

But the insistent demand for affection without the traditional supporting structure has dangers of its own. The pioneering sociologist Edward Westermarck observed that "marriage rests in the family and not the family in marriage." The corollary used to be that the family existed for many practical purposes beyond love. To base

it so heavily on love—including the variable pleasures of sexual love—is to weaken the stability.

Mother's kiss

A related danger is to romanticize and sentimentalize the family. From the Greek tragedians to the modern psychoanalysts, men have known that the family, along with being a source of immense comfort, is also a place of savage battles, rivalries, and psychological if not physical mayhem. Psychoanalyst R. D. Laing says that the "initial act of brutality against the average child is the mother's first kiss." He finds it hurtful that a child is completely at the mercy of his parents, even to having to accept affection. Laing's colleague, David Cooper, calls the nuclear family the "ultimately perfected form of non-meeting" and, in a new book called *The Death of the Family,* demands its abolition. These are extreme views, but it may be better to face the fierce aspects of family life than to expect only bliss. There is something of the disillusioned lover in many people who today are trying to live outside the conventional family.

Dissatisfied with the traditional family setup, or simply unable to cope with it, Americans by the thousands are seeking alternatives. One that has most captured the imagination of youth and that has an almost religious appeal to members of the counterculture is a family structure that is as old as antiquity: the commune. Utopians from Plato onward have visualized children as not being raised in traditional families but in various communal organizations; the instinct that pulls man toward a tightly knit "nuclear" family has often been counterbalanced by the dream of escaping from it.

Only five years ago, there were perhaps a hundred "intentional communities" in the U.S., founded mostly by religious fundamentalists, utopian socialists or conscientious objectors. Today, as an outgrowth of the hippie movement, there are about 3,000, a third of which are in rural settings. "There are farms everywhere now, and we might go in any direction on compass to find warm bread and salt," writes Raymond Mungo in *Total Loss Farm*. Although Vermont, Oregon, California and New Mexico are still the favored states, some new commune clusters are cropping up in what Mungo calls "the relatively inferior terrain and vibration of Massachusetts and points south and west, and the huge strain of friendless middle America."

Most of the new communards are fleeing what they regard as the constriction, loneliness, materialism and the hypocrisy in straight society and the family life on which it is based. Yet some of the same old problems reappear—for example, the tug of war between individualism and submission to the group. One contributor to the *Whole Earth Catalog* summed up his own experience. "If the intentional community hopes to survive, it must be authoritarian, and if it is authoritarian, it offers no more freedom than conventional society. Those communes based on freedom inevitably fail, usually within a year."

But when they fail, their members often go on to join other tribes, now that there is a network of communes available to them. Benjamin Zablocki, a Berkeley sociologist who has visited more than 100 communes in the past six years, insists: "The children are incredibly fine. It's natural for children to be raised in extended families, where there are many adults." Yet in spite of the talk of extended families, the extension in the new communes does not reach to a third generation. Indeed, the "families" have a narrow age span, and it is possible that the children have never seen an adult over 30.

Deformed monstrosity

Writes Brandeis' Sociologist Philip Slater, in *The Pursuit of Loneliness:* "It is ironic that young people who try to form communes almost always create the same narrow, age-graded, class-homogeneous society in which they were formed. A community that does not have old people and children, white-collar and blue-collar, eccentric and conventional, and so on, is not a community at all, but the same kind of truncated and deformed monstrosity that most people inhabit today."

Some communes actually form compromises with the nuclear family. Nowhere is this point better made than at Lama, a contemporary commune 18 miles north of Taos, N. Mex., which was re-visited last week by Correspondent David DeVoss after an absence of 19 months.

"We work together—we collectively grow and distribute the crops, but we go back to our individual nests at night," explains Satya De La Manitov, 28, who has now moved from a tepee into a still unfinished A-frame house that took him $1,500 and twelve months to build. Most couples are in their upper 20s, are married, have children, own their own homes, have a deep respect for property rights and believe in the value of honest toil. Although the concept of complete sexual freedom retains its followers, it plays only a minor role in Lama society today. Indeed, reports DeVoss, "were it not for their long hair, predilection for grass and rejection of the American political system, Lama residents could pass for solid, middle-class citizens."

Most of today's communes are in the cities, and they indeed do have appeal for many middle-class citizens. To Ethel Herring, 30, married to a Los Angeles lawyer and active in Women's Lib, a city commune seemed the answer to growing frustrations, which culminated when she realized that she was spending $60 to $70 a week for baby sitters; the Herrings had no live-in grandparents or nearby relatives to care for their children while Ethel was attending her frequent feminist meetings. In effect, she says, "we were suffering from the nuclear family setup."

With six other sympathetic couples in similar circumstances, the Herrings scouted around and finally found a U-shaped, six-unit apartment building in southern Los Angeles. They purchased it last September, and converted it into a successful, middle-class (most of the men are lawyers) city commune. Knocking out walls and doors, they built interjoining apartments and a communal nursery, TV room and library. "The apartments open up so that the kids' rooms can run into each other," Ethel explains, "and yet there is still plenty of privacy for adults."

The families share their services, following a schedule that calls for each couple to do all of the cooking and housework for one week. "That's KP once every six weeks per couple, which keeps everybody happy," says Ethel. Her husband, for instance, has curtailed his practice so that they can spend one day a week at home on child-care and cooking duty. Says Ethel. "The truth is that most men are deprived of a close relationship with their children, and our men are finding out what they've been missing. It's groovy."

Disillusionment with the traditional family has led to other alternative life-styles. In Boston, David, 36, a divorced architect, and Sarah, 29, a researcher for a consulting firm, have an "arrangement"; like an increasing number of other American couples, they live together in David's Cambridge walkup apartment in a "marriage" that has endured solidly for two years without benefit of legal sanction. They sometimes join David's ex-wife and his son, Jonathan, 5, for dinner. Bubbly, attractive Sarah still maintains her own apartment and sometimes spends a few days there.

Both Sarah and David are convinced that their relationship is superior to a conventional marriage. It is the legal tie, they believe, that is the subtle influence in making a marriage go sour. "On the small scale," says David, "there's no difference, except that you know you could call it off when you want to. That makes you more careful and considerate. You don't say subconsciously, 'Oh, she's always going to be there.' So you make that little extra effort." Only under one circumstance would Sarah and David consider a legal marriage: if they decided to have children.

Doubts about conventional family life have also led to the growth of another phenomenon: the "single-parent family." No longer fearful about complete ostracism from society, many single girls who become pregnant now choose to carry rather than abort their babies and to support them after birth without rushing pell-mell into what might be a disastrous marriage.

Population explosion

Judy Montgomery, 21, is a major in political science at the University of Cincinnati. She lives in the exclusive suburban area of Indian Hill with her parents and her son Nicky, 16 months. She became pregnant at 19 but did not want to get married. "I think having a mother and a father are important for a child, but Nicky can be raised so he isn't scarred. There are now substitutes in society that will allow him to grow up fatherless. I have no feeling of guilt. My only real hassle is with guys I meet who are interested in me, and I say, 'Oh, I have to go home and take care of my kid.'"

Liberalized adoption laws are also making it possible for single and divorced women to have children and to set up housekeeping without the necessity of a father. Ruth Taylor, a secretary at a hospital in suburban Warrensville township, near Cleveland, was divorced shortly after her daughter, Kelley, was born three years ago. Because she did not want the girl to grow up as an only child, she adopted a little boy who was listed as a "slow learner" by the agency (there was a three-year waiting list for normal Caucasian children). But in the year that she has had Corey, 2, the boy's personality and intelligence have blossomed.

To Ruth, adopting a child is the answer for both single and married people who have decided to forego children because of their concern about the population explosion. "Form a family with what has already been provided," she suggests. "That way you will be helping to solve the problem."

The re-examination of the traditional family and the desire to try other forms have also produced some bizarre experiments. In La Jolla, Calif., Michael, an ocean-ographer, and his artist wife, Karen, both 27, had been married for four years when Michael met Janis, who was studying at the Scripps Institute of Oceanography. Janis often came to study at Michael and Karen's apartment, and a strong attachment developed. When Michael took off on a field trip to Antarctica, the two women became good friends and decided that because they both liked Michael, all three ought to live together. Last May the trio formalized it all with an improvised wedding ceremony attended, incidentally, by other trios.

As the three were leaving for a summer session at the University of Oregon, they were delighted to learn that Karen was pregnant. "We'll all take turns caring for it," says Janis, "just as we share all the house-hold chores. That way each of us has time for things we like to do best."

There are other far-out experiments. One group, living at Sandstone, a handsome complex of houses near Los Angeles, has varied in size from three to twelve adults, and currently consists of only five: three men and two women. Says Barbara Williamson, a member of what she calls the "intentional" family: "It's a smorgasbord. It's so much more exciting to have nine different dishes than just one." The group has had no children yet because it wants to stabilize its "marriage" first.

Such eccentric arrangements obviously have no meaning for the vast majority of people, except perhaps as symptoms of an underlying malaise. Thus, while some sociologists and anthropologists make their plans for the reordering of the social struc-ture, most are more immediately concerned with removing—or at least alleviating—the stresses of the nuclear family.

Emancipated women

Psychologist Richard Farson, for one, believes that the increased emphasis on the role of the family "as an agent for human development and personal growth" will again make the family important in the field of education. "Parents will not necessarily teach the children," he says. "That is probably quite unlikely." But the family itself may become a learning unit, stimulated by new programs and new processes (like cartridge TV) that are even now being introduced into the home by industry. This, he feels, will help strengthen the nuclear family "by involving people in all kinds of interesting mutual experiences of learning."

While some fear that Women's Lib is a threat to the family, many experts believe that its more sensible goals could strengthen it. As women become increasingly emanci-pated—by child-care centers and equal-employment practices—they could have more time for intellectual and emotional fulfillment. Thus although their housekeeping role may diminish, they could become less frustrated and better wives. Though the idea is still shocking to many, some experts feel that certain women are better mothers if they are not with their children all day.

The Pill and abortion are obviously part of a loosening of morals that undermines the family in some ways; but these developments, too, can have their positive effects by reducing the number of pregnancies that lead to hasty and ill-considered marriages, and by allowing couples to put off having children until they are older and have had time to enjoy themselves, to travel and to grow up themselves. The reduction in unwanted pregnancies will also lessen the number of children who are rejected even before they are born and the financial hardship brought on by unplanned large families.

Adds Psychoanalyst Rollo May: "Even the growing frequency of divorce, no matter how sobering the problems it raises, has the positive psychological effect of making it harder for couples to rationalize a bad marriage by the dogma that they are 'stuck' with each other. The possibility of finding a new lover makes it more necessary for us to accept the responsibility of choosing the one we do have if we stay with him or her."

If the experts have their way, the nuclear family can be further strengthened in the future. Margaret Mead, for example, believes that many bad starts can be avoided if marriage can be postponed. She proposes a kind of universal national service that will take adolescents out of the nuclear home (where they apparently do not fit in), train them and keep them occupied until they are more mature. "We need something to allow those people who don't go to college to grow up without committing themselves to a marriage."

Instead of traditional marriages, Mead would also encourage a "two-step marriage" for young people. During the first phase, which would, in effect, be a trial marriage, the young couple would be required to agree not to have children. If a stable relationship developed and the couple decided to have children, a second license would be obtained and another ceremony performed.

Business, too, has a responsibility to relieve some of the stress on the contemporary family, according to Psychologist Urie Bronfenbrenner. In a report to last week's White House Conference on Children, he urged business to create flexible work schedules, cut back on travel, on transfers and on social obligations that keep parents away from their children. Bronfenbrenner also feels that large

corporations should concern themselves with "where and how their families live," and with more part-time positions, better maternity leave, day-care centers and family recreation plans.

Another suggestion of the report, which urges that businesses "adopt" groups of young people to give them the opportunity to see adults at work, has already been tried by a few firms. At the White House conference, delegates saw a film about a highly successful program set up by Bronfenbrenner's colleague, David Goslin, of the Russell Sage Foundation. It showed children from the Detroit public-school system spending three days at the Detroit *Free Press,* learning to relate to the newspapermen and what they were doing, and saying things like "You know, in school you learn a subject, but here you meet people."

In Bronfenbrenner's view, meeting people —especially people of different ages—is all-important to the preservation of the family. Parents now spend their time with other parents, he suggests, children with children, the young with the young and the old with the old. To end this segregation, which is particularly acute in suburban living, Bronfenbrenner and others recommend planning by architects for community clusters where children, their parents and the elderly can intermingle, each group bringing its experiences, knowledge and support to the other. University of Michigan's John Platt visualizes clusters he calls "child-care communities" which resemble communes: in addition to enlarged recreational and shopping facilities, they would include centralized schoolrooms, dining rooms (for both adults and children) and kitchens.

Gypsy caravan

For all of the family's ills, the U.S. is still probably the most marriage-and-home oriented nation in the modern world. In the

1960s the number of U.S. families grew at a greater rate than the population; 87% of Americans live in families that include both parents. While the divorce rate is rising, so is the rate of remarriage among divorced people. Thus, the nuclear model will undoubtedly remain the basic family structure in the U.S. But that does not mean that it will function as a healthy institution unless ways are found to strengthen its concept and spirit.

A man's family used to be his fate; he could scarcely change it. In the modern U.S., people think easily of changing their family, like their occupation or their home. The result is psychologically unsettling and yet this changeability has obviously become a part of American life and the family will have to adjust to it. Theologian Sam Keen (*Apology for Wonder*) suggests that one should boldly take the notion of the family as a center for mobility: "It should be thought of like a gypsy caravan. You have that point of stability in the caravan, but it is continually moving and each member of it goes out to forage for food and then catches up with it."

That vision will probably never replace the image—and the dream—of the snug, permanent hearth, even suitably expanded by "clusters." But it may be closer to the reality of American life.

Conclusion

The recent trend which is perhaps most encouraging to the family is the rising national attention which it has received. Though conflicting and inclusive, this attention at least signifies that the family no longer is taken for granted.

SUMMARY

In small, primitive societies, the family is often the only social institution providing for a range of individual and societal needs. In modern, complex societies, education, religion, and social control are performed by outside agencies. The primary functions of the family in modern societies are socialization, providing affection and companionship, and sexual regulation. Although modern societies have numerous formal institutions dedicated to socialization, primary responsibility falls to the family, and children spend their most impressionable years within the family circle. How well the family performs this function is the subject of much debate. A few societies have experimented with alternate routes to socialization (the collective nurseries of the USSR, China, and the Israeli kibbutzim). In modern societies the family is the main source of warmth and companionship for both children and adults, who may have few opportunities for intimacy outside the family. Sexual regulations, which in America are tied to both religion and the law, enable societies to assign responsibility for children.

Not all Americans live in the two-parent family we consider normal; there are numerous variations in family organization. In describing family patterns, sociologists distinguish between *kin,* a person's relatives, and *family,* a kin group that lives together and functions as a unit, and between the *consanguine* family, biological relatives, and the *conjugal* family, relatives through marriage. The characteristic pattern of family organization in America, the *nuclear* family, which consists of a couple and their children, is most typical of the middle class. *Extended* families, which consist of a couple, their children, and one or more other relatives, are often found in the lower classes. In the past, American families—like most families around the world—were *patriarchal.* However, today many families are becoming *egalitarian:* husband and wife share authority and privileges. Nearly all contemporary Americans are *neo-*

local: married couples set up house on their own. Descent in this country is *bilateral:* children feel they are equally related to their father's side of the family and their mother's side. Children in the United States also inherit from both parents. Thus American norms emphasize the importance of the conjugal, rather than the consanguine, family. Many sociologists feel that the major variations in American family organization—from reliance on the extended family to female-headed households—are largely the result of social class differences.

Although Americans marry for love and believe mate selection is a personal decision, we tend to marry people who are like us in socioeconomic, racial, religious, and ethnic background *(homogamy).* However, a few subcultures in this country do prescribe *endogamy* (marriage within a certain group). The emphasis on romantic love and sexual attraction in our culture is sometimes a source of disappointment for married couples who feel the romance should continue forever, and it is not always a good basis for choosing a marriage partner.

The emotional quality of marriage varies greatly. In the working class, spouses tend to expect less in the way of companionship from one another; a wide range of companionship forms have been identified in the upper-middle class, varying from "conflict-habituated" to total commitment. Researchers have found that sex is less important to married people than advertisers and movie makers seem to believe. One in every four marriages in this country ends in divorce, because of such reasons as economic hardship, personality conflicts, adultery, and alcoholism, together with broader factors of instability in American society.

Today the family institution is in a state of some disarray. Demographic changes and the fact that motherhood is no longer a lifetime career are primary pressures for change in the woman's role. The isolated, child-centered family, whose primary function is bearing and socializing children, is subject to much social stress. The commune, an attempt to create a new kind of extended family (without kin ties), is one family alternative which presently is widely discussed.

GLOSSARY

Bilateral descent   Descent through both the male and female line. (page 218)

Conjugal family   A family unit formed by marriage, centering on the husband-wife relationship rather than the relationship with biological relatives. (page 213)

Consanguine family   A family unit consisting of biological relatives. (page 213)

Egalitarian family   A form of family organization in which the husband and wife regard each other as equal in authority and privileges. (page 217)

Endogamy   The custom requiring marriage in one's own group. (page 226)

Exogamy   The custom requiring a person to marry outside his own group. (page 226)

Extended family   A family unit that consists of a nuclear family plus one or more relatives living together. (page 214)

Family group   A relatively permanent group of two or more people who are related by blood, marriage, or adoption, live together, and cooperate economically. (page 212)

Family of orientation   The family into which an individual is born and in which the major part of his socialization takes place. (page 207)

Family of procreation   The family formed by an individual when he marries and has children. (page 207)

Homogamy   Marriage between individuals of similar socioeconomic, racial, ethnic, and religious background. (page 226)

Kin group   A group of people who are related by common ancestry or origins, not all residing in a common household. (page 212)

Matriarchal family   A form of family organization in which the mother is dominant. (page 217)

Matrilineal descent   Descent through the female line. (page 218)

Matrilocal residence   The custom for a married couple to reside in the wife's parental household or community. (page 217)

Monogamy   Marriage which involves one husband and one wife at the same time. (page 228)

Neolocal residence   The custom for a married couple to reside apart from either spouse's consanguine relatives. (page 218)

Nuclear family   A unit of family organization consisting of a couple and their children. (page 213)

Patriarchal family   A form of family organization in which the father is dominant. (page 216)

Patrilineal descent   Descent through the male line. (page 218)

Patrilocal residence   The custom for a married couple to reside in the husband's parental household or community. (page 217)

SUGGESTED READINGS
AND RELATED RESOURCES

I   READINGS IN SOCIOLOGY

Becker, Howard, and Reuben Hill, eds. *Family, Marriage and Parenthood.* 2d ed. Boston: D.C. Heath, 1955. An extensive collection of essays by behavioral scientists, this book includes a typology of family systems, the social functions of the family, the implications of the customs surrounding betrothal, husband-wife interaction, and a section on marital and family problems.

Farber, Bernard. *Family: Organization and Interaction.* San Francisco: Chandler, 1964. This book would be a good follow-up for students interested in further pursuing many of the aspects of the family covered in this chapter.

Frazier, E. Franklin. *The Negro Family in the United States.* Abr. ed. 1939. Reprint. Chicago: University of Chicago Press, 1966. First published in 1939, this study of the Negro family in America, from slavery through the first third of the twentieth century, has become a classic.

Goode, William. *World Revolution and Family Patterns.* New York: Free Press, 1963. Goode believes there is a worldwide trend toward the conjugal family; he analyzes changing family patterns from data collected in Africa, Arabic Islam, the West, China, Japan, and India.

Kephart, William. *The Family, Society, and the Individual.* Boston: Houghton Mifflin, 1966. Kephart discusses the family from historical, sociological, and psychological perspectives. This book could be used as a basic introduction to the study of the family.

Miller, Daniel, and Guy Swanson. *The Chang-ing American Parent.* New York: John Wiley, 1958. This empirical study points out the differences in the means and the normative content of socialization among American social classes.

Sears, R., E. Maccoby, and H. Levine. *Patterns of Child Rearing.* New York: Harper & Row, 1957. This study is based on data collected from 379 American mothers on how they rear their children; it points out differences and similarities of patterns of socialization.

Winnicott, Donald. *The Family and Individual Development.* New York: Basic Books, 1965. In his discussion of socialization Winnicott emphasizes that the maturation process for the individual is almost wholly dependent on the environment created by the family.

Young, Michael, and Peter Willmott. *Family and Kinship in East London.* London: Routledge & Kegan Paul, 1957. In this study of a working-class community, it was found that extended family relationships were still quite strong, and that family members felt obligated to remain in the same neighborhood and find jobs for relatives.

Articles and Papers

Chamblis, Rollin. "Married Students at a State University." *Journal of Educational Sociology* **34**, 9 (May 1961):409–416.

Glick, Paul. "The Family Cycle." *American Sociological Review* **12**, 2 (April 1947):164–174.

Nelson, Joel I. "Clique Contacts and Family Orientation." *American Sociological Review* **31**, 5 (October 1966):663–672.

Parsons, Talcott. "The Kinship System of the Contemporary United States." *American Anthropologist* **45**, 1 (January–March 1943):22–38.

Pitts, Jesse R. "The Family and Peer Groups." In *The Family,* edited by N. W. Bell and E. F. Vogel. New York: Free Press, 1960.

Spiro, Melford. "Is the Family Universal?" *American Anthropologist* **56** (October 1954): 839–846.

Strauss, Murray A. "Conjugal Power Structure and Adolescent Personality." *Marriage and Family Living* **24**, 1 (February 1962):17–25.

II RELATED RESOURCES
Nonfiction

Bowlby, John. *Child Care and the Growth of Love.* Middlesex, England: Penguin, 1957. This concise presentation of how maternal deprivation affects the emotional growth of a child and his behavior as an adult was prepared for a United Nations Commission. The book discusses ways to prevent maternal deprivation.

Lewis, Oscar. *Five Families.* New York: Mentor (Paper), 1959. This study focuses on the daily life of five families who represent a cross-section of Mexico today.

Mace, David, and Vera Mace, eds. *Marriage East and West.* New York: Doubleday, 1960. Primarily a descriptive work, this study compares the values, customs, and functions related to marriage in the Orient and the West. The Maces document the change in Western society toward the "democratic family."

Wickes, Frances. *The Inner World of Childhood.* New York: Signet Books (Paper), 1968. The crucial relationship between parent and child is examined in this book; it emphasizes the influence this relationship exerts on the child's relationships outside the family.

Fiction

Faulkner, William. *As I Lay Dying.* Middlesex, England: Penguin (Paper), 1963. The successive episodes in the death and burial of Addie Bundren are recounted in this novel by various members of the family circle. As the story unfolds, the members of the family reveal their desires, fears, and rivalries.

Markandaya, Kamala. *Nectar in a Sieve.* New York: Avon (Paper), 1954. This is a story of a simple woman of India, her husband and children, and their struggle to survive against nature, changing times, and poverty.

Styron, William. *Lie Down in Darkness.* New York: Signet Books (Paper), 1960. This is the story of Peyton Loftis, the daughter of a wealthy Virginia family, and her desperate search for love and understanding. It revolves around Peyton's life with her family—her indulgent father, her stern mother, her pathetic sister—and the men who were a part of her search for identity.

Puzo, Mario. *The Godfather.* New York: G. P. Putnam's Sons, 1969. This novel provides an interesting view of a family subculture as one son after another is persuaded to take an active part in saving the dwindling fortunes of a Mafia family.

Paton, Alan. *Too Late the Phalarope.* New York: Charles Scribner's Sons, 1953. The son of a white South African family has an affair with a black girl, and the family closes in upon itself. An excellent example of the pressure toward conformity exerted upon an individual by a primary group.

Films

The Crowd (Silent). King Vidor, 1929. Lower-middle-class family life in a New York apartment house is poignantly portrayed in this film classic.

Goodbye, Columbus. Stanley Jaffe, 1969. This story of a young Jewish girl's first love affair illustrates how a middle-class family can determine values for its children—even when the children try to break away.

The Graduate. Mike Nichols, 1967. The hero of Mike Nichols's film is an alienated college graduate; the story focuses on his perception of his family's way of life, at a time when he is caught in the panic of his own self-discovery.

7 Social Stratification

No society has ever been studied that is without some system of stratification. Stratification *is a social pattern based on the ranking of individuals and social positions in terms of the distribution of the desirable elements, both material and emotional, which society has to offer. Sociologists believe that human social stratification is primarily socially devised, and is an inevitable accompaniment to the basic features of social organization. Many believe that it also has a biological basis, however, and they point to the basic forms of stratification that exist in other primate communities. As a matter of fact, some sort of stratification can be found in all higher animal communities. There is a pecking order in chickens, an organization of hunting packs in wolves or lions, and a division of all such communities into leaders and followers.*

In many obvious ways, both people and animals are differentiated genetically. Some are smart, some are retarded, some are strong and some are weak, some are large and some are small. They are further differentiated within their lifetimes by other biological factors. Some are old, some are young, some are healthy and some become ill or crippled by accidents. Out of nothing more than these various biological differentiations, there will arise a hierarchy in animal communities. At the top are the males in their prime, followed by the immature males, the females in their prime, the immature females, the old of both sexes, the ill of both sexes, and the very young. This is a hierarchy based on the ability to survive, with the most able at the top and the least able at the bottom. The leaders, by superior strength, force cooperation and obedience from the rest of the group.

*When we speak of human social stratification we mean something much more complex than a hierarchy based on sheer physical power. Humans have increased their capabilities to survive by creating complicated forms of social organization, with a wide-ranging division of labor which soci-*ologists call social differentiation. *Such organization improves the efficiency of man's attempt to master the environment. People are assigned positions in the social order on the basis not only of their biologically inherited assets and physical strengths, but also on the basis of their achievements in life. Leadership and power over others is not given just to strong men, but also to men who, for example, have earned the respect of their fellow men through good works: a wise judge, a good governor, an able chief.*

Stratification and inequalities are inherent in social life, then, not only because of inborn differences among individuals (and innate differences in physical environment—for example, rich deposits of natural resources among groups and nations); they are also inherent because social positions of unequal importance seem to be necessary for the smooth functioning of human social organization. A certain amount of inequality also results simply from the ever fluctuating conditions of life, which bring good luck to some, bad luck to others.

Sociologists have been interested in social stratification for a long time, for a variety of reasons. Just knowing what the desirables are in a society tells us a good deal about that society. If we know where a person ranks in the stratification scale, the research findings that have accumulated enable us to tell much about that person, including his life style, his chances for a successful marriage, and his outlook on life itself. Finally, knowledge of the stratification system or structure of a society tells us a great deal about stability and change in that society.

1 THE DISTRIBUTION OF DESIRABLES

All systems of social stratification are built on the natural inequality between men. All men may be *created* equal in terms of human rights, according to the Constitution, but from the minute they are born, they are faced with inequality. This is because the supply of the desirable things is limited, so that there is inevitably some degree of unequal distribution.

Sociologists have singled out three principal categories of desirables which are especially important for social stratification—wealth, power, and prestige. These are sometimes called the "rewards" of society, but that term can be misleading to the beginning student, since it may imply that those who have these rewards have somehow done something to deserve them, that they accompany merit. However, that is not always the case. For example, a young man may be born to inherit a fortune already in trust for him, so that no action of his own can possibly influence the time or amount of his inheritance; a child born to a king has prestige at birth, and power as soon as he is old enough to exercise it. So we must realize that social rewards are not necessarily given for good behavior, although of course they may be; frequently they are given to the person who happens to be in the right social position. It might be more accurate to call these society's assets, rather than rewards.

WEALTH

Wealth in a general sense means not only money, but all the economic assets of a society—the material products, land and natural resources, and productive labor services. Some of the things called "wealth" may be valuable because of the hours or skill of labor that went into making them, some because of aesthetic or even emotional reasons, some because they will bring future economic rewards. The pyramids of the Egyptians were valued because of the innumerable hours of slave labor and the engineering skills it took to build them; also because they held valuable art and literary treasures, and because they were sacred. They would be less valued if built today because with modern construction techniques they could be built quickly, with far less labor. Diamonds are valuable because of their scarcity and beauty. A letter autographed by George Washington is valuable because it is rare, and has historic, patriotic, and sentimental appeal. Land is valued in the degree to which it can be utilized to bring other economic rewards. Wealth is often defined as stored labor, but actually it can represent the storage of other valuable assets as well, such as beauty, sentiment, knowledge, or future economic opportunity.

Everyone would like to possess wealth, but some people always go without. The inequality of wealth distribution exists on an international scale. In Haiti, the annual per capita income (average income per person) is $80, while in the United States it is fifty times that, $3,910. Such inequalities among nations are partly based on differing amounts of natural resources in the territory claimed by each country, partly on the varying successes of different economies, and partly

Elaborate vaults are required to protect material assets. In addition to using the cash-storing facilities of banks, individuals frequently rent safe deposit boxes to store other forms of wealth such as jewelry, securities, and important legal documents. *(Photo by H. Armstrong Roberts)*

on the possession, or lack of, armed might and other kinds of power which allow some countries to appropriate the commodities they want from weaker nations.

The same inequality of wealth distribution is continued within the boundaries of our own country, and it is patterned by place of residence, by race, by education, by occupation, and by many other variables. To demonstrate the regional inequalities, consider the fact that the per capita income in Mississippi is $2,561 a year, while in Connecticut it is $4,807, or nearly twice as much. Furthermore, figures show that per capita income is now increasing much more rapidly in the southwestern and western states than it is in the East and the South.

Looking at the racial pattern of unequal distribution of wealth, we find that only 9.5 percent of whites have incomes that were below the figures designated by the federal government as poverty levels, while 31 percent of nonwhites fell into that category. The median family income in 1972 was $10,236 for a white family; $7,117 for a Mexican-American family; $5,279 for a black family; and less than $2,000 for an Indian family. These income differences are even more significant when you remember that the family size of whites is on the average the smallest of all the groups, so that the lower incomes of nonwhites generally must meet the needs of more people.

Other figures indicate the degree of inequality in the distribution of wealth even more dramatically. There are 5.3 million poor families in the United States, and 12.2 percent of our population has an income below the poverty level. Yet the average household income in Clayton, Missouri, an exclusive suburb of St. Louis, is $36,777! Many other similar communities, such as Westport, Connecticut, and Fairfax, Virginia, have average household incomes of well over $20,000 a year. The wealthiest 5 percent of families in this country receive about 20 percent of the total income.

The novelist F. Scott Fitzgerald said, "Let me tell you about the very rich. They are different from you and me," to which Hemingway is supposed to have made the sarcastic reply, "Yes, they have more money." But sociologists confirm the truth in Fitzgerald's observation that wealth affects personality and behavior. Possession of wealth alone is not enough to guarantee a high social status, and wealth may not always be able to buy power and prestige, although often it can do all of these things, but wealth does affect the nature of one's relationships with others in the society. It improves one's chances of doing well in nearly every field of endeavor; it even improves one's chances of living to a ripe old age. Many of these advantages will

FAMILIES BY INCOME LEVEL IN THE UNITED STATES: 1971

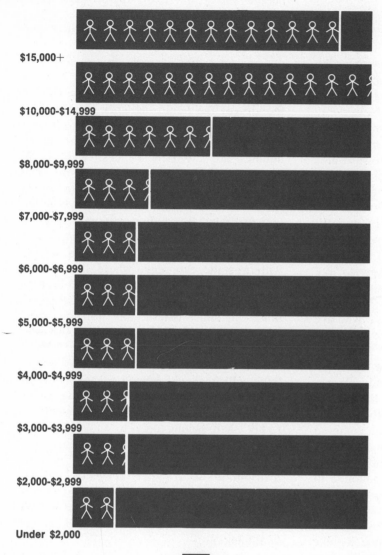

$15,000+

$10,000-$14,999

$8,000-$9,999

$7,000-$7,999

$6,000-$6,999

$5,000-$5,999

$4,000-$4,999

$3,000-$3,999

$2,000-$2,999

Under $2,000

each   represents one million families

In 1971 as many families had incomes over $10,258 a year as had incomes below that level; so in 1971 our median income was about $10,000.

SOURCE: U.S. Bureau of the Census, *Current Population Reports,* "Consumer Income," series P-60, no. 83, July 1972 (Washington, D.C.: Government Printing Office).

be discussed later in more detail in "The Consequences of Stratification." Wealth also evokes certain characteristic kinds of social behavior, such as the need and desire of the rich to set themselves apart from the not-so-rich masses. An extreme example of the latter

effect of wealth can be seen in Howard Hughes. In his younger days, when he was only moderately rich, he was often seen out in society, and photographed in night clubs with a beautiful movie star on his arm. The richer he got, the more secluded his life became, so that today only a handful of people can be sure he is really alive.

If wealth affects its possessors, the lack of wealth has an even greater effect. For example, the anthropologist Oscar Lewis felt that the conditions of poverty generate a sub-culture, that is, a set of values and behavior patterns unique to the poor. Basing his views on comparative studies in Mexico, New York, and Puerto Rico, Lewis suggests that the "culture of poverty" includes such characteristics as a fatalistic attitude toward life, a lack of initiative and achievement motivation, and strong feelings of alienation, helplessness, dependence, and inferiority.[1]

In our society, the incidence of poverty shows a marked pattern; the have-nots are not distributed at random. Figures show that the poor of America are likely to live in a city, to belong to a family that consists of more than five persons, and to have no male head of the household. People who are over sixty-five and under sixteen comprise more than 55 percent of the poor. Poverty is also common among those who are nonwhite and those who have little education— every year of schooling adds dollars to an annual income. As we examine these facts, we begin to see the emergence of a common denominator. Generally speaking, those who are limited in what they are able to consume are those who are less productive in economic terms. They are too old or too young to work, their employment is severely limited by lack of education or by discrimination, or they must stay at home to take care of dependent children; these people are seldom economically productive, at least as measured in our American market system. In our society, the amount a family consumes is tied to the value of what the family produces. Or to put it another way, wealth in the form of income is our society's reward for economic productivity. Of course,

not all unproductive people are poor; many people have inherited wealth and never worked for a living.

It should be stressed here that this norm, while it may seem quite natural to us, is *not* universal. For example, in a society with an extended rather than a nuclear type of family organization, wealth may result from the ties of the family network. In the Trobriand Islands, the richest man is the one with the most brothers-in-law and the largest families are the richest ones; whereas in America, the largest families are more likely to be the poorest ones. In our society, which is based on the experience and expectation of a continually expanding economy, the common belief is that wealth is something a person can—and must—earn. But in a society with a static economy, where the amount is limited and the limitations are broadly known, wealth is more likely to be something one must inherit, and not something tied to personal achievement. As another variation, in societies organized on a communal basis, wealth is considered to be something which should belong to all people as they need it—"from each according to his abilities, to each according to his needs"— rather than belong only to those who are economically most productive.

Other aspects of the problem of unequal distribution of a society's wealth are discussed in "The Consequences of Stratification" later in this chapter, and also in chapter 8: Ethnic and Racial Minorities, and chapter 9: Education.

POWER

Of the three categories of desirables important to social stratification, power is the hardest to measure with any demonstrable accuracy. Most studies on power represent nothing more than an average of guesses about where that power is located; many forms of power are so well concealed that only its holders are aware of its location.

We should distinguish here between two kinds of power—personal and social. An indi-

1. Oscar Lewis, *A Study of Slum Culture* (New York: Random House, 1968). See also Charles A. Valentine, *Culture and Poverty* (Chicago: University of Chicago Press, 1969).

THE TERRIBLE PEOPLE

People who have what
they want are very fond
of telling people who haven't
    what they want that they
    really don't want it.
And I wish I could afford
to gather all such people
into a gloomy castle
    on the Danube and hire
    half a dozen capable
    Draculas to haunt it.
I don't mind their having
a lot of money,
and I don't care how they
    employ it,
But I do think that they
damn well ought to admit

they enjoy it.
Some people's money is
merited,
And other people's is inherited,
But wherever it comes from,
They talk about it
as if it were something
you got pink gums from.
This may well be,
But if so, why do they not
relieve themselves of
the burden by transferring
    it to the deserving poor
    or to me?
Perhaps indeed
the possession of wealth
is constantly distressing.
But I should be quite willing

to assume every curse
of wealth if I could
    at the same time
    assume every blessing.
The only incurable troubles
of the rich are the troubles
that money can't
    cure,
Which is a kind of trouble
that is even more troublesome
if you are poor.
Certainly there are lots
of things in life
that money won't buy, but
    it's very funny—
Have you ever tried to
buy them without money?

From *The Face Is Familiar* by Ogden Nash, by permission of Little, Brown and Company. Copyright, 1933, by Ogden Nash.

vidual has *personal power* when he is able to choose the direction and quality of his own life, and when he can avail himself freely of the things society offers. In practical terms, in our society, this generally means belonging to the dominant culture of the group and having an adequate amount of money to purchase goods and services. Poor people, minority groups, the very young and the very old, and immigrants who can't speak English usually have little personal power. They cannot pursue goals of their own choosing nor live in the way they wish; instead their lives are dictated by the limitations of their circumstances and the whims of other members of society.

Since personal power is so closely related to possession of wealth, the unequal distribution of wealth guarantees the unequal distribution of personal power. There have been increasing attempts in this country to provide various kinds of personal power for all citizens, regardless of their ability to purchase it for themselves. Free legal assistance, civil rights legislation, tenants' as-sociations for those who live in government-subsidized housing projects, and birth control clinics for the poor are all mechanisms whereby the poor can broaden their personal power and increase their freedom of choice. We believe that everyone should have personal power over his own life. To the reader, perhaps that sounds obvious, because we take for granted the ideals of our culture. But other periods in history, and other cultures, have viewed personal power quite differently. Many groups have, at one time or another, been deprived of personal power— the young, the poor, women, minority groups, and persons in a slave status. The concept of universal personal power is a twentieth-century idea.

Another kind of power is *social power*, which means the capacity to make decisions which shape and direct social life— for the entire society, the local community, or even a small group. It is this kind of power, the power to guide the lives of others, that is so hard to identify. Making lists of the powerful is practically a national hobby in America. *Esquire* magazine publishes several articles every year telling its readers who has power in government, in business, in education, and even in the radical movement; *Fortune* magazine tries to identify the most powerful men in the business world, presumably for the convenience of its readers who might have to deal with them. *New York* magazine tells us annually who are the ten most powerful men in New York City (and why) as well as who wields the power in the worlds of education, art, and politics. Newspapers run long columns about which government officials are really the most powerful and which local businessmen are able to influence City Hall in the direction they wish. All these lists have at least one thing in common—it is difficult to tell whether they are right or wrong.

Sociological studies of power have become quite common in the last two decades. Many have focused on a particular community or complex organization. An early approach to sociological research in this area was to ask interviewees to name the people they believed had the power in the community or organization. When the results of these lists were averaged, those named most often were regarded as being the major powerholders and were called the "power structure." This method, called the reputational method of status determination,[2] has proven to be quite successful in determining symbolic power and prestige, which are primarily reflections of the way others in society see a person. But the reputational method cannot reveal whether those reputed to be powerful actually exercise power. Such studies, then, can tell us something important about the stratification and functioning of the community: they can tell us which people are commonly *thought* to be powerful.

A more recently developed method of studying power is to observe the actual decision-making processes, analyzing the personal interactions which occur to reveal who actually wields the power. This is sometimes called the behavioral approach.[3] In important areas of power, however, this course is rarely open to sociologists, because decisions of great social importance are nearly always made secretly or in private. An investigator might question those people reputed to be powerful about the extent of their power, but there is no way of demonstrating the accuracy of their comments, and one can think of many reasons, both conscious and unconscious, that a person might have for misleading the investigator.

The subject of power, who holds it, and how it is exercised, produces a good deal of professional disagreement. This is due to differences in ideology among sociologists, as well as to the difficulties lying in the way of accurate research. Some sociologists maintain that social power in America is concentrated in the hands of a very few people, whose backgrounds are so similar that they tend to act in concert. For example, C. Wright Mills set the number of important social powerholders at no more than three hundred.[4] Other sociologists believe that in our country social power is exceptionally fragmented, divided among many groups and individuals, and that decisions that are workable can only be made when all these power sources come into some sort of balance and agreement.[5] Sociologists generally agree, however, that fewer and fewer social decisions—in politics, business, communica-

2. See Floyd Hunter, *Community Power Structure* (Chapel Hill: University of North Carolina Press, 1953); and Lloyd Warner, Marchia Meeker, and Kenneth Ellis, *Social Class in America* (New York: Harper Torchbooks, 1960), pp. 73–78.

3. See William Spinrad, "Power in Local Communities," *Social Problems* 12 (Winter 1965):335–356; and Nelson W. Polsby, *Community Power and Political Theory* (New Haven: Yale University Press, 1963).

4. C. Wright Mills, *The Power Elite* (New York: Oxford University Press, 1959), p. 10.

5. For example, see Talcott Parsons, "The Distribution of Power in American Society," in Parsons, *Structure and Process in Modern Society* (New York: Free Press, 1960).

tions, education, and other fields—are being made at the local level and more at the national or society-wide level. National organizations and the federal government now are the prime locations of power.

Sociologists also agree that all formally stated power structures can be misleading; the real power may lie elsewhere. This is true in all areas where power is exercised, including the government. There is often a difference between who is *supposed* to be powerful and who *really* is. For instance, presidents of large corporations can turn out to be mere figureheads, whose function is mainly to look impressive, whereas decisions about the running of the company are made by some energetic junior executives in alliance with a few of the directors. There is reason to believe that some important national decisions, which are popularly supposed to be made by the people's elected representatives in the legislature, are actually made by certain powerful career military men and big business executives, whose names and faces are largely unknown to the general public.

Power may on occasion exist independently of wealth—not all rich men are powerful and not all powerful men are rich—but generally the two categories show a high degree of association. Wealth can sometimes help to buy power, as evidenced by the acknowledged fact that a career in national politics has become to a large extent the prerogative of the rich: note, for example, the Kennedy brothers, the two Rockefeller governors, Senator Percy, and Governor Reagan, to name only a few men who were millionaires and became politically powerful. On the other hand, power is often used to acquire wealth. How many legislators and major executives retire in poverty?

PRESTIGE

The third category of desirables that is important in social stratification is prestige. *Prestige* may be defined as the favorable evaluation and social recognition that a person receives from others. This is the subjective dimension of social stratification. There are many kinds of prestige, such as public recognition and fame, respect and admiration, honor, and esteem. Often the term *esteem* is used only to refer to an evaluation of the personal qualities of an individual, or how well he performs a certain role. A good janitor can thus be held in high esteem but he will not have great prestige.

There are a variety of ways to gain prestige. Acts of kindness, generosity, bravery, creativity, or extraordinary intelligence are usually rewarded by the granting of prestige by the beholders. Sometimes money can buy prestige, and sometimes power can demand it, or at least its outward appearance. Prestige usually comes, however, from holding a high social position; and in our society it comes especially from being employed in certain occupations, such as that of physician, scientist, or lawyer.

An interesting clue to the basis of prestige in America is the poll taken annually by the Gallup organization, which asks a representative group of the population the question, "Which prominent man (or woman) do you admire or esteem the most?" From the responses, we can deduce that for Americans, power gives prestige; the president nearly always heads the list, and former Senator Margaret Chase Smith, virtually the only woman to hold national political power over an extended period of time, was a perennial winner in the woman's section. We also grant prestige for personal accomplishment, as can be seen from the fact that recently several astronauts have made the list. Personal conduct is another source of prestige. Ethel Kennedy, who had never been on the list before, was number one in 1968 because of public admiration for her bravery and strength when her husband was assassinated; Mrs. Martin Luther King, Jr., was also on the list that year for the same reason. It is interesting to note that in our society, so often criticized for being excessively materialistic, wealth alone does not give prestige. Men like J. Paul Getty or H. L. Hunt, richer than anyone on the list, have never made it.

The basis of prestige varies from group to group and society to society, for to win prestige one usually must act in accordance with accepted norms and subscribe to commonly held values. In a religious group, a member might win for the strength of his faith, that is, his ability *not* to ask unanswerable questions; yet in a group of intellectuals, it is this very questioning that can bring great prestige. When we speak of a person's prestige in a community or society, it refers to a sort of average and does not necessarily mean that everyone in the society grants the same amount of prestige to a given person.

We might illustrate the different bases of prestige with a case history. Benjamin Spock held a position of great prestige in American society, first because of his occupation as a physician and later because of his fame and success as an adviser to millions of parents on child care. When he began to take part in political activities, his prestige status was changed for many people. To a certain group of Americans, his prestige was greatly lowered because of his involvement with "hippies" or "those radicals," because of his arrest and conviction on conspiracy charges (the conviction was later overthrown, but it was not, of course, removed from memory), and because of his freely expressed antimilitaristic sentiments. These people saw him as a "troublemaker" first and a physician second, and his prestige lowered in their minds accordingly. However, to another group Spock was raised in prestige, because of what they interpreted as moral integrity and courage—for them, these convictions gained him new prestige which, when added to his occupational status, put him even higher on the scale than before.

TOPIC 2 SOCIAL STATUS AND STATUS RANKING

Status in general sociological usage is defined as a position in the social structure of an organized group or society. Each status carries with it a set of rights and responsibilities, that is, a set of roles which describe how the status holder should act, and each status often entitles the status holder to an allotted share of society's assets (for further discussion of this definition of status role see chapter 2). However, when discussing stratification the term is used in a more specialized way to mean a *ranked* position in a social hierarchy or stratification system. It is also used to mean a person's general or total standing in society, a combination of his known statuses. This usage is closely related to the concept of social class discussed in topic 3, and also to the common usage of the term—for example, when we say that a person is of high status.

Each person acquires his general status initially from his family. Children, by and large, do not have a status position which is different from their families. In addition, most wives acquire their status position from their husbands. Thus it is apparent that for some purposes it is the family unit and not the individual which is the basic unit in social stratification.

HOW STATUS IS RECOGNIZED

Since so much of social life is based on the ranking of social positions, the accurate identification of an individual's total social status is quite important. This has become a problem especially in modern urban societies, where many of the people we meet, and about whom we must make quick judgments as a basis for social action, are unknown to us. There are two aspects to this problem of status recognition. First, there must be general agreement about the system of ranking, and second, there must be some common signals which identify the correct status level of an unknown individual.

Suppose that you are at a large party, and a man you have never seen before comes up to you and says, "Hello, I'm Dr. Smith — call me John," and then starts a conversation about how much he likes your hostess's potato salad. If you are concerned with social status, as most of us are, you realize that you must respond to him, and the way in which you respond — the degree of your friendliness — should be governed primarily by the ranking of his status in relation to you. If he has a higher status, you should be respectful; if he is an equal, you should be friendly and chatty; if he is an inferior, the correct behavior may be distant formality. Presumably you already know your own status, but what is his?

Your first and most important clue is that of his occupation, which gives him a certain status. By a little deft questioning, you can find out whether Dr. Smith is an M.D. or a Ph.D., whether he is a general practitioner or a specialist, whether he practices in an expensive private hospital or a public one, and

where his office is located. All of these answers will aid you in fixing his status. If you discovered that he is a brain surgeon at a private hospital with offices in the best part of the city, you would assign him a high status. Your decision is based in large part on a system of ranking you acquired as part of your socialization: you learned that a doctor was respected because you observed doctors being treated with more respect than were other people, or because your parents told you how wonderful they were, or because you watched television programs that depicted doctors as high status persons. Even if you were unaware of the fact that some kinds of doctors have a higher status than others, you would still know the general category of status to which a doctor belongs.

It should be stressed here that there is no single society-wide ranking system that is *always* followed; it differs somewhat from community to community and individual to individual — there is no scorecard that tells all the answers. For example, in New York, the occupation of doctor is not so high a status as it is in Topeka, Kansas. This is because New York has many highly paid workers of other sorts — businessmen, entertainers, tycoons of all kinds — whereas in Topeka, a doctor is probably at the very top of the economic scale. Personal bias also affects ranking. For example, suppose you are a devout member of a religious group that believes in faith healing rather than medical cures. In that case, you would downgrade Dr. Smith's status accordingly, because you would consider him misguided or even a fraud. Or if you were a research scientist who was working in a highly sophisticated and theoretical branch of biophysics, you might feel that the doctor was not "a man of science" but a mere technician, who should be ranked only a few steps above a good automotive mechanic. On the other hand, if a friend's life was saved by emergency brain surgery last year, you would probably grant Dr. Smith a very high status level.

Another important element in status ranking is that it is greatly influenced by the extent of the ranker's knowledge about the status being ranked. For example, when you knew nothing more about Dr. Smith than that he had an M.D., you weren't sure where to rank him; he might have been a small-town general practitioner, and low in status for a doctor, or a world-renowned pioneer of surgical techniques, which would put him far up the ladder. Or suppose you met someone who said he was an ichthyologist; if you didn't know what the word meant, you wouldn't know where to place him. You would have the same problem with someone who called himself "an assistant to the head of the department of removal and disposal of labor-generated industrial debris"— you couldn't be sure whether he was an important corporation executive or the man who sweeps the floor of the factory at night.

In spite of such prejudices, differences in personal experience, or lack of knowledge, there is surprising agreement in our society in regard to many key elements—such as prestige—in status ranking of individuals and occupations.

But now that you have discovered Dr. Smith's occupation, and you have made your judgment about the relative rank of that occupation, you are still faced with one more problem. Is Dr. Smith really what he claims to be? After all, the status of doctor is a high one, which entitles the holder to a variety of social privileges, and many people might like to claim it falsely as their own, just to enjoy those privileges, even if only for the length of one party. But if the system of stratification is to be maintained, it is important to be able to check on the truth of a person's status claims.

There are two principal ways that we can do this. The first is to look for symbols that confirm the person's status, and prove his claim either true or false; we will discuss these below. The other way is to observe how the supposed Dr. Smith interacts with other people. How do they treat him? What do they say about him? How does he behave toward them? This method of observing the way an individual is treated by other members of the group is akin to the behavioral method of status determination used by sociologists which was discussed in the last topic. It is used by ordinary people every day, as they carefully, though sometimes unconsciously, interpret the signals contained in patterns of social behavior.

Returning to our example, you will be able to get some idea of Dr. Smith's status by watching what happens to him during the party. It is a general rule that at a party the guest with the highest status will get the most attention from the host, the greatest number of refills of his plate and glass, the most comfortable (and visible) chair to sit in, and probably also the most people to listen to his stories. The other guests will be allotted their share of desirables at the party—respect of the host, food, comfort, appreciation of their jokes—in accordance with their respective levels of status. However, to be absolutely sure of an individual's status ranking, it is necessary to observe his behavior and the treatment he is accorded in several different groups. It is conceivable that Dr. Smith could be treated as a low status guest at the party because all of the other guests are older and even more successful brain surgeons. Yet his ranking in the society at large is a high one.

STATUS SYMBOLS

It is not always possible to evaluate a person's status by watching his interactions with others who know him, for we often meet strangers in some neutral and impersonal setting. And it is usually impossible for a man to prove to you that he is really a doctor by taking you with him to the hospital to watch him perform an operation, or to convince you of his wealth by showing off his bank book and stock certificates. But his status might be identified by what sociologists call the *status symbol*. A status

Possession of wealth in itself does not confer high social status. Money must be translated into socially recognized symbols. The man who drives a Rolls Royce, orders perfectly iced champagne, and flashes several dozen credit cards conveys a different message about his social rank than a man who drives a Volkswagen, drinks beer, and carefully pays his check in small bills and change. *(Photos by H. Armstrong Roberts)*

symbol can be anything—a possession, a style of dressing, a manner of speech—that represents to others a certain status level.

If someone were in the lowest status level, he obviously wouldn't want to go to all the effort of constructing a symbol of his low status; but one might make the effort to present a high status to the world and to protect that status from being underevaluated. So the farther up the status ladder you

go, the more status symbols you will find. However, it is also true that at the higher levels status symbols get harder and harder for outsiders (that is, people of a markedly different status level) to interpret, or even, in some cases, to notice. Take the example of male attire at work. The difference between the blue workshirt, and the white shirt, tie, and suit is something that everyone can understand. The white shirt, the confining jacket—both say that their wearer does intellectual work, with more prestige and a higher salary than manual labor; therefore, they are status symbols. Most people also recognize the difference between the suit that cost $59.95 in the bargain basement, and the one that cost $200 at the best men's shop in town; this also symbolizes a difference in economic status, since it is assumed that the wearer of the more expensive suit has more money. But not too many people can recognize the difference between a suit that came from a good men's store and one that was made to measure by a custom tailor. Only people of a fairly high social class even know what signs to look for to tell them apart.

Dress is a very popular method of symbolizing status. Of course, dress may symbolize other things as well: the doctor's white jacket symbolizes his occupation and the status due him on its account; the dress made of handprinted fabric from Indonesia symbolizes cosmopolitanism in its wearer, and possibly also the income needed to take a trip to such a faraway place. Cowboy boots and a ten-gallon Stetson hat tell us that the wearer comes from the Southwest.

What is true of dress is true of thousands of other items. A house, a neighborhood, a rug, a choice of words, a breed of dog, a car, a picture on the wall—all these can symbolize a certain status to those who know how to read the signs. We are all skilled at reading and interpreting the symbols that belong to our particular status level, although it is often done so unconsciously that it escapes our attention.

Of course, it is possible for a status symbol to mislead, in the same way that a person might lie about his occupation at a party. A status symbol may be used by a person who does not in truth possess the status. For example, it is quite common for a family to buy a car or a piece of furniture for the living room that it can barely afford, so as to give the impression of a greater wealth status. The typical executive in a large organization may spend money and behave in a way that is more suitable to the next status level above him than the one he currently occupies; he hopes that this will convince his superiors that he should be promoted. As long as he does get the promotion, the raise in salary will presumably cover the extravagance.

Because status symbols can be adopted by those outside the appropriate status group, the most functional symbol is one that is hard to fake. Thus symbols of high status are well hidden. They are expensive. They change frequently, because it takes time for an outsider to recognize the change, and it may take more money than he can afford to keep up with the changes. This explains the faddist aspect of the status symbol—one year, high status people have Yorkshire terriers, and the next year they all have Lhasa apsos.

THE RANKING OF SOCIAL POSITIONS

Now let us turn from the individual's general status or rank to discuss the ranking of the social positions themselves, particularly occupational positions. Why is it that some occupations rank much higher than others?

One factor is the personal characteristics and skills which are required to adequately fill a given status. Thus the status of the college professor is high because people believe that one must be intelligent to teach complex subjects to others, and intelligence is valued in our society. The status of an assembly line worker is lower, because it is thought to require less intelligence and leadership. An assembly worker's greatest assets are a high tolerance for boredom, attention for detail, and perhaps manual dexterity, and we don't consider these qualities as very valuable.

Another factor in status ranking is the amount of training or preparation the status requires, the highest statuses being those which call for the greatest preparation.

A third factor is the social function of the status—that is, the importance the status has for the larger society. This is one reason a judge holds a higher status, and makes more money, than the bailiff of the court. It is also a reason men have traditionally held a higher status than women. In the course of a man's work or career, he may affect the larger events of society (social power), whereas the woman's sphere of influence is more limited to her home and the members of her family. As more women work outside the home, or if we develop a greater appreciation of the social importance of the family, we can expect to see a gradual upgrading of the status of women.

Statuses which rank high in these three respects are usually rewarded with relatively large amounts of wealth, privilege, and power. Wealth and power, in turn, become additional important factors which the members of society use in ranking status and granting prestige.

STATUS HIERARCHIES IN THE UNITED STATES

It is no accident that most of the examples we have given so far pertain to occupational status, for in the United States, it is the most important of the *status hierarchies*. A man's occupation is the single most important factor in determining his overall social position, as well as that of his wife and children. The chart on page 264 shows the way that many common occupations are ranked. You can see that the general tendency is for the occupations that pay best to be at the top of the list, and those with the lowest remuneration to be at the bottom. But this order is not always followed strictly. A Supreme Court Justice, in the number one occupational position, makes $62,500 a year, which is probably less than is earned by a successful physician or lawyer who works in a big city like New York, or a director of a large corporation, or the owner of a successful factory. The status of the Justice is due to his important function in our society, and to the years of education and training he must have before he can reach the Supreme Court. His status is also due in part to his uniqueness, for after all, only nine persons in the entire country can occupy that position.

An interesting study was made, comparing the occupational status ranking of previous decades with that of the present time. Robert Hodges, Paul Siegel, and Peter Rossi found that there has been very little change in the rankings since 1925.[6] A comparison of studies made of the very same occupations in 1947 and 1963 showed an almost perfect .99 correlation. (For an explanation of correlation, see box on page 265.) The only changes noticeable were a slight increase in the status of scientific occupations and a slight drop for "culturally oriented" occupations. Furthermore, Rossi undertook another study, with Alex Inkeles, comparing the status levels of certain occupations in six different countries—the United States, Germany, Great Britain, New Zealand, Japan, and Russia.[7] They found a high level of correspondence in all the countries. This shows that there may be a certain occupational hierarchy dictated by modern industrialism.

Occupation, however, is not the only important status hierarchy in the United States. There is a ranking of status based on skin color: white, yellow, tan, brown, and black. There is a ranking by annual income, from rich to poor. There is a ranking by religion: Protestants are higher than Catholics and Jews, and Episcopalians are at the highest level among the Protestant group. We have already mentioned that males have a status rank above

6. Robert W. Hodges, Jr., Paul M. Siegel, and Peter H. Rossi, "Occupational Prestige in the United States," *American Journal of Sociology* 70 (November 1964): 286–302.

7. Alex Inkeles and Peter H. Rossi, "National Comparisons of Occupational Prestige," *American Journal of Sociology* 61 (January 1956):329–339.

DISTRIBUTION OF PRESTIGE RATINGS

	1963		1963		1963
U.S. Supreme Court Justice	94	Owner of a factory that		Traveling salesman for a	
Physician	93	employs about 100 people	80	wholesale concern	66
Nuclear physicist	92	Building contractor	80	Plumber	65
Scientist	92	Artist who paints pictures that		Automobile repairman	64
Government scientist	91	are exhibited in galleries	78	Playground director	63
State governor	91	Musician in a symphony		Barber	63
Cabinet member in federal		orchestra	78	Machine operator in a factory	63
government	90	Author of novels	78	Owner-operator of a lunch	
College professor	90	Economist	78	stand	63
U.S. representative in		Official of international labor		Corporal in the regular army	62
Congress	90	union	77	Garage mechanic	62
Chemist	89	Railroad engineer	76	Truck driver	59
Lawyer	89	Electrician	76	Fisherman who owns his own	
Diplomat in the U.S. Foreign		County agricultural agent	76	boat	58
Service	89	Owner-operator of a printing		Clerk in a store	56
Dentist	88	shop	75	Milk route man	56
Architect	88	Trained machinist	75	Streetcar motorman	56
County judge	88	Farm owner and operator	74	Lumberjack	55
Psychologist	87	Undertaker	74	Restaurant cook	55
Minister	87	Welfare worker for a city		Singer in a nightclub	54
Member of the board of		government	74	Filling station attendant	51
directors of a large		Newspaper columnist	73	Dockworker	50
corporation	87	Policeman	72	Railroad section hand	50
Mayor of a large city	87	Reporter on a daily newspaper	71	Night watchman	50
Priest	86	Radio announcer	70	Coal miner	50
Head of a department in a		Bookkeeper	70	Restaurant waiter	49
state government	86	Tenant farmer—one who		Taxi driver	49
Civil engineer	86	owns livestock and		Farm hand	48
Airline pilot	86	machinery and manages		Janitor	48
Banker	85	the farm	69	Bartender	48
Biologist	85	Insurance agent	69	Clothes presser in a laundry	45
Sociologist	83	Carpenter	68	Soda fountain clerk	44
Instructor in public schools	82	Manager of a small store in		Sharecropper—one who	
Captain in the regular army	82	a city	67	owns no livestock or	
Accountant for a large		A local official of a labor		equipment and does not	
business	81	union	67	manage farm	42
Public school teacher	81	Mail carrier	66	Garbage collector	39
		Railroad conductor	66	Street sweeper	36
				Shoe shiner	34

SOURCE: Robert W. Hodges, Paul M. Siegel and Peter H. Rossi, "Occupational Prestige in the United States, 1925-1963," *American Journal of Sociology* 70 (November, 1964):286-302.

This chart shows the results of a national survey conducted in 1961 to determine the prestige ranking of various occupations. The figures were arrived at by averaging thousands of responses. These rankings differ very little from those of a similar study made in 1947.

that of females. Another biologically based hierarchy is that of age, and it is interesting that the age hierarchy in modern societies is similar to the one for apes: those in the prime of their maturity, the immature, then the very old, and finally the very young. There is an educational hierarchy, with those who have earned graduate degrees at the top and those who never went to school at the bottom. People who are married have a higher status than those who are either single or divorced; people who live in cities rank above those who live on a farm. Although family background is not so important in America as it is in many countries, there is still a hier-archy based on parentage, with native Anglo-Saxons at the top, and the foreign born and those of non-European extraction at the bottom.

STATUS INCONSISTENCY AND THE MASTER STATUS

It can be seen that everyone belongs to a number of status hierarchies, based on a variety of criteria. It has been found that most people exhibit a marked degree of status consistency; that is, people are at the same level in different hierarchies. A man with high occupational rank usually has a high income rank as well, because of the close

---

CORRELATIONS

Statisticians express relationships between two or more variables by using *correlation*. Correlation is expressed as a scale ranging from −1 to +1. A correlation of either −1 or +1 means that one variable can be used to perfectly predict another variable. If there is a +1 correlation between Factor A and Factor B, then A increases as B increases; with a −1 correlation, Factor A increases as Factor B decreases. A correlation of 0 means there is no relationship between the two factors. In actual scientific research, correlation coefficients of +1, −1, or 0 are rare; most correlations fall between +1 and −1.

It is important to note that if a study reveals a correlation between two factors, that correlation does not necessarily prove that the factors have a direct cause-and-effect relationship; the factors may be influenced by other factors not included in the study. Let's consider an example.

BIRTH CONTROL PILLS

A Survey made in March 1970. Question: "Do you think birth control pills should be made available free to all women on relief of child-bearing age?"

INCOME OF RESPONDENTS	YES	NO	NO OPINION
$15,000 & over	63	26	11
$10,000-$14,999	62	31	7
$7,000-$9,999	56	35	9
$5,000-$6,999	52	39	9
$3,000-$4,999	45	35	20
Under $3,000	37	40	23

SOURCE: *Gallup Opinion Index*, Report no. 57 (Princeton, N.J.: Gallup International, March, 1970), p. 5.

In this example, the correlation between income and attitudes toward free birth control is .185, indicating a very slight positive correlation; that is, there is a slight relationship between a respondent's income and his tendency to answer yes to the question—the greater his income the more likely he is to answer yes.

But these statistics are only as accurate as the data they represent, and one should always read and analyze tables such as this one carefully. How representative is the sample of people chosen to be questioned? Was the question asked clearly? Could the question have been interpreted differently by different respondents? Could there be some reason that many people would not want to answer it truthfully? Do the answers reflect any other attitudes than the one being tested? These questions are clues to some of the other factors that may influence the correlation between income and attitudes found in this study.

interrelationship between wealth and prestige. Because of this advantage, he is able to get married and to move to a good neighborhood in a city. He needed the initial advantages of high status in education, color, and parentage in order to achieve his high occupational rank. Although the various levels may not show an exact correspondence—the very same person may not be number one in every status hierarchy—it is generally true that the people in any given quarter of one status rank will be in the same quarter of the other status ranks. This is the meaning of *status consistency*.

There are numerous cases, however, where a person ranks very high in one category and low in another. This is called *status inconsistency,* and it sometimes creates a serious social problem, both for the individual and for those who must decide how they should behave toward him. Status inconsistency is often the result of an individual's social mobility, whereby the help of education and great personal ability he has risen above the handicaps of color or parentage to achieve a high occupational status. The classic example is that of black physicians.[8] We can now add the even more inconsistent example of the black Supreme Court Justice, Thurgood Marshall; occupationally, he is in the very top status, while racially he is at the bottom level.

Another kind of status inconsistency is that which is built into certain occupations, because they have high prestige with relatively low incomes. The minister is a good illustration of this. Ranked quite high occupationally, he makes much less money than do congressmen, lawyers, dentists, airline pilots, and bankers, to name a few of those who have lower occupational status. Obviously, the average minister cannot afford to live in a way that accords with his occupational status.

Status inconsistency is a difficult problem to resolve. An individual with inconsistent statuses generally claims as his overall level the highest level he has attained, while other people tend to treat him as a member of the lowest status group to which he belongs. For example, the black doctor wants to be given the general status of his occupation, whereas most of the people he meets will be inclined to assign him the lower status of a black man. This often makes the individual feel cheated of his just reward and therefore angry and hostile toward society. The social critic Eric Hoffer has suggested that most social and political revolutions are caused or led by status inconsistent people; he gives the example of the Biblical prophets, who were members of a low peasant class by birth but became allied with the ruling elite by their education as scribes.[9] There is some limited sociological evidence to support Hoffer's idea; for example, persons of inconsistent status are more likely to support liberal and radical movements than are persons of consistent status.[10]

The sociologist Everett Hughes has pointed out that one way status inconsistency is resolved is when everyone agrees that certain status rankings are more important than others.[11] In America, status ranking by race carries great weight. The man who is both black and a doctor, which makes him status inconsistent, will be regarded by society as belonging to the black status rank rather than the doctor's. Hughes calls this the *master status,* meaning that his status as a black dominates whatever other status rankings he may attain. In cases where income and occupation conflict, the master status is determined by wealth status. When a young man from the Rockefeller family becomes a

8. For a discussion of this problem see Everett Hughes, "Dilemmas and Contradictions of Status," *American Journal of Sociology* 50 (1945):353–359.

9. Eric Hoffer, *The Ordeal of Change* (New York: Harper & Row, 1967), pp. 82–89.

10. Seymour M. Lipset, *Political Man* (New York: Doubleday, Anchor Books, 1963), pp. 249–261.

11. Everett Hughes, "Dilemmas and Contradictions of Status."

schoolteacher, he is status inconsistent, but his master status is that of a rich man. In many European countries, family background is a master status and a poor prince is still treated as a prince. In America, such a man's status would be determined by his new income level primarily, with his status as an aristocrat subordinate to that.

A PROBLEM IN STRATIFICATION

The study of stratification is often complex, as we have seen, since many factors must be accounted for when ranks and statuses are measured. One way to better understand the elements involved is to undertake a project to measure some form of stratification. We discussed the National Opinion Research Council rating of occupational prestige and noted that there was no significant change in ratings from the 1947 to 1963 studies. (See figure below.) Below is a project designed to find out if your fellow students agree with the ratings of ten of the occupations, and what criteria they use in assigning such ratings.

Even if you and your class do not perform this project, study the proposal carefully, for the procedures it outlines and the questions it raises are helpful in understanding sociological methods of research.

DIRECTIONS FOR THE INTERVIEWER

Before the interview

1. Prepare for yourself a working copy of Sheets I and II below (be sure your respondent does not see this sheet):

Sheet I   List of Occupations
For each job listed, please pick out the statement which best gives *your own personal opinion* of the *general standing* that such a job has.
1. Excellent standing
2. Good standing
3. Average standing
4. Somewhat below average standing
5. Poor standing

Radio announcer
Civil engineer
Building contractor
Janitor
Physician
Mail carrier
Airline pilot
Clerk in store
Truck driver
Shoe shiner

(Be sure your respondent does not see this sheet.)

Sheet II Sample of Occupations
N.O.R.C.

Occupation	Rank	(1947) Score	(1963) Score
Physician	1	93	93
Civil engineer	2	86	84
Airline pilot	3	86	83
Building contractor	4	80	79
Radio announcer	5	70	75
Mail carrier	6	66	67
Clerk in store	7	56	59
Truck driver	8	59	54
Janitor	9	48	44
Shoe shiner	10	34	33

Interviewer's Results
Rank   Score

2. Choose any TEN students, being sure *not* to interview people presently registered for this course. Also, do not choose your respondents (the people to be interviewed) from homogeneous groups such as fellow fraternity members, dorm residents, etc. All interviewing is to be done without other people being around to "kibitz." You and your respondent should complete the short interview as privately and as free from interference as possible.

THE INTERVIEW

3. Having gotten a willing respondent, hand him the copy of Sheet I, give him a pencil and a blank sheet of paper and have him read the opening statement on Sheet I. Next, have him write the number next to each occupation which he thinks reflects his own personal opinion. If he asks "what do you mean by general standing?" or seeks clarification, *do not* say any more than words which mean the same as "general standing." In other words, do not suggest to him money, prestige, glamour, or anything. Be sure to collect Sheet I and the paper with the rankings on them.

4. After he has completed assigning a value to the list of ten occupations, ask him the following—*being sure to ask the question exactly as written here:* "You have assigned a value of_____ (the value he assigned) to the occupation of mail carrier and a value of_____ (the value assigned) to civil engineer. What is it in your mind that made you feel this way?" Be prepared to write down answers on a separate sheet of paper, and attach it to his previous answers. If he answers something like: "That's how I feel" or "just because," or some equally useless answer, feel free to ask him to be more specific. Note: if by some odd chance he assigned the same values to the two occupations (mail carrier and civil engineer), select some other occupation to which he assigned a different value and ask him the same question as above.

5. Now say the following to your respondent (exactly as written here): "I am going to describe to you a certain kind of person. This person is a man with a college degree, who earns $28,000 a year. He lives in the suburbs with his wife and children, is a family man, and attends church regularly. He is a member of La Cosa Nostra [a Mafia organization], working as an accountant, keeping the books."

How would you rate this occupation?

Why did you give it the rank you did?
Did you have any difficulty in deciding on the rank?

Be sure to write down his answers to these questions also. Next, complete nine other interviews in the same way.

After the interviews

6. This step requires some simple computations. Each occupation has been given a score by ten different people of from 1 to 5. For each occupation, count the number of 1's, 2's, 3's, etc. Then multiply as follows:

Rating	*Multiply by*
excellent:	5
good:	4
average:	3
somewhat below:	2
poor:	1

For example, suppose a building contractor received 5 excellents, 2 goods, 1 average, 2 somewhat below, and no poor grades.

$$
\begin{aligned}
5 \times 5 &= 25 \\
2 \times 4 &= 8 \\
1 \times 3 &= 3 \\
2 \times 2 &= \underline{4} \\
& 40
\end{aligned}
$$

Now, divide the total by 5 (40/5) = 8 × 10 = 80. This is the score assigned by your ten respondents for the occupation of building contractor. Do this for each occupation. On Sheet II, list your results. The rank of each occupation is determined by its score. The occupation receiving the highest score ranks 1, the lowest score ranks 10, and so on.

7. If a difference appears between what you have recorded and the original N.O.R.C. ratings, and the difference is *one rank, or 8 or more points,* consider that difference meaningful.

a. Are there any meaningful differences? What are they? Can you offer any explanation, thoughts, suggestions, ideas, theories, etc., to account for these differences?

b. In comparing the two lists, how do you account for the stability?

8. Given your respondents' answers from item 4 above (when you asked him to justify the values he assigned to the two occupations):

a. Summarize what you see as the main types of answers.

b. From an analysis of these answers, what can you say about the criteria of prestige of occupations in the United States?

c. What ranks were given to the Cosa Nostra occupation? How much agreement was there among your respondents on ranking this occupation? Using sociological ideas about occupational ranking, how might you account for the rankings this occupation received?

9. Most of you were probably able to conduct these interviews very easily and were able to get your college respondents to answer your questions willingly. This, of course, is not an accident. Rather, we can say that your interviewing, and the questions you ask, are "legitimate" in the eyes of your respondents. Suppose, however, you were assigned to do some interviewing in a lower class suburban neighborhood. Your respondents are to be married women. The interview must be conducted in private, since you want to be sure that no one else is listening and may possibly influence her answers. The interview you will conduct is to be identical with the one in this assignment. Do you anticipate being able to get willing respondents as easily as you got willing college respondents? Once you may have contacted some respondents who were willing to be interviewed, do you think the "flow" of the interview would go as smoothly as it did with your college respondents? In sum, what do you think would stand in the way of (1) your ability to get willing respondents, and (2) a flowing interview?

10. Looking over your experiences with these ten interviews, what hints or instructions would you give to someone who had never had any interview experience and was going to do this assignment?

TOPIC

3 SOCIAL CLASS AND STATUS GROUPINGS

We have seen in the preceding section that a single individual or family occupies many different statuses, and that some of them may conflict with others. In general, however, statuses tend to be relatively consistent. They also form a relatively consistent pattern in society as a whole. People of approximately the same general status get lumped into a category together, and there is only a limited number of such categories in each society. These categories, called *strata* or *stratification levels,* can range from being rather loose aggregates of individuals who have nothing more in common than certain shared characteristics that can be similarly ranked, to cohesive groupings of persons who interact together, share the same beliefs and attitudes, and are conscious of

House type provides a fairly obvious criterion of social class membership. A lower-class family would not normally live in an old Victorian mansion; an upper-middle class family would not be found in an isolated and dilapidated wood-frame structure; and an old and aristocratic family would probably not choose a new suburban development home. Type of dwelling is of course related to place of residence, the area where one chooses or can afford to live. *(Photos r.: H. Armstrong Roberts) (Photo l.: Charles Harbutt, Magnum)*

belonging to their group. Most strata in modern societies fall somewhere between these two extremes—they are not merely the artificial creation of the sociologist, but neither are they highly organized and immediately identifiable by society.

Such strata are often called *status groupings* or *social classes,* particularly when they are more than just artificial categories. The term *social class,* given its modern importance by Karl Marx, is often used to mean a status grouping which is based on economic criteria—wealth and access to the means of production. Thus we have Marx's famous class distinction between the bourgeoisie, or those who own the means of production, and the proletariat, the workers who have nothing but their labor power. The meaning of social class has been extended by frequent use, however, so that it now generally means the same as status grouping—people with similar status level and some degree of similarity of behavior and values.

CLASS DIVISIONS

The number of generally recognized social classes or status groupings varies from society to society. So do the differences between the classes (whether in income, power, or prestige), the ease of recognition of a class structure, and the amount of movement of people between classes (social mobility). We speak of greater class divisions in a society, when the "distance" between classes is great, the awareness of class is high, and the social mobility is low.

At the one extreme is India, where until recently the caste system of social classes was formally defined. Caste divisions were further reinforced by legal means: stepping outside the caste boundaries was a punishable offense. There were four major castes, but well over a thousand subcategories had been established, each with its own traditional occupation, place of residence, and pattern of behavior with other castes. An Indian (or at least an Indian of Hindu religion—Moslems have no place in the caste system) knew from very early childhood what caste he belonged to, and he soon learned to recognize the characteristic marks and dress that identified members of other caste groups. At the other extreme is the United States. Class divisions in America tend to be quite blurred: the differences between classes is not so great, the awareness of class is not so high, and there is more social mobility than in India and most other nations of the world. This is not to say that class divisions do not exist in the United States, however. The cherished myth of a "classless society" is still believed by many people, but one of the outstanding contributions of sociologists in the first half of this century was to point out the role that class divisions and inequality still play in our society—a society which values the ideal of classlessness.[12]

How much class consciousness and social mobility exist in America will be discussed in the next two topics. Here we shall discuss what the major class divisions are, and the somewhat different life styles by which each division is characterized.

Some sociologists prefer to use only three class categories: the upper class, middle class, and lower class. Lloyd Warner, the author of a classic study of American social stratification published as "The Yankee City Series" in the 1940s, established six categories, dividing each of the major classes into an upper and lower level.[13] Warner's system of class division is the one still used most frequently by sociologists, although it is common to find some special variation in each different research project. For example, the study by Harold Hodges, which is reported in the abridgment accompanying this chapter, uses only five classes, omitting the distinction between lower-upper and upper-upper classes. Some additional useful differentiations of the middle class have been introduced by other sociologists, who speak of the "blue-collar middle class," "white-collar middle class" and "professional middle class."

12. Charles H. Page, *Class and American Sociology* (New York: Schocken Books, 1969).

13. Warner et al., *Social Class in America.*

DETERMINING CLASS DIVISIONS

How do we determine the major class divisions, and who is a member of which class? All sociologists agree that there *are* social classes here, but they differ on what criteria are best used to distinguish among them. The problem is that class differences are a matter of degree on several different status dimensions; there are no clear-cut and sharp distinctions as there often are, for example, in determining who is and isn't a member of a certain organization. Since every class represents an average of status traits, there are also millions of individual variations within each class.

Sociologists have established many quantitative measures for class membership, and these indicators have been used widely; they are, however, subject to many limitations. Suppose, for example, that the amount of annual income is made the prime factor, and lower-middle-class income is defined as being between $6,500 and $8,500. Now look at some examples that fall within this category. You have the forty-year-old foreman of an assembly line in a factory; the young recent college graduate who is teaching in public school in a big city; a wholesale meat salesman of sixty who is past his earning prime but not quite ready to retire; and a widow who collects that amount of income from yearly dividends of the American Telephone and Telegraph stock that her husband left her. It is obvious that these four have very little in common aside from their income figure, and yet they would all be placed in the same status category.

Nevertheless, there do exist some statistical indicators of social class which have some degree of validity. Warner's "Index of Status Characteristics" uses six different criteria: occupation, amount of income, source of income, house type, residential location, and amount of education. August Hollingshead constructed a rather similar type of multiple-item index.[14] An ingenious device for the same purpose, but not very valid, is S. F. Chapin's Living Room Scale.[15] It consists of an evaluation of the kind of furnishings and decorative objects, and their condition, that are found in a family's living room; the scale can be filled out by a researcher in about five minutes and has the advantage of requiring no direct information from the person being studied.

Statistically, it is much easier to categorize the upper and lower class than the middle. The extremes of very high and very low incomes are relatively easy to establish; so are the extremes of luxury housing and dwellings without adequate room or sanitation. The lower class stands out in its marked lack of education; occupationally, too, it is distinct, filling the jobs that call for very few skills. So in a sense what we have is a rather clearly defined class at either end of the spectrum, plus all the people who fall in between—the heterogeneous and statistically difficult to characterize middle class.

CLASS AND LIFE STYLES

Having a large income and living in a mansion in the best part of town does not guarantee membership in a high social class; one must also share the general life style that is associated with that class. Class differences in life style are hard to measure accurately, and yet we are all aware that they exist. For example, a typical worker in a Ford body plant might spend his Saturday night watching television and drinking beer with his brother, neighbor, and cousin, while his wife and theirs sit in the kitchen drinking coffee and talking about the children. But that is not how the president of the Ford Motor Company spends his Saturday night, and if he did, people would be surprised.

In the Hodges abridgment, many descriptive illustrations of these class differences are mentioned. As you read, notice especially the differences in attitudes and values from

14.   August B. Hollingshead and Frederick C. Redlich, *Social Class and Mental Illness* (New York: John Wiley, 1958), pp. 387–397.

15.   Stuart F. Chapin, "A Quantitative Scale for Rating the Home and Social Environment of Middle Class Families in an Urban Community," *Journal of Educational Psychology* 19 (February 1928):99–111.

Here we see evidence of two different life styles of American social classes. The upper-middle or upper-class group on the top is attending the opening of an art exhibition. The people in the group on the bottom are in shirt-sleeves and wear enthusiastic expressions as they root for the home team; Hodges says that such spectator sports are especially popular with the lower and lower-middle classes. (Photos by Ken Heyman)

class to class. The middle class aspires to improve its social position; the upper class doesn't need to, and the lower class doesn't have much reason for hope. The middle class encourages its children to be creative and independent; the lower classes want them to be "good," that is, to behave themselves. The upper class tends to treat religion as primarily a social function, while to the others, especially the lower classes, it is more likely to be a matter of real substance. Many other such distinctions can be drawn.

These class differences are perpetuated from generation to generation. In the family, in peer groups, at school (higher classes send their children to private schools which will socialize them to different norms and values from those of the public school), the children are taught the behavior which accords with their class. Even in public school, there is evidence of differential socialization. For example, it has been found that teachers often expect less in the way of academic achievement from lower-class students, and give them less encouragement to prepare themselves for careers requiring expensive educations their parents could not afford, or careers which would remove them from the surroundings of their family and friends. (This is discussed in more detail in chapter 9.)

HAROLD M. HODGES, JR.
A Contemporary Study of Social Class in the Metropolis

From "Peninsula People: Social Stratification in a Metropolitan Complex," in Clayton Lane, ed., *Permanence and Change* (Cambridge, Mass.: Schenkman, 1969), pp. 5–36.

Introduction

This article was published in 1962, as a partial report on a research project that had already been going on for six years.

It was Hodges' belief that the classic studies of social stratification, such as Warner's "Yankee City" and Hollingshead's "Elmtown," pertain to a vanishing America, the small and stable community of yesterday's memory. America today is a nation of city-dwellers and suburbanites, who move frequently and must create their own stability. Hodges chose to focus his study on the area of metropolitan and suburban San Francisco, using a variety of study techniques such as questionnaires, clinical tests, and in-depth interviews. Hodges cautions the reader of this article: "The class portraits which follow must be recognized for what they are: mere partial vignettes, tapping what appear to be certain class-related characteristics among given people at a given time. They cannot be safely generalized to the whole of the American population. Some distinctions will seem ruthlessly pat and others make-shift and tentative. The vast majority of the conclusions are based on statistical examina-tion of empirical evidence; others are more impressionistic, deriving from analyses of tape-recorded interviews, responses to open-ended questions, and Rorschach protocols. The reader, lastly, must con-stantly remind himself that tags of identity, no matter what their technical validity, are forever in danger of glossing over a central truth: however else we might define or categorize him, every last person on earth is an individual, unlike any other human who has ever existed."

Lower-lower class:
despair, anger, apathy

Of every six Peninsula families, at least one inhabits this lower-most position in the class hierarchy. Occupationally, the man at this level is an unskilled "lower-blue-collarite"; but his employment is characteristically sporadic and marginal, his marketable talents are few, and he is the last to be hired and the first to be fired. He entered the labor arena in his middle teens after dropping out of school just short of the eighth grade, he was still a teenager when he married (a legal formality bypassed by at least one "husband" in ten at his class level), and he fathered the first of his four or five children before he was old enough to vote. He had achieved social and legal adulthood at an age when his upper-middle-class contemporaries faced another five years of schooling and celibacy.

If his marriage has endured—and the odds are just short of even that it has not or will not—he is likely to find that it is strife-ridden; he rarely admits an abiding love for his wife and his children, and he is plagued by in-law troubles.

The lower-lower-class Peninsula dweller lives in cramped quarters, enjoying at best a minimal level of sanitation. Although the monthly family income of the LL—about $250—is the most he has ever realized (more than two wives in three at this level are gainfully employed outside the home), it is consumed more rapidly than it is earned. Only occasional items in his household have not been purchased on an installment plan, and he is perennially in debt.

Virtually every one of the LL's major life goals has somehow been thwarted or stifled. It may be hypothesized that the "cultural deficiency" which inhibits so many LLs is due in the main to (1) a set of values and traditions "inherited" from his three in four grandparents who came from rural or village areas and/or (2) a simple adaptation on the part of a vulner-able and insecure person to what must cer-tainly seem an omnipotent and brutal environment. Perhaps the greatest incum-brance is the LL's pervasive sense of close-ness to kin. Despite the frequency of bitter husband-wife conflicts, the LL seems especially fearful of venturing beyond the familiar confines of his family group; although he "neighbors" more frequently and intimately than those in other levels, he derives the greater part of his psychic support from intimate interaction with relatives: from visits to taverns, front-porch gossip, and watching the fights on tele-vision with brothers, brothers-in-law, or same-sex cousins. In consequence, he is more unwilling than any to leave "home" for better employment opportunities, he possesses an abiding sense of loyalty toward kinfolk (an unwritten code of mutual aid prescribes that near relatives come to one another's unstinting assistance in times of trouble), and, perhaps most importantly, his network of lower-class convictions,

habits, and life styles is consistently reinforced and insulated by his like-minded
relatives. The latter, predictably, live nearby,
almost half of all LLs—in comparison to
one in ten middle-class Peninsulans—claim
close relatives living within a four-block
radius of their own dwellings.

It is the LL who most readily concurs
that "the wife's place is in the home"
(with LL wives in hearty accord!), that the
husband should "run the show" and that
the child is ideally obedient, quiet, and
even servile to parental dictates. The errant
baby or child is punished with dispatch and
often with harshness for "being bad"—for
toilet accidents, messiness, crying, fighting,
and above all, sassing or talking back.

For many LLs, particularly the elderly,
the most effective way of coping with life
appears to be a reaction blended of apathy
and resignation. They belong to few or no
formal organizations except for the Roman
Catholic or Baptist churches. Some of the
younger LLs are disinterested members of
trade unions and a sparse handful of the
older still claim memberships in fraternal
orders, but for most social life is limited
to relatives and occasional neighbors.
Nor is the LL ego-involved in his community. "Girlie" and movie magazines,
the television and comic sections of the
newspaper: these are among his rare links
with the larger world of affairs. His, it
seems evident, is a fatalistic what-can-
I-do-about-it, why-bother, universe; he
has retreated into the comfortable worm-like
sanctuary of the cocoon.

Upper-lower class:
Marlboro man . . . or milquetoast?

In many telling and predictable ways the
upper-blue-collarite (approximate statistical
markings: he comprises one-third of the
Peninsula's residents, completed 10 to 11
years of schooling, reaps a $5,500–$6,500
annual family income, and occupies a semiskilled or skilled occupational status) is less
like the white collarites just above him

than he is like his LL peers. Thus, the UL
is like the LL—only "less so"—in his proclivity for authoritarian, anomic,
misanthropic, and patriarchal values; he is
almost as intolerant of Mexican-Americans,
Oriental-Americans, and Negroes, and is
even more anti-Semitic.

But undue stress on the similarities between
those in the two blue-collar levels might
belie the even more numerous dissimilarities
which amply warrant the conclusion that
the UL inhabits a class level distinctly
his own. In contrast to the LL, the UL seems
infinitely more confident and ebullient;
he is less concerned with his self image
among strangers and, unlike the LL, rates
himself as aggressive and friendly rather
than shy and uncomfortable with strangers.
By way of amplification, the UL is the
apparent personification of the "Marlboro
Man": he describes himself as "strong
and silent," "tough-minded," and
"manly"; he is less forgiving than any of
"sissiness" in men and boys; his favorite
movies and television shows are horse operas;
John Wayne and Clark Gable are his professed ideals. He is far and away the most
avid outdoorsman, hunter, and fisherman,
the heaviest of smokers. He likes beer, and
poker is his card game.

Yet in a puzzling reversal of form, the UL
is apparently plagued by "status concern."
One of life's most important goals, he
declares, is "raising one's social position";
and most vital of all in choosing a career
(even more vital than income and job satisfaction) is the prestige which attaches to
it. Neighborhood status competition is also
of disproportionate concern to the UL;
and he more than any would admit to
"extreme disappointment" were his similarly circumstanced neighbors to acquire
newer and bigger cars, extensively remodel
their homes, or buy their wives expensive
furs. Somewhat perversely, too, this
self-styled he-man is likelier than the male
at any other level to help his wife with
such womanly domestic chores as grocery

shopping, dishwashing, and tablesetting.

The UL's leisure-time pace is less restricted than the LL's; not so given to such passive entertainment as movies and television, he is an ardent baseball, boxing, and wrestling fan, bowler, and do-it-yourself addict. Likelier than the LL to entertain friends he met at work, more than four in five of his and his wife's most intimate acquaintances are classifiable as ULs. And when he and his wife do act as hosts, they eschew bridge, rarely serve hard liquor, and tend to break up into all-male or all-female gossip groups. The UL is more active in clubs than the LL; he tends to prefer such veterans' organizations as the American Legion or V.F.W. and occasional fraternal orders (in particular the Elks); she is especially active in the P.T.A. and in auxiliaries to her husband's clubs.

Lower-middle class:
puritanism, frugality, and the Bible

If his UL next-door neighbor stands out as a distinct sort, so does this salesman, clerical worker, foreman, lathing contractor, and proprietor of the corner drug store. In a real sense his social class level is the most variant and unique of all; yet in another, concrete context, he represents that most illusive of all animals: the "typical" American.

His is what has been called the "level of the common man." And though barely one in three Peninsula-dwellers are members of his class, his common-ness is not a qualitative matter, but a quantitative one. For he is the mythical average man in many ways. His traits include an annual income of between $8,000 and $9,000, a high school diploma, and a tract home in the suburbs. The LM is virtually the "common denominator" that purveyors of the mass media speak of so fondly. Take, for example, his consumption preferences in four of the media. "His" magazines — *Life, Reader's Digest, Saturday Evening Post,* and *Ladies' Home Journal;* his television menu —

Perry Mason, The Untouchables, Gunsmoke, Jack Benny, and Groucho Marx; his pet comic strips — Gasoline Alley, Dixie Dugan, Mary Worth, Dick Tracy, and Joe Palooka; his cinema preferences — for five successive years, his favorite movie stars were rated first in "box-office appeal" by *Variety* — all have time and again been recognized as national favorites.

A person who is puritanical is one who is "extremely or excessively strict in matters of morals and religion"; this would seem an apt description of the LM. At no other level was there such rigid insistence upon toeing the ethical and sexual line: upon righteous conduct and conformance with accepted standards of goodness and honesty. "Sex" is a naughty word to many a LM, and he is less at home than most with an off-color joke. In a somewhat related sense, he expresses the greatest degree of fear that his own son or daughter might depart from the appropriate sex role — that his son might be thought a sissy or his daughter a tomboy and unladylike.

If puritanism is a central LM trait, so is the "Protestant Ethic." The characteristic LM belief that hard work, frugality, saving for a rainy day, and proving oneself in the marketplace are virtues: these are characteristic of the LM. A third major component value system is religiosity; it is a dominant motif in his life. He claims the most frequent church attendance (half his numbers attend weekly), active memberships in church-related clubs, Bible reading, and beliefs that biblical precepts are of paramount importance for children and adults alike. Like the blue collarites, his ranks include more Roman Catholics than adherents of any other single faith; yet in a relative sense the most characteristic LM denominational preference is Methodist.

Less "organization prone" than the UMs, the LM still belongs to many clubs; but his favorites are the fraternal order (especially the Elks, Shriners, Masons and Oddfellows), the chamber of commerce, and assorted religious auxiliaries. He, more than any, is a baseball aficionado, and it is his sons who provide the bulk of Pony and Little League rosters. But no one is more of a homebody than the LM; he spends more time than any at the family dinner table, on family vacations and weekend auto trips, and barbecuing and gardening in the back yard. His, in fact, is the sole level where husbands claim greener thumbs than wives.

In a stark economic context he is this era's "forgotten man." Most consequentially, his is the only level where the value of the "real" dollar has actually shrunk; to purchase basic staples he, unlike the majorities in other class levels, must work longer hours in the 1960s than he did in the 1950s. In the critical dimension of power, too, his lot appears to be worsening; in the battle of giant vested interests his chamber of commerce is certainly no match for the N.A.M. on the one hand and the A.F.L.-C.I.O. on the other.

Upper-middle class:
tomorrow's American

If the Peninsula's LM approximates the "average" American, his peer in the next-highest status niche may be said to depict the American of tomorrow. It is well documented that yesterday's UM Peninsulan was the first to adopt what have now become nation-wide fancies: the split-level ranch home, the Ivy-League style in men's clothes, the sports car, the barbecue addiction, and the hi-fi craze, to mention the more obvious.

Scarcely one subject in seven, characteristically the professional, semi-professional, independent businessman, or corporate employee who has gone a year or two beyond his A.B. degree, belongs to the UM level. Yet his numerical insignificance is abundantly offset by his disproportionate influence.

What are the distinctive qualities of the UM? No one word describes it. But the words flexible, trusting, democratic, tolerant, and nondogmatic come most quickly to mind. Thus, though by several measures the most

"child-centered" of all subjects, the UM parents appeared to be less anxious and more easy-going in the sphere of child-rearing and disciplining. They are more tolerant and understanding of children's tantrums, messing, fighting, and sassing. Deviates, too—delinquents, homosexuals, and drug addicts as well as such lesser norm-flouters as people who swore, drank excessively, professed atheism, or engaged in extra-marital affairs—incurred less wrath from UMs than from those at other levels.

Almost three-fifths of the UMs were, in terms of their parents' class levels, "upward mobile." And the key to their mobility, especially if they were 45 or younger, was the college diploma. "Education" and "career"—and the two are indissolubly linked—may be said, in fact, to be the most focal UM concerns. At the family dinner table, at parties, in terms of values they would instill in their children, "career" crops up again and again as a central UM value. And when he is not talking "shop," it appears, the man at this level is talking education—especially to his children. Even as early as the kindergarten-primary years, he apprehensively scans his children's school performances less for signs of social adjustment than for indications of academic competence. Where, at lower levels, the parents might stress toughness and obedience, or morality, frugality and religiosity, the UM parent urged his children to attain top academic marks and win out in classroom competition.

It is unquestionably at this level that "organization proneness" most emphatically prevails. It is not, however, the lodge or fraternal order that the UM joins, but the service club: Rotary, especially, and the likes of Kiwanis, Lions, professional societies, and the big-city chambers of commerce. UM wives, too, are the most avid clubwomen. They prove likeliest to pack the seats at neighborhood improvement meetings, to belong to garden, alumnae, and bridge clubs, and to campaign vigorously for charitable enterprises. What is more, she, like her husband, is frequently elected president of some such group. And her children, too, are elected to school offices more frequently than others and belong to more such organizations as Boy Scouts and Girl Scouts.

The UM is not very "religious." He takes his religion more socially than literally, more ceremoniously than moralistically. It is into three denominations in particular that the UM respondents have elected to move: Presbyterian, Episcopalian, and Congregational. While the matter of marriage is relevant, it should be noted that the broken-marriage rate is lowest of all at the UM level: less than one marriage in ten had been dissolved by divorce, separation, desertion, or annulment.

UMs were plainly more sophisticated and more discriminating than any but the uppers in the arena of leisure. The fine arts—ballet, opera, symphonic music, the theater, poetry, literature and graphic art— drew their most enthused devotees from the UM class. They read more books. They rarely attended motion pictures, but when they did they typically preferred foreign and art fare or sophisticated comedy; representative of their favorite stars were Greta Garbo, Marlene Dietrich, Audrey Hepburn, Cary Grant, Jack Lemmon, Alec Guinness, Jimmy Stewart, and Peter Sellers. Their television tastes were similar to their cinematic: they rarely watched television and the one half who did watch on other than special occasions averaged less than 20 minutes a night in front of their sets.

Upper class:
eccentricity, ancestor worship, and insouciance

Numerically insignificant—less than one in every five hundred Peninsula families is listed in the *Social Register*— the upper class is nonetheless highly influential as a reference group: a membership to which many aspire and which infinitely more consciously or unconsciously imitate.

The ranks of the upper class are only rarely characterized by conspicuous and showy consumption: costly debuts, mansions, hosts of servants, gala parties, glittering limousines and furs; this is the rare but publicized side of the coin. Not opulence and certainly not ostentatious display, but more nearly "inconspicuous" consumption—tweeds, flat shoes, battered stationwagons, quiet parties. There is, of course, a minority "jet set" which boasts a faster, more public, life, and there are many in the U ranks who are ultra-fashionable in the realms of clothes, homes, and cars, and others still who boast chauffeurs and $100,000 homes. But the upper class cannot be legitimately assessed in such terms.

However conservative or however flamboyant, the U is heavily addicted to a seemingly unending chain of parties big and small, dances, charity balls, first nights at the theater and opera, and frequent sorties to the Sierra ski slopes, resort homes at Lake Tahoe or the beach, and his box seats for the baseball games. He drinks more frequently—and more heavily—than those at other levels, but he is less given to smoking. When he entertains, he is likelier to host bigger parties than the UMs—or smaller; for most typically he and his wife will entertain another couple with dinner followed by bridge or dominoes. He likes formality: white-tie affairs, and at work, dark or banker's gray suits with vests. His wife often prefers simple and basic black.

The U is likeliest of all to live in the city. He attended school at either Stanford, California, Yale, or Harvard (his mean educational attainment is equal to that of the UM). She was likelier than he to have gone to a private school and thence to Stanford, California, Vassar, or a two-year finishing school in the East. Fewer Us attend church than those at any other level. More than half are nominally Episcopalians, but fewer find themselves at church on Sunday than for weddings.

The U is in many ways more akin to the lower than the middle classes. Like the LL, he is more tradition-oriented, and like the Ls in general, he claims to be tougher-minded, more introvertive, and in accord with the ideals that husband and parents should be dominant. He is less permissive than the UM parent toward infants and children, and like the L favors obedience and quietness. Even more than the UM, the U appears to be at home among others, more insouciant and at ease no matter what his current social surroundings. Not quite so flexible and democratic, certainly not as gregarious and empathic, he seems in many ways the most non-conforming and individualistic of all Peninsulans. Much of his social life and public decorum is rigidly straitjacketed by custom, yet he is frequently given to eccentricities which are rare at other levels: to a curious blend of formality and casualness, diffidence and outspoken candor, of reverence and irreverence toward tradition.

Conclusion

In undertaking this study, Hodges' main concern was to try to discover whether or not social status distinctions such as occupation, income, and prestige levels are associated with distinctive cultural patterns and personality types. He succeeded in identifying five distinct class-based subcultures or life styles that existed in the San Francisco metropolitan region. These groups differed not only in occupation and income, the class distinctions which first come to mind, but also in such far-ranging areas as basic values and attitudes, personalities and dispositions, and cultural interests and recreation.

We must stress once again the caution that Hodges himself gave at the outset of the article. These are not hard and fast lines of division, and the classes which are described here are not definite and easily identified groups of people. They tend rather to be loose and constantly fluctuating clusters of people within a broad continuum. We must avoid the dangers of caricature and stereotype, of rigid adherence to the distinguishing class factors described here, for these factors were true only of one place at one time; other cities, or San Francisco in other decades, may be stratified quite differently. For example, what we today call middle-class values may in the future be found infrequently in the middle class but perhaps quite commonly in the lower classes. This flow of class distinctions from one group to another is already evident with such formerly middle-class possessions as automobiles and television sets.

TOPIC 4 SOCIAL MOBILITY

Social mobility is the term used to refer to the movement of an individual from one status to another. In common usage, social mobility has a favorable connotation of improvement, of moving upward. However, upward mobility is only one of the three major kinds of social mobility. An individual may also move to a lower status (downward mobility) or to a new and different status that is approximately equal to his old one (horizontal mobility).

The phenomenon of social mobility is exhibited by all societies, but not in the same degree. As we shall see, there are certain conditions which favor great social mobility, and others that tend to restrict it. We

Brown Bros.

C. Wright Mills (1916–1962) felt that the sociologist should not be content with merely studying society; he ought also to play a significant role in changing it. It was his conviction that American life was in need of radical reconstruction, and that it was up to this society's intellectuals, especially those with a training in sociology, to point the way. Through his writings and his teaching career, he was a major founder of the movement known as radical sociology. Influenced by both Marx and Weber, Mills concentrated on the study of the classes created by American industrial bureaucracy. His best-known works are *The Power Elite* (1956), *White Collar* (1951), and *The Sociological Imagination* (1959). *(Brown Bros.)*

should stress here that one should *not* assume that social mobility is always beneficial. On the contrary, there is evidence that mobility sometimes has undesirable consequences both for the society and the individual.

OPEN AND CLOSED SOCIETIES

Stratification systems in societies may be compared in terms of the ease and frequency of changes in rank position, or the degree to which members are permitted to attain higher statuses through their own achievements. A perfectly open society, which exists only in theory, would be one in which every individual could achieve the status for which his natural talents, abilities, and inclinations

best suited him. Statuses which can be gained by some direct effort of the individual, often through competition, are called *achieved statuses*. The best examples are most occupational positions in modern societies. An open society would not be a society of equals; there would still be inequality, but it would be based solely on merit.

A completely closed society, also purely theoretical, would be one in which every individual was assigned a status at birth, or at a certain age, which he could never change, either for better or worse. Such statuses are called *ascribed*. The usual basis of ascribed status is parentage; a child inherits the social class of his father or mother. But status assignment could be based on some other factor—for example, the region in which the child was born, or the time or circumstances of the child's birth. We see an example of the influence of this latter factor from time to time; the Dionne children achieved fame, a certain kind of prestige, and gifts of money because they were born as a set of five—an unusual occurrence. In a completely closed society, no individual action, no outstanding merit or scandalous misconduct, could alter one's ascribed status.

All societies range between the extremes of open and closed; they consist of both achieved and ascribed statuses in varying proportions. An example of a rigidly stratified, relatively closed society is that of India before the time of Gandhi, when the caste system was legally enforced. Yet even this society afforded some examples of mobile individuals. For instance, a talented individual could occasionally marry into a higher caste, or acquire patronage and the means of an education and a better occupation from someone of a higher caste. Such an individual, and certainly his children, would move into that higher caste. Sometimes even whole groups could be mobile, and the exact hierarchical ranking of the many castes has often been revised to account for such a change. By accident of low birthrate or faulty geographical distribution, there may not be enough individuals of the right caste to perform a certain necessary function of service—not enough warriors to make up an army, for example. What happens then is that another caste (a lower one—a higher one would not be interested) is given the opportunity to adopt that occupation. As members of the lower caste take up the new occupation, they acquire the higher status that goes with their work. With many members of the caste becoming upwardly mobile, the entire caste eventually takes on the improved status, and even those who did not move into the new work benefit from it.

Where does the United States fit on the open to closed continuum? It has traditionally been called the "land of opportunity," meaning specifically the opportunity for social mobility in an upward direction. However, a study made at the end of the fifties by Seymour M. Lipset and Reinhard Bendix, entitled *Social Mobility in Industrial Society,* indicates that the United States today probably offers neither more nor less opportunity for social mobility than does any other industrial society.[16] It is just as easy to climb the social ladder in Great Britain, or West Germany, or Russia, as it is here. Still, along with these and some other modern countries, we do occupy a position toward the top of the scale of social mobility. This and other studies have indicated that a fully industrialized, bureaucratically organized society is the most open, and the United States is one of a small handful of such societies. The most closed society is likely to be a preindustrial, or agricultural, society that is organized on the basis of kinship.

KINDS OF MOBILITY

Earlier, we listed the three kinds of mobility—upward, downward, and horizontal. Although all three kinds will be found more often in an open society than in a closed one, there are certain factors in the open society

that may favor one kind of mobility over another.

Upward mobility

Thomas Fox and S. M. Miller undertook a research project with the object of identifying the basic determinants of mobility, in many different nations.[17] Their research identified two main factors that seem to encourage a high degree of upward social mobility: a large educational enrollment and an advanced stage of development of an industrial economy. As a society becomes more and more industrialized, the unskilled and low-salaried jobs at the bottom of the occupational status rank are slowly eliminated, for these are the jobs than can most easily be performed by machines. On the other hand, more jobs are added at the middle and upper levels, to manipulate and control the flow of machine-produced goods and information. The vertical mobility resulting from such system changes is usually called *structural mobility.* As these opportunities become available, they remain useless unless the children of lower-level parents can be educated so that they have the knowledge and training that will equip them for these higher positions. Compulsory public education and the opportunity for low-cost, unrestricted college attendance provide this necessary second factor. This is one reason education has become such an important institution in modern society.

Once a society has provided the conditions that will permit, or perhaps actually encourage, upward mobility, the next question is: which individuals from the large lower-level population are going to seize the opportunity? We have some answers to this question from statistical comparisons of upwardly mobile and nonmobile individuals.[18] Typically, the upwardly mobile man lives in a city;

16. Seymour M. Lipset and Reinhard Bendix, *Social Mobility in Industrial Society* (Berkeley: University of California Press, 1959).

17. Thomas G. Fox and S. M. Miller, "Economic, Political and Social Determinants of Mobility: An International Cross-sectional Analysis," *Acta Sociologica* 9 (1965):76–93.

18. Lipset and Bendix, *Social Mobility in Industrial Society,* pp. 73–74.

Programs such as this Head Start class try to provide greater educational opportunity for members of low status groups, by giving them an early introduction to the skills they will need to compete successfully in school. *(Photo by George W. Gardner)*

he was either the only child of the family, or else had only one sister or brother; in his home, his mother was the dominant influence; he acquired more education than did either of his parents; he married relatively late and often into a status level slightly above his own (the classic example is marrying the boss's daughter); he deferred having children for several years after marriage and limited his family to two children. We can generalize to say that this pattern speaks of the conservation of resources, the intentional limiting of obligations and responsibilities outside of work and career to a manageable minimum. The individual who follows such a life pattern often exhibits not one but two aspects of upward mobility: he is mobile in generational terms, achieving a higher social class for himself than that of his parents (*intergenerational* mobility) and he is mobile in personal terms (*intragenerational* mobility), advancing his social level throughout the course of his career.

We might illustrate upward mobility with a real-life case, that of Arthur Goldberg. He was born into a low social level, for his father was a Jewish immigrant from Russia, a peddler of fruits and vegetables. Goldberg was not typical of the upwardly mobile individual in one respect, for he came from a large family and was the twelfth and last child. But in other characteristics he follows the pattern we have mentioned. He came from a large city, Chicago; his mother was the strongest influence on his home life; he struggled to get a good education, ending up with a graduate degree in law; he married only after his education was finished, and to a girl whose parents had a higher status than his did (she was well-educated also, and worked for a time when they were first married, another frequent occurrence in upwardly mobile families); he had only two children. Goldberg was generationally mobile, in that as a lawyer he achieved a higher status than his father did as a peddler. He was personally mobile too,

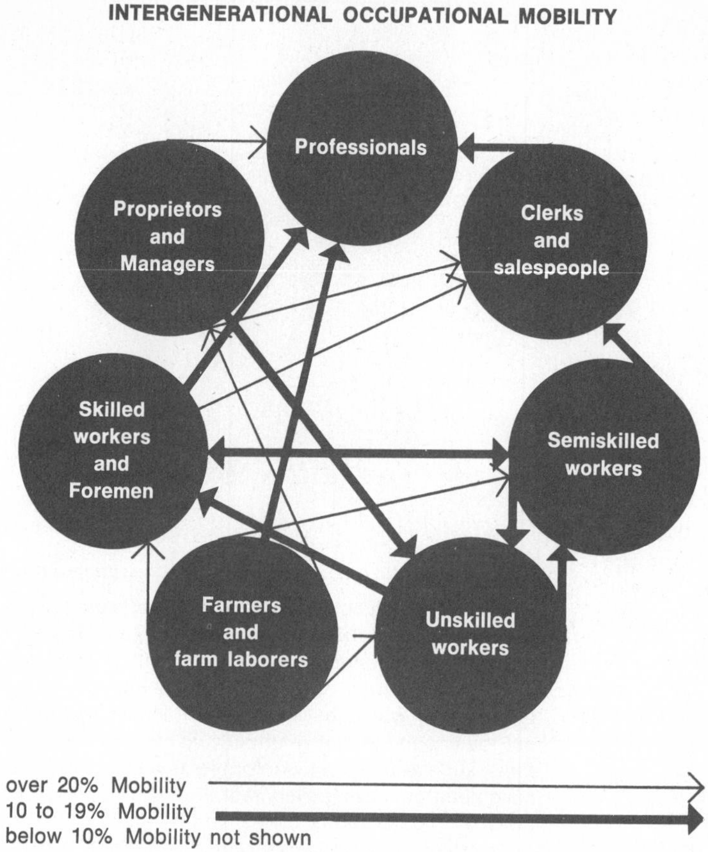

INTERGENERATIONAL OCCUPATIONAL MOBILITY

over 20% Mobility
10 to 19% Mobility
below 10% Mobility not shown

This chart diagrams the frequency and direction of social mobility from one generation of a family to another. Note that the children of unskilled and semiskilled workers are the least likely to move out of their fathers' occupational status rank.

SOURCE: Adapted from NORC sample of 1,334 Men in 1947. Published in Reinhard Bendix and Seymour M. Lipset, eds., *Class, Status and Power,* (New York: Free Press, 1953), pp. 424–425. Originally published in National Opinion Research Center, "Jobs and Occupations: A Popular Evaluation," *Opinion News,* vol. 9 (September 1, 1947).

going from the level of private lawyer to counsel for an international labor union, and then on to cabinet member and the number one occupational level, Justice of the Supreme Court.

Downward mobility

Common sense might suggest that the conditions which lead to downward mobility are simply opposites of those mentioned as encouraging upward mobility. In some cases this is true. For example, being born into a very large family is sometimes a cause of downward mobility, as the family cannot provide education and other advantages for all the children, and some must fall down to the next level. Sometimes this natural problem is aggravated by customs such as primogeniture (favored, for instance, by the English aris-

tocracy), whereby the lion's share of the parents' possessions passes to the firstborn male of the family. This assures that the family fortune and power will remain concentrated in the hands of the one heir rather than become the diluted inheritance of many children, but it also means that all the other children will fall to a lower social status than that of their parents and their favored brother.

Likewise, failing to get an education, marrying very young, and raising a large family can all cause downward mobility. But some situations are more complex, and a simple reversal of upward mobility factors will not lead to downward mobility. We have said that living in a city is a cause of upward mobility; the research of Fox and Miller showed that living in a city also caused downward mobility. In other words, city life is conducive to mobility of all kinds, whereas those who live in small towns are generally less mobile. We must be careful, therefore, to distinguish between factors which prevent upward mobility and those which produce downward mobility.

Horizontal mobility

The third kind of mobility is that of moving from one status to its equivalent. Little research has been done in this area, so the causes of horizontal mobility are not as well known. One obvious explanation is simple personal inclination. A college graduate with a degree in chemistry had planned to work in the research department of a large chemical company, but after a year he finds that the work seems dull and repetitive, with no improvement in sight. He quits and becomes a professor of chemistry at a nearby university instead. He likes the job and the people he works with. His mobility involves no essential change of status, because the two occupations are at roughly the same level; it was simply a move to a more congenial job.

It has been observed within large organizations that horizontal mobility may be caused by manipulation from higher levels of the bureaucracy, and it may be designed to serve as a camouflage for lack of upward mobility. Offering an employee who is expecting a promotion a new job in another office may distract his attention from the fact that the new job is not really at a higher level than his old one, and thus keep him content. On occasion, politicians use the same strategy. For example, following the Civil War when black Americans demanded an improvement in their status, they were offered the concept of "separate but equal"; in most cases it proved to be a horizontal change only, with low status for blacks still the prevailing norm.

CONSEQUENCES OF SOCIAL MOBILITY

It is often assumed that social mobility is an unqualified good. Research does not support this assumption. Mobility can have

Brown Bros.

Thorstein Veblen (1857–1929) was an early and forceful critic of modern commercial society in America. Trained as an economist, he turned to writing speculatively regarding the effects technology and industrial bureaucracy would have on society. He also pointed out the economic motive underlying many social customs, such as women's conformity to fashion and the male habit of shaving every morning. The social functions of "conspicuous consumption" and "conspicuous waste" of economic resources were analyzed in his most famous work, *The Theory of the Leisure Class* (1899). *(Brown Bros.)*

serious disadvantages, both for the mobile individual and for the society.

It is easy to understand that downward mobility can cause stress for the individual, and studies bear out this fact; for example, Warren Breed found that suicide rates are markedly higher among the downwardly mobile than either the nonmobile or those who are mobile in other directions.[19] But what is not always realized is that upward mobility can also cause great stress. Mobility has been linked to schizophrenia and psychoneurosis.[20] Mobile persons exhibit more prejudice against

19. Warren Breed. "Occupational Mobility and Suicide among White Males," *American Sociological Review* 28 (April 1963): 179–188.

20. A. B. Hollingshead, Robert A. Ellis, and E. Kirby, "Social Mobility and Mental Illness," *American Sociological Review* 19, no. 5 (October 1954):577–583.

people of low status than do nonmobile individuals at the same level. Mobility puts a great strain on the relationship between parents and children. Allison Davis undertook a study of the effect of upwardly mobile parents on their children. He found that

In training their children toward upward mobility, such parents really teach the child that he must become superior to them. The child who accepts this orientation must learn early not to fly in the face of authority. He must become a "diplomat in aggression" with his parents as he will later need to be with his social class superiors. The aggressive feelings he may have toward his parents must be transformed into competitiveness and initiative. He must learn how to impress and how to become accepted by persons more powerful than he. He must be able to give up the identity he derived from his family and become identified with a group whose ways he has not yet learned. He cannot learn from his parents the folkways, mores, norms, and values of this reference group, yet he must know them to be accepted in the social circles to which he aspires. Sometimes the task is too great—the child may move downward in his search for identity, choosing radical groups, identifying with out groups, marrying "out," or giving up the effort to form any identity at all.[21]

Many studies of the effects of mobility have focused on a crucial question: the conflict between the norms and values of the social class to which one was socialized in childhood, and those of the social class into which the mobile individual moves. This problem exists no matter what the direction of the mobility; it is often just as hard for an upper-class person to learn the correct behavior and acquire the value system of the middle class, as it is for a middle-class individual to move to the upper class.

Mobility can also have disadvantages for the society at large. High rates of mobility may mean that many individuals will be moving too fast and too frequently to be assimilated into their new levels, leading to the possibility of serious social strain. Moreover, a society with great visible social mobility, and especially a society like ours that attaches a high value to upward social mobility, has the problem of arousing expectations in many individuals who will not be able to fulfill them. Everyone wants to be upwardly mobile, but only a small proportion of the population can actually succeed in this goal. The phenomenon of rising expectations has surely played a role in the recent increase in civil strife in this nation. However, a recognition of the stresses of mobility may be changing our values, with job satisfaction slowly being substituted for job advancement.

But it would be just as bad for the society if mobility were extremely low. The closed society would soon become so inefficient that it would be unworkable. Parentage is no guarantee of capability, as a look at the history of any hereditary monarchy will show. A father of extraordinary ability may have sons of only mediocre talents, and vice versa. So there must be a way for high-born oafs to sink into obscurity, and for talented men of lower classes to rise to positions of power and influence; a closed society is too extravagant of human resources. It does not encourage achievement from everyone.

Another drawback of very low mobility is that it leads to resentment or despair, or even open aggression on the part of those who are forever trapped at the bottom of the system. Although most people, even in a society as open as ours, will not succeed in becoming upwardly mobile, the fact that it is a possibility serves as a source of hope and contentment for many lower status individuals.

It is interesting to speculate about a future society based almost entirely on merit.[22]

21. Thomas E. Lasswell, *Class and Stratum* (Boston: Houghton Mifflin, 1965), p. 108, summarized from Allison Davis, "Personality and Social Mobility," *The School Review* 65 (Summer 1957):134–143.

22. Michael Young, *The Rise of Meritocracy* (New York: Random House, 1959).

Think of the psychological consequences on those persons of lowest status who were at the bottom because they knew, and everyone could rightly conclude, that they truly lacked merit! They could not justifiably complain about the inequities of "the system"; there would be no hope for future advancement. Based on recent trends, however, we are not moving toward that state of affairs very rapidly. Several studies have indicated that in recent decades the United States has moved very slowly, if at all, toward a more open society.[23] Indeed, the amount of vertical mobility in the United States today is only a very small percentage of what it would be if people born at all levels had a truly equal chance to attain any given status.

23.   These studies are summarized in Gerhard E. Lenski, *Power and Privilege* (New York: McGraw-Hill, 1966), p. 415.

TOPIC

5 THE CONSEQUENCES OF STRATIFICATION

We have already pointed out in this chapter many instances of the widespread influence of social stratification on society and on daily human existence. In this final section we shall discuss more fully the far-reaching consequences of the uneven division of society's resources.

Some evidence has been presented above to show the effect of social class membership on a person's life style. Where and at what a person works, the values he believes in and tries to live by, the activities and interests of his leisure time, the visible and tangible proofs of esteem he receives from other members of the society—these are all directly associated with social status. But that is not the limit of status influence. Status also helps to determine how long a person lives, whether he will be sick or well, and whether or not he can exercise freedom of action and choice. We refer to these basic conditions as *life chances*—the probability that an individual will attain or fail to attain important goals and experiences in life.

The consequences of stratification for society also have been the subject of much study and concern to sociologists. Two persistent themes, which will be discussed below, are (1) the degree and nature of class consciousness, and (2) the disruptive presence of class conflict.

LIFE CHANCES

We have already emphasized the fact that a key to the best and most favorable life chances is wealth, and that when wealth is unequally distributed, life chances will be also. In our country, the richest 10 percent of the population receives an estimated 27 percent of the total national income, while the poorest 10 percent of the people receive only 1 percent;[24] so there is no question that the poor-

24.   Editors of *Fortune, The Changing American Market* (Garden City, N.Y.: Hanover House, 1955), p. 262.

Two-thirds of the arrests made in every major city of the United States take place among only about two percent of the population, from the segment where the infant mortality rate is as much as four times higher than in the city as a whole; where the death rate is 25 percent higher; where life expectancy is ten years shorter; where classrooms are the most crowded and turbulent and the dropout rate is high; where many of the children live in broken homes; and where alcoholism and drug addiction are prevalent. A lower-class criminal's chances of being apprehended by the law are significantly greater than those of a middle- or upper-class offender. (Leonard Freed, Magnum)

est segment of our population cannot afford to buy those life chances which have price tags. The welfare system is designed to compensate for this inequality by providing free medical care, food, and additional income to cover the purchase of necessities like clothing and adequate housing. Thus it may be argued that the inequity of wealth distribution does not affect the life chances of America's poor in any significant way. But statistics show a different story; the system does not actually provide this basic equality. In the first place, the welfare program does not in fact result in any actual redistribution of wealth. Gabriel Kolko has pointed out that the poorest people contribute through taxes more

than enough to pay for the total amount they receive from welfare. He gave as an example figures from the national budget of 1955. Welfare expenditures that year were 4,026 billion dollars, but families with incomes under $4000, who pay about 20 percent of the total collected federal income tax, paid more than this in income taxes. Kolko concluded: "Welfare spending has not changed the nature of income inequality, nor raised the standard of living of the lowest income classes above what it would have reached if they had not been subjected to federal taxes."[25]

25.   Gabriel Kolko, *Wealth and Power in America* (New York: Frederick A. Praeger, 1962), p. 39.

Statistics also show that social class has a high correlation with mortality rates. The most reliable comparisons are those between whites, who can be designated as the higher status group, and blacks, with a lower social status. The Census Bureau estimates that a newborn white male can expect to live to be 66½ years old; his nonwhite counterpart will have a life expectancy of only 60 years. There are similar discrepancies between white and black female children. The mortality rate for female white babies in the first year of their lives is 1.6 percent. For black female babies, the rate is twice as high, 3.2 percent. The chance that the baby's mother will die in childbirth is four times as great if she is black than if she is white. National average infant mortality is 2.2 percent, for American Indians it is 3.2 percent, and for Mexican-Americans it is 3.9 percent.

Other statistics point up the class-linked health problems of the low status American. There is an increased incidence of heart disease, diabetes, and tuberculosis among the poor. Malnutrition is also common; one estimate is that thirty-seven million Americans have incomes too low to provide themselves with a nutritionally correct diet.[26] Malnutrition in expectant mothers is highly correlated with premature and still births, and can cause permanent brain damage, and stunted physical and mental development in these mothers' offspring. The United States Public Health Service says that one out of every three children in poor families is so anemic that he should have immediate medical attention. Some industrially caused diseases, such as black lung and cancer produced by asbestos particles, are found only among those unskilled workers of low status who must work in such health-hazardous industries. Low status people not only fall ill more often, but they have less to spend for medical attention. For example, a survey in California showed that Mexican-Americans made 2.3 visits to a doctor per year, compared with 5.6 for other residents of the state.[27]

In addition to illness, low status Americans have more accidents. Household accidents, such as carbon monoxide poisoning (often caused by space heaters that are needed to keep substandard dwellings warm in the winter), lead poisoning from flaking paint, fires, and falls, occur much more frequently in lower-class homes. The victims of industrial accidents come almost entirely from the lower classes. Residents of lower-class neighborhoods are also more likely to be the victims of crimes of violence at home and on the streets.

Social class also affects one's treatment by the law. Lower-class criminals are more likely to be caught because they lack the education and the money to evade the pursuit of law enforcement officials. Once caught they cannot afford the best legal assistance. When they appear in court, their shabbier appearance and their life history, which typically includes quitting school, unemployment, divorce, and signs of apparent irresponsibility, may antagonize or prejudice the judge, who in all likelihood himself comes from the middle or upper class and shares the norms and values of his class. Consequently, statistics show that the lower-class criminal is more likely to receive the maximum penalty. He has the additional penalty of having to wait for his trial in a jail cell rather than the comfort of his home, because he cannot afford to pay the bond posted to insure his reappearance. It has also been shown that criminals, whatever the class of their origin, who are able to steal enough money to acquire the prestige of high wealth and power status, will be treated more leniently if caught than those that steal a lesser amount

26. George McGovern, Senator from South Dakota, *The Food Gap: An Interim Report*, U.S. Congress, Senate Committee on Labor and Public Welfare, 91st Cong., 1st sess., August 1969.

27. *New York Times Encyclopedic Almanac 1970* (New York: New York Times Co., 1969), p. 301.

and thus are unable to buy "respectability."[28]

One final observation can be made about differing life chances. A study by Morris Axelrod indicates that low status individuals are typically deprived of the opportunity for, and the benefits of, social participation. They tend to have fewer friends, to know fewer of their neighbors and co-workers, to join fewer organizations, and just generally to have fewer social contacts of any kind.[29] In a literal sense, the low status individual is a social outcast.

CLASS CONSCIOUSNESS

There are two important aspects of the phenomenon of *class consciousness*. The first is the recognition of the existence of a system of social stratification and of one's own location within it. The second is the awareness of some shared goals, or interests in common, with other members of the same status group or class. Both depend to a large extent on the degree to which each major status grouping is a real social system rather than just a loose statistical grouping.

There is little doubt that in small and even medium-sized communities across the nation, class groupings exist as real and important social entities. People choose friends, wives, employees, and associates from members of their own social stratum, and this results in a group which shares values, attitudes, and interests and whose members are known to one another. Further, in these relatively personal and small-scale residential settings, there develop powerful class barriers to many kinds of relationships outside of one's class. A factory worker knows principally factory workers and others of about the same occupational standing, and he has little contact with members of other classes, especially those who are far from his own level. The

Culver Pictures, Inc.

Karl Marx (1818-1883) believed that social class structure was the single most important influence on the character of a society. He viewed all human history as a story of inevitable conflict between different social classes, classes which were formed mainly on the basis of economic factors. The great influence of Marx's views on world society in the past century cannot be denied; massive social changes in Russia, Eastern Europe, China, and many developing countries reflect the influence of Marx's interpretation of the social order. Although many of his economic theories have fallen into disrepute and his view of history has been criticized, Marx is still read and appreciated by sociologists for his insights into social structure. His best-known works are *The Communist Manifesto* (with Friedrich Engels, 1848) and *Das Kapital* (1867). *(Culver Pictures, Inc.)*

president of that factory may lead an even more insulated existence, because his power and his wealth serve as a screen behind which he can hide from contact with members of other classes.

In metropolitan areas, it is much more difficult to identify class groupings, which are as real and concrete as those in a small town. Nevertheless, the fact that persons

28.   See Edwin H. Sutherland, *White Collar Crime* (New York: Dryden, 1949).

29.   Morris Axelrod, "Urban Structure and Social Participation," *American Sociological Review* 21 (February 1956).

are evaluated in very similar ways in all parts of the nation, that there are many objective bases of evaluation (for example, wealth), and that our national communication media are patterned somewhat along class lines, enables us to speak meaningfully of society-wide status groups. Furthermore, the elite in our society do comprise a relatively closed group of persons who share a large number of mutual acquaintances and even intimate associations.

Compared with other countries, America has a rather low degree of class consciousness; this reflects in part the prevailing ideology that values the classless society. Our society is not classless, but our belief that it is often keeps us from noticing class distinctions. One study showed that approximately 20 percent of Americans, when asked the question, "Which social class do you think you belong to?" were unable to place themselves in any social class.[30] When a choice of social classes was listed at the end of the question, there was a much better response, but the response was not an accurate reflection of reality. Of those who answered, 80 percent said they were members of the middle class, a far higher proportion than would have been arrived at by objective measures.

Other reasons for the relatively low class consciousness in American society are the widespread belief in opportunities for upward mobility, which perhaps makes us seem more equalitarian than we really are, and the pluralism in American life—racial, religious, ethnic, and regional differences—which often cross-cut and even submerge class differences. (See chapters on Ethnic and Racial Minorities and Religion.) Another factor, which has assumed great importance in the past few decades, is the leveling influence of our national patterns of consumption. The level of the working-class standard

of living has shown steady improvement, permitting members of the working class to consume goods which until now have been identifying marks of the middle class. This is especially true in housing, automobiles, good clothing, and durable goods ranging from television sets to household gadgets.

Although Americans have trouble identifying their own class, there is evidence that we are somewhat more class conscious when it comes to identifying the class of other people. In a remarkable experiment Dean Ellis asked subjects to count from one to twenty, while he recorded their voices. By using numbers, Dr. Ellis eliminated clues like vocabulary, grammar, patterns of speech, idioms which would have appeared if the subjects had spoken sentences. Then he gave them Warner's standardized test to obtain an objective classification of their status level. When he played the tapes and asked other subjects to guess the speaker's social category, he found that the estimates matched the actual social class of the speaker in more than two-thirds of the cases![31]

Some societies put a great deal more stress on class in their national system of values, and that stress may not always be related to the real class conditions in each society. China is an example of a contemporary society of this sort. Children are taught recognition of classes in school, along with a value system that labels certain classes as "good" and others as "bad." The "good" and "bad" judgments are assigned by the government and do not necessarily reflect the life chances or real condition of these classes. Russia is also a class conscious country, and visitors there find that they are often asked about their class membership; to the Russians, it is an important part of social identity.

Since awareness of the social class structure is so limited in the United States, the feeling of shared class interest is not wide-

30. Neal Gross, "Social Class Identification in the Urban Community," *American Sociological Review* 18 (1953):398–404.

31. Dean S. Ellis, "Speech and Social Status in America," *Social Forces* 45 (1967):431–437.

spread either. It seems to be strongest in the upper class and the working class. There are, however, periods in which there is an increased awareness of common class interests. Strikes of national importance sometimes have this effect on the working class. Examples of such strikes are the steelworkers' strike in 1959, the strike at General Electric in 1969–1970, and numerous automotive strikes. These have all evoked feelings of interests shared with others, which may be expressed in terms of class distinctions. Under normal conditions, Americans do not often generalize to the extent of seeing class interests. For example, if an American has troubles or disagreements with a boss, a man in the loan department at the bank, a cab driver, or a welfare department official, he usually sees it as a personal matter, not as a sign of conflicting class interests.

CLASS CONFLICT

It is undeniable that members of the same economic class do have similar interests, whether they recognize the fact or not. It is in the interest of the owners of factories to keep wages low, while it is in the interest of the workers to make them higher. It is in the interest of middle-class shopkeepers to boost prices on food and clothing and other frequently purchased items, but that is against the interests of the other two classes. It has been theorized that many shared interests of one class will conflict with the shared interests of other classes, with the result that the classes will become hostile toward each other. This is called *class conflict*.

The concept of class conflict was elaborated by Karl Marx. He began his *Manifesto of the Communist Party* by saying:

The history of all hitherto existing society is the history of class struggles.
Freeman and slave, patrician and plebeian, lord and serf, guildmaster and journeyman, in a word, oppressor and oppressed, stood in constant opposition to one another, carried on an uninterrupted, now hidden, now open

fight, a fight that each time ended, either in a revolutionary reconstruction of society at large, or in the common ruin of the contending classes.[32]

Marx thought that the blame for the constant disorganizing changes of society could be laid on the capitalists, whose changes in the production system brought about corresponding changes in society. One such change was the devaluation and degradation of the work of the common man; now in competition with machines, he needed to labor longer hours at work that was more boring. Thus the interests of the two classes were in radical opposition to each other. Marx pointed out the dangerous social alienation of the workers:

The proletarian is without property; his relation to his wife and children has no longer anything in common with the bourgeois [capitalist] family relations; modern industrial labor, modern subjection to capital, the same in England as in France, in America as in Germany, has stripped him of every trace of national character. Law, morality, religion, are to him so many bourgeois prejudices, behind which lurk in ambush just as many bourgeois interests.[33]

Finally, Marx predicted that the ultimate result of such class conflict would be the victory of the proletariat, and then the establishment of a truly classless society.

Formerly, Marx was read principally as an ideologist, the father of Communist thought and doctrine, and for this reason he had enthusiastic supporters and bitter enemies. But today he is being read more and more as a sociologist rather than as a political thinker. There is much keen observation and understanding of social systems in general, and the industrial type of social organization in particular, in the works of Marx.

32. Karl Marx and Friedrich Engels, *Communist Manifesto* (Baltimore: Penguin Books, 1969), pp. 79–80.

33. Marx and Engels, *Communist Manifesto*, p. 92.

Marx defined two types of class conflict. One was the unconscious struggle for power and control of the economy, which he said existed at all times. The other was open warfare, which occurs when the lower classes become class conscious and realize that they must stand together to fight for their interests. In our world today, we can see examples of both kinds of class conflict. In poor and developing nations, such as many Latin American countries, the possibility of actual revolutionary conflict, such as that which took place in Cuba, is very great. Where the economy is more fully developed and stable, as it is in the United States, class conflict is largely unconscious. The conflict which takes place in our society is seldom expressly based on class cleavage, though this in fact may often be its underlying cause.

LEE RAINWATER
The Lessons of Pruitt-Igoe

Abridged from "The Lessons of Pruitt-Igoe," *The Public Interest*, Summer 1967, pp. 116–123. Copyright © 1967 by National Affairs, Inc.

Introduction

This article is based on a study Professor Rainwater made of a public housing project in St. Louis. The Pruitt-Igoe Housing Project was built in 1954 and houses approximately 10,000 low-income people. When it began it was considered a model of its kind; today it represents the worst of ghetto living. The 2,000 families who live there, all blacks, are ones who can find no other adequate housing within their means; if they had a choice they would live elsewhere. Rainwater selected this project to study not because it was typical, but because "it condenses into one 57-acre tract all of the problems and difficulties that arise from race and poverty, and all of the impotence, indifference, and hostility with which our society has so far dealt with these problems." It draws a clear portrait of the life style of the urban lower classes in America.

THE LOWER CLASS ADAPTATION

The observer who examines the lower class community in any detail perceives an almost bewildering variety of difficulties that confront its inhabitants. But if one wishes to move from simple observation to understanding and on to practical action, it is necessary to bring some order into this chaos of troubles, problems, pains, and failure. That is, one must move from a description of *what* lower class life is like to an understanding of *why* it is that way.

Let us start with an inventory of behavior in the lower class community that middle class people think of as hallmarks of the "tangle of pathology" of slum and ghetto worlds:

High rates of school dropouts
Poor school accomplishment for those who do stay in
Difficulties in establishing stable work habits on the part of those who get jobs
High rates of dropping out of the labor force
Apathy and passive resistance in contact with people who are "trying to help" (social workers, teachers, etc.)
Hostility and distrust toward neighbors
Poor consumer skills—carelessness or ignorance in the use of money
High rate of mental illness
Marital disruptions and female-headed homes
Illegitimacy
Child abuse or indifference to children's welfare
Property and personal crimes
Dope addiction, alcoholism

Destructiveness and carelessness toward property, one's own and other people's

All of this behavior is highly disturbing to middle class people—and most of it is even more disturbing to the lower class people who must live with it. It is not necessary to assume that all lower class families engage in even some of these practices to regard such practices as hallmarks of the pathology of the lower class world. Lower class people are forced to live in an environment in which the probability of either becoming involved in such behavior, or being the victim of it, is much higher than it is in other kinds of neighborhoods.

Behavior of this kind is very difficult for most middle class observers to understand. If, however, this behavior is seen in the context of the ways of life lower class people develop in order to cope with their punishing and depriving milieu, then it becomes much easier to understand. Much of the social science research dealing with lower class life in general, or with particular forms of deviant behavior such as juvenile delinquency, has sought to place these kinds of behavior in their contexts. As a result of these studies, we now understand that the "unreasonable" behavior which so often perplexes outsiders generally arises as a logical extension of the styles of life that are available to lower class people in their efforts to adapt to their world.

The ways people live represent their efforts to cope with the predicaments and opportunities that they find in the world as they experience it. The immediately experienced world of lower class adults presents them with two kinds of problems:

1. They are not able to find enough money to live in what they, and everyone else, would regard as the average American way. Because of inability to find work or only work at very low pay, they learn that the best they can hope for if they are "sensible" is despised housing, an inferior diet, and very few pleasures.

2. Because of the poverty, they are constrained to live among other individuals similarly situated—individuals who, the experience of their daily lives teaches them, are dangerous, difficult, out to exploit or hurt them in petty or significant ways. And they learn that in their communities they can expect only poor and inferior service and protection from such institutions as the police, the courts, the schools, the sanitation department, the landlords, and the merchants.

It is to this world that they must adapt. Further, as they grow up, they learn from their experiences with those around them that persons such as they can expect nothing better. From infancy on, they begin to adapt to that world in ways that allow them to sustain themselves—but at the same time often interfere with the possibility of adapting to a different world, should such a different world become available to them. Thus, in Pruitt-Igoe, eight-year-old girls are quite competent to inform the field worker that boys and men are no damn good, are not to be trusted, and that it isn't necessary to listen to or obey your mother because she's made such a mess of her life.

We know from sociological studies of unemployment that even stable middle or working class persons are likely to begin to show some of these lower class adaptive techniques under the stress of long-term unemployment. In the lower class itself, there is never a question of responding to the stress of sudden deprivation, since a depriving world is often all that the individual ever experiences in his life, and his whole lifetime is taken up in perfecting his adaptation to it, in striving to protect himself in that world and to squeeze out of it whatever gratification he can.

STRATEGIES FOR SURVIVAL

It is in terms of these two cardinal characteristics of lower class life—poverty and a potentially destructive community— that lower class individuals work out their strategies for living.

In most of American society two grand strategies seem to attract the allegiance of its members and guide their day-to-day actions. These are the strategies of the good life and of career-success. A good-life strategy involves efforts to get along with others and not to rock the boat; it rests on a comfortable family environment with a stable vocation for husbands which enables them to be good providers. The strategy of career-success is the choice of ambitious men and women who see life as providing opportunities to move from a lower to a higher status, to "accomplish something," to achieve greater than ordinary material well-being, prestige, and social recognition. Both of these strategies are predicated on the assumption that the world is inherently rewarding if one behaves properly and does his part. The rewards of the world may come easily or only at the cost of great effort, but at least they are there for the individual who tries.

In slum worlds, little in the experience that individuals have as they grow up sustains a belief in a rewarding world. The strategies that seem appropriate are *strategies for survival*.

Three broad categories of lower class survival strategies can be observed. One is the strategy of the *expressive life style*. In response to the fact that the individual derives little security and reward from his membership in a family which can provide for and protect him, or from his experiences in the institutions in which he is expected to achieve (first the school, later the job), individuals develop an exploitative strategy toward others. This strategy seeks to elicit rewards by making oneself interesting and attractive. In its benign forms, the expressive style is what attracts so many middle class people to the lower class — the fun, the singing, the dancing, the lively slang, the spontaneous gratification of impulse. But underneath the apparent spontaneity, the expressive style of lower class people is deadly serious business. It is by virtue of their ability to manipulate others by making themselves interesting and dramatic that the individual has an opportunity to get some of the few rewards that are available to him — whether these be gifts of money, a gambling bet won, the affections of a girl, or the right to participate in a community of peers, to drink with them, bum around with them, gain status in their eyes. While the expressive style is central to preserving the stability and sanity of many (particularly younger) members of the lower class, the pursuit of expressive and self-dramatizing goals often results in behavior which makes trouble for the individual both from his own community and from representatives of conventional society. Dope addiction, drunkenness, illegitimacy, "spendthrift behavior," lack of interest in school on the part of adolescents — all can arise in part as a result of commitment to a strategy of "cool."

When the expressive strategy fails — because the individual cannot develop the required skills or because the audience is unappreciative — there is a great temptation to adopt a *violent strategy* in which you force others to give you what you need. The violent strategy is not a very popular one among lower class people. There is little really cold-blooded violence either toward persons or property in the slum world; most of it is undertaken out of a sense of desperation, a sense of deep insult to the self. Yet this strategy does not seem as distant and impossible to them as it does to the most prosperous.

Finally, there is the *depressive strategy* in which goals are increasingly constricted to the bare necessities for survival (not as a social being, but simply as an organism). This is the strategy of "I don't bother anybody and I hope nobody's gonna bother me; I'm simply going through the motions of keeping body (but not soul) together." Apparently this strategy of retreat and self-isolation is one that is adopted by more and more lower class men and women as they grow older, as the payoffs from more expressive strategies begin to decline.

HOPES AND ASPIRATION

And along with these survival strategies, lower class people make efforts to move in the direction of the more conventional strategies of the good life or (occasionally) of career-success. One can observe in the lives of individual families (or in whole groups, during times of extraordinary demand for lower class labor) a gradual shift away from the more destructive components of these survival strategies. It is from observations such as these, as well as from interviews about lower class people's hopes and aspirations, that one learns that lower class styles of life are pursued, not because they are viewed as intrinsically desirable, but because the people involved feel constrained to act in those ways given the deprivations and threats to which they find themselves subject. *The lower class does not have a separate system of basic values. Lower class people do not really "reject middle class values." It is simply that their whole experience of life teaches them that it is impossible to achieve a viable sense of self-esteem in terms of those values.*

Conclusion

Americans like to think of their country as the "land of opportunity." Even if they do not believe that every person has the same chance to become president, Americans usually think that anyone with talent and persistence can find some degree of success. Therefore, lower class people whose way of living often seems less serious-minded, or more violent, are seen as inferior people who have rejected the chance for success that is offered to them. Professor Rainwater attempts to dispel this view. His study reveals that many people at the lower level end of the stratification scale are forced to live in a community so hostile that their energies cannot be directed toward achievement. They must concentrate all their efforts on merely staying alive.

SUMMARY

All societies have some system of stratification, a social pattern based on ranking individuals and social positions in terms of the desirable things that society has to offer, particularly wealth, power, and prestige. *Wealth* refers to all the economic assets of a society: the material products, land and natural resources, and productive labor services. While possession of wealth in itself is not enough to guarantee high social position, wealth improves one's life chances by providing access to a variety of socially desirable commodities. The distribution of wealth is patterned by place of residence, race, education, and occupation. In our society the poor are concentrated in urban areas, among the nonwhite, those with little education, and among the very old and young. The patterns found among those living in poverty reflect the lack of *personal power,* the ability to choose the direction and quality of their own lives. Sociologists have also tried to identify those individuals with *social power,* the capacity to make decisions which direct and shape the lives of others. They have tried to identify the power-holders by the reputational method, through asking individuals to identify community influentials, and by the behavioral approach, observing the actual decision-making processes and analyzing patterns of personal interaction. Often those people who are supposed to wield power are not those who are found to be truly powerful. Some sociologists believe that in America power is concentrated in the hands of a very few people; others maintain that social power is exceptionally fragmented, divided among many groups and individuals. *Prestige* is a more subjective dimension of stratification. Favorable social recognition varies from group to group, for it often is based on behavior which is in accordance with accepted group norms and values.

In terms of social stratification, a person's *status* refers to his ranked position in the social hierarchy. A person's social status depends on evaluations made by others with whom he comes into contact. His position is often expressed through such *status symbols* as possessions, style of dress, or manner of speech. A person's general status usually depends heavily on his occupation, which in turn is ranked in terms of its utility to society and the amount of training or education that it requires. Ranking is also carried out in terms of race, income, religion, sex, age, and education. In general an individual who ranks high in one area will also rank high in other areas: his status is consistent. Status inconsistency occurs when a person's various rankings do not coincide (e.g., high occupational prestige and low income). Such situations may be socially resolved by making one rank the dominant or master status (e.g., a person is classified primarily in terms of his race rather than his occupation).

People of approximately the same general status are combined in status groupings or *social classes*. Sociologists have used a variety of criteria to distinguish among social classes: occupation, amount and source of income, house type, residential location, and amount of education. These factors can be measured relatively objectively and are easiest to identify at the upper and lower extremes. It is more difficult to measure the differences in life-style that are associated with each social class: differences in the way that members of each class spend or use their money, and differences in the values and at-titudes shared by each stratum. Such differences are perpetuated from generation to generation through the socialization process.

In all societies there is some degree of *social mobility* as individuals move from one status to another. In an *open society* an individual can achieve his status through personal effort and competition. In a *closed* society status is ascribed or assigned at birth and is difficult to change. Most stratification systems are based on a mixture of achievement and ascription. Upward mobility appears to be easiest in societies with a large educational enrollment and an industrial economy. Upwardly mobile individuals generally try to conserve their resources consciously and to limit their obligations and responsibilities outside of their career. Downward mobility is sometimes caused by failing to get an education, marrying very young and raising a large family, and by being born into a large family that cannot provide advantages for all the children. Horizontal mobility consists of moving from one status to its equivalent, and often involves a change of jobs. Whether the mobility is up or down, the mobile individual can experience conflict between the norms and values of the social class in which he was socialized and those of the social class into which he moves. A social system that emphasizes mobility, such as we have in the United States, may be strained in trying to assimilate many mobile individuals and in trying to fulfill the expectations that it arouses in members of the population.

The probability that an individual will attain his goals in life is affected by his social status at birth. Mortality, illness and accidents, draft liability, treatment by the law, and opportunity for social participation are all directly influenced by one's social class. The traditional belief that America is a classless society often prevents us from noticing class differences and from being conscious of our own position in the class hierarchy. However, members of the same economic stratum do have similar interests. Karl Marx theorized that the shared interests of one class will conflict with those of other classes. In societies where class consciousness and a sense of oppression are heightened among the lower classes, the result may be open class warfare. In highly developed and stable economies, such as that of the United States, conflict is seldom expressly based on class cleavage, though such cleavage may be an important underlying cause.

GLOSSARY

Achieved status A position in society which can be gained by an individual's own achievements. (page 280)

Ascribed status A position in society to which members are assigned by criteria beyond their control, usually parentage, age, and sex. (page 280)

Class conflict Hostility between classes due to their different interests. (page 291)

Class consciousness Recognition of a system of social stratification and of one's location within it; awareness of some shared goals or interests in common with other members of the same status group. (page 289)

Class divisions The perceived and real differences between the classes of a society. (page 271)

Esteem The favorable evaluation that a person receives from others concerning his own unique qualities, or how well he performs a certain role. (page 257)

Life chances The probability that an individual will attain or fail to attain important goals and experiences in life. (page 286)

Master status The status which dominates others and thereby determines a person's general status level in the case of status inconsistency. (page 266)

Personal power The ability to control one's own life. (page 255)

Prestige The favorable evaluation and social recognition that a person receives from others. (page 257)

Social class (or **Status grouping**) A grouping of persons with similar status levels and some degree of similarity of behavior and values. (page 271)

Social differentiation The result of specialization of roles, positions, and groups within a society. (page 250)

Social mobility The movement from one status to another, either upward, downward, or horizontal. This can be measured intergenerationally (one generation to another) or intragenerationally (within an individual's own lifetime). (page 279)

Social power The capacity to control or influence the actions of others, whether they wish to cooperate or not. (page 255)

Status 1. A position in a social system that carries with it a set of rights and responsibilities. (page 258)
2. A ranked position in a social system. (page 258)
3. A person's general or total social standing in society. (page 258)

Status consistency The general tendency for people in any given quarter of one status rank to be in the same quarter of other status ranks. (page 266)

Status hierarchies The order in which statuses are ranked. (page 263)

Status inconsistency A combination of statuses embodied in one person which are of unequal ranking. (page 266)

Status symbol A conspicuous possession, style of dress, manner of speech, etc. which denotes that its owner belongs to a particular status level. (page 261)

Strata (or **Stratification levels**) A unit or category in a status hierarchy. (page 269)

Stratification A social pattern based on ranking individuals and social positions according to the distribution of the material and emotional desirables which society has to offer. (page 249)

Structural mobility Vertical mobility resulting from changes in the social or economic system. (page 281)

Wealth All the economic assets of a society—the material products, land and natural resources, and productive labor services. (page 251)

SUGGESTED READINGS AND RELATED RESOURCES

I   READINGS IN SOCIOLOGY

Hodges, Harold. *Social Stratification: Class in America*. Cambridge, Mass.: Schenkman Publishing, 1964. A good general introduction to social stratification in the United States; contains a full discussion of class-based life styles.

Keller, Suzanne. *Beyond the Ruling Class: Strategic Elites in Modern Society*. New York: Random House, 1963. Drawing upon classical and contemporary theories, the author writes about the elites in society which formulate, realize, and, sustain its social goals and social order. Keller rejects the model of a central power elite or ruling class.

Kolko, Gabriel. *Wealth and Power in America*. New York: Praeger (Paper), 1962. An important study of America's social and economic structures within the framework of its failure to solve the problems of poverty, maldistribution of wealth, and the resulting disparities between the classes. Kolko rejects the notion that the United States is becoming more egalitarian in the distribution of wealth and income.

Leinwand, Gerald, ed. *Poverty and the Poor*. New York: Washington Square Press (Paper), 1968. Provides a graphic description of poverty, with essays on suggested solutions to this problem.

Lenski, Gerhard. *Power and Privilege: A Theory of Social Stratification*. New York: McGraw-Hill, 1966. A major contribution to the theory of social stratification. Lenski develops a theory that stratification mainly results from the different ways power is exercised in social life. The book is unique in that it compares social stratification in all major types of societies from the most primitive to the advanced industrial.

Lipset, S. M., and R. Bendix. *Social Mobility in Industrial Society*. Berkeley, Calif.: University of California Press (Paper), 1966. An influential work in this field which questions whether the United States is as open and mobile a society as is commonly claimed.

Maclay, George, and H. Knipe. *The Dominant Man*. New York: Delacorte Press, 1972. An exploration of the pecking order in human society. The authors explore questions related to how people adjust to varying levels of dominance and the struggle that determines authority structures of societies.

Mills, C. Wright. *The Power Elite*. New York: Oxford University Press (Paper), 1959. An absorbing description of the life styles and social dynamics of the people with the most prestige, power, and wealth in America. Mills draws conclusions which have raised great controversy.

Rosenberg, Bernard, ed. *Thorstein Veblen*. New York: T. Y. Crowell (Paper), 1966. One of the best introductions to Veblen's writings about the leisure class and the American business enterprise. It is specifically written for the undergraduate who is not necessarily majoring in sociology, and contains excerpts and explanations from Veblen's best known book, *The Theory of the Leisure Class,* first published in 1889.

Tumin, Melvin. *Social Stratification*. Englewood Cliffs, N. J.: Prentice-Hall, 1967. Although this book demands some prior knowledge of sociology, undergraduate students will find it an excellent introduction to social stratification. Good critique of the functionalist theory of stratification which argues that stratification exists because it is beneficial for social organization.

Warner, W. Lloyd. *American Life: Dream and Reality*. Chicago: University of Chicago Press (Paper), 1962. This thoughtful discussion of social life in America deals not only with the observable facts, but also with the dreams, myths, and ideologies by which Americans interpret the past and look to the future. Warner did pioneering work in the study of social stratification.

Articles and Papers

Cohen, Bernard P. et al. "Reactions to Inequity." *Acta Sociologica* 12, 1 (1969):1–12.

Coser, Lewis A. "The Sociology of Poverty." *Social Problems* 13, 2 (Fall 1965):140–148.

Davis, Kingsley, and W. E. Moore. "Some Principles of Stratification." *American Sociological Review* 10 (1945):242–249.

Duncan, Otis Dudley. "The Trend of Occupational Mobility in the United States." *American Sociological Review* 30, 4 (August 1965):491–498.

Fox, Thomas G., and S. M. Miller. "Economic,

Political and Social Determinants of Mobility: An International Cross-Sectional Analysis." *Acta Sociologica* **9** (1965):76–93.

Hodges, Robert W., Paul M. Siegel, and Peter Rossi. "Occupational Prestige in the United States." *American Journal of Sociology* **70** (November 1964):286–302.

Kohn, Melvin L. "Social Class and Parent-Child Relationships: An Interpretation." *American Journal of Sociology* **68**, 4 (January 1963): 471–480.

Leggett, John C. "Uprootedness and Working Class Consciousness." *American Journal of Sociology* **68**, 6 (May 1963):682–692.

Leslie, Gerald R., and Richard F. Larson. "Prestige Influences in Serious Dating Relationships of University Students." *Social Forces* **47**, 2 (December 1968):195–202.

Mills, C. Wright. "The Middle Classes in Middle-Sized Cities." *American Sociological Review* **11**, 5 (October 1946):520–529.

Tumin, Melvin. "Some Principles of Stratification: A Critical Review." *American Sociological Review* **18** (1953):387–394.

Wrong, Dennis H. "The Functional Theory of Stratification: Some Neglected Considerations." *American Sociological Review* **24**, 6 (December 1959):772–782.

II SOME RELATED RESOURCES
Nonfiction

Agee, James. *Let Us Now Praise Famous Men*. New York: Ballantine (Paper), 1966. A sensitive description of the life of white tenant farmers during the depression.

Birmingham, Stephen. *Our Crowd*. New York: Dell (Paper), 1968. A description of newly rich Jews in New York City, and the difficult and superficial adjustment they make to the way of life of the wealthy.

_____. *The Right People*. New York: Dell (Paper), 1969. An interesting portrayal of the super-rich and their way of life.

Huber, Richard. *The American Idea of Success*. New York: McGraw-Hill, 1971. Huber moves beyond the money definition of success to examine what has been the philosophy of achievement for middle-class Americans.

Lundberg, Ferdinand. *The Rich and the Super-Rich*. New York: Bantam (Paper), 1969. An interesting and readable interpretation of America's upper-class control of corporations, legislation, and governmental action.

Packard, Vance. *The Hidden Persuaders*. New York: McKay, David, 1957, Pocket Books (Paper), 1958. Packard has studied the techniques used to advertise and sell products in America and examined the appeal of some of the best-selling products, including their status appeal.

_____. *The Status Seekers*. New York: McKay, David, 1959, Pocket Books (Paper), 1961. In this book Packard describes the American search for status symbols and cites the possessions that currently lend social status.

Fiction

Dreiser, Theodore. *An American Tragedy*. Cleveland and New York: World Publishing, 1946. A story of a lower-class boy driven to murder by his overwhelming desire to become part of upper-class society.

Lewis, Sinclair. *Main Street*. New York: Signet (Paper), 1950. A classic depiction of the middle-class life style in America at the turn of the century.

Warren, Robert Penn. *All the King's Men*. New York: Random House, 1960. First published in 1947. This novel depicts that part of American politics which is not concerned about the people, but only with obtaining more power and wealth.

Films

All the King's Men. Robert Rossen, 1949. Based on Robert Penn Warren's Pulitzer Prize novel of the same name, this film portrays the life of Willie Stark, a backwoods politician who was transformed into a power-grabbing governor.

An American Tragedy. Josef von Sternberg, 1931. The theme and characters of this film, based on the Dreiser novel, revolve around class and economic conflict.

Marat/Sade. Peter Brook. Adapted from Peter Weiss's play of the same name, this film provides the viewer with a sense of the social and class conflicts which arose during and after the French Revolution.

Room at the Top. Jack Clayton, 1959. Based on John Braine's novel of the same title, this film tells the story of a man seeking wealth and power. It is followed by the film *Life at the Top,* which portrays the same central character ten years later. He has obtained wealth, prestige, and power, and is still unhappy.

8 Ethnic and Racial Minorities

It has been speculated that the very earliest
human societies were so homogeneous that, like
primitive tribes today, they never experienced
minority groups that had different physical or
cultural traits. However, the oldest written records
of civilization do speak of minorities and raise the
question of how they should be treated. There were
minorities in ancient Egypt and Babylon, and the
Old Testament of the Bible furnishes so complete a
description of minority-group relations that it could
almost serve as a textbook on the subject.

A minority group is any recognizable ethnic,
racial, or religious group in a society which suffers
some disadvantage due to prejudice or discrimination.
Minorities are the product of migration. Changing
conditions of environment or economics, the hostile
policies of a new ruler toward some faction of his
subjects, signs of a coming war—such situations
lead people to leave their homes in a society where
they are part of the cultural majority and migrate in
search of a better or more congenial city or country
to live in. There are numerous historical examples of
this occurrence. When the mouth of the Euphrates
River silted up and the once fertile lands along
its banks became the desert they are today, the
residents of the cities of Akkad and Babylon were
forced to move to the Persian Gulf. When oil was
discovered at the turn of this century and coal lost
its predominance as a fuel, hundreds of people left
the mining towns of Pennsylvania and Kentucky
to look for work in other states. After the abortive
revolution in the Dominican Republic in 1965, many

of those who took part in it had to leave the country. Sometimes a migration is forced, as was the case with American slavery. When a migrant group settles in a new location, unless they are quickly assimilated into the new culture, they will constitute a minority group. The people who already live there will be conscious of the newcomers as being somehow "different," and they will treat them in certain ways that acknowledge these differences. The minority group in turn will respond to this special treatment in certain characteristic ways.

In modern times, the negative aspects of minority group relationships are often in the news—the riots, conflicts, strife, and bloody wars. Often when new people enter relatively closed social groups, tension results. If the newcomers display social and cultural differences as they compete for the scarce goods of their new country (jobs, housing, schooling, for example) this tension can reach a breaking point.

But when minority groups migrate into other societies, they also can bring with them valuable new information, new ideas, new energy and competence, thus providing their adopted society with a cultural transfusion. For example, when the Arameans migrated to Assyria around 1100 B.C., they brought writing based on an alphabet instead of pictures, as well as the innovations of pen, ink, and papyrus. When the Assyrians adopted these inventions, their general culture, and the very rise of the Assyrian Empire, was advanced significantly.

The waves of immigration into the United States have meant that our society has been heavily and continuously enriched with new ideas and skills. During the Nazi regime of the 1930s many of Europe's best minds left the universities there and emigrated to America, bringing to this country remarkable intellectual and artistic gifts: Einstein in science, Thomas Mann in literature, and Arnold Schoenberg in music are three famous examples.

We will begin this chapter by looking at some of the larger minority groups in our society. Then we will consider the subject of prejudice and discrimination—how and why they develop, their consequences for society, and especially their shape and character in modern America. In the third topic, we examine the ways in which the dominant society may choose to behave toward a minority, and in the concluding topic we look at the ways in which minority groups respond to the dominance of others.

1 ETHNIC AND RACIAL GROUPS

For a minority group to be viewed and treated as such, the individuals in the group must have significant things in common which can be distinguished by the members both of the minority group and of the dominant society. People with *O* negative type blood are a minority, but they are not treated as a minority group in the social sense of the term: first, because blood type is not considered a significant social category; and second, because blood type is a characteristic that only a trained laboratory technician can recognize.

Examples of common differentiating factors which do lead people to think in terms of "we" and "they," are language, customs of child rearing, style of dress, skin color, hair texture and style, stature, and religious practices. These factors can be divided into two general groups: (1) those which are biologically caused, such as skin color, stature, and hair texture; and (2) those which are socially caused, such as hairstyle, dress, and language.

Groups with distinctive social and cultural characteristics are called ethnic groups; groups with distinctive physical characteristics are called racial groups. We will see that race is often intertwined with ethnicity.

ETHNIC GROUPS

It is difficult to develop a clear definition of ethnic groups. Some people use the term to denote all people from a certain geographical area, such as the Irish. Sometimes the term ethnic is used to mean people who speak the same language or have the same religion. A common sociological definition, and the one which we shall use, is that an *ethnic group* is any group which is socially differentiated, has

developed its own subculture, and has "a shared feeling of peoplehood."[1]

An important factor in the way an ethnic group is defined is the recognition by others of some social difference. For example, the Italian-Americans are called an ethnic group, because certain general traits in the Italians who immigrate here set them apart from the dominant American society and from other cultural groups. Among these traits are speaking Italian, belonging to the Roman Catholic Church, cooking certain traditional foods, and being emotionally expressive. In some European countries—let's say France—where the people have the opportunity to meet many more Italians than we do in America, "Italian" by itself is no longer perceived as referring to a single group, because it is too general a category to them to be socially significant. The French are aware of the northern Italian group, the southern Italians, and the Sicilians, and each of these groups is viewed as having specific characteristics. In Italy, these categories are too broad to be meaningful, and people may be distinguished on the basis of regional dialect, local customs, and certain physical characteristics, such as hair and eye color.

In a true ethnic group, recognition of social differences comes not only from outsiders, but also from the members of the group. They perceive themselves as different, and outsiders are regarded as incompatible or "not of our people." In groups with definite ethnic identities a strong attempt is made to prevent

1. Milton M. Gordon, *Assimilation in American Life: The Role of Race, Religion and National Origins* (New York: Oxford University Press, 1964), p. 24.

A traditional kind of Jewish culture is still preserved by members of the Hasidic Sect. These children are being taught to read Hebrew in a school associated with their synagogue. Their teacher wears a long curl over each ear, an identifying mark of the male Hasidim. *(Capa, Magnum)*

group members from having primary relationships with people who are not of the same ethnic type. Within the ethnic group there sometimes develops a social system, distinct from that of the larger society, which socializes members to the subculture of the group. Strong sanctions may enforce the ethnic group's pattern of socialization, which deals with all stages of the life cycle: birth, educa-

tion, marriage, and death. The social and cultural bond which holds such groups together may be in part racial, religious, or linguistic. But more generally it is a basic sense of ancestral identification with a specific portion of mankind—the special feeling of "my people" which sets one's group apart from all others.

It is possible for the individual members of what is considered to be one ethnic group to have dissimilar cultures in many respects. An example of this can be seen in the case of the Jews. They are considered an ethnic group, both by others and by themselves. But what is it exactly that they have in common? It is not race. Their racial origins (called *Semitic*) are exactly the same as those of the Arabs; the Jordanian Jew and the Jordanian Arab look exactly alike. European Jews have intermarried with gentiles so frequently that Semitic features do not distinguish them from other Europeans. Jews do not necessarily have religion in common; the practices and beliefs of Jews vary greatly; some who identify themselves as Jews are no longer practicing or believing members of the Jewish religion. In addition, Jews have no single culture in common: a Russian, Polish, or German Jew has an entirely different culture from a Syrian or Moroccan Jew. This lack of cultural similarity has created great problems for the nation of Israel, where these cultural groups are trying to live together. Sociological studies have verified that the European Jews are prejudiced against the "Oriental" Jews (those from North Africa and the Middle East) and consider them culturally primitive.[2]

What, then, do Jews have in common that makes them an ethnic group? We might say that their bond is their feeling of shared peoplehood — of Jewishness. Jews are people who regard themselves as descendants of that biblical group of exiles and wanderers who received the Ten Commandments. They are people who remember their ancestors as a group who have been discriminated against, sometimes persecuted, often pursued by powerful enemies all over the world for more than two thousand years. This is another demonstration of the fact that ethnicity is predominantly a set of cultural, social, and psychological attributes that certain people share, mainly because of common background and tradition.

RACIAL GROUPS

The concept of *race,* like ethnicity, is a very difficult one to define. It is based on observable physical differences among people resulting from inherited biological characteristics. The task of trying to set up a scientific classification of the races has fallen to the physical anthropologists and biologists. They have classified skin colors, measured heads, and even counted pieces of hair. The result has been a number of different systems of racial classification, from a system of three races to one of thirty-nine, and even more. As the biologist Theodosius Dobzhansky puts it, "it should always be kept in mind that while race differences are objectively ascertainable facts, the number of races we choose to recognize is a matter of convenience."[3]

The most commonly used system divides the world's population into three major racial groups — Caucasian, Mongoloid, and Negroid. Classification is based on a combination of physical characteristics such as hair texture, eye shape, and skin color. (See the accompanying diagram of racial groups for a more detailed breakdown.) There are also racial groups which do not easily fit into any one of these three categories because they are mixtures of two or more of the basic races; examples of such groups would be many Polynesians and Latin Americans. It should be pointed out that classification of two people in the same racial group does not necessarily mean that they are closely related in any meaningful way. The bushman of Africa and the black American are both classified as Negroid peoples, yet the two groups are vastly dissimilar, both socially and physically. The bushmen have very short stature; they have a unique ability to store fat in their thighs and buttocks for later need; and their culture is a nomadic one, centered around the constant search for food in a semi-desert. The similarities between the two groups consist mainly of the color of their skin, hair, and eyes.

2. S. N. Eisenstadt, "The Process of Absorption of New Immigrants in Israel," *Human Relations* 5 (1952): 223–246.

3. Theodosius Dobzhansky, *Mankind Evolving: The Evolution of the Human Species* (New Haven: Yale University Press, 1962), p. 266.

RELATIONSHIP OF HUMAN RACES

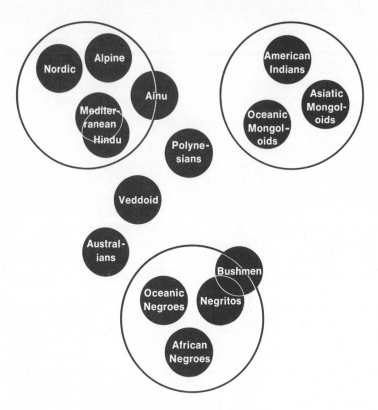

SOURCE: A. L. Kroeber, *Anthropology* (New York: Harcourt Brace Jovanovich, Inc., 1948).

The most common system of racial classification is to divide mankind into three basic racial groups: Mongoloid, Negroid, and Caucasian. Groups such as the Ainu of Japan, the Polynesians, and the natives of Australia represent a mixture of two or even three of the groups.

The differences in physical characteristics found in the various racial groups of mankind were probably due to the fact that the requirements of climate and environment in different areas tended to select out these characteristics. The dark skin of the Negro protects him from the burning rays of the sun; the relative lack of body hair facilitates the cooling action of evaporation when he sweats. The Eskimo (a Mongoloid) has a compact frame and a tendency to put on fat which helps insulate him in his cold climate.

At one time it was thought that in the early stages of man's development each racial group was "pure"—that is, unmixed with any of the characteristics of other races. Today some scientists believe that a pure race has never existed and that every racial group has always had some sprinkling of genes for other, nontypical physical characteristics. Certainly there is no pure race, or racial type, in the modern world, for there has been some degree of intermarriage in every group. For example, in Sweden, which we often think of as a society composed of purely Nordic racial types (a subcategory of Caucasians), all blue-eyed blonds, a survey based on records of physical characteristics of army draftees showed that this type was actually a very small minority.[4] Only 7 percent had blond hair, whereas 90 percent had hair in various shades of brown. Blue eyes were dominant, but one out of every seven men had eyes of another color, including dark brown.

The common definition of racial group is as much social and cultural as biological. Although it is true that we can sort many people out as being members of a group which has a specific combination of inherited physical characteristics, it is also true that racial identity can often be due more to cultural than to biological assignments. Why do we classify the singer Barbara McNair as a black? She has straight hair, light skin, and a straight nose—in looks, she is almost identical to, let's say, a girl from southern Italy. We call her a black because of her cultural or ethnic background, not her physical appearance. She may call *herself* a black either because society defines her that way, or because she shares the black ethnic heritage, or both.

Thus it can be seen that in real life racial and ethnic groups overlap in large part, and this is sometimes a source of confusion. American blacks and American Orientals form relatively distinct racial groups in our society, and for the most part they are also ethnic groups. However, there are some individuals who belong to the groups racially but not ethnically—for instance, a Japanese-American whose family has lived among Caucasians for two or three generations and who feels few remaining ties to the Japanese subculture and traditions. And it is fair to say that there are many individuals—for example, those who are 75 percent Caucasian—who may be blacks or Orientals ethnically but not racially, strictly speaking. In fact, when people are classified as members of one or another race according to such percentages, they are in reality classified according to a social, not racial, definition.

It is also possible for an ethnic group to include more than one race. We would call the people of India an ethnic group, though they represent at least two racial groups (some anthropologists put it at a much higher figure): the Caucasian Hindus and the Negroid-Caucasian mixture found in the Veddoids. The Irish nation is composed of two different subraces of Caucasians—the tall, fair Anglo-Saxons and the shorter, darker skinned Celts, who are related to the Welsh and the gypsies.

A final question about race—and one which has been studied for a long time—is whether or not the obvious physical variations among the races are accompanied by more subtle differences in such areas as level of intelligence and emotional makeup. The studies made offer almost no firm conclusions. Because of the great degree of racial intermixing, it is of course impossible to study anything close to pure racial types. In addition, such studies are made extremely difficult by the problem of separating culturally learned behavior from biologically inherited behavior, and by the problem of how to measure quantitatively emotional and intellectual characteristics.

After the Frenchmen Alfred Binet and Theodore Simon developed in 1905 one of the first modern intelligence tests that promised to measure level of intelligence objectively, sociologists used this test and its successors to compare racial and ethnic abilities. Results of tests administered in the early decades of this century indicated that there was wide variation among the various ethnic and racial groups in what was thought to be intelligence. In recent years social scientists have been reexamining this and similar evidence, and they have concluded that it is misleading. The problem is that all the tests used to measure intelligence, while remarkably accurate in predicting intellectual success, were developed around the social, cultural, and academic values of the dominant and educated middle-class culture. Taking the test requires some mastery of the English language, especially the version of it spoken by

4. Study cited by James W. Vander Zanden, *American Minority Relations: The Sociology of Race and Ethnic Groups*, 2d ed. (New York: Ronald Press, 1966), p. 42.

white middle-class Americans. Even parts that are supposedly nonverbal, such as the matching of shapes or colors, still require language understanding in order to comprehend the instructions. Moreover, some of the "right" answers to the questions are right only for the dominant middle-class culture which is making up and giving the test. James Vander Zanden gives an example from the National Intelligence Test:

One such sentence reads, _____ should prevail in churches and libraries; the correct answer is silence. But in the southern Negro church, silence is neither the rule nor the ideal. The worshippers are expected to respond, to participate actively and audibly; in fact, a church service characterized by silence might well be considered a failure. Accordingly, many southern Negro children might be expected to answer this question incorrectly.[5]

Actually, what is being tested may not be innate intelligence at all, but rather the ability to perform in a special social and intellectual manner. This is borne out by the fact that lower-class black children score *on the average* a few points lower than white children, but when middle-class black children are compared with middle-class white children the difference appears to be erased.

Some tests have been developed recently which overcome some of these cultural biases by relating the questions to situations which are familiar to black children. However, high performance on these tests still requires skill in test taking in a formal, academic context, a skill which is more likely to be possessed by white children (because of their socialization) than by black children. The ability to read "the King's English" accurately and easily, plus an understanding of the importance of following directions, is also required, and these things too are socially learned factors which may not be a direct reflection of innate intellectual ability.

5. Vander Zanden, *American Minority Relations*, pp. 46–47.

Today, the great majority of social scientists who have studied the evidence believe that there are probably no significant inborn or inherited differences in levels of intelligence among the various racial groups.

With regard to emotional makeup, the answer is even more difficult to determine. Stereotyped generalizations about racial personality and "character" abound, based mostly on casual observation by another racial or ethnic group. There may be some differences between racial groups in personality types; however, personality is even more difficult to measure than intelligence and there is very little hard data to study. Even if differences are observed between the average members of various racial groups (certainly not all members of each group share all traits), they are probably culturally learned and are not inborn biological differences in character. They represent a typical collection of attitudes and responses to social situations – much like national character, which was discussed in chapter 4.

MINORITY GROUPS IN AMERICA

In every large American city, you will find certain sections that house different ethnic groups. Most cities contain a "Little Italy," a predominantly Jewish suburb, an inner-city black section, or a "Chinatown." Papers and magazines are published in this country in every European language; and one can find groceries that sell the ingredients for any kind of ethnic dish. In America you will find not only the Greek and Russian Orthodox churches, but also the Serbian, Armenian, Albanian, Bulgarian, Syrian, and Ukrainian Orthodox churches. The Irish here celebrate St. Patrick's Day, the Italians, Columbus Day. In Lorain, Ohio, you can watch people dancing the Hungarian *chardas;* in Gallup, New Mexico, a performance of the Zuni Rain Dance; and in Delano County, California, the Mexican Hat Dance. We are a country with literally hundreds of well-established ethnic minorities. We will take a closer look at five of these, each with its own specific problems in adjusting to American life—the blacks, the Jews, the Puerto Ricans, the Mexican-Americans, and the Indians.

Blacks

There are nearly 25 million black Americans today, representing about 11 percent of the population. This figure actually shows a decrease in percentage terms since the early days of our country, for at the time of independence, blacks made up slightly more than 20 percent of the total population of the thirteen colonies. Blacks are born at a higher rate, and die younger, than whites, with the result that the black population is younger, on the average, than the white population. In 1971 the average age for whites was 28.6 years; for blacks it was 21.3 years.

Black households are usually larger than white ones, averaging 4.38 members, as compared to 3.62 members for white households. One out of every three black households is headed by a woman rather than a man, whereas the figure is only one out of eleven for whites. The greater number of fatherless households helps to explain why blacks also have a lower median family income than whites—the figures are $10,670 for whites and $6,440 for blacks.

Patterns of residence for blacks have been changing rapidly since the time of World War II. At its close, more than 80 percent of all blacks lived in the South; now the figure has dropped to about 50 percent, and the migration north and west is still continuing at the rate of 4 percent a year. Fifty-two out of every one hundred blacks live in a central city (only twenty-seven out of one hundred whites do) and another thirteen of that hundred live in metropolitan areas but outside the central city. The image of the black man as farmer and rural resident is giving way to the new reality, that of the black as an urban man. The abridgment from *Tally's Corner* (see chapter 5) presents a picture of one kind of urban culture; the abridgment in this chapter by Kenneth Clark analyzes some important elements of that culture.

E. Franklin Frazier (1894–1962) has given us a penetrating analysis of the culture, social position, and problems of the American black. He is best known for his studies of the black family and the influence of family life on social behavior; for example, he pointed out the dominance of the female in black family life, and the consequences which that dominance has for the children. His interest in ecology, community studies, and stratification helped him to view black Americans in the wider context of modern urbanized society. Frazier's principal works are *The Negro Family in the United States* (1939) and *Black Bourgeoisie* (1955).

Traditionally, black Americans have had comparatively little sense of ethnic identity and group solidarity as expressed by efforts to preserve and develop their ethnic cultural heritage. This is largely due to the special conditions of slavery. But recently blacks, especially urban blacks, have developed a strong interest in their culture, background, and ethnic bonds. This new mood is expressed in many ways. The "natural" hair styles and dashikis, the emphasis on "soul food" as a cultural cuisine, the influence of organizations like the Black Panthers and the Black Muslims, the slogans "Black is Beautiful" and "Black Power"—these are all signs of a great and continuing change in the black community. The black experience in America will be discussed more fully in topics 3 and 4.

Jews

There are about six million Jews in the United States. Approximately half of them live in New York City; the rest are concentrated in the larger cities of the Northeast and the Far West. It has been true for many centuries (largely because in many countries they were prohibited from owning land) that Jews tend to be oriented toward urban life.

Statistics show that on the average, Jews reach a fairly high level of educational attainment, hold jobs of high occupational status rank, and have incomes somewhat above the level of the national average. Jews today do not usually have large families, but they tend to have particularly strong family ties. Their divorce rate is very low, and they generally feel a deep sense of involvement with their families, including relatives outside the immediate nuclear family, even though at the same time they have a high rate of residential mobility.[6] Jews are frequently professional men—lawyers and doctors—or independent merchants and manufacturers, often in business with a family member. The fact that they are underrepresented in America's large corporations may be due more to discrimination against Jews by the dominant society than to any personal disinclination of Jews to take such jobs. The popular stereotype portrays Jews as clannish, preferring to stick with their own kind, and statistics support this view, for Jews have always ranked high in sense of ethnic identity and solidarity. They tend more than most other groups, for example, to have strong sanctions against marriage outside the group.

Certainly Jews in America have been the victims of prejudice and discrimination, and they have been denied many kinds of opportunities. A number of residential areas and social organizations are closed to them; many private secondary schools and colleges have either refused to accept Jewish students, or held unacknowledged low quotas for them; the biggest businesses in the country discriminate against them, especially at the executive level. In spite of such difficulties, most Jews have achieved great success in this society. How have they overcome the handicaps of the minority group? One clear answer has been provided by Gerhard Lenski, who suggests that it is because the values and goals of the Jewish ethnic group actually correspond closely to those of the white Anglo-Saxon Protestants who are the dominant group in American society.[7] In this respect, the present day Jewish subculture has benefited from a very long tradition of literacy, concern for personal achievement, and skill in the marketplace.

Puerto Ricans

There are nearly a million and a half Puerto Ricans in the United States, so they constitute a sizable ethnic minority. Most of them live in New York City and its satellite cities, such as Newark and Jersey City. Other concentrations of Puerto Rican population can be found in and around Chicago, Cleveland, and Philadelphia.

The Puerto Ricans have many of the same problems as the Afro-American Negro—they tend to be low in educational, occupational, and income status. They are additionally handicapped by the fact that they speak Spanish rather than English, which they must learn after they come here. This creates employment barriers, and causes difficulties for the children, who must attend school and try to learn their lessons in a strange language. They are for the most part practicing Catholics and tend to have a high birthrate and large families. The average family is one child larger than the average black family. The com-

---

6. Gerhard Lenski, *The Religious Factor* (New York: Doubleday, Anchor Books, 1963), chap. 5, pp. 212–259.

7. Gerhard Lenski, *The Religious Factor*.

bination of all these factors has resulted in very little upward mobility among Puerto Ricans.

By any standards, the Puerto Ricans live a marginal existence in our society. Typically they stay within their own neighborhoods, where the tradesmen speak their own language. In fact, they are often unlikely to have even a nodding acquaintance with anyone outside the Puerto Rican community. Although many people mentally classify them with Afro-Americans because of their skin color, which ranges from light brown to pure black, they have little in common with Afro-American Negroes, and can no more fit into that subculture than they can into the dominant one. They have almost no political power; many can't even vote. There are few organizations in Puerto Rican communities except for the Catholic church; and there are few people who have had the training, education, or experience that would enable them to develop into effective leaders of the group.

So, in terms of many criteria, the Puerto Ricans rank as one of the most disadvantaged of our ethnic groups; only the American Indians have a lower living standard. One reason for this is that a major motivation for Puerto Rican migration to this country is economic problems at home; thus Puerto Ricans tend to be very poor on arrival. In addition, Puerto Ricans are the most recent immigrants to this country; they have not yet had time to adjust and adapt to the point where they can function in our society with any success. Another reason may be that they often have very little feeling of commitment to American society. Since their goals are mainly economic ones, a large number have come to this country for the express purpose of accumulating enough money to go back home and build a house, open a business, or buy a farm; thus many do not have a strong motivation toward fitting into American society. There is a growing indication, however, that the young people born here and now reaching their mid- and late teens, the second-generation Puerto Ricans, are beginning to feel more of a sense of involvement in American society.

Mexican-Americans

The Mexican-American minority is growing faster than any other ethnic group in the United States. Approximately 5 million are concentrated in the Southwestern states—82 percent in Texas and California alone. Traditionally Mexican-Americans have been a rural people. They have held over half the agricultural labor jobs in both California and Texas, and they have served as the backbone of the migrant labor force in recent decades. However, as agriculture becomes increasingly mechanized and the demand for farm labor shrinks, millions are moving to urban areas and are swelling the *barrios,* Mexican slum neighborhoods, of cities like Albuquerque, Los Angeles, Phoenix, and Denver. About 80 percent of the Mexican-American population now lives in these urban enclaves. Unlike most ethnic ghettos that developed as a new minority appeared quite suddenly in a city and settled in inexpensive, central housing districts, many *barrios* were the original settlements around which Anglo or white communities were later built. Nonetheless, like other minorities, Mexican-Americans have often been barred from full participation in the wider community.

Although segregation laws against Mexican-Americans have never existed officially, many still find it difficult to be admitted to certain neighborhoods and public places in the Southwest: swimming pools, barbershops, and movie theaters sometimes have rules excluding Mexican-Americans from their facilities or limiting them to certain sections. Their participation and representation in local, state, and federal politics has been extremely low—illiteracy and inability to read English have prevented many from voting. Job opportunities have also been restricted. The majority work as unskilled or semiskilled labor in factories and packing plants, or in service jobs as maids, waitresses, and delivery men. Their unemployment rate is almost twice that among Anglos, and over a third live below the poverty line. Despite a median family income that is slightly higher than among blacks, the extremely large size of most Mexican-American families and the disproportionate number of dependent children in the population sharply limit the share of income available to each Mexican-American.

Like Puerto Ricans, Mexican-Americans have been impeded in their efforts to improve their socioeconomic standing by a language barrier. Often children enter school unable to speak English. Although new bilingual education programs are being established in many areas, until recently there have been regulations in some Southwestern schools, which, in an attempt to force the learning of English, forbid the speaking of Spanish. This system has undoubtedly contributed to the high dropout rate among Mexican-Americans. They average 8 years of schooling—two less than blacks and four less than whites. In some areas only 25 percent of the Mexican-American population reportedly can speak English fluently. Recent trends show some improvement, however, as younger people are acquiring more education than their parents. Many are now enrolled in colleges and universities throughout the Southwest.

Most Mexican-Americans originally came to this country voluntarily, unlike the blacks, and many still maintain social and cultural ties to Mexico. As with the Puerto Ricans, the Catholic church often plays an important role in their daily lives, and helps to shape their social and cultural outlook. In comparison with both Puerto Ricans and blacks, a higher percentage of Mexican-Americans have achieved a large measure of success in American life. There are many Mexican-Americans in the Southwest who have "made it," and who are fully accepted by the dominant society.

Most Mexican-Americans live within a separate and relatively closed community, and they have been slow to develop aggressive leadership. Recently, however, perhaps inspired by successes of the Black Power movement, Mexican-Americans have taken a new and sometimes militant interest in politics. They have founded a "Chicano" political party, achieved representation at national party conventions, and have launched their own civil rights movement, *la causa* (the cause), emphasizing pride in the Mexican-American heritage and calling for solidarity among all Spanish-speaking Americans. As among other minority groups, the leaders of the Chicano movement are now faced with the question of whether Mexican-Americans should strive toward becoming fuller members of mainstream American culture or toward maintaining a separate cultural identity.

American Indians

American Indians are possibly the most neglected of all our minorities. We do not even know precisely how many Indian Americans there are. Estimates range from 650,000 to 1 million. This confusion reflects the fact that many are part of the least visible groups in our society—the unemployed and the homeless—who elude census takers. A statistical glimpse into the facts of Indian life indicates that they are probably the poorest and most marginal group in America today. They earn 80 percent less than most other Americans, their unemployment rate is almost ten times the national average, and their infant mortality is three times higher than in the rest of our society. Fifty percent of Indian school children are dropouts; and despite recent government efforts to provide better homes, a large number of families live in substandard housing, often without electricity or plumbing. The impact of these conditions on Indian Americans is revealed in the high level of alcoholism, divorce, various diseases such as tuberculosis, and perhaps most tragically, in a teen-age suicide rate that is one hundred times higher than among whites.

Indian Americans are members of a widely varied group that includes a number of distinct cultures. As legal wards of the federal government their situation among minorities has been somewhat unique. Often federal policies have treated every tribe alike, without regard for distinctions in their heritage of styles of life. During the nineteenth century, the government tried to transform Indians into small farmers, and by providing allotments of land to individual Indians, destroyed tribal organization based on communal ownership. Through the system of off-reservation boarding schools conducted by the Bureau of Indian Affairs, an attempt was made to prepare Indian children for life outside the reservation. Yet most chose to return home rather than move to white communities. The high dropout rate and low achievement and self-confidence levels among Indian children indicate that our present system of dividing responsibility among local public, private, and federal schools has not been successful in meeting the needs of Indian children for positive cultural identity. New efforts are now being made to establish schools controlled by tribal boards of education that can serve as centers of community life and will include Indian values and tradition in the school curriculum.

The Red Power movement and the increasingly militant demonstrations made by Indians in various parts of the country indicate deep dissatisfaction with their exclusion from the material benefits of the wider society and unwillingness to accept judgments and regulations imposed on their daily lives by the dominant culture. Like many other ethnic minorities today, they are demanding social participation on their own terms and are refusing to accept unequal treatment passively.

Fifty thousand American Indian families live in grossly substandard homes ranging from tarpaper shacks to abandoned automobile bodies to hillside caves. Not until 1961 were Indians included in plans for public housing projects. On many reservations the home improvement programs have helped to replace some of the more ramshackle dwellings. However, among the Rosebud Sioux, 375 of these new homes have been judged defective. Many have crooked walls, roofs that leak, and over a fourth are without toilets, plumbing, cupboards, cabinets, or sinks. (Martin J. Dain, A.A.I.A./Magnum)

HERBERT J. GANS
The Birth of a Jewish Community

Abridged with permission of the Macmillan Company from "The Origin and Growth of a Jewish Community in the Suburbs: A Study of the Jews of Park Forest" in *The Jews: Social Patterns of an American Group*, ed. Marshall Sklare. © Copyright by The Free Press of Glencoe Corporation, 1958.

Introduction
In 1949, Herbert Gans studied social relationships within a new, middle income housing project. In the course of the study,

he began to notice that among the small percentage of Jewish residents of the project, a real sense of community was emerging. In this paper, he traces the steps in that process, and describes the way that Jewish people preserve and pass on to the next generation a feeling of Jewishness. This community illustrates the successful existence of cultural pluralism in American society.

Park Forest is a garden-apartment housing project located thirty miles south of Chicago. The project, privately developed, was started in 1947, when the Chicago housing shortage was at its height. The first tenants moved in on August 30, 1948, and for two years they continued to come in as new sections of the village were completed. By November 1949, there were 2,000 families — nearly 8,000 people — renting garden apartments at $75 to $100 per month. One hundred and forty-one of these families were Jewish. Of these, about thirty had not been in the village long enough to have relations with the other Jewish families; another fifteen were "mixed marriages," with both husband and wife having rejected any identification as Jews; and the remainder, approximately one hundred families (including a few mixed marriages), 5 percent of the project, formed a fledgling "Jewish community."

In Park Forest the accent is on youth; the project naturally attracted the people most sorely pressed for housing: veterans with children. The men average thirty to thirty-five years of age, the women somewhat less (anyone over forty is generally considered old). Most of the men are at the beginning of their careers, in professional, sales, administrative, and other business fields. (Only four of the men interviewed owned their own businesses.) Although not long removed from the GI Bill of Rights, they were in 1949 already earning from $4,000 to $10,000 a year — most of them

perhaps around $5,000. Few of the men, and few of the wives even, are without some college experience, and educationally the Jews as a whole stand even higher than the rest of the Park Forest community. Ninety percent of the Jewish men interviewed have college training, 60 percent hold degrees, and no less than 36 percent have graduate degrees.

The Jews of Park Forest dress as do the other Park Foresters, enjoy similar leisure-time activities, read the same newspapers, look at the same movies, hear the same radio programs — in short they participate with other Park Foresters in American middle class culture. They observe few traditional Jewish religious practices; the village's isolation from synagogues and kosher food shops has probably discouraged observant Jews from becoming tenants, and brought problems to those few who did.

Not only do Park Forest Jews live like other Park Foresters, they live with them. Whereas most American cities have "neighborhoods" dominated by one ethnic group or another — in atmosphere and institutions if not in numbers — this is not true of Park Forest. Most Park Foresters live in what are called "courts" — *culs de sac* surrounded in circular fashion by twenty to forty two-story garden apartments. Each "apartment" is actually a house, built together with five or seven others into a single unit. Privacy is at a minimum and each court is almost an independent social unit. Many of the Park Foresters find all their friends in their own court — but this is not the case with the Jews. The Jewish families are scattered all over the village, and only rarely are two Jewish families to be found in adjacent apartments. Yet in just one year, a Jewish community consisting of informal groups of friends, a B'nai B'rith lodge, a National Council of Jewish Women chapter, a Sunday School, and even a Board of Jewish Education had emerged.

How did this happen?

From the very beginning it seemed to be important to Jewish Park Foresters to "recognize" whether or not any of their neighbors were Jewish. And the widespread labeling, in America and Europe, of certain Mediterranean-Armenoid facial features as "Jewish," plus the monopolization of certain surnames by Jews, has resulted in a stereo-typical formula of recognition, used by Jews and non-Jews, which is accurate more often than not.

One early resident related: "I saw Mrs. F. in the court a couple of times . . . I thought she looked Jewish. With me, there's no mistaking it. Then someone told me her name, and I went up to talk to her. Finally we talked about something Jewish, and that was it."

"Jewish mannerisms" were also used to establish, or at least guess at, the other person's Jewishness. "The woman across the street, her actions were typical New York, so we recognized them as Jewish immediately . . ." People very skillfully explored each other through conversations, attempting to discover whether the other person was Jewish or not, and offering clues to their own Jewishness. "She's been told I'm Jewish, and I know she's Jewish, we haven't discussed it, but she uses Jewish expressions she wouldn't use in front of other people." Others turned the conversation to favorite foods: "It was a slow process, we told them what kind of food we like, corned beef, lox . . ." Sometimes there are no symbols or formulas which can be applied, and people find out by accident: "I asked before Passover if they wanted macaroons, and we found out."

Barely had this informal network of friendships and acquaintances sprung up among the first Jews moving into Park Forest (it did not, of course, preclude friendships with non-Jewish neighbors — though these, as we shall see later, were rather different in quality from the friendships with Jews), when two formal Jewish organizations were set up — a chapter of the B'nai B'rith and a chapter of the National Council of Jewish Women. Both enrolled only about forty members — those who, for various motives and reasons, were "organization-minded," and those, especially women, who had no Jewish neighbors and wanted to meet Jews from other parts of the village.

Both almost immediately found a purpose: "doing something" about the Jewish children of the growing Park Forest community. And through them steps were soon taken to establish the single most important Jewish institution in Park Forest: the Sunday school.

Eventually a steering committee of four men and four women was formed to proceed with the organization of a Sunday school. While the administrative organization and the budget were being prepared, largely by the men, the school's curriculum was left to a young Chicago rabbi who had become interested in Park Forest. Quite unexpectedly to some, he supported the women in their rejection of a congregation, and formulated instead a Sunday school that would involve the parents in their children's Jewish education: "As we train the children," he told the parents, "you will have to train yourselves . . . You'll have to move toward a community center and a synagogue eventually . . ." The parents' major contribution would be to prevent such inconsistencies as would be apt to arise from not practicing at home the content of the Sunday school curriculum.

The focus of Park Forest's problem — and conflicts — lies in the family. The Sunday school, much as other Jewish institutions, is recognizably an ethnic rather than a religious institution — more correctly, an American reaction to an ethnic situation — which transmits ethnic behavior and identity; the Jewish home, however, is run by American middle class behavior patterns. The women feared that the contradictions between the traditional Jewish home, whose features are now incorporated in the Sunday school curriculum, and the American home, which embodies their primary present-day values, would lead to family tensions. So, although they wanted their children to learn about traditional Jewish life, they did not want it brought home.

The situation in Park Forest, then, is that many parents reject involvement in the cultural-religious aspects of the Jewish tradition for themselves as adults, while they demand that their children involve themselves to the extent of learning about this tradition, without, however, getting so involved as to wish to practice it. The fruit of this might well be a Judaism that ends rather than begins with Bar Mitzvah.

Why, however, did the parents want the children to go to Sunday school at all?

First, and quite important, was the fact that children, in contrast to the parents of Park Forest, having found their friends within the court without concern for ethnic origin, would see their non-Jewish friends leave for school on Sunday mornings. As one mother explained: "Our kids want to get dressed up and go to church too. The Sunday school (the Jewish one) will give them something to do." A few children were actually sent to the Protestant Sunday school a couple of times, but the over-whelming majority of the parents found this intolerable, so the pressure from the children was translated into parental demand for a Jewish Sunday school.

Second, and this is perhaps the more important reason, the parents wanted to send their children to Sunday school because they wanted to make them aware of their ethnic identity, to acquaint them with Jewishness through Jewish history and customs. (Quite frequently, this explanation was complemented by the qualification, ". . . so that later he can choose what he

wants to be." The notion that the Jewish child would have a choice between being Jewish or not Jewish, a decision he would make in adolescence or early adulthood, was voiced even by parents who admitted their own continuing confusion as to how to act, and as to the identity they had and wanted to have.)

But why become aware of ethnic identity and of "Jewish customs"? Because parents want their Jewish identity explained to their children, often as a defense against hardships they might run into because they are Jews. Representative of this rather widespread sentiment was the comment: "A Jewish child, he's something different, he's never one of the boys in a Gentile group, even if he's the best guy, he's one of the outsiders, the first to get abused, and if he doesn't know why, it's going to be a shock. It's part of his training, the Sunday school, he needs it."

A number of parents of six- and seven-year-olds were particularly clear in their hopeful expectation that Sunday school would supply the children with answers about their identity. It seems to be at that age that questions first develop in the children's play groups as to what they are, in terms of religion or nationality. Sometimes the children are stimulated by a remark made in school or kindergarten, sometimes by something overheard in parents' conversation. One child may thus discover that he is Protestant, and that there are also Catholics and Jews. He brings this infor-mation to the group, which then tries to apply these newly discovered categories to its members. Soon the children come home and ask their parents what they are, and are they Jewish, and perhaps even "Papa, why do I have to be Jewish?" Here the Sunday school is asked to come to the rescue. One father reported of his son now in Sunday school: "He can probably tell me more than I can tell him."

Uninterested as Park Foresters may be in

"the Jewish heritage," they are nevertheless very much Jews. Clearly and unmistakably, that is, they remain both matter-of-factly and by conscious design, members of identifiably Jewish groups. This Jewish group may be another Jewish couple with whom they spend much of their time; it may be a regular and more or less stable group which gathers, in full or in part, almost every weekend and on special occasions. These groups make up the informal Jewish community, the "spontaneous" community that did not require professionals and organizers to be created.

For the most part, this informal community exists at night. In the daytime, when only housewives and the children inhabit Park Forest, the Jewish housewife participates in the general court social life. She interrupts her household duties to chat with a neighbor, while "visiting" over a morning cup of coffee or while watching the children in the afternoon. In most cases there is no distinction here between the Jewish and the non-Jewish housewife; they belong together to the bridge and sewing clubs that have been established in many courts. Women have little to do; they talk about it in the afternoons.

At night, however, in the social relations among "couples," the Jewish husband and wife turn to other Jews for friendship and recreational partnership. As one person summarized it: "My real close friends, my after-dark friends, are mostly Jewish; my daytime friends are Gentile." It is easy to explain the tendency to find friends in one's own group, even when this takes one from one's own front door, as it does in Park Forest. As the Park Foresters say, "It's easier being with Jews"—it is psychologically more accommodating, and there is less strain in achieving an informal, relaxed relationship with other Jews: "You can give vent to your feelings. If you talk to a Christian and say you don't believe in this, you are doing it as a Jew; with Jewish friends you can tell them point blank what you feel."

There are many Jewish Park Foresters who reject these in-group attitudes as "chauvinistic," and when asked about their friends, are quick to reply that they do not distinguish between Jews and non-Jews in choosing friends. Yet as one said: "The funny thing is, most of our friends are Jewish even though we say we don't care." And to quote another: "I think we should try to have friends that aren't Jewish. I don't like the fact that all my friends are Jewish."

But these Jewish Park Foresters, too, feel that they differ from the majority of the non-Jewish Park Foresters—and not only because their friends are Jews. These feelings have a basis in Park Forest reality. The Jews are distinguished by a feeling of "social consciousness," by concern over political and social problems, by a tendency toward a humanistic agnosticism, and by an interest in more "highbrow" leisure activities: foreign films, classical music, the fine arts, and in general the liberal intellectual-aesthetic leisure culture of America, and perhaps the Western world. There seem to be proportionately more Jews than non-Jews in Park Forest who participate in this culture. Jews who seek other people with whom they can share these attitudes and interests tend to find other Jews. This culture—which includes an important proportion of Park Forest's Jews—itself is largely devoid of Jewish content, and the Jews who come together in it would seem to do so not primarily because they are Jews but because they share a culture. When Jewish problems are discussed by these people (and they are discussed), they are seen from a generalized world view, rather than from an in-group perspective.

Park Forest is a new and growing community; it has changed since this study was made, and will continue to change in the future as its present tenants are replaced by others or decide to stay and settle down. Nevertheless, the Jewish community has already become oriented around a number of elements which are unlikely to change.

Whereas their parents were not only socially "clannish" but culturally different from their non-Jewish neighbors, the adult Jews of Park Forest are "clannish" but culturally not very different. (Or, rather, their cultural distinctiveness, when it exists, is not along Jewish lines.) Their adjustment to American society and their present status can be described as one of cultural assimilation and continued social distinctiveness. Thus, the Jews of Park Forest remain an ethnic group, albeit different from the parental one.

It is this feeling of Jewish togetherness, to sum up, which provides the impetus for child-orientation, for the parents' insistence on a Sunday school, and the unending attempt to indoctrinate the child with a sense of Jewishness.

Conclusion

The Jews in Park Forest were basically quite similar to their gentile neighbors. The Jews were scattered throughout the community and their life style was similar to that of other residents in the project; yet the Park Forest Jewish community created a variety of special organizations and developed into a strong informal clique. To Gans, these organizations and cliques were set up in response to a number of specific problems that are special to the Jews as an ethnic group. All the ethnic groups in America face certain problems to which they must respond in one way or another; each group finds its own way to respond. In the Clark abridgment later in this chapter we will see some responses that blacks have made to more severe problems of discrimination. An interesting contrast between the blacks and the Jews is that while the blacks handled their problems in individual ways, the Jews turned toward the Jewish community or toward their children.

TOPIC

2 PREJUDICE AND DISCRIMINATION AGAINST MINORITIES

In nearly every situation, we find some sort of prejudice or discrimination. When a man says, "My school is the best in the state," he is exhibiting a prejudice. To hire a new employee because he graduated from the same college that you did is discrimination. Such behavior may lead to misunderstanding and disappointments, but it does not constitute the

kind of major social pattern to be discussed here because it is relatively random and may affect only a few individuals. Here we shall take up the problems which arise when prejudice and discrimination are systematically applied by members of the dominant society toward a minority group. We will also discuss the causes and manifestations of both prejudice and discrimination, and consider how these attitudes are, or can be, changed.

PREJUDICE

The Latin root of the word prejudice means "judging before." *Prejudice* consists of judging — people, things, or situations — on the basis of preconceived stereotypes or generalizations. A prejudice may be either positive, such as the belief that Harvard graduates make the best business executives, or negative, such as the belief that all people on welfare are lazy.

Given the human inclination to generalize, a certain amount of prejudice, in the broadest sense of the word, is probably inevitable, and indeed functional in many situations. If you are a woman walking down the street, about to be attacked by a man with a knife, and you see two men nearby who might help you, one muscular and tall, the other skinny and shorter than you are, which one will you run toward to ask for protection? Of course you will choose the tall, muscular man. It is quite possible that he is terrified of men with knives, that he faints at the sight of blood, or that he is the kind of person who doesn't want to get involved with someone else's troubles. It is also possible that the short skinny man is very brave and has a black belt in judo. Yet the circumstances call for a prejudgment, without knowing anything more about the men than their relative sizes.

The same kind of decision comes up almost daily in a less dramatic way. When a business executive hires a secretary, or a college freshman fills out the form describing the kind of roommate she would prefer to have, or a family chooses which suburb to live in when they move to a new city, they are all operating on the basis of some prejudice, or preformed stereotype.

Prejudice becomes a problem when the preformed judgment remains unchanged even after facts show it to be inaccurate. To return to our example, suppose you recognize the face of the skinny man and remember that you saw him win the world championship in judo

the night before on television. Then at the moment you make your decision about which way to run, you would think, "I know that big muscular men are often better fighters than short skinny men, but this particular short skinny man has proven himself to be a good fighter, so I would be safe if I ran to him." In other words, you would discard your prejudice when it no longer fit the situation. But some people are unable to do this. They have believed for so many years that a skinny man can't be a good fighter and have been so thoroughly convinced it must be true, that they simply can't accept any evidence to the contrary. Such people would still run to the bigger man, because they make their decisions on the basis of their prejudices even when they conflict with the obvious facts.

The social problem of prejudice, then, is not so much the prejudgment, which can in many cases be a necessary condition for social interaction — for example, when we have to make some assumption about how to treat people we have just met and to decide what to expect from them. Rather it is the failure to discard that prejudgment in the light of additional evidence. The white college graduate who assumes, on meeting an American Indian, that the Indian has less education than he does, is prejudiced, in the sense that he has made a prejudgment based on a generalization. But the generalization is a reasonable one, because statistics show that on the average American Indians complete only six-and-a-half years of school. Suppose, however, that he is told by a third person that the Indian has a Ph.D. in computer science, and he still persists in treating the man as if he had an inferior education, then his prejudice is a social problem, and his attitude will certainly be resented by the Indian in question. In common usage, the word prejudice is usually meant to refer to this kind of biased, inflexible thinking, rather than to all forms of prejudgment.

Prejudgment against ethnic or racial minorities is always a learned attitude. No one is born with a prejudice. He learns it from his social experience, his parents, at school or church, from his friends, or from the books he reads. A whole system of prejudices may be built into a culture, as is true in racist societies. A white child growing up in South Africa, for instance, learns prejudice against blacks from nearly all his social experiences, for it is an integral part of his culture. Many prejudices are based on the differences caused by social stratification. A prejudice against members of the League of Women Voters, or young people who have long hair, is the result of socialization to the standards of behavior, dress, and taste of one's own social class. Prejudice can also be a quite personal reaction to the specific experiences of one's own life. A girl can become prejudiced against soldiers after she has been jilted by one. Most widely held prejudices are a result of all these forms of social learning.

Studies by a number of investigators have shown that certain groups of people are more likely to be prejudiced against minority groups than others. Economic competition can lead to prejudice. Lower-class whites are usually more prejudiced against blacks (who are for the most part confined to low status occupations) than against whites of higher social class, because lower-class whites compete with blacks for jobs. For the same reason, prejudice against Jews is common among the higher classes of gentiles.[8] Some sociologists have theorized that in general low status groups are more prone to prejudice than high status groups.[9] This is partly because the prejudice boosts their own low social status and social power; if another group is placed lower than themselves, they have in effect raised their status. It may also be due in part to a scapegoat mechanism whereby the low status groups put the blame on their disadvantaged situation on someone else.

Certain personality types also seem to be associated with the formation of prejudice. A study by T. W. Adorno in the late 1940s purported to find that many prejudiced persons have an "authoritarian" personality.[10] Another study found that the prejudiced or intolerant person is characterized by an unwillingness to accept authority, by an interest in physical activity and health, and by an emotional rather than a rational approach to problem solving.[11] Psychologists have pointed out a correlation between feelings of insecurity or anxiety and prejudiced attitudes. Even if these research findings were more conclusive than they are (owing to the difficulties in studying such a complex subject), it would be important to keep in mind that they do not mean that an authoritarian person will always be prejudiced, or that a high status person will never be prejudiced. However, certain social situations seem to teach and reinforce prejudice better than others.

DISCRIMINATION

We usually speak of prejudice and discrimination as an inseparable and natural pair. They generally occur together, but it is important to understand that they are two separate concepts. Prejudice refers to an attitude, an internal feeling. *Discrimination* means unfair or unequal treatment that is accorded to people or groups; it is not an attitude, but an action or type of behavior based on an attitude.

The two need not always occur together. It is possible to be prejudiced but not translate that prejudice into an action of discrimination. A prejudiced person may believe that Orientals are inferior and yet, because of a commitment to democratic ideals, be willing to allow Orientals to live in his neighborhood, vote for the president, and compete freely for all jobs. The reverse is also possible—dis-

8.   Robin M. Williams, Jr., *Strangers Next Door* (Englewood Cliffs, N.J.: Prentice-Hall, 1964), pp. 53–54.

9.   Robert K. Merton, *Social Theory and Social Structure* (New York: Free Press, 1957), pp. 121–194.

10.   T. W. Adorno et al., *The Authoritarian Personality* (New York: Harper, 1950).

11.   Eugene Hartley, *Problems of Prejudice* (New York: King's Crown Press, 1946).

The Jim Crow system that developed toward the end of the nineteenth century increasingly hemmed in and controlled the actions of black people, particularly in their contacts with whites. Public facilities ranging from rest rooms to buses to beaches were declared off-limits to blacks. The laws were so numerous and conflicting that it was often difficult to know just what behavior was in fact legal for blacks in a specific situation. Given the power to legally control the actions of blacks, many whites were encouraged to be openly aggressive. After 1900, race riots became increasingly common in both North and South. Under these conditions blacks adopted a strategy of apparent compliance and superficial obsequiousness. *(Photo by Ken Heyman)*

crimination without any feelings of prejudice. For example, company officials may be aware of the fact that Miss Smith has the ability to perform the duties of a vice-president with great competence and yet still refuse to promote her to that position, because they are afraid that their clients might not like to deal with a female executive. Of course, it is true that this excuse—"I don't have anything against Miss Smith personally, but it would ruin my business if I promoted her"—is often used as an excuse for discriminatory actions that do in fact stem from a personal prejudice.

Many forms of discrimination are the simple outcome of attitudes of prejudice. It is also true that discrimination can lead to, or cause, prejudice. If, through discriminatory practices, a group of people is denied the opportunity to get an adequate education, then others may begin to view them as intellectually inferior; eventually the fact that their deficiency is the result of a policy of discrimination may be forgotten altogether. Prejudice and discrimination are mutually reinforcing, each one intensifying the other.

There are many different kinds and levels of discrimination. Many kinds of discrimination have been legal at one time or another in

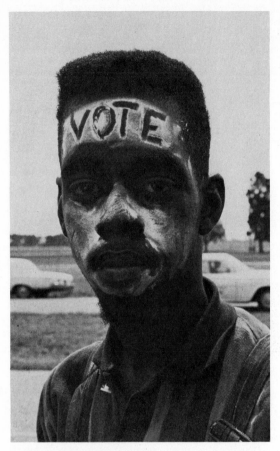

In the face of stubborn white resistance to laws forbidding discrimination against black voters, Civil
Rights organizations adopted a more radical form of
direct action through an intensive drive to register
black voters in rural counties of the deep South.
Despite hostility and threats of violence, blacks indicated their refusal to accept subordination passively,
and continued their efforts throughout the early 1960s.
The tactics of direct action made it possible for ordinary citizens to participate in the Civil Rights Movement and played a central role in the passage of a
comprehensive Voting Rights Act in 1965. *(Bruce
Davidson, Magnum)*

our country, as evident, for example, in voting
restrictions. In most of the thirteen original
colonies, the right to vote was given only to
white males over twenty-one who owned land
or a house; this meant that the poor, the nonwhite, the young, and women were all dis-

criminated against. By the time the Constitution was written, legal discrimination against
the poor was remedied. After the Civil War,
it was no longer legal to discriminate directly
against black people in voting—though many
more subtle discriminatory practices remained.
In the early twentieth century, the discrimination against women as voters was eliminated.

Sometimes discrimination can be made legal
by disguising the true purpose of a law that
in effect is discriminatory. In many southern
states which were strongly opposed to letting
blacks vote, the laws against blacks voting,
although repealed, were replaced by laws requiring some test of reading ability as a qualification for voting. The end result was the same
exclusion of black voters, since few blacks
were able to pass the required test. Another
example can be seen in the requirement of
many Arab countries that American and
European visitors submit a baptismal certificate as "proof of identity" before they can
be issued a visa to enter the country, or immigrate there. Since baptism is not a practice
of the Jewish religion, no Jew will be able to
present the necessary certificate, and will be
legally kept from entering the country. A
close examination of the laws of many countries will show that a number of them are
written in such a way that certain groups gain
an advantage over others, while others are
restricted in their activities.

Informal patterns of discrimination can be
found in every aspect of daily life. The anti-
black business employer simply turns down
black applicants for a job, on the grounds that
they are "not qualified," and ignores black
customers until they give up and go elsewhere.
Many schools, businesses, employment agencies, and real estate agents employ even more
subtle means of discrimination. The admissions officer of a school may have in mind a
personal quota of blacks or Jews and will
accept no more than that number. Employment agencies may use code phrases in their
written job descriptions, such as "Employer

will not make any twelve o'clock appointments"—which the employees of the agency know means that he will not hire an Indian, or an Oriental, or a black. Rental agents may tell a Puerto Rican couple that the apartment has already been taken, and then rent it to a white applicant. Actually, most of the discrimination that members of minority groups face in the United States today is of this more informal, rather than legal, type.

ETHNICITY AND STRATIFICATION

In the last chapter we observed how society is stratified along lines of racial and ethnic groups. These patterns of stratification result in part from discrimination and prejudice. Though ethnic groups may be ranked in a status hierarchy, they are only one factor among many in determining each person's social class position. Education, occupation, place of residence, and many other rankings must also be taken into account. Perhaps the most accurate way to describe the connection between ethnic group membership and overall social status is to say that ethnic origin will not determine social class but that it will determine the approximate range of social classes which will be open to a particular individual. A Mexican-American, for example, is less likely to be able to achieve the very highest social status. A black has a more than average likelihood of being in the lower social classes.

Several studies have been made to try to determine the status ranking of ethnic groups in America.[12] It is interesting to speculate about the reasons for some of these ratings. Generally speaking, all Caucasian groups have higher status than Mongoloid or Negroid groups. A notable exception is that of the Russians; their low status can probably be accounted for in political terms, for this study was done at the height of the Cold War. (In

12. Emory S. Bogardus, *Social Distance* (Yellow Springs, Ohio: Antioch Press, 1959).

UNEMPLOYMENT RATES BY RACE*

Year	White	Nonwhite
1960	4.9	10.2
1965	4.1	8.1
1969	3.1	6.4
1970	4.5	8.2
1971	5.4	9.9

*Unit of measure: percent

Statistical Abstract of the United States, 1972, p. 351.

FAMILIES BY INCOME LEVEL*

	White		Nonwhite	
Year	Under $3000	$10,000 and over	Under $3000	$10,000 and over
1960	13.4	30.9	36.4	10.8
1965	10.2	41.4	27.3	15.8
1969	7.3	52.5	18.9	27.3
1970	7.5	51.6	20.1	28.2

*Unit of measure: percent

Statistical Abstract of the United States, 1972, p. 527.

PROPORTION OF WHITES AND NONWHITES BELOW POVERTY LEVEL IN THE UNITED STATES*

Year	White	Nonwhite
1960	17.8	55.9
1965	13.3	47.1
1969	9.5	31.1
1970	9.9	32.0
1971	9.9	30.9

*Unit of measure: percent

Statistical Abstract of the United States, 1972, p. 539.

These three tables record recent inequalities between the white and nonwhite populations of the United States. For the last eleven years unemployment among nonwhites has been greater and has fluctuated more than that among whites; nonwhite incomes have increased at a slower rate; and more nonwhites have continued to receive incomes below the poverty line, despite a recent drop in number.

countries where the dominant group is Mongoloid, Caucasians may have the lowest status.) But how do we explain the fact that the very lowest group on the scale, the Indians, are Caucasians? Politics probably also influenced the very low status of the Koreans, as the Korean War had ended only three years before the study was made. But why do the Turks rank so low? It could just be the result of unfamiliarity, or it could be a kind of secondhand prejudice picked up from the eastern European immigrants, many of whom consider the word "Turk" to be a synonym for "barbarian."

CHANGING PATTERNS OF PREJUDICE AND DISCRIMINATION

Patterns of prejudice and discrimination always lead to social problems. They cause social and psychological problems for the minority group that is their target and, sometimes, create guilt and anxiety in members of the dominant society. They cause the waste of valuable human resources. No society can afford to put deliberate limits on the achievements of a sizable segment of its population; therefore, wherever prejudice and discrimination exist, so do pressures to bring about a change.

The elimination of discrimination requires social change. It is useful to distinguish between two different kinds of social change. One is planned or enacted change, where, for example, laws are passed which alter some social situation. The other is natural or crescive change, which comes about without any deliberate planning, but simply as the result of small adaptations to changing circumstances.

In America today, both planned and natural change are affecting old patterns of discrimination and segregation. Planned change is only demonstrably effective in the area of discrimination, not in the area of prejudice. Laws can regulate behavior, but it is almost impossible for them to control attitudes or feelings. In the last decade, many laws have been passed outlawing discriminatory behavior. It is illegal to discriminate against minority groups in education, employment, and housing. However, enforcement of these laws presents problems.

It is hard to prove that a family was turned down by the owner of an apartment building because they are black, or that a worker did not get the job he applied for because he is Jewish. Proof takes a lot of work, and even when it is established, long and costly court cases are necessary to enforce antidiscrimination laws. The government has undertaken the work and expense of this kind of enforcement, but its resources are not great enough to pursue every case. If a policy of strict enforcement is followed, in time it will be easier to carry out, because social sanctions will force people to conform to the law.

Other kinds of change are even more difficult to accomplish. As members of minority groups gradually achieve higher occupational positions, their changing conditions will tend to modify the attitudes others hold toward them. More and more blacks are getting at least a high school education, which gives them a chance of obtaining more prestigious jobs at higher salaries. Gradually the stereotypes of blacks will change to reflect their improved circumstances. There is reason to believe that something like this has already happened in the case of the Jewish minority group. In several generations they have made great gains in educational, economic, and occupational status, and this, apparently, has somewhat lessened the prejudice against them.

One popular theory is that attitudes of prejudice can be changed by increased contact with the minority group. In some cases this does appear to work, but increased contact is by no means a universal cure. For example, one study found that of 106 white boys who attended an interracial camp for four weeks, 28 came home with a significantly lower degree of prejudice, but 27 became significantly *more* prejudiced.[13] Sometimes the contact simply serves to reinforce existing stereotypes and thus strengthens prejudice.

13. Paul H. Mussen, "Some Personality and Social Factors Related to Changes in Children's Attitudes toward Negroes," *Journal of Abnormal Psychology* 45 (1950):423–441.

MALCOLM X
Mascot

Excerpt from *The Autobiography of Malcolm X* by Malcolm X with the assistance of Alex Haley. 1965, Grove Press Inc., pp. 23–28. Reprinted by permission of Grove Press, Inc. Copyright © 1964 by Alex Haley and Malcolm X. Copyright © 1965 by Alex Haley and Betty Shabazz.

Introduction

Malcolm X spoke for the black community in strong and uncompromising terms. Although many could not share his Muslim religious beliefs, they could identify with his struggle to triumph over his own background to become an articulate leader and forceful champion of his people.

In this excerpt Malcolm X relates how he awakened to the cold and devastating facts of what it means to be black in America. As a youngster he lived with a white family and was one of the few blacks in his junior high school. Although he was well liked at home and popular at school, Malcolm was always conscious of his separateness and the often unconscious prejudice that kept him from being accepted as simply another human being.

I noticed again how white people smelled different from us, and how their food tasted different, not seasoned like Negro cooking. I began to sweep and mop and dust around in the Swerlins' house, as I had done with Big Boy at the Gohannas'.

They all liked my attitude, and it was out of their liking for me that I soon became accepted by them—as a mascot, I know now. They would talk about anything and everything with me standing right there hearing them, the same way people would talk freely in front of a pet canary. They would even talk about me, or about "niggers," as though I wasn't there, as if I wouldn't understand what the word meant. A hundred times a day, they used the word "nigger." I suppose that in their own minds, they meant no harm; in fact they probably meant well. It was the same with the cook, Lucille, and her husband, Duane. I remember one day when Mr. Swerlin, as nice as he was, came in from Lansing, where he had been through the Negro section, and said to Mrs. Swerlin right in front of me, "I just can't see how those niggers can be so happy and be so poor." He talked about how they lived in shacks, but had those big, shining cars out front.

And Mrs. Swerlin said, me standing right there, "Niggers are just that way...."
That scene always stayed with me.

It was the same with the other white people, most of them local politicians, when they would come visiting the Swerlins. One of their favorite parlor topics was "niggers." One of them was the judge who was in charge of me in Lansing. He was a close friend of the Swerlins. He would ask about me when he came, and they would call me in, and he would look me up and down, his expression approving, like he was examining a fine colt, or a pedigreed pup. I knew they must have told him how I acted and how I worked.

What I am trying to say is that it just never dawned upon them that I could understand, that I wasn't a pet, but a human being. They didn't give me credit for having the same sensitivity, intellect, and understanding that they would have been ready and willing to recognize in a white boy in my position. But it has historically been the case with white people, in their regard for black people, that even though we might be *with* them, we weren't considered *of* them. Even though they appeared to have opened the door, it was still closed. Thus they never did really see *me*....

Many youngsters from the detention home, when their dates came up, went off to the reform school. But when mine came up—two or three times—it was always ignored. I saw new youngsters arrive and leave. I was glad and grateful. I knew it was Mrs. Swerlin's doing. I didn't want to leave.

She finally told me one day that I was going to be entered in Mason Junior High School. It was the only school in town. No ward of the detention home had ever gone to school there, at least while still a ward. So I entered their seventh grade. The only other Negroes there were some of the Lyons children, younger than I was, in the lower grades. The Lyons and I, as it happened, were the town's only Negroes. They were, as Negroes, very much respected. Mr. Lyons was a smart, hard-working man, and Mrs. Lyons was a very good woman. She and my mother, I had heard my mother say, were two of the four West Indians in that whole section of Michigan.

Some of the white kids at school, I found, were even friendlier than some of those in Lansing had been. Though some, including the teachers, called me "nigger," it was easy to see that they didn't mean any more harm by it than the Swerlins. As the "nigger" of my class, I was in fact extremely popular —I suppose partly because I was kind of a novelty. I was in demand, I had top priority. But I also benefited from the special prestige of having the seal of approval from that Very Important Woman about the town of Mason, Mrs. Swerlin. Nobody in Mason would have dreamed of getting on the wrong side of her. It became hard for me to get through a school day without someone after me to join this or head up that—the debating society, the Junior High basketball team, or some other extracurricular activity. I never turned them down.

And I hadn't been in the school long when Mrs. Swerlin, knowing I could use spending money of my own, got me a job after school washing the dishes in a local restaurant. My boss there was the father of a white classmate whom I spent a lot of time with. His family lived over the restaurant. It was fine working there. Every Friday night when I got paid, I'd feel at least ten feet tall. I forget how much I made, but it seemed like a lot. It was the first time I'd ever had any money to speak of, all my own, in my whole life. As soon as I could afford it, I bought a green suit and some shoes, and at school I'd buy treats for the others in my class—at least as much as any of them did for me.

English and history were the subjects I liked most. My English teacher, I recall— a Mr. Ostrowski—was always giving advice about how to become something in life. The one thing I didn't like about history class was that the teacher, Mr. Williams, was a great one for "nigger" jokes. One day during my first week at school, I walked into the room and he started singing to the class, as a joke, " 'Way down yonder in the cotton fields, some folks say that a nigger won't steal." Very funny. I liked history, but I never thereafter had much liking for Mr. Williams. Later, I remember, we came to the textbook section on Negro history. It was exactly one paragraph long. Mr. Williams laughed through it practically in a single breath, reading aloud how the Negroes had been slaves and then were freed, and how they were usually lazy and dumb and shiftless. He added, I remember, an anthropological footnote on his own, telling us between laughs how Negroes' feet were "so big that when they walk, they don't leave tracks, they leave a hole in the ground."

I'm sorry to say that the subject I most disliked was mathematics. I have thought about it, I think the reason was that mathematics leaves no room for argument. If you made a mistake, that was all there was to it.

Basketball was a big thing in my life, though. I was on the team; we traveled to neighboring towns such as Howell and Charlotte, and wherever I showed my face, the audiences in the gymnasium "niggered" and "cooned" me to death. Or called me "Rastus." It didn't bother my teammates or my coach at all, and to tell the truth, it bothered me only vaguely. Mine was the same psychology that makes Negroes even today, though it bothers them down inside, keep letting the white man tell them how much "progress" they are making. They've heard it so much they've almost gotten brainwashed into believing it — or at least accepting it. . . .

The summer of 1940, in Lansing, I caught the Greyhound bus for Boston with my cardboard suitcase, and wearing my green suit. If someone had hung a sign, "HICK," around my neck, I couldn't have looked much more obvious. They didn't have the turnpikes then; the bus stopped at what seemed every corner and cowpatch. From my seat in — you guessed it — the back of the bus, I gawked out of the window at white man's America rolling past for what seemed a month, but must have been only a day and a half.

When we finally arrived, Ella met me at the terminal and took me home. The house was on Waumbeck Street in the Sugar Hill section of Roxbury, the Harlem of Boston. I met Ella's second husband, Frank, who was now a soldier; and her brother Earl, the singer who called himself Jimmy Carleton; and Mary, who was very different from her older sister. It's funny how I seemed to think of Mary as Ella's sister, instead of her being, just as Ella is, my own half-sister. It's probably because Ella and I always were much closer as basic types; we're dominant people, and Mary has always been mild and quiet, almost shy.

Ella was busily involved in dozens of things. She belonged to I don't know how many different clubs; she was a leading light of local so-called "black society." I saw and met a hundred black people there whose big-city talk and ways left my mouth hanging open.

I couldn't have feigned indifference if I had tried to. People talked casually about Chicago, Detroit, New York. I didn't know the world contained as many Negroes as I saw thronging downtown Roxbury at night, especially on Saturdays. Neon lights, nightclubs, poolhalls, bars, the cars they drove! Restaurants made the streets smell — rich, greasy, down-home black cooking! Jukeboxes blared Erskine Hawkins, Duke Ellington, Cootie Williams, dozens of others. If somebody had told me then that some day I'd know them all personally, I'd have found it hard to believe. The biggest bands, like these, played at the Roseland State Ballroom, on Boston's Massachusetts Avenue — one night for Negroes, the next night for whites.

I saw for the first time occasional black-white couples strolling around arm in arm. And on Sundays, when Ella, Mary, or somebody took me to church, I saw churches for black people such as I had never seen. They were many times finer than the white church I had attended back in Mason, Michigan. There, the white people just sat and worshiped with words; but the Boston Negroes, like all other Negroes I had ever seen at church, threw their souls and bodies wholly into worship.

Two or three times, I wrote letters to Wilfred intended for everybody back in Lansing. I said I'd try to describe it when I got back.

But I found I couldn't.

My restlessness with Mason — and for the first time in my life a restlessness with being around white people — began as soon as I got back home and entered eighth grade.

I continued to think constantly about all that I had seen in Boston, and about the way I had felt there. I know now that it was the sense of being a real part of a mass of my own kind, for the first time.

The white people — classmates, the Swerlins, the people at the restaurant where I worked — noticed the change. They said, "You're acting so strange. You don't seem like yourself, Malcolm. What's the matter?''

I kept close to the top of the class, though. The top-most scholastic standing, I remember, kept shifting between me, a girl named Audrey Slaugh, and a boy named Jimmy Cotton.

It went on that way, as I became increasingly restless and disturbed through the first semester. And then one day, just about when those of us who had passed were about to move up to 8-A, from which we would enter high school the next year, something happened which was to become the first major turning point of my life.

Somehow, I happened to be alone in the classroom with Mr. Ostrowski, my English teacher. He was a tall, rather reddish white man and he had a thick mustache. I had gotten some of my best marks under him, and he had always made me feel that he liked me. He was, as I have mentioned, a natural-born ''advisor,'' about what you ought to read, to do, or think—about any and everything. We used to make unkind jokes about him: why was he teaching in Mason instead of somewhere else, getting for himself some of the ''success of life'' that he kept telling us how to get?

I know that he probably meant well in what he happened to advise me that day. I doubt that he meant any harm. It was just his nature as an American white man. I was one of his top students, one of the school's top students—but all he could see for me was the kind of future ''in your place'' that almost all white people see for black people.

He told me, ''Malcolm, you ought to be thinking about a career. Have you been giving it thought?''

The truth is, I hadn't. I never have figured out why I told him, ''Well, yes, sir, I've been thinking I'd like to be a lawyer.'' Lansing certainly had no Negro lawyers—or doctors either—in those days, to hold up an image I might have aspired to. All I really knew for certain was that a lawyer didn't wash dishes, as I was doing.

Mr. Ostrowski looked surprised, I remember, and leaned back in his chair and clasped his hands behind his head. He kind of half-smiled and said, ''Malcolm, one of life's first needs is for us to be realistic. Don't misunderstand me, now. We all here like you, you know that. But you've got to be realistic about being a nigger. A lawyer—that's no realistic goal for a nigger. You need to think about something you *can* be. You're good with your hands—making things. Everybody admires your carpentry shop work. Why don't you plan on carpentry? People like you as a person—you'd get all kinds of work.''

The more I thought afterwards about what he said, the more uneasy it made me. It just kept treading around in my mind.

What made it really begin to disturb me was Mr. Ostrowski's advice to others in my class—all of them white. Most of them had told him they were planning to become farmers. But those who wanted to strike out on their own, to try something new, he had encouraged. Some, mostly girls, wanted to be teachers. A few wanted other professions, such as one boy who wanted to become a county agent; another, a veterinarian; and one girl wanted to be a nurse. They all reported that Mr. Ostrowski had encouraged what they had wanted. Yet nearly none of them had earned marks equal to mine.

It was a surprising thing that I had never thought of it that way before, but I realized that whatever I wasn't, I *was* smarter than nearly all of those white kids. But apparently I was still not intelligent enough, in their eyes, to become whatever *I* wanted to be.

It was then that I began to change—inside.

Conclusion

Malcolm's experience illustrates one of the most basic features of racial prejudice —the inability to perceive and judge minority group members as individuals. Despite outstanding personal qualities, Malcolm's ambition to pursue his goals in life came into conflict with stereotyped notions of what blacks can appropriately do and become in life. By blocking efforts to achieve occupational success, society often leaves the minority individual with the option of giving up his goals altogether or of achieving material success through crime or other deviant means. Malcolm's criticism of white

society was directed at the limitations placed on the black man's efforts to fulfill his potential as a human being. His criticism of white society was inspired by the insidious effects of racism that destroy the self-respect of American blacks. His approach to the "Negro problem" which he called "the white man's problem" was directed at heightening black militancy, solidarity, and racial pride.

TOPIC

3 PATTERNS OF ASSIMILATION AND EXCLUSION

Societies have chosen to treat minority groups in their midst in a number of ways. The particular pattern utilized in each society depends in large part on the value system and other elements of social organization in that society. It also depends on the kind and degree of difference displayed by the minority group and the emotional responses which their differences evoke. Within a single society, different treatment may be accorded to different minority groups. This can be seen in our own society, where the French, German, or Irish ethnic groups have not been subjected to the same enduring discriminatory treatment as blacks, Mexican-Americans, or American Indians.

We may divide the patterns of intergroup relations into broad categories which represent polar positions: assimilation and exclusion. *Assimilation* consists of those processes directed toward bringing the minority groups to full and equal status in the dominant society. Integration, amalgamation, and cultural

pluralism are major patterns of assimilation which will be discussed here. *Exclusion* refers to those processes directed at preventing or minimizing assimilation. Examples of exclusionary patterns to be discussed here are annihilation, expulsion, and segregation.

Most societies have a mixture of assimilation and exclusion patterns. This is partly due to the fact that within the same society different policies and attitudes are maintained toward different groups. It is also because patterns of assimilation are often held more as ideals than as practices, the actual practice being one of diffuse discrimination and prejudice.

PATTERNS OF ASSIMILATION

If a society highly values equality and freedom for all individuals, then it is likely to try to respond to the presence of ethnic groups within it in a manner which provides for as much assimilation to the dominant culture as the groups desire. There are three major patterns that fall in this general category.

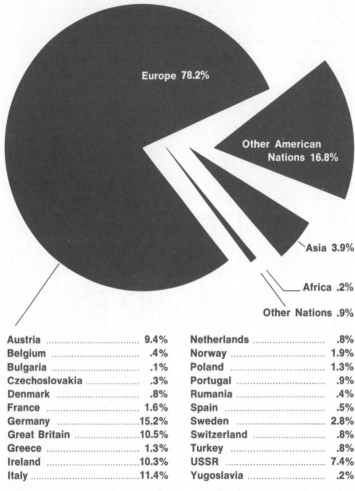

IMMIGRATION TO THE UNITED STATES: 1820-1971

Europe 78.2%

Other American Nations 16.8%

Asia 3.9%

Africa .2%

Other Nations .9%

Austria	9.4%	Netherlands	.8%
Belgium	.4%	Norway	1.9%
Bulgaria	.1%	Poland	1.3%
Czechoslovakia	.3%	Portugal	.9%
Denmark	.8%	Rumania	.4%
France	1.6%	Spain	.5%
Germany	15.2%	Sweden	2.8%
Great Britain	10.5%	Switzerland	.8%
Greece	1.3%	Turkey	.8%
Ireland	10.3%	USSR	7.4%
Italy	11.4%	Yugoslavia	.2%

SOURCE: U.S. Immigration and Naturalization Service Annual Report, 1971.

We speak of the United States as a "melting pot"; this chart shows the many different nations and areas of the world which have contributed to the United States population.

Integration

Integration is an ideal of American society, but one which we often fail to achieve: it means to blend fully the culture and social structure of the incoming group into that of the dominant society. The concept of the melting pot is simply another way of describing integration. Obviously, if the dominant society is to maintain its general character and social organization, it will have to be the minority group that yields most of its cultural attributes. However, there is always some influence in the other direction as well. The English language has been greatly enriched by words learned from our minority groups, and we have come to enjoy their foods as well—we eat almost as much pasta here as they do in Italy!

NUMBER OF IMMIGRANTS TO THE UNITED STATES BY REGION OF ORIGIN

Years	Europe	Asia	South America	Africa
1820–1971	35,630,398	1,782,711	7,641,268	82,317
1951–1960	1,325,640	153,334	996,944	14,092
1961–1970	1,123,363	427,771	1,716,374	28,954
1971	91,509	98,062	171,680	5,844

Statistical Abstract of the United States, 1972, p. 92.

Until the late nineteenth century, most immigrants to America came from northwestern Europe—from England, Ireland, Scotland, France, and Germany. From 1880 to 1920, the majority of newcomers were from Italy and eastern Europe. In recent decades immigration has been relatively low, because of strictly limited quotas.

Two forms of integration may be distinguished. The first consists of conformity to existing life, in our case to American life. In this kind of integration, the new immigrant is supposed to alter his actions, values, and attitudes, so that they conform with the dominant type of American culture—that of the white Anglo-Saxon Protestant. From this point of view, the most "successful" immigrants are those from countries like England, Ireland, and Scandinavia.

The second form of integration is what might be called the true melting pot. This type involves a complete intermixing of the dominant culture with all the different cultures of the immigrants, with the result that a truly new, uniquely American culture is developed. The city is the "pot" where the blending of cultures takes place. The integration of the immigrants of the late nineteenth and early twentieth centuries took place mainly in the large cities of the Northeast, such as Boston, New York, and Philadelphia, where the pressures of physical closeness, combined with the large numbers of immigrants that arrived each year, helped to make these cities into cosmopolitan centers. Yet there is much evidence that America is still a long way from the melting pot ideal.[14]

Integration occurs more readily in some circumstances than in others. W. Lloyd Warner and Leo Srole, using the material from the "Yankee City" study, suggested that integration is more likely to take place easily and quickly when the minority is fairly similar to the dominant society in both cultural and biological traits.[15] Thus light skinned English-speaking Protestant groups integrate most easily into American society (the English, Scotch, and Canadians, for example) and dark skinned peoples who do not speak English and are not Christian integrate with most difficulty. It is interesting to note that Warner and Srole found that ease of integration is closely associated with the numerical status ranking of ethnic groups, with the highest status ethnic groups also being those that integrate most easily into our society.

Other factors that affect the ease of integration have been identified. Other things being equal, the larger the incoming ethnic group is, the harder it is for it to become integrated into the dominant culture. If the group is far away from its homeland, it integrates more easily than when its members can make frequent trips back and forth, which tend to reinforce its native culture. A group with a relatively high level of education and income, or prestige, integrates quite rapidly. This is probably due to two reasons: the natives accept them more readily, and they are better able to adapt to their new circumstances. A good example of this might be the German Jews who came to the United States during

14. Nathan Glazer and Daniel Patrick Moynihan, *Beyond the Melting Pot* (Cambridge, Mass.: M.I.T. Press, 1963).

15. W. Lloyd Warner and Leo Srole, *The Social Systems of American Ethnic Groups* (New Haven: Yale University Press, 1945), pp. 285–286.

the 1930s. They were for the most part integrated very rapidly. They came in small numbers, over a long period of time (about a decade). They were far away from home, and moreover, knew that they couldn't return. They were, as a group, high in educational and occupational status—professors, merchants, musicians. They were Caucasians, like the dominant group in this country. It should be noted also that many of the immigrants had unique talents that were highly desired by this country; for this reason they were for the most part welcomed by the dominant society. Two adverse factors acted to slow down their assimilation. One was that they were not Christian, and therefore not members of the dominant religious group, and the other was that they tended to move into neighborhoods that housed many other European Jews; integration takes place faster when the newcomers are scattered evenly throughout the native population.

Although integration does provide a harmonious way for minority groups to live in a society, it is not an unqualified benefit. One problem, of course, is that the immigrants often resist the process. They naturally regard their own native cultures as valuable and preferable, and they are reluctant either to conform to the dominant culture here, or to disappear in the melting pot. The parades, celebrations, and festivals that each ethnic group in America continues to hold indicate the desire to retain ethnic identity. Pressures toward integration may create a situation of serious strain for these people, and thus be dysfunctional.

Another dysfunction is the loss of diversity. As was discussed in the chapter on culture, strong subcultures constitute a kind of natural resource for a society. When a change is needed, or some great social strain pervades the country, then differing subcultures provide models of new ways of thinking and doing. They are, so to speak, our substitutes warming the bench, ready to be sent into society in times of failure or need. This important resource is lost when everyone becomes alike.

Amalgamation

Integration refers to a social and cultural merging; *amalgamation* means the *biological* merging of the new ethnic group with the native population. Some degree of amalgamation always occurs when two groups live together, but it is rare for amalgamation to be the dominant pattern of relationships. This is illustrated very clearly in the case of black-white relationships in America. There are many blacks in this country who have some Caucasian genes. But marriage and reproduction between blacks and whites have generally never been socially approved; intermarriage is not common, and the two races remain physically different. True amalgamation can be seen in Hawaii and in Polynesia, where Caucasians, Negroes, and Mongoloids have intermarried so frequently that the three races have in large part melded into one group that is a mixture of all three.

Obviously, amalgamation is not a useful solution for all interrelationship problems of all ethnic groups. The amalgamation of Arabs and Jews in the Middle East would not solve their problems, because they are already virtually indistinguishable from one another physically. Their differences are social, not biological.

Cultural pluralism

Cultural pluralism is a pattern in which the dominant or native group allows newcomers to achieve full participation in society, without discriminating against them, and at the same time allows them to maintain many of their cultural and social differences. In certain major respects, America can be regarded as a pluralistic society. We allow most immigrant groups to start their own churches and maintain their own religious affiliations. A Greek immigrant, for example, is free to join the Greek Orthodox church; he is not required to become a Protestant. He can continue to eat lamb *shashlik* instead of cheeseburgers. At the same time, he usually must learn English, must adopt our style of dress at work, and must conform to a number of our

RACIAL COMPOSITION OF THE UNITED STATES
(in percentages)

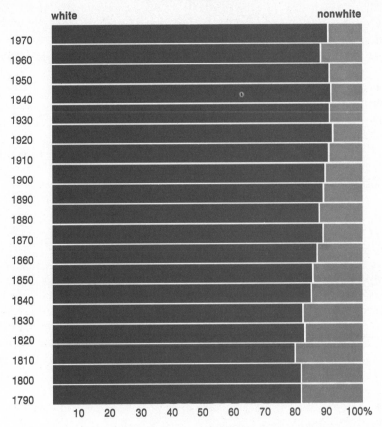

SOURCES: U.S. Bureau of the Census, *Historical Statistics of the United States* and *Statistical Abstract of the United States, 1972* (Washington, D.C.: Government Printing Office).

It is interesting to note that in 1790, nonwhites composed almost 20 percent of the total population; today they account for only 12 percent.

social customs if he is to function well in this country.

Cultural pluralism is a difficult pattern to maintain. If society is to function as a unit, it must be culturally unified to some degree. To be workable, cultural and especially linguistic pluralism must always be limited to a rather small number of groups; at the same time these groups must achieve a rather high level of integration into the overall society in terms of basic values and commitments. If every ethnic group in America spoke only its own language, our society would be paralyzed by communication problems. If we had many different basic values and were committed to different goals it would be difficult for any state or government to form and maintain its authority, or even to arrive at a course of action that would be satisfactory to a significant proportion of the nation.

A good example of pluralism can be seen in Switzerland. Both German and French are spoken everywhere, and usually Italian as well. As long as an individual speaks one of these three languages, he can participate fully as a citizen. There is little discrimination

Like many other ethnic groups in American society, various Slavic peoples have maintained much of their distinctive cultural tradition. While women no longer ordinarily wear the traditional forms of dress, such displays are encouraged at festivals celebrating religious and national holidays. Typically, as the children of various immigrant groups have become more integrated into American society, ties with their parent's ethnic group grow weaker and may be expressed only at special ethnic events. A heterogenous society such as ours faces the problem of how to maintain the best of the past while adapting to changing conditions, and how to encourage respect for cultural differences while preserving the integration of our society. *(Bill Anderson, Monkmeyer)*

because someone speaks the wrong language. In the same way, one is free to choose between the Protestant and the Catholic churches, both of which have equal status. The French-speaking Catholics and the German-speaking Protestants live together in relative harmony, neither one dominating the other. But this situation cannot be extended indefinitely. If the Swiss accorded the same treatment to a hundred other ethnic groups, or even to ten more, their country would become hopelessly fragmented.

Some sociologists consider cultural pluralism to be a stage in the process of integration, rather than an end in itself. By allowing immigrants to retain some aspects of their ethnic group identity, rather than merge totally with the dominant group, a society cushions the shock for them and helps them function effectively in their new circumstances. In time,

this link between the old life and the new may become unnecessary and will gradually be dropped. This has often been the case in America. Third- and fourth-generation Irish, for example, may only think of their Irishness once a year, on St. Patrick's Day. Yet their great-grandfathers were never fully integrated and remained a distinct minority unit within the bounds of the larger society. However, our earlier example of Switzerland indicates that pluralism is indeed possible and may exist for centuries without ever turning into true integration. In the foreseeable future, though the trend toward full integration of most groups seems quite strong, the United States will undoubtedly continue to be characterized by some measure of ethnic pluralism. The abridgment by Herbert Gans in this chapter presents an example of successful cultural pluralism.

PATTERNS OF EXCLUSION

Patterns of intergroup relations whose goal is full or partial exclusion have been by far the most commonly observed type throughout history. Obviously the dominant group, which is already holding the social power in the society, is reluctant to share it. Immigrants are often feared as potentially disruptive influences, and keeping them isolated and powerless is seen as a social necessity.

We saw in the last topic that prejudice and discrimination in general lead to the exclusion of many minority group members from the rights and privileges of full citizenship and participation. The exclusionary patterns to be considered here are those relatively extreme forms in which discrimination and prejudice become highly organized and focused, and are often a deliberate policy agreed upon by the society.

Annihilation

The most extreme of the exclusion patterns is annihilation, whereby the dominant group causes the death of minority group members in large numbers. In other words, a society eliminates the problem of getting along with a minority by eliminating the minority. Sometimes this is a deliberate and explicit policy of the leaders of the society. The most infamous modern example is Hitler's "solution" to the presence of Jews in German society, which was to round up an estimated six million Jews and systematically exterminate them. This is by no means the only example of annihilation in modern times; the "Stalin Purges" in Russia in the 1930s reportedly killed even more people. In the 1960s a political purge in Indonesia took an estimated one million lives.

Unfortunately, these are not isolated examples; all through history various societies have resorted to this brutality. Some of them made a habit of it, such as the ancient Assyrians and the nineteenth century Turks, both of whom established a policy of butchering as many of the residents of a conquered city or country as they could find. Other societies have resorted to it only on occasion. The white settlers of America often deliberately practiced genocide (the destruction of a whole racial or ethnic group) against the native Indians. At one time or another, every colony paid a bounty for Indian heads or scalps. This genocidal policy was carried on over a much longer period and was more successful than Hitler's. Estimates are that Hitler killed about 60 percent of the Jews in all the territory under his control,[16] whereas the whites in America killed more than 75 percent of the Indians.[17]

In some cases, annihilation is more accidental than purposeful. It is not the result of planned action or warfare, but of the uncushioned clash between two cultures. We can illustrate accidental annihilation with our example of white settlers and native Indians. Only a fraction of the American Indians who died were deliberately shot or scalped: many of them died because the whites took away the land where they hunted for food, and because whites killed in large numbers (for sport) the buffalo that were the main source of food and clothing for the Plains Indians. The Indians were highly susceptible to the new diseases the whites brought with them, and to the white man's whiskey. The guns which the Europeans sold them, or which they captured, made their own tribal wars suddenly much more lethal. We might say that basically the Indians died because their society became so disorganized in trying to deal with the European culture and technology to which they were suddenly introduced, that their society could no longer provide them with the necessary support.

When one group chooses to annihilate another one, there is usually a special kind of motivation involved. Many of the factors which produce this behavior are the same as those listed by Gordon Allport in his study of racial violence (see the Allport abridgment

16. Brewton Berry, *Race Relations* (Cambridge, Mass.: Riverside Press, 1951), p. 201.

17. Horace M. Kallen, "On Americanizing the American Indian," *Social Research* 25 (1958), p. 470.

in chapter 13). The people have been worked up by hate or fear (for example, the Europeans believed that the Indians meant to annihilate them). Also there has been some depersonalization of the victim group, which allows people to forget that they are killing real human beings like themselves.

Expulsion

Expulsion (forcing people to leave their homes and the dominant society) is a second form of exclusion that has been historically prevalent. Expulsion may be nearly as costly in terms of lives lost as annihilation. Often the minority group is extremely reluctant to leave its home, and a show of force is necessary to convince its members that they must go. The same social attitude which leads the dominant group to choose to expel the others will probably keep them from being too concerned over the consequences of the move. The minority group's trip to the "new home" may be an ordeal of hardship and suffering. For example, when the Cherokees were forced by Army troops, in the 1830s, to move from their native area in Georgia to a reservation in Oklahoma, over four thousand of the ten thousand who made the trip died along the way; the Cherokees called it "the Trail of Tears."[18] Many more Cherokees died after they settled in their Oklahoma reservation, because their culture was not suited to deal with the problems of life there. Many times, of course, no provision is made for a new home for those being expelled. A common biblical example is that of the Jews, who were turned out into the uninhabitable desert more than once.

Partition

A more peaceful form of expulsion is *partition,* which occurs when a country is reorganized politically to try to make national groups correspond with ethnic ones. Sometimes the two groups involved arrive at this solution

18. Marion L. Starkey, *The Cherokee Nation* (New York: Alfred A. Knopf, 1946), p. 283.

themselves. This was the case in the partitioning of India in response to the troubles between Hindus and the large Moslem minority. The Hindus remained in control of most of India. The Moslems were given a slice of the western part of the country (West Pakistan) together with a small piece of land in the eastern corner (East Pakistan), where they could live unmolested in their own autonomous Moslem state. It is instructive to note that this "solution" has not stopped widespread discrimination against the outside group within each country, and it has led to a continuing state of conflict between the two nations. Sometimes partition is imposed from outside. An example of this occurred in Palestine, which was divided by the British (who claimed its ownership at the time) into two separate countries, one for Arabs and one for Jews.

Clearly, partition is not an ideal solution. It means that many people have to relocate, so that they can live in the section which has been given over to their group; this always causes bad feelings and social disorganization. It is also nearly impossible to agree on a plan of division that is absolutely fair to everyone. Experience shows that partition may generate hostilities that last for years. The Jordanians and the Israelis, twenty years after the partitioning of Palestine, are at war with one another, and the war is due in large part to unresolved problems of partition. The Catholics and Protestants in Ireland, who partitioned their country along religious lines in 1921, don't get along together any better than they did before the division took place. Riots, bitterness, and threats of war still erupt quite frequently as a result of conflict between the two religious groups. The evidence indicates that partition is not a permanent solution to the coexistence of differing ethnic groups.

Segregation

Segregation may be considered as a kind of partitioning within a society, where the boundaries are not so much political as they

Within cities, minorities are segregated into specific, usually less affluent neighborhoods. In New York City 80 percent of the black population live in the 26 officially designated poverty areas. These areas are increasing and "urban blight" continues to spread as whites move out of the poverty areas, often out of the city altogether and into the suburbs. *(Photo by Steve Salmieri)*

are social, and perhaps also legal. Segregation can be defined as the involuntary separation of residential areas, services, or other facilities on the basis of the racial or ethnic characteristics of the people using them. The fully segregated minority group is forced to live in one particular town, or one part of town; they may be legally prohibited from leaving there except to go out to work (this is the literal meaning of a ghetto). They are not allowed to attend the same churches or the same schools as the dominant group, or to participate in the government, or to form any kind of intimate relationship with members of the dominant group. Sometimes these restraints are legal, and sometimes they involve the use of sanctions that are outside the law, such as mob violence or economic reprisals.

The effect of segregation is to keep the minority group available but in a nonparticipant social status. It is a social pattern that is usually found in cases where the dominant society for some reason dislikes and distrusts the minority group, but needs its talents or labor services. A typical example of this situation can be seen in seventeenth-century Persia. In 1605, a whole community of Armenians was "invited" to migrate to Isfahan (the invitation consisted of surrounding the town and cutting off its water supply). They were settled there under the protection of the Shah, who needed their highly developed skills and artistry to help with the speedy construction of his beautiful new capital city. But they were forced to live in only one part of the city, were not allowed to vote, could not own property anywhere in the country outside the section of Isfahan allotted to their use, could not remain outside their houses after a certain hour of the evening, and were of course not allowed to intermarry with the Persians. The descendants of the early Armenians still live in Isfahan today. There are no more laws which enforce their segregation, but extralegal social sanctions still serve to keep the pattern much the same as it used to be.

Segregation has also been the dominant pattern of relations between blacks and whites in America, but it was not that way originally. The blacks were brought here as slaves because they were needed as a source of labor, particularly in the agricultural South. In colonial America, the dominant pattern of discrimination was against slaves, and not against blacks in general. There were several ways by which slaves could become free, and once they were free they enjoyed all the rights and privileges of any colonial citizen. Increasingly, however, in the eighteenth and early nineteenth centuries, laws were passed which discriminated against all blacks, both slaves and free men. This occurred when the southern plantations became "big business," greatly dependent upon the cheap and stable labor force of slaves. Laws forbidding intermarriage between blacks and whites were designed to prevent the needed slave laborers from achieving freedom through marriage; other laws took away the right of blacks to vote and to be educated. Sometimes laws were even passed requiring that free slaves be banished. Thus all blacks gradually came to be placed in a segregated and debased status.

In America, therefore, patterns of segregation were developed to help ensure the continued dominance of whites over blacks, in order to preserve the economic resource of slave labor. The laws were also meant to create a barrier against uprising or rebellion by blacks, which the whites feared. The segregation of blacks has proved an especially enduring pattern because of the obvious and unchangeable difference in skin color. If an Armenian learned the language and customs, and wore the dress of the Persians, he could probably pass for one; the difference between black and white is much more difficult to overcome.

A looser pattern of segregation developed after the Civil War. Under certain circumstances, close relationships between blacks and whites were permitted, and many activities could be shared based on the assumption that facilities could be separate but equal. In recent years this pattern of segregation has broken down substantially. Blacks now go to the same schools, attend the same movies, and ride in the same bus seats as white people do. But there is still some resistance among whites to integrated housing and integrated eating facilities, and interracial dating and marriage.

Today, strict segregation of races is fading in our society, but there still remain diffuse patterns of discrimination which are often quite resistant to change. There has been a marked degree of assimilation of blacks into the mainstream of American society; there has also been an increase in conflict, especially on the part of those many blacks who, though no longer legally segregated, continue against their will to lead lives outside of the mainstream.

4 MINORITY GROUP REACTIONS TO DOMINANCE AND DISCRIMINATION

It is the actions of the dominant society which largely define the patterns of intergroup relations, for their dominance gives them the power to enforce their will on the minority group. But all human relationships are two-way streets, and the actions of the dominant group will be in some measure influenced by the nature of the response these actions elicit from the minority group. We will examine some of these responses and look also at some of the psychological reactions a minority group may develop in response to being dominated.

PASSIVE ACCEPTANCE

One course open to minority group members is simply to accept the situation as it is. They can passively accommodate themselves to their subordinate position and make the best of it. The classic example of acceptance is Uncle Tom, the black servant in the novel *Uncle Tom's Cabin*. He was resigned to the fact that he would always be a white man's servant, and he therefore tried to behave in a way that would make his servitude as comfortable for him as possible. He did as he was told, never caused trouble, and was faithful to his master's interests. Because of this compliant behavior, he was well treated by his master, and he actually succeeded in achieving some of his personal goals.

Accepting one's subordinance does not necessarily mean that one gives up all hope of personal satisfaction or happiness. Oppressed minorities have developed many skillful techniques for dealing with members of the

dominant society that will permit them to manipulate the situation in some way that is to their advantage. A traditional technique is flattery. This often takes the form of excessive deference or humility, which plays on the vanity of the dominant person. Uncle Tom's bowing, his repeated phrase "Yes sir, yes sir," are forms of flattery which gained him favor and privilege. Another technique is playing the clown, or "acting dumb." This insures that the dominant group will make only minimal demands on the minority group, because they will believe that the minority group is not capable of very much.

Both of these forms of acceptance are good examples of working the system. The minority group in this case accepts the rules of the system—the main one being the social norm that makes their inferiority expected—and then actually uses these rules to accomplish its own private goals. Some of the remarkable achievements of blacks in our society can be viewed as resulting in part from some such working of the system, in a shrewd and skillful way.

Acceptance may seem the easiest response for a minority group to make, easy in the sense that it promotes intergroup harmony, but those who adopt it often pay for outer peace by inner turmoil. It is impossible to accept the role of an inferior and at the same time maintain much self-respect. Total acceptance leads to self-hatred and a wide variety of accompanying pathological emotional responses. To appear to accept personal inferiority while secretly believing otherwise is also an enormous strain, since it calls for a whole lifetime of carefully concealing true inner feelings.

The response of passive acceptance tends to support the continuance of a pattern of dominance, discrimination, and exclusion. The dominant society sees no reason to change because it appears to them that the minority is satisfied with the situation. The minority is unable to change or to improve its position, partly because the members of the group believe that it is impossible. Acceptance leads to self-limitation. Suppose that there is an intelligent and successful Jewish lawyer in Chicago who is told by his business associates that he has such a keen understanding of the intricacies of municipal government that he ought to be the next mayor. They suggest that he run for the office. He says, "Don't be ridiculous, Chicago would never elect a Jewish mayor." So he doesn't run and the city doesn't have an opportunity to elect a Jewish mayor, since there is no Jewish candidate on the ballot. As a result of his acceptance of exclusion, his prediction has not been challenged. Even if the others talk him into running, his feeling that it is impossible for him to be elected will be communicated to potential supporters, campaign workers, and voters, in a hundred different subtle little ways. His lack of self-belief is likely to cause him to lose the election and his prediction to come true. We call this the *self-fulfilling prophecy*, meaning that things tend to work out in a certain way because everyone is convinced that that's the way they are going to work out. This doesn't mean that you can always do exactly what you think you can, because obviously there are other factors involved—the Jewish lawyer might have lost the election even if he had believed he could win. But it does mean that people's beliefs about the outcome of a given social situation are a factor influencing that outcome.

AGGRESSION AND ACTS OF VIOLENCE

Another possible response to dominance is aggression. This may take the form of physical violence against the dominant group. The savage raids on white settlements which the Apaches made in the late nineteenth century are a good illustration of this response. The inner-city riots of the last several years here in America are also rooted in feelings of hostility and aggression on the part of the minority black group against the dominant white society. This can be a very dangerous kind of behavior, because those who are caught in such acts of aggression will be severely punished, perhaps even killed, by the dominant group.

Usually the minority looks for a safer way to display its aggression. Verbal expressions of hostility and aggression are common. Minority group members may shout threats at passersby or write them on walls. They may even write them in books: consider the aggression that is expressed in the title of the book by black author Julius Lester—*Look Out Whitey, Black Power's Gonna Get Your Mama*. Jokes can also be used to express aggression, by making the attitudes and actions of the dominant group objects of ridicule. It is especially satisfying when the joke is told in such a way that members of the dominant group join in the laughter, unaware that they are laughing at themselves.

Psychologists have pointed out that automobile drivers may use their cars as emotional outlets. An interesting example of a black laborer in Texas expressing aggression against the dominant group, without fear of reprisal, is quoted by Charles S. Johnson in a study of black segregation and response:

I drive in a way that makes it look like I'll run over them if they walk in front of me when I have the right. I act like I don't see them. I have had some of them to curse at me for this, but I just laugh at them and keep on driving.[19]

Another common form of aggression is expressed in the way that work for the dominant group is performed. This is one reason slavery can be a rather uneconomical form of

19.   Charles S. Johnson, *Patterns of Negro Segregation* (New York: Harper, 1943), p. 303.

labor. Slaves in the South sometimes had "accidents" that ruined the crops or killed the livestock. A cook may burn the family's dinner on a special occasion, or break a valuable dish. The Indian factory worker may bungle his job, causing a slowdown of the assembly line. Quitting may be a way to express hostility also. The stereotype of the handyman from a minority group who just doesn't show up the day after payday is an example of this. His behavior is not merely irresponsibility; it is also an act of aggression against his employer, for whom it causes difficulty and annoyance.

Sociologists have theorized that many crimes committed by minority group members may be related to aggressive responses to the dominant society. When a minority group member steals money from a higher status person at gunpoint, he is doing more than just trying to improve his economic condition; he may also be behaving aggressively toward a member of the dominant group.

Sometimes the minority group is fearful of the consequences of any direct expression of aggression against the dominant group, and so such feelings are directed against others instead—for example, against other members of the same minority group. This may be one reason rates of crime and violence are relatively high in some ethnic neighborhoods. A man's pent-up feelings of aggression that were generated on the job by the actions and the attitudes of his majority group boss, come out in what seems to him a safer way when he beats up his wife that evening, or stabs a friend in an argument over a poker game, or gets into a street fight with a stranger of his own group who gave him "the bad eye." Another possible target for this aggression is a member of another minority group, who is just as powerless.

SELF-SEGREGATION

When a minority group somewhat voluntarily tries to keep itself separated from the dominant society, we call it self-segregation. Unable to find any satisfactory way to conduct their relationships with members of the

Washington, D.C. was not the only city to experience race riots in the 1960s. It has become evident that these occurrences cannot be dismissed as senseless eruptions or isolated events that receive no support from the ghetto community. Surveys conducted for the President's Kerner Commission indicated that these riots are a form of social protest, involving a substantial minority of the community. Many more were sympathetic bystanders, and still more believed that the riots were helpful to the black struggle. *(Burt Glinn, Magnum)*

dominant society, they try to eliminate contacts with those outside the minority group. The simplest form of self-segregation is avoidance. Another man interviewed by Charles Johnson explained why he chose avoidance:

I found that the best way to get along with white folks is to just be pretty careful and come in contact with them as little as possible. There are times when you have to take a lot of things. Those things that you can avoid, you ought to. I am not a white folks' nigger, and I try to keep out of trouble. I know, though, that I am in the south, and I know they can make it hard for me, so I just try to attend to my business and see if I can dodge a lot of trouble.[20]

Note the differences between this man's avoidance reaction, and the acceptance reaction we discussed earlier. He says that he is no "white folks' nigger," meaning that he does not accept his own inferiority. He stays apart because he knows that he does not want to act like an inferior when that is required, and that this failure will lead to trouble for him.

In terms of occupation, self-segregation may mean working in areas that are overlooked or not favored by the dominant group. An example is the Chinese immigrants who went into the laundry business, where they were not competing with the native whites. Booker T. Washington advocated this course of action for the black, suggesting that he specialize in agriculture and craftsmanship, doing the kind of work that whites preferred to avoid rather than trying to compete with them for their jobs.[21] Another kind of occupational self-segregation is to own or work in a neighborhood business that caters only to other minority group members. In big cities like New York and Chicago, a number of such businesses can succeed and prosper—a travel agency selling tickets for trips back home to the West Indies, a restaurant that special-

izes in "soul food," a grocery that sells the ingredients for Chinese cooking, a newspaper printed in German with news from the old country.

This type of self-segregation can work only for a limited number of people and can provide only limited rewards. It is unfortunate but true that the best opportunities usually exist in the dominant society—the most rewarding jobs, the nicest houses, the best schools. So the self-segregation response can lead to further handicaps for the minority group that restricts itself to choosing from the limited opportunities of its own subculture.

A recent trend has been for some minority groups to seek acceptance in occupational areas but to choose social and residential segregation. Today, many blacks who formerly would have preferred to move from a segregated neighborhood to an integrated one are likely to want to stay in an all-black neighborhood. In New York's Harlem, new apartment buildings have gone up to house the middle income blacks who want to stay there. In Boston's North End, many blacks who achieve financial success choose to buy one of the old houses there and renovate it, rather than move to another neighborhood.

The most extreme form of self-segregation is *separatism,* where the minority group aspires to set up a totally independent society of its own. It may try to do this within the geographical and political bounds of the dominant society, or it may plan to migrate, or it may work for partition. Such separatism was the great dream of many American and some European Jews, who began the Zionist movement. Their dream came true when Palestine was partitioned and the Jewish state of Israel came into being. This is one of the very few successful examples of separatism. The country of Liberia in Africa represents another experiment in separatism. It was colonized by a group of freed American slaves, under the sponsorship of the American government, which did no more than arrange for them to go there. This was the first back-to-Africa movement, around 1825. The first hundred years

---

20. Johnson, *Patterns of Negro Segregation,* p. 269.
21. Booker T. Washington, *The Future of the American Negro* (Boston: Small and Maynard, 1902).

of this colony were very hard ones, as the American blacks, descendants of many different African tribes, had much trouble in adjusting to the climate and the environment, and had neither the capital nor the technology needed to develop the country's economy. They also had problems in getting along with the native tribes already living there, who were not too enthusiastic about the whole scheme. It is only in recent years that Liberia has made strides toward achieving a satisfactory standard of living.

In the 1960s, there began a new back-to-Africa movement, initiated by black Americans, who bought land in countries of central Africa and established agricultural and handicraft communes there. However, most participants admit that these experiments have not been successful, due primarily to the enormous differences between African and black American culture. Leaders of African nations, like Tom Mboya, have warned American blacks that Africa cannot be the solution to their problems.[22]

The concept of separatism has received renewed interest lately, and many minority groups have formulated plans for their own societies. Some American Indians want part of their land back, to establish their own sovereign nations again. Many black power advocates are suggesting separate black states, either in the South or in Africa. History shows that separatism is a very difficult policy to turn into a satisfactory reality—but some minorities feel it is their only hope for ever achieving real equality.

ACCULTURATION

The fourth major type of response to dominance is when a minority group member tries to blend into the majority by taking on as many of the cultural characteristics of that dominant group as possible. This is called *acculturation*. He learns the language, adopts

22. Tom Mboya, "The American Negro Cannot Look to Africa for an Escape," *New York Times Magazine*, 13 July 1969, pp. 30–40.

the dress, practices the customs, and after a while no one can tell that he is not a member. In fact, acculturation may lead in time to full assimilation when the individual becomes integrated socially as well as culturally.

When the minority is a racially determined one, it is more difficult for its members to acculturate, since their biological differences will always be evident. However, some individuals in whom racial physical characteristics are not strongly marked, may be able to appear to be members of the dominant group. This is often called "passing."

There are many different degrees of passing. It can be for a single occasion, such as gaining admittance to an all-white social event. It can be confined to a single aspect of one's life. A man might pass at work, to improve his employment opportunities, but return home at night to his own group. A black girl might pass when she is out with a white escort but not when she is with a black one. Passing can also be spending an entire lifetime as a member of an ethnic group into which one was not born.

We usually think of passing in connection with blacks, but there are many other examples of passing as well. A European Jew may change his name in America from Lefkowitz to Lewis, or if he has obviously Semitic features, he may claim to be a non-Jewish descendant of Middle-Eastern parents.

For many European ethnic groups, acculturation is simply a matter of dropping old customs, simplifying names with an obvious "foreign" sound, and moving out to the suburbs to lead the all-American life. An illustration of such acculturation can be seen in a Cleveland suburban community of second- and third-generation Poles and Czechs. All the houses are built in the housing-development colonial style, with brass eagles over the door, on streets named for presidents. If you look closely as you drive along, you will see that on many of the mailboxes the last syllable of the owner's name has been neatly painted out, a concrete symbol of the way he has broken a tie with his ethnic group.

Joseph Rudenski has become Joe Ruden, and Robert Marcowiak is now Bob Marco.

The decision to acculturate is always a painful one in some respects. It involves turning away from an entire heritage, one that may have a great deal of emotional meaning and connection. It also means cutting oneself off from the support of the rest of the ethnic group, or at least those who can't or won't try to acculturate. It is quite typical for the acculturator to be bitterly blamed by his parents, brothers and sisters, aunts and uncles, for his actions in repudiating the family name, history, language, and cultural traditions. For example, the daughter of strict Orthodox Jewish parents who adapts to the prevailing culture and ends up marrying a Gentile may be cut off from her family; in some cases, they even hold a funeral service and pronounce her dead, as a formal expression of their intention never to see her again and as a symbol of the gap that has been created between parent and child.

We might note here the presence of a countertrend to acculturation that makes itself felt particularly among the better educated and more successful descendants of well-integrated ethnic minorities. The children and grandchildren of these groups may, when they grow up, deliberately begin to cultivate a stronger sense of their ethnic past. They take courses in college to learn the language of their grandparents; they master the art of cooking some of the national dishes; or they revive in their homes some of the old customs.

Acculturation without significant social assimilation and acceptance often generates serious psychological problems for minority group members. This situation occurs when the minority accepts the values, attitudes, and customs of the dominant society, identifying with it rather than with their own group, yet are still rejected or unaccepted by the dominant group. The black psychologist Frantz Fanon wrote a book, *Black Skin, White Masks,* which explores the various problems, both social and psychological, which are inherent in this kind of cultural and mental assimilation that is unaccompanied by any social acceptance.

EMOTIONAL RESPONSES TO DOMINANCE

In our discussion of the social responses to dominance and discrimination we have already touched on some of the common emotional characteristics developed by members of minority groups. One common personality characteristic associated with the response of acceptance is self-hatred. Another, produced by attempts at acculturation, is a sense of alienation from one's own group. Members of a minority group may also develop an excessive sensitivity about prejudice and discrimination, and see every failure or rejection in their lives as a result of persecution by the majority. In its most extreme form, this type of reaction comes very close to the mental illness called paranoia, and may be a great handicap in most social relationships the minority group member undertakes.

One of the most common emotional responses is to avoid or escape from the reality of the situation. It has been suggested that some ethnic minority groups typically have high rates of alcoholism and drug addiction for this reason. They also have high rates of mental illness, which is due in part to the strain of their deprived situation. The sad fact is that for some minority group members, the world of addiction or fantasy may be an improvement over their real world. This desire to escape from, or ignore, the real world is one of the most serious handicaps of minority groups in terms of achievement in the dominant society.

We should not overlook the role which emotional response to a situation of prejudice or discrimination plays in the development of many character types which become associated with various groups. S. I. Hayakawa gives a good example of the way this works:

The distinguished French abstract artist Jean Hélion once told the story of his life as a prisoner of war in a German camp, where, during World War II, he was compelled to do forced labor. He told how he loafed on the job, how he thought of device after device for avoiding work and producing as little as possible—and since his prison camp was a farm, how he stole chickens at every opportunity. He also described how he put on an expression of good-natured imbecility whenever approached by his Nazi overseers. Without intending to do so, in describing his own actions, he gave an almost perfect picture of the literary type of the southern Negro of slavery days. Jean Hélion, confronted with the fact of forced labor, reacted as intelligently as southern Negro slaves and the slaves reacted as intelligently as Jean Hélion. 'Laziness,' then, is not an 'inherent quality' of Negroes or of any other group of people. It is a response *to a work situation in which there are no rewards for working, and in which one hates his taskmasters.*[23]

SOME FUNCTIONS OF INTERGROUP CONFLICT

When two ethnic groups continue to live together within the same society but have not yet arrived at a stable pattern of coexistence, they are quite likely to exhibit the kind of relationship we call conflict. Riots, lynchings, sit-ins, demonstrations, lawsuits contesting legal discrimination or seeking to uphold it— these are all part of a pattern of conflict within a society. In some segments of American society today, conflict is the type of relation-

ship that prevails between blacks and whites.

Obviously, open and bitter conflict between ethnic groups in one society is a potential source of destruction and breakdown. It can jeopardize national unity and endanger the existence of the whole community, even bringing it to the brink of civil war, as in Northern Ireland today.

Yet it is also true that some conflict between ethnic groups may have a certain social value. One positive function of conflict is that it helps to develop what sociologists call *group consciousness,* which means an awareness of belonging to a group and a sense of group identity. It seems that in the course of battling "them," people develop a stronger sense of who "we" are.

Sociologists have pointed out that ethnic group conflict may be a sign of an improving relationship between the two groups, as well as a force which speeds further improvement. Indulging in conflict, with its potential risks, can be interpreted as indicating that both groups have a sense of strength and security, that they feel they can afford to run the risks of conflict. Another value is that participating in the conflict, like any kind of social participation, sometimes strengthens the ties of individuals to the social order. It may also lead the conflicting groups into some kind of communication, enabling them later to deal with their differences in a more realistic way.

Finally, conflict makes it impossible for people to ignore the fact that a problem exists, and that a solution is needed. Thus conflict generates pressures that help to bring about its resolution.

23. S. I. Hayakawa, *Symbol, Status, and Personality* (New York: Harcourt Brace Jovanovich, 1963), pp. 14–15.

KENNETH B. CLARK
The Psychology of the Ghetto

Introduction

Kenneth B. Clark is a black psychologist who has devoted much of his professional life to a study of the ways in which American patterns of racial segregation and discrimination affect members of minority groups. In this excerpt from his famous book Dark

Ghetto, *he examines some of the ways in which low-income blacks in central city ghettos have responded to dominance, and points out the harm that some of these responses have brought to the self-image and self-esteem of blacks in this country. Although his piece deals mainly with the problems that blacks face in a white man's world, the emotional responses he discusses can be found among all minorities who are discriminated against.*

It is now generally understood that chronic and remediable social injustices corrode and damage the human personality, thereby robbing it of its effectiveness, of its creativity, if not its actual humanity. No matter how desperately one seeks to deny it, this simple fact persists and intrudes itself. It is the fuel of protests and revolts. Racial segregation, like all other forms of cruelty and tyranny, debases all human beings—those who are its victims, those who victimize, and in quite subtle ways those who are merely accessories.

The victims of segregation do not initially desire to be segregated, they do not "prefer to be with their own people," in spite of the fact that this belief is commonly stated by those who are not themselves segregated. A most cruel and psychologically oppressive aspect and consequence of enforced segregation is that its victims can be made to accommodate to their victimized status and under certain circumstances to state that it *is* their desire to be set apart, or to agree that subjugation is not really detrimental but beneficial. The fact remains that exclusion, rejection, and a stigmatized status are not desired and are not voluntary states. Segregation is neither sought nor imposed by healthy or potentially healthy human beings.

Human beings who are forced to live under ghetto conditions and whose daily experience tells them that almost nowhere in society are they respected and granted the ordinary dignity and courtesy accorded to others will, as a matter of course, begin to doubt their own worth. Since every human being depends upon his cumulative experiences with others for clues as to how he should view and value himself, children who are consistently rejected understandably begin to question and doubt whether they, their family, and their group really deserve no more respect from the larger society than they receive. These doubts become the seeds of a pernicious self- and group-hatred, the Negro's complex and debilitating prejudice against himself.

The preoccupation of many Negroes with hair straighteners, skin bleachers, and the like illustrates this tragic aspect of American racial prejudice—Negroes have come to believe in their own inferiority. In recent years Negro men and women have rebelled against the constant struggle to become white and have given special emphasis to their "Negroid" features and hair textures in a self-conscious acceptance of "negritude"—a wholehearted embracing of the African heritage. But whether a Negro woman uses hair straightener or whether she highlights her natural hair texture by flaunting *au naturel* styles, whether a Negro man hides behind a neat Ivy League suit or wears blue jeans defiantly in the manner of the Student Nonviolent Coordinating Committee (SNCC), each is still reacting primarily to the pervasive factor of race and still not free to take himself for granted or to judge himself by the usual standards of personal success and character. It is still the white man's society that governs the Negro's image of himself.

Fantasy protections

Many Negroes live sporadically in a world of fantasy, and fantasy takes different forms at different ages. In childhood the delusion is a simple one—the child may pretend that he is really white. When Negro children as young as three years old are shown white- and Negro-appearing dolls or asked to color pictures of children to look like themselves, many of them tend to reject the dark-skinned dolls as "dirty" and "bad" or to color the picture of themselves a light color or a bizarre shade like purple. But the fantasy is not complete, for when asked to identify which doll is like themselves, some Negro children, particularly in the North, will refuse, burst into tears, and run away. By the age of seven most Negro children have accepted the reality that they are, after all, dark skinned. But the stigma remains; they have been forced to recognize themselves as inferior. Few if any Negroes ever fully lose that sense of shame and self-hatred.

To the Negro child the most serious injury seems to be in the concept of self-worth related directly to skin color itself. Because school is a central activity at this age, his sense of inferiority is revealed most acutely in his lack of confidence in himself as a student, lack of motivation to learn, and in problems of behavior—a gradual withdrawal or a growing rebellion. The effects of this early damage are difficult to overcome, for the child who never learns to read cannot become a success at a job or in a society where education and culture are necessary. In addition, there is the possibility that poor teaching, generally characteristic of the ghetto schools, tends to reinforce this sense of inferiority and to give it substance in the experience of inferior achievement. The cycle that leads to menial jobs and to broken homes has then begun; only the most drastic efforts at rehabilitation can break this cycle.

Teen-age Negroes often cope with the ghetto's frustrations by retreating into fantasies related chiefly to their role in society. There is, for example, a fantasy employed by many marginal and antisocial teen-agers, to pretend to knowledge about illicit activities and to a sexual urbanity that they do not, really, have. They use as their models the petty criminals of the ghetto, whose colorful, swaggering style of cool bravado possesses a peculiar fascination.

Some pretend falsely to be pimps, some to have contacts with numbers runners. Their apparent admiration of these models is not total but reflects a curious combination of respect, of contempt, and, fundamentally, of despair. Social scientists who rely on questionnaires and superficial interviews must find a way to unravel this tangled web of pretense if their conclusions are to be relevant.

Among the young men observed... fantasy plays a major role. Many of these marginal, upward-striving teen-agers allowed others to believe that they were college students. One young man told his friends that he was a major in psychology. He had enrolled in the classes of a Negro professor with whom he identified, and he described those lectures in detail to his friends. The fact is that he was a dropout from high school. Another youngster who said he was in college planned to become a nuclear physicist. He spoke most convincingly about his physics and math courses and discussed the importance of Negroes' going into the field. Within a year, however, he had been dropped for non-attendance from the evening session of the municipal college at which he was enrolled. He had not taken a first course in physics and had not been able to pass the elementary course in mathematics. He explained this failure in a complicated story and reported that he now intended to get a job. Later he described his new job in the executive training program of a high-status department store downtown. He was saving for college where he would continue with nuclear physics. He carried an attaché case to work each day. But the truth was that he was not in an executive training program at all; he had a job as a stock clerk. Yet the fantasy was one of performance; there was truth in his dreams, for if he had been caught in time he might have become a scientist. He did have the intellectual potential. But as a Negro, he had been damaged so early in the educational process that not even the surge of motivation and his basic intelligence could now make his dreams effective. His motivation was sporadic and largely verbal; his plans were in the realm of delusion. To some, this form of social schizophrenia might seem comic, but a more appropriate response is tears, not laughter.

Sex and status

In Negro adults the sense of inadequate self-worth shows up in lack of motivation to rise in their jobs or fears of competition with whites; in a sense of impotence in civic affairs demonstrated in lethargy toward voting, or community participation, or responsibility for others; in family instability and the irresponsibility rooted in hopelessness.

But, because, in American life, sex is, like business advancement, a prime criterion of success and hence of personal worth, it is in sexual behavior that the damage to Negro adults shows up in especially poignant and tragic clarity. The inconsistency between the white society's view of the Negro as inferior and its sexual exploitation of Negroes has seemed to its victims a degrading hypocrisy. Negroes observe that ever since slavery white men have regarded Negroes as inferior and have condemned interracial marriage while considering illicit sexual relationships with Negro women appropriate to their own higher status. The white man in America has, historically, arranged to have both white and Negro women available to him; he has claimed sexual priority with both and, in the process, he has sought to emasculate Negro men. Negro males could not hold their women, nor could they defend them. The white male tried to justify this restriction of meaningful competition with the paradoxical claim that Negro males were animal-like and brutish in their appetites and hence to be feared and shunned by white women.

The ironic fact has been that, given the inferiority of their racial status, Negro males have had to struggle simply to believe themselves men.

Certain Negro women of status who have married white men report that their choice was related to their discovery that the Negro men they knew were inferior in status, interests, and sophistication and hence unsuitable as partners. Many problems of race and sex seem to follow this principle of the self-fulfilling prophecy. The Negro woman of status may see the Negro male as undesirable as a sexual partner precisely because of his low status in the eyes of whites.

The emerging, more affirmative sexual pride among Negro males may have as one of its consequences an increasing trend toward more open competition between white and Negro males for both white and Negro females. One of the further consequences would probably be an intensification of hostility of white males toward interracial couples and toward the white female participants, reflecting the desire on the part of the white male to preserve his own competitive advantage. One would expect him then to employ his economic and political power — without suspecting the fundamental basis of his antagonism — to maintain the inferior status of the Negro male for as long as possible. An important level of racial progress will have been reached when Negro and white men and women may marry anyone they choose, without punishment, ostracism, ridicule, or guilt.

The Negro matriarchy and the distorted masculine image

Sexual hierarchy has played a crucial role in the structure and pathology of the Negro family. Because of the system of slavery in which the Negro male was systematically used as a stud and the Negro female used primarily for purposes of breeding or for the gratification of the white male, the only source of family continuity was through the female, the dependence of the child on his mother. This pattern, together with the continued post-slavery relegation of the Negro male to menial and subservient status, has made the female the dominant person in the Negro family. Psychologically, the Negro male could not support his normal desire for dominance. For the most part he was not allowed to be a consistent wage earner; he could not present himself to his wife and children as a person who had the opportunity or the ability to compete successfully in politics, business, and industry. His doubts concerning his personal adequacy were therefore reinforced. He was compelled to base his self-esteem instead on a kind of behavior that tended to support a stereotyped picture of the Negro male — sexual impulsiveness, irresponsibility, verbal bombast, posturing, and compensatory achievement in entertainment and athletics, particularly in sports like boxing in which athletic prowess could be exploited for the gain of others. The Negro male was, therefore, driven to seek status in ways which seemed either antisocial, escapist, or socially irresponsible. The pressure to find relief from his intolerable psychological position seems directly related to the continued high incidence of desertions and broken homes in Negro ghettos.

The Negro woman has, in turn, been required to hold the family together; to set the goals, to stimulate, encourage, and to protect both boys and girls. Her compensatory strength tended to perpetuate the weaker role of the Negro male. Negro boys had the additional problem of finding no strong male father figure upon which to model their own behavior, perhaps one of the reasons for the prevalent idea among marginal Negroes that it is not masculine to sustain a stable father or husband relationship with a woman. Many young men establish temporary liaisons with a number of different women with no responsibility toward any. Among Negro teen-agers the cult of going steady has never had the vogue it seems to have among white teen-agers; security for Negroes is found not in a relationship modeled after a stable family — for they have seen little of this in their own lives — but upon the relationships they observed in their own home: unstable and temporary liaisons. The marginal young Negro male tends to identify his masculinity with the number of girls he can attract. The high incidence of illegitimacy among Negro young people reflects this pervasive fact. In this compensatory distortion of the male image, masculinity is, therefore, equated with alleged sexual prowess.

Conclusion

It is possible for discrimination to produce certain benefits for its victims. The desire to advance oneself, to prove one's equality or superiority, or to improve a prejudiced society are all conceivable reactions to social injustices. Understandably, these reactions are rare. And it is inevitable that people who are discriminated against will be damaged in some way by their experiences. In this abridgment Kenneth Clark discusses various responses to prejudice and discrimination. All of the responses are pathological; they create still further damage to the victims of discrimination. Clark does not cover all the pathological reactions to discrimination that have been observed. Can you think of others?

SUMMARY

For ethnic, racial, or religious groups to be viewed and treated as minority groups, the members of these groups must have significant things in common which can be distinguished by individuals in the larger, dominant society and by members of the minority groups themselves. Racial groups are distinguished by particular physical characteristics such as skin color, stature, and hair texture. Ethnic groups are distinguished by social and cultural characteristics. Ethnicity is predominantly a shared sense of "peoplehood," a set of psychological, social, and cultural attributes that have developed through common experiences and tradition. In fact there is considerable overlap between racial and ethnic distinctions. A racial group may share a common ethnic heritage, or one ethnic group may contain several races; racial identity can often be due more to cultural than to biological assignments. The physical differences between the world's major races—Caucasian, Mongoloid, and Negroid—probably evolved in response to distinct climatic and environmental conditions. However, the subsequent mixing of the races has made it impossible to isolate any "pure" racial population and has made classification in terms of physical characteristics difficult. The problems of separating culturally learned behavior and environmental influences from biologically inherited traits makes any distinctions in terms of intelligence or personality extremely uncertain.

While each minority group in the United States has had a different set of experiences, to some extent they have all suffered disadvantages due to prejudice and discrimination. Social problems develop when preconceived stereotypes or generalizations are used to judge people despite evidence that shows these judgments to be inaccurate. Such prejudgments are learned during the socialization process along with other culturally patterned perceptions and attitudes. Many studies have indicated a correlation between prejudice and social status and personality type. Insecure, anxious, and authoritarian personalities are more likely to be prejudiced. Prejudice seems to be learned and reinforced better in certain social conditions, such as those associated with low social status.

When prejudiced attitudes are translated into action, into unfair or unequal treatment of certain individuals, we speak of *discrimination*. Prejudice and discrimination need not always occur together, but usually the two are mutually reinforcing. Discrimination may be legally and formally built into a social system,

as slavery was in the United States before the Civil War. However, even when such practices are not legally sanctioned, informal patterns of discrimination may be found in every aspect of daily life. Patterns of stratification in a society are partially the result of prejudice and discrimination against certain racial and ethnic groups. While ethnic origin does not determine social class, it does determine the approximate range of social classes that will be open to a particular individual. In general, nonwhite groups in our society are concentrated in low status occupational and income groupings.

In our society today, both planned and natural change are affecting old patterns of discrimination and segregation. Discrimination in education, employment, and housing have now been outlawed, although enforcement of new laws continues to be a problem. Prejudice, however, cannot be regulated through laws, and attitudes toward minority group members will probably change slowly as minority groups achieve higher socioeconomic standing and gradually overcome traditional stereotypes.

Within the same society different policies and attitudes are maintained toward different groups. Intergroup relations are usually a mixture of *assimilation*, processes directed toward bringing the minority groups to full and equal status, and *exclusion*, processes directed at preventing or minimizing assimilation. Patterns of assimilation include 1) *integration*, which may involve conformity to the actions, values, and attitudes of the dominant culture or a complete blending of the dominant and minority cultures; 2) *amalgamation* or the biological merging of an ethnic group with the native population; and 3) *cultural pluralism* which allows minority groups to participate fully in society while maintaining their cultural and social differences. Patterns of exclusion result from extreme prejudice and discrimination and include 1) *annihilation*, the deliberate execution of minority group members in large numbers; 2) *expulsion* or forcing a group to leave their homes and the dominant society; 3) *partition,* a more peaceful form of expulsion which occurs when a country is reorganized politically to make national groups correspond with ethnic ones; and 4) *segregation,* a kind of partitioning within society in terms of social or legal boundaries. In America, segregation developed to ensure the continued dominance of whites over blacks and has been the primary pattern of relations between the two groups.

Minority groups have responded to these patterns of dominance and discrimination in a variety of ways: 1) *passive acceptance* or submission to domination; although such acceptance may be a superficial conformity to the demands of the dominant group, it leads to self-limitation and supports the existing pattern of dominance; 2) *aggression,* physical or verbal expressions of hostility toward the dominant group; 3) *self-segregation,* voluntary separation or avoidance of the dominant group; and 4) *acculturation* or adoption of the cultural characteristics of the dominant group. Patterns of dominance also produce certain emotional responses in subordinated individuals. Self-hatred, alienation from one's group (due to acculturation), and avoidance or escape are not unusual reactions. When ethnic groups within a society have not developed a stable pattern of coexistence, they are likely to come into conflict. While conflict is a potential source of social breakdown, it can also serve to develop group consciousness and a sense of equal strength and it may generate pressures that will force people to deal with problems in the social system.

GLOSSARY

Acculturation The modification of a group's or individual's culture caused by acquiring traits of another culture with which the group or individual has contact. (page 343)

Amalgamation The biological merging of an ethnic or racial group with the native population. (page 332)

Annihilation The process by which a dominant group causes the deaths of minority group members in large numbers. (page 335)

Assimilation The process by which a minority group is absorbed into the dominant society. (page 329)

Cultural pluralism The social pattern in which the dominant group allows newcomers to achieve full participation in society, without discriminating against them, and at the same time allows them to maintain many of their cultural and social differences. (page 332)

Discrimination Unfair or unequal treatment that is accorded to people or groups. (page 320)

Ethnic group Any group which is socially distinguished from other groups, has developed its own subculture, and has a shared feeling of peoplehood. (page 303)

Expulsion A form of exclusion in which minority group members are forced to leave the country. (page 336)

Group consciousness An awareness of belonging to a group and having a sense of group identity. (page 345)

Integration The fusion of minority and majority groups which takes place through the spreading and sharing of cultural and social traits. (page 330)

Minority group Any recognizable ethnic, racial, or religious group in a society which suffers some disadvantage due to prejudice or discrimination. (page 301)

Partition The political reorganization of a country along racial, ethnic, or religious lines. (page 336)

Prejudice Judging of people, things, or situations on the basis of preformed stereotypes or generalizations. (page 319)

Race A subgroup of the human species characterized by physical differences which result from inherited biological characteristics. (page 305)

Segregation The establishment of separate residential areas, services, and other facilities to which people are involuntarily restricted on the basis of racial, ethnic, or religious characteristics. (page 336)

Self-fulfilling prophecy A false belief regarding a social situation which, because one believes it and acts upon it, actually becomes true. (page 340)

Self-segregation A process by which a minority group somewhat willingly tries to keep itself separated from the dominant society. (page 341)

Separatism A form of self-segregation in which a minority group aspires to set up a totally independent society of its own. (page 342)

SUGGESTED READINGS AND RELATED RESOURCES

I READINGS IN SOCIOLOGY

Banton, Michael. *Race Relations*. New York: Basic Books, 1967. Banton analyzes international race relations through detailed comparisons and historical studies.

Frazier, E. Franklin. *The Negro in the United States*. Rev. ed. New York: Macmillan, 1957. This description of the structure of the American black community traces its development from colonial days to the present.

Ginzberg, Eli. *The Negro Potential*. New York: Columbia University Press (Paper), 1965. Ginzberg's concise and factual study is concerned with the problems and potential of black Americans in the areas of education, job skills, and economic power.

Glazer, Nathan, and Daniel Moynihan. *Beyond the Melting Pot*. Cambridge, Mass.: M.I.T. Press (Paper), 1963. This documented analysis is a well-written account of the various ways in which minority groups have adapted to life in New York City.

Gordon, Milton. *Assimilation in American Life*. New York: Oxford University Press, 1964. The effects of religion, class, and nationality are the center of interest in this analysis of the process of assimilation in the United States.

Handlin, Oscar. *The Newcomers*. New York: Doubleday, Anchor (Paper), 1962. Handlin writes about the immigration problems of blacks and Puerto Ricans coming into the United States, and compares and contrasts their situation to that of earlier groups of immigrants, such as the Irish, Germans, Italians, and Jews.

Hughes, Everett C., and Helen M. Hughes. *Where People Meet*. New York: Free Press, 1952. This is a useful general survey of the ways in which different ethnic and racial groups come into contact with and influence each other.

Lewis, Oscar. *La Vida: A Puerto Rican Family in the Culture of Poverty, San Juan and New York*. New York: Random House, Vintage, 1968. A readable book in which Lewis reports the results of his study of the Puerto Rican culture in San Juan and its transformation into a subculture in New York City.

Myrdal, Gunnar. *An American Dilemma*. New York: Harper & Row, 1962. This is a revised edition of Myrdal's classic 1944 study of black Americans.

Rose, Peter. *They and We: Racial and Ethnic Relations in the United States*. New York: Random House, 1964. A simply written introduction to minority group relations. Rose focuses upon the processes of conflict and accommodation among ethnic groups in the United States.

Sklare, Marshall. *America's Jews*. New York: Random House, 1971. A comprehensive examination of the Jewish community in the United States.

Thomas, W. I., and F. Florian Znaniecki. *The Polish Peasant in Europe and America*. New York: Alfred A. Knopf, 1927. This pioneering study, which used many personal documents, such as diaries and journals, as a major source of information, emphasizes how personally disorganized an individual can become when he moves from his own culture into one that is foreign and sometimes hostile.

Van den Berghe, Pierre. *Race and Ethnicity — Essays in Comparative Sociology*. New York: Basic Books, 1970. An examination of race relations, applying theoretical and integration skills to cross-cultural and comparative studies in Mexico, Guatemala, South and East Africa.

Vander Zanden, James. *American Minority Relations*. New York: Ronald Press, 1966. This basic book will serve as a good resource for the further study of minority relations and the sources of prejudice and discrimination in America.

Williams, Robin M. *Strangers Next Door.* Englewood Cliffs, N.J.: Prentice-Hall, 1964. Based on an eight-year study, this carefully researched book documents intergroup and minority relations in America.

Articles and Papers

Cothran, Tilman C. "The Negro Protest Against Segregation in the South." *Annals of the American Academy of Political and Social Science,* January 1965, pp. 65–72.

Davis, F. James. "The Effects of a Freeway Displacement on Racial Housing Segregation in a Northern City." *Phylon* **26**, 3 (Fall 1965):209–215.

Eisenstadt, S. N. "The Process of Absorption of New Immigrants in Israel." *Human Relations* **5** (1952):223–246.

Francis, E. K. "The Nature of the Ethnic Group." *American Journal of Sociology* **52**, 5 (March 1947):393–400.

Gordon, Milton M. "Social Structure and Goals in Group Relations." In *Freedom and Control in Modern Society,* edited by Morroe Berger. Theodore Abel, and Charles H. Page. New York: Van Nostrand, 1954.

Heer, David M. "Negro-White Marriage in the United States." *Journal of Marriage and the Family* **28** (August 1966).

Holloway, Ralph S. "School Desegregation in Delaware." *Social Problems* **4**, 2 (October 1956): 166–172.

Lieberson, Stanley. "Residential Segregation and Ethnic Assimilation." *Social Forces* **40** (1961).

Lohman, Joseph D., and Delbert C. Reitzes. "Notes on Race Relations in a Mass Society." *American Journal of Sociology* **58** (November 1952):240–246.

Silberstein, Fred B., and Melvin Seeman. "Social Mobility and Prejudice." *American Journal of Sociology,* November 1959.

Tomasson, R. F., and L. D. Savitz. "The Identifiability of Jews." *American Journal of Sociology* **64**, 5 (March 1959):468–475.

Wheeler, Raymond H., and Jack C. Ross. "Structural Sources of Threat to Negro Membership in Militant Voluntary Associations in a Southern City." *Social Forces* **45**, 4 (June 1967): 583–585.

Williams, Robin M., Jr. "Unity and Diversity in Modern America." *Social Forces* **36**, 1 (October 1957).

Youngquist, Wayne. "Wooden Shoes and the One-third Hypothesis." *Wisconsin Sociologist* **6**, 1 (Spring–Summer 1968):21–24

II   RELATED RESOURCES
Nonfiction

Baldwin, James. *The Fire Next Time.* New York: Dell (Paper), 1963. In this absorbing autobiography Baldwin describes what he had to do to survive in his segregated community in New York's Harlem, and discusses possible future racial problems.

Cleaver, Eldridge. *Post-Prison Writings and Speeches.* New York: Random House, Vintage (Paper), 1969. Written after his release on parole from prison, this collection of Cleaver's essays and speeches analyzes the turning points in the black movement which led him and others to become black revolutionaries.

Du Bois, W. E. B. *The Autobiography of W. E. B. Du Bois.* New York: International Publishers (Paper), 1969. Writing in his ninetieth year, Du Bois reviewed the changes in his life; he became a black social scientist but ended as a Communist living in Africa because of the racial oppression he encountered in America.

————. *The Philadelphia Negro: A Social Study.* New York: Schocken Books (Paper), 1967. Published in 1899, this classic study is the first empirical study of blacks in American society.

Jackson. T. A. *Ireland, Her Own.* New York: International Publishers, 1947. This study of Ireland documents its history from the first subjugation by the English over eight hundred years ago to the partition in 1921 which brought about a temporary truce with the British.

Jones, LeRoi. *Home.* New York: Apollo (Paper), 1966. Through essays written during a five-year span (which includes the Cuban Revolution, the Birmingham bombings, the Harlem riots, and the assassination of Malcolm X), Jones describes the transformation of his view of America and his role as a black man in this society.

Mayerson, Charlotte, ed. *Two Blocks Apart.* New York: Avon (Paper), 1967. Through interviews with two seventeen-year-old boys—Juan Gonzales and Peter Quinn—Mayerson illustrates the differences in life styles and expectations of a lower-class Puerto Rican teen-ager and a middle-class white teen-ager living only two blocks apart.

Momaday, N. Scott. *The Way to Rainy Mountain.* New York: Ballantine Books (Paper), 1970.

As a Kiowa Indian, Scott Momaday tells the story and legends of his people through the recollections of his childhood.

Report of the National Advisory Commission on Civil Disorders. New York: Bantam Books (Paper), 1968. In this factual report, the commission concludes that rioting by minority groups is the result of a social system with built-in prejudice and discrimination which allows too few remedies for degradation and poverty.

Sartre, Jean-Paul. *Anti-Semite and Jew.* New York: Grove Press (Paper), 1962. Sartre writes about the characteristics of an anti-Semite, and the reasons this prejudice is developed within an individual and a society.

Stalvey, Lois M. *The Education of a Wasp.* New York: William Morrow, 1970. A moving account of a middle-class, white, Anglo-Saxon Protestant housewife and her family who discover the anguish of discrimination.

Wright, Nathan. *Black Power and Urban Unrest.* New York: Hawthorn Books (Paper), 1967. Wright explains "Black Power" as part of a larger movement toward black leadership in the black communities and in the struggle for civil rights and economic development.

Fiction

Chesnutt, Charles. *The House Behind the Cedars.* New York: Collier (Paper), 1969. First published in 1900. Chesnutt was the first black novelist to write about the interracial tensions in what he perceived as a white-dominated society.

Fuchs, Daniel. *Summer in Williamsburg.* New York: Basic Books, 1961. A novel about life among ethnic villagers, the Hasidic Jews of Brooklyn, New York, the story describes the strong sense of community which pervades the neighborhood where the author grew up.

Gordon, Noah. *The Rabbi.* Greenwich, Conn.: Fawcett (Paper), 1968. This absorbing novel portrays the conflicts which arose for a young Rabbi married to a non-Jew.

Grass, Günter. *Dog Years.* Greenwich, Conn.: Fawcett, 1969. Grass's perceptive novel describes Hitler's Germany and the causes for the mass murders of millions of Jews.

Malamud, Bernard. *The Fixer.* New York: Dell, Mayflower Books (Paper), 1968. In this story, based on an actual incident of anti-Semitism in turn-of-the-century Russia, the protagonist is accused of committing a ritual murder.

Momaday, N. Scott. *House Made of Dawn.* New York: Signet (Paper), 1969. The life of quiet desperation led by the American Indian is portrayed in Momaday's novel. It depicts the plight of the Indians, who have become outsiders in their native land.

Films

A Raisin in the Sun. Daniel Petrie, 1961. This is Lorraine Hansberry's study of the attempt of a lower-middle-class black family to move away from the Chicago slums, and the prejudice which they thus encountered.

Intolerance (Silent). D. W. Griffith, 1916. In this film classic Griffith attacked, through four separate stories, intolerance and bigotry in all periods of history.

One Potato, Two Potato. Larry Peerce, 1964. This provocative film portrays the problems of an interracial marriage.

The Learning Tree. Gordon Parks, 1969. The setting of this film is the South; the plot revolves around the life of a black teen-age boy and the prejudice he encounters there.

9. Education

Learning is a process that takes place all through life, as an individual undergoes various social and personal experiences that alter his behavior and his attitudes. In this book we will make a distinction between the broader learning experience called socialization, which means the general process of learning social behavior patterns and the cultural content of one's society, and education. As the term will be used in this chapter, education means a set of processes which are specifically and purposely directed toward inducing learning.

Formally directed learning experience, or education, is one of the very old and important institutions of society. In the first part of this chapter, we will discuss the functions of education in society, the reasons that the institution has come into being. Then we will talk about some of the effects that our educational system has on our society, with particular emphasis on the connection between education and social stratification. In the final section, we will look at some specific educational systems—the primary school, the secondary school, and the college—and at the appropriate role behavior for those who teach and those who learn in them. We will close with a brief look at the modern college campus, and at its social, cultural, and intellectual atmosphere.

1 THE SOCIAL FUNCTIONS OF EDUCATION

Educational organizations vary widely. Think of the contrast between a Summerhill school where the children roam about freely and attend only the lessons that interest them, and a French lycée, where the children must memorize long passages of plays written by Racine in the seventeenth century, spend several hours a day on written exercises, and be prepared to accept a disciplinary whack if they fail at these tasks. Yet in spite of these enormous differences, both schools fulfill the same basic functions within their society. The methods, perhaps even the goals, of individual schools vary, but the educational functions are essentially the same.

We can summarize the social functions of the institution of education under four headings: (1) to transmit the society's culture; (2) to help the individual select social roles and teach him how to perform them; (3) to integrate into the cultural mainstream various individual and group subcultures and identities; and (4) to serve as a source of social and cultural innovation.

One point we should make here is that there is a great difference between the functions of the institution of education and the functions of a specific organization. We have listed above the functions of the institution of education. But a specific educational organization, George Washington Elementary School, for example, has other functions. It functions as a source of employment for teachers, cafeteria workers, and janitors; it functions as a babysitter for working and busy mothers; it functions as a provider of hot lunches for children who may get no other meal all day. These functions will not concern us in this chapter; our focus will be on the institution of education.

Not every educational organization necessarily serves all four of these functions, for a school may concentrate on one and deemphasize or even ignore the others, in a form of educational specialization. For example, a college like Missouri Valley College, with a student body of about nine hundred and no courses given at the graduate level, has only a minor concern for societal innovation, but concentrates on the other aspects of the educational function. On the other hand, the Rockefeller Institute for Medical Research, a school in New York for doctors and medical researchers, concentrates on innovation and all but ignores social integration. Most schools place varying emphases on the four social functions, depending in part on their positions in the educational hierarchy which extends from nursery school to postdoctoral institutes.

CULTURAL TRANSMISSION

We can separate the transmission of culture into two different (although related) aspects—the transmission of cultural knowledge, and the transmission of cultural attitudes, values, and norms. The transmission of cultural knowledge is the function of education that is most familiar to everyone. This broad term, cultural knowledge, includes language, mathematical systems, and scientific and technological discoveries. The importance of this function of education is not the same for every society. In an industrialized and complex society like ours, with a system whose operation depends on the capabilities of many different specialists, it is of vital importance that the coming generations learn much of our accumulated cultural knowledge. Because this knowledge is so extensive, the task takes many years, and also requires both specialized teachers (such as the fourth grade science teacher) and specialized educational organizations which teach only certain fields of knowledge (such as a school of engineering). In societies that have less cultural knowledge than ours, where there are few specialists and a simple form of social organization, the transmission of knowledge is a minor aspect of education.

In the narrowest sense, the transmission of cultural knowledge is simply vocational training. This is true of most primitive societies. Among the Mbuti Pygmies of Africa, a father teaches his son how to make an arrow shaft so it will be straight, how to attach the arrowhead securely, and how to shoot the finished arrow at a moving target. In the same way, vocational high schools in America teach boys how to repair automobile engines or run a drill press. The Pygmy boy learns how to be a hunter, and the American boy learns how to be a mechanic; both have thus been equipped with some skills based on technical knowledge that will help them survive and succeed in the competitive conditions of their lives.

However, we need not define the transmission of knowledge in so restricted a way. A person may learn *how* to learn, how to discover, how to create. This kind of education has a broader purpose, but it is still basically the transmission of a skill that is a part of the society's culture.

Transmission of cultural knowledge is like the tip of an iceberg. It is the small part of education that everyone sees. All the activities of the school—the reading of textbooks, homework, tests, grades, and report cards—focus our attention on this aspect, and many students understandably assume that it is

the sole function of their education. When we say someone is "doing well" in school, we usually mean that he is getting good grades and learning the information presented in the formal classes. However, there is much more for the student to learn than just cultural knowledge. He must also learn the values and attitudes of his culture.

Most of this learning takes place informally, but within the formal setting of the classroom. In primary schools, children may be explicitly instructed in certain cultural norms and values. The teacher will say "Don't tell lies." But such learning is likely to occur less obviously than this. For example, the book the children use in learning to read may include a story about the trouble a little girl gets into when she tells her mother a lie. The teacher may never comment on the obvious moral of the story, but the children will nevertheless draw the conclusion that it is bad to lie.

As a student reaches higher levels of education, he learns more and more about the definition of the culture he lives in. When an English class reads *Moby Dick* in high school or college, they are learning a number of things that have the main value of helping them understand American culture. They learn that we value literature as an art form, and that we consider reading a novel to be an aesthetic experience. They learn about the effects of the use of language in communication, and how words can evoke emotional responses; for example, they notice the way the opening sentence, "Call me Ishmael," tells them about the man who speaks. They learn something about the traditions of our society and of the particular subculture of nineteenth-century, seafaring New Englanders. In trying to understand the meaning of Captain Ahab's pursuit of the white whale, they come to learn something about American attitudes toward good and evil. The teacher may discuss some of the points with the class; others will be left for the students to draw their own conclusions. In either case, the result will be an increased awareness of

American cultural attitudes and values, and a greater understanding of that culture as a whole. This kind of cultural awareness is an important function of the educational experience.

SELECTING AND TEACHING SOCIAL ROLES

Our society is deeply committed to the necessity for occupational specialization. This brings with it several problems which the social system must find some way to solve. First, we must have facilities for teaching all the different specialties. Second, we need some way of ensuring that the supply of people trained in each specialty is roughly equal to the demand. Too few qualified people mean the job will go undone; too many mean unemployment. Both may create serious social problems. Third, we must find some way of matching the talents and abilities of individuals with the requirements of the specialty, so that each job is filled by a person capable of performing it successfully. We touched on educational specialization, the first of these problems, above; here we will look at the way the other two problems are handled.

The schools have been reasonably successful at ensuring that an adequate supply of trained people exists to fill job openings. Secondary schools and colleges choose their course offerings with this in mind. When the demand for one specialty (mechanical drawing, for example) drops, the number of those courses will be reduced or perhaps eliminated altogether. New ones will be offered to keep pace with the new technology. When public schools fail in this task, private institutions, or private businesses, often step in to fill the gap and meet the demand for a specific kind of training. A good example can be seen in the business schools which teach typing and shorthand to secretaries, and the schools that offer courses in computer programming, a relatively new and rapidly expanding occupational specialty.

Severe shortages of trained personnel do not occur often in any field. When they do, it is usually not because of inadequate facilities and programs for training, but for some other social reason. For example, shortages of teachers and nurses occur when their pay is very low in relation to the amount of training their jobs require; shortages of servants occur because the work is considered degrading.

Often, however, too many people compete for certain job openings. This is an especially serious problem in times of rapid technological change, such as the present. A new invention can reduce almost overnight the number of people needed in a job. For example, many bookkeepers and accountants lost their jobs when computers began to handle payrolls and routine accounting chores. Of course, new jobs were created for computer technicians and programmers, but that is no help to the bookkeepers who don't know how to program a computer.

A certain amount of this kind of difficulty is probably inevitable in any vital society. In some cases, institutions other than education must solve it. The government can give the bookkeepers unemployment compensation while they learn new skills, or the company can pay to have the bookkeepers retrained as programmers, rather than hire new employees. But part of the solution must come from educational institutions. They must make longer-range plans to anticipate obsolescence—for example, they must analyze those occupations which machines could easily perform. A school may also help keep a rough balance between supply and demand in the various occupational specialties by teaching people more than one area of competence and by teaching them how to learn, so that if, in the future, they must be retrained it will not be too difficult to do.

It is one thing to know that five thousand new teachers will be needed in 1978 and to provide educational facilities to train them. It is another to select which five thousand individuals they will be. Of course, in our society, the ultimate decision of whether or not to prepare for and accept a job as a teacher is in the hands of the individual. Yet the school is involved in this decision, in two ways. It gives advice and assistance in career planning to those of appropriate age. In more subtle ways, it also serves to channel the individual into certain careers.

Both high schools and colleges have departments specifically concerned with career guidance. The high school may employ one or more guidance counselors to discuss career possibilities with each student and make recommendations. These recommendations normally are based on a study of the individual's school record, and perhaps also on the results of special tests of ability and interest that the counselor administers. Colleges usually maintain placement bureaus, where students can obtain information about various careers and job openings. In many cases, recruiters for government and industry may come there to interview interested students.

The formal guidance program is only one way in which educational institutions help determine who takes what job. Actually the process begins almost from the moment the child first enters primary school. As soon as children begin to read and write, to add and subtract, the school starts testing and then grading them. Those who do well on the tests are given an "enriched" program. They may be placed in a class that goes faster and covers more material; they may have a chance to take extra courses, such as a foreign language. Perhaps the teacher will give them additional independent projects—books to read, or reports to make—because from their superior performance she has concluded that they are capable of learning more than most of the other children. Those students who do poorly on the tests are sometimes placed in classes of "slow learners"; although students in these classes often receive special remedial and individualized attention, they are not expected to learn as much as the other children and so not as much academic material is taught to them. In short, school children are filtered into different levels or sometimes different tracks according to their academic performances.

In time, the low rated students may feel that they cannot succeed at anything which requires much education or specific academic knowledge. One might also say that they have accepted the roles to which they were guided. When they are old enough, they find jobs as manual laborers, or waitresses, and they "drop out" of school, as we like to say. With each additional year of education, another group leaves the system. The high school dropouts, the high school graduates, the college dropouts, the M.A.'s, and finally at the end of the road, the M.D.'s and the Ph.D.'s—each will fill different occupational categories, and so the selection is made.

It is a workable system, but not necessarily the best one imaginable. For one thing, it has put a very high premium on certain characteristics, such as a good rote memory and test-taking ability, which may not be so useful in many high status occupations as, say, imagination or leadership. Another problem is that certain children may be channeled into a low educational achievement level, not because of their personal inability, but because of their membership in a low ranked social class, racial minority, or ethnic group. (We will discuss this phenomenon more fully in topic 2.) Also, this system is a great handicap to those who acquire motivation to do well in school only later in their educational careers; by the time they do get interested, they have already been labeled as low achievement students.

We have centered our discussion of the teaching of roles on occupational roles, but the school does teach other kinds of roles as well. It instructs children in their roles as citizens of their country, and in their roles as children or young people. It also, of course, teaches them how to perform the role of student which they are obliged to assume while they are at school.

SOCIAL INTEGRATION

In a pluralistic and widely heterogeneous society like that of the United States, social integration is a most important function of

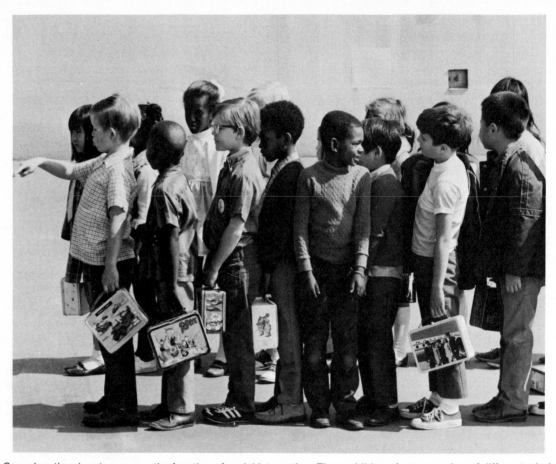

Our educational system serves the function of social integration. These children, from a number of different ethnic and racial groups, are learning a common culture through the time they spend together at school, both in and out of the classroom. *(Ralph Crane,* Life Magazine © *Time Inc.)*

the institution of education. Our population is large; we come from a number of dissimilar backgrounds, each with its own special values and attitudes that may not be shared by the majority of people. This variety, of course, is one of the hallmarks of our society. We have the freedom of choice that pluralism offers, and we have opportunities (created by our diversity) for social renewal and innovation. However, without some kind of cohesion and integration, our society would splinter into thousands of independent factions unable to cooperate with each other in a larger pattern of organization. Education helps to provide the social integration that keeps America bound together in a functioning social system.

The most basic way in which education integrates our population is to teach us all the same language. Each year thousands of first graders come to school unable to speak English—in New York and California, the children of Puerto Rican and Mexican immigrants; in Cleveland, Detroit, Chicago, and Pittsburgh (where steel mills and factories have offered employment for many newcomers to America), children who speak only Ukrainian or Polish or Croatian. There are other pockets of ethnic groups all over the country—Cubans in Florida, Germans in Pennsylvania, Scandinavians in Minnesota and Wisconsin, and Chinese and Japanese on the West Coast. By the time these children leave our public schools they are able to speak and understand English, which is a most important step in bringing them closer to the cultural mainstream.

In addition to sharing a language, so that communication can be relatively free and extensive, a cohesive nation must share a certain fund of experience. Perhaps you have noticed the bond that a common experience creates between individuals. For example, suppose you go away to college, and you meet someone there, in the mass of strange faces, who played in a band that competed in the Tri-State Music Festival the same year your band did. You feel more of a connection to him, even though you never met him before, than you do with the other strangers. You can see the same thing happen between fifty-year-old women who discover that they went to the same college, or thirty-year-old men who reminisce together about the messages they used to read with their Captain Midnight decoder rings.

Education gives people many shared experiences. All day long, the third grade class does the same thing together. They read the same book, take the same test, play the same games at recess. We sometimes make the mistake of assuming that childhood everywhere is very much like our own, that every child plays baseball, jumps rope, and knows "Hey Diddle Diddle." We may not think it unusual to hear that a little girl who came here from Japan has never heard of the story of Cinderella, but it comes as a surprise to read about a whole class of ninth graders in a California public school who have no idea how the story of Cinderella comes out.

Knowing the story of Cinderella is not in itself very significant socially, but having some fund of shared experience does induce cohesion. Also, shared experience leads to shared attitudes and values which are even more meaningful in terms of social integration. For example, the fact that we all had to undergo a certain number of years of school attendance gives all of us, even those who hated every minute of it, the sense that an education is somehow a valued commodity— this is a shared social value. Many other such values come from our shared educational experiences.

Another aspect of social integration is an awareness of the fact that we share attitudes and experiences with others in our society. This may be called a *sense of cultural identity;* it is necessary for social cohesion, as the sense of self is necessary for a well-integrated personality.

A strong feeling of cultural identity is an especially important element of nationalism, the creation of which the modern nation-state and formal education are major mechanisms. This can be seen in emerging nations all over the world today, and especially in Africa and Asia. In these nations formal and directed education is often used to promote nationalistic feelings and to dilute all influences that are alien to the national culture.

Along with nationalism comes patriotism, another important ingredient of the modern nation-state. Patriotism can be the natural result of living together and sharing experiences over a long period of time. Or it can be explicitly taught in the schools, as it is in the United States and every other modern society. The morning recital of the Pledge of Allegiance to the flag, the bulletin board pictures of the president, the playing of "The Star-Spangled Banner" before an assembly or a basketball game—these devices teach patriotism to all our school children.

American education is strongly oriented, especially in the primary schools, toward the function of social integration. (This is not so true of more homogeneous nations, like Japan or England.) This function in America was formerly concerned mainly with integrating the many immigrants who came here, but in the last two decades immigration to this country has decreased significantly, and now only a small percentage of our population are recent immigrants. Today a slightly different kind of social integration is aimed at—the full inclusion of the poor, the black, and the disadvantaged, in the mainstream of our society.

INNOVATION

Societies need innovations of many kinds, and educational organizations are a prime source of innovation. This is particularly true in a complex, technological society. Since innovation is so necessary to progress in societies, there must be some system which encourages its development. Our society has chosen to incorporate much of that function within educational organizations, particularly in colleges and universities.

The most familiar example of innovation within universities is the research and development activity of professors and graduate students. Such activity is stimulated and sup-

ported by government funds and grants from private businesses and foundations. Often research projects are designed to answer specific questions ("How can we keep metal from melting when it encounters the heat of friction generated by high speeds?" or "How can employees be motivated to help the company increase its profits?") that arise in society during the pursuit of our goals (sending a rocket to the moon or improving business efficiency). This kind of activity is called *applied research,* and is contrasted with *basic research,* which is not concerned with an immediate practical result, but rather with investigating fundamental facts, processes,

Research is an important aspect of the university's function in society. Laboratories there not only train the next generation of scientists, they also make many significant technological advances. *(Hugh Rogers, Monkmeyer)*

and phenomena. A large amount of basic research also goes on at colleges and universities.

Some critics of our educational system believe that our universities are too much involved with the function of social and technical innovation, that this is impairing their ability to perform the other educational functions. Professors may be hired solely for their ability to do research; classes on an introductory level are then either taught badly by that research worker, or handed over entirely to overworked graduate students. The result may be that the university does poorly in its function of cultural transmission.

On the other hand, the current focus of interest on research in our universities can be defended from several points of view. In our highly industrialized, knowledge-oriented society, innovation of this kind is necessary to social viability. Even though most of the students are not personally involved with the work of the research projects, they benefit from the consequent atmosphere of increased intellectual stimulation they give to the whole university. From a practical viewpoint, we must also remember that research projects attract funds to the university. These funds often permit additional benefits—more instructors, expanded course offerings, or a noted expert in residence for a semester—for the whole student body. Corporations will often give large gifts to universities that have contributed useful research results. For better or worse, the economy of a modern American university is very dependent on the existence of its research programs.

The kind of innovation we have been primarily discussing leads to the production of new technology, to scientific advances, to the acquisition of new or more extensive information about the way things work. Just as important, though, is another kind of innovation, the production of new ideas. And nowhere is this more important than in the field of social innovation.

Traditionally in Western history, the university has been a major source of innovation in ideas. The traditional attitude of the university scholar or intellectual is openness, a willingness to investigate and consider new ideas, the ability to compare and examine conflicting opinions. The academic life is deliberately designed to encourage such innovation. However, some people question how well the modern institution of higher education can continue to serve this function. They point to the increasing bureaucratization of such institutions, and suggest that nowadays there is very little difference between being employed by a large university or by General Motors. Employees in both situations must comply with an elaborate set of rules and regulations, wade through tons of paperwork, maneuver to acquire power, and remember not to upset the *status quo*.

There is some truth in these observations, as we shall discuss in topic 3. Nevertheless, it is still true that universities foster social innovations and that they provide probably the most hospitable climate available for innovators to live and work in. Also, they can pass on to their students attitudes and skills which lead to innovative thought. Education can help the individual to step aside from his cultural web for a moment, and to evaluate it, as we are trying to do here: this is the necessary first step for intelligent and meaningful change.

EDGAR Z. FRIEDENBERG
High School in America

"High School in America" by Edgar Z. Friedenberg, from *The Dignity of Youth and Other Atavisms* by Edgar Z. Friedenberg, Dalhousie University. First published in *Commentary*, Vol. 36, November 1963.

Introduction

Edgar Friedenberg is one of the best known sociological critics of the American educational system. He has studied it closely over a period of years, and in general has been quite critical of what he has seen.

His books have been widely read and discussed by both academic and general readers. This selection comes from The Dignity of Youth and Other Atavisms, *and was written in 1963. Although many of Friedenberg's conclusions are controversial, his work demonstrates the value of logical observation and analysis of modern institutions and patterns of culture.*

The modern high school: a profile

Not far from Los Angeles, though rather nearer to Boston, may be located the town of Milgrim, in which Milgrim High School is clearly the most costly and impressive structure. Milgrim is not a suburb. Milgrim is an agricultural village which has outgrown its nervous system; its accustomed modes of social integration have not yet even begun to relate its present, recently acquired inhabitants to one another. So, though it is not a suburb, Milgrim is not a community either.

Milgrim's recent, fulminating growth is largely attributable to the rapid development of light industry in the outer suburbs, with a resulting demand for skilled labor. But within the past few years, further economic development has created a steady demand for labor that is not so skilled. In an area that is by no means known for its racial tolerance or political liberalism, Milgrim has acquired, through no wish of its own, a sizable Negro and Puerto Rican minority.

Estimates of the proportion of the student body at Milgrim who are, in the ethnocentric language of demography, non-white, vary enormously. Some students who are clearly middle-class and of pinkish-gray color sometimes speak as if they themselves were a besieged minority. More responsible staff members produce estimates of from twelve to thirty percent. Observations in the corridors and lunchrooms favor the lower figure. They also establish clearly that the non-whites are orderly and well behaved, though somewhat more forceful in their movements and manner of speech than their light-skinned colleagues.

What is Milgrim High like? It is a big, expensive building, on spacious but barren grounds. Every door is at the end of a corridor; there is no reception area, no public space in which one can adjust to the transition from the outside world. Between class periods the corridors are tumultuously crowded; during them they are empty. But at both times they are guarded by teachers and students on patrol duty. Patrol duty does not consist primarily in the policing of congested throngs of moving students, or the guarding of property from damage. Its principal function is the checking of corridor passes. Between classes, no student may walk down the corridor without a form, signed by a teacher, telling where he is coming from, where he is going, and the time, to the minute, during which the pass is valid. A student caught in the corridor without such a pass is sent or taken to the office; there a detention slip is made out against him, and he is required to remain after school for two or three hours. He may do his homework during this time, but he may not leave his seat or talk.

There is no physical freedom whatever at Milgrim. During class breaks, the lavatories are kept locked, so that a student must not only obtain a pass but find the custodian and induce him to open the facility. Indeed Milgrim High's most memorable arrangements are its corridor passes and its johns; they dominate social interaction. "Good morning, Mr. Smith," an attractive girl will say pleasantly to one of her teachers in the corridor. "Linda, do you have a pass to be in your locker after the bell rings?" is his greeting in reply. There are no more classifications of washrooms than there must have been in the Confederate Navy. The common sort, marked just "Boys" and "Girls," are generally locked. Then there are some marked, "Teachers, Men" and "Teachers, Women," unlocked. Near the auditorium are two others marked simply, "Men" and "Women," which are intended primarily for the public when the auditorium is being used for some function. During the school day cardboard signs saying "Adults Only" are placed on these doors. Girding up my maturity, I used this men's room during my stay at Milgrim. Usually it was empty; but once, as soon as the door clicked behind me, a teacher who had been concealed in the cubicle began jumping up and down to peer over his partition and verify my adulthood.

He was not a voyeur; he was checking on smoking. At most public high schools, students are forbidden to smoke, and this is probably the most common source of friction with authorities. It focuses, naturally, on the washrooms which are the only place students can go where teachers are not supposed to be. Milgrim, for a time, was more liberal than most; last year its administration designated an area behind the school where seniors might smoke during their lunch period. But, as a number of students explained to me during interviews, some of these seniors had "abused the privilege" by lighting up before they got into the area, and the privilege had been withdrawn. No student, however, questioned that smoking was a privilege rather than a right.

The concept of privilege is important at Milgrim. Teachers go to the head of the chow line at lunch; whenever I would attempt quietly to stand in line the teacher on hall duty would remonstrate with me. He was right, probably; I was fouling up an entire informal social system by my ostentation. Students on hall patrol also were allowed to come to the head of the line; so were seniors. Much of the behavior that Milgrim depends on to keep it going is motivated by the reward of getting a government-surplus peanut butter or tuna fish sandwich without standing in line.

What adults generally, I think, fail to grasp even though they may actually know

it, is that there is no refuge or respite from this: no coffee break, no taking ten for a smoke, no room like the teachers' room, however poor, where the youngsters can get away from adults. High schools don't have club rooms; they have organized gym and recreation. A student cannot go to the library when he wants a book; on certain days his schedule provides a forty-five minute library period. "Don't let anybody leave early," a guidance counselor urged during a group-testing session at Hartsburgh, an apparently more permissive school that I also visited. "There really isn't any place for them to go." Most of us are as nervous by the age of five as we will ever be, and adolescence adds to the strain; but one thing a high-school student learns is that he can expect no provision for his need to give in to his feelings, or swing out in his own style, or creep off and pull himself together.

The little things shock most. High-school students—and not just, or even particularly, at Milgrim—have a prisoner's sense of time. They don't know what time it is outside. The research which occasioned my presence at Milgrim, Hartsburgh, and the other schools in my study required me to interview each of twenty-five to thirty students at each school three times. My first appointment with each student was set up by his guidance counselor; I would make the next appointment directly with the student and issue him the passes he needed to keep it. The student has no *open* time at his own disposal; he has to select the period he can miss with least loss to himself. Students well-adapted to the school usually pick study halls; poorer or more troublesome students pick the times of their most disagreeable classes; both avoid cutting classes in which the teacher is likely to respond vindictively to their absence. Most students, when asked when they would like to come for their next interview, replied, "I can come any time." When I pointed out to them that there must, after all, be some times that would be more convenient for them than others, they would say, "Well tomorrow, fourth period" or whatever. But hardly any of them knew when this would be in clock time. High-school classes emphasize the importance of punctuality by beginning at regular but uneven times like 10.43 and 11.27, which are, indeed, hard to remember; and the students did not know when this was.

What is learned in high school, or for that matter anywhere at all, depends far less on what is taught than on what one actually experiences in the place. The quality of instruction in high school varies from sheer rot to imaginative and highly skilled teaching. But classroom content is often handled at a creditable level and is not in itself the source of the major difficulty. Both at Milgrim and Hartsburgh, for example, the students felt that they were receiving competent instruction and that this was an undertaking the school tried seriously to handle. I doubt, however, that this makes up for much of the damage to which high-school students are systematically subjected. What is formally taught is just not that important, compared to the constraint and petty humiliation to which the youngsters with few exceptions must submit in order to survive.

But far more of what is deeply and thoroughly learned in the school is designed to keep the heart from raising awkward, heartfelt issues—if design governs in a thing so subtle. It is learned so thoroughly by attendance at schools like Milgrim or even Hartsburgh that most Americans by the time they are adult cannot really imagine that life could be organized in any other way.

First of all, they learn to assume that the state has the right to compel adolescents to spend six or seven hours a day, five days a week, thirty-six or so weeks a year, in a specific place, in charge of a particular group of persons in whose selection they have no voice, performing tasks about which they have no choice, without remuneration and subject to specialized regulations and sanctions that are applicable to no one else in the community nor to them except in this place. Whether this law is a service or a burden to the young— and, indeed, it is both, in varying degrees—is another issue altogether. So the first thing the young learn in school is that there are certain sanctions and restrictions that apply only to them; that they do not participate fully in the freedoms guaranteed by the state, and that *therefore, these freedoms do not really partake of the character of inalienable rights.*

Of course not. The school, as schools continually stress, acts *in loco parentis;* and children may not leave home because their parents are unsatisfactory. What I have pointed out is no more than a special consequence of the fact that students are minors, and minors do not, indeed, share all the rights and privileges—and responsibilities—of citizenship. Very well. However one puts it, we are still discussing the same issue. The high school, then, is where you really learn what it means to be a minor.

For a high school is not a parent. Parents may love their children, hate them, or like most parents, do both in a complex mixture. But they must nevertheless permit a certain intimacy and respond to their children as persons. Homes are not run by regulations, though the parents may think they are, but by a process of continuous and almost entirely unconscious emotional homeostasis, in which each member affects and accommodates to the needs, feelings, fantasy life, and character structure of the others. This may be, and often is, a terribly destructive process; I intend no defense of the family as a social institution. But children grow up in homes or the remnants of homes, are in physical fact dependent on parents, and too intimately related to them to permit their area of freedom to be precisely defined. This is not because they have no rights or are entitled to less respect than adults, but because intimacy conditions freedom and growth in ways too subtle and continuous to be defined as overt acts.

After the family, the school is the first social institution an individual must deal with—the first place in which he learns to handle himself with strangers. The school establishes the pattern of his subsequent assumptions as to what relations between the individual and society are appropriate and which constitute invasions of privacy and constraints on his spirit—what the British, with exquisite precision, call "taking a liberty." But the American public school evolved as a melting pot, under the assumption that it had not merely the right but the duty to impose a common standard of genteel decency on a polyglot body of immigrants' children and thus insure their assimilation into the better life of the American dream.

The first thing the student learns, then, is that as a minor, he is subject to peculiar restraints; the second is that these restraints are general, not limited either by custom or by the schools' presumed commitment to the curriculum. High-school administrators are not professional educators in the sense that a physician, an attorney, or a tax accountant are professionals. They do not, that is, think of themselves as practitioners of a specialized instructional craft, who derive their authority from its requirements. They are specialists in keeping an essentially political enterprise from being strangled by conflicting community attitudes and pressures. They are problem-oriented, and the feelings and needs for growth of their captive and unenfranchised clientele are the least of their problems; for the status of the "teen-ager" in the community is so low that even if he rebels, the school is not blamed for the conditions against which he is rebelling. He is simply a truant or a juvenile delinquent; at worst the school has "failed to reach him." What high-school personnel become specialists in, ultimately, is the *control* of large groups of students even

at catastrophic expense to their opportunity to learn. These controls are not exercised primarily to facilitate instruction, and particularly, they are in no way limited to matters bearing on instruction. At several schools in our sample boys had been ordered —sometimes on the complaint of teachers— to shave off beards. One of these boys had played football for the school; he was told that, although the school had no legal authority to require him to shave, he would be barred from the banquet honoring the team unless he complied. Dress regulations are another case in point.

The effects on the students are manifold. The concepts of dignity and privacy, notably deficient in American adult folkways, are not permitted to develop here. The school's assumption of custodial control of students implies that power and authority are indistinguishable. If the school's authority is not limited to matters pertaining to education, it cannot be derived from its educational responsibilities. It is a naked, empirical fact, to be accepted or contraverted according to the possibilities of the moment. In such a world, power counts more than legitimacy; if you don't have power, it is naive to think you have rights that must be respected.

Yet, finally, the consequence of continuing through adolescence to submit to diffuse authority that is not derived from the task at hand—as a doctor's orders or the training regulations of an athletic coach, for example, usually are—is more serious than political incompetence or weakness of character. There is a general arrest of development. An essential part of growing up is learning that, though differences of power among men lead to brutal consequences, all men are peers; none is omnipotent, none derives his potency from magic, but only from his specific competence and function. The policeman represents the majesty of the state, but this does not mean that he can put you in jail; it means, precisely, that he cannot—at least not for long. Any person—especially if he does not like them or is afraid of them—is tempted to claim diffuse authority and snare the youngster in the trailing remnants of childhood emotion which always remain to trip him. Schools succumb to this temptation, and control pupils by reinvoking the sensations of childhood punishment, which remain effective because they were originally selected, with great unconscious guile, to dramatize the child's weakness in the face of authority.

Thus the high school is permitted to infantilize adolescence; in fact, it is encouraged to by the widespread hostility to "teen-agers" and the anxiety about their conduct found throughout our society. It does not allow much maturation to occur during the years when most maturation would naturally occur. Maturity, to be sure, is not conspicuously characteristic of American adult life, and would almost certainly be a threat to the economy. So perhaps in this, as in much else, the high school is simply the faithful servant of the community.

Conclusion

Many observers of our nation's high schools are concerned with issues directly related to the educational experience. They think in terms of special programs, class size, student–teacher ratios, and up-to-date equipment. Edgar Friedenberg deals with a more basic and potentially more important issue. He wants to know how the teachers and administrators in the high school relate to the students. Friedenberg's findings are dismaying. The students in Milgrim High School are treated with little respect. It is impossible to generalize accurately from one case to the majority of high schools, but Friedenberg implies that Milgrim is not unique. Do you agree?

In the last section of his report Friedenberg makes two interesting, and controversial, suggestions. First, he suggests that Americans have a hostile attitude toward youth. He claims that this hostility accounts, at least in part, for the harsh treatment that the students receive in school. Friedenberg's second hypothesis is that one of the unconscious aims of the high school teachers and faculty, and of the entire society, is to prevent the maturation of the teen-age students. He cites no evidence to support this claim: Friedenberg does not write in a careful, scientific fashion. But what he says is insightful, controversial, and thought-provoking.

TOPIC

2 EDUCATION AND SOCIETY

The way a society handles the education of its young people has a great influence on many of its broad social patterns. We noted in the last section that the content of education is highly important to the continuation and development of the social system. The manner in which formal education is conducted is also highly significant. So is the question of which people formal education reaches most effectively and frequently in a society.

In this section, we will consider some of the effects, many of them not explicit or intended, of the educational system in the United States.

Of prime concern in this topic is the way that education is related to the process of stratification. We have discussed already the ways in which schools at all levels act as filtering mechanisms, directing young people into certain roles and occupations that will be of great importance to them for the rest of their lives. This is certainly one of the intended functions of our educational system. An inevitable corollary of such filtering is that the level and type of education an individual achieves bestows upon him a certain status rank; thus the school plays an important role in determining his life chances. Moreover, there is much evidence that status ranks are not bestowed impartially, or strictly on the basis of inherent ability and talent. Some people are much better endowed by their family background with those attributes which lead to success in the educational system.

In order to orient ourselves in this area, we will start with a look at some basic statistics relating to educational trends in the United States. These can help to answer such questions as who is getting how much education, and they can also point out future trends in educational enrollment and attainment. Then we will talk about the general relationship between education and stratification, bringing up a special problem of our society, currently the focus of much concern and attention—the connection between our educational system and the unequal social positions of minority groups. In a final section, we will consider the effect of education on social values and attitudes, pointing out the ways in which the educational system can be a force for social change as well as a conservative influence.

EDUCATIONAL TRENDS IN THE UNITED STATES

All the statistics concerning education in the United States point to the same conclusion; more and more people are getting more and more years of education. For the school year 1959–1960, the total enrollment in all American educational institutions was 46 million persons; ten years later it had grown to 58 million, more than a 25 percent increase. In part, of course, this reflects the fact that there are simply more young people in the country. However, there is evidence that the increased enrollment is also the result of increased educational participation. For example, the greatest rate of enrollment increase in the 1960s has been at the college level, where it jumped from 3½ million to 7½ million students. Primary schools are growing more slowly, showing only a 13 percent increase over this same decade.[1]

The figures concerning numbers of high school graduates are perhaps the clearest demonstration of the trend in this century toward mass or universal education. In 1900, the number of people graduating from high school was 95,000. The total number of people of graduating age was 1,500,000. This means that only about 7 percent of the young people were finishing high school then. By 1920, this figure was 17 percent, and by 1940, it had soared to 50 percent. Today, the vast majority of people, about 80 percent, in the appropriate age group graduate from high school. A statistic which also serves to dramatize the distance we have come along the road to universal education is that today ten times more students enter college than graduated from high school at the turn of the century. In 1965, 54 percent of all high school graduates enrolled in college, compared with 34 percent in 1940.

Not everyone who goes to college gets a degree, but the number of college graduates is increasing rapidly. In 1900, 30,000 people received college degrees. By 1920 the figure had grown to only 54,000, but by 1940, the figure was 217,000, and it climbed to 497,000 in 1950. In 1968, 867,000 degrees were conferred by colleges, and the figure for 1970 is about 1 million. A significant point also is that

1. Unless otherwise noted, all statistics in this chapter come from the public reports of the U.S. Department of Health, Education and Welfare.

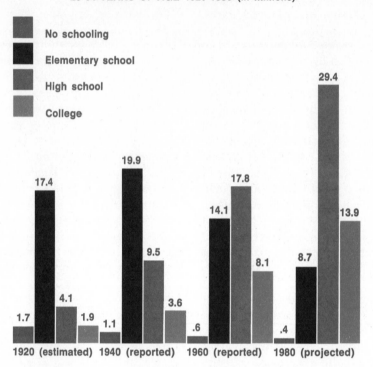

EDUCATIONAL ATTAINMENT OF MALE POPULATION
25-64 YEARS OF AGE 1920-1980 (in millions)

■ No schooling

■ Elementary school

■ High school

■ College

1920 (estimated)   1940 (reported)   1960 (reported)   1980 (projected)

SOURCES OF DATA: *1950 Census of Population,* vol. 1, U.S. Summary; *1960 Census of Population,* vol. 1, part 1, U.S. Summary; U.S. Bureau of the Census, *Current Population Reports,* series P-20, no. 91.

The educational level of the population has been rising rapidly. By 1960 the average man between 25 and 64 years of age had a high school education. By 1980, more than half will have finished high school and a quarter will be college graduates.

the proportion of advanced degrees is increasing. Today nearly one-quarter of the total college degrees are master's and doctor's degrees, representing at least one more year of education beyond the bachelor's degree.[2]

Another way to measure the trend toward more education for more people is to compare the figures for the educational attainment of the current labor force with those of the past. In 1952, 42.8 percent of the total labor force

reached at least the level of 4 years of high school education; the median number of school years completed was 10.9. Today 62.1 percent of the labor force has a high school education or better, and the median number of school years completed is 12.3.[3] In other words, the average worker in this country has a high school education.

Universal education

This trend toward mass education, which has been a feature of the past fifty years, is largely taken for granted today, but it actually

2. Out of a total of 866,548 college degrees awarded in 1968, 176,749 were master's degrees and 23,089 were Ph.D.'s. Source: U.S. Office of Education, as cited in *New York Times Encyclopedic Almanac 1970* (New York: New York Times Co., 1969), p. 517.

3. Figures from the U.S. Department of Labor, as cited in *New York Times Almanac 1972.*

NUMBER OF COLLEGE DEGREES CONFERRED
(per thousand population) in the United States: 1870-1970

SOURCES: U.S. Bureau of the Census, *Historical Statistics of the United States* and *Statistical Abstract of the United States, 1970* (Washington, D.C.: Government Printing Office).

The overall trend in American education has been a steady increase in the percentage of the population receiving college educations. The sharp rise after World War II was encouraged when government benefits for GIs helped to send many men to college; the subsequent drop was due in part to a drop in the proportion of the population that was of college age.

constitutes a new and quite radical social experiment, one which no other society has undertaken on such a scale. The traditional view of education was that it was a special privilege of the elite. This view was prevalent until quite recently in European countries such as England and France, where the best (and the longest) educations were reserved for a small number of students who could pass highly competitive examinations when they were eleven or twelve years old. Standards in such schools are high, training is rigorous, and there is much room in the curriculum for subjects with no immediate or practical utility, such as ancient languages.

In the United States education has tended to be viewed more as the right of every individual than as the privilege of the few. Universal education has long been an ideal in this country, but we have only had the resources to put it into practice in recent years. Such a policy means, of course, that there must be some relaxation of the traditional academic standards to accommodate a wide variety of abilities and experience. This necessity is especially marked in secondary schools and colleges. The lowering of certain standards, along with a reorientation of the curriculum toward subjects useful to a greater number of students, began in the 1920s, which was the time when enrollment started its process of rapid expansion.

Within the last fifteen years, this lowering of standards has been a subject of widespread concern. At the time the first Russian satellite was launched, in 1957, there was a great public outcry that education for all was leading to a poor quality of education. Subse-

---

**MEAN, MEDIAN, AND MODE
THE ARITHMETIC MEAN**
is a single number used to summarize a set of measurements made on members of some group. In other words, it is an average for a group. It is obtained by taking the sum of the individual measurements for the entire group and dividing it by the number of members in the group. For example, consider a group of three people, each holding an amount of money. One person has $3.00, another $5.00, and the third $7.00. If we sum these amounts of money and divide by three (the number of people in the group) we shall have

$$3 + 5 + 7 = 15 \frac{15}{3} = \$5.00$$

The mean amount of money for the group is $5.00.

THE MEDIAN is another kind of average. It is the number that represents the middle figure in a group. For example, if the number of years of schooling for a group of eight people is 5, 5, 6, 7, 7, 10, 11, and 12 years, the median years of schooling for the group is 7 years. The median is obtained by finding the figure that has the same number of measurements above it as below it. In our example there are three measurements above and three below the figure 7.

THE MODE is a third kind of average. It is the most frequently found measurement in a group of measurements. For example, if the number of children per family in a group of eight families is 1, 2, 2, 2, 3, 3, 4, and 9, the mode is the most frequently listed number, or 2.

The arithmetic mean, the median, and the mode, are three different kinds of averages. There are other kinds of averages, such as the geometric mean or the harmonic mean, but these are not much used by sociologists. Of the three discussed, the arithmetic mean is the most commonly used.

---

quently, attempts have been made to upgrade the level of public education, primarily through the support of government subsidies, especially in the fields of math, science, and foreign languages.

At about the same time, more people began turning to private schools in a search for higher educational standards. Enrollment in private schools increased dramatically. However, this has not been an altogether successful solution, and there is some question as to whether the average private school does indeed offer an education of higher quality than many public schools. One problem is that many private schools do not have the financial resources to secure the best teachers and provide adequate facilities. Another issue is that the private school solution can only be adopted by those parents who can afford the high tuition at these institutions. Most private schools have increased the number of scholarships available, but for the most part, a private school education is still the prerogative of the rich.

Today in public education the problem remains of balancing the standards of academic excellence with the necessities of universal education. Racial minorities and the economically disadvantaged members of society have been demanding greater educational opportunity, especially in high school and college, with special classes and curricula to compensate for their learning handicaps and open enrollments to guarantee that they do not suffer from discrimination in admissions policies. At the same time, many segments of the population have been asking for an improved quality of education, pointing to the all-too-frequent cases of college freshmen who cannot spell and can read only with difficulty. This indicates that there is a continuing conflict of social values, with *both* academic excellence and universality of education seeming desirable. The schools have inaugurated many new programs in an effort to achieve each of these worthy aims. For example, many public grade schools now offer a foreign language, starting in the fourth or fifth grade, to those students whose performance so far indicates that they can cope with the demands. Junior highs and high schools in many cities are specialized, with some being largely vocational and others college preparatory. Sometimes certain big city high schools maintain a staff and curriculum of exceptional quality, and city-wide competitive exams are given to determine who should be admitted. In cities and towns that have a college or university, arrangements are made for especially interested and able high school students to take college courses in their senior year. At the same time, many school systems and colleges have set up pilot and experimental programs designed to reach the low achievers. These programs are fast becoming a regular part of American education.

EDUCATION AND STRATIFICATION

The most visible connection between education and stratification is education's effect on occupation and income. If you turn back to the chart in chapter 7 that ranks occupations according to their status, you will see that the occupations which rank highest, such as Supreme Court Justice and physician, are occupations with a prerequisite of a bachelor's degree, at least, if not an advanced degree in law or medicine or science. Similarly, the low status occupations, like street sweeper and shoe shiner, are ones which require virtually no formal education, not even the ability to read and write. You may remember from chapter 7 that one determinant of an occupation's rank is the special training, or education, that it requires. Therefore, in general, those with the greatest amount of education will have occupations of the highest status.

The same is true of education in relation to income. The more education a man has, the greater his income is likely to be. Men who make under $2,000 a year have completed a median number of 8.4 school years. Those who make incomes of over $25,000 a year have completed a median 16.3 years.[4] Another study shows that men who hold advanced degrees (master's or doctorates) had, in 1966, median earnings that were 42

Black students must overcome a number of obstacles in their efforts to obtain a high school or college diploma. In addition to inadequate facilities and discriminatory educational policies, they are handicapped by a social background that often provides inadequate preparation in the skills and values needed for academic success. The black student who has successfully completed a college career must still confront the inequalities that exist outside school *(Photo by H. Armstrong Roberts)*

percent higher than those of men who held only a bachelor's degree.[5] The gap between those with a high school and those with a college education is about the same. Over a lifetime, the difference in earnings because of educational level can be enormous. One estimate is that workers with a high school diploma earn $56,000 more during their working life than those who have one to three years of high school.[6]

So it is clear that the amount of education one receives has a direct bearing on his future social class standing. What is not always so

4. *Statistical Abstract of the United States: 1966* (Washington, D.C.: Government Printing Office, 1966), table 157, p. 115.

5. *New York Times Almanac 1970*, p. 542.

6. *Statistical Abstract of the United States: 1971* (Washington, D.C.: Government Printing Office, 1971), p. 111.

EDUCATION AND INCOME

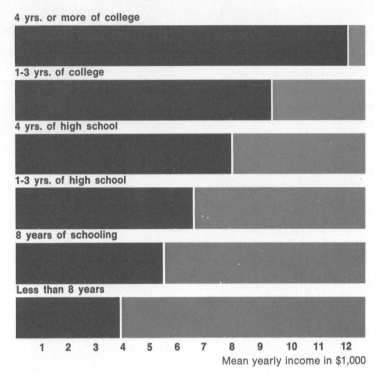

4 yrs. or more of college

1-3 yrs. of college

4 yrs. of high school

1-3 yrs. of high school

8 years of schooling

Less than 8 years

1   2   3   4   5   6   7   8   9   10   11   12

Mean yearly income in $1,000

SOURCE: U.S. Bureau of the Census, *Current Population Reports*, series P-60, no. 56.

There is a direct relationship between the number of years a person has attended school and his yearly income. For those who have eight years of schooling, the mean income is just over $5000 a year; for a high school graduate it is about $8000; and for a college graduate it is well over $12,000.

clear, but is just as true, is that the chances to acquire the kind of education which leads to high school status are not equally distributed in the general population. What are the factors that enable a student to graduate from college? (1) He must have the desire to attend and to remain until graduation. (2) He must have a scholastic record that qualifies him for admission, and scholastic ability and preparation adequate for successful performance in college. (3) He must be able to afford the tuition and to defer his gainful employment. Young people from low status families have less chance to meet all three of these requirements.

Regarding the first requirement, the lower-class child generally has less motivation for college attendance than does the middle- and upper-class child. In fact, the social pressure to conform to the standards of his class and his peer group work against his going to college. The norm of his class is to enter the full time labor force at age seventeen or eighteen.[7] In addition to this handicap, it is likely that the lower-class child will have less personal desire to obtain an education. The socialization of the middle-class child teaches him to value education and academic excellence, but

7. S. M. Miller, "The Outlook of Working-Class Youth," in *Blue Collar World: Studies of the American Worker*, ed. Arthur P. Shostak and William Gomberg (Englewood Cliffs, N.J.: Prentice-Hall, 1964).

the lower-class child does not always share this value. Also, the socialization of the lower-class child does not usually give him the kind of self-discipline needed to want to undertake such a demanding commitment, with a reward that is years in the future — what sociologists call the *deferred gratification pattern.*

The lower-class child is also handicapped in terms of scholastic preparation and performance, the second of the three requirements. The schools are staffed and directed largely by individuals from the middle class, and there is clear evidence that doing well in school requires certain attitudes and skills that are taught in middle-class homes but not in lower-class ones. For example, class participation is much more difficult if a child has not practiced verbal skills in communicating with adults. The middle-class child is encouraged to communicate freely and to formulate his thoughts in conversation. The lower-class child is not encouraged to do so. The way questions are asked, both informally during class and formally on tests, reflects middle-class habits of speech and thought, and often puzzles the lower-class child. "Good" behavior — which in the school world means not being too boisterous, showing the inclination to work independently at one's own desk, carrying out assigned responsibilities on time — is something the typical middle-class child has already learned at home but the lower-class child often has not.

This initial disadvantage is one aspect of the lower-class child's inadequate preparation for academic success. Another is that it is all too likely that the quality of education in the public school he attended was comparatively poor. A poor community of lower-class residents cannot afford a first-rate school system. On the other hand, suburban communities with a high proportion of middle-class residents of substantial incomes, such as Shaker Heights in Cleveland and Spring Branch in Houston, are willing and able to spend the money for good schools. Even in

"Do you realize, young man, what C-minus can mean in terms of lifetime earnings?"

Drawing by Lorenz: ©1970 The New Yorker Magazine, Inc.

This father's concern may be exaggerated, but it is statistically true that those who get the best grades in school have the best chance to earn the highest incomes.

big city school systems, it is common for the best teachers and the most resources to be concentrated in schools serving middle-class neighborhoods.

The third requirement for getting a college education is the ability to afford it. Even at state-supported schools, tuition plus room and board is likely to come to around $1,800 a year, though it is considerably lower than this in the growing number of community and junior colleges. To go to a top-rank private college like Harvard or Swarthmore (which will give the student higher status and an income that averages about $4,000 a year more than that of a state university graduate[8]) will cost about $5,000 a year. So it is

8. *New York Times Almanac 1972.*

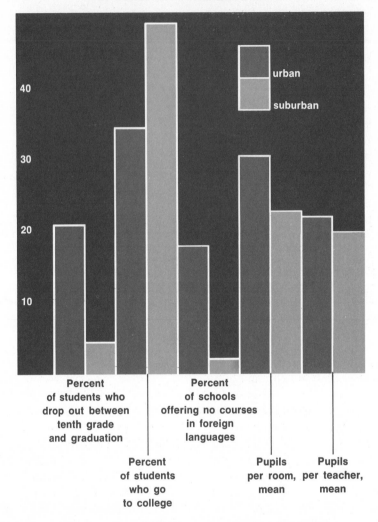

**URBAN AND SUBURBAN SECONDARY SCHOOLS
BY SELECTED CHARACTERISTICS***

urban

suburban

40

30

20

10

**Percent
of students who
drop out between
tenth grade
and graduation**

**Percent
of schools
offering no courses
in foreign
languages**

**Percent
of students
who go
to college**

**Pupils
per room,
mean**

**Pupils
per teacher,
mean**

*Based upon figures for schools in the northeastern United States only.

SOURCE: U.S. Commission on Civil Rights, *Racial Isolation in the Public Schools:
Appendices* (Washington, D.C.: U.S. Government Printing Office, 1967).

obvious that the cost of a college education will be less of a burden on the more affluent families, who also will find it easier to obtain credit if they must borrow. We must remember, too, that the tuition costs are only a part of the total cost of sending a person to college, which postpones his entry into the labor force and keeps him dependent on the family financially; they must buy his clothes, pay his doctor bills, and otherwise support him, whereas the eighteen-year-old who has a full-time job is already self-supporting. Lower-class families may not be able to afford this additional burden; and they may need his contribution to the family finances. Also, since on the average lower-class young people

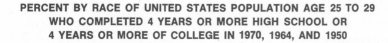

**PERCENT BY RACE OF UNITED STATES POPULATION AGE 25 TO 29
WHO COMPLETED 4 YEARS OR MORE HIGH SCHOOL OR
4 YEARS OR MORE OF COLLEGE IN 1970, 1964, AND 1950**

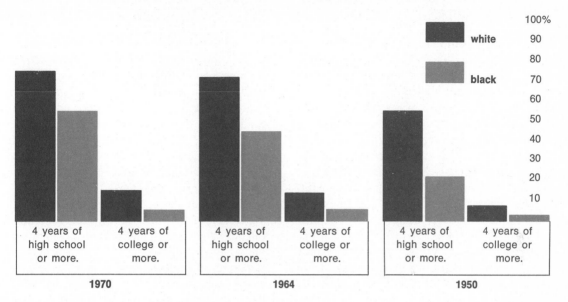

SOURCE: U.S. Department of Commerce, Bureau of the Census.

The number of American blacks receiving high school education today is greater than ever before. Although their percentage is approaching that of high school educated whites, the difference between the percentages of blacks and whites receiving college education is still great.

marry earlier, it is more likely that they will have a family of their own to support.

So the total picture adds up to a cycle that gives the best educational opportunities to those already of highest status, who then keep their status because of the benefits of their education. It takes a great deal of determination on the part of the lower-class child to break out of his cycle of restricted educational opportunity (and resultant lowered life chances) in order to acquire the education that is the key to upward social mobility.

EDUCATION AND MINORITY GROUPS

In the section above we have shown how educational opportunity is unevenly distributed in a system which works to the disadvantage of the lower-class child. When such a child is also a member of a minority group, the problem is even more severe. In addition to all the handicaps mentioned above, which as a member of low income and low status groups he shares with other such individuals, he has several additional problems. The first is the problem of racial segregation in the school systems, and the other is the problem of his adjustment to, and acceptance in, the school systems which are dominated by members of other races.

Segregated schools

Schools serving only or mainly children of minority groups are, on the average, of lower quality than those which serve white children. Classes are larger, facilities and buildings are inadequate for the current numbers of students (and may be outmoded or dilapidated as well), and libraries are too small. Such problems discourage many of the best qualified teachers from wanting to work in these schools, so the staff is likely to have lower than average training and enthusiasm. Segregation, then, usually means inferior education for the minority group.

Many public school systems in our country have had policies of segregation based on local law. This is called *de jure* or legalized segregation. De jure segregation was made illegal by a Supreme Court decision of 1954, and since then the number of segregated school systems has dropped. However, it would be a mistake to believe that they no longer exist. Enforcing desegregation is a costly and not always very successful obligation of the federal government; by a combination of withholding funds for educational subsidies and initiating suits against the local governments and their officials, the federal government has often had to coerce to bring about compliance with the law. Black civil rights leaders have spoken out repeatedly to demand that the government not relax its enforcement.

An even more complex problem is presented by what is called *de facto* segregation. Because they have lower incomes, and because they often are discriminated against when they try to rent or buy in white neighborhoods, minority groups have a limited choice of residence, even in big cities. Hence, racial minorities usually live clustered together in certain ghetto-like areas of a community. Public schools in this country are based on neighborhood lines, and because these minority groups live in geographical separation and even isolation from the dominant group of whites, the schools they attend usually have few white children. The result is *de facto* (from the facts) segregation, even though no legal barrier to integrated schools exists. This problem occurs particularly in primary schools; secondary schools and especially colleges usually draw their students from more than one neighborhood and thus tend to have a more representative sampling of the total population.

This second kind of school segregation is much more difficult to combat. Since residen-

tial patterns cannot easily be changed, the only way around *de facto* segregation is to modify or abolish the neighborhood character of schools. Some communities have reorganized the traditional primary school system to accomplish this purpose. For example, a town large enough to have three primary schools no longer has three neighborhood schools for grades one through six. Instead, it has one school for grades one and two, another for grades three and four, and the third for grades five and six. That way all the children of the same age group attend the same school, thereby achieving a more balanced racial mixture.

This and similar solutions involve transporting a certain number of children to schools outside their local neighborhood, which produces much opposition to them. Parents are reluctant to have their six- and seven-year-olds bussed across town because the ride is tiring for them; they may get lost or confused about which bus to take; and they cannot come home for lunch. In neighborhoods with a strong local identity there is usually great resistance to the idea, because it tends to weaken that identity. People often move to a neighborhood because they want to make friends within the particular group of people who live there, and they want to see their children do the same. Therefore, bussing, or the change away from neighborhood schools, seems to threaten their whole life style. Even parents of children who stand to gain the most from being bussed into an area with better schools are sometimes afraid of the threat to their sense of community or group identity.

Teaching the minority group student

Many of the problems that the minority group child encounters in the course of his educational experience are based on the social attitudes of the dominant group. Two principal factors in the educational difficulties of minority group students are: (1) lack of understanding of the students' various subcultures, and (2) prejudice, either conscious or unconscious, against their minority group.

The problems of understanding the culture and attitudes of minority groups such as Puerto Ricans, blacks, Indians, and Mexican-Americans can be very complex. For example, a basic problem is that of language. It is not uncommon for Puerto Rican and Mexican-American children to start first grade without knowing more than a few words of English, the language in which all their classes will be taught. Black children, especially in urban ghettos, may have accents which the teachers cannot understand and vocabularies they do not know. The frustrations of this situation may cause the child to view school as a place where he cannot possibly hope to succeed, and so he may give up trying, or even attending. Until recently, the typical grade school reading book dealt with situations in the life of a white, middle-class, small-town American family. To the black child in Chicago's South Side, or the Mexican-American in southern California, these people seem nearly as strange and exotic as a family of bushmen or Eskimos.

Educators have become increasingly aware of this problem and a corresponding attempt is being made to use educational materials which are more relevant to members of minority groups. Many elementary reading materials now portray blacks and Orientals as frequently and positively as whites, have illustrations of urban sights and situations, and attempt to depict the world of childhood in a realistic way. Frequently the educational materials (for example, programmed readers) are designed so that they deemphasize the competitive aspects of learning, such as test taking and classroom performance, so common in the traditional approach. A child is encouraged to compete only against his own past performance and is rated from this perspective.

But the poverty culture continues to work against the child, in a thousand little details of school life. A child with no father and a mother who works nights to support the family cannot produce his parents for the meeting of the P.T.A., which may be embarrassing or distressing for him; also the teacher will be unable to confer with his family about problems that arise at school. Because of lack of communication with members of the subcultures, the teacher, typically white and middle class, may not know how to motivate minority group children to want to do well in school. She may not even be able to tell what effect she has had, for a Mexican-American or an Indian boy may feel that his pride does not permit him to display any receptivity to her admonitions or fear of her threats, an attitude she may misread as "not caring" or "displaying defiance." A Puerto Rican child, who is accustomed at home to an atmosphere of high emotional content and expression, can be hurt and disappointed by the apparent reserve and coldness of a teacher who may herself think that she is trying to reach out to him.

It is very hard for a grade school child from a lower-class family to learn to adjust to the different attitudes and expectations that he meets at school. Even after he learns outwardly to adjust, he still may feel uncomfortable in the school environment, because of the many strains it puts on him. The cultural difference of minority group students is a major reason black students ask for their own dormitories and dining halls at many colleges. While there are many reasons given for these separatist experiments, certainly one important reason is that it is much less of a strain— for anyone—to live and eat with people of similar cultural background.

Minority group students must also cope with the handicapping effects of prejudice. Some of their classmates may display prejudice against them, which is a disturbing and frightening experience. Even more serious in its effect on their education is the prejudice of a teacher. If for some reason a teacher has formed an opinion that blacks, or Puerto Ricans, or Mexican-Americans, or Indians are an inferior group, this may affect his classroom behavior. He may show an open and conscious prejudice—denying the child extra help or the chance to participate in some educationally enriching experience, ignoring his raised hand during class discussions, grading his test answers more strictly than those of the other students. Or the prejudice may be largely unconscious and work in subtler ways. For example, a prejudiced teacher may assume that the black child with a C in math is doing as well as can be expected, whereas when the white boy sitting next to him gets a C, the teacher is concerned that he does not do better. The white boy gets extra problems and instructions about the parts that confuse him; his parents are called in and urged to push him a little more; and he is made to understand that everyone expects him to study harder and do better. The result is that he learns more math than the black boy, who might be just as capable. The prejudiced teacher may neither ask nor expect a very high level of achievement from children of minority groups, and he often passes along this attitude to the children themselves.

There is overwhelming evidence of the unfortunate results that all of the educational disadvantages discussed above have on minority group children. The median educational level for all white adults over 25, in 1970, was the completion of 12.2 school years; for black adults it was only 9.9 years. Of white people, 16 percent between 25 and 34 have completed college; only 7 percent of blacks in that age group have college diplomas.[9] The high school dropout rate for Mexican-Americans is 50 percent, and they have only completed 7.1 years of schooling on the median. Of American Indians, 60 percent have less than an eighth grade education, and 10 percent of those over 14 have had no education whatsoever.[10] By referring back to the statistics on education in relation to income,

occupation, and social class, we can see that these minority groups are likely to remain in low status positions as long as they face such educational disadvantages.

EFFECTS ON VALUES AND ATTITUDES

It is clear that our educational system is closely connected with the existing pattern of social stratification—in fact, it supports it to a great degree. But the relationship is not as simple as it may seem, for education may also bring about changing attitudes toward inequalities, which may in time lead to changes in the pattern of stratification. Education gives people the opportunity to understand more about the way the social system works; for example, this is what you are learning right now. With such an understanding, one can better evaluate, and then perhaps change, some of his own cultural attitudes.

The effects of education on values and attitudes is an area in which many sociological studies have been made. One such study, by Burton Clark, concluded that education tends to make an individual more tolerant, more democratic, and "more politically and culturally involved."[11] In the area of political involvement, he found that college graduates are twice as likely to belong to some political club or association as high school graduates, and four times as likely as those with only a grade school education. Another study, by Hanan Selvin and Warren Hagstrom, supports Clark's suggestion that education is positively correlated with democratic attitudes.[12] They did a survey of attitudes toward the granting of civil liberties which indicated that every year of college makes a person more libertarian in his outlook (meaning, more in favor of legally granting widespread civil liberties). Of the freshmen in his sample, 21 percent had

9. *Statistical Abstracts 1971*, Table 165, p. 110.
10. *New York Times Almanac 1970*, p. 301.

11. Burton R. Clark, *Educating the Expert Society* (San Francisco: Chandler Publishing Co., 1962), p. 27.
12. Hanan C. Selvin and Warren O. Hagstrom, "Determinants of Support of Civil Liberties," *British Journal of Sociology* 11 (March 1960):51–73.

highly libertarian attitudes; the figure for sophomores was 29 percent; for juniors 34 percent; and for seniors 40 percent. Other studies have shown that those individuals with the least education are the ones most apt to construct rigid social categories (stereotypes) in dealing with other people, and that education decreases prejudice against racial and ethnic minorities.[13]

The pollster Louis Harris recently has summarized the evidence from his opinion polls on this matter:

In the regular surveys which the Harris organization has conducted on a monthly basis over the past seven years, the impact of education in forming people's attitudes has also proven to be decisive. On the key issues of the day, those with least education tend to hold a harder line on U.S. foreign policy, favoring a 'fortress America' view, and are keenly suspicious of 'too much involvement' abroad. The college educated, by contrast, are more in favor of limiting the use of American military power abroad, and are much more inclined to commit the nation's resources to international organizations and agreements with the communist world.

On racial matters, educated whites are far more amenable on the subject of integration than the less well educated. Concerning young people and their tastes and styles, the college educated are far more open minded than the less well educated.[14]

From all these sources of data, we can conclude that education does have some effect on changing social values and attitudes. It appears that a most important factor here is whether or not an individual gets a high school education. There is some evidence to indicate that there is, on the average, a much bigger difference between the attitudes of those with only a grade school education and those with a high school education, than there is between high school and college graduates.[15] Thus a high school education may be somewhat more important than a college education in its effects on attitude change.

Other studies show that college has a greater effect while the student is on the campus than it does in the long run. For example, a study of Bennington College graduates indicated that twenty-five years after graduation, most of the women had substituted the values of their inherited social class or background for the ones they had acquired while in college.[16] The exceptions to this rule were those who had married men who shared the college-acquired values, or those who had established careers based on them. In other words, a person may be convinced of the need for a change in his social values and attitudes by his educational experience, but if he does not take some step to incorporate this change into the circumstances of his later life, so that the new values are continually reinforced, the value changes brought about during his college years are likely to be short-lived.

In considering these studies of value change in college it is important not to overlook the fact that only a selected group of the population attends college. It may well be that those who attend college are disposed more toward value change at the time they enter than those who do not attend, and that the effect of college on attitude and values may not be quite so great as several of these studies have indicated.

13.   Daniel J. Levinson, "Ethnocentrism in Relation to Intelligence and Education," in T. W. Adorno et al., *The Authoritarian Personality* (New York: John Wiley, 1964), p. 287; Gordon W. Allport, *The Nature of Prejudice* (New York: Doubleday, 1958), p. 406; Gordon W. Allport and B. M. Kramer, "Some Roots of Prejudice," *Journal of Psychology* 22 (1946):9–39; and Samuel Stouffer, *Communism, Conformity and Civil Liberties* (New York: John Wiley, 1966), pp. 90 and 96.

14.   "Many Feel Undereducated," *New York Post,* 30 April 1970.

15.   Gabriel A. Almond, *The American People and Foreign Policy* (New York: Harcourt Brace Jovanovich, 1950), p. 129.

16.   Mervin B. Freedman, "Studies of College Alumni," in *The American College,* ed. Nevitt Sanford (New York: John Wiley, 1962), chap. 25, pp. 847–886.

3 THE ORGANIZATION OF EDUCATION

The basic organization of American education has remained more or less unchanged for well over a century. Although we have at times modified our ideas about the goals and methods of education—from mildly elitist to universal (and even compensatory) education, from memorization to participatory learning—there have been few major changes in organization. In the last decade many pressures have been developing for change in this area. Some observers predict that the question of how, and how much, to change the organization of our educational system will be one of the most prominent social issues of the next several years.

In this section we will discuss educational organization at all levels, together with the roles of teachers and students. In addition we will take a look at the current social environment on college campuses.

PRIMARY AND SECONDARY SCHOOLS

Like all organizations, schools have an interlocking system of specialized roles and responsibilities. Within a single public school is the teaching staff, which is directly responsible for the education of the children, and an administrative staff—the principal and all his assistants—to see that the activities of the teachers are coordinated efficiently. The principal is responsible to a superintendent, an administrative official whose duty is to coordinate the activities of all the schools at the various levels in the district. The superintendent is hired by, and is responsible to, a school board, or a Board of Education. The board members are customarily elected by the voters of the district; in some cases, they are appointed by an elected city official, such as the Mayor.

Private schools have the same general organization at the level of teacher and principal. Then the next link in the chain of responsibility is the organization which sponsors the school—the Catholic church if it is a parochial school, or the Board of Trustees if it is an independent private institution. About six-and-a-half million children attend private and parochial elementary and secondary schools, compared with about 45 million who attend public schools.[17]

Both public and private schools are closely connected with government. The largest part of the financial resources of public schools comes from local government, covering such things as teachers' salaries, buildings, and equipment. Today, state and federal governments as well are increasingly involved in public education, partly for the purpose of balancing out regional inequities. They provide funds to serve hot lunches to all children, to strengthen teaching in certain critical areas such as math and science, to buy textbooks and school supplies for low-income students, even to construct new schools. In addition, a number of special programs have been established and funded by the federal government to combat the social problems of low-income, disadvantaged, and minority groups. Examples are the Head Start and Upward Bound programs, the adult education programs to

17. Bureau of the Census, U.S. Department of Commerce, *Current Population Reports,* series P-20, no. 199 (Washington, D.C.: Government Printing Office, 1970).

help dropouts acquire high school diplomas or teach new skills to the unemployed, and the bilingual programs now being tried in Boston, New York, and several California cities, where Spanish-speaking children are taught most of their lessons in their native language while they are learning English.

Private schools also receive some government funds, although they are principally supported by tuition fees and private donations. They get money to help in the bus transportation of their students, and in feeding those from low-income homes. Government money for private schools has been for many years a controversial issue; one reason is that the majority of private schools are church schools, and some people believe that government support of them is a violation of the principle of separation of church and state. The current attitude seems to be that it is acceptable for the government to provide what might be termed "fringe benefits," but not to contribute directly to its budget—though this attitude is in the process of changing toward much greater flexibility in the use of public funds.

Of course, since nearly every elementary and secondary school in America gets some kind of government funds, they have also had to accept a certain amount of government supervision, perhaps even control. For example, government agencies set standards that educational institutions must meet. They influence the choice of course offerings, since pressure is felt to teach subjects that will receive government subsidies. They certify the competence of teachers. They insist on adherence to certain policies, such as desegregation, as a condition for financial support.

From the government's point of view, the school provides an excellent opportunity to implement the social programs and policies of a particular administration. Integration of black and white Americans is carried out largely through the agency of the school; so is the program of compensatory help for disadvantaged children. Public health agencies

The new educational technology has changed the face of many classrooms, but it has not as yet altered the basic organization of our educational system. In deciding how much emphasis to place on programmed and computer-assisted instruction, the makers of educational policy will have to consider and carefully define the objectives of public education. Should we emphasize programmed instruction to teach specialized skills and knowledge in precise behavioral terms; or would we cultivate personal freedom and autonomy in a less structured environment?

use the school as a means of achieving widespread vaccination and immunization against epidemic diseases. It should be pointed out that central government aims do not always coincide with those of the local educational system, as in cases where desegregation is forced on reluctant schools.

A feature of public school organization which is very hotly debated today is the question of *community control* of the school staff and policies, particularly in urban neighborhoods where racial and ethnic minorities predominate. Community citizens, the parents of children in the schools, complain that the schools are not responsive to their particular needs and requests, to their opinions about what and how their children need to be taught. Racial and ethnic minorities would like to see more adjustment of the schools to their own values and customs and ways of thought. The issue arouses much emotion, because a successful education, as we have seen, is the key to upward mobility for low status groups of all kinds.

Another complaint of the community is that their influence as voters is too far removed from the actual day-to-day operation of the public schools. In some public school systems the only way a citizen can have a say in the educational system through the ballot box is by his vote for the mayor. Every post within the school system itself is filled by appointment rather than election. In a small and homogeneous community, this might not be a serious problem, but in a large city with many different racial and ethnic groups, it is a source of real dissatisfaction.

So on one side we have the parents, who want more of a voice in the running of their neighborhood schools. They want to be consulted about what courses will be offered, which new teachers will be hired and which old ones ought to be fired, and what kind of disciplinary action will be taken against students. At the secondary level, they are joined in their demands by the students themselves, who would also like to participate in the making of major decisions about their schools.

On the other side, most teachers and school administrators seem opposed to the granting of greater community control over the public schools, on the grounds that a certain degree of professional and technical knowledge is needed to make important decisions about educational methods and policies, and that it is essential to keep "politics" out of the schools. Frequently, municipal officials are also against it, because they have learned that centralization is the cheapest and most efficient way to administer the schools, and fear that local control will lead to higher educational costs and a strain on their already very empty pocketbooks. Also, it is generally true that in any situation involving a proposed transfer of some kind of power, those who have the power are reluctant to give it up.

The conflict between parents in the community and the officials of the school and municipal government has sometimes been bitter, especially in the larger cities, and could possibly damage the interests of everyone involved. In the past few years, we have seen strikes by teachers, strikes by students, protests, rallies, and demonstrations by both sides, and several confrontations that have led to physical violence. One of the most unfortunate developments in the situation is that at times it has been expressed as a racial issue, of blacks against whites. It has caused deep and dangerous division in many of our big cities, and remains a threat to the stability of the educational system, perhaps of the entire community.

HIGHER EDUCATION

The organization of a college or university differs in certain significant respects from that of lower level educational systems. First, there is a more pronounced hierarchical organization of the teachers, with more money and privileges for those at the top. This introduces an element of competition that is not as prevalent in primary and high school teaching staffs. Another difference is that the faculty has much more autonomy. The administration—president, treasurer, deans, registrar—sticks closely to administrative concerns, such as raising and allocating funds; admitting, processing, and expelling students; and building new dormitories and classrooms. Unlike school principals, a college president makes little effort to act as a direct supervisor of the teaching staff. Decisions about the curriculum, the division of teaching responsibilities, and the hiring of new teachers are generally left to the faculty members.

A third difference is that the ultimate responsibility for decisions about the operation and the policies of the school is often less clear than it is in other institutions. State-supported colleges and universities, of course, must account to state legislators and the governor about the way they use funds. In a private college, the president is responsible to a Board of Trustees, which decides basic

During the past decade, the routine of academic life has been repeatedly interrupted by protests on college campuses. The activist mood began to develop as students participated in the civil rights movement during the early 1960s. About one-third of American college students have participated in demonstrations against U.S. military policy, existing ethnic or racial policies, or administrative policies of a college. Most of these activists attend high-quality institutions, have above average grades, high status socioeconomic backgrounds, and expect academic or professional careers. *(Photo by H. Armstrong Roberts)*

policy—an organizational pattern similar to that of business corporations. In both cases, new board members are usually chosen by the old ones when a vacancy arises. However, in a business, the board must eventually account to the stockholders, who provide the funds for the operations of the company and have the power to remove unsatisfactory officials by a majority vote. The trustees of a private college have no clear responsibility to any group. The funds which the board oversees come from tuition fees, government grants, and gifts from individuals (especially alumni) and other organizations. Because of this diversity of financial support, the board cannot be completely influenced by any one source. Usually there is no way to remove trustees from office except by the weight of outspoken public disapproval that forces them to resign.

This kind of organization, like all organizations, has both its advantages and disadvantages. It helps to prevent the college from becoming dominated by some small special-interest group. For example, it is difficult for a business, by giving the college millions of dollars, to dictate a curriculum which will produce individuals suited for nothing but employment in that company. On the other hand, the Board of Trustees, because of its independence, can become an autocratic group that fails to respond to the needs of either the students or the employees of the college.

The position of students

Two very important questions about the organization of higher education today are: (1) To what extent should the college control the students? and (2) To what extent should the students control the college?

It has been customary for the college to see itself as standing *in loco parentis,* meaning in the place of the parents. Therefore it has made the same sort of rules governing the students' conduct that a parent might make. It has told them when to be home at night, what clothes to wear on certain occasions, and what kind of relationships to have with members of the opposite sex.

In recent years, the college has been less and less successful in achieving this kind of control over the student body. Students have protested and petitioned, but what has been even more effective is that they have refused, sometimes through existing student governments, sometimes informally but in large numbers, to observe the social rules of their campus. The school, meeting so much resistance and difficulty, has gradually withdrawn from many areas of the students' lives. It is now typical for the college to leave decisions about wearing apparel, weekends off campus, and courtship activities to the students' own choice.

It is interesting to speculate about the reasons students suddenly became so resistant to college control of their social lives. It may be simply a part of the whole trend toward greater personal power for everyone; the young see no reason why they should have less than their elders. It has also been suggested that the colleges have failed to keep up with changes in social attitudes and permissiveness: many students have complained that college social rules were much more restrictive than the ones they were used to at home. It is also probable that part of the difficulty is due to the change in the composition of the student body. Until after World War II, college students were a fairly homogeneous group, mostly of middle-middle and upper-middle-class and white Anglo-Saxon backgrounds. The enormous increases in college enrollments are indicative of widened educational opportunity, and many college students now come from other backgrounds. This means that it would probably be impossible to get the students to agree on any one set of social rules, because their past experiences have been too diverse.

Many of these factors may also be involved in current student demands for more control over the university. Students ask that courses be made more "relevant" to their interests and point of view; that academic policies be made not by the administration alone but by a consensus of the whole college, including the student body; and that the college concern itself more fully with the major issues of the day, such as racial integration, defense spending, and the pollution of the environment. They are often joined in these demands by many of the faculty members who would like to see fewer decision-making powers centralized in the administration and board of trustees. The question of the degree to which students should control or influence the policies of the college is one that has not yet been resolved on most campuses, and we can expect to see further debate and dissension over this issue in the next few years.

STUDENT ROLES

The role of the student is a relatively easy one to learn. At the early stages of formal education, the role of the student is primarily defined by the school officials — teachers and principals. They usually define a student as one who listens in class, does his homework, does not cause disruptions, and tries his best to learn what is being taught him. This definition really describes the behavior they expect and approve of for a person filling the position, or status, of student. As children get older they play a much larger part in defining their own student role, and the norms change. In high school, for example, a student who was as anxious to respond in class as a first grader is, or who commented enthusiastically on how much he liked school and his teacher, as elementary school children often do, would *not* be playing the commonly accepted role of student. Although the accepted role model is mainly defined by student peer groups, it is interesting to note that even the teachers sometimes accept it as the norm; it is quite common for teachers to discourage the over-eager high school student, by means of subtle disapproval tactics. On the other hand, a characteristic of the modern school system is that the students' peer group norms run counter to the norms of the teachers and administrators, particularly in the area of academic achievement.

For the older student in many public high schools, there is a certain degree of role conflict. To play his role properly, he must not appear too industrious, or too eager to succeed. Yet he must somehow put in enough effort to learn something from his classes and pass the course, for the student who flunks is not only an academic failure but a social failure as well. He has misinterpreted his role, and it may have serious consequences for his future, in terms of earning power, occupational status, and social life style.

The attitude of the teacher toward his students also has certain built-in conflicts. A teacher is expected to treat his students impartially, and even impersonally. He is generally expected to exercise a certain disciplinary authority over them. Yet at the same time he is expected to *teach* them, and in many cases, this may call for some personal rapport with a student or group of students, as well as a measure of sympathy and affection in his feelings toward them. It is often difficult to balance these conflicting role demands successfully. The abridgment by Edgar Friedenberg presents one view of the roles of teachers and students in high schools today.

We have already mentioned in chapter 4 that peer groups are a very important socializing agent. This is especially true during adolescence, and therefore most studies of peer group relationships have focused on junior high and high school students. At this age, peer group membership is a powerful factor in social stratification; the group to which one belongs determines status. In the late 1950s, James S. Coleman made a study of students in ten different high schools to determine the qualities or achievements that influenced group membership opportunities and conferred high status. He found that:

The variation among schools was not nearly so striking in this research as the fact that, in all of them, academic achievement did not count for as much as other activities. In every school the boy named as best athlete and the boy named as most popular with the girls was far more often mentioned as a member of the leading crowd, and as someone to "be like," than was the boy named as the best student. And the girl named as best dressed, and the one named as most popular with boys, was in every school far more often mentioned as being in the leading crowd and as someone to "be like," than the girl named as the best student.

The relative unimportance of academic achievement ... suggests that these adolescent subcultures are generally deterrents to academic achievement. In other words, in these societies of adolescents those who come to be seen as the "intellectuals" and who come to think so of themselves are not really those of the highest intelligence but are only the ones who are willing to work hard at a relatively unrewarded activity.[18]

Student protests

The numerous student protests that occurred on many college campuses during the late 1960s led several social scientists to investigate the nature of such protests, who participates in them, and why. One study examined the student protests that occurred during the first half of 1969 on 232 college campuses.[19] More than 215,000 students were involved in protests at the 232 schools studied; 3,652 of these students were arrested. But the study contradicts the popular image

18. James S. Coleman, "The Adolescent Sub-culture and Academic Achievement," *American Journal of Sociology* 65 (January 1960):342.

19. *Summary Report on Student Protest* (Chicago: Urban Research Corp., 1970).

of student protest as violent, disruptive, and militant. Of the protests studied, 76 percent were entirely free of violence or destruction of any kind, and 60 percent caused no disruption of campus life. Only 6 percent of the protests involved "nonnegotiable" demands. Only about a quarter of the students who participated in protests had an organizational or ideological affiliation with the New Left. There was no one part of the country that was either more or less likely to experience student protests. However, one significant influencing factor was discovered. Schools whose student bodies had high scholastic aptitude and achievement were much more likely to face protests than other schools.

The study also threw some light on the question of why students protest, and why students are willing to risk arrest or expulsion to participate in a protest. A significant 42 percent of the protests revolved around the students' requests for more control over decisions that affect them intimately, such as decisions on curriculum changes, and campus rules and regulations. In other words, the students may in large part be protesting what they sense as their own lack of power.

Who are the student activists? The accompanying abridgment by Seymour Martin Lipset summarizes some research on this question and suggests answers which should dispel some prevalent misconceptions.

SEYMOUR MARTIN LIPSET
The Activists

"The Activists" by Seymour Martin Lipset from *The Public Interest,* No. 13 (Fall 1968), pp. 39–51. Copyright © by National Affairs, Inc., 1968.

Introduction

In this selection, Lipset looks at the phenomenon of student activism in a broad sociological context. He discusses the factors in the social environment of the university which lead to activism in both conservative and radical politics. He also mentions elements of modern American culture that favor such activism. Then he surveys the studies made of the personality, attitudes, and behavior patterns of various activist groups. The conclusions Lipset reaches about the political activists are surely different from the many stereotypes that have emerged in the last few years.

Any effort to account for the rise of student activism in the United States during the 1960's is faced with the fact that we are obviously dealing with a world-wide phenomenon. This, in turn, suggests that the sources of political activism among students must essentially be found in politics itself — in the changing world-wide climate of political opinion. Students as a stratum are more responsive to political trends, to changes in mood, to opportunities for action than almost any other group in the population. They also are the most easily mobilizable stratum; ideas which arise as a response to a given issue may move readily among them, and may move them more readily, since they have fewer responsibilities in the form of commitments to families and jobs.

The American university

The modern American university has become a place of assembly and major occupational outlet for many of the brightest people who seek to be innovative, who wish to be free of the ideological restrictions and materialistic commitments that they believe are inherent in the corporate and professional worlds. It is an institution where "liberalism" in politics and "modernism" in culture has become an established, if unofficial, ideal. It is not surprising, then, that evidence drawn from a variety of surveys of student attitudes indicates that colleges do have a "liberalizing" effect on young people. Samuel Stouffer pointed out over ten years ago that the conservatives who attack the universities for "corrupting" young people were correct, from their political and moral standpoint. Nor is it only the young students who are so influenced.

Changes in the backgrounds and opinions of increasing numbers of college faculty have undoubtedly been as marked as, if less noticed than, those of the students. Before the 1930's, the American professoriate was not known especially for having strong political views, or for engaging in political action. This changed somewhat during the depression, with the identification of the New Deal with reliance on academic expertise. But since the war particularly, various segments of the population with strong liberal views, which hitherto played very little role in university life, finally moved in a massive way onto the campus. This has been most visible in the enormous growth in the number of liberal Jewish faculty, but many of the non-Jews who have been attracted to university life have similar views.

The shift to the left in the opinions of faculty, and of other intellectuals as well, is, of course, not simply explained by the changing composition of the stratum. It also reflects a heightened resentment among humanistically-inclined, "general" intellectuals toward the increased emphasis on intellectual technology and expertise, toward the decline of the status of diffuse intellectualism in the social and political arena.

But if faculty helps to create a climate of opinion that encourages students to move to "the left," it is ironic that some of the sources of student malaise stem from the fact that changes in the role of this very faculty have contributed to making the situation of being a student less attractive than it once was. With increasing size and greater pressures on faculty to do research, publish, and take part in "public service" activities, the faculty at the leading institutions increasingly gives a larger proportion of its ever more limited time to graduate research students and pays relatively little attention to undergraduates. So, in an odd way, the emergence of the university as a major liberal institution of our society has *reduced* the informal influence of students within the university, as compared with thirty or forty years ago. This development is not simply or even principally a function of the growth of the university; it reflects even more the increased "professionalization" of the faculty, the extent to which "teaching" as such has declined as the main identification of the role of being a professor.

A youth culture

There are components of American values that make adults reluctant, even when they have good cause, to sharply call students or youth to task. Rather they like to encourage youth and students to take independent, new positions. This ties in with the part of the American self-image that assumes that the United States is a progressive country, one that accepts reform and change. And the truism that the youth will inherit the future is linked with the sense that the youth are the bearers of all those "progressive" ideas that will dominate the future.

The tensions within the university system are also increased by the fact that the increasing amount of time required for educational development inherently means the prolongation of adolescence. Although physiologically mature, and often above the age legally defined as adult, students are expected to refrain from full involvement in the adult world. Dependency is, of course, built into the very essence of the university system. The American university, in particular, with its stress on frequent examinations, emphasizes this relationship even more than does that of most other countries. Hence, the student who leaves home to attend the university finds that he remains in a highly controlled situation, even while society is urging him to become independent.

It may also be argued that student activism is the most recent expression of the need of youth to have a separate culture of their own. The student stratum, as such, has always tended to create a whole array of age-group symbols, which set it apart from others in society, and from adults in particular. The changes in the political role of the university increasingly make politics a particularly critical source of self-expression. The institution itself may be nonpartisan, but its professors fulfill ever-growing roles as party activists, commentators on events, advisers, consultants, and researchers on policy matters. Many students are thus in centers of great political significance, but have little or no share in the political status of the institution. In addition, although most of the faculty political involvement is generally on the left of the spectrum in the United States, it also occurs within the "establishment." Hence, if it is to express a sense of separate identity, student politics as part of the student culture must be outside of, and in opposition to, the politics of most of the adults.

The powerful 2 percent

The university campus is an ideal place in which to be a radical activist. Many universities have tens of thousands of students concentrated in a small area. It takes only a small percentage of these massive student bodies to make a large demonstration. Thus, in 1965–1967, although opinion polls indicated that the great majority of American students supported the Vietnam War and that anti-war sentiment within the group was no greater than in the population as a whole, the campus opposi-

tion was able to have an inordinately great impact because it could be mobilized. During 1967–1968, as the country as a whole turned increasingly critical of the war, campus opinion—both student and faculty—has moved to a majority anti-war position. This has placed the student anti-war activist groups in a very strong moral position, comparable to the one held earlier by the civil rights organizations; their goals, if not always their means, are approved by the community within which they operate.

It remains true, as Herbert Marcuse pointed out recently, that the majority of the students in all countries are politically quiescent and moderate in their views. According to national surveys of student opinion taken by the Harris Poll in 1965 and the Gallup Poll in 1968, approximately one-fifth of the students have participated in civil rights or political activities (17 percent in 1964–1965, the year of the Berkeley revolt, and 20 percent in 1967–1968, the year of the McCarthy and Kennedy campaigns). The radical activist groups generally have tiny memberships. Students for a Democratic Society (SDS) claims a total membership of about 30,000 out of a national student body of 7 million, of which about 6,000 pay national dues. A Harris Poll of American students taken in the spring of 1968 estimates that there are about 100,000 radical activists, or somewhere between 1 and 2 percent of the college population. A Gallup survey also conducted in the spring of 1968 reports that 7 percent of male students indicate that they will refuse to go, if drafted. Given that the activists are such a small minority, the question must be raised as to who are they, and what are the factors that contribute to activist strength?

The influence of parents

The major conclusion to be drawn from a large number of students in the United States and other countries is that *left-wing students are largely the children of left-wing or liberal parents.* The activists are more radical than their parents; but both parents and children are located on the same side of the spectrum. Conversely, studies of those active in conservative student groupings, such as the Goldwaterite Young Americans for Freedom (YAF), indicate that they are largely from right-wing backgrounds.

Among faculty students, there are clear-cut correlations between academic disciplines and political orientations. *On the whole, those involved in the humanities and softer social sciences, or in the more pure theoretical fields of science, are more likely to be on the left than those in the more practical, applied, or experimental fields. Such variations, however, would appear to be more a product of selective entrance into different disciplines than of the effects of the content of the fields on those pursuing them as students or practitioners.* Thus, studies of entering freshmen—i.e., those who have not yet taken a single lecture—report the same relationships between intended college major and political attitudes as are found among seniors, graduate students, and faculty.

The relationships between academic fields and political sympathies are also linked to the finding that the leftist activists within American universities tend to come from relatively well-to-do backgrounds as compared to the student population generally. A comparison by Braungart and Westby of the delegates to conventions of SDS and YAF also indicated that *the left-wingers come from somewhat more affluent backgrounds than the rightists.* The majority of the latter are the children of conservative businessmen and professionals, but they include a significant proportion (one-fifth to one-third) from working-class origins, a group almost unrepresented among the SDS delegates.

Black students, of course, constitute a major exception to the pattern of political passivity, or conservatism, among students of relatively deprived backgrounds. To them, the gains made before they came of age appear empty. And on the major campuses of the nation, the growing minority of black students have found themselves in a totally white-dominated world, facing few—if any—black faculty, and incorporated into a white student body whose liberal and radical wing turned increasingly, after 1964, from involvement with civil rights to activity directed against the Vietnam War. The concern with Black Power has, consequently, won growing support among black students. They have been among the major forces initiating sit-ins during the 1967–1968 school year at schools as diverse and separated as San Francisco State College, Columbia, Boston, and Northwestern universities, and at many predominantly Negro institutions as well. However, as Charles Hamilton has pointed out, black-student protest differs considerably from that of the more affluent white radicals in that the politics of the former is much more *instrumental,* directed toward realistic, achievable goals, whereas that of the latter is inclined to be *expressive,* more oriented toward showing up the "immorality" of the larger society than to securing attainable reforms.

The radical traditions

The political traditions and images of certain universities also may play an important role in determining the orientations of their students and faculty. In the United States, Madison and Berkeley have maintained a fairly long record as centers of radicalism. The University of Wisconsin image goes back to before World War I, when the strength of Progressive and Socialist politics in the state contributed to the university's political aura. Berkeley is a particularly interesting case in point. The San Francisco Bay area has a history, dating back to the turn of the century, as one of the most liberal-left communities in the nation. A history of student activism during the 1930's by Hal Draper credits Berkeley with one of the largest reported anti-war demonstrations of the time. Various pieces of data pertaining to the Berkeley campus since the end of World War II point up the continuity of that university as a center of leftism. In his Memoirs, George Kennan reports his puzzlement, as of 1946, that his West Coast academic lecture audiences, and those at Berkeley especially, tended to be much more sympathetic to the Soviet Union than those at other universities. Berkeley was the only large university in the country to sustain a major faculty revolt against restrictive anti-Communist personnel policies in the form of the loyalty oath of 1949–1950. The data collected by Paul Lazarsfeld, in a national opinion survey of the attitudes of social scientists, conducted in 1954 to evaluate the effect of McCarthyism on universities, indicated that the Berkeley faculty was the most liberal of any of the schools sampled in this study.

In stressing that involvement in leftist student activism is a function of the general political orientation which students bring to the university, it is not being argued that changes in attitude do not occur. Universities clearly do have a liberalizing effect, so that there is a gradual shift to the left. However, if we hold pre-university orientation constant, it obviously will make a difference which university a student attends, what subjects he decides to major in, who his friends are on the campus, what his relations are with his teachers of varying political persuasions, what particular extra-curricular activities he happens to get involved in, and the like. There is also a special aspect of university life that enhances the chances that certain groups of students will be more likely to find satisfaction in intense political experience. Various students suggest that mobility, particularly geographic mobility, where one becomes a stranger in an unfamiliar social context, is conducive to making individuals available for causes that invoke intense

commitment. *Thus, new students, or recent transfers, are more likely to be politically active than others*. The various Berkeley studies emphasize this. Local students, or those relatively close to home are less likely to be active than those who are a considerable distance from their home communities. In Berkeley, Madison, and other university centers, the activists have come disproportionately from the ranks of the migrants.

Personality traits and activism

Some of the recent research by psychologists seeks to go beyond the analysis of factors which seem to have a direct impact on political choice. They have also sought to account for political orientation and degrees of involvement by examining personality traits. Thus, they have looked at such factors as variation in the way different groups of students have been reared by their parents, i.e., in a permissive or authoritarian atmosphere, as well as investigating family relationships, student intelligence, sociability, and the like. Such studies have reported interesting and relatively consistent differences between the minority of student activists and the rest of the student population. At the moment, however, these findings are unconvincing, in large part because the extant studies do not hold constant the sociological and politically relevant factors in the backgrounds of the students.

But if we cannot conclude that the differences in the family structures of committed leftists and rightists are causally related to the side of the spectrum which they choose, that they have been reared differently should mean that they vary in their personality traits and consequently political styles. David Riesman has pointed out that conservative student activists seem to be afraid of the emotion of pity and compassion, that they find a concern for the "weak" threatening. Conversely, the leftists, more likely to have been raised in female-dominated families, are more prone to be open expressively toward "feminine" concerns.

In evaluating the growing body of research on the characteristics of leftist activists by psychologists, it is also important to note whether these activists are being compared with other activists or, as often is done, with data from the bulk of the student population, that is, the passive majority. Leftist activists should properly be compared with conservative activists, and with those involved in nonpolitical forms of campus activity. The limited efforts in these directions indicate that *some of the characteristics which have been identified as those of leftist activists, such as greater intelligence, characterize the involved generally. Both leftist and conservative activists, as well as moderates involved in student government, are drawn from the ranks of the academically talented in the United States.*

Conclusion

In seeking to explain the recent increase in student activism, Lipset has tried to find changes within the university that have put increased strain on college students. He believes that the growing emphasis on research within the university has detracted from the time that teachers are willing to spend with students, and is one source of "student malaise." He also points to the movement toward the political left among college faculty. When teachers express discontent with our society, the students who are exposed to them are more likely to become political activists. Finally, Lipset refers to the strain on students of the increased time that must be devoted to getting an education. The added time in school prevents students from achieving adult status as quickly as they would like.

These new strains can lead to a variety of consequences, and student activism is only one of them. The key point of Lipset's argument is that there is a greater probability today that any student will become an activist, but in the latter part of his article he also tries to identify the special characteristics of those students who actually become activists.

SUMMARY

Despite enormous differences in the methods used by specific educational institutions, they all share certain basic social functions. 1) *Cultural transmission* involves transmission of knowledge and skills that are part of a society's culture; more informally but no less significantly, it also involves transmission of the culture's attitudes, values, and norms. 2) By *helping individuals to select and learn social roles,* the school attempts to ensure an adequate supply of trained people to fill needed social functions or occupations. In an effort to match the talents and abilities of individuals with the requirements of specialized occupational roles, the school channels children into different areas of study and places them at distinct academic levels. 3) The school attempts to promote *social integration* in our heterogeneous society by teaching us all the same language, and by providing us with a fund of common experiences and with a sense of cultural identity. 4) Educational organizations are also a prime source of *innovation.* Through research and development activities within universities, ideas are generated and new scientific and technological advances are stimulated.

The trend toward mass education in our society has led to a conflict between the need to maintain academic excellence and the belief that everyone should receive greater educational opportunity. A wider range of vocational and academic courses, and specialized programs for both high and low achievers have been initiated in an effort to balance these demands. Not only does the amount of education received bear directly on an individual's future social standing (occupation and income), but educational opportunity and level of achievement are in themselves influenced by a child's social class. Socialization patterns in the lower class do not motivate children to excel academically and do not usually teach the kind of self-discipline, or deferred gratification, that is needed for commitment to a lengthy and demanding academic training period. Nor have lower-class children generally learned the verbal skills and standards of behavior that are emphasized in most schools. Opportunity to pursue a college education may be further limited by the inferior quality of schools in lower-class areas and by financial limitations.

When a lower-class child is also a member of a minority group his educational opportunities are even more severely restricted. Although *de jure,* or legalized, segregation has been outlawed, many communities still maintain officially, if not legally, segregated school systems. *De facto* segregation, resulting from segregated residence patterns, continues to promote racial imbalance in schools throughout the country. Proposals to overcome this pattern by bussing children to schools outside their neighborhoods have aroused much opposition, particularly in neighborhoods concerned with maintaining a strong local identity. In general, schools serving minority groups are lower in quality than those which serve middle-class white children. Not only are facilities inferior, but failure on the part of teachers to understand the students' various subcultures, prejudice against minority group students, and lack of communication between the school and families of students all serve to compound the problems of minority group students. These disadvantages are reflected in a high dropout rate that in turn limits the level of eventual socioeconomic achievement. However, while our educational system supports our system of stratification to some degree, there is also evidence that education may help to change social attitudes and values by making individuals more tolerant and democratic.

Although the basic organization of American education has remained relatively unchanged for decades, recent trends indicate that the federal and state governments are becoming increasingly involved in both public and private schools. Although local governments contribute the largest share of financial resources, many federal and state programs, such as Head Start and various bilingual and adult education programs, are attempting to correct regional inequities. In return for government subsidies, schools have had to accept a certain amount of government supervision, particularly in the areas of curriculum, teacher certification, and adherence to a policy of desegregation. Government aims do not always coincide with those of the local community, and many neighborhoods are demanding greater control over school policies in their own areas. Racial and ethnic minorities in particular would like schools to be better adapted to their own values and ways of thought. Teachers and school administrators, on the other hand, believing that professional and technical knowledge is needed to make important decisions about educational methods and policies, are often opposed to greater community control. In many urban areas, this conflict has been expressed as a racial issue.

At the university level, decision-making powers have traditionally been centered in the administration and an independent board of trustees. However, college students, sometimes joined by faculty, have increasingly come to demand a larger voice in academic policies and have resisted college control of their private and social lives. Contrary to popular stereotypes, student protests have not usually been violent or disruptive. They are most likely to occur among student bodies with high scholastic aptitude and achievement. For the most part, students seem to be protesting their own lack of power. These efforts are one aspect of the more general attempt made by most older students to define their own roles. In many cases they look to their peers for new role models. When the norms of their peer group run counter to the norms of teachers and administrators, students may experience a certain degree of role conflict in balancing academic and social demands.

GLOSSARY

Applied research Research designed to provide answers for the solution of some immediate practical problem. (page 364)

Basic research Research designed to build knowledge of fundamental facts, processes, and phenomena. (page 364)

Community control The ability of members of a community to influence the actions of public institutions serving their neighborhoods. (page 385)

De facto school segregation Segregation of schools due to the residential patterns of minority groups. (page 380)

De jure school segregation Segregation of schools based on law. (page 380)

Deferred gratification pattern The postponing of immediate pleasures in order to better prepare for later life. (page 377)

Education A set of processes specifically and purposely directed toward inducing learning. (page 357)

Learning The process by which an individual's thoughts, feelings, and behavior are changed as a result of new experience. (page 357)

Sense of cultural identity Awareness of an identity with attitudes, values, and experiences shared by members of one's group or society. (page 363)

SUGGESTED READINGS AND RELATED RESOURCES

I READINGS IN SOCIOLOGY

Becker, Ernest. *Beyond Alienation: A Philosophy of Education for the Crisis of Democracy.* New York: George Braziller (Paper), 1969. Becker examines the past and present condition of education and sets forth a program for the future based on his social philosophy of man and society.

Becker, H. S., B. Greer, E. Hughes, and A. L. Strauss. *Boys in White.* Chicago: University of Chicago Press, 1961. This is a pioneering attempt to study how medical students feel about their training, their doctor-teachers, and the pinnacle profession they are entering.

Brim, Orville. *Sociology and the Field of Education.* New York: Russell Sage Foundation (Paper), 1962. This concise sociological study of the educational system, its aims, and the roles of the people within its structures can serve as a basic resource for the beginning student.

Buckman, William W., and Stanley Liehrer. *Conflict and Change on the Campus: The Response to Student Hyperactivism.* New York: New York School and Society Books, 1970. The authors explore backgrounds of student disenchantment and offer a response to the conflict of "lawlessness vs. learning."

Caplow, Theodore, and Reece McGee. *The Academic Marketplace.* New York: Doubleday, Anchor (Paper), 1965. Two sociologists analyze from a fresh perspective the university as an institution. They discuss areas such as the salary question, the publish-or-perish phenomenon, and the haggling which results from a faculty vacancy.

Clark, Burton. *Educating the Expert Society.* San Francisco: Chandler, 1962. A look at the relationships between some of the dominant characteristics of modern societies, such as high fertility, technological change and mass education, and the educational establishment that develops to meet society's needs.

Coleman, James. *The Adolescent Society.* New York: Free Press, 1961. Coleman examines the status systems and norms of teen-agers attending ten high schools in widely varied communities. He attributes the differences between the high schools and their students to the different value systems within those subcultures which influence the leadership, attitudes, and achievements of the adolescent members.

Crain, Robert. *The Politics of School Desegregation.* New York: Doubleday, Anchor (Paper), 1969. Crain analyzes the political processes by which public schools are being desegregated in both southern and northern cities. He also discusses the problems which arise from attempts at desegregation and their implications for the future.

Friedenberg, Edgar. *Coming of Age in America.* New York: Random House, Vintage (Paper), 1965. An analysis of the conflicts which arise between adolescents and the secondary school's role of teaching mass cultural values. The author approaches his study and the students from a personal perspective; in his view mass education as it is practiced today cripples individual growth.

Jencks, C., and D. Riesman. *The Academic Revolution*. New York: Doubleday, 1968. An excellent and extensive sociological and historical analysis of trends in American higher education.

Koerner, James. *Who Controls American Education?* Boston: Beacon Press (Paper), 1969. In this critical study, Koerner perceives American education as being controlled by small administrative groups within the school systems, state departments of education, and the National Education Association, at the expense of the students and communities that these groups are supposed to serve.

Litcher, S., E. Rapien, F. Seibert, and M. Sklansky. *The Dropouts*. New York: Free Press, 1968. This study describes the experiences and treatment of intellectually capable students who drop out of high school.

Newcomb, T., and E. Wilson, eds. *College Peer Groups*. Chicago: Aldine, 1966. This authoritative collection of studies focuses on the various peer groups found on college campuses and the ways in which these peer groups influence students during their college years.

Riesman, David. *Constraint and Variety in American Education*. Lincoln, Nebr.: University of Nebraska Press, 1958. Riesman's study can serve both as an introductory essay in the sociology of American education and as a stimulating analysis of education's leadership and the forces that constrain freedom in secondary schools and colleges.

Sexton, P. *The American School: A Sociological Analysis*. Englewood Cliffs, N.J.: Prentice-Hall, 1967. A concise introduction to the major issues in the sociology of education; Sexton has assembled the essential thought and findings of many experts in the field.

Stinchcombe, Arthur. *Rebellion in a High School*. Chicago: Quadrangle Books (Paper), 1969. The relevance of traditional teaching is criticized by Stinchcombe, who sees as one of the main sources of dissension within the high schools the difference between what the student knows about society and what the school teaches about society.

Wallace, Walter. *Student Culture: Social Structure and Continuity in a Liberal Arts College*. Chicago: Aldine, 1966. This innovative and documented study describes and analyzes the processes by which students entering a small Midwestern liberal arts college become assimilated into the local "campus culture." Wallace compares their rapid socialization to socialization in other organizations which inculcate values and norms into newcomers within a few short months.

Articles and Papers

Anderson, Margaret. "Education in Appalachia: Past Failures and Future Prospects." *Journal of Marriage and the Family* **26**, 4 (November 1962):443–446.

Clark, Burton R. "The 'Cooling Out' Function in Higher Education." *American Journal of Sociology* **65**, 6 (May 1960):569–576.

Coleman, James S. "The Adolescent Sub-Culture and Academic Achievement." *American Journal of Sociology* **65** (January 1960).

Folger, John K., and Charles B. Nam. "Trends in Education in Relation to the Occupational Structure." *Sociology of Education* **38**, 1 (Fall 1964):19–33.

Halsey, A. H. "The Changing Functions of Universities." In *Education, Economy and Society,* edited by A. H. Halsey, Jean Floud, and C. Arnold Anderson. New York: Free Press, 1961.

Katz, Fred E. "The School as a Complex Social Organization." *Harvard Educational Review* **34**, 3 (Summer 1964):428–455.

Peters, R. S. "Reason and Habit: The Paradox of Moral Education." In *Moral Education in a Changing World,* edited by W. R. Niblett. New York: Humanities Press, 1963.

Sewell, W. H., Archie O. Haller, and Murray A. Strauss. "Social Status and Educational and Occupational Aspiration." *American Sociological Review* **22** (1957):67–73.

Shepherd, John. "An Experiment in Increasing the Educational Television Audience." *Journal of Broadcasting* **10**, 1 (Winter 1965–66):55–66.

Turner, Ralph H. "Sponsored and Contest Mobility and the School System." *American Sociological Review* **25**, 6 (December 1960):855–867.

Wallace, Walter L. "Peer Influences and Undergraduates' Aspirations." *Sociology of Education* **38**, 5 (Fall 1965):375–392.

II RELATED RESOURCES

Nonfiction

Barzun, Jacques. *The American University: How It Runs, Where It Is Going*. New York: Harper & Row (Paper), 1970. Written from the point of view of a professor-administrator, Barzun's analysis provides the reader with suggestions for changing the role of university teachers, as well as with many ideas as to how a university should be run.

Bourges, H., ed. *The French Student Revolt*. New York: Hill and Wang (Paper), 1968. This controversial book contains essays by the leaders of the May 1968 student revolt in France, which was joined by workers and which seriously threatened the Gaullist government. The essays describe the conditions in France that led these leaders to their radical activism.

Conant, James. *Slums and Suburbs*. New York: McGraw-Hill, 1961. In this authoritative commentary, Conant contrasts the inequalities of expenditures, teaching personnel, and facilities which favor suburban schools over slum schools in our cities. Conant also offers many suggestions for overcoming these inequalities.

Fader, Daniel N. *The Naked Children*. New York: Macmillan, 1971. A description of the many barriers to be overcome with ghetto children before they are capable and ready to learn reading, writing, and arithmetic.

Frankel, Charles. *Education and the Barricades*. New York: W. W. Norton (Paper), 1968. Frankel argues that the major causes of dissension in the universities lie beyond the campus, in the issues of Vietnam, racial conflict, and an unresponsive government. But he also perceives that dissension is caused by a lack of real communication between students, faculty, and the administration.

Holt, John. *How Children Fail*. New York: Dell (Paper), 1964. Holt discusses why children fail to learn in our present educational system, and gives guidelines for the correction of these failures.

Hutchins, Robert. *The Learning Society*. New York: Mentor (Paper), 1969. Hutchins criticizes our educational establishment for training students, rather than teaching them and relating to them as persons. He presents alternatives that would allow the university to be an agent for change, rather than a guardian of the status quo.

Kohl, Herbert. *36 Children*. New York: Signet (Paper), 1968. This case history of Kohl's year of teaching in a Harlem school describes how his radical departure from traditional teaching methods allowed his children to develop their previously stifled potentials.

Miller, M., and S. Gilmore, eds. *Revolution at Berkeley*, New York: Dial Press, 1965. This collection of essays discusses the causes and implications of the student revolt at the University of California at Berkeley in 1964.

Fiction

Kaufman, Bel. *Up the Down Staircase*. New York: Avon (Paper), 1968. This is a sympathetic and delightful novel of a young teacher's experience in an urban school and what she learned from the children she was supposed to be teaching.

Kolb, Ken. *Getting Straight*. New York: Bantam (Paper), 1970. A highly entertaining satiric novel of a 28-year-old graduate student's search for his place in society. The novel emphasizes that the content of most teaching courses is irrelevant to the subjects and children to be taught.

Salinger, J. D. *The Catcher in the Rye*. New York: Signet (Paper), 1962. A country prep school for boys is the setting for Salinger's depiction of sixteen-year-old Holden Caulfield's search for himself.

Films

Getting Straight. Richard Rush, 1970. A film based on Ken Kolb's novel, described above.

Up the Down Staircase. Robert Mulligan, 1967. This film is based on Bel Kaufman's novel of the same name, described above.

10. Religion

Religion is an institution—that is, a formal and stabilized way of pursuing a socially important activity—that exists in every human society. Because religion is an institution found in all societies, it is usually assumed to meet some basic need of man. Yet no other institution shows such rich variety of forms as does religion. This variety is one factor that has led to the conclusion that religion, in addition to its sacred and spiritual aspects, is a social *institution, shaped by the culture and environment of each society. When we study religion, therefore, we must recognize these two elements, which are separate but closely interrelated—the universal human impulse toward religion, with its spiritual basis, and the social form in which it is expressed and institutionalized.*

Religion is commonly thought of as a field of study for the theologian and the philosopher, who try to assess the meaning and value of different beliefs. However, the sociologist is also interested in religion. The sociologist does not attempt to judge the value of the beliefs of any religion; instead, he attempts to determine religion's role in the social system as social behavior and as a cultural fact. The sociologist wants to know how religious beliefs and practices affect the political organization, the stratification or the population composition of a society, and how such basic social processes as socialization, institutionalization, and adaptation in turn shape religion. In addition, he is interested in religion as a set of meanings and beliefs and in the relationship of these to other values and ideologies in a society.

1 RELIGION AS AN INSTITUTION

Both sociologists and theologians agree that the term *religion* can be used to refer to widely differing behavior. Because it appears in such a variety of forms, religion is not easy to define precisely. Webster's dictionary says that religion is "the service and adoration of God or a god as expressed in forms of worship, in obedience to divine commands...and in the pursuit of a way of life regarded as incumbent on true believers." This definition is too narrow to cover many known forms of religious behavior and experience. A better definition for the sociologist is the one given by Emile Durkheim in his book *Elementary Forms of the Religious Life:* "Religion is a unified system of beliefs and practices relative to sacred things, uniting into a single moral community all those who adhere to those beliefs and practices."[1] A modern and even broader definition states that religion is a socially recognized way of entering into a relationship with the aspects of reality that are nonrational or nonempirical.[2]

THE VARIETIES OF RELIGION

We are all more or less familiar with the form that religion has taken in modern Western society. There are three principal religious groups of historic importance—the Catholics, the Protestants, and the Jews. All are *monotheistic* (believe in one god only), and all have church organizations, rituals of worship, sacred writings containing principles and beliefs, and some form of ministry or priesthood. Christianity is currently the world's largest religion, with 925 million believers.[3] Judaism is the smallest of the world's major religions, with about 13½ million followers.

The religion with the second largest group of followers, after Christianity, is that of Islam (its members are called Moslems, Muslims, or Mohammedans) with 493 million adherents. It is also a monotheistic religion, and is, in fact, very similar in its structure to Christianity; for example, the prophet Mohammed, the interpreter of Muslim religion, has much in common with Jesus Christ, the interpreter of Christian religious doctrine.

The Hindu religion, practiced primarily in India and Pakistan, is *polytheistic,* believing in many gods, and is a rather loose association of hundreds of local religious cults. In India each village, and each caste, has its own special god and honors him or her on feast days; a certain location, either a temple or a sacred well, tree, or field, will be reserved especially for purposes of worship. The gods of other communities or castes may also be worshipped because they are thought to be especially powerful, or to govern an especially important aspect of life, such as harvesting or childbirth. In spite of the ways Hinduism differs from monotheistic religions, in its basic outline Hinduism is still familiar to Westerners, because it centers on

1. Emile Durkheim, *The Elementary Forms of Religious Life* (1912; New York: Free Press, 1947), p. 47.
2. Thomas F. O'Dea, *The Sociology of Religion* (Englewood Cliffs, N.J.: Prentice-Hall, 1966), pp. 1–2.
3. All statistics on world religious membership are from *Britannica Book of the Year* (Chicago: Encyclopaedia Britannica, 1969).

Three times a day—sunrise, midday, and sunset—a Moslem *muezzin* (a kind of priest) mounts the tower at the mosque and calls the faithful to prayer. The people need not enter the mosque but may conduct their devotions outside, sometimes using prayer rugs to kneel on. They all face toward Mecca, the birthplace of the prophet Mohammed. *(Marc and Evelyne Bernheim, Rapho Guillumette)*

the worship of a god in a certain prescribed way.

The other major religions of the world today—Buddhism, Confucianism, Shintoism, and Taoism—are somewhat different.[4] They do not involve a god figure; instead some ethical, moral, or philosophical principle becomes the center of worship. Confucianism, Buddhism, and Taoism, the religions of southeastern Asia, are all systems for achieving some kind of moral or spiritual excellence. The means of such an achievement— the "way" of Buddha, the laws of Confucius—become the focus of the religion. Shintoism, practiced largely in Japan, is a system of rituals and rules of conduct which

4. For a discussion of non-Western religions, see Charles J. Adams, ed., *A Reader's Guide to the Great Religions* (New York: Free Press, 1965).

serve to glorify one's ancestors. It makes the element of duty to one's parents, which is present in many religions, including Christianity, the center of religious feeling and devotion. Confucianism has no priesthood, but the others all have some specialized group that carries out most of the religious obligations and functions as a conserver of religious values. All have established rituals and sacred scriptures.

These major world religions have long histories—the Hindu religion, probably the oldest, originated over six thousand years ago—and have had many centuries in which to evolve into complex and sophisticated systems of belief and behavior; yet they are "modern" in the sense that they have adapted to conditions of twentieth-century life over most of the globe. This "modern" quality

Every Hindu tries to go at least once in his lifetime to bathe in the sacred waters of the Ganges River. Funerals also take place along its banks. Hindus favor the custom of cremation rather than burial; the ashes of the deceased are then scattered in the Ganges as a symbol of the soul's immersion in the sacred. *(Lynn McLaren, Rapho Guillumette)*

plant) as both a god and an ancestor. The totem is nearly always something important to the community as either a food source or a dangerous predator. Characteristics of totemism are the learning and performing of special dances that mimic the *totem* animal; the wearing or making of costumes and other totemic symbols; the ritual of community banquets in which the totem animal is consumed; and the celebration of some form

makes their beliefs and values fairly easy to understand. In surveying the religions of more primitive societies, it is sometimes more difficult to truly understand the beliefs and practices involved.

A common form of religion among primitive peoples, found in societies widely separated by time and space, is what sociologists call *totemism*. Totemism is the worship and veneration of an animal (or in rare cases, a of communion with the animal. It is a highly complex religion, but one difficult for the modern mind to understand. Sociologists are especially interested in totemism because it is generally the basis for some kind of clan organization which may govern an individual's place of residence, occupation, and choice of marriage partner. Totemism is still practiced in the culture of the Australian aborigines, and among certain New Guinea clans. It was common among the American Indian tribes of the plains and the northwest United States; a small survival of it can still be seen in the hunting society to which all males of the Blackfoot Indian tribe belong. Some sociologists have suggested that totemism was probably the first religion, and that other forms of religious organization have evolved from it.[5]

Primitive religions often include *rituals* of sacrifice, dancing, feasting, and gathering to observe important days. Rituals are frequently conducted by a priesthood, sometimes limited to members of one family or clan. Inevitably, rules evolve governing some aspects of the conduct of the believers. Usually the activities have great significance to the whole community and are directly related to other social functions. For example, courtship, initiation ceremonies, and political processes within the clan are interwoven with totemic rituals. The choice of a dance partner could be a symbol of the choice of a marriage partner; the privilege of killing or catching or handling the totem might be a sign of social power. And, of course, in a society where existence is always in danger and most of one's daily activities revolve around the simple struggle for survival, dancing and feasting would have a special meaning because of their contrast with daily life.

An early source of specific details about religious beliefs and practices in primitive societies is *The Golden Bough*, a book published first in 1890 by Sir James Frazer, a British anthropologist.[6] Frazer laboriously collected every report made by other observers on the magic, religion, and science of primitive or early historic cultures. It was Frazer's contention, and that of a number of scholars who followed him, that a society passed from magic to religion to science as it grew more enlightened. He regarded religion as a survival of the primitive: a form of superstition, an institution linked to ignorance and confusion, always in conflict with science and with the magic rites it supplanted.

Many social scientists who study religion today emphasize a different point of view. They are interested in the psychological necessity for religion and the functions of religion in society.[7] Apart from its important psychological and social aspects, they regard religion not as a step on the road to a system of scientifically accurate explanations of the way the world works, but as a system for dealing with another kind of reality. This reality is the transcendental, otherworldly supernatural reality which is neither scientific nor unscientific, but stands apart from both concepts. It is different from, and not necessarily in conflict with, the scientific world.

Both magic and science can serve some of the same functions as religion, and it is not always easy to make distinctions between them. Magic and religion often have similar rituals and practices, and they are both non-scientific systems for dealing with reality. The chief difference is that the goals of *magic,* unlike most goals of religion, are concrete, specific, and immediate. Magic rituals are performed to cause some desired change in the environment—to bring rain, to banish sickness, to right an injustice. Religion's goals are more spiritual and transcendental—spiritual harmony, inner peace, security, and salvation. In most primitive societies,

5. See Emile Durkheim, *The Elementary Forms of Religious Life.*

6. James George Frazer, *The Golden Bough*, abridged ed. (New York: Macmillan, 1943).

7. For example, see Kingsley Davis, *Human Society* (New York: Macmillan, 1948), p. 529.

Membership of the Major Religions of the World

Religion	North America[1]	South America	Europe	Asia	Africa	Oceania[2]	Total
Total Christian	214,258,000	150,426,000	442,006,000	61,473,000	42,056,000	14,055,000	924,274,000
Roman Catholic	126,468,000	147,219,000	226,303,000	47,622,000	28,751,000	4,107,000	580,470,000
Eastern Orthodox	3,675,000	47,000	114,103,000	2,819,000	4,956,000	84,000	125,684,000
Protestant	84,115,000	3,160,000	101,600,000	11,032,000	8,349,000	9,864,000	218,120,000
Jewish[3]	6,035,000	705,000	4,025,000	2,460,000	238,000	74,000	13,537,000
Moslem	166,000	416,000	13,848,000	374,167,000	104,297,000	118,000	493,012,000
Zoroastrian			12,000	126,000			138,000
Shinto	31,000	116,000	2,000	69,513,000			69,662,000
Taoist	16,000	19,000	12,000	54,277,000			54,324,000
Confucian	96,000	109,000	55,000	371,261,000	9,000	57,000	371,587,000
Buddhist	187,000	157,000	8,000	176,568,000			176,920,000
Hindu	55,000	660,000	160,000	434,447,000	1,205,000	218,000	436,745,000
Others, including primitive or none	83,595,000	21,638,000	176,865,000	363,189,000	180,329,000	3,605,000	829,221,000
TOTAL	304,439,000	174,246,000	636,993,000	1,907,481,000	328,134,000	18,127,000	3,369,420,000

[1] Includes Central America and West Indies. [2] Includes Australia and New Zealand. [3] Includes total Jewish population, whether or not related to the synagogue.
SOURCE: Reprinted from the *1971 Britannica Book of the Year*, published by Encyclopaedia Britannica, Inc.

There are more Christians in the world than there are believers in any other religion. The largest unified religious body is the Roman Catholic church; although the Moslem and Hindu religions have nearly as many followers, they are split into many different sects.

magic and religion cannot really be separated into two institutions, but are rather two facets of the single process of dealing with the unknown. In modern societies they are usually more separate, but all religions include an element of magic, and in everyday practice religion and magic are still intermingled, as, for example, when the devout Christian prays for specific favors from God: help with a problem, or the protection of a loved one.

Science, like magic and religion, tries to furnish explanations for the unknown; but it is concerned only with the natural world and uses methods which are empirical and quantifiable. Science explains the rise of the tides by laws of gravity that can be demonstrated and have been observed to be constant and unchanging. Science may sometimes supplant religious explanations, as was the case when Galileo demonstrated that the earth revolved around the sun, rather than the other way around, as Catholic church doctrine had explained it. Often scientific explanation is worked into the existing religious explanations; this has been the trend of most interpretations of biblical events such as the Creation and the Flood.

THE ELEMENTS OF RELIGION

In comparing various religions, certain common factors begin to emerge, so that one can identify the elements of the institution of religion. There are four basic and necessary elements of religion: (1) the creation of the sacred; (2) the establishment of rituals; (3) the establishment of a system of beliefs; and (4) the formation of an organization of believers.

The creation of the sacred

The creation of the sacred is the basic religious impulse. A sacred item is something set apart from everyday life and deserving of special respect and reverence. That which is sacred has some special power or force and cannot be understood or comprehended by reason alone. It is a potential source of both good and evil influences. It demands from those who recognize it a special commitment or obligation of a moral nature. It arouses feelings both of great attraction, because of its desirability, and of dread, because of its powers.

Many different things can be made sacred: objects such as an altar, a bone, a wooden cross; a location such as a grove of trees, a spring, or a cave; a time such as sunrise, or the day of the equinox; an animal such as the cow, or a rattlesnake. Sometimes that which is made sacred is connected with the unusual or the unpredictable, such as erupting volcanoes or rivers that periodically flood a country. Other common objects of sacred beliefs are the scene of an unusual event, a person of rare abilities, or the date of some strange and significant occurrence.

Sociologists theorize that religion began with the creation of the sacred within a family unit or clan, based on the particular experiences of its members. As we mentioned above, one such sacred item is a family's totem animal. As one family in a community grew more powerful, perhaps its sacred objects were adopted by others in that community. This seems to be the way most cult religions, the Hindu religion, and the religions of Ancient Greece and Rome evolved. A religion may also accept the sacredness created by a single unusual individual; Christianity accepts the sacredness created by Christ and Islam accepts that created by Mohammed.

The establishment of ritual

The establishment of ritual was probably the second step in the creation of religion. Ritual consists of certain patterns of behavior toward the sacred. It prescribes some course of action for dealing with, or relating to, the sacred. For example, by holding certain ceremonies along the banks of the Nile, the Egyptians felt that they were able to help (or symbolically take part in) the annual flooding that brought needed water and soil to the fields. Ritual is also a way of safeguarding the sacred, of protecting it from contamination by the everyday or the ordinary.

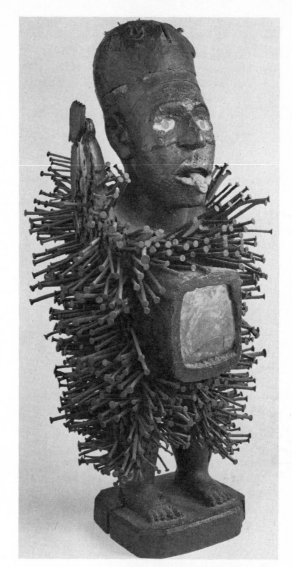

Unlike Western religious idols, this Bakongo magical figure does not represent a god or spiritual being. He is not worshipped, but rather is used for specific, concrete purposes. Nails are driven into the figure to seal an agreement, to drive out pain from a particular part of the body, or to harm an enemy. The box in the figure's abdomen is sealed by a mirror that reflects the sun and thus drives off evil spirits. *(The Brooklyn Museum)*

For example, a sacred chalice or cup is not used every day for drinking water, but only on certain days of feast or celebration, when it is filled with special wine and passed from one person to another.

Ritual is a means of organizing the believers of any given religion, as it brings them together in a group. And ritual is a way of alleviating dread of the sacred, and its power, because ritual is acknowledged to be the "right" way to behave toward the sacred. By worshipping the crocodile in formal ceremonies, certain African tribes who shared their environment with these frightening animals felt they were protecting themselves from attack.

Ritual can itself become sacred, through its connection with and its symbolization of the sacred. The paraphernalia of ritual—the herbs or potions used, the clothes worn by the participants, the place where ritual is conducted—come to be regarded with the same reverence as the initial sacred object. That is why a church, the scene of the ritual of worship, is sacred.

Another significant aspect of ritual in religion is that it usually evokes some kind of collective behavior, which plays an important part in the religious experience. In fact, Emile Durkheim theorized that perhaps the institution of religion is actually a product of collective behavior. When clans or tribes gathered together, they probably feasted, drank, danced, and by their unaccustomed numbers induced a reaction of crowd behavior, through which the individual lost his sense of separateness and isolation as he was swept along in the excitement.

The system of religious beliefs

The system of religious beliefs is the element of religion that has undergone the most development. In primitive religions the main function of systems of belief was to relate the sacred objects to the religious rituals, and to justify and protect the sacred. They also helped to explain the role of the sacred objects to the members of the religion and thus connect these objects to their lives and problems. The Old Testament provides an example of how this is done. In the Bible God is portrayed as a superhuman figure that

can be understood in human terms. Thus the abstract concept of God is transformed into a symbol that religious members can identify and deal with. Belief systems have also served to explain the meaning and purpose of rituals. The Moslem, for instance, learns that he must wash before evening prayers because physical cleanliness is a symbol of moral cleanliness and one must always appear before God morally clean. With this knowledge, the ritual of washing becomes more meaningful.

As religions have evolved, the significance of sacred objects and rituals has declined in importance. All the modern religions place much less emphasis on them than do primitive religions, and their importance continues to lessen. For example, the role of ritual in Catholic church ceremonies has diminished through the years and the practice of most Protestant religions, which grew out of Catholicism, requires a greatly reduced number of rituals and sacred objects.

As sanctity and rituals were deemphasized in religion, the system of beliefs was developed and refined. Most modern systems of religious beliefs go far beyond merely supporting the other elements of religion. Modern religions include beliefs, such as the equality of all men, which are considered to be of great worth and not to be violated; in this sense such beliefs have become sacred, although they are not considered "holy" by religious members. These beliefs are important not only to the religions but also to the nonreligious affairs of a society, for they are often translated into constitutions, political ideology, and educational doctrine.

The organization of believers

The organization of believers is necessary to assure the continuity and effectiveness of the religious experience. Conducting the rituals, constructing places of worship, choosing specialists such as priests, monks, and ministers to cultivate and safeguard the sacred, all call for some kind of organization. The organization called the Second Methodist Church in Great Falls, Montana, builds the church building; it selects and pays the minister; it buys the hymnals and the organ; it recruits the choir. All these things are necessary so that the believers in that religion can go to church on Sunday morning and have a sense of the religious experience. This does not mean that all religions have organizations like the churches of today. In primitive societies, the village meeting place is the scene of religious worship, and the headman of the village usually serves as the high priest or chief organizer of religious activity. Religious organization is not separate, but is an integral part of the total community organization. The earliest forms of worship, the religions that began within family groups, were probably conducted by the head of the family, within the family dwelling place, and as a part of family life.[8] The modern trend has been toward increasing religious specialization, with priesthoods, churches, and other purely religious institutions carrying most of the responsibility for dealing with the sacred. (We will discuss the social organization of religion further in topic 2.)

Sociologists have observed that elements of religion also occur in secular aspects of life. For example, to many people the flag of their country is sacred; a ritual prescribes its handling; and strong ideological beliefs are connected with it. Sociologist Milton Yinger suggests that we should not construct two categories, the religious and the secular, but rather should imagine a continuum, with the nonreligious at one end, and the highly religious at the other end. The church would be located far down at the sacred end, but still contain certain elements of the secular, such as the bureaucracy of its hierarchy. The state or nation would be located near the secular end of the continuum but still contain features which are almost sacred, such as the flag, our Declaration of Independence, and certain formal rituals of government. The extremes at each end of the continuum represent ideals rather than any actual reality.[9]

Ritual in particular is a characteristic often found in secular institutions and behavior. The Japanese make a ritual of drinking tea. There is a ritual involved when a group of American students graduates from college. Bureaucracies may have many work-oriented rituals. Sociologists speculate that ritual may serve many of the same functions in secular institutions that it does in religious groups. For example, the elaborate ritual with which contemporary America surrounds the election of its presidents—the primaries, the national conventions, the campaigning all over the nation, and the kissing of babies—helps to magnify its importance and protect the presidency and the government from seeming too routine, too commonplace. It helps to organize the candidate's supporters into a unified group; it gives many citizens a chance to feel that they are participating or in some way entering into a relationship with the candidate, when they shake hands with him at their local shopping center; it assures everyone that the "correct" procedures are being followed and that therefore the best man will indeed win.

RELIGION AND THE HUMAN CONDITION

Why does man need religion? So durable an institution must surely meet some basic psychological needs of man and be rooted in some fundamental problems of the human condition. Scholars have suggested many answers to this question, which we may summarize under the following points.

(1) Religion provides support and consolation that help to overcome man's fear of the unknown, and his anxiety about the

8. Fustel De Coulanges, *The Ancient City* (Magnolia, Mass.: Peter Smith, 1959).

9. See J. Milton Yinger, *Sociology Looks at Religion* (New York: Macmillan, paper, 1963).

future. Because the world is an unpredictable place in which to live, man feels anxious and fearful of its dangers. Religion provides significant emotional support in helping him to face life's uncertainties. Most religions also offer specific reassurance and hope about the final unknown, death, by defining a supernatural afterlife.

(2) Religion serves to give human existence a meaning and a purpose. The question of the ultimate "why?" is perhaps the hardest question for men to answer, but religion can help to provide an answer by defining supernatural forces and God-given origins. Part of man's search for the meaning of life is really a search for absolute moral meanings and standards, and these can also come from religion. Thus religion may serve as a kind of yardstick for mankind in evaluating actions, goals, ideals and ideas, even society itself.

(3) Religion provides men with the opportunity to transcend the "self" and the everyday reality of the present. Man seems to desire some kind of relationship with the "other," or that which goes beyond the known limits of daily life. The keen awareness of human limitations also leads to a desire to escape from the confines of the self, the purely human. Religion helps here in two ways. First, its doctrines and beliefs regarding the sacred "otherness" or "beyondness" give man a sense of some relationship with, and understanding of, these things. Second, religion fosters and encourages the transcendental emotional experience, the feeling of stepping outside or above oneself. Many rituals of religious observance have this as their basic purpose; repeated incantations, frenzied dances, fasts, and the taking of drugs such as peyote, are examples.

(4) Religion helps give man a sense of identity. While religion helps one transcend the self, it also helps to define the self, to answer the basic human question, "Who am I?" Religion establishes a sense of what it is to be human, by helping man to accept the limitations of the human condition,

and also by celebrating the successes of man over the forces of uncertainty and adversity. All religions, however much they may stress the powers of the supernatural, also emphasize the power and capability of man to decide and direct his own destiny.

A second way in which religion helps to give man a sense of identity is through membership in specific religious organizations. Religious membership provides a stronger bond of identity than most other organizations because of the sharing with others of "ultimate" and deeply felt values and beliefs. The theologian Will Herberg conducted a study during the 1950s which concluded that one of the most significant sources of identity in American society is membership in one of the three basic religious groups—Protestants, Catholics, and Jews.[10]

(5) Religion can help the individual during the crises of certain transitional stages in life. All religions take note of the basic and important events of a lifetime: birth, puberty, marriage, and death. Around these important events a system of rituals grows up which anthropologists refer to as "rites of passage."[11] These major transitions are times of special strain on the individual going through them and on those who are emotionally close to him, such as his family and friends. Religious rites of passage—weddings, baptisms, funerals—help to ease the strain of these difficult periods. Sometimes they give consolation, as in the case of rituals surrounding dying and death. Sometimes they give guidance and instruction to help the individual cope with his new role and understand its demands; the rites of passage concerning puberty and marriage (bar mitzvahs and weddings) both have this function.

It should be noted, however, that religion is not the only institution that can meet many of the needs we have outlined. An ethical system that is not specifically religious can give

10. Will Herberg, *Protestant, Catholic, Jew* (New York: Doubleday, 1955).
11. For a further discussion see Joachim Wach, *Types of Religious Experience: Christian and Non-Christian* (Chicago: University of Chicago Press, 1952), p. 42.

moral meaning to life; so can a strong occupational commitment. Ties to other groups such as a family, a neighborhood, a work organization, or a nation can help to give people a sense of identity. Social movements stimulated by secular causes can give a person the feeling of self-transcendence. Thus, certain of the functions of religion can be provided by alternative institutions and social structures. However, no other institution, except the family, is so specifically geared to the problems of the meaning and value of life, or historically so successful in creating strong allegiance in followers.

Another way that sociologists have answered the question of "why does man need religion?" is by considering the importance of religion for society—the *social* functions of religion. Some of these will be discussed in the next topic.

TOPIC

2 THE ORGANIZATION AND COHESIVE FUNCTIONS OF RELIGION

The relationship between religion, a social institution, and the total sociocultural system is a complex one. As Thomas F. O'Dea puts it:

There is, however, a two-way relationship here. Not only do social conditions affect the rise and spread of ideas and values, but ideas and values once institutionalized in a society affect the actions of men. Hence the sociology of religion must not only study the effects of social structure upon religion, but also the effects of religion upon social structure.[12]

There are two general ways in which something can affect a sociocultural system. One way acts to support and maintain the system; the other may serve to change it. When Karl Marx said that religion was the opiate of the masses, he was indirectly making reference to the supportive or cohesive aspect of the institution of religion. He contended that religion lulled individuals into accepting the conditions of their society, removing their incentive to demand change, and should thus be considered an active ally of the established social order, an antirevolutionary agent.[13] Most sociologists of religion also have emphasized that religion is a force of social cohesion and a support for the established system of social organization and control—for the status quo.

But religion may also serve as a divisive force—a rallying point to which the disaffected may gather to attack the other institutions of society and seek social change. History furnishes many examples of this process. The Protestant Reformation may

12. Thomas F. O'Dea, *The Sociology of Religion*, p. 55.

13. Karl Marx and Friedrich Engels, *The Communist Manifesto* (Baltimore: Penguin Books, 1969).

have begun as a purely theological reform of Catholic church doctrine, but it quickly attracted many of those whom society had alienated, and in time it became a prime agent of many far-reaching social changes — such as the decline of the feudal system and the rise of an industrial society — well outside the province of religion.

THE EVOLUTION OF RELIGIOUS ORGANIZATION

In the early stages of human society, religion was presumably practiced by the family group in the home. The sacred objects were those with special meaning to the family — the well that furnished precious water, the site of burials, the relics of ancestors. The ritual was devised by family members. The god, or god-substitute, which they worshipped was one that protected and supported the members of the family, and it was thought to reside either in the home or on land owned by the family. This family orientation of religion was still dominant in the early days of the Roman civilization, when each family had its own special gods, some of whom were later borrowed by the whole society. It still exists in the form of Shintoist shrines that are a feature of many Japanese homes, where the family's ancestors are worshipped, in the family chapels sometimes built by wealthy Catholics, in the family possession of ikons (religious images which may be worshipped), among the Eastern Orthodox believers.

Later, the unit of religious organization became the tribe or the village, but religion was an integral part of other social institutions. Religious worship and observance, the safeguarding and preservation of the sacred, the continuity of rites and rituals, were the concerns of every member of the family or the tribe. The head of the family, and later the head of the village, usually attended to administrative details; he was also assigned the task of learning, and then teaching to his successor, the correct way to perform all the religious rituals. But he was not considered any more religious than other members of the group; he carried on the same nonreligious functions as the others and he was not a true religious specialist.

In such a society, the question of religious choice or preference virtually never arose. There was only one religion in each community. Children were taught its beliefs and rituals from a very early age. The religion was inseparable from the social organization of home, family, and community, and it played a part in nearly every aspect of life. Planting, harvesting, hunting, entering adulthood, marrying, falling ill, building new houses, preparing and eating food — almost every activity was linked to some religious ritual or belief. Religion was a daily connection with the spiritual dimension of the world, an integration of that "otherness" with ordinary life. To renounce one's religion would be to destroy all of one's social existence.

However, the trend of human history has been toward differentiation and specialization, and the institution of religion is no exception. Gradually religion has become a separate institution with its own specialized organizations, bringing about significant and far-reaching changes in the position of the religious element in society: (1) certain people adopted religion as a full-time vocation; (2) there came to be a division between religious and secular (nonreligious) activity; and (3) participation in religious activity became to some degree voluntary.

The development of an occupational position of priests was probably the first step in the specialization of religion. As beliefs became more sophisticated, and rituals more complicated, certain individuals — priests — began to specialize in interpreting and explaining them. The priest could no longer divide his attention among many concerns, but had to give full time to the service of the religion. Eventually religions developed

These men are part of the hierarchy of the Catholic church; they are members of the General Council of the Commission for Latin America. The council meets to discuss such problems as raising funds for schools and missionary programs, recruiting priests, and competing with other denominations and ideologies for the support of the public. (V. Rastelli, LIFE Magazine © Time Inc.)

whole hierarchies of officials to administer the affairs of the religious group. For example, the Episcopal church in America, with 3½ million members, has several hundred bishops and thousands of ministers.

The creation of a full-time priest led to a second change, the separation of sacred and secular activities. The priests were now specialists and were no longer always considered competent to give leadership and guidance in other fields. Where formerly the village headman decided when and what to plant in the spring, and then conducted a religious ritual as a part of the planting, the two aspects—the secular planting and the religious ritual—were now divided. The chief gave planting instructions and then the priest held religious ceremonies at the proper time. The priests, of course, had a personal interest

in this separateness, because it gave them a kind of job security (they alone could perform the needed religious rituals). The separation also helped to keep their religious organizations free of all outside influences. On the other hand, as religion was compartmentalized, its influence over the secular was weakened.

Once the religious and the secular were firmly established as two separate worlds, a third change, voluntary participation in religion, was inevitable. When religion and secular activities were intermixed, the only way a person could avoid involvement with religion was to give up living, because all activities were touched by religious ritual and significance. With separation, one could choose between accepting and rejecting religious experience (one could either include the ritual or not). This later opened the way for choice between religious denominations (one could choose from a variety of rituals).

Religious organizations were born to meet the needs of groups of believers for order and stability. Contemporary sociologists generally divide religious organizations into two categories: church and sect.

A *church* is the sociological name for a stable and institutionalized organization of religious believers. A church has an accepted administration and clerical hierarchy, a fixed body of doctrine or dogma which usually covers most ordinary human situations, and an established form of ritual. Like any other organization, it also has a certain social base from which it draws its members and supporters.

The church often does not demand from its members a great deal of active participation. Members subscribe to, and support, the body of beliefs of the church, but the majority of the religious duties are performed by the specialized officials of the organization. The church may be integrated closely with other social institutions—the government, the school, the family—and embrace almost all members of society, in which case it sometimes is called an *ecclesia*. Or it may be one of a number of religious organizations that are considered socially acceptable in society, in which case sociologists call it a *denomination*. In either case, a church normally will try to cooperate with, and preserve, the established and dominant social order. An example of this trend is the biblical injunction to "render unto Caesar that which is Caesar's."

A *sect* is less formally organized than a church. It may have few or no officials, and many religious duties fall on the shoulders of the members. They may run religious affairs, recruit and instruct new members, conduct services of worship and other rituals, and even interpret the will and the commands of the sacred. Because the members must

perform more of the work, it is clear that they must have a higher sense of commitment to the organization than do members of a church. Typically those who join a sect are of lower occupational and educational status than those who join a church. They are likely to be dissatisfied with their positions in life, which probably encourages them to commit themselves more fully to religion.

The sect is generally characterized by a strong emphasis on belief, and a concern for the depth and purity of religious feeling. Increased faith and fervor take the place of established organization. The sect will often conflict with other social institutions over this question of belief because the sect is against compromise on such issues; and it can be considered a more revolutionary kind of organization because it would rather try to change the whole world than change its own beliefs. Whereas the church expects to obtain new members primarily from inheritance (that is, the children of present members become members), the sect is more dependent on conversions as a source of new members.

Although we have drawn a clear distinction between the concepts of church and sect, the difference is not always so distinct in practice, for sects may gradually become institutionalized and turn into churches. Groups of members dissatisfied with the doctrine or dogma of the church may break away to found a new sect. Sects may exist even within the framework of a church. For example, many orders of monks have most of the typical characteristics of a sect—avoidance of formal organization patterns, a strong commitment to beliefs, and a need for conversion to obtain new members—even though they are a part of the Catholic church, the most highly organized kind of ecclesia.

Religious officialdom refers to priests, ministers, and other full-time religious workers. Probably when religions were first developing into specialized organizations a single priest could handle all the religious duties. In today's complex religious organizations, religious hierarchies have many of the characteristics of bureaucracies. They are large and complex organizations concerned with the administration of church affairs. The Catholic church has a pyramid of religious officials—pope, cardinals, archbishops, and so on, right down to the neighborhood curate—and is, perhaps, the best example of this kind of religious bureaucracy. But every church has one. Sects may have religious officials but they usually have not become so institutionalized that they are patterned along bureaucratic lines.

RELIGION AS A FORCE OF SOCIAL COHESION

Theologians view religion as a vehicle for man's individual quest for salvation. Sociologists, on the other hand, have tended to see religion as a strong force of social cohesion and many have rated that its most important function. Emile Durkheim virtually ignored all other aspects of religion, and suggested that all forms of worship were actually a way to worship the community. He suggested that the totem was actually the society, with its great power to accept or reject, support or destroy the solitary individual.[14] While modern sociologists might disagree with such an extreme position, Durkheim's theory does explain many of religion's contributions to society. These contributions to, or positive functions for, society may not, of course, always be evaluated as "good" by various ethical theories and political ideologies. Such an evaluation must rest on the value one places on the society as a whole, and the desirability of maintaining it.

The functions of religion for social cohesion may be summarized in five points:

(1) Religion renders the society's basic norms and values more important and also more acceptable. The existence and observance of social norms is the foundation of all social organization and of a sense of community, and religion usually supports these norms and values. It often makes them sacred; it gives them moral meaning; it consoles people for the sacrifices they must make when individual wishes conflict with societal values, such as in time of war.

In our society, showing respect for one's parents is a behavioral norm. You are taught it at home (not surprisingly, by your parents) and at school. This social norm is made sacred for both Christians and Jews by the Old Testament commandment, "Honor thy father and thy mother, that thy days may be long upon the land which the Lord thy God giveth thee." As the word of God, this norm has been made sacred. The norm which prohibits sexual relationships between people married to other partners is made sacred by the commandment, "Thou shalt not commit adultery." The same is true of many other social norms. By this connection with the sacred, norms and values become even more important and significant—they are integrated into a system of moral and religious meaning—and conformity to them is strongly encouraged.

(2) Religion emphasizes the basic similarity of all human beings. Much of the appeal of religion, as was noted in the last topic, is directed toward certain elements of the human condition—anxiety in the face of the unknown or unfamiliar; regret over past mistakes and lost opportunities; fear of death; the desire to transcend the limits of body and self; the need for love and acceptance from others. Through the institution of religion, we are made aware that such feelings are not singular but universal. Such an awareness creates a strong sense of community and "belonging"—as the words of a spiritual put it, "We're in the same boat, brother, and if you shake one end you're going to rock the other." Along with this feeling of shared interests comes a realization of man's dependence on man, which per-

14. Emile Durkheim, *The Elementary Forms of Religious Life*, p. 383.

haps is the basis for all social organization. It is important to note again that religions can also be very divisive—emphasizing the uniqueness and superiority of their own group.

(3) Religion helps reconcile individuals to the hardships and inequities of a society, and helps those who have become alienated from the social system to readjust to it. It has been observed that religious belief and commitment are more common among the poor than the rich, among the oppressed rather than the oppressors. Although there are a number of reasons for this phenomenon, one important factor is that the poor and the oppressed are in need of some stronger tie to the social system that has placed them at the bottom. These people need alternative sources of rewards for social cooperation, since they are not being well compensated in the usual ways for their participation in society. Religion can provide that reward. Every religion offers its followers the chance, by observing its precepts, to achieve a high *moral* status, which can to some degree offset their low *social* status. Some religions meet this problem by stressing the equality of all those who believe in them; others actually regard their believers as a special elite. Religion also approaches the problem from the other direction as well—that is, by affecting the behavior of those who are favored by the social system. If the favored gloat too much in their superiority, or badly abuse their wealth and power, the system will become even less acceptable to those at the bottom. Consequently religion advocates charity, mercy, kindness, the sharing of one's blessings with the less fortunate, the renunciation of pride and vanity. Such conduct helps to ease the dissatisfactions of the poor and the powerless, even though it may do nothing for their actual condition.

(4) Religion binds the community together in certain rituals of worship and in observance of the sacred powers. Many rituals and forms of worship require common participation, and thus serve to bring the group together. Once people are congregated for religious rituals or worship, the emotional contagion of the crowd, evoked by the ritual, also welds them more closely together. When people have jointly shared an important occasion, experience forms a bond between them. This is more true of the small homogeneous communities with a single religious organization, found in primitive societies, than it is of a complex and pluralistic society like ours. Today people worship in many different groups, in different places, and in different ways; they may even worship on different days—Friday morning for Black Muslims, Friday evening for Jews, Saturday for the Seventh Day Adventists, and Sunday for Catholics and most Protestants. Yet in a sense Black Muslims, Jews, Adventists, Catholics, and Protestants are united by their common worship of God and their presence at whatever ritual they have chosen. People frequently express a feeling of identity with other "churchgoing, God-fearing folk." But, though a belief in religion results in a unity, a belief in the superiority of one ritual or sacred tradition over another can be the cause of serious division in religiously heterogeneous societies. This may be expressed as a running feud between the two churches in a little town, or a bloody war between Catholics and Protestants, or the extermination of one entire religious group. However, even this intergroup conflict is essentially an outgrowth of the cohesion established by religion within a group of believers.

(5) Religion offers support when other social organizations are undergoing change and stress. It has been observed that the membership figures of religious denominations vary in relationship to other prevailing social conditions. In times of war, or great social upheaval, such as that caused by the onset of the Industrial Revolution, more people join the established churches and more new sects are founded than in times of social stability. O'Dea explains this function of religion:

Durkheim used the term anomie *to characterize that state of social disorganization in which established social and cultural forms break down. He spoke of two aspects of this breakdown. There is loss of solidarity; old groups in which individuals find security and response tend to break down. There is also loss of consensus; felt agreement (often only semi-conscious) upon values and norms which provided direction and meaning for life tend to break down. While Durkheim saw this as two sides of one process of social disorganization, he showed that the two sides could become disorganized at different rates of speed. The result of the process is a condition of relative isolation and "normlessness" for individuals which Durkheim called anomie.*

Social patterns emerge because men have need for them, and when such patterns disintegrate, men seek ways out of their predicament—out of the confusion and anxiety which result. Since the experience of anomie is frustrating, men may go over to aggression against real or imagined sources of their difficulties. Moreover, they may try the various means of escape which their situation offers them: pleasure-seeking, alcohol, drugs, or similar things. Finally, they may engage in a "quest for community" and a search for new meaning. From such quests, movements develop which offer new values and new solidarities. Such movements may be religious, or they may be quasi-religious, offering less-than-ultimate values and relationships.[15]

Religion as an agent of social control

The function of religion in promoting the maintenance and cohesion of a society can be illustrated by considering the specific use of organized religion in the performance of one of a society's chief "maintenance processes," social control. Religion poses a threat of punishment, reinforcing the sanctions of secular society, to those who deviate from social norms. We have already briefly explained in chapter 3 the system of sanctions by which society enforces conformity to its norms. Secular society can offer only the rewards and punishments of other human beings and the social system. The institution of religion adds another dimension to those sanctions, that of the supernatural. Those who comply with the commandments and conform to the social norms are promised some kind of reward which is beyond the ability of humans to bestow—divine assistance in times of crisis, invulnerability to the danger of enemies and hostile forces, or eternal life after death. Those who deviate from the norms are threatened with supernatural punishments, such as constant bad fortune or everlasting torture after death. Thus religion greatly extends the scope of sanctions on behavior and reinforces the society's system of social control.

We might point out that religion also offers a more complete or extensive method of controlling deviance, because it adds a sort of supernatural "detective" power. In society, deviance is noticed and subject to negative sanctions only when the deviant actually commits some positive act of deviance which is both seen and reported to the community by some other person. As Howard Becker has stated, the concept of social deviance includes both the role of the deviant and the role of those who object to his behavior.[16] (Deviance will be more fully discussed in chapter 12.) The institution of religion sometimes eliminates the necessity for anyone to play the role of observer or objector, for it can extend control to cases where deviance is neither seen nor reported by another person; God, or whatever other supernatural power the religion believes in, sees the deviation and will punish the deviant. In fact, some religions go so far as to exert some control over mere thoughts of deviance that never result in an actual deviant act. Planning to kill someone, or imagining his death, will evoke religious punishment even though the intended victim is never harmed. Thus religion is a major influence on those internalized social norms that we call conscience.

15. Thomas F. O'Dea, *The Sociology of Religion*, pp. 56–57.

16. Howard Becker, *The Outsiders,* ed. Lewis B. Whitman (New York: Free Press, 1966), pp. 8–9.

Religion also provides a way for a deviant individual to atone for his deviance. When one has committed a deviant act and has been apprehended in that act, one is publicly branded as a deviant. This creates a strain on the individual, and is a potential danger to the society, because the deviant may choose to reject the normative system which has rejected him, and live altogether outside the society. Obviously, if very many people elected that course of action, society would collapse. Religion eases this situation by providing a way for the deviant to atone for his behavior and be reaccepted into society. There may be a ritual of purification that he must perform, or an ordeal he must undergo; in many modern religions the deviant undertakes some relatively mild form of penance, such as additional church attendance, limited fasting, or the denial of some customary pleasure or comfort.

This system is highly efficient, because the deviant knows exactly how to go about the atonement, and society knows exactly when to reaccept him as a member of the community. Thus the social stress is minimized and social control is maintained. The very act of the atonement serves to reemphasize to the deviant the value of the social system and to draw him securely back into it.

Religion and expressive culture

Another important cohesive force in society is expressive culture, particularly literature and the visual arts (painting and sculpture). Through the arts, the values and beliefs of a society are expressed and interpreted; in some cases religion dictates their precise form. Expressive culture has been closely associated with religion for a long time. In fact, the earliest known artistic attempts of prehistoric man, the small figurines used in cult ceremonies and the murals on walls in the south of France, are believed to have been an attempt in part either to express worship, or to magically capture the powers of the sacred.[17]

17. E. H. Gombrich, *The Story of Art* (Greenwich, Conn.: Phaidon, 1961).

A Renaissance artist sculpted this portrait of the infant Jesus and Mary. The haloes and the wise expression on the child's face serve to increase the feeling of sanctity in the viewer; Mary's look of motherly tenderness helps to personalize the sculpture. *(The Metropolitan Museum of Art)*

The association between religion and expressive culture has varied throughout history. From the tenth to the seventeenth century, life in all Europe was centered around the Catholic church, and the relationship between religion and expressive culture was extremely close. The church was the primary source of support for the arts and artists. Most of the art and literature of that time was religious or was for religious use. Architects designed churches; sculptors carved altars and sacred objects.

Painters created art works that illustrated biblical stories and undoubtedly inspired faith and religious feeling. Literature taught religious values and beliefs.

In their use of artistic works, the organized institutions of religion face two dilemmas. First, the representation of the sacred may itself become sacred, so that people worship the picture and not the spirit. This is considered to be the biblical sin of idolatry. Some religions, such as Islam, and to a limited extent, Judaism, have forbidden all pictorial representations of religious subjects, to avoid the possibility of idolatrous practices. The second dilemma of religion when it turns to art is that the graphic representations of religious subjects may serve to devalue the mystery and awe that religion dictates should surround them. In spite of their halos, Mary and the baby Jesus in many paintings look very much like any other mother and child. Although this helps people identify with their emotions and actions, at the same time it makes the holy quite human.

In the eighteenth century, as religion became less central to European society, expressive culture turned to secular areas for subject matter, audience, and financial support, for the expressive arts always mirror the central concerns of a society. The modern era has often been categorized as a time in which the influence of religion is waning. Today, although religion plays a much less important role in expressive culture, its impact is still quite marked. Many of the modern artists whose works fill our museums often treat religious subjects. Many works of modern literature are rich in religious content and meaning. For example, Ernest Hemingway's Nobel Prize winning novel *The Old Man and the Sea* is filled with religious symbolism. *Finnegans Wake,* an avant-garde work, and John Updike's *Couples,* a modern best seller, also exhibit the strong influence of religious meanings. Thus even with the growing secular trend in the arts, religious topics and themes are popular and important. The exposure of society's members to religious values through expressive culture is another way in which religion helps to maintain the social bond.

RELIGION AND PRIMARY RELATIONSHIPS

Religion has a great influence over the way an individual conducts his most intimate relationships with other people, particularly primary relationships within the family.

Many social institutions tend to depersonalize relationships. The common forms of social organization, role playing, and the patterning of responses all exert pressures on us to view others in *situational* rather than in *personal* terms. Obviously this is necessary if we are to maintain a complex society. Role playing is an efficient way to establish and maintain a large number of workable relationships. If we responded to each person we met as a total person, it would consume too much of our time and emotional energy.

Yet no one would deny that we lose something by this impersonality. Being regarded as nothing more than a social unit may make a person feel undervalued and something less than human. The institution of religion serves as a counterbalance to the forces of depersonalization in society. It has been pointed out by many theologians that all the major religions of the world today contain some principle or rule analogous to the Golden Rule of Christianity: "Do unto others as you would have them do unto you." Religious doctrine puts a constant stress on the understanding and acceptance of all human beings, complete with their frailties and errors, and it emphasizes the need for love and respect between individuals.

Religion stresses the importance of primary relationships; in fact, it suggests in a sense that all relationships be primary ones, with full communication and acceptance. This focus on primary relationships can be seen in all contemporary religions, so that we can hypothesize one of the major functions of the institution of religion. A large number of all religious laws and principles are specifically slanted toward the conduct of primary

Much Catholic ritual and belief centers around Mary, the mother of Jesus. She has inspired much of the religious art and architecture in the Western world. In Mexico, Mary is often depicted as the Indian Virgin of Guadalupe, the patron saint of all Mexicans. Many homes include a small shrine in her honor, and the family may often gather there to offer prayers and light candles. *(Photo by Ken Heyman)*

relationships with friends, lovers, husbands, parents, and children.

Religion and the family

The influence of religion on primary relationships is most notable within the family group. The institution of religion is intimately interconnected with that of the family. As mentioned, religion probably began as a family activity. It is interesting to note the family orientation of the divinities of most religions. Deities may be husband and wife, like Siva and Kali in the Hindu religion; they may be brother and sister, like Artemis and Apollo in the ancient Greek religion; or they may be both at once, as in the case of the Egyptian brother-sister husband-wife pair, Osiris and Isis. Parent-child relationships are also prominent, as seen in the Christian religion in God the father and Jesus the son. The worship of a mother figure is thought by some researchers to be the very oldest form of religion, and is strongly reflected in the prehistoric religious art found by archeologists. The cult of the mother is still represented today in the worship of many of the Hindu goddesses, and in the Catholic worship of Mary, the mother of God. The most common type of deity, however, is the father figure, who both loves and chastises his children, the believers.

To Sigmund Freud, the domination of fatherlike deities was not surprising. Freud felt that man created religion in an attempt to overcome the anxieties he naturally felt living in a world which he could not control. During his nearly helpless infancy and childhood, man develops an almost complete dependence on his parents. Freud believed that the feelings toward parents, developed during these formative years, are in adulthood transferred to the supernatural.[18]

The family is thus deeply embedded in religious belief. In fact, the family has become, to a limited extent, a sacred institution by its connection with the sacred beings. It is difficult to predict the decline of the family as an institution without envisioning an accompanying decline of all of the world's religions, because of the close connection between the two institutions.

What effect does religious belief, affilia-

tion, or participation have on family life? These answers can be given in largely empirical terms. Religious affiliation certainly has an effect on the choice of a marriage partner, for the majority of all marriages are between people of the same religious faith. This is in part the result of church doctrine, which makes partners of the same faith desirable if not required; it may also be due to the fact that a religious denomination is a social acquaintance group, so it is easier to meet people of the same denomination. The fact that religious affiliation is also connected with social class membership is another factor favoring marriage between partners of the same faith.

Statistics also show that there is a difference in family stability among members of various religious denominations. Of the three main faiths in the United States, Protestants have the highest rate of family breakups, and Catholics have the lowest. This difference may result in part from beliefs regarding divorce that are taught within the two churches. The abridgment by Gerhard Lenski within these pages discusses other effects of religion on family cohesion and solidarity.

---

18. Sigmund Freud, *The Future of an Illusion,* rev. ed. J. Strachey, trans. W. D. Robson-Scott (New York: Doubleday, Anchor, 1964).

GERHARD LENSKI
Religion and Family Ties

Introduction

A large-scale and important investigation of the effects of religious belief on social behavior was conducted by Gerhard Lenski, and his book has become a classic in the field. The Religious Factor, *published in 1961, is the result of an empirical study carried out over a period of years in Detroit, Michigan. Lenski investigated many different connections between religion and*

social behavior—its effects on group ties, economic capabilities, political affiliation, and educational achievement. In this excerpt, Lenski discusses the effects affiliation with specific religious denominations has on the family.

Strength of loyalty to the kin group

In the great majority of simpler, preliterate societies, life is organized around the kin group. Economic, political, educational, and even religious activities are largely performed within the context of the kin group, which is typically a moderately large organization involving a substantial proportion of the people with whom the average individual comes in contact in the course of daily life.

However, as societies develop and technology advances, more and more functions become separated from the kin group and are taken over by highly specialized institutional systems. Hence, in the modern industrial society the kinship system is only one among a multitude of specialized institutions, and in this setting it is constantly obliged to compete with other institutions for the time, energies, and loyalties of individuals.

Migration

One of the best indicators of the importance attached to the family and kin group by modern Americans is their willingness, or unwillingness, to leave their native community and migrate elsewhere. Migration of this type generally involves a physical separation of the individual from those relatives with whom he has the closest ties. He may take some of these relatives with him, but rarely all of them. A man usually migrates in response to the lure of economic or vocational opportunities; hence we may regard migration as an indicator of the importance he attaches to the kin group when its ties compete directly with the prospect of more money or a better job.

Pooling the results of four separate surveys in the Detroit area, it appears that Catholics are the most likely to be natives, and Negro Protestants the least. The specific figures for the four groups were as follows:

White Catholics	43%
Jews	31%
White Protestants	26%
Negro Protestants	7%

Of special interest in this connection were those persons who had no relatives in Detroit, except their immediate family living in the same dwelling unit. These are generally the people who have most completely severed their ties with the extended kin group. The 1952 survey indicated that 20 percent of the white Protestants fell in this category, compared with only 10 percent of the Catholics and Negro Protestants, and 6 percent of the Jews. This pattern of total separation from the kin group was especially pronounced among middle-class white Protestants. Fully 29 percent of this group reported no relatives living in the community other than those in the dwelling unit itself. This contrasted with only 9 percent of the middle-class Catholics and none of the middle-class Jews. Among members of the working class, 20 percent of the Jews, 15 percent of the white Protestants, 10 percent of the Catholics, and 8 percent of the Negro Protestants were "alone" in the community.

It is interesting to speculate about the significance of these findings for our findings on vertical mobility. Sociological research on vertical mobility makes it abundantly clear that spatial mobility facilitates, or at least normally accompanies vertical mobility. If this is true, then people whose ties with kin bind them to their community of birth are necessarily at a disadvantage in the competition for advancement. This factor may well contribute to the different rates of mobility for Catholics and white Protestants.

Relatives vs. neighbors

In the 1952 survey there were other indications that the attraction of the kin group is stronger for Catholics than for Protestants. The study showed that the more frequently members of a group visit relatives, the less frequently they visit neighbors. Jews were the most likely to visit relatives every week; Negro Protestants were the least likely. Comparing white Protestants and Catholics, the former were more likely to visit neighbors on a weekly basis, while the latter were more likely to visit relatives.

Other indices of family solidarity

Another distinctive feature of the white Protestants was the small number who had relatives outside the immediate family (e.g., grandparents) living in the same dwelling unit. This was especially evident in the middle class, where only 5 percent of the white Protestants reported this pattern, compared with 14 percent of the Jews and 16 percent of the Catholics. If we had the data required to eliminate from consideration those married couples who had no parents still alive, the differences between the groups would undoubtedly be even larger.

In the 1958 survey we gave respondents the following list and asked them to indicate which two had the greatest influence on their religious beliefs: (1) Friends; (2) Teachers; (3) Husband, wife, children; (4) Parents; (5) Ministers, priests, or rabbis; (6) Books; (7) TV or radio. As might be expected, parents and clergy were cited more often than other categories. However, for the purpose of the present analysis, we were especially interested in the relative influence of friends and family. It was our prediction that the influence of friends (item 1) would be greater among Protestants than among Catholics, and the influence of family (items 3 and 4) greater among Catholics than among Protestants. This prediction was supported by the data.

Finally, in the 1957 survey, Detroiters were asked whose political opinions had the greatest influence on how they voted: their close friends, family members, religious leaders, union leaders, business leaders, nationality group leaders, or party leaders. Roughly one-fifth of the sample cited either close friends or relatives. Of the white Protestants who did so, 30 percent cited friends, and 70 percent family members. For both Catholics and Negro Protestants, the comparable figures were 22 and 78 percent. For Jews the figures were 50 percent for each category.

By all these criteria it seems clear that Catholics are more highly involved in their kin group and value them somewhat more than white Protestants. Or, to look at the data the other way around, white Protestants seem more involved in, and favorably disposed toward, groups and social ties where the bond of kinship is absent. In the case of the Jewish and Negro Protestant groups the evidence is less clear, but seems to indicate that the Jews resemble the Catholics in this respect, while the Negro Protestants tend toward the white Protestant pattern.

Divorce and the immediate family

Not only are ties with the extended family weaker among white Protestants than among Catholics, this is also apparently true of ties with the immediate family. For example, Protestants, both white and Negro, were much more likely to have been divorced than either Catholics or Jews. The differences were not very great if we compared only persons currently divorced, since divorced Catholics are much less likely to remarry than Protestants. Fifty percent of the Catholics on our sample who had ever been divorced had not remarried, compared with 26 percent of the white Protestants, and 14 percent of the Negro Protestants. However, more important for our present discussion is the fact that of the 206 Catholics in our 1958 survey who had ever married, only 8 percent had ever been divorced, compared with 16 percent of the 247 White Protestants, and 22 percent of the 94 Negro Protestants. The Jewish families had the lowest divorce rate of all, with only 4 percent of the 26 Jewish respondents who had ever married reporting a divorce.

Although the interpretation of these figures is complicated somewhat by the differing views of the seriousness of divorce taken by the various religious groups, one point is clear. The immediate family relationship is less durable among Protestants than among Catholics, a fact undoubtedly associated with differing attitudes toward the immediate family. Also of significance is the fact that Catholics remarry after divorce so much less often than Protestants. This means that if Catholics derive any rewards at all from family life they are under greater pressure than Protestants to make their first marriage work. This too must have some effect on the pattern of social relationships within the nuclear family. One would expect Catholics (especially those who are better educated and strongly committed to their faith) to make vigorous efforts to achieve harmonious and rewarding relationships within the family, since the alternatives are so serious and so threatening.

Familialism and vertical mobility

Before leaving the subject of kin-group loyalty, it is necessary to reconsider the relationship between this type of loyalty and vertical mobility. If weak familial ties facilitate upward mobility, how then may we reconcile the strong familial ties of the Jewish group with their obvious economic success? This is a question which deserves an answer.

Unfortunately, there is no obvious answer to this problem. One might argue that Jews have advanced in the economic realm despite their strong family ties, and this may well be correct. However, it is not a very satisfying explanation—it seems too much of an effort to beg the question.

Happily, there is an alternative explana-tion which is more satisfying and also more intriguing. This explanation is based on the thesis that strong familial ties are only a liability for those who work for firms which the family group does not control. In contrast, such ties may prove an *asset* for those who work for family owned and operated firms. Under these conditions the demands of the work group and the family group are much more nearly co-ordinated and time spent with relatives may greatly advance the individual's economic interests. In view of the high incidence of family owned and operated businesses in the Jewish group, the strength of family ties, which may prove an occupational liability for most members of other groups, may prove a definite asset in the case of the Jews. Although the present study affords no systematic evidence to support this line of reasoning, the logic of the argument seems sound enough to indicate the need for further study of this question.

Conclusion

One of the most interesting aspects of Lenski's work is his strategy for determining the strength of loyalty of members of different religious faith to their kinship groups. Lenski was not satisfied with one indicator of family attachment; he sought evidence from various aspects of life, ranging from migration to divorce rates. The use of various criteria for kinship loyalty makes Lenski's argument much more convincing.

3 RELIGION AND SOCIAL STRUCTURE IN THE UNITED STATES

Religious attitudes and institutions in this country stem from the long Judeo-Christian tradition which has been the major religious influence on most of the Western world. But the development of religious institutions here has also been shaped by other social factors—by the structure of other institutions, such as the government, by cultural values such as toleration and optimism, and by modes of social organization, especially our pluralism and diversity. Therefore, much of our religious organization and many of our beliefs are uniquely American.

GENERAL CHARACTERISTICS OF RELIGION IN THE UNITED STATES

The most outstanding feature of American religious life is its variety. There are 236 different organized religious denominations in the United States at the present time.[19] This diversity, which reflects a basic cultural stress on pluralism, is due in large measure to two historical factors.

First, the United States was founded on the principle of separation between church and state. This principle is written into our Constitution and has been faithfully followed. Unlike England, Italy, and many other countries (including, at first, some of the original thirteen American colonies), America has no official religion. Moreover, the government does not intervene to support any

19. Lewis B. Whitman, ed., *Yearbook of American Churches, 1972* (New York: Council Press, 1972).

one religion or to suppress another. Some people feel that recent interpretations of the separation law go to extremes; for example, many communities have protested the ruling against prayers in public schools. Yet the rigor with which this provision of our political system has always been followed is largely responsible for the religious diversity we enjoy today.

Second, religious toleration was established early in the nation's history, even before it was guaranteed by the Bill of Rights. Although our country was in large part founded by religious dissenters, in most of the early settlements there was no religious tolerance; the dissenters wanted to make their own religion the official or dominant one. But due to many different factors each group was forced to tolerate the others—the new colonies came to include many different sects of Protestant dissenters; no one group could really dominate the others; and there was no existing central source of religious organization and power. By the late eighteenth century, this policy of tolerance had become such an essential part of the society that it was written into the Constitution. In the accompanying abridgment, Milton Yinger comments on the significance of religious pluralism in modern American society.

There are several other characteristics of religious beliefs and organization that are specific to our society. One is the underlying optimism of our religious beliefs. Religions which put a high premium on mortification of the flesh, feats of self-denial, and the need for complete self-sacrifice, are not common here. Likewise, American religious beliefs focus more clearly on the positive rewards of the religious life—security, peace of mind, spiritual peace, an afterlife—than on the penalties for religious weakness, such as damnation and hellfire. Peter Berger has suggested that this positive aspect of American religion is due in part to religious diversity. Each church is competing for members with others, and therefore its doctrines must be appealing. Berger expresses it in the language of the marketplace:

Again, putting it in a somewhat oversimplified way, the "product" of the religious institution must be "saleable." It is one thing to threaten a captive audience of medieval peasants with hellfire and damnation. It is quite another thing to market a doctrine of this sort in a population of suburban commuters and housewives. In other words, the "needs" of the consumer clientele must now be taken into consideration.[20]

One other characteristic of American religion which should be mentioned is its freedom from anticlericalism—the dislike, distrust, and suspicion of priests and ministers which is prevalent in many other countries. Anticlericalism is especially marked in countries where the church was once a part of the feudal system, owning much of the land and other valuable property. In such instances, members of the clergy constituted a wealthy and oppressive upper class, thus earning the dislike of the common people. This has been much less true in America.

Membership in religious groups

In 1971, there was reported to be a total membership of 131 million persons in the 236 religious bodies in the United States.[21] This amounted to about 63.2 percent of the total population, and may be compared with a membership percentage of 16 percent in 1850, 36 percent in 1900, and 49 percent in 1940. Thus there has been a notable increase in church membership in this country, and many experts point to an accelerated "revival" of religious interest following World War II. This relatively sharp postwar increase in church membership has now leveled off.

Experts disagree on the meaning of this growth in religious affiliation. There is no convincing evidence of a revival of supernatural beliefs or the infusion of religious values into our daily lives. Much of the increased religious activity would seem secular in nature to the religious person of a few years back, though the rapid growth of such groups as the Pentecostal sects seems to indicate a parallel growth of a more intense and supernatural form of religion. There has very recently been a rising interest in religion on the part of young people, but this has almost always been channeled outside the established churches. One expression of this interest is the formation of various communal religious groups. And despite increased religious activity, there has been a long-term trend of declining ratios of clergymen to total population and declining per capita financial support of churches.

What are the largest organizations in America? If we divide all churches into the three "faiths"—Protestant, Catholic, and Jews—then Protestants are the most numerous, with approximately 70 million believers. However, if we consider the figures by the specific denomination, then Roman Catholics are far in the lead, with almost 48 million members. The chart in the accompanying figure gives membership figures for some major denominations. Several interest-

20. Peter Berger, "Religious Institutions," in *Sociology: An Introduction,* ed. Neil J. Smelser (New York: John Wiley, 1967), p. 375.

21. Lewis B. Whitman, *Yearbook of American Churches, 1971.*

RELIGIOUS AFFILIATION
IN THE UNITED STATES

Roman Catholic	48,215,000
Baptist	25,001,000
Methodist	11,221,000
Lutheran	8,574,000
Jewish	5,870,000
Episcopalian	3,286,000
Mormon	2,037,000
United Church of Christ	1,961,000
Greek Orthodox	1,950,000
African Methodist Episcopal	1,166,000
Assembly of God	1,065,000
Presbyterian	958,000
Seventh-Day Adventist	420,000
Jehovah's Witnesses	389,000
Salvation Army	327,000
Unitarian	265,000
Black Muslim	250,000
Pentecostal Church of God	115,000
Mennonite	89,000

SOURCE: *Yearbook of American Churches, 1972.*

Roman Catholics are by far the largest unified religious body in the United States. The next groups on the list—Baptists, Methodists, and Lutherans—are divided among several different church organizations. The figure for Jewish affiliation represents the total ethnic group population rather than actual church membership.

ing points can be noted. We can see that the Roman Catholics are slightly more than twice as numerous as the next largest group, the Baptists. When we take into account that the figure for Baptist membership actually includes at least fifteen different denominational organizations—the American Baptist Association, the Conservative Baptist Association of America, the Free Will Baptists, the General Baptists, and so on—then we realize that Roman Catholics are far and away the largest single unified religious group in the country. The next largest single group is the United Methodist church, with 11 million members (in our chart, they have been combined with another Methodist organization), so that it is less than one-fourth as large as the Roman Catholic church. The influence and dominance of the Episcopal church seems

especially remarkable in view of its relatively small number of members. Not everyone is aware of the size of the Greek Orthodox church, which must be classed as one of our larger religious groups. When one adds to this figure the members of the Bulgarian, Armenian, Syrian, Serbian, and Russian branches of that church, the total number of Eastern Orthodox believers comes to well over 3 million, which makes them a sizable influence on American religious life.

Of course, figures on the membership of American churches are not always reliable. There is a tendency for the churches themselves to exaggerate their membership to some degree for this competitive reporting. A further difficulty arises from the fact that not all denominations even try to keep careful records of membership. Also, they may have varying criteria for membership. Some churches count only active members of a congregation, but others count all those who have been baptized or confirmed. When the question, "What is your religion?" is asked, there is also a problem of different definitions of religious affiliations. To some people affiliation means total involvement and participation in the church organization; for others, affiliation means a personal commitment to the beliefs of a religion without any involvement in the organization of the church; and some respondents may identify their religion as the one practiced by parents or relatives or the ethnic group to which they belong. For example, many people who identify themselves as belonging to the Jewish religion actually mean to convey only an ethnic identity and not an active religious belief.

The Census Bureau has tried several experiments to develop reliable figures in this area. Although the question of religious affiliation has never been included in a regular census, it has been asked in at least one large survey, that made by the Bureau in 1957. People were asked "What is your religion?" and 96 percent reported some religious affiliation. However, these figures, which are considered among the most reliable we have, still tell us nothing about the degree of involvement or commitment which lay behind the answer. The uncertainty in turn adds to the difficulty of predicting trends of growth.

However, some basic trends can still be identified. As mentioned earlier, the fastest growing denomination in America today is the Pentecostal church. The Black Muslims have also shown a phenomenal rate of growth; they have only been in existence for about forty years, and probably had a membership of less than 50,000 until the sixties, when their membership expanded rapidly. Most of the older established denominations are growing very slowly, if at all, and in fact are constantly concerned with recruitment of new members.

Several other interesting statistics relating to religious affiliation in American life bear mentioning. Statistics show that slightly more women than men are church members; 5 percent of the males reported no religion as compared with only 2 percent of females in a Gallup survey. There are regional differences in religious affiliation, with Jews, Catholics, Episcopalians, and Unitarians, for example, being heavily concentrated in the Northeast. Methodists and Baptists are concentrated in the South and Midwest. Jews and Catholics are more likely to be urban residents, while the greatest majority of rural residents are Protestants. Fertility rates are highest among Baptists, even higher than among Catholics, whose beliefs prohibit artificial birth control. This high rate is no doubt due in part to the fact that Baptists often live in rural areas, where large families are more common, and in part because about half of all Baptists are blacks, an ethnic group with a high fertility rate. The lower rate for Catholics may be because they are a largely urbanized group, and that factor counterbalances the dictates of their beliefs. The lowest birthrates are for Jews and Presbyterians, two groups which rank high in class level.

RELIGION AND SOCIAL STRATIFICATION

The institution of religion almost always has a strong influence on the larger social structure of the society which, in turn, sustains and shapes it. This is evident in the relationship between religion and social stratification. This connection has been investigated in some detail by sociologists, and a few of the more significant findings will be reported in this section.

The status of religious denominations

A society may have dozens of religious groups within it, but one particular religion normally has the highest status, and the others are ranked in orderly fashion below it. In Great Britain the highest status religious group is the Church of England; in India it is the Brahmin caste of Hinduism; in America it is the Episcopal church. Generally, the religion with the highest status is the one to which the leaders and the upper stratum of the society, the elite, belong. The relationship between the elite and the status of religion flows two ways. People who belong to lower status religions may be denied the necessary opportunities to advance to the elite, whereas on the other hand, certain religions may have high status because of their connection with the elite. If membership in the elite changes, the highest status religion may change. A demonstration of this can be seen in the varying status ranks of Catholicism and Protestantism during the sixteenth and seventeenth centuries in England. When Catholic monarchs were on the throne, Catholicism was the highest status religion, but it lost status when the Church of England became the religious group to which English monarchs must belong.

Religion and occupation

There appears to be no direct connection between religious affiliation and any specific occupation (except, of course, for religious vocations) but research has shown several more generalized links between employment and religion in the United States. Both Jews and Protestants have, on the average, greater career success than do Catholics. Protestants have a greater degree of upward mobility in occupational status than Catholics, in spite of the fact that Catholics are more likely to live in cities, a circumstance which normally favors upward mobility.[22] According to Gerhard Lenski:

When White Protestants were compared with Catholics who began life at the same point in the class system, the former rose to (or stayed in) the ranks of the upper-middle class more often than the latter. At the opposite extreme, Catholics wound up in the lower half of the working class more often than Protestants three out of four times. Differences were especially marked among sons of middle-class men and farmers.

Unfortunately, there were not enough Jewish males in our sample to permit analysis, but the heavy concentration of Jews in the middle class, and even the upper-middle class, found in all recent studies, indicates their rapid rise in [the] economic system. Only a generation or two ago a substantial proportion of American Jews were manual workers.[23]

Lenski ranks Jews as the most occupationally successful group, followed by white Protestants, Catholics, and then black Protestants. He also found that Jews were more likely than any other group to be self-employed.

A relationship between religion and occupational success, which was originally hypothesized by Max Weber in his book *The Protestant Ethic,*[24] has been the subject of much study and controversy. Weber sug-

gested that because the Protestants believe in hard work as valuable and as personally fulfilling, Protestants have developed a favorable attitude toward work, and have thus achieved greater worldly success. Lenski's study tended to support Weber's theory. He gave various men a list of values related to work and asked them to rank the importance of these values in their jobs. A positive correlation was found between occupational success (especially in terms of upward mobility) and the choice of a value which was expressed as follows: "The work is important and gives a feeling of accomplishment." This value is a very simplified statement of Weber's classic definition of the Protestant ethic. Lenski found that 52 percent of white Protestants put this value at the top of his list, compared with 48 percent of Jews and 44 percent of Catholics, and roughly this same relationship held even when comparing persons of the same social class level.

Religion and income

Statistics show a clear link between religious affiliation and income level in America. In a recent study it was found that 57 percent of Episcopalians and 56 percent of Jews had incomes greater than $10,000, whereas only 24 percent of Baptists fell into this income group.[25] Although every religion includes people from all income levels, the overall membership of various denominations reveals differences of average income levels.

Why are Episcopalians and Jews more successful financially than Baptists and Jehovah's Witnesses? Some of the answers may lie, as Max Weber suggested, in the acceptance or rejection of the Protestant ethic which underlies the whole capitalistic structure of our economy. Other factors enter into the picture. The Episcopal church is an offshoot of the Church of England; many of its members are of English ancestry, and people of English extraction belong to

22. Thomas G. Fox and S. M. Miller, "Economic, Political and Social Determinants of Mobility: An International Cross-sectional Analysis," *Acta Sociologica* 9 (1965):76–93.

23. Gerhard Lenski, *The Religious Factor* (New York: Doubleday, Anchor, 1963), pp. 84–85.

24. Max Weber, *The Protestant Ethic and the Spirit of Capitalism* (London: George Allen and Unwin, 1930).

25. *Gallup Opinion Index* (1970).

INCOME LEVELS OF RELIGIOUS DENOMINATIONS IN THE UNITED STATES

	$7,000+	$5,000-6,999	$3,000-4,999	Under $3,000	Undesignated
Jewish	69	14	9	6	2
Catholic	47	23	16	12	2
Protestant	38	21	19	20	2
Episcopalian	55	20	14	9	2
Presbyterian	50	19	17	12	2
Lutheran	49	20	15	15	1
Methodist	42	21	17	18	2
Baptist	26	21	23	28	2

SOURCE: *The Gallup Opinion Index*, No. 44, (Princeton, N.J.: Gallup International, February, 1969), pp. 22 and 32.

the highest status ethnic group in America. People of Italian, Irish, and middle European descent, who are often Catholic, are handicapped by a lower ethnic status, and sometimes also by a lack of knowledge of the language. Difference in opportunity due to ethnic group also accounts for Lenski's findings that white Protestants are considerably more successful economically than black Protestants.

Another possible factor in the financial success of certain religious groups is the regional strength of the various denominations. Most Episcopalians live in the northeastern United States, where income levels are generally high. The Baptists are most numerous in the South and the Midwest, where income levels are lower. The Baptist church also has many members in rural communities, whereas Episcopalians are more likely to live in cities—and city residents have higher income levels than country people.

Religion and education

Religious affiliation is also closely related to educational motivation and level of achievement. There is a measurable difference in the average educational level reached by members of different religious groups. The statistics in this area roughly correspond to those regarding income level because of the close association between education and income which we have noted before. A young person has the best chance of going to college if his parents are Jews or Episcopalians,

or if they subscribe to no religion. The lowest educational levels of major denominations are found among the Baptists.[26]

Lenski turned up another significant finding in regard to education and religion, and that is a large difference in the dropout rate among students of various religions. In his study, only 29 percent of Jews had ended their education by dropping out of the highest grade level they had achieved, rather than finishing the year out. For Protestants, the figure was 39 percent, and for Catholics it was 52 percent. As Lenski points out, this difference is certainly significant, and it may be another clue to the greater financial and occupational success of Jews and Protestants. They could be more highly motivated for achievement in job or school. Another explanation, which Lenski advances, is that Catholics are likely to come from larger families, which tend to have more pressing financial burdens and a crowded home situation which may inhibit studying.

Another link between religion and education is the existence of schools run by religious groups. Both Catholics and Jews in most American cities have the option of going to schools operated by their religious institutions rather than by the city government. Slightly more than one-third of all Catholic children go to Catholic schools; the proportion of Jewish children attending Yeshiva schools is not so high but is still significant. This difference of educational

26. *Gallup Opinion Index* (1970).

RANK ORDER OF
MAJOR RELIGIOUS GROUPS IN THE UNITED STATES
BY INCOME AND EDUCATION

Income	Education
Jewish	Episcopal
Episcopal	Jewish
Presbyterian	Presbyterian
Catholic	Methodist
Lutheran	Other Protestants
No religion	Lutheran
Methodist	No religion
Baptist	Catholic
Other Protestants	Baptist

SOURCE: Donald J. Bogue, *Population of the United States* (New York: Free Press of Glencoe, 1959).

The same three groups—Jews, Episcopalians, and Presbyterians— lead in both income level and educational attainment. This helps to account for the high social status associated with membership in these denominations.

background may also account for many other stratification differences among religious groups. Certainly parochial schools and yeshivas impart certain special norms and values, pertaining to religious beliefs, to the children attending them, and this difference may influence social performance in many areas. There is also a possibility, supported by the research of educational specialists, that these religious schools put more stress on socialization to religious values and less on the teaching of vocational skills than do the public schools, so that their students may be handicapped in the competition for employment opportunities.[27]

Religion and social class

Since religion is so closely linked with status and with levels of education and income, it follows that there must be a correlation between religious affiliation and social class in general. In the abridgment in topic 3 of chapter 7, Harold Hodges specified some pairings

of social classes and certain religions. In the accompanying chart showing rank order of religious groups by income and education other such correlations between religion and social class are pointed out.

Perhaps an even more significant class difference concerns religious *participation* rather than membership. Both those of very low social class and those of very high social class tend to be uninvolved with religion as measured by church attendance. The reasons for this are not altogether clear. Some sociologists suggest that people of high social class are not attracted to the Christian religion because it is based on a premise of total equality among all members.[28] A more commonly suggested reason for upper-class lack of involvement is that the upper-class person is less in need of the social benefits of the institution of religion—religion simply serves less of a social function in his life because he has so many other alternatives.

The nonparticipation of the lowest classes

27. Will Herberg, *Protestant, Catholic, Jew*, p. 233.

28. Thomas F. O'Dea, *The Sociology of Religion*, p. 55.

may be traced to an attitude of suspicion toward all influences and agencies outside the home and the immediate family. Hodges suggests that it is also due to a feeling of helplessness or apathy that makes it seem useless to try taking any positive actions toward the outside world. The lower classes tend not to participate in *any* organized groups outside the home.

The majority of religious participants come from the upper-lower and the lower-middle classes. Here both involvement with the church and belief in its doctrines are the strongest. The upper-middle class also contains a high proportion of church members, but studies have indicated that for those people religion is often more a matter of formality and of social desirability, rather than emotional conviction.[29]

Religious beliefs and stratification

An interesting dilemma arises when we pose religious tenets and beliefs against the reality of social stratification. The Christian religion has as one of its central tenets the absolute equality of all those who accept its beliefs. The Old Testament contains many stories about the temptations inherent in assuming high worldly status and the conflict of high status with religious conviction and experience. The New Testament goes even further, enjoining believers to give up both power and wealth. Taking a vow of poverty is specified as a way to display religious faith and commitment, and also to increase it. The Christian church was conceived as a classless institution.

29. See Charles Y. Glock and Rodney Stark, *Religion and Society in Tension* (Chicago: Rand McNally, 1965).

But as we have seen, in reality it is not classless. Religious institutions contain many internal class distinctions, and at the same time they both initiate and perpetuate class distinctions and social stratification in our society. Why does this happen, when it is in direct conflict with religious beliefs? The answer lies in the fact that stratification, as we noted in chapter 7, is a universal and deeply ingrained social pattern. For example, every religious group believes in its own rightness and value and attempts to make itself stable and continuous. Stability and continuity come from institutionalization, which necessarily involves much internal stratification, such as the establishment of a hierarchy of administrative officials, and the successful adaptation to the values and social patterns of the larger society, which is always highly stratified.

The significance of this dilemma can be seen in the history of the Christian church. It began as a relatively classless sect and eventually became a stratified institution, the Catholic church. Protestantism was inspired by religious beliefs which were in part a reaction to this stratification; it, too, was at first a relatively classless sect. In time it also became institutionalized, and then the inevitable reaction led to the formation of other sects, such as Calvinism and Methodism. The process continues today.

So we must view religion as having a very mixed function in regard to stratification—in addition to supporting the existing system of stratification in a society, its ideology and beliefs sometimes serve as a threat to the entrenched distinctions between classes and statuses.

J. MILTON YINGER
Religious Pluralism in America

Abridged with permission of the Macmillan Company from *Sociology Looks at Religion* by J. Milton Yinger. © J. Milton Yinger, 1963.

Introduction

Milton Yinger is a leading scholar in the area of the sociology of religion; he published several books on the subject of religion in the 1960s. This selection comes from Sociology Looks at Religion. *It provides an excellent summary of the consequences of religious pluralism in our society, some of which are touched on in this topic. Yinger also suggests possible dysfunctions of our present approach to pluralism and postulates an alternative approach that might be preferable. Although he is dealing here specifically with* religious *pluralism, many of the points he raises are equally applicable to ethnic and racial diversity in our society.*

What are the consequences for the total society of continued identification with separate ethnic-religious groups? This leads us into one of the central questions of contemporary sociology: How does a complex, urban society manage to exist as a healthy system; how does it establish and maintain a sufficient level of integration and consensus to maintain order and carry through the necessary accommodations among its heterogeneous peoples? It cannot rely on what Durkheim called the "mechanical solidarity" of a relatively undifferentiated community; and a free society resists an integration that is imposed by coercion. Does it not, therefore, at the least require consensus on its fundamental values, on religion, which is often thought to be the source of integration at the deepest level? Can it afford to be indifferent to the continued vitality of ethnic-religious groups which divide a society in important ways?

On this question we are confronted again by a paradox: the integration of a complex and heterogeneous society requires both basic commonalities and freedom to be different. These are readily granted as important values of American society: but they are not always recognized as functionally necessary patterns for a heterogeneous, changing society. There are, of course, a great many common elements in Protestantism, Catholicism, and Judaism — elements that have been increased in the last several decades. The classicist in each tradition insists that the reduction of distinctiveness is a loss, and from his point of view it is. His point of view, however, is unlikely to prevail. The reduction, particularly, of the parochial, the exclusive, the claims of absolute truth seems inevitable in our kind of society. It is dysfunctional in a mobile and diverse society to have a group of religions, each of which claims some kind of ultimate superiority; the elements of Protestantism, Catholicism, and Judaism which sponsor such claims are disruptive. Claims by Protestants that the Bible is the final and literal truth, by Catholics that theirs is the only true church, by Jews that they are the chosen people can only exacerbate the divisions of a society. (The believer will say, "But these are the truth." Such a view is never disproved: but it may become a meaningless claim to another generation.)

In a diverse society in which absolute religious claims are asserted, three things may happen: (1) the society will be split seriously; or (2) the differences will be reduced; or (3) the traditional religious assertions will lose force, while a new unifying system of beliefs and actions will be developed, often around national and patriotic themes. All three of these things are happening in the United States, the last being perhaps the strongest tendency. "The American Way of Life" becomes the operative faith to a substantial degree. Those who wish to relate the national faith to one of the traditional religions are free to do so, provided they do not challenge any of the basic premises of Americanism. Emphasis on religious variation thus tends to shift the burden of integration to other parts of the social system — particularly to the sentiments of nationalism. If this interpretation is correct, universalistic religions may face self-defeating limits to the insistence upon their differences.

The other side of the paradox also requires examination. On the contemporary scene, in fact, the need for a common core of values is doubtless more readily granted than the need for diversity. The latter, therefore, requires special emphasis. The integration of any society, however homogeneous it may seem to an outsider, is pluralistic; it requires the harmonizing of different individual roles and different groups. The vast complexity of a modern society extends pluralism to an extraordinary degree. The constant interaction of people with different national and religious backgrounds, with different occupations and different levels of education, makes mutual tolerance, as the minimum degree of accommodation, a vital necessity. A century ago, John Stuart Mill observed that a diversity of religious views was essential to a free, heterogeneous society, to minimize any authoritarian tendencies in the church and to maximize the autonomy of religious influences from other centers of power. Contemporary political sociology, drawing on a long tradition, has documented the importance of a strong network of private associations, standing between the individual and the state, if democracy is to thrive. A vigorous group of partially competing religious organizations may be among the most significant of such associations. Their importance to the members lends them strength to counter the opposite dangers of lack of meaningful attachments in a changing world on one hand and the threat of domination by the state on the other. The fact that our major religious divisions cut across such other lines as class, occupation, and race, helps greatly to prevent the cumulative reinforcement of dividing forces that can split a society into warring segments.

The point of view just expressed is, I believe, widely supported. Yet it leaves problems unexplored that deserve our attention. I would like to conclude therefore, by raising some questions that are usually kept muted. Is the continuing separation of American religious subcom-munities—to the degree that this exists—a good thing? Is pluralism the best arrangement for a complex society? Are signs of the weakening of the internal cohesion of the traditional groups, intermarriage particularly, unhappy indicators of a loss of strength and fervor? These are, of course, value questions; and in the paragraphs that follow, I will take a frankly evaluative position.

For the most part, those who take a liberal view of American society support religious pluralism. Distinctive religious traditions, all free to develop in their own ways, are essential to the religious quest and to a democratic society. To the individual they represent freedom and yet a significant tie to his own heritage. To the society they represent the kind of competing points of view that help to maintain flexibility, because there is no official religion to give undue sanctity to our imperfect human institutions.

There is some conservative challenge to this view. Some Catholics believe that a genuinely healthy society and full individual salvation are possible only when all men have returned to the one true church. Most Catholics who take this view have learned patience in the American scene, indicating a kind of qualified acceptance of pluralism. Some Protestants look upon Catholics and Jews as at least slightly un-American and wonder why they are so recalcitrant in becoming Methodists or Baptists or Presbyterians.

Now I am much closer to the liberal than to the conservative view. I am not, however, entirely happy with pluralism as it is usually described and would like to comment on some of its possible dysfunctions. I think one can argue that emphasis on distinctive pluralistic traditions implies a measure of religious stagnation and isolation. The best way to justify continued separation is to point to different origins, histories, and traditions. To some degree, American religious groups are like our Indian tribes:

they lose their liberals to the "secular" world, because the emphasis on preservation of distinctiveness is inherently backward-looking. The churches "boom" in this day of upsetting change and continual crisis; but the messages they preach are tuned to an earlier time, so the people are "secular-ized"—indifferent and unbelieving and religiously ill informed—even while they participate in the "boom."

Is there any way out of this dilemma? I would like to suggest a possible road by introducing the concept of "contemporary pluralism," in contrast to the more familiar "historical pluralism." The latter might be briefly defined in these terms: Preservation of ties to the religious community (and ethnic group—for some of the same questions arise in this area) of one's parents is good; respect its traditions: a free society must encourage this in the name of tolerance, flexibility, and individual freedom. I would argue that there is more than a little nostalgia and sentimentality connected with this idea. These qualities are often heightened by those professionally identified with a group, whose preservation as a distinctive entity is necessary for their professional existence. They are also heightened by persons working in the field of intergroup relations and other liberally minded individuals who, again with generous motives, support and encourage group-identity as a way of developing mutual respect and tolerance.

To continue to promote religious and ethnic separation in a new context, when the tie to the earlier situation has been broken, may be unwise. Perhaps the necessary pluralism today is not a process whereby

each of us binds his children to the ancestral religious groups, while teaching them to respect the rights of others who are different. Perhaps we need to open up interaction and choice among several contemporary efforts to struggle with the human condition, each a hybrid, each a product of religious contact and growth.

We cannot cling to the culturally and religiously integrated patterns of the past. If we think we are doing so, we hide the loss of their vitality and the emergence of competing systems of value (nationalism as a religion, for example). The inherent rigidity of historical pluralism obscures the new problems faced by men today, for which we need vital contemporary religious thought and action.

Conclusion

Yinger argues that the highly valued tradition of religious pluralism in America is an important factor in religion's loss of influence in American life. Religious groups have been too separated and too competitive with one another. He feels that if religion is to play a more important role in our society, it must move away from its past diversity, with each group claiming to be the best. Yinger is sensitive, however, to the positive features of religious pluralism, and feels that much of it can be preserved at the same time that the various religions unite around a new set of contemporary orientations and values. Religion is thus faced with one of the basic dilemmas of all social institutions: how to preserve the best of the past while adapting to changing conditions.

4 RELIGION AND SOCIAL CHANGE

So far this chapter has focused primarily on the important way that religion functions to support and reinforce the organizational patterns of a society. This is probably the most important function of religion; certainly it is the one most analyzed by sociologists. But we should not lose sight of the fact that religion need not always support the status quo. Religion may also stimulate conflict and open the door to social change. A church or sect can gather together a large number of society's discontented citizens and give them a community of interest, the power of organized numbers, and a ready-made base from which to alter the prevailing social structure. This was true in the Protestant Reformation, one of the most far-reaching changes in the modern world.

The institution of religion itself, and its functions in society, have been modified as religion has adapted to its increasing separation, over the last few hundred years, from a large area of social and cultural life — a process known as secularization. In this topic we will discuss both change within religion, and religion's role in social change.

PROTESTANTISM AND THE RISE OF CAPITALISM

During the sixteenth century the entire character of European society was altered. The emergence of a new religion, Protestantism, was a major factor in bringing about this change. Two aspects of the Protestant movement, which affected every sphere of European life, had an especially great impact. First was the ability of the movement to bring together diverse forces in society. Second was the support the Protestant ethic gave to the newly developing capitalistic system.

In 1500 all the countries in Europe still had basically feudal social systems. The economy was agricultural and the barter system was common (money was scarcely used in many areas). Only a small percentage of the population lived in cities and people rarely moved. There was no middle class and almost no social mobility.

The entire Western world was Catholic, and the Catholic church did much to bolster the social system. Its own organization was a close parallel to the feudal type of organization found in the secular world. The church had large agricultural land holdings, profitably leased to tenant farmers. Church doctrine supported class distinctions, and church officials, themselves members of the upper classes, saw to it that the doctrines were rigorously applied. Papal edicts and threats of excommunication helped more than one king defend his throne against rebellion and uprising.

By 1600, much had changed. An economy of trade and manufacture was growing steadily; and with it, cities began to expand and to occupy a significant position in national affairs. The size of the middle class was greatly increasing as more and more opportunities occurred for making a business profit without a large capital investment in land. Charles I of England found that, unlike his predecessors, he could not save his throne, or his life, by relying on the support of the Catholic church. The feudal system was breaking up.

An important reason for the disintegration of feudalism was the rise of Protestantism. Protestantism began as a doctrinal dispute among a group of clergymen in a remote part of Germany. As it grew, it began to attract all those who were unhappy under the existing social system. Social dissenters from the city and from the country, from the lower and upper classes and from the capitalistic and feudal segments of Europe were united by their Protestant religious beliefs. Protestantism gave them a single, emotionally charged cause around which they could rally their forces. Changes might have come anyway, without the help of the Protestant movement, but they would have come much more slowly, since those who desired change were scattered and divided among a number of different segments of the public. It was the cohesive power of religion that brought all these people together and increased their ability to influence the restructuring of society.

Protestantism was an especially effective agent of change in the economic sphere of European society. In fact, the rapid emergence of a capitalistic system in Western Europe from the feudal system was closely associated with the growth of Protestantism. In his famous study *The Protestant Ethic and the Spirit of Capitalism*,[30] Max Weber pointed out the close connection between the values of the Protestant religion and those necessary for success in a capitalistic industrial system. Belief in the value of hard work as a kind of salvation exercise, belief that worldly prosperity is a mark of God's favor, belief in the exercise of free will—all of these religious attitudes of Protestantism helped foster the rise of an economic system demanding hard work, thrift, initiative, competition, and acquisition.

Weber's concentration on the role of Protestantism in the growth of capitalism has attracted both support and criticism. Some critics have felt that religious ideas were not transferable to other activities, that theology could not influence market behavior. Others have stated that it was actually the growth of capitalism which encouraged the emergence of Protestantism, that the power of the new capitalists was so great that they could influence the establishment of a church which supported their financial activities.

Actually, many forces were at work. No doubt the beliefs of Protestantism did have some positive effect on the emergence of capitalism; *The Protestant Ethic* presents a convincing argument. It also seems to be true (Weber himself, in fact, believed that it was) that the growth of capitalism supported and encouraged the growth of Protestantism. Thus, a new religious system and new economic system emerged at approximately the same time. Each supported the other's needs, and each encouraged the other's growth.

RELIGION IN MODERN SOCIETY: SECULARIZATION

Like all social institutions, religion has had to adapt itself to the changing conditions of the modern world. In the view of many scholars, religion's adaptation has been a long, continuous decline in influence as compared to other institutions, especially the state or central political institutions. Peter Berger, in supporting this view, suggests that the only important sphere of influence religion retains today is within the family — that is, on a personal level.[31] Religion has been separated from government, from education, and from the marketplace. As Milton Yinger points out, religion is no longer the primary cohesive force in society. This is still certainly an important function of religion, as we noted in topic 2, but today religion is being somewhat displaced in this area by nationalism and other secular and political ideologies.

Thus a large area of social and cultural life —beliefs and practices, basic values, patterns of behavior, and institutional functions—have become increasingly separated from religious or spiritual influences. This is the trend known as *secularization*. (The opposite of secularization would be sacralization, when social and cultural life would become more religious and sacred in character.)

Not only has religion declined as an institution, but religious norms and values have lost much of their force in the modern world.

30. Max Weber, *The Protestant Ethic*.

31. Peter Berger, "Religious Institutions," p. 373.

Located in a commercial district of the city, next to stores selling groceries and hardware, this storefront church makes religion a part of everyday life rather than an isolated experience. *(Henry Monroe, DPI)*

Many people have noted that the supernatural quality has been fading from religious observances; that important days in religious calendars are no longer holy days, but simply holidays; that the symbols of heaven and hell, sin and salvation, have lost much of their importance to many people; and that moral rules concerning interfaith marriage, divorce, and sexual activities, originally enforced by religious sanctions, have been relaxed. Religious belief in general has become more a matter of personal, rather than social, convictions.

The religious organizations themselves have changed quite markedly. Some have become bureaucratic organizations, with large national staffs, many specialized departments, and efficient procedures for record keeping and financial management. At the same time, a growing interest in conducting secular, practical affairs has developed within or through the church. Many graduates of theology schools pursue careers side by side with people trained in other professions, such as social work, teaching, city planning, and public administration. In such ways as these, the distinction between secular and sacred has become increasingly blurred.

These changes in religious organizations have done much to keep the church an active institution in American life. Over the last one hundred years there has been a great increase in that proportion of our population which belongs to and is involved with organized religion. In a 1966 survey, 44 percent of the sample questioned reported having attended at least one religious service during the week before the interview.[32] This figure has remained about the same in the annual surveys done since then. But as we noted in the section on church membership, this church activity is often quite secular in character. Religious practice and belief is commonly recommended for its practical advantages — mental health, better family life, or national loyalty. Studies have indicated that churches, especially in middle-class suburban areas, often serve as voluntary associations which meet social as much as religious needs.

There is no convincing evidence that the high amount of church activity represents a widespread revival of supernatural beliefs, or a resurgence of a religious way of life. On the contrary, as Peter Berger has noted: "If commentators on the contemporary situation of religion agree about anything, it is that the supernatural has departed from the modern world."[33] Indeed, the most important aspect of secularization may be the end of belief in

32. Lewis B. Whitman, *Yearbook of American Churches, 1968,* p. 228.

33. Peter Berger, *A Rumor of Angels* (New York: Doubleday, 1969), p. 1.

In recent decades the distinction between secular and sacred has become increasingly blurred. In an effort to make religion a more vital and relevant force in modern life, many religious groups have gone out into the community to establish family, youth, and counseling centers that are not necessarily committed to a particular denomination but are dedicated to the principles of brotherhood and peace. In a drug prevention center such as this, there is little effort to teach formal Christian dogma. Rather, members are encouraged to rebuild their personal lives around broad religious principles. *(Bethel Agency)*

a transcendental being and the removal of supernatural sanctions from secular beliefs and institutions. But we do not know how extensive or enduring the cultural effects of this decline of the supernatural will be, or if this decline will continue.

Like most social trends, secularization is accompanied by trends acting in opposition to it. One such countertrend in American life is the vitality of religious sects, such as the Pentecostal groups, among the working and lower-middle classes. Another is the growing interest in religious ideas among college students, whose enrollment in religion courses has been rising after years of decline. A third force is the hippies' attempts to create life styles based on supernatural values and beliefs, especially those of the Eastern religions.

Whether trends like these will grow to such proportions that secularization will be slowed down, or even reversed, remains to be seen. The sociologist Robin Williams has noted that: "Neither mass religiosity nor complete secularism appear to be permanent historical possibilities."[34] There is good reason to believe that religion will never be at the center of modern societies, as it has been in almost every past society. But religion may become more important to modern man in lending emotional support, giving a deeper meaning to his values, and helping him to express ultimate concern and commitment.

34. Robin Williams, *American Society* (New York: Random House, 1960), p. 383.

SUMMARY

Religion is present in all human societies and is a socially recognized way of entering into a relationship with the aspects of reality that are nonrational or nonempirical. It is expressed and institutionalized in a variety of ways. The world's three major religions — Christianity, Islam, and Hinduism — are all monotheistic, have church organizations, rituals of worship, sacred writings containing principles and beliefs, and some form of priesthood. Other major religions do not center on a god figure, but rather on some ethical, moral, or philosophical principle. Many preliterate societies practice *totemism,* the worship of an animal as both a god and an ancestor. The totem selected is usually something particularly important to the culture, and totemic ritual normally involves some form of communion with the animal. Totemism generally provides the basis for some type of clan organization which may govern an individual's place of residence, occupation, and choice of marriage partner.

Whatever the form of expression, religion, like magic, provides a nonscientific system for dealing with transcendental, supernatural reality. Unlike magic, however, the goals of religion are spiritual rather than concrete, specific, and immediate. In primitive societies magic and religion cannot usually be separated into two institutions. Religion is similar to science in that it tries to furnish explanations of the unknown, but science is concerned only with the natural world and uses methods which are empirical and quantifiable.

All forms of religion have four basic elements in common. 1) Sociologists theorize that religion began within the family or clan with the *creation of the sacred,* something set apart from everyday life and associated with special power or force. 2) The second step was probably the *establishment of ritual* or patterns of behavior toward the sacred. Ritual brings believers together in a group, and by evoking collective behavior, helps the individual to lose his sense of isolation. 3) As sanctity and rituals were deemphasized, a *system of beliefs* became dominant. 4) The *organization of believers* became necessary to assure the continuity and effectiveness of religious experience.

Religion helps to meet a variety of basic psychological needs in man. It may provide a sense of support and consolation which assists man in overcoming his fear of the unknown; it may provide human existence with meaning and purpose; it may provide an opportunity to transcend the "self" and the everyday reality of the present; or it may strengthen an individual's sense of identity and help to ease transitions through the stages of life. Religion also serves certain social functions. As a cohesive force, it helps to maintain the established social system. As a divisive force, it may help to effect social change, a process exemplified in the Protestant Reformation.

Although religion began as an integral part of other social institutions, first the family and then the tribe or village, it has gradually become a separate institution with its own specialized organization. Development of a specialized hierarchy of full-time religious leaders was probably followed by separation of sacred and secular activities. Subsequently, participation in religious activity became voluntary. Sociologists distinguish two forms of contemporary religious organizations. A *church* is a stable and institutionalized organization with an established clerical hierarchy and a fixed body of dogma. A *sect* is less formally organized and religious responsibilities may be handled by the members themselves rather than by specialized officials. Because absolute commitment to sect beliefs are emphasized, the sect may conflict with other social institutions. Sects are usually a more revolutionary force than are churches, which normally try to cooperate with and support the established social order.

Religion acts as a force for social cohesion by giving a society's norms and values moral support, by emphasizing the basic similarity among all human beings, by reconciling individuals to the hardships and inequities of society, by uniting the community through ritual worship, and by providing stability and support for individuals during times of social upheaval. Religion functions as an agent of social control by threatening deviants with supernatural punishment; it also minimizes social stress by providing deviants with a means of atonement and reintegration into society. Religion also stimulates the expression and interpretation of society's values and beliefs through literature and the visual arts. Finally, religion functions to counterbalance the forces of depersonalization in society by stressing the importance of primary relationships and the need for communication in all human relationships. Many religions are structured around the image of the family; deities may be represented as father or mother figures. Through its connection with sacred beings, the family has become almost a sacred institution. Religious beliefs often govern marriage and family patterns.

The separation of church and state and the

high degree of religious toleration permitted have encouraged development of a wide variety of denominations in the United States. The Protestant, Catholic, and Jewish faiths are the largest religious organizations in our society; Pentecostal and Black Muslim faiths are probably the fastest growing. Despite the Christian belief in the absolute equality of all individuals, religious institutions contain many internal class divisions. Often a denomination is associated with a particular stratum of society from which it draws most of its members. Correlations have been found between religion and occupational, income, and educational levels, with Jews and Protestants showing greater financial and occupational success.

Yet members in both the highest and lowest social classes tend to participate less in church activities. Some sociologists have stressed a connection between economic success and acceptance of the Protestant ethic which stresses hard work and views worldly prosperity as a mark of favor. Max Weber theorized that the growth of Protestantism in the sixteenth century was the major stimulus in the growth of the capitalistic system. In the modern world, however, society has become increasingly secularized as religion has become separated from government, education, and from basic values and patterns of behavior. Religious belief has become a matter of personal, rather than social, conviction.

GLOSSARY

Anomie A social situation in which established norms and values break down or conflict. (page 416)

Church A stable and institutionalized organization of religious believers. (page 414)

Denomination One of a number of religious organizations considered socially acceptable by a society. (page 414)

Ecclesia A church which is integrated with other social institutions and embraces almost all members of a society. (page 414)

Magic A set of actions, usually highly ritualistic, that are believed to bring about some desired change in the environment. (page 405)

Monotheism The belief that there is only one god. (page 402)

Polytheism The belief that there is more than one god. (page 402)

Religion A system of beliefs and practices concerning ultimate reality and the sacred. (page 402)

Religious officialdom Full-time workers in a religious organization. (page 414)

Religious ritual Formalized behavior, usually of a symbolic nature, oriented toward the sacred. (page 405)

Sacred, the A culture trait or object which is set apart from everyday life and which evokes great respect and reverence. (page 406)

Science An approach to the problem of human knowledge which utilizes quantifiable and objective methods. (page 406)

Sect An exclusive group of religious believers which tends to ignore or repudiate the established order and place emphasis on faith and fervor. (page 414)

Secularization A trend in which many aspects of life become increasingly separated from religious or spiritual connections or influences. (page 437)

Totemism A complex of beliefs organized around a totem, an object worshipped as a god and an ancestor. (page 404)

SUGGESTED READINGS
AND RELATED RESOURCES

I READINGS IN SOCIOLOGY

Berger, Peter L. *A Rumor of Angels: Modern Society and the Rediscovery of the Supernatural.* New York: Doubleday, 1969. Berger states that the belief in the supernatural is the only way man can grasp the true meaning of many of his experiences in life; religion is of great significance, even in this age of science and secularism.

_____. *The Sacred Canopy: Elements of a Sociological Theory of Religion.* New York: Doubleday, 1967. Berger views religion as a social product and develops a sociological theory of religion drawing on analyses of both ancient and contemporary religions.

Durkheim, Emile. *The Elementary Forms of Religious Life.* New York: Collier (Paper), 1961. First published in 1915. Durkheim developed the theory that religion is a product of the social conditions of man and viewed the collective consciousness of society as the source of religion.

Fontinell, Eugene. *Toward a Reconstruction of Religion: A Philosophical Probe.* Garden City, N.Y.: Doubleday, 1970. A presentation of ideas of why and how religion must be reconstructed if it is to survive and truly serve modern man.

Frazier, E. Franklin. *The Negro Church in America.* New York: Schocken (Paper), 1969. Frazier writes about the very important role that the church has played in black society and culture in America.

Glock, Charles Y., and Rodney Stark. *Religion and Society in Tension.* Chicago: Rand McNally, 1965. Glock and Stark examine the strains and contradictions between religious values and modern culture; their study is based on a great deal of information from survey research.

Herberg, Will. *Protestant, Catholic, Jew.* New York: Doubleday, Anchor, 1960. This book is particularly interesting for its history and comparison of the three major United States religious faiths. Herberg argues that religious involvement is important to Americans, but that the type of religion is relatively unimportant.

Lenski, Gerhard. *The Religious Factor.* New York: Doubleday, Anchor, 1963. This famous study, carried out in Detroit, considers the effects of religious beliefs and participation upon attitudes toward work, family life, education, politics, and other subjects.

Needleman, Jacob. *The New Religions.* Garden City, N. Y.: Doubleday, 1970. This work describes the teachings and practices of the new predominantly Oriental religions. Needleman examines areas where traditional religion has failed and how the new Eastern religions offer an alternative.

O'Dea, Thomas. *The Sociology of Religion.* Englewood Cliffs, N.J.: Prentice-Hall (Paper), 1966. O'Dea's concise book is a very good introduction to the historical and contemporary study of the sociology of religion. It is one of the best resources for students who want an overall perspective, rather than detailed analysis of this area of study.

Rosenberg, Stuart E. *The Search for Jewish Identity in America.* New York: Doubleday, Anchor (Paper), 1965. Rosenberg studies the religious and cultural changes in the American Jewish community brought about by life in the United States.

Vernon, Glenn. *Sociology of Religion.* New York: McGraw-Hill, 1962. For students interested in a more detailed explanation of the topics covered in chapter 10, this book would be a good resource.

Weber, Max. *The Protestant Ethic and the Spirit of Capitalism.* Translated by Talcott Parsons. New York: Charles Scribner's Sons, 1958. The most famous of Weber's works, this book explains how widespread acceptance of Protestant values encouraged the growth of European capitalism.

Yinger, J. Milton. *Sociology Looks at Religion.* New York: Macmillan, 1963. Yinger covers, in a very readable manner, a wide range of questions in the sociology of religion. He discusses, for example, the functions of religion as the agent of social change and as the basis for group identification.

Articles and Papers

Bellah, Robert N. "Religious Evolution." *American Sociological Review* **29**, 3 (June 1964):358–374.

Berger, Peter. "Religious Institutions." In *Sociology: An Introduction,* edited by Neil J. Smelser. New York: John Wiley, 1967.

Dillingham, Harry C. "Protestant Religion and Social Status." *American Journal of Sociology* **70**, 4 (January 1965):416–422.

Glock, Charles Y., and Benjamin B. Ringer, "Church Policy and Attitudes of Ministers and Parishioners on Social Issues." *American Sociological Review* **21**, 2 (April 1956):148–156.

Goldstein, Sidney. "Socio-Economic Differentials Among Religious Groups in the United States." *American Journal of Sociology* **74**, 6 (May 1969):612–631.

Goode, Erich. "Social Class and Church Participation." *American Journal of Sociology* **72** (July 1966):102–111.

Greeley, Andrew M. "Influence of the 'Religious Factor' on Career and Occupational Plans of College Graduates." *American Journal of Sociology* **68**, 6 (May 1963):658–671.

Hammond, Phillip E. "Religion and the 'Informing' of Culture." *Journal for the Scientific Study of Religion* **3,** 1 (October 1963):97–106.

Jordan, Robert H. "Social Functions of the Churches in Oakville." *Sociology and Social Research* **40**, 2 (November–December 1955):107–111.

McNall, Scott G. "The Sect Movement." *Pacific Sociological Review* **6**, 2 (Fall 1963):60–64.

Williams, Robin M., Jr. "Religion, Value-Orientations and Intergroup Conflict." *The Journal of Social Issues* **12**, 3 (1956).

Wilson, Bryan R. "An Analysis of Sect Development." *American Sociological Review* **24** (February 1959):3–15.

II   RELATED RESOURCES
Nonfiction

Allport, Gordon W. *The Individual and His Religion: A Psychological Interpretation.* New York: Macmillan, 1960. Allport attempts to explain the origins of the need for religion, the functions of religion for the individual in various phases of life, and the nature of doubt and faith.

Altizer, Thomas, and William Hamilton. *Radical Theology and the Death of God.* Indianapolis: Bobbs-Merrill (Paper), 1966. This collection of essays, by two leaders of the "God is dead" movement, emphasizes an active humanistic approach to religion rather than the passive, theological one.

Callahan, Daniel, ed. *The Secular City Debate.* New York: Macmillan (Paper), 1966. This book is a collection of critiques—positive and negative —of Harvey Cox's book, *The Secular City.*

Cox, Harvey. *The Secular City.* New York: Macmillan (Paper), 1965. Cox examines the phenomena of urban secularization and the breakdown of traditional religion from both a sociological and a theological perspective.

Fromm, Erich. *Psychoanalysis and Religion.* New York: Bantam (Paper), 1967. Fromm writes about the basic human needs which underlie all theological doctrines as well as psychoanalytic theories and approaches. He views some religious doctrine, especially that which emphasizes "adjustment" to society, as impeding the self-realization of man.

Marty, Martin. *The New Shape of American Religion.* New York: Harper & Row, 1959. Marty analyzes the religious situation in America from a Christian point of view. He discusses the superficiality of much of contemporary religion and points out new theological resources in the United States.

Raab, Earl, ed. *Religious Conflict in America.* New York: Doubleday, Anchor (Paper), 1964. This collection of essays deals with religious conflicts from the perspectives of theologians, historians, and sociologists.

Smith, Huston. *The Religions of Man.* New York: Harper & Row (Paper), 1964. Smith describes the history of the seven largest world religions, and provides a good introduction to the study of religion.

Fiction

Greene, Graham. *The Power and the Glory.* New York: Viking Press (Paper), 1958. This is a story of a Mexican priest who, although a drunkard and living in sin, continues to do good works during the anticlerical revolution in Mexico.

———. *A Burnt-Out Case.* New York: Viking Press (Paper), 1967. This is a story of a European architect who ends up in tropical Africa because of a spiritual dilemma.

Hesse, Herman. *Siddhartha.* New York: New Directions (Paper), 1957. This novel is about a Brahmin's son, Siddhartha, and his search for self-realization as a man and as a disciple of Buddha.

Films

The Cardinal. Otto Preminger, 1963. This is the story of an Irish-American youth who becomes a priest and rises to the eminent position of cardinal in the Roman Catholic church.

Elmer Gantry. Richard Brooks, 1960. A revivalist minister who uses people's need for religion for his own purposes is the protagonist of this poignant story.

Exodus. Otto Preminger, 1960. Preminger's film depicts the exodus of a group of Jews from Europe to Israel after World War II. It depicts Israel's struggle for independence from British control and the tensions that arose between the Arabs and the Jews.

11. Population and Ecology

Not so very long ago, the study of populations was considered a province not of sociologists, but of mathematicians, economists, and politicians. In the seventeenth and eighteenth centuries it was sometimes called "political arithmetic." One of the first men to formulate a comprehensive theory of population growth and change was the English clergyman and economist, Thomas Malthus. He published a classic essay on the subject in 1798 exploring the causes and consequences of population growth.[1] With the rise of sociology there developed an increasing awareness that population size and composition are not due to biological and economic factors alone, but are also greatly influenced by social factors. In addition, sociologists began to realize that the size, composition, and underlying trends of population exert in turn a most important molding influence on personality, social organization, and culture. So the study of population —technically called demography*—has become today one of the most highly developed and important fields of sociology, though it continues to span several disciplines.*

Many serious thinkers feel that overpopulation is the greatest threat to our modern way of life, potentially more dangerous even than atomic weapons or hostile ideologies.[2] The rate of world

1. Thomas R. Malthus, *An Essay on Population* (New York: E. P. Dutton, 1914).

2. For a discussion of this point of view, see Lincoln H. Day and Alice Taylor Day, *Too Many Americans* (Boston: Houghton Mifflin, 1964).

population growth in recent years has been unprecedented in human history. But more precisely, the problem is not the size of the population as such, but the rate of population growth in relation to economic growth and social conditions. Population experts suggest that the pressures of the world's rapidly expanding population may first cause an unpleasant deterioration in both the physical and social environments — indeed, they say this is already happening — and then may lead to the horrors of famine and disease, the natural checks on population growth throughout history. Not everyone agrees that the situation is already so perilous, especially in the United States, but there is general agreement that the consequences of overpopulation could some day be a very serious problem. This lends an air of urgency to the sociological study of populations, their growth, composition, trends, and the relationship of these factors to the larger society.

Equally urgent at the present time is the need for more knowledge about the broader relationships between man and his environment, which are the focus of ecology. *Closely related in many ways to demographic study, ecology was once an important area of study in American sociology, then fell into decline, and recently has been resuming an important position. While much of sociology is limited to the study of structures and processes of cultural and social systems, ecology looks specifically at how these systems relate to the biological and physical environments.*

1 THE STUDY OF POPULATIONS

The scientific and quantitative study of population, or demography, is a fairly recent phenomenon. This is partly due to the fact that early workers in the field had to deal with figures that were very unreliable, some of them established as much by guess or hunch as by scientific enquiry. Most countries of the world now regularly collect population figures, though they are still far from perfect, especially in the developing countries. Another factor in the growth of demography as an area of study has been the development of the electronic computer, which has made analysis of the data much easier and faster, as well as more accurate. Today the study of demography is based firmly on an empirical foundation, that is, on reasonably accurate and thoroughly analyzed data. Indeed, it is probably the most well developed special field of sociology in this respect.

HOW POPULATION DATA IS COLLECTED

The single most important source of demographic data is the *census,* a periodic head count of a population which usually includes in addition data about such individual characteristics as age, sex, marital status, income, family size, and so forth. In most countries only the central government has the resources necessary to conduct such a count, and the authority to enforce the cooperation of the citizens. Census taking began long ago. The Romans tried to count the number of residents in their Empire; England's famous *Domesday Book* is the report of a national census undertaken, for tax purposes, at the order of William the Conqueror in 1086. However, it is only in modern times that census taking has been on a regular basis. In the

United States, the requirement of a census of "all free Persons, including those bound to Service for a Term of Years, and excluding Indians not taxed," was established in the Constitution as a responsibility of the new government. The first census was taken in 1790, and there has been one every ten years since that date.

A census is an enormous and a very costly undertaking, yet almost every country agrees that the benefits of an accurate census justify the cost and effort. In all the wealthier, more highly developed nations, censuses are taken periodically as a matter of course. In some nations in the world today, though, census data is still either very skimpy or nonexistent. In the poorer and less developed countries, despite the fact that good demographic data are desperately needed to permit the wisest possible use of scarce resources, insufficient money and lack of skilled personnel make census taking especially difficult. The United Nations and some of the wealthier nations, including the United States, England, France, and Sweden, have given valuable assistance to help poorer countries improve their census. But accurate and adequate census data are still lacking for many nations.

The United States census is presently conducted by means of questionnaires. Traditionally the forms have been filled out by door-to-door census takers, asking questions of each household. In the 1970 census, questionnaires were mailed to people in some areas with a request to fill them out on their own and mail them back in.

It is the aim of the U.S. census to gather information about age, sex, residence, marital status, race, and income of each person in the entire country. A representative sampling

The Bureau of the Census has developed elaborate and precise methods for keeping track of our population growth. The balance between birth and death rates, immigration and emigration are the critical factors in determining the net rate of increase. However, demographers are interested in more than a simple numerical count. They use information from the census and from government records of vital statistics to analyze how the population is distributed in terms of geographic location, race, sex, age, occupation, and a number of other categories. Birth and death rates vary among different segments of the population. The rates shown here merely indicate an average for the population as a whole. *(U.S. Department of Commerce, Bureau of the Census)*

of the population is selected for more detailed questioning concerning occupation, housing, and education. On the basis of this sample, figures are estimated for the entire population.

As a check on the accuracy of the census, a Post-Enumeration Survey is undertaken, which uses complex techniques to systematically and accurately recount a very small sample of the population. This survey is then compared with the national census; the comparison provides an estimate of the degree of error, if any, in the census. It is usual for the census to undercount the population by a small percentage.

In addition to the census, demographers

have another major source of valuable data in the government records of vital statistics — births, deaths, marriages, and international migrations. These statistics vary in their accuracy and comprehensiveness. In some countries, such as Sweden, vital statistics have been accurately collected for well over a century. In the United States, it was not until 1933 that every state in the union required the keeping of such records, and in a few rural areas, some births still go unregistered. Demographers use these statistics to gain continual knowledge of the patterns and nature of demographic changes taking place in the population. Vital statistics, when combined with census data, give the vital rates which describe how and why changes in population occur. The data are also used to keep the census figures up to date (adding births and immigrants into the population; subtracting out deaths and emigrants), and to predict future population changes.

THE TABULATION AND USES OF CENSUS DATA

It was only with the 1960 census in this country that widespread use of the computer became a feature of the census, and it has proven an invaluable aid to the counting and analysis of census data. The use of computers does much to speed the processing of the data collected by the census takers. The end product of the census is a set of tables, many of which are published for public use. The United States Census is reported in many volumes according to geographic units. For each unit the most useful cross-classifications of the residents are shown in tables. For example, for any state or metropolitan area a table will show the number of men and women who are single (that is, who have never married), married, widowed, and divorced. This is a cross-classification of sex by marital status. Many other pieces of information collected in the census are similarly reported.

An example will illustrate the way census data can be used by a government. The city

INTERPRETING CORRELATIONS

This chart is an example of the way in which the correlation between ecological statistics may be shown visually. A sampling of states was chosen, and data on the murder rates and expenditures for education were assembled for each of the states. The two variables were then plotted on the chart. If a perfect positive correlation existed between the two (that is, if, in every case, the more a state spent for education, the higher its murder rate), then every point would fall exactly on a line running from the lower left to the upper right of the chart. If a perfect negative correlation existed (that is, if the more a state spent on education the lower the murder rate, as there is more reason to expect), all the points would fall exactly on a line running from the upper left to the lower right. If no correlation existed at all, the points would be scattered all over the chart.

In this instance, as in almost all others in real life, the data are neither perfectly correlated nor totally uncorrelated. So we must determine how closely the data approach perfect positive or negative correlation. To do this we imagine that we have drawn a straight line across the chart in such a way that the distance between all the points and the line is as small as possible. Pearson's correlation coefficient, or "r," is a measure of correlation based upon this line. It measures the degree to which the actual points conform to this "line of best fit." Like other measures of correlation it ranges from plus one (perfect positive correlation) to minus one (perfect negative correlation), with zero indicating no linear correlation.

In this example "r" turns out to be −.457, indicating that there is a slight negative correlation between murder rates and educational expenditures in the states sampled. That is, the less a state spent on education, the higher was its murder rate, on the average.

As with some other measures of correlation, "r" may be squared to obtain the proportion of variation in one variable that is associated with or "explained by" the other. In our example, we would square "r" to find out what proportion of variation in a state's murder rate is "explained by" expenditures for education. In this case $r^2 = .2088$, or 20.88 percent. So we can say that, statistically, about 20 percent of the variation in murder rates seems to be associated with variation in educational expenditure. About four-fifths of the differences in murder rates between states appear to be associated with other factors.

A CAUTION

As in the example of correlation used in chapter 6, we should not interpret these results too blindly. In the first place, we should look carefully at the sample states. In this case they are ten states drawn randomly from all the fifty states. When a random sample includes 20 percent of any large population (ten out of fifty states) we may expect that the sample will be highly representative, and in this case, the sample includes states from all regions of the country in approximately the correct proportions.

Second, we should examine the instrument used to collect the data. The educational data is standardized by the U.S. Census Bureau, so it may be assumed to be reasonably accurate. The murder rates, however, may contain a number of sources of bias. If the murder rates had been based upon convictions or arrests for that crime, they would have been influenced by the efficiency of the courts and the police of those particular states. In this case the murder rates are based upon murders known to the police, so we must consider bias that may have been introduced by faulty reporting, the different legal definitions of murder in the different

states, and the inaccuracy of the cause of death findings of the coroners of the states. The rates may probably be taken to be roughly accurate.

In the third place we should look for "intervening variables" that may serve to distort the statistical relationship between the two variables. For example, the highest murder rate in our sampling was in Nevada. Since one of the major industries of that state is tourism, it is entirely possible that a large proportion of the murders committed

there involve nonresidents. The state's educational system, of course, cannot be expected to have much effect upon visitors to the state. Some of the other variables that might also affect the murder rate are the proportion of the state population living in urban areas, the size and efficiency of the police force, the social class composition of the state, the murder laws of the state, and the laws of the state regarding the sale, ownership, and bearing of arms.

CORRELATING ECOLOGICAL STATISTICS

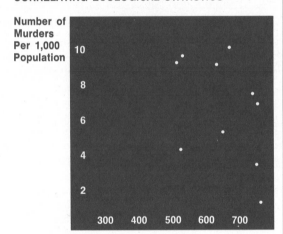

Average state expenditure per pupil

of Milwaukee wants to know how many children will be enrolled in primary school each year for the next decade, because it must plan ahead to raise money and to contract for new schools if they are needed, hire more teachers, add buses and drivers, and so on. So tables reporting the census data for Milwaukee residents are examined; they show how many children living in Milwaukee are five years old, four years old, three years old, and so on. The number of married women of child-bearing age will also be noted; this figure can be used, along with estimates of the average number of children born each year and

the average family size, to predict the approximate number of children who will be born in time to attend school by the later years of the decade.

Governments at all levels—municipal, state, and federal—utilize population figures not only to help plan educational facilities, but also to provide care for the elderly, build adequate public housing, and calculate the number of men that will be eligible for the draft. The data are used wherever planning and decision making require information that is objective and accurate. A good census is a kind of national look in the mirror.

However, it is not only to governments that the figures are useful. When the figures are released to the general public, they have applications in other areas as well. Hospitals use them to determine the size of the patient load to be expected in the future; guidance counselors use them to steer young people into careers that are uncrowded; corporations use them to determine where to locate a new factory or office. Manufacturers and businessmen analyze them to determine the probable size of the markets for their products. For example, Johnson and Johnson might use the figures to predict the number of babies that will be born in the next decade, thus providing an estimate of the size of the market for baby oil. The publishers of *Sports Illustrated,* who know that their readers are mainly drawn from men between the ages of 20 and 35, can estimate how many potential new readers there will be for their magazine. And, of course, the census is probably the richest mine of data for all sociologists, but especially for demographers and ecologists.

Most census data are reported by geographic units with politically defined boundaries, such as states, counties, or municipalities, since most political and business planning is done in terms of these units. From time to time minor difficulties arise in comparing one census with the next as a result of political boundary changes. (For example, the boundaries of the United States itself changed recently with the statehood of Hawaii and Alaska.) Such problems can usually be resolved with relatively simple adjustments, however.

A useful unit of population analysis which is not based on a political boundary is the *census tract.* This is a unit resulting from the division of an urban area into a group of smaller, well-defined units which usually contain from 3,000 to 6,000 people. Wherever possible, the division is made on the basis of natural boundaries such as rivers or parkland, as well as based on social and economic characteristics. Since generally the same tracts are used for every census, it is possible to see how these city "neighborhoods" change

and develop. The census tract is especially important for ecological analysis, which we will discuss in topic 3.

POPULATION AND SOCIETY

One of the most important reasons for population study is to better understand the nature of society. The relationship between populations and societies is one in which the influence travels both ways: the composition and size of the population affect the society, and the society in turn affects the population.

How do the characteristics of a population influence a society? We can see some answers by comparing our country in 1790, at the time of the first census, to our country today. In 1790 there were only about four million American citizens; there was a large country to explore and settle and the average density of population was about five persons per square mile. The largest city, Boston, had fewer than twenty thousand residents; 95 percent of the population lived on farms or in rural areas.

Death and disease were much more a part of the life of every man and woman. Life was a far more chancy affair: probably something like one infant in five could be expected to die before having a first birthday; nearly half of all children born would fail to live to be adults; orphanhood and widowhood were much more common than now; epidemics were a constant threat.

Fertility was very high: having babies was a much bigger component of a woman's life; she spent a large percentage of her life being pregnant, but she ran a higher risk of losing her babies and also of being sterile.

Old people were a very small percentage (less than 5 percent) of the total population; children less than fifteen years of age made up about 45 percent of the total population—there were more dependents per worker.

In 1970, the United States was the fourth largest nation in the world, with a population of approximately 205 million persons;[3] 70

3. Estimated figure from Dennis Wrong, "Portrait of a Decade," *New York Times Magazine,* 2 August 1970.

POPULATION DENSITY, BY COUNTIES: 1960

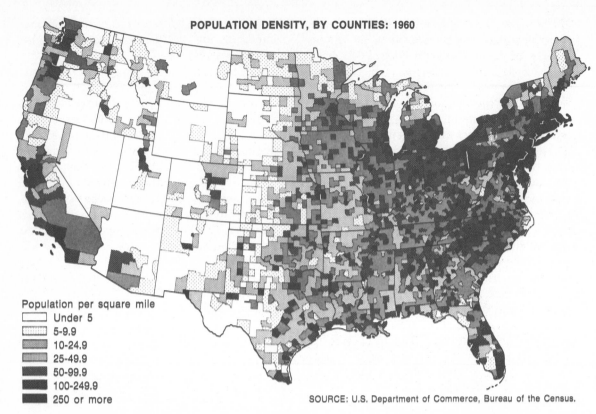

Population per square mile
- ☐ Under 5
- ▦ 5-9.9
- ▨ 10-24.9
- ▩ 25-49.9
- ▤ 50-99.9
- ▥ 100-249.9
- ■ 250 or more

SOURCE: U.S. Department of Commerce, Bureau of the Census.

Our population is becoming more and more concentrated around urban areas in the Northeast, Southwest, and West. How do you think this will affect the distribution of political power, of goods, and of services?

percent of the population lived in urban areas and there were five cities with over a million residents (New York, Chicago, Los Angeles, Philadelphia, and Detroit). The density of settlement had climbed to over fifty persons per square mile. In contrast to 1790, a major concern today is overcrowding, not settling new territory.

Death and disease are still a central part of our lives (in fact the diseases that increase with age, such as heart disease and cancer, have increased greatly since 1790), but a much higher percentage of babies live to adulthood. Some scholars have suggested that this has had a beneficial effect on child rearing: the child of today receives more care and attention in the home, especially before the age of six.[4] This is because attitudes are

geared more to the fact that each child will most likely live to adulthood.

The role of women has changed, partly because of lower rates of fertility, smaller families, and lower rates of infant mortality. Many more women today hold jobs outside the home; women are more able to secure an education on an equal basis with men. There are many more years in a woman's life after her children have left home.

Today, persons over sixty-five make up about 10.7 percent of the population. This has led to the need for vast retirement and nursing care facilities, and consequent segregation of the elderly. It has also led to the problem of deciding what attitude society should take toward so large a group with a reduced potential to be productive.

We can also see that society influences the size and composition of the population. We have already touched on several instances.

4.   Philippe Ariés, *Centuries of Childhood* (New York: Alfred A. Knopf, 1962).

Our population did not increase as rapidly as it was expected to in the decade of the sixties because of demographic and social changes which caused a drop in the birthrate. The change was in part technological, due to the discovery of the birth control pill, a more effective and acceptable contraceptive than any previously available. It was also partly a result of attitudes. The average age at marriage did not continue to decline; changed attitudes toward working wives and mothers caused more women either to postpone or to limit their families and to take their place in the work force instead; the amount of education considered appropriate for children has risen at the same time as the costs of education so that the actual cost of having children has increased.

Social factors affect the population in other ways as well. Health care and technological advances may increase the proportion of elderly in the population; many social customs affect the incidence of sickness and death and access to the means of prevention and cure. Other social factors, such as the desirability of a particular society as a place to live and the nature of immigration laws, will affect the number and composition of the migrants coming into the group, thus influencing population growth.

2 POPULATION COMPOSITION AND CHANGE

Population composition refers to such significant biological or social characteristics as (1) sex; (2) age; (3) race; (4) place of residence; (5) marital status; (6) size of household; (7) occupation; and (8) income. The distribution of many of these characteristics has been discussed in earlier chapters: income in the chapter on stratification, race in the chapter on ethnic and racial minorities, marital status in the chapter on the family. This is an indication of how important demographic data can be to the sociologist, whatever the area of his specialization.

In this topic, we will look at the two most fundamental population characteristics—sex and age—and at the basic factors of population growth and decline: fertility, mortality, and migration.

SEX RATIO

The census figures on the number of males and the number of females in a population are usually expressed in terms of a sex ratio (SR), measuring the number of men per 100 women. If the sex ratio is 100, then the numbers of men and women are equal. If it is over 100 (SR = 105), there are more men than women; if the sex ratio is less than 100 (SR = 87), there are more women than men.

In the United States more boys are born than girls—about 106 boys for every 100 girls, a sex ratio at birth of 106.[5] However, although boys start out in greater numbers than girls, they gradually lose their lead as the result of a higher death rate among males. For the United States population as a whole, the sex ratio is 95, meaning there are 95 males for every 100 females. When the sex ratios are examined at each age level, a gradual decrease in the sex ratio with every decade of the life

5. Unless otherwise noted, all statistics on American population used in this chapter are drawn from *Statistical Abstract of the United States: 1971* (Washington, D.C.: Government Printing Office, 1971).

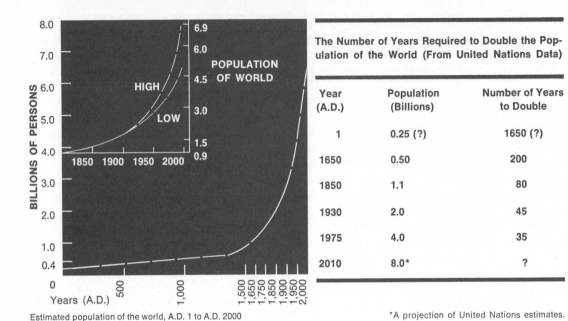

Estimated population of the world, A.D. 1 to A.D. 2000

The Number of Years Required to Double the Population of the World (From United Nations Data)		
Year (A.D.)	Population (Billions)	Number of Years to Double
1	0.25 (?)	1650 (?)
1650	0.50	200
1850	1.1	80
1930	2.0	45
1975	4.0	35
2010	8.0*	?

*A projection of United Nations estimates.

SOURCE: Harold F. Dorn, "World Population Growth: An International Dilemma," *Science* 135 (January 22, 1962) pp. 283-290.

This chart shows that the world population is not only increasing, but increasing at a constantly growing rate. It took an estimated 1650 years for the population to double the first time, but the next doublings took fewer and fewer years. From 1930 to 1975 it will double, and from 1975 it will double again in only 35 years.

span is revealed, until by the time of old age, women far outnumber men, with a sex ratio of 72. This pattern is made clear also by an analysis of death rates. At every age, males suffer higher mortality rates than do females. This has led many to conclude that females are physically stronger than males in a biological (not a muscular) sense. It is noteworthy, also, that this biological superiority of women is found in all human populations except those where girls begin having babies at a very early age and continue having babies frequently throughout their childbearing years.

Although the sex ratio is about even under natural conditions, it can be unbalanced by a variety of social factors. For example, until the present day, combat and other physically dangerous activities have been the province of men, and the victims have been mostly taken from the male population. Even today war and occupational hazards take a heavier toll of men than of women. A growing country, as America was in the nineteenth and early twentieth centuries, will typically have more men than women, because it is most commonly the males who are willing and able to leave their families and undertake the risk and adventure of migration to a new country. An immigrant community with a high sex ratio may have increased adjustment problems, for family building will be handicapped if there is an excess of men of marriageable age.

Sex ratios may be unbalanced regionally for much the same reasons. In our country, Alaska, which is still in many respects a frontier, has a sex ratio of 132. As a general rule, most cities in economically advanced nations have a low sex ratio (that is, they have slightly more women than men) compared with rural areas. This is mainly due to the urban employment opportunities, such as the huge clerical force required by modern bureaucracy, which tend to attract more women. In cities dominated by heavy industry, however, males often predominate. This higher sex ratio is also true of many cities in developing countries such as India.[6]

It should be pointed out that the concern over a balanced sex ratio is primarily due to our commitment to the ideal of monogamous marriage (with only one wife and one husband) for everyone. A sex ratio that is unbalanced in either direction means that some people will be unlikely to obtain spouses.

AGE

One important reason for the government's interest in age statistics is the link between age and economic productivity, the ability to produce goods and services needed by others. Also, with national pension and health insurance plans for those over 65, the government must be able to provide the funds needed to implement those plans.

In our industrialized society, the young and the old cannot always be economically productive citizens. On the farm, children and grandparents could help with some of the chores. But their skills and abilities do not allow them to compete for jobs in factories and offices, and now we have even passed laws expressly prohibiting their participation in many forms of employment. Thus the people in these age categories become dependent upon the productivity of others in the country. If the number of such dependents becomes too large in relation to the number of producers, the country may have serious economic problems.

An examination of census figures shows that in 1970, 45 percent of the population was either under the age of 18 or over 65 and could therefore be presumed to be relatively nonproductive citizens. Ten percent of the population was between the ages of 18 and 24, which means that many of them were in college or undergoing some sort of vocational

6.   Statistics concerning the populations of foreign countries are taken from the United Nations, *Demographic Handbook, 1969.*

training or business apprenticeship. We can assume that a number of the people in this age category were still dependent on someone else for all or most of their financial support. If roughly half of them were nonproductive, it would raise the total percentage of the dependent population to 50 percent. In the developing countries today such a high percentage of dependents is often a serious barrier to economic advancement; in an industrialized society like ours, it is probably an impediment to economic growth but is not regarded as a serious problem.

The United States has historically been a country of young people. Before World War II, birthrates and death rates both were high, meaning that most of the population was concentrated in the early decades of the life span. This trend gradually slowed down during the twentieth century, and then revived again after World War II, with the great postwar baby boom. The 1970 census shows that the trend of the future will probably once again be a decrease in youthfulness, as a result of the newly declining birthrates. It will be interesting, especially to sociologists, to see if the coming rise in the average age of the American population will have any dampening effect on the orientation toward youth that dominates so much of our culture at the present time. It will, however, be some years before the actual raising of the average age level, the result of the present decline in birthrates, shows up.

When we compare the age distribution of our population with that of some of the developing nations, we see how lucky we are. Frank Notestein explains:

In our population only a little more than one-fourth are children under age 15, whereas in Asia, for example, about four persons of each ten are in that generally unproductive group. The rearing of children, of course, is the soundest investment that a nation can make, and in our case the investment is a particularly good one, for at current rates of survival more than 95% of those born will live to at least age 15 and more than 60% will live to age 65. But in the Far East the investment is much more precarious; a conservative estimate is that a smaller proportion of those born live to age 15 there than live to age 65 in the U.S. Probably more than 40% of the children in the Far East never reach the productive years of life.[7]

POPULATION CHANGE

When we speak of a population, it is important to remember that we are referring not to some fixed and stable entity but to a constantly changing group. Populations can either increase or decrease very rapidly (although during the past 250 years, most populations have tended to increase markedly), and their entire composition may also change. The decennial census (that taken every ten years) is a measurement of the population at one particular time; it is rather like a still photograph, capturing just one frozen moment of a continuous action. It is the task of the demographer to try to piece together, using vital statistics, some explanation of the events that took place before the census, and those that can be expected to take place after the census, so that we can understand the single picture that we see.

In discussing population analysis it is important to recognize the difference between the *analysis* of data, and *predictions* based on that data. Analysis of census data showed that the population of the United States increased by 18.6 percent from 1950 to 1960. A prediction made in the sixties based on an analysis of that increase was that in 1970 our population would be 220 million. However, this prediction was too high because there was a substantial drop in the birthrate during the last few years of the decade. Thus, predictions are based on the analysis of existing data, but they must at the same time include judgments of possible future changes which

7.   Frank W. Notestein, "Population," *Scientific American,* September 1951, p. 31. Copyright © 1951 by Scientific American, Inc. All rights reserved.

POPULATION OF UNITED STATES: 1800 TO 1970

Year	Resident population
1800	5,308,483
1850	23,191,876
1900	75,994,575
1950	150,697,361
1970	203,211,926

Statistical Abstract of the United States, 1972, p. 5.

Our population has increased almost 40 times since 1800. Advances in medical science, agricultural technology, and in the means of production and transportation have all helped to reduce the death rates, and to prolong life.

may not be suggested by the existing data. A prediction which essentially represents an extension of present known trends is called a *projection.*

Three elements are together entirely responsible for population growth or decline, and therefore are the key to explaining past changes and to predicting future ones. They are: (1) fertility (birthrate); (2) mortality (death rate); and (3) migration.

Fertility

The rate of *fertility,* the rate at which births occur in a population, depends on both biological and social factors.

The most important biological factor is the number of women of childbearing age in the population. Usually demographers pick ages, such as 14 to 44, or 15 to 49, which correspond roughly to the limits of childbearing years and then count how many women (potential bearers of children) there are in that age range. Calculating that women could have an average of from fifteen to twenty children during the time they are in this category, we may come up with a figure that represents the maximum number of births in the population that are biologically possible. This is often called the *fecundity rate.*

Another biological factor is the general health of childbearing women. If, for example, women live under conditions of severe famine, their ability to conceive and bear children will be biologically limited; or if an epidemic of rubella (German measles) strikes a community, birthrates will drop because of the number of pregnancies that end in miscarriages.

Important social factors are the attitudes people have toward reproduction. There has never been a society whose actual fertility rate was anywhere near the level of its fecundity rate, so we conclude that every society puts some kinds of limitations on its natural fertility. Kingsley Davis and Judith Blake have placed these social limitations in three categories. The first covers the factors affecting exposure to intercourse, such as age of marriage, norms of premarital behavior, or the value of chastity. The second group consists of factors that influence exposure to conception and includes practices of contraception and ideals of family size. The last group consists of factors affecting the actual birth and survival of the infant, such as abortion and infanticide.[8]

Davis and Blake take care to point out that not all social attitudes which control fertility do so purposely. For example, in our society it is the norm to limit parentage to married people. This limitation has the effect of decreasing the fertility rate. But that is a side effect of the norm, not its purpose; the norm is meant to ensure that children are brought up in a stable family with both a father and a mother.

The greatest influence on a society's fertility rate, however, is its social attitudes toward reproduction. For the greater part of human history, man has been struggling against high mortality rates and the problem of underpopulation, so that the underlying norms of most societies encourage reproduction at as high a rate as possible. The biblical injunction to "be fruitful and multiply" is reinforced by a number of social norms. It is only relatively recently that the situation has changed.

8.   Kingsley Davis and Judith Blake, "Social Structure and Fertility: An Analytic Framework," *Economic Development and Cultural Change* 4 (April 1956): 211–235.

The medical advances which prolong life, the technological discoveries that have enabled us to cope more safely with the hostilities of our natural environment, and the results of the fruitfulness of many generations have combined to create a large population. A high fertility rate is no longer desirable. The problem is that basic social attitudes have not yet completely shifted to encourage fewer births, and so we are currently trying to deal with a problem which our norms are making more serious every day.

Today, signs indicate that a change in attitudes toward reproduction, making the task of limiting the population easier, is taking place. There is a statistical increase in the number of users of contraceptive techniques, as well as in the number of abortions performed. In the early 1970s, several states began to liberalize their abortion laws; and a 1973 Supreme Court decision placed severe limitations on the power of the state to regulate abortion. The belief is growing that only two children — or even one or none — is an acceptable and a responsible family size. Most concrete of all the signs in this direction is a definite drop in the birthrate for the last several years. After World War II there was a sharp increase in births in America, but the rate for first births has remained level for several years and people have been having fewer second, third, and fourth children.

Birthrates are commonly expressed in terms of the annual number of births per 1,000 of the total population; this is called the *crude birthrate*. By counting the number of births per 1,000 women of a specific age group, such as 20–24, we get the *age-specific birthrate*. A further refinement is to limit the group to married women of that age, thus arriving at an *age-specific marital fertility rate*. Detailed vital statistics about births and mothers are needed to figure these two more specific fertility rates, and so such figures are available only in countries where record keeping is quite sophisticated. They are often not available in developing countries that badly need accurate figures to plan their modernization.

Fertility rates are never the same throughout all segments of a society. In the United States, for example, there are definite class differences in fertility rates, which are caused by the varying class attitudes toward reproduction and family size, and variations in knowledge and availability of safe and effective means of controlling fertility. Lower-class families are larger than those of the middle and upper classes. Also, rural birth-rates are nearly always higher than urban ones; Catholics have higher fertility rates than do either Protestants or Jews; blacks have higher fertility rates than whites (although this differential is more a reflection of class differences than racial differences as such). An understanding of these kinds of differential fertility rates helps demographers predict future trends. For example, predictions of population growth must always take into account changes in religion and ethnicity which may be occurring.

Mortality

Fertility may often involve some compromise between individual goals (such as the desire for a large family, the freedom of childlessness, or the pursuit of sexual fulfillment), and social goals (such as limiting or increasing the population). Mortality is a less complicated social element since personal health and long life are goals of individuals and societies alike. The major issue which decides the level of mortality rates is the extent of a society's willingness, and ability, to mobilize its resources to achieve the goal of good health and long life for its citizens.

Our country spends a great deal of money and human resources in programs designed to investigate and control the causes of death in America. We have, in fact, given the health and long life of our population a higher financial priority than fertility. The result has been a steady increase in life expectancy. The average length of life for an American is now about 71 years. In 1900 it was only 50 years,

and in 1850, it was 41 — so we can see what progress has been made. Decreasing a mortality rate does have many social effects, because a lengthened life-span means more people are able to be productive longer and more people are economically dependent during a longer old age. We have made impressive gains in this area, but American levels of mortality are by no means the lowest in the world.

An increase in the life-span increased the *average* life-span. That is, more people are living longer, but there is no evidence to show that we have lengthened or will significantly lengthen the possible life-span of all men. What we can do is help more people to achieve that possible life-span.

Mortality rates vary among different segments of the population, as do fertility rates. For example, the highest rates are found among the lower classes, a fact which may be attributed mainly to environmental and health conditions. There are several different ways to measure mortality.

(1) *The crude death rate,* like the crude birthrate, measures deaths per 1,000 general population. The crude death rate is not a very precise tool for predicting future trends or population sizes, because it does not tell the ages of those who die.

(2) *Age-specific death rates* are calculated by dividing the population into age spans of various sizes, usually one year or five years, and then counting the incidence of deaths per 1,000 members of each group. This is a much more revealing figure than the crude death rate. From it we can see that the first year of life is a high risk period, and then there is a sharp decline in the death rates. The lowest rates are for those in the age group of six to twelve years old, and then the rates slowly climb with each year, until by age sixty Americans reach again the risk level of the first year of life. Then the rates climb much more rapidly as one advances into old age. The age-specific death rate for infants is usually regarded as the best indication of a

CRUDE INFANT MORTALITY RATE FOR TWENTY COUNTRIES: 1930 and 1965

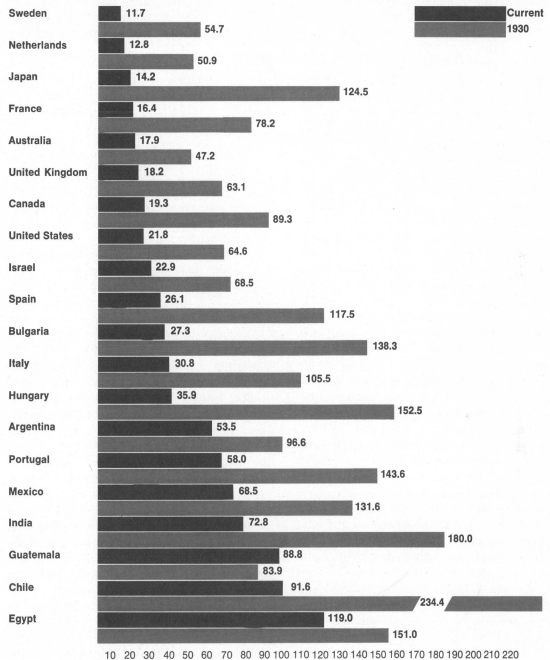

SOURCE: Dennis H. Wrong, *Population and Society* (New York: Random House, 1967), p. 30. United Nations, *Demographic Yearbook*, 1971.

The crude infant mortality rate has declined in almost every country largely because of advances in medical care and sanitation. It is interesting to note that the United States has a rate higher than a number of other countries.

population's health level and medical welfare facilities. Special attention is given the *neonatal mortality rate,* the age-specific death rate for the group of those under one month of age, for that is the period of greatest hazard.

The age-specific rate for those under one year is generally referred to as the *infant mortality rate.* Although the rate of infant mortality in the United States is low by international standards of comparison, it is by no means the lowest in the world (see the accompanying chart for a complete tabulation). Our rate is about 27, whereas in Sweden it is only 12, and in the Netherlands 14. Japan, Australia, France, and Great Britain also have lower rates than we have. At the other end of the scale are Egypt with 119 and Chile with 114; if we could make accurate calculations for countries like Indonesia, India, the Congo, and China, we might find their rates to be even higher.

(3) *Life tables* are a measure of survival rates of those born at any given time; it is from life tables that life expectancies are calculated, and they are also the basis of life insurance actuarial tables. A life table is a complicated statistical device which summarizes the mortality experience of a population of the various ages at a single point in time. It tells how many of a given group of newborn babies would still be alive at each successive year of their existence, given existing levels of mortality. Of course, such tables are theoretical projections, not actual records, and are thus subject to change as the age-specific mortality rates vary due to technological advances or changes in social attitude.

(4) *Life expectancies* tell us how many more years the average person of any given age can be expected to live if current mortality levels prevail. We see a much greater variation of life expectancy at early ages from country to country; this reflects the progress in certain societies in combating the diseases of infancy and childhood. As the ages increase, there is less variation in life expectancy, and the expectancy for a 70-year-old

LIFE EXPECTANCY IN UNITED STATES: 1920 TO 1970

Year	Life Expectancy
1920	54.1
1930	59.7
1940	62.9
1950	68.2
1960	69.7
1970	70.8

Statistical Abstract of the United States, 1972, p. 55.

Life expectancy refers to the mean number of years of life remaining at any given age. As this table shows, life expectancy at birth has increased by 16.7 years since 1920. In other words, infants today are far more likely to reach the age of 70 than infants 50 years ago.

man is nearly the same in every country. This indicates that we have not as yet been successful in doing much about the fatal diseases of middle and old age.

Migration

Migration is the movement of people from one geographic area to another. It was discussed in chapter 8, Ethnic and Racial Minorities. When people leave a country, it is called emigration; when they enter, it is immigration. Migration can be the cause of great population fluctuations. Generalizations concerning the direction, magnitude, and composition of streams of migration are not perfect; nevertheless, certain patterns appear with considerable regularity and are therefore noteworthy.

William Peterson, an expert on the study of population, has made a useful list of different categories of migration as an aid to studying its effects. He distinguishes five types:[9]

(1) *Primitive migration* is the travel of those who wander freely over some roughly defined territory, hunting animals or foraging for plants. There are still some nomadic tribes left in the world but modern governments

9. William Peterson, *The Politics of Population* (New York: Doubleday, 1964).

find them a great inconvenience and try to suppress this form of migration. The United States government stopped the migration of Indian tribes in this country by restricting them to the reservations. The governments of Iran, Afghanistan, and Pakistan try to control the periodic wanderings of the Kurds, Bakhtiari, Qashqai, and Baluchi tribes by breaking up their tribal organization. Some sociologists suggest that the moves of American workers following their jobs can be considered comparable to primitive migration.

(2) *Forced migration* is the compulsory transfer of people from one country or region to another. Trading in slaves is an example of forced migration; so was the partial colonization of Australia by convicts. In the late nineteenth century, the Czarist government of Russia used forced migration to relocate whole villages of Jews.

(3) *Impelled migration* is the movement of people from one country to another caused by extremely difficult social conditions, but which an individual can, if he wishes, choose not to follow. Examples of this type are the exodus of Jews from Nazi Germany during the thirties, the emigration of the Irish during the potato famine, the flight of any population before a conquering army, and the departure of the Pilgrims from England.

(4) *Free migration* is the movement of peoples motivated by an individual desire for adventure or a search for improved living conditions and social circumstances. The immigration of Europeans to America in the nineteenth century is the classic example of free migration. Virtually no free international migration is permitted in the world today.

(5) *Controlled migration* is a variant of free migration; it has the same motivation but takes place under limitations prescribed by the government. The United States now controls immigration here, by setting annual quotas, based on country of origin and a system of priorities which gives first consideration to moves which reunite family groups or bring the country badly needed skills. The current quota is 170,000 immigrants per year, although the actual number of migrants is probably somewhat higher, since certain United States territories, such as Puerto Rico, have the privilege of unlimited immigration.

It must be recognized that migration is not always permanent. In voluntary (free) migration, men often go alone, with the intention of returning home after they have "made good." Sometimes the migrant finds that he is unable to adjust to his new country, and so he gives up the venture and returns home. Changed social conditions at home can bring about the return of forced or impelled migrants. One study of world population movement found that 30 percent of the immigrants who entered the United States between 1821–1924 returned to their original countries.[10] Unless the return rate is taken into account, it is difficult to estimate the exact effect of migration on population size and composition.

Another problem to demographers is the incomplete state of migration records, especially in regard to emigration. The United States, for example, keeps no official count of emigration. One way to determine an approximate number is to use the immigration records of other countries, since they normally specify the country of the immigrant's origin. Our census figures do include the numbers of people presumably living in America who were foreign born, or born here to foreign parents. This group, sometimes called the foreign-stock population, currently amounts to about one-fifth of our total population. The subject of migration is discussed more fully in chapter 8, Ethnic and Racial Minorities, and chapter 14, Community and Economic Change.

TRENDS IN WORLD POPULATION

The rate and nature of past population growth in America and Western Europe, where reliable census figures extend over

10. A. M. Carr-Saunders, *World Population* (New York: Oxford University Press, Clarendon, 1936), p. 49.

PROJECTED POPULATION GROWTH OF THE FIFTEEN LARGEST NATIONS

	1968 (millions)	1985	% of growth
China (Mainland)	730	964	32.1
India	524	808	54.4
Soviet Union	238	289	21.4
United States	201	253	25.8
Indonesia	113	184	62.8
Pakistan	110	224	103.7
Japan	101	121	5.05
Brazil	88	143	62.5
Nigeria	63	85	39.9
West Germany	58	62	6.9
Gt. Britain	55	62	12.7
Italy	53	60	13.2
France	50	58	16.0
Mexico	47	84	78.8
Philippines	36	64	77.8

SOURCE: United Nations, *Demographic Yearbook: 1971* and *World Population Prospects.*

The population of the United States and Western Europe will grow relatively slowly in the next several decades—an average of about 15 percent. However, the average for the Asian nations on this list is 51 percent, and other Third World nations will also grow rapidly.

several centuries, have been carefully studied. The pattern of this population growth can be summarized as follows:

Premodern populations maintain stability of numbers by balancing high, though fluctuating, death rates with high birth rates. As they begin to experience the effects of modernization, improvements in nutritional and health standards reduce mortality while fertility remains high and rapid growth ensues. Later, urbanization and other social changes associated with the more 'mature' stages of industrialism create pressures favoring smaller families, and the birth rate falls, once again approaching balance with the death rate, but at low (though fluctuating) rather than high levels.[11]

It was once thought that this pattern was universal, that it was a model of demographic change applicable to all societies. However, recent research and the experience of developing countries indicate that this model of demographic transition may be simply one possible pattern out of many. Human attitudes and social factors seem to be too variable for there to be any one universal pattern.

A useful classification of societies by stage of population growth has been developed by the Population Division of the United Nations.[12] It divides all countries into the following five categories:

1. Countries with high birthrates and high death rates. This is the pattern of most

11. Dennis H. Wrong, *Population and Society* (New York: Random House, 1967), pp. 18–19.

12. United Nations, Department of Economic and Social Affairs, *The Future Growth of World Population,* Population Studies, no. 28 (New York: United Nations, 1958).

primitive societies, which may still be found today in some of the areas of Central Africa, Asia, and Latin America most remote from outside influence.

2. Countries with high birthrates and declining but still fairly high death rates. Examples of this type can be found in the countries of northern and eastern Africa, and in the majority of Asian nations. China may be tentatively included in this group, although lack of data on birth and death rates makes its classification uncertain.

3. Countries with high birthrates and fairly low death rates. This is the pattern of maximum population growth, and was characteristic of the United States and Europe in the nineteenth century. Today we find this pattern principally in some parts of Asia and in many countries of Latin America.

4. Countries with declining birthrates and fairly low death rates. This is the situation which now exists in some Asian countries such as Taiwan and the Republic of Korea, and in some South American nations such as Chile and Argentina.

5. Countries with low or fluctuating birthrates and low death rates. This is called the modern pattern, and is characteristic of the United States, Canada, most of Europe (including the Soviet Union), Japan, Australia, and New Zealand.

Countries with growth patterns of types (2), (3), and (4) are all growing so fast that their social and economic development is impeded. At this time, many of these countries are taking steps to slow down the rate of their population's increase; they are being assisted in this effort by the United Nations and some of the wealthier countries such as Sweden and the United States. However, the task is an immensely difficult and expensive one. Consider the problem of reaching the 500 million peasants in India alone to inform them about, and provide them with, safe and effec- tive modern contraceptives. A massive effort will be required if the rate of population growth is to be brought under control. It is encouraging that some of the largest and even some of the poorest developing countries have recognized and accepted the challenge. India, Pakistan, China, the United Arab Republic, Kenya—these and many others are starting to develop national family planning programs.

The recent decrease in the birthrate in America and many countries of Western Europe is cause for a more optimistic outlook on the control of population growth, and some sociologists feel we may already have seen the end of the population explosion. Donald Bogue is one who has opposed the pessimistic predictions regarding the threat of overpopulation.[13] He asserts that the population crisis will be over by the next century for several reasons. He has noted that in developing countries political leaders have begun to favor birth control, and in many countries small families are beginning to be preferred. Increased support for research is making available more kinds of contraception that may easily be taught and made available; information about them is being spread around the world. Along with this growing concern for fertility control, Bogue also reports a leveling off of progress in death control.

But many well-known sociologists and demographers would not agree. While downward trends in fertility may be appearing in some developing countries, in most places they are no more than a start, and often fail even to keep up with declines in mortality. What must be clearly recognized is that even cautious optimism will not justify ignoring this problem, which concerns all humanity. For a further discussion of the problems and potential dangers of rapid population increase, see the abridgment "The World's Exploding Population" by Paul R. Ehrlich.

13. Donald J. Bogue, "The End of the Population Explosion," *Public Interest* 7 (Spring 1967):11–20.

PAUL R. EHRLICH
The World's Exploding Population

Abridged from *The Population Bomb* (New York: Ballantine Books, 1969), pp. 17–35.

Introduction

Paul Ehrlich is a Professor of Biology at Stanford University, and the author of a recent controversial book, The Population Bomb. *In this book, Ehrlich predicts some of the consequences to human society, and even human existence, of the constantly expanding population of our modern world. He also gives timetables for the occurrence of some dire events, unless present trends are stopped. Not all students of population agree with all of the conclusions that Ehrlich reaches. However, there is no doubt that Ehrlich is deeply concerned with some of the most perilous problems facing humanity today. Few indeed would disagree that the present high rates of population growth are continuing to add substantially to the sum total of human misery.*

Americans are beginning to realize that the undeveloped countries of the world face an inevitable population-food crisis. Each year food production in undeveloped countries falls a bit further behind burgeoning population growth, and people go to bed a little bit hungrier. While there are temporary or local reversals of this trend, it now seems inevitable that it will continue to its logical conclusion: mass starvation. The rich are going to get richer, but the more numerous poor are going to get poorer. Of these poor, a minimum of three and one-half million will starve to death this year, mostly children. But this is a mere handful compared to the numbers that will be starving in a decade or so. And it is now too late to take action to save many of these people.

In a book about population there is a temptation to stun the reader with an avalanche of statistics. I'll spare you most, but not all, of that. After all, no matter how you slice it, population is a numbers game. Perhaps the best way to impress you with numbers is to tell you about the "doubling time"—the time necessary for the population to double in size.

It has been estimated that the human population of 6000 B.C. was about 5 million people, taking perhaps one million years to get there from 2½ million. The population did not reach 500 million until almost 8000 years later—about 1650 A.D. This means it doubled roughly once every thousand years or so. It reached a billion people around 1850, doubling in some 200 years. It took only 80 years or so for the next doubling, as the population reached 2 billion around 1930. We have not completed the next doubling to 4 billion yet, but we now have well over 3 billion people. The doubling time at present seems to be about 37 years. Perhaps the meaning of a doubling time of around 37 years is best brought home by a theoretical exercise. Let's examine what might happen on the absurd assumption that the population continued to double every 37 years into the indefinite future.

If growth continued at that rate for about 900 years, there would be some 60,000,000,000,000,000 people on the face of the earth. Sixty million billion people. This is about 100 persons for each square yard of the Earth's surface, land and sea. A British physicist, J. H. Fremlin, guessed that such a multitude might be housed in a continuous 2000-story building covering our entire planet. The upper 1000 stories would contain only the apparatus for running this gigantic warren. Ducts, pipes, elevator shafts would occupy about half of the space in the bottom 1000 stories. This would leave three or four yards of space for each person. I will leave to your imagination the physical details of existence in this ant heap, except to point out that all would not be black. Probably each person would be limited in his travel. Perhaps he could take elevators through all 1000 residential stories but could travel only within a circle of a few hundred yards' radius on any floor. This would permit, however, each person to choose his friends from among some ten million people! And, as Fremlin points out, entertainment on the worldwide TV should be excellent, for at any time "one could expect some ten million Shakespeares and rather more Beatles" to be alive.

Could growth of the human population of the Earth continue beyond that point? Not according to Fremlin. We would have reached a "heat limit." People themselves, as well as their activities, convert other forms of energy into heat which must be dissipated. In order to permit this excess heat to radiate directly from the top of the "world building" into space, the atmosphere would have been pumped into flasks under the sea well before the limiting population size was reached. The precise limit would depend on the technology of the day. At a population size of one billion people, the temperature of the "world roof" would be kept around the melting point of iron to radiate away the human heat generated.

Of course, population growth is not occurring uniformly over the face of the Earth. Indeed, countries are divided rather neatly into two groups: those with rapid growth rates, and those with relatively slow growth rates. The first group, making up about two-thirds of the world population, coincides closely with what are known as the "undeveloped countries" (UDCs). The UDCs are not industrialized, tend to have inefficient agriculture, very small gross national products, high illiteracy rates, and related problems. That's what UDCs are technically, but a short definition of undeveloped is "starving." Most Latin American, African, and Asian countries fall into this category. The second group consists in essence, of the "developed countries" (DCs). DCs are modern, industrial nations, such as the United States, Canada, most European countries, Israel, Russia, Japan, and Australia. Most people in these countries are adequately nourished.

Doubling times in the UDCs range around 20 to 35 years. Examples of these times are Kenya, 24 years; Nigeria, 28; Turkey, 24; Indonesia, 31; Philippines, 20; Brazil, 22; Costa Rica, 20; and El Salvador, 19. Think of what it means for the population of a country to double in 25 years. In order just to keep living standards at the present inadequate level, the food available for the people must be doubled. Every structure and road must be duplicated. The amount of power must be doubled. The capacity of the transport system must be doubled. The number of trained doctors, nurses, teachers, and administrators must be doubled. This would be a fantastically difficult job in the United States—a rich country with a fine agricultural system, immense industries, and rich natural resources. Think of what it means to a country with none of these.

Doubling times for the populations of the DCs tend to be in the 50 to 200 year range. Examples of 1968 doubling times are the United States, 63 years; Austria, 175; Denmark, 88; Norway, 88; United Kingdom, 140; Poland, 88; Russia, 63; Italy, 117; Spain, 88; and Japan, 63. These are industrialized countries that have undergone the so-called demographic transition—a transition from high to low growth rate. As industrialization progressed, children became less important to parents as extra hands to work on the farm and as support in old age. At the same time they became a financial drain—expensive to raise and educate. Presumably these are the reasons for a slowing of population growth after industrialization. They boil down to a simple fact—people just want to have fewer children.

This is not to say, however, that population is not a problem for the DCs. First of all, most of them are overpopulated. They are overpopulated by the simple criterion that they are not able to produce enough food to feed their populations. It is true that they have the money to buy food, but when food is no longer available for sale they will find the money rather indigestible. Then too, they share with the UDCs a serious problem of population distribution. Their urban centers are getting more and more crowded relative to the countryside. This problem is not as severe as it is in the UDCs (if current trends should continue, which they cannot, Calcutta could have 6 million inhabitants in the year 2000). As you are well aware, however, urban concentrations are creating serious problems even in America. In the United States, one of the more rapidly growing DCs, we hear constantly of the headaches caused by growing population: not just garbage in our environment, but overcrowded highways, burgeoning slums, deteriorating school systems, rising crime rates, riots, and other related problems.

There are some professional optimists around who like to greet every sign of dropping birth rates with wild pronouncements about the end of the population explosion. They are a little like a person who, after a low temperature of five below zero on December 21, interprets a low of only three below zero on December 22 as a cheery sign of approaching spring. First of all, birth rates, along with all demographic statistics, show short-term fluctuations caused by many factors. For instance the birth rate depends rather heavily on the number of women at reproductive age. In the United States the current low birth rates soon will be replaced with higher rates as more post-World War II "baby boom" children move into their reproductive years. In Japan, 1966, the Year of the Fire Horse,

was a year of very low birth rates. There is a widespread belief that girls born in the Year of the Fire Horse make poor wives, and Japanese couples try to avoid giving birth in that year because they are afraid of having daughters.

But it is the relationship between birth rate and death rate that is most critical. Indonesia, Laos, and Haiti all had birth rates around 46 per thousand in 1966. Costa Rica's birth rate was 41 per thousand. Good for Costa Rica? Unfortunately, not very. Costa Rica's death rate was less than 9 per thousand, while the other countries all had death rates about 20 per thousand. The population of Costa Rica in 1966 was doubling every 17 years, while the doubling times of Indonesia, Laos, and Haiti were all above 30 years. Ah, but, you say, it was good for Costa Rica—fewer people per thousand were dying each year. Fine for a few years, perhaps, but what then? Some 50 percent of the people in Costa Rica are under 15 years old. As they get older, they will need more and more food in a world with less and less. In 1983 they will have twice as many mouths to feed as they had in 1966, if the 1966 trend continues. Where will the food come from? Today the death rate in Costa Rica is low in part because they have a large number of physicians in proportion to their population. How do you suppose those physicians will keep the death rate down when there's not enough food to keep people alive?

One of the most ominous facts of the current situation is that roughly 40 percent of the population of the undeveloped world is made up of people *under 15 years old*. As that mass of young people moves into its reproductive years during the next decade, we're going to see the greatest baby boom of all time. Those youngsters are the reason for all the ominous predictions for the year 2000. They are the gunpowder for the population explosion.

It is, of course, socially very acceptable to reduce the death rate. Billions of years of evolution have given us all a powerful will to live. Intervening in the birth rate goes against our evolutionary values. During all those centuries of our evolutionary past, the individuals who had the most children passed on their genetic endowment in greater quantities than those who reproduced less. Their genes dominate our heredity today. All our biological urges are for more reproduction, and they are all too often reinforced by our culture. In brief, death control goes with the grain, birth control against it.

In summary, the world's population will continue to grow as long as the birth rate exceeds the death rate; it's as simple as that. When it stops growing or starts to shrink, it will mean that either the birth rate has gone down or the death rate has gone up or a combination of the two. Basically, then, there are only two kinds of solutions to the population problem. One is a "birth rate solution," in which we find ways to lower the birth rate. The other is a "death rate solution," in which ways to raise the death rate — war, famine, pestilence — *find us.* The problem could have been avoided by *population control,* in which mankind consciously adjusted the birth rate so that a "death rate solution" did not have to occur.

Conclusion

Ehrlich provides a very pessimistic picture of the world's future. By projecting present rates of population growth into the future he shows how dangerous the population explosion could be. One must ask if these projections are really what we must look forward to. Do you think they are?

More important, though, are the trends that exist now. *The population of the world doubles approximately every 37 years, and Ehrlich indicates that there is no convincing evidence that this trend is easing. In your own judgment, is this a good or a bad thing? Should anything be done about it (which is not being done now)? If so, what?*

The study of ecology began in the nineteenth century as a branch of biology. Ecology is a branch of science concerned with how living things, both animate and inanimate, are related to their environment, and the changes that are produced in both the organisms and the environment as they adapt to one another. Charles Darwin's theory that organisms change and evolve in response to their living conditions greatly stimulated the growth of ecology as a field of study.[14] Ecologists even- tually were able to depict in general terms the complex web of relationships between living things and their environment. This web is called the *ecosystem.*[15]

In 1893, Emile Durkheim conceived of a "social morphology" to study the relation- ships of population and environment to social structure. But not until about fifty years ago did American sociologists begin to study seri- ously the applications ecology had to their own discipline. They recognized that social

14. Charles Darwin, *On the Origin of the Species by Means of Natural Selection* (New York: D. Apple- ton, 1873).

15. Otis Dudley Duncan. "Social Organization and the Ecosystem," in *Handbook of Modern Sociology,* ed. Robert E. L. Faris (Chicago: Rand McNally, 1964), p. 37.

Robert Park (1864–1944) was one of the most influential figures in the development of American sociology. It was largely due to his leadership that the sociology department of the University of Chicago made so many outstanding contributions to the science of sociology during the 1920s and 1930s; this prominent school also trained many young sociologists who later became influential in their own right. Park's primary interest was in the field of urban studies, especially urban ecology. However, he is best remembered not for any work of research, but as the author of the classic sociology textbook, *Introduction to the Science of Sociology* (1921).

behavior, after all, is essentially a form of adaptation to environment, and human beings both cooperate and compete among themselves, and with other life forms, in ways similar to the animals studied by the biological ecologist.[16] Sociological interest was spurred by the fact noted even by biological ecologists that man's evolution is mostly social and cultural, rather than physical, and therefore falls outside the province of biology and the natural sciences.

The ideas of ecology were first introduced into American sociology by Robert Park of the University of Chicago. The University

of Chicago dominated the field of American sociology during the years between World Wars I and II, and much of the sociological work done at this school was ecological in orientation.[17] Foremost in this work were the studies of ecological patterns and processes in cities, which are discussed below. Although the term ecology is often associated with the Chicago school of thought, it is used in a general sense in sociology today to mean the study of the relationship between social organization and the natural and material environments, and especially of the way in which social organization represents an adaptation to those environments.

Sociological ecologists pay less attention to specifically cultural facts of social organization (such as norms and values) than do other sociologists, though they are interested in the spatial distribution of social and cultural phenomena. For example, ecological studies have been made of the way many kinds of social facts, like mental illness or suicide, are distributed throughout the population. Other studies have defined certain areas of concentrated activity—areas of work, play, residence, and commerce. In preparing studies and gathering data, sociological ecologists use many of the techniques and working methods of demographers and share research sources with them. The two fields are closely related, both in their subject matter and in their scientific approach to quantifying human relationships and behavior.

URBAN ECOLOGY

Urban ecology has long been an important field of investigation within sociology, and many of the studies carried out by ecologists have been a valuable aid to the formation of theories about urban life and the planning of urban communities. Urban ecologists have singled out a number of basic ecological processes which occur in urban areas. Examples of such processes are:

(1) *Concentration and Dispersion.* All cities

16.   See George A. Theodorson, ed., *Studies in Human Ecology* (New York: Harper & Row, 1961).

17.   See Robert E. L. Faris, *Chicago Sociology, 1920–1932* (San Francisco: Chandler Publishing, 1967).

are a function of population concentration, the ecological process in which individuals tend to cluster where conditions are favorable. Throughout much of its history the United States has had a dispersed or scattered population, especially in the period of development when isolated rural farmsteads were common. Today, we can see concentration and dispersion occurring simultaneously, as some persons leave rural areas for the city while others leave the city to settle in less dense suburban areas.

Population concentration is measured by the ratio of population to land area. The newer cities of the western United States are much more dispersed, that is, they have more land area per person than the older industrial cities in the east.

The terms *centralization* and *decentralization* are sometimes used to refer specifically to the concentration or dispersion of economic, governmental, and service functions rather than population. Centralization is the tendency of retail businesses, industry, banks, educational and recreational and other facilities to congregate in the central and most accessible sections of an urban area. The central business district is the clearest example of centralization. It is the focus of transportation and communication in the urban area and is therefore the area most easily reached by shoppers and workers. This advantage results in higher density and land values.

If a central district becomes too dense and congested, however, and the land and other costs become too high, economic activities may be decentralized, relocated to secondary centers or subcenters located in outlying areas. The process of decentralization is occurring today in every metropolitan area in the United States. Industries are leaving the central cities in search of more space; retail businesses are following the population to the suburbs. As this happens, metropolitan areas spread, becoming so large that the edge of one area starts to overlap the area adjacent to it, forming what are called *megalopolises*. (Jean Gottman discusses one of these mega-

The great population density of modern cities leads to crowded and congested conditions everywhere; traffic jams like this one are a daily frustration of urban life. Yet this density also produces economic and social opportunities not found anywhere else. *(Henry Monroe, DPI)*

lopolises in the accompanying abridgment.)

(2) *Ecological Segregation.* Ecological segregation is the process in which areas of the city become specialized in types of land use, services, or population. The most obvious example is the gradual establishment of certain areas as residences for specific minority groups, but there are many other kinds of segregation. There are places where childless couples or single people live, such as the apartments in Cleveland's "Gold Coast." Public housing projects, such as the Pruitt-Igoe Project in St. Louis, segregate those with low incomes. Chicago's Old Town and New York's Greenwich Village are two examples of areas segregated on the basis of certain life styles popular among artists, bohemians, and the young. Ecologists have noted that economic facilities which provide certain types of services also tend to cluster together into specialized areas. For example, government offices are often found within a few blocks of

The suburbs provide millions of Americans with more privacy and living space than they could have in the city. Sociological studies show that housing developments like this one usually develop definite subcultures of their own, and that they maintain their distinctive identities for many years. *(Georg Gerster, Rapho Guillumette)*

each other: the courts are near to the jail; the State Employment Office is next door to the welfare agencies. Ecological segregation also can be seen in the "industrial parks" with their rows of small manufacturing concerns, in the entertainment districts where theaters and restaurants are grouped together, in the

central business district with all of the large department stores, and in suburban shopping centers.

Segregated areas which emerge without planning and as a result of ecological processes are sometimes called *natural areas,* to distinguish them from administrative or political areas having more artificial boundaries.

A useful, quantitative way of identifying urban residential areas has been widely tested in recent years. Called social area analysis, it uses census tract data in classifying areas according to three factors: "social rank" (measured by level of occupation and income); "urbanization" (measured by fertility rates, women in the labor force, and the percentage of single family dwellings); and "segregation" (measured by the spatial isolation of ethnic or racial groups). These three factors help to describe the way in which people sort themselves out in cities.

(3) *Invasion and Succession.* These concepts have been borrowed directly from biologists. Invasion refers to the entrance of one group into the territory of another. The colonization of America by Europe was an invasion of the territory of the American Indian. In ecological succession one social group or type of land use replaces another as the dominant group or use in a certain area. Succession can be well illustrated on the neighborhood scale. Let's consider Cleveland's Hough area. Once an open hunting territory for the Indians, it became farmland for the colonists. As city centers were established, the farms gave way to city houses—first small ones spread far apart, then, as things grew more crowded, larger ones squeezed closer together. Finally the proximity to the city center attracted the wealthy, who built expensive town houses or brownstones. Then the neighborhood began to deteriorate, the wealthy left, and their places were taken by poorer and disadvantaged people, who were attracted by the bargain prices of the large old houses. These were broken up into multiple family dwellings, then into apartments and rooming houses.

These pictures contrasting Boston as it appeared in the early nineteenth and twentieth centuries and as it appears today are clear examples of urban change and evolution. The old Faneuil Hall building, whose steeple was once a prominent landmark, is now dwarfed by the modern government buildings and cultural center behind it. The harbor has been filled in so that automobiles may take the place of boats. *(New York Public Library Picture Collection, Bettmann Archive, Center Photo Service)*

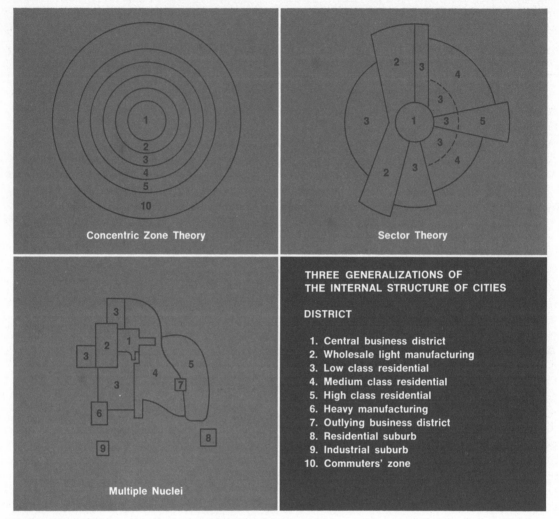

These diagrams represent the three major patterns of urban growth.
SOURCE: Charney D. Harris and Edward L. Ullman, "The Nature of Cities," *The Annals of the American Academy of Political and Social Sciences* 242 (November 1945).

Eventually the deterioration became so bad that many buildings were condemned, and for a while they then furnished a home for those on the fringes of society—drug addicts, drifters, vagrants, the very poor, and the homeless. Recently many buildings have been torn down or completely renovated as a new cycle of invasion and succession begins.

Urban spatial structure

Urban ecologists have also been much interested in explaining the overall spatial struc-

ture of cities. Several different models have been developed. The first work in this area was done by Ernest Burgess in the 1920s, using Chicago as a model.[18] It is called the concentric zone pattern. In the heart of the city is the business district; ringed around it are zones of light manufacturing, of lower-class residences, and of family-owned middle-class houses. Generally speaking, the

18.   Robert E. Park, Ernest W. Burgess, and Roderick D. McKenzie, *The City* (Chicago: University of Chicago Press, 1925), chap. 2.

status of the resident increases the farther out from the center he lives. Central zones have high proportions of foreign stock, a high sex ratio, and high rates of crime of all types. Outer zones contain more homeowners, and more members of the middle class. Upward status mobility is expressed in moves out from the city center. Also, as the size of the urban area increases new zones are added around the outside, and the status rank of all the old zones moves down one notch.

Originally, Burgess thought that the concentric zone pattern might be universal, and other researchers found that it could be demonstrated in some other cities, such as St. Louis.[19] However, further study indicated that many cities did not fit the pattern. It appears that the model is most applicable to cities that grew rapidly during the period of massive European immigration. In the late thirties, a new model was suggested, by Homer Hoyt, called the sector pattern.[20] This features the same type of outward movement, but along pie slice sectors out from the center rather than in concentric zones. The hypothesis is that the original city center is divided into various districts, such as business, industrial, and low- and middle-class housing. Each of these sectors then expands outward in a line or a V from the center, usually following the main transportation routes. This pattern was roughly demonstrated empirically in Minneapolis, San Francisco, and Richmond, Virginia.[21]

A third and more refined model is that of multiple nuclei; this was formulated by Harris and Ullman in the 1940s.[22] It holds that early in a city's history, certain outlying subcenters of business, commerce, and residence are established. Each separate subarea then expands in any available direction, perhaps in a concentric or sectorial fashion. This model does not assume that growth radiates from one central business district; rather it assumes that there are many minor business clusters or nuclei. Boston shows many characteristics of this kind of pattern.

Actually, no city's structure and growth can be explained fully by any one of these models, although they are all valuable in pointing out certain tendencies and patterns. They have also generated a great deal of continuing interest in the spatial structure of cities. Today urban ecologists, together with scholars from the fields of geography, economics, and the new discipline of regional science, are developing and testing much more elaborate models with the help of computers. These newer models all contain elements of the basic patterns developed by the early ecologists. Many also try to incorporate a wider range of noneconomic social and cultural factors and thus more closely approach the extreme complexity of the real world.

GENERAL HUMAN ECOLOGY AND THE ECOSYSTEM

Except for work on urban ecology, American sociology has not been strongly oriented toward this branch of science. One noteworthy exception is the pioneering book on *Human Ecology* written in 1950 by Amos Hawley.[23] Quite recently there has been an upsurge of interest in ecology, however, due partly to a growing general concern with the pollution of the environment. A number of sociological ecologists are attempting to analyze social patterns from the perspective of the *ecological complex* or *ecosystem*. Otis Dudley Duncan, one of the leading ecologists and a former student of Hawley, suggests that the ecosystem consists of four main elements: population, organization, environment, and technology (referred to sometimes by the acronym POET). The work of sociological

19. Stuart A. Queen and David B. Carpenter, *The American City* (New York: McGraw-Hill, 1953), p. 101.

20. Homer Hoyt, *The Structure and Growth of Residential Neighborhoods in American Cities* (Washington, D.C.: Federal Housing Administration, 1939).

21. Homer Hoyt, p. 115.

22. Chauncy D. Harris and Edward L. Ullman, "The Nature of Cities," *Annals of the American Academy of Political and Social Science* 242 (November 1945):7–17.

23. Amos H. Hawley, *Human Ecology: A Theory of Community Structure* (New York: Ronald Press, 1950).

The increasing density of population, the by-products of developing technology, and lack of control over our environment have created many problems for our cities. In the photos above smog shrouds Los Angeles; in New York garbage piles up and it is difficult to find a way to dispose of it; in Cleveland a few years ago the Cuyahoga River burned because it was full of litter and debris. *(The Plain Dealer, Cleveland; Arthur Leipzig, Fred Lyon, Rapho Guillumette)*

ecologists is focused on the complex interplay between these elements.

An example of this complete interrelationship has been suggested by Duncan in an analysis of the smog problem in the Los Angeles basin of southern California.[24] During and after World War II, which brought a large influx of population and industry to the Los Angeles area, residents began to notice a blue-gray haze which reduced visibility and caused irritation of the eyes and nose. As the smog became worse, it led to more serious health problems, as well as damage to plant life. Scientists eventually discovered that smog results when sunlight converts certain by-products of combustion, particularly those in automobile exhaust, into toxic chemicals. The problem is magnified by atmospheric conditions in the area which frequently prevent the polluted air from rising into the atmosphere, and by a ring of mountains which traps the air in the Los Angeles area:

The problem, severe enough at onset, was hardly alleviated by the rapid growth of population in the Los Angeles area, spreading out as it did over a wide territory, and thereby heightening its dependence on the already ubiquitous automobile as the primary means of local movement. Where could one find a more poignant instance of the principle of circular causation, so central to ecological theory, than that of the Los Angelenos speeding down their freeways in a rush to escape the smog produced by emissions from the very vehicles conveying them.[25]

One important area of ecological research is the relation between population density and human behavior. There is a good deal of experimental evidence from animal studies

Many of the changes man makes in his natural environment turn out to have unforeseen side effects. Farmers have cleared this land of grass, boulders, and trees so they can plant crops; when it is left unplanted the wind takes much of the best soil off because there is nothing left to anchor it down.

which indicates that severe overcrowding produces serious pathological behavior such as suicide and cannibalism, sexual breakdown, and mental illness. Researchers in many different disciplines are trying to find out if human overcrowding can cause similar effects. Some of this work has recently been discussed in such popular books as Desmond Morris's *The Human Zoo*.[26] The evidence that is so far available indicates that extremely high densities of population do play a significant role in personal and social pathologies among human beings.

THE PLANET AS AN ECOSYSTEM

We are finally beginning to realize that man's relationship with his natural environment is just as important and meaningful as his relationship with his social environment; it is also just as difficult to control. Like all

24. Otis Dudley Duncan, "From Social System to Ecosystem," *Sociological Inquiry* 31, no. 2 (Spring 1961): 140–149, reprinted in *Urbanism, Urbanization and Change: Comparative Perspectives,* ed. P. Meadows and E. H Mizruchi (Reading, Mass.: Addison-Wesley, 1969), pp. 87–95.

25. Otis Dudley Duncan, "From Social System to Ecosystem," p. 91.

26. Desmond Morris, *The Human Zoo* (New York: McGraw-Hill, 1969).

other animals, our very lives are dependent on an adequate supply of fresh water, clean air to breathe, and a food supply provided by green plants capable of making carbohydrates from the sun's energy. We also need a certain amount of habitable space in which to live and carry on our life activities. Until now we have behaved as if we lived on a planet with inexhaustible resources of all these necessities, but we are presently finding out that the limits are in sight. Our air, our water, and our soil are all becoming polluted with chemicals and garbage, and it is conceivable that we may push this pollution past the earth's natural ability to regenerate itself. Ironically, many of our attempts to improve upon nature have exactly the opposite effect. For example, some scientists hypothesize that the building of dams for irrigation has the long-term result of damaging the land; this might help to explain why the Middle East, once the home of the great ancient civilizations that grew crops by damming the Tigris and Euphrates rivers, is today a virtual desert. Today we are aware that the fertilization of crops to improve their yield actually upsets the balance of life in nearby water sources. There is even a possibility that by turning green land into cities and destroying much of the sea's plant life by pollution, we will lower the oxygen content of the atmosphere to such an extent that we will no longer be insulated from the sun's rays and the earth will someday become unbearably hot in the daytime and cold at night, as is the moon.

Even if we do not agree with the direst predictions of some scientists, we can see that as the world's population increases, we will all have to be more careful to conserve our natural resources, or succeeding generations may find themselves paying a very high price for our neglect.

JEAN GOTTMAN
Megalopolis

Jean Gottmann, *MEGALOPOLIS: The Urbanized Northeastern Seaboard of the United States.* © 1961 by The Twentieth Century Fund, New York. First published November, 1961. First M.I.T. Press Paperback Edition, February, 1964.

Introduction

A phenomenon of the mid-twentieth century has been the emergence of the megalopolis—an interdependent cluster of large metropolitan areas. This reading selection is taken from a book written in 1961 about the ecology and population distribution of the megalopolis that stretches along the eastern seaboard of the United States from Boston to the Virginia border. Some writers have jokingly labeled this megalopolis "Boswash." Scholars have identified over a dozen other megalopolitan areas which have emerged in different parts of the United States.

POPULATION AND ECOLOGY

The Northeastern seaboard of the United States is today the site of a remarkable development—an almost continuous stretch of urban and suburban areas from southern New Hampshire to northern Virginia and from the Atlantic shore to the Appalachian foothills. The processes of urbanization, rooted deep in the American past, have worked steadily here endowing the region with unique ways of life and of land use. No other section of the United States has such a large concentration of population, with such a high average density, spread over such a large area. And no other section has a comparable role within the nation or a comparable importance in the world. Here has been developed a kind of supremacy, in politics, in economics, and possibly even in cultural activities, seldom before attained by an area of this size.

An urbanized area with a nebulous structure

As one follows the main highways or railroads between Boston and Washington, D.C., one hardly loses sight of built-up areas, tightly woven residential communities, or powerful concentrations of manufacturing plants. Flying this same route one discovers, on the other hand, that behind the ribbons of densely occupied land along the principal arteries of traffic, and in between the clusters of suburbs around the old urban centers, there still remain large areas covered with woods and brush alternating with some carefully cultivated patches of farmland. These green spaces, however, when inspected at closer range, appear stuffed with a loose but immense scattering of buildings, most of them residential but some of industrial character. That is, many of these sections that look rural actually function largely as suburbs in the orbit of some city's downtown. Even the farms, which occupy the larger tilled patches, are seldom worked by people whose only occupation and income are properly agricultural. And yet these farm areas produce large quantities of farm goods!

Thus the old distinctions between rural and urban do not apply here any more. Even a quick look at the vast area of Megalopolis reveals a revolution in land use. Most of the people living in the so-called rural areas, and still classified as "rural population" by recent censuses, have very little, if anything, to do with agriculture. In terms of their interests and work they are what used to be classified as "city folks," but their way of life and the landscapes around their residences do not fit the old meaning of urban.

In this area, then, we must abandon the idea of the city as a tightly settled and organized unit in which people, activities, and riches are crowded into a very small area clearly separated from its nonurban surrounds. Every city in this region spreads out far and wide around its original nucleus; it grows amidst an irregularly colloidal mixture of rural and suburban landscapes; it melts on broad fronts with other mixtures, of somewhat similar though different texture, belonging to the suburban neighborhoods of other cities. Such coalescence can be observed, for example, along the main lines of traffic that link New York City and Philadelphia. Here there are many communities that might be classified as belonging to more than one orbit. It is hard to say whether they are suburbs, or "satellites," of Philadelphia or New York, Newark, New Brunswick, or Trenton. The latter three cities themselves have been reduced to the role of suburbs of New York City in many respects, although Trenton belongs also to the orbit of Philadelphia. Thus an almost continuous system of deeply interwoven urban and suburban areas, with a total population of about 37 million people in 1960, has been erected along the Northeastern Atlantic seaboard. It straddles state boundaries, stretches across wide estuaries and bays, and encompasses many regional differences.

Megalopolis — main street and crossroads of the nation

There are many other large metropolitan areas and even clusters of them in various parts of the United States, but none of them is yet comparable to Megalopolis in size of population, density of population, or density of activities, be these expressed in terms of transportation, communications, banking operations, or political conferences. Megalopolis provides the whole of America with so many essential services, of the sort a community used to obtain in its "downtown" section, that it may well deserve the nickname of "Main Street of the nation." And for three centuries it has performed this role, though the transcontinental march of settlement has developed along east–west axes perpendicular to this section of the Atlantic seaboard.

In recent times Megalopolis has had concentrated within it more of the Main Street type of functions than ever, and it does not yet seem prepared to relinquish any of them. Witness, for example, the impact of the Federal government in Washington, D.C., as it tightens up over many aspects of national life; the continued crowding of financial and managerial operations into Manhattan; New York's dominance of the national market for mass communication media, which resists all attempts at erosion; and the pre-eminent influence of the universities and cultural centers of Megalopolis on American thinking and policy-making. Megalopolis is also the country's chief facade towards the rest of the world. From it, as from the Main Street of a city, local people leave for distant travel, and to it arriving strangers come. For immigrants it has always served as the chief debarkation wharf. And just as passing visitors often see little of a city except a few blocks of its Main Street, so most foreign visitors see only a part of Megalopolis on their sojourns in the United States.

Just as a Main Street lives for and prospers because of the functions of the whole city, rather than because of any purely local advantages of its own, so is Megalopolis related to the whole United States and its rich resources. In general, Megalopolis itself was blessed only moderately by nature. It has no vast expanse of rich soils (there are some good soils but more poor ones), no special climatic advantages (its cyclonic climate is far from ideal), and no great mineral deposits (though there are some). In these respects it cannot compare with the generous natural potential of the Middle West or Texas or California. But it does excel in locational advantages— deep harbors of a drowned shoreline, on which its principal cities were early established, and a connecting-link relationship betwen the rich heart of the continent

and the rest of the world. By hard work man has made the most of these locational resources, the most outstanding ones in an otherwise average natural endowment. As a result, early in its history Megalopolis became a dynamic hub of international relations, and it has maintained and constantly expanded that role to the present day. It is now the most active crossroads on earth, for people, ideas, and goods, extending its influence far beyond the national borders, and only as such a crossroads could it have achieved its present economic pre-eminence.

Megalopolis as a laboratory of urban growth

Modern technology and social evolution provide increasing opportunity in urban pursuits on the one hand, and on the other steadily improving means of producing more agricultural goods with less manpower. The forces at work in our time, coupled with the growth in population, are, therefore, bound to channel a rising flow of people toward urban-type occupations and ways of life. As this tide reaches more and more cities they will burst out of old bounds to expand and scatter all over the landscape, taking new forms like those already observable throughout Megalopolis. This region serves thus as a laboratory in which we may study the new evolution reshaping both the meaning of our traditional vocabulary and the whole material structure of our way of life.

Tomorrow's society will be different from that in which we grew up, largely because it will be more urbanized. Nonagricultural ways of life will be followed by more and more people and will occupy much more space than they ever did, and such changes cannot develop without also deeply modifying agricultural life and production. So great are the consequences of the general evolution heralded by the present rise and complexity of Megalopolis that an analysis of this region's problems often gives one the feeling of looking at the dawn of a new stage in human civilization. The author has visited and studied various other regions of the world but has not experienced such a feeling anywhere else. Indeed, the area may be considered the cradle of a new order in the organization of inhabited space. This new order, however, is still far from orderly; here in its cradle it is all in flux and trouble, which does not facilitate the analyst's work. Nevertheless, a study of Megalopolis may shed some light on processes that are of great importance and interest.

For the better or for the worse?

Urban growth in general has been discussed and condemned on moral grounds for a long time. Such debate is expectable and desirable, but on the whole history has shown the condemnation to be unjust, as can be seen by a brief review of some of the consequences of crowding.

Contrasts between rich and poor, for example, are especially striking in the crowded communities of cities. These may exist in rural areas too, but there they are diluted by scattering and veiled in greenery. The growth of urban pursuits (industries, trade, services) sharpens the contrasts by condensing them into a smaller area. Rich and poor live within short distances of one another and mix together in the streets in a way that often arouses righteous indignation. It seems brutally amoral to witness destitution neighboring on elegant sophistication, poverty mixing with prosperity. And yet, alas, a growing city's environment can hardly escape offering such sights. For many centuries there was an enormous difference between the advancement possible in trade and industry on the one hand and in farming on the other (though modern farm mechanization and subsidies to agriculture have substantially increased the profit possibilities of farming), and so to rise

economically within the span of one lifetime has traditionally been easier in cities than in rural areas. The affluence of those who have so risen draws to the city large groups of humbler people, who come there to profit by the local abundance of money and the volume of spending and to serve the wealthier. In contrast to the more conservative "open" country, the "closed-in" city offers a more dynamic environment, socially and economically.

Crowding of population within a small area creates shortages of various resources, and most of the crowded people are bound to suffer in some ways because of the shortages. To alleviate them, to make crowding more bearable and the population happier, ways and means of constantly better distribution must be found. Otherwise no lasting growth can develop, and the whole enterprise will soon be doomed. From the struggle against such shortages have come some of mankind's most important advances. In the arid areas of the Middle East, for example, early civilization arose when people first congregated around the main springs and permanent rivers. As the settlement grew, the supply of both water and irrigable land became scarce. To insure survival of the people a proper distribution system had to be achieved, and rules and regulations had to be set up and accepted. Thus organized society, ruled by law, was born. Because authorities were needed to enforce law, political power arose, and people organized themselves to avoid more oppression than was necessary. Everywhere, the more crowded people have become in cities the more they have craved both security and freedom. Modern political life and its concepts of liberty, self-government, and democracy are the products of urban growth, the inheritance of cities in process of growth and development—places such as Jerusalem, Athens, Rome, Bruges, Florence, Paris, London, to mention only those that have been most studied by historians. And the same places, or similar urban centers, have contributed most of our scientific and technological developments, either because people there were struggling to solve problems or because urban societies make possible a leisurely enough elite, some of whose members can devote themselves to disinterested research and a search for a better understanding of the universe.

Thus urban crowding and the slums and mobs characteristic of it may be considered growing pains in the endless process of civilization.

In the same way, the picture of Megalopolis is not as dark as the out-spoken pessimists and frequent protests would seem to paint it. Crowded within its limits is an extremely distinguished population. It is, *on the average,* the richest, best educated, best housed, and best serviced group of similar size (i.e. in the 25-to-40-million-people range) in the world. The area is still a focus of attraction for successful or adventurous people from all over America and beyond. It is true that many of its sections have seen pretty rural landscapes replaced by ugly industrial agglomerations or drab and monstrous residential developments; it is true that in many parts of Megalopolis the air is not clean any more, the noise is disturbing day and night, the water is not as pure as one would wish, and transportation at times becomes a nightmare. Many of these problems reflect the revolutionary change that has taken place as cities have burst out of their narrow bounds to scatter over the "open" countryside. In some ways this suburban sprawl may have alleviated a crowding that had threatened to become unbearable, for residential densities of population per square mile have decreased. But new problems have arisen because of the new densities of activities and of traffic in the central cities and because the formerly rural areas or small towns have been unprepared to cope

with the new demands made upon their resources. New programs are needed to conserve the natural beauty of the landscape and to assure the health, prosperity, and freedom of the people. In spite of these problems, however, available statistics demonstrate that in Megalopolis the population is on the average healthier, the consumption of goods higher, and the opportunity for advancement greater than in any other region of comparable extent.

Thus the type of urban growth experienced here generates many contrasts, paradoxes, and apparently contradictory trends. It calls for debate and naturally excites passionate opinions for and against it. Are its results for the better or for the worse? It is not for our generation to moralize on the matter, but to strive to make the out-come be for the better, whatever obstacles may be in the way. Megalopolis stands indeed at the threshold of a new way of life, and upon solution of its problems will rest civilization's ability to survive. In the search for such solutions there will be found no easy keys to success, no "gimmicks" or "open-sesames." Solutions must be thought out, ironed out, and constantly revised in the light of all the knowledge that can be acquired by all concerned.

Conclusion

As our population grows, patterns of human organization must change. Gottman suggests that in Megalopolis we are witnessing "the cradle of a new order in the organization of inhabited spaces." The author claims that the key features of "Boswash," the megalopolis that stretches from Boston to Washington, will be the characteristics of most other communities in the years to come. Do you think that our nation will be very different when almost all Americans live in this new form of ecological habitat?

SUMMARY

The scientific and quantitative study of population, or demography, is concerned with the size and distribution of population and the factors that affect it. Most demographic data are based on the *census,* a periodic head count of a population which includes data about age, sex, marital status, income, family size, and similar characteristics of population members. The accuracy of census questionnaires is checked through detailed recounts of a very small sample of the population. Census data are supplemented by government records of vital statistics: births, deaths, marriages, and international migration. Such data are used by the government and by numerous private organizations and businesses for a variety of planning purposes. Usually information is reported by geographic units with politically defined boundaries. The *census tract,* resulting from division of an urban area into smaller, well-defined units often based on natural boundaries, is especially important in ecological research.

The nature of a society both determines and is in turn determined by size and composition of its population, as reflected, for example, in death, disease, and fertility rates. Demographers are concerned especially with sex and age ratios. The proportion of males and females in a population will affect both marriage patterns and fertility rates. The age distribution of a population can affect a country's economic productivity. Societies with a high percentage of young and old people will have a lower proportion of economically productive members, and a large number of persons who are economically dependent on them.

Demographers are concerned not only with analysis of data, but also with the prediction of population changes based, in part, on projections of existing trends. Changes are affected by fertility (birthrate), mortality (death rate), and migration. Fertility depends on biological factors such as the number and health of childbearing women in a population, and on social factors such as attitudes toward reproduction. The *crude birthrate,* or number of births per 1,000 women in a population, can be refined by examining the birthrate among women of a specific age and marital status (*age-specific birthrate* and *age-specific marital birthrate*). Within a society these rates vary in terms of social class, race, religion, and place of residence.

Fertility rates are largely influenced by personal considerations such as the desire for a large family, together with social policies. Mortality rates are affected by a society's willingness and ability to mobilize its resources to achieve the goal of good health and long life for its citizens, and by the level of medical technology. In America there has been a steady increase in the *average life expectancy,* the average number of years a person at birth can expect to live. This change has increased the number of economically dependent persons in our country. Mortality rates are highest among the lower classes, reflecting poorer environmental and health conditions. Our *infant mortality rate,* the age-specific rate for those under one year, is relatively high among Western industrialized societies. This rate is generally considered the best indicator of a population's health level and medical welfare facilities. Specific information about a society's mortality patterns are provided by *life tables,* a measure of survival rates of those born at any given time.

Population fluctuations may be caused by migration, or the movement of people from one geographic area to another. Five types of migration have been distinguished: 1) *primitive migration,* in which people follow the movement of food animals; 2) *forced migration,* the compulsory transfer of people from one country or region to another; 3) *impelled migration,* caused by extremely difficult social or economic conditions; 4) *free migration,* movement motivated by a desire for adventure or a search for improved living conditions; and 5) *controlled migration,* free migration under governmentally prescribed conditions such as quotas.

It has traditionally been thought that pre-industrial societies maintained population stability by balancing high birthrates with high death rates, while in modernizing societies population growth exploded as death rates were suddenly lowered and birthrates remained high; fully urbanized societies achieved stability once again through a lowered birthrate. It now appears that there are many variations of this pattern. Despite recent decreases in the birthrate of many industrialized countries, the problem of overpopulation remains an immediate and global concern.

The relationship of population and environment to social structure has been studied by sociological ecologists. Focusing on the ecology of urban communities, they have identified a number of processes: 1) *Concentration and dispersion* occur as people migrate from rural areas to the city while others leave the city for the suburbs; as urban areas spread and overlap *megalopolises* are formed. 2) *Ecological segregation* is the process in which natural areas of the city become specialized in types of land use, services, or population. 3) *Invasion and succession* refer to the entrance of one group into the territory of another. Urban spatial structure has been explained in terms of the *concentric zone model* in which the central business district is ringed by progressively higher status areas; the *sector model* in which pie-slice zones fan out from the center; and the *multiple nuclei* model in which outlying subcenters of business, commerce, and residence expand and merge. As concern over man's relationship with his environment has increased, sociologists are beginning to focus on the interrelationship of population, organization, environment, and technology as an ecosystem, and on the relation between population density and human behavior.

GLOSSARY

Age-specific birthrate   The number of live births per 1,000 women of a specified age group. (page 457)

Age-specific death rate   The number of deaths per 1,000 persons in a specified age group of a population. (page 458)

Age-specific marital fertility rate   The number of live births per 1,000 married women of a specified age group. (page 457)

Census   The counting and collection of data about a population, usually involving a count of every person. (page 447)

Census tract   A small subdivision of an urban area, usually including from 3,000 to 6,000 people, which is created to make easier the tabulation and analysis of population data. (page 451)

Centralization   The concentration of economic, governmental, and service functions. (page 469)

Concentration   The ecological process in which individual and social units tend to cluster where conditions are favorable. (page 468)

Controlled migration   Migration which takes place within government restrictions. (page 461)

Crude birthrate   The number of live births per 1,000 persons in a population within a given time period, usually a year. (page 457)

Crude death rate   The number of deaths per 1,000 persons in the population during a given period, usually a year. (page 458)

Decentralization   The dispersion of economic, governmental, and service functions. (page 469)

Demography   The study of population size, composition and distribution, and patterns of population change. (page 445)

Dispersion   The scattering of population and social units; the opposite of concentration. (page 468)

Ecological segregation   The process in which certain areas of a city become specialized in type of land use, services, or population. (page 469)

Ecology   The study of the interrelationships between organisms and their environment. (page 446)

Ecosystem (or **Ecological complex**)   The web of interrelationships between living things and their environment. (pages 467 and 473)

Fecundity   The potential capacity of the females of a population to have children. This figure represents an estimate of the maximum number of births biologically possible in the population. (page 456)

Fertility The frequency of births in a population. (page 456)

Forced migration Compulsory transfer of people from one region or country to another. (page 461)

Free migration The movement of peoples motivated by an individual desire for adventure or a search for improved living conditions and social circumstances. (page 461)

Impelled migration The movement of people from one country to another due to social conditions, wherein the individual may choose not to leave. (page 461)

Infant mortality rate Age-specific death rate for infants under the age of one. (page 460)

Invasion A process involving the movement of one type of population or land use into an area already occupied by a different type of population or land use. (page 470)

Life table A statistical table that presents the death rate and life expectancy of each of a series of age-sex categories over a period of time. (page 460)

Megalopolis A concentration of two or more metropolitan areas which have grown and spread until they overlap one another. (page 469)

Migration The movements of individuals or groups from one geographical area to another. (page 460)

Natural area A territorial area with some common unifying characteristic which emerges through ecological processes. (page 470)

Neonatal mortality rate Age-specific death rate for infants under one month of age. (page 460)

Primitive migration Movement of a population to follow food sources. (page 460)

Sex ratio The number of males per 100 females in a specified population. (page 453)

Succession The replacement of one type of occupancy of an area by another type; the completion of the process of invasion. (page 470)

SUGGESTED READINGS AND RELATED RESOURCES

I READINGS IN SOCIOLOGY

Beshers, James. *Population Processes in Social Systems*. New York: Free Press, 1967. An introductory book, but somewhat theoretical, on the role of population in societies.

Duncan, Otis Dudley. *Metropolis and Region*. Baltimore: Johns Hopkins Press, 1960. A lengthy and sophisticated discussion of metropolitan ecology, with descriptions of the intraregional relationships of fifty major U.S. cities.

Falk, Richard. *This Endangered Planet*. New York: Random House, 1971. Falk analyzes war, overpopulation, depletion of resources, and deterioration of the environment, and discusses philosophical, political, and economic means to avert catastrophe.

Freedman, Ronald, ed. *Population: The Vital Revolution*. New York: Doubleday, Anchor, 1964. A nontechnical survey of the most important population trends of modern times, this collection of essays on population studies will be of interest to both students of population and laymen.

Hauser, Philip, ed. *The Population Dilemma*. Englewood Cliffs, N.J.: Prentice-Hall (Paper), 1969. This collection of essays by economists and students of population concentrates upon the consequences and problems of rapid population growth.

Hawley, Amos. *Human Ecology: A Theory of Community Structure*. New York: Ronald Press, 1950. A pioneering work, Hawley's book pulls together a general theory of human ecology.

Hertzler, J. O. *The Crisis in World Population*. Lincoln, Nebr.: University of Nebraska, 1961. A study of social problems which are related to population growth, such as food supply, migration, and family planning.

Nam, Charles. *Population and Society*. Boston: Houghton Mifflin, 1968. This book can serve as a follow-up for students interested in doing a research exercise in analyzing population and its relationship to the social and economic aspects of society.

Petersen, William. *The Politics of Population*. New York: Doubleday, 1964. This book is a readable study of population growth and family planning and the reactions and adjustments they involve.

Schnore, Leo. *The Urban Scene: Human*

Ecology and Demography. New York: Free Press, 1965. This collection of Schnore's articles compares the populations and environments of American urban and suburban areas.

Theodorson, George, ed. *Studies in Human Ecology.* New York: Row, Peterson, 1961. This is one of the most complete collections of articles in the field of human ecology.

Wrong, D. H. *Population and Society.* New York: Random House, 1961. Wrong clearly defines the major aspects and concerns of population analysis and its relation to society.

Articles and Papers

Bogue, Donald J. "The End of the Population Explosion." *Public Interest* **7** (Spring 1967): 11 – 20.

Brown, L. A., and J. C. Belcher. "Residential Mobility of Physicians in Georgia." *Rural Sociology* **31**, 4 (December 1966):439–448.

Burrus, John Newell, and C. A. McMahon. "An Analysis of Selected Demographic Aspects of Autopsied Cases in Certain Southeastern States and Counties." *Southern Quarterly* **1**, 1 (October 1962):1–12.

Davis, Kingsley. "The Unpredicted Pattern of Population Change." *Annals of the American Academy of Political and Social Science* **305** (May 1956):53–59.

Deevey, Edward S., Jr. "The Human Population." *Scientific American* **203**, 3 (1960):194 – 204.

Duncan, Otis D. "Social Organizations and the Ecosystem." In *Handbook of Modern Sociology,* edited by R. L. Faris. Chicago: Rand NcNally, 1964.

Gibbs, Jack P., and Leo F. Schnore. "Metropolitan Growth: An International Study." *American Journal of Sociology* **66** (1960):160 – 170.

Hauser, Philip M. "The Chaotic Society: Product of the Social Morphological Revolution." *American Sociological Review* **34**, 1 (February 1969):1 – 19.

Lindgren, Herbert. "Perception Changes of Farm Immigrants Before and After Migration." *Rural Sociology* **34**, 2 (June 1969):223 – 227.

Mayer, Kurt B. "Developments in the Study of Population." *Social Research* **29**, 3 (Autumn 1962):293 – 320.

Robinson, W. S. "Ecological Correlations and the Behavior of Individuals." *American Sociological Review* **15**, (June 1950):351 – 357.

II SOURCES OF POPULATION DATA

Donald J. Bogue. *The Population of the United States.* New York: Free Press, 1959. An encyclopedic work designed to serve as a reference book for social scientists. Although the statistics are somewhat dated, the discussion of the issues in population studies is still relevant.

Millbank Memorial Fund. *Emerging Techniques in Population Research.* Proceedings of the 1962 Annual Conference, New York, 1963. This is only one of a constantly expanding series of volumes financed and published by the Fund. They include topics such as population growth, fertility, migration, and industrialization, and usually concentrate on a particular part of the world, such as southern Asia.

United Nations, Department of Social Affairs, Population Division. *The Future Growth of World Population.* Population Studies, no. 28. New York: United Nations, 1958. Contains projections of the population of the world, of countries and regions, and discusses the reasons for growth and decline. More recent projections may be found in later Population Division publications.

United Nations, Statistical Office. *Demographic Yearbook.* New York: published annually. Contains basic data on the social, economic, and occupational characteristics of most of the member nations. The data from the Warsaw Pact Nations are frequently very outdated, but it is still the best source for comparative international population statistics.

Catalog of U. S. Census Publications, 1790– 1945. Washington, D.C.: Government Printing Office, 1950. The original catalog is cumulative, and supplements are issued annually. It is a convenient guide to Census Bureau publications and is divided into broad subject areas, such as agriculture, population, and housing.

U.S. Bureau of the Census. *Census of the Population, 1970.* Washington, D.C.: Government Printing Office, 1971. This is the complete report of the decennial census and comes in several volumes, each devoted to one subject area. It contains detailed statistics on every aspect of the census.

U.S. Bureau of the Census. *Current Population Reports.* Especially the series P-20, P-25, and P-60. Washington, D.C.: Government Printing Office. These reports are issued at irregular intervals between censuses to update census data on particular subjects. They are issued in pamphlet form and are available from the Superintendent of Documents, U.S. Government Printing Office, Washington, D.C.

U.S. Bureau of the Census. *Historical Statistics of the U.S. (Colonial Times to 1957)*. Washington, D.C.: Government Printing Office, 1958. Supplement, 1958–1962. A two-volume set containing most of the information given in the Statistical Abstracts since 1790.

U.S. Bureau of the Census, *Statistical Abstract of the United States*. Washington, D.C.: Government Printing Office, published annually. This summary of vital statistics and population characteristics contains statistics from the Department of Commerce and other government agencies.

U.S. Department of Health, Education and Welfare. *Vital Statistics of the United States, Annual Report*. Washington, D.C.: Government Printing Office. A detailed account of births, deaths, and marriages by state, region, age, sex, and race. This information may be updated by referring to *Monthly Vital Statistics Report,* published by the National Center for Health Statistics.

III RELATED RESOURCES
Nonfiction

De Bell, Garrett. *The Environmental Handbook*. New York: Ballantine (Paper), 1970. This book was compiled for the "first national environmental teach-in" on 22 April 1970. It consists of essays on the "meaning of ecology," and proposes actions which could help to prevent further deterioration of our environment.

DuBos, René. *So Human an Animal*. New York: Charles Scribner's Sons (Paper), 1968. DuBos' book, which won a 1969 Pulitzer Prize, deals with the dehumanizing aspects of man's environment and the prospects for man's future.

Ehrlich, Paul. *The Population Bomb*. New York: Ballantine (Paper), 1968. Ehrlich warns of overpopulation and diminishing food supplies, and also writes of two other dangers to man's environment—air and water pollution.

Handlin, Oscar. *The Uprooted*. New York: Grossett & Dunlap (Paper), 1957. Through an historical perspective, Handlin writes about the migration of Europeans who eventually made up the American people.

Morris, Desmond. *The Human Zoo*. New York: McGraw-Hill, 1969. An interesting and readable comparison of man's biological and social evolution with that of the other animals. As in Morris's other books, the emphasis is upon the interrelationship between biology and social behavior.

————. *The Naked Ape*. New York: Dell, 1967. In this book Morris studies man as an animal and compares man's origin, living habits, and survival instincts to those of the rest of the animal kingdom.

Reid, Leslie. *Sociology of Nature*. Baltimore: Penguin (Paper), 1962. Reid applies some of the principles of social ecology to a study of animal life.

Fiction

Shute, Nevil. *On the Beach*. New York: Signet (Paper), 1958. This novel is set in Australia after an atomic war. Shute depicts the responses of certain individuals and the adjustment of the community as a whole to the threat of destruction by radioactive fallout.

Steinbeck, John. *In Dubious Battle*. New York: Viking Press, 1936. Steinbeck depicts the intense struggles of the American people for justice and survival during the Depression.

Whyte, William H. *The Last Landscape*. New York: Doubleday, Anchor (Paper), 1968. The effects environment has on human relations are the subject of this book in which Whyte suggests possible ways to develop a more livable environment.

Films

America America. Elia Kazan, 1963. A fictional story of a Greek youth who tries to escape oppression and emigrate to America.

The Covered Wagon. James Cruze, 1923. This classic film is about the American migration movement to the West.

On the Beach. Stanley Kramer, 1959. An adaptation of Nevil Shute's novel of the same name, which hypothesizes what would happen to the survivors of a nuclear holocaust.

Weekend. Jean-Luc Godard, 1968. This film is a vision of the consequences of man's selfish disrespect for life.

III

Order and Change in Society

12. Deviant Behavior and Social Control

Human social life depends on the willingness of its members to follow certain rules and to regulate their behavior in accordance with certain norms. A society can only survive and function as long as most of the people follow most of the rules.

When social rules exist it is inevitable that on certain occasions, for a variety of reasons, some people are going to break some of the rules: they are going to be deviant. If one rule is broken once, very little harm is done to the society as a whole. However, if many rules are broken frequently, the very existence of the society is in danger. Therefore the society must evolve some way of enforcing conformity with the rules—a process called social control.

In discussing deviance and the mechanisms by which society controls it, we will begin by defining deviance and mentioning some of the types of deviance that occur most frequently. Next we will look at causes of deviant behavior. The third topic focuses on how the deviant is regarded by others and by himself, and the way deviance affects or alters his subsequent social experiences. Then we will discuss the ways and means at society's disposal as it attempts to control social deviance. The concluding topic touches briefly on how episodes of deviant behavior affect the successful operation and continuation of social systems.

(Santi Visalli, Photoreporters)

1 THE NATURE OF DEVIANCE

We can roughly define *deviance* as the process of breaking the rules and norms of society. A deviant can be a traitor to his country, a woman who refuses to put a nickel in the parking meter while she is at the grocery store, or a maniac who murders a dozen strangers for no apparent reason. It is hard to construct exact definitions or categories to cover all these varieties of deviance; in studying the subject, sociologists have developed a number of different approaches. We will discuss several of the major ones here.

DEFINING DEVIANCE

One way to define deviance is to say that it means "not average"; if you are like most other people, you are normal, and if you're not, then you are a deviant. In addition to the problems inherent in trying to arrive at a measurement of "average" this approach has a major drawback. Many kinds of unusual behavior are socially approved and do not violate any social rule. For example, it is not normal behavior for a man to send his wife flowers every day, but it is acceptable behavior to which there is no social objection. The same is true of writing with your left hand, or eating ice cream for breakfast; such actions are not average, but neither are they deviant. The social definition of deviance, then, implies more than just statistical abnormality.

A more common approach to defining deviance is through a medical analogy.[1] Conformity may be considered healthy or functional,

[1]. See Robert K. Merton, *Social Theory and Social Structure* (New York: Free Press, 1957); and Talcott Parsons, *The Social System* (New York: Free Press, 1951).

promoting the stability of the social system. Deviance then would be pathological or dysfunctional behavior, disrupting social stability and organization. This definition, too, has serious drawbacks. It is very difficult to determine what a healthy society is, much less, what contributes to such health. Also, sociologists have observed that deviance has some positive value for society (as we shall discuss in topic 5); in some cases it may actually serve to improve social functioning.

Even the simple definition of deviance as the failure to obey group rules leaves many questions unanswered. Which rules do we mean? Does it matter who breaks them, or why they are broken, or when they are broken? There are hundreds of examples to show that such conditions do influence the social definitions of deviance. A prostitute may solicit openly on the street one day without being bothered by the police; if she does it a day after the newspapers feature a story on corruption in the police department, she will be taken off to jail. Her behavior would be identical on both days, and yet it would be socially defined quite differently, and with very different consequences, on the two occasions. A thief who steals a car for an evening's ride is viewed, and treated, differently from one who steals it to sell to an unsuspecting purchaser. A derelict who murders another derelict will be treated much more leniently than the derelict who murders a wealthy man under the very same conditions. A wife who has extramarital sexual relations will be viewed with more disapproval, and considered more deviant, than the man with whom she was involved.

So we must conclude that the definition of

Deviant actions by certain individuals can make others aware that some social rules are bad or contradict other more important rules. The non-violent sit-ins by blacks in the 1960s thus pointed out the unfairness of segregation laws, thus changing some of the laws. *(Wide World Photos)*

deviance changes according to social circumstances. Howard Becker comments upon the relativity of deviance in writing about people who break the rules of one group by conforming to the rules of another:

Social rules are the creation of specific social groups. Modern societies are not simple organizations in which everyone agrees on what the rules are and how they are to be applied in specific situations. They are, instead, highly differentiated along social class lines, ethnic lines, occupational lines, and cultural lines. These groups need not, and in fact often do not share the same rules. The problems they face in dealing with their environment, the history and traditions they carry with them, all lead to the evolution of different sets of rules. Insofar as the rules of various groups conflict and contradict one another, there will be disagreement about the kind of behavior that is proper in any given situation.[2]

Becker has suggested that deviance should not be defined as a quality that is contained within a certain act; instead it is the outcome of social interactions between the person who commits the act and those who call the act deviant. We will discuss the significance of this concept, called labeling, in topic 3.

TYPES OF DEVIANCE

It is clear that deviants may be treated in a variety of ways, based on the attitudes members of society have about the specific act of deviance involved, and the apparent motivation for the act. The man who says he killed his wife when the gun he was showing her

2.   Howard S. Becker, *The Outsiders* (New York: Free Press, 1963), p. 15.

went off accidentally will probably be prosecuted for manslaughter, perhaps receiving only a suspended sentence; whereas the man who admits he shot his wife deliberately during a quarrel is likely to serve a long prison term. A man who has plotted his wife's death for months will probably draw the severest sentence the law can give. Some of the distinctions society makes between types of deviance are very useful for sociological study. Four major types are:

(1) *Aberrant behavior versus nonconforming behavior.* This distinction was originally made by Robert Merton.[3] The aberrant deviant is one who basically accepts the validity of the rules but breaks them for some personal advantage. Most types of criminal activity fit into this classification. So do such deviations as extramarital affairs, lying to one's employer, or failing to observe work quotas. The aberrant deviant always hopes to remain undetected. He often agrees that the rule he is breaking is a good one, and he may be opposed to its violation by others; he simply believes that his case constitutes an exception for some reason.

The nonconforming deviant is different; he usually hopes to attract attention to his rule-breaking behavior. He breaks the rule because he believes it is a bad one, one which no member of the society ought to have to observe. He hopes that by breaking it he can cause the rule to be changed. Thus nonconforming deviance is often an act of conscience and is the result of a commitment to some social ideal. Civil disobedience, as it has been practiced by black Americans and by antiwar protesters, is an example of nonconforming behavior. Another example would be an unmarried couple who live together openly because they do not believe in the institution of marriage.

(2) *Socially approved deviance versus socially disapproved deviance.*[4] In some cases,

breaking the rules may not bring social disapproval. At times, those who establish the official rules or regulations of the social system do not truly represent the sentiments or needs of the system's members, and consequently, unpopular laws, such as the Prohibition Amendment, are passed. When members of the system ignore or violate these laws their deviance may be approved by other members. In bureaucracies, those who create the rules may also create so much "red tape" that it is only through breaking the regulations that the organization can operate.

Rules can also be broken without disapproval when the deviant action can be justified by pointing to a higher cause. For example, Napoleon broke a number of France's legal and moral rules as he rose to power, but he justified this by making France the most powerful country in the world for a short period of time.

(3) *Inability to conform versus failure to conform.*[5] An insane or ill person may break many rules, because he is physically or mentally incapable of conforming to them. This kind of deviation, which sometimes is beyond anyone's power to correct (except, of course, by curing the person who is sick), is usually viewed with relative tolerance. Steps will probably be taken to restrain the deviant, such as putting him in a mental hospital, but he will not be held personally responsible for his deviations. A person who is capable of conforming but fails to do so, on the other hand, must usually accept the full responsibility for his deviance. A murderer who is judged to have been of "sound mind" at the time he committed the act will face a long prison term; if he is judged to have been insane, he may be hospitalized instead. It is often very hard to make the distinction between the two categories. Some psychological theorists believe that all antisocial acts are the result of real inability to behave any differently in the given

3. Robert K. Merton, "Social Problems and Social Theory," in *Contemporary Social Problems*, Robert K. Merton and Robert A. Nisbet, eds. (New York: Harcourt Brace Jovanovich, 1966), pp. 808–811.

4. See Edwin H. Sutherland, *White Collar Crime* (New York: Holt, Rinehart and Winston, 1967).

5. Fred Davis, "Deviance Disavowal: The Management of Strained Interaction by the Visibly Handicapped," in *The Other Side*, ed. Howard S. Becker (New York: Free Press, 1964), pp. 119–137.

situation at the given time; surely we have all had the experience of knowing that we ought to do something and yet for some reason just cannot make ourselves do it. But too broad a definition of the inability to conform makes the concept of personal responsibility meaningless.

(4) *Individual deviance versus group deviance*.[6] Some kinds of deviance are the result of a single individual acting alone; others are the act of a group as a collective or corporate entity. A corporation is deviant, for example, when it breaks laws about price fixing or monopolistic trade practices. Group deviance raises some complex questions about the responsibility of the individual. When is an individual acting in his own behalf, and when in behalf of the corporation? Different answers to this question will lead to very different consequences—a group is not punished in the same way as an individual. Assessing the degree of involvement and responsibility in cases of group deviance presents difficult social, legal, and moral questions, and this is one reason the distinction between group and individual deviation is an important one to make. The adjacent abridgment describes an instance of group deviance within an aircraft factory.

We are all skilled in making the distinctions outlined here, although we may not realize that we are doing it. An employer offers a responsible position to an ex-convict whose crime was armed robbery; the traffic policeman does not issue a ticket to the speeder who is taking a sick child to the hospital; the boy who doesn't want to come home on time is punished more severely than his brother who is late because he is not able to tell time. It is our almost unconscious awareness of these fine distinctions that helps keep the system of social regulation a functional and viable force.

6. See Herbert Block and Arthur Niederhoffer, *The Gang* (New York: The Philosophical Library, 1958).

JOSEPH BENSMAN AND ISRAEL GERVER
The Crime of Tapping

From "Crime and Punishment in the Factory: The Function of Deviancy in Maintaining the Social System," in the *American Sociological Review*, Vol. 28, August 1963, pp. 588–598.

Introduction

This selection presents a study of an airplane factory where the norms of workers encourage the breaking of an important work rule. It demonstrates the situation described by Howard Becker, where conformity to one group's rules entails deviance according to the standards of a second group. The question of punishment in such cases is a complex one, and within the factory studied, a delicate balance had been achieved between enforcement of the law of the organization and support for group members, so that the rule breaking, a necessary part of keeping up production, could continue.

The research was carried out in an airplane factory employing 26,000 people in the New York metropolitan area. One of the authors was a participant observer from September 1953 through September 1954. He gathered his data in the daily course of work while working as an assembler on the aileron crew of the final wing line. No special research instruments were used; the ordinary activities of workers along the line were observed and noted as they occurred, and recorded daily. All aspects involved in the use of the tap were discussed in the context of the work situation when they were relevant and salient to the personnel involved, and without their realizing that they were objects of study.

The tap and its functions

The tap is a tool, an extremely hard steel screw, whose threads are slotted to allow for the disposal of the waste metal which it cuts away. It is sufficiently hard so that when it is inserted into a nut it can cut new threads over the original threads of the nut.

The use of the tap is the most serious crime of workmanship conceivable in the plant. A worker can be summarily fired for merely possessing a tap. Nevertheless, at least one-half of the work force in a position to use a tap owns at least one.

The tap is defined as a criminal instrument, primarily because it destroys the effectiveness of stop nuts. Aviation nuts are specifically designed, so that, once tightened, a screw or bolt cannot back out of the nut under the impact of vibration in flight. Once a nut is tapped, however, it loses its holding power and at any time, after sufficient vibration, the screw or bolt can fall out and weaken the part it holds to the wing and the wing itself.

In addition, the use of a tap is an illegal method of concealing a structural defect. If the holes, for example, were properly drilled and the nuts were properly installed, the use of the tap would be unnecessary. Whenever a tap is used, there are indications of deviations from standards. Furthermore, such deviations make subsequent maintenance of the airplane difficult since maintenance mechanics have no records of such illegal deviations from specifications.

The tap, then, is an illegal tool, the use or possession of which carries extreme sanctions in private organizational law, but which is simultaneously widely possessed and used despite its illegal status. The problem of such a pattern for the meaning of private organizational law is to account for the wide acceptance of a crime as a means of fulfilling work requirements within a private organization, the aircraft plant.

The socialization of the worker

To most workers entering an aircraft plant the tap is an unknown instrument. The new worker does not come into contact with the tap until he finds it impossible to align the holes in two skins. In desperation and somewhat guiltily as if he had made a mistake, he turns to his partner (a more experienced worker) and states his problem. The experienced worker will try every legitimate technique of lining up the holes, but if these do not succeed, he resorts to the tap. He taps the new thread himself, not permitting the novice to use the tap. While tapping it he gives the novice a lecture on the dangers of getting caught and of breaking a tap in the hole, thereby leaving telltale evidence of its use.

For several weeks the older worker will not permit his inexperienced partner to use a tap when its use is required. He leaves his own work in order to do the required tapping and finishes the job before returning to his own work. If the novice demonstrates sufficient ability and care in other aspects of his work he will be allowed to tap the hole under the supervision of a veteran worker. When the veteran partner is absent, and the now initiated worker can use the tap at his own discretion, he feels a sense of pride. In order to enjoy his new found facility, he frequently uses the tap when it is not necessary. He may be careless in properly aligning perfectly good components and then compensate for his own carelessness by using the tap.

Sooner or later he inevitably runs into difficulties which he is technically unprepared to cope with. When his partner and mentor is not available, he is forced to call upon the assistant foreman. If the situation requires it, the foreman will recommend the tap. If he has doubts about the worker's abilities, he may even tap the hole himself. In doing this, he risks censure of the union, because as a foreman he is not permitted to handle tools.

While the foreman taps the hole, he also lectures on the proper and technically work-manlike ways of using the tap: "The tap is turned only at quarter turns . . . never force the tap . . . it has to go in easy or it's likely to snap . . . if it snaps, your ass is in a sling and I won't be able to get you out of it."

The foreman warns the worker to make sure "not to get caught, to see that the coast is clear, to keep the tap well hidden when not in use, and to watch out for inspectors while using it." He always ends by cautioning the worker, "It's your own ass if you're caught."

When the worker feels that he is experienced and can use the tap with complete confidence, he usually buys his own, frequently displaying it to other workers and magnanimously lending it to those in need of it. He feels himself fully arrived when a foreman borrows his tap or asks him to perform the tapping. The worker has now established his identity and is known as an individual by the higher ups.

Once the right to use the tap is thus established, the indiscriminate use of it is frowned upon. A worker who uses a tap too often is considered to be a careless "botcher." A worker who can get his work done without frequently using a tap is a "mechanic," but one who doesn't use the tap when it is necessary does not get his own work done on time. Proper use of the tap requires judgement and etiquette. The tap addict is likely to become the object of jokes and to get a bad work reputation among workers, foremen and inspectors.

Agencies of law enforcement

The enforcement of the plant rules of workmanship devolves upon three groups: foremen, plant quality control and Air Force quality control. The ultimate and supreme authority resides in the latter group. The Air Force not only sets the blueprint specifications, but also and more impor-tantly, can reject a finished airplane as not meeting specifications.

There were only two Air Force inspectors to a shop at the time of these observations, so that it was almost impossible for Air Force inspectors to police an entire shop of over 2,000 men. As an Air Force inspector walks up the line, it is standard procedure for workers to nudge other workers to inform them of the approach of the "Gestapo." When tapping is essential and when it is known that Air Force inspec-tors are too near, guards of workers are posted to convey advance notice of this approach to any one who is actively tapping. This is especially true when there are plant drives against the use of the tap.

Despite the Air Force inspectors' high authority and the severity of their standards, they are not sufficiently numerous to be considered the major policing agency for detecting and apprehending violators of the rules of workmanship. Plant quality control is the actual law enforcement agency in terms of the daily operations of surveillance. There are approximately 150 plant in-spectors to a 2,000 man shop. They work along the assembly line along with the workers.

There is a general understanding that workers are not supposed to use a tap in the presence of plant inspectors. At various times this understanding is made explicit. The inspector frequently tells the workers of his crew: "Now fellas, there's a big drive now on taps. The Air Force just issued a special memo. For God's sakes, don't use a tap when I'm around. If somebody sees it while I'm in the area, it'll be my ass. Look around first. Make sure I'm gone."

At other times the verbalization comes from the worker. If a worker has to use a tap and the inspector is present, he will usually wait until the inspector leaves. If the inspector shows no sign of leaving, the worker will tell him to "Get the hell outa here. I got work to do and can't do it while you're around."

If the worker knows the inspector he may take out the tap, permitting the inspector to see it. The wise inspector responds to the gesture by leaving. Of course, a worker has already "sized up" the inspector and knows whether or not he can rely upon him to respond as desired.

When there is an Air Force-inspired drive against the tap, the inspectors will make the rounds and "lay the law down": "I want no more tapping around here. The next guy caught gets turned in. I can't cover you guys any more. I'm not kidding you bastards. If you can't do a decent job, don't do it at all. If that s.o.b. foreman of yours insists on you doing it, tell him to do it himself. He can't make you do it. If you're caught, it's your ass not his. When the chips are down, he's got to cover himself and he'll leave you holding the bag!"

For about three or four days thereafter taps disappear from the public view. The work slows down, and ultimately the inspectors forget to be zealous. A state of normal haphazard equilibrium is restored.

The role of the foreman

In rare cases an inspector will catch a worker using the tap, reprimand him and turn him over to his foreman. The foreman then is forced to go through the procedure of reprimanding the errant worker. The foreman becomes serious and indignant, primarily because the worker let himself get caught. He gives the worker a genuine tongue lashing, and he reminds him once again that he, as foreman, has to go to bat to save the worker's neck. He stresses that it is only because of *his* intervention that the worker will not lose his job. He states, "Next time be careful. I won't stick my neck out for you again. For God's sakes don't use a tap, *unless it's absolutely necessary.*"

The worker is obliged to accept the reprimand and to assume the countenance of true penitent, even to the extent of promising that it won't happen again. He will say, "Awright, awright. So I got caught this time. Next time I won't get caught." Both the foreman and worker play these roles even though the worker tapped the hole at the specific request of the foreman. The most blatant violation of the mores in such a situation is when the worker grins and treats the whole thing as a comic interlude. When this happens, the foreman becomes truly enraged, "That's the trouble with you. You don't take your job seriously. You don't give a damn about nothing. How long do I have to put up with your not giving a damn!"

The public ritual therefore conceals an entirely different dimension of social functions involved in the use of the tap. It is inconceivable that the tap could be used without the active or passive collusion of the foreman. As noted, the foreman instructs the worker in its use, indicates when he wants it used, assists the worker in evading the plant rules, and when the worker is caught, goes through the ritual of punishment. These role contradictions are intrinsic to the position of the foreman.

The pressures "to get work out" are paramount for the foreman. There is a relatively high turnover among foremen. In the last analysis, production records are the major consideration in supervisory mobility. All other considerations, e.g., sociability, work knowledge, personality, etc., are assumed to be measured by the production chart.

In this context the foreman, vis-a-vis the ticklish question of the tap, is compelled to violate some of the most important laws of the company and the Air Force. Crucial instances occur at times when the Air Force institutes stringent anti-tap enforcement measures. When key holes do not line up it may be necessary, as an alternative to using the tap, to disassemble previous installations. The disassembling and reassembling may take a full eight hours before the previously reached work stage is again reached. The production chart for that eight-hour period will indicate that no work has been done. In such a situation the worker may refuse to tap a hole since he risks endangering his job. The foreman also may be reluctant to request directly that the worker tap a hole. To get the work done he therefore employs a whole rhetoric of veiled requests such as "Hell, that's easy . . . you know what to do . . . you've done it before." "Maybe you can clean out the threads," or "Well, see what you can do."

If the worker is adamant, the foreman will practically beg him to do the *right* thing. He will remind him of past favors, he will complain about his chart rating and of how "top brass doesn't give a damn about anything but what's on the chart." He usually ends his plea with: "Once you get this done, you can take it easy. You know I don't work you guys too hard most of the time."

If the veiled requests and pitiful pleadings don't produce results, the foreman may take the ultimate step of tapping the hole himself. He compounds the felony, because he not only violates the rules of workmanship but also violates union rules which specifically state that no foreman can use a tool. To add insult to injury, the foreman further has to borrow the tap in the midst of an anti-tap drive when taps are scarce.

From the viewpoint of production the use of the tap is imperative to the functioning of the production organization, even though it is one of the most serious work crimes.

Summary

From the point of view of the actors involved, the major definition of "deviancy" takes on another dimension. The major crime for the actors involved is the lack of respect for the social ceremonialism surrounding the tap. The worker who allows an inspector to see him possessing or using a tap threatens the defenses of the inspector and is likely to be reprimanded for not being careful. He is likely to find it harder to "sell" his work to that inspector. He gets a bad reputation and is thought of as a "character." Similarly, in talking to an inspector the worker who casually mentions illegal workmanship is told by this inspector not to mention it. Finally, a worker who grins while being reprimanded for the use of the tap, is likely to be bawled out for lack of awareness of the seriousness of his act and his flippant attitude. The foreman is likely to threaten him with a withdrawal from the circle of protection given by the foreman to apprehended criminals.

The worker is taught the proper techniques of tapping, and he is taught the situations for which use of the tap is appropriate. Misuse of the tap (using the tap as a substitute for lining up holes and for careless workmanship) is frowned upon by supervisors. Using the tap as a substitute for less severely defined illegal techniques of workmanship is also frowned upon.

The worker who uses the tap promiscuously is subject to a wide variety of informal controls. He is kidded and teased by other workers. Inspectors become sensitive to his action, and when he is caught, he is reported and bawled out, primarily because of his reputation and not so much for the use of the tap in a specific situation. The foreman rides him unmercifully and tends to become more sensitive to all his faults of workmanship. If he persists in abusing the use of the tap, he ultimately gets transferred to another foreman who is short of men. The floating worker is presumed to be a botcher by the very fact of his being transferred.

In no case, however, are formal actions, which involve the possibility of dismissal, taken against the worker. This is because, in writing up a worker for abusing the tap, the foreman would risk the danger of bringing into the open and into official and public channels the whole issue of the use of the tap. In punishing promiscuous tappers by official means, the foreman might risk losing opportunities to have the tap used in situations which are advantageous to him. Moreover, in bringing serious charges against the deviant tapper, the foreman might find that workers necessarily would be hesitant to use the tap in situations the foreman regards as necessary.

The use of such controls results in a new definition of crime and its function at the behavioral level. A "crime" is not a crime so long as its commission is controlled and directed by those in authority toward goals which they define as socially constructive. A violation of law is treated as a crime when it is not directed and controlled by those in authority or when it is used for exclusively personal ends.

Conclusion

Deviance has been defined as rule breaking. But what happens if conflicting rules are applied to certain types of behavior? This was the case in the airplane factory. Production was supposed to remain high, but one of the prerequisites for maintaining high production was not supposed to be used. This conflict led to the development of a new "informal" rule which came to govern the situation. The new rule was that the tap could be used if its use went undetected. Society often acts to reduce conflict in this way; new norms are continually emerging from the specific circumstances of social interaction in changing situations.

TOPIC
2 BECOMING DEVIANT

We have discussed what deviance is; the next step is to look at the deviants themselves. Why do some people break the rules of society? Or it might seem more logical to ask why some people obey the social rules. The very fact that we look at deviance rather than conformity as the quality that needs explaining is an indication of the tremendous power of social organization, and of the degree to which most people accept social rules.

Social scientists have developed a variety of theories in an attempt to explain the causes of deviant behavior. The fact that there are so many different theories to explain deviance does not necessarily mean that some are right while others are wrong. Deviance may be anything from the persistent failure to greet a neighbor passed on the street to a lifetime career of crime, so there will be no single factor to explain such varied phenomena. In addition, most theories are closely tied to the focus of the discipline in which they were developed: psychologists develop theories concentrating on psychological factors, sociologists develop theories concentrating on social factors. Each of the theories we will discuss here may be very useful for explaining some kinds or aspects of deviance.

It is especially important in discussing theories of deviance to remember that social scientists deal with general causes and not with causes specific to the act of a given individual. Many people can be in a situation that encourages deviance and yet maintain their conformity. As with most human behavior, there is an element of human variation that cannot be measured. We can say with some certainty that certain types or groups of people will be most likely to exhibit signs of deviant behavior, but we can rarely predict which individuals of that group will be the deviants. For example, we know that underprivileged teenagers commit a relatively high number of deviant acts; but this is not to say that all underprivileged teenagers are deviant, or that we can tell which underprivileged teenagers will be deviant.

The search for the origins and causes of deviant behavior has been conducted on three different levels. Some scholars find the origin of deviance to be biological; they feel that certain organic weaknesses are primarily responsible for much deviant behavior. Psychologists, along with many of the general public, attribute deviance to personality maladjustments. Sociologists feel that, although biological and psychological problems can influence a person's tendency to be deviant, we may achieve a much fuller understanding of why people break rules through a knowledge of the social environment of the deviant.

BIOLOGICAL CAUSES OF DEVIANCE

Many kinds of deviant behavior have been carefully studied to see if biological factors may be involved. For example, several researchers have tried to establish a connection between body structure and criminality. A nineteenth-century Italian, Cesare Lombroso, suggested that criminals were biologically less advanced than law-abiding citizens.[7] The American anthropologist Ernest Hooten concluded in 1939 that criminals were genetically and physically degenerate human beings.[8] American psychologist William Sheldon, in a book published in 1949, stated that body type could be linked to criminal intent, and that the same genes that produce a stocky body type (the mesomorph) also produce an inclina-

tion to break social rules.[9] Regarding these studies, sociologist Albert Cohen has stated: "No conclusions can be drawn, because so much of the research has been so shoddy."[10]

However, the search for biological factors continues as an important area of research. In the 1960s two scientists, Menachem Amir and Yitzchak Berman, published a paper in which they reported that a high percentage of men who had committed crimes of violence were found by laboratory tests to have a chromosome abnormality, a combination of chromosomes that rarely occurs.[11] Further investigation has supported this observation: for example, tests revealed Richard Speck, who was convicted of killing seven nurses in Chicago, to have this abnormality.[12] There is as yet no proof that the abnormal chromosome actually causes the violent behavior of the deviant, and it has been shown that not all criminals have the abnormality. It is, however, quite possible that there is a genetic factor involved in some kinds of deviant behavior, that some men born with such genetic factors are more prone to commit violent crimes than is a normal person. Much more research must be done before we can draw any firm conclusions. Albert Cohen feels that it is reasonable to expect "that the linkages of biology to the various forms of deviance will be as various, indirect and remote as its linkages to the varieties of conforming behavior."[13]

PSYCHOLOGICAL CAUSES OF DEVIANCE

Both psychologists and sociologists have suggested that certain types of personalities are more often associated with deviant be-

7.   See Cesare Lombroso, *Crime: Its Causes and Remedies* (Boston: Little, Brown, 1918).

8.   Ernest A. Hooten, *Crime and the Man* (Cambridge, Mass.: Harvard University Press, 1939).

9.   William H. Sheldon, *Varieties of Delinquent Youth* (New York: Harper & Bros., 1949).

10.   Albert K. Cohen, *Deviance and Control* (Englewood Cliffs, N.J.: Prentice-Hall, 1969), p. 53.

11.   Menachem Amir and Yitzchak Berman, "Chromosomal Deviation and Crime," *Federal Probation* 34 (June 1970):55–62.

12.   Richard D. Lyons, "Ultimate Speck Appeal May Cite Genetic Defect," *New York Times* (22 April 1968).

13.   Albert K. Cohen, *Deviance and Control*, p. 54.

havior than are others. One hypothesis is that some people are less able to control inner impulses or are less able to structure their behavior in an orderly way. For example, some people are unable to defer gratification in the present for some future benefit. The possibility of future benefit is the basis of much conformity. Becker says that the "normal" person is able to control his deviant impulses by thinking about what will happen if he carries them out; he does not want to risk damaging his image as a normal person.[14] Some people have trouble restraining these impulses because they lack a sense of identity, so that they have no real commitment to themselves. Others are unable to perceive the link that exists between their failure to restrain the impulse and the later consequences of being a deviant; they don't clearly see the cause-and-effect relationship. Or they may view themselves as worthless and feel that it doesn't matter what happens to them. All these psychological problems may weaken an individual's ability to cope with or control his deviant impulses.

A popular psychological explanation of deviance suggests that it is a form of aggression toward others and toward society produced by frustration of the individual. When a person has a need that is not fulfilled he becomes frustrated and vents his frustration in aggression. The amount of frustration is based on the strength of the needs, impulses, or wishes obstructed in various situations, and the degree of aggression is related to the amount of frustration. This is called the *frustration-aggression theory*.[15] The frustration may be poverty, or lack of affection, or prejudice; in fact, it can be widely enough defined so that it will cover just about any situation. Albert Cohen has remarked that "no mechanism has been used to explain so much deviant behavior as the frustration-aggression hypothesis, and it is

as popular in common sense thinking as it is in the professional literature."[16]

Psychological explanations are very useful, but they cannot serve as the sole explanation for deviance. Psychological explanations emphasize the characteristics of individual personalities that motivate those individuals to act in deviant ways. Sociologists are interested in deviance from a slightly different point of view. They want to explain how culture and social structure help motivate people to be deviant, and to determine what deviant acts they commit. Are some social environments more conducive to deviance than others? Why do deviants break some rules and not others?

SOCIAL CAUSES OF DEVIANCE

Some sociologists have been increasingly inclined to look at deviance as an attempt by an individual to adapt to his social environment, rather than as something inherently pathological. They start from the premise that a deviant is basically the same sort of human being as the conformist. He is searching for the same things—gratifications, reassurances, social relationships—as everyone else. What differs about him is that he formulates his goals in deviant terms and tries to achieve them by deviant means. To these sociologists, deviance is not just a desire to be "bad" or to injure society; instead, it is an effort to achieve some personal or social goal (which may or may not be a socially approved one).

All social theories about the causes of deviance hypothesize that certain social situations produce pressures toward deviance. An early and influential theory is the one advanced by Robert Merton in 1938.[17] Building on Durkheim's general concept of *anomie* (a social condition in which values are absent or confused), Merton suggests that deviance is likely to be the result of a strain between

14.   Howard Becker, *The Outsiders*, pp. 27–28.

15.   See John Dollard, Leonard W. Doob, Neal E. Miller, O. H. Mowrer, and Robert R. Sears, *Frustration and Aggression* (New Haven: Yale University Press, 1939).

16.   Albert K. Cohen, *Deviance and Control*, p. 58.

17.   Robert K. Merton, "Social Structure and Anomie," *American Sociological Review* 3 (October 1938): 672–682.

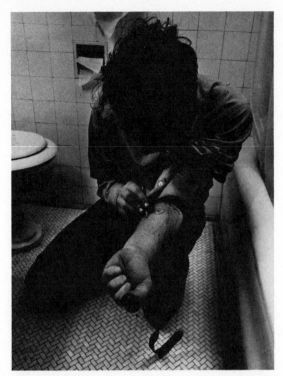

Heroin addiction is concentrated in slum communities, among those under 30. The typical addict is usually initiated by a friend. He is taught how to prepare and inject or how to ''snort'' the drug; but once the sense of euphoria and numbness has set in, the addict is fairly indifferent to others. In contrast to marijuana, the use of heroin is largely an individual activity. *(Michael Hanulack, Magnum)*

the culture and the social structure of a society; between the culturally prescribed goals and the socially approved ways of obtaining or achieving these goals. Ideally, everyone in a society believes in the goals valued by his society, and he believes that he can obtain them by following the prescribed methods. But social change, or some cultural imbalance, or widespread social inequality, may affect either a belief in the importance of society's goals or the availability of opportunities for achieving them, or both.

In American society one of the strongest and most important societal goals is the attainment of financial success. This goal is taught to all Americans: rich and poor, black and white. The socially approved way to attain this success is through getting an education, finding a good job, and working hard. But not all Americans can get the needed education or job. The goal is still desirable to these people, but it is unattainable. The result is social strain or anomie.

Merton listed four different types of adaptation to such social anomie. Accepting the goals and rejecting the means of achievement prescribed by society he called *innovation:* for example, a person might decide to steal money to buy a house in the suburbs, rather than earn it. A person who accepts the means but rejects the goals becomes a *ritualist,* an example of which is a hospital admitting clerk who asks a seriously ill person to fill out long forms before he can be given a bed at the hospital; the clerk thus carefully follows the rules but loses sight of the goals of the hospital — to care for the sick. Rejection of both the goals and the means, Merton called *retreatism;* this reaction is what we see in alcoholics and drug addicts. The final possibility is *rebellion,* which means rejecting both ends and means and substituting new ones in their place. This is the solution of the revolutionary.

A good description of the social strain and anomie faced by some adolescents was given by Richard Cloward and Lloyd Ohlin in their book *Delinquency and Opportunity.* They discuss the situation in which:

Efforts to conform, to live up to social expectations, often entail profound strain and frustration. For example, a boy of fourteen may desperately wish to become a man, and certainly we should agree that this is a proper goal for him. Yet the very fact that he wants so much what the society at large wants for him produces problems of adjustment, for ours is not a society that eases the transition from childhood to adulthood. We have thrown up difficult obstacles to the achievement of adult status except after the young have endured long years of waiting and training. But during the years of preparation, they become more and more impatient to be what we have urged them to be. This impatience with the enforced occupancy of a half-child, half-adult status frequently bursts forth and finds expression in dissidence and protest. Thus efforts to be what one is supposed to be sometimes lead to aberrant behavior. Reaching out for socially approved goals under conditions that preclude their legitimate achievement may become a prelude to deviance.[18]

In *Delinquency and Opportunity,* Cloward and Ohlin further elaborated on Merton's view of deviance. They pointed out that deviance, like conformity, is learned behavior. The occurrence of strain or anomie will not cause deviance, as Merton implied; for a person to learn how to be deviant, there must be "opportunity structures" where this learning can take place. For example, a ghetto child who has no opportunity to achieve an education or financial success will be frustrated, but that frustration will not cause him to steal or to become a drug addict. In *Manchild in the Promised Land,*[19] Claude Brown describes his life as a black child living in Harlem. He was unsuccessful in school but did not become a truant or a thief until he was taught how by some neighborhood boys. He had to learn how to forge absence notes, how to avoid truant officers and the police, and how to rob stores before he became deviant. Without the opportunity structure for deviance to be learned and reinforced, Brown might never have committed these deviant acts.

The work of Cloward and Ohlin, especially in its emphasis on the subculture of delinquent groups, was influenced by the theories which focus on deviance as it is taught culturally. It seems logical to suppose that deviance, like all other forms of human be-

havior, is only rarely "invented" by the individual; it is much more likely that it is learned through the process of cultural transmission—by observation, by reading or hearing about it. Of course, most social institutions are geared to teach conformity to social norms, but sometimes, due to the attitudes of the teachers, legitimate social institutions may instruct young people in deviance rather than in conformity. For example, a mother teaches her daughter conformity for the most part, and she may tell her repeatedly she must obey all the laws of the community. Yet when the mother gets a parking ticket while they are shopping in the city, she may say "Oh, I'll just throw it away; they'll never know the difference." In other words, she may tell the girl that certain kinds of deviance are acceptable. Schoolteachers, the mass media, church groups for young people can on occasion transmit attitudes supporting deviance rather than conformity. In fact, teachers and ministers, both entrusted with the teaching of social conformity, are sometimes found today teaching nonconformist deviance, as they have been since the time of Socrates and St. Paul, in observation of what they consider to be some higher moral law or social ideal.

There are also illegitimate groups in which the teaching of deviant attitudes and behavior is a basic goal. The best example of this is the delinquent street gang in which young boys are taught to steal cars, to disobey their parents and teachers in a variety of ways, and to apprentice themselves to adult criminals. The deviant subcultures of the drug addict, the pickpocket, the homosexual, and others also serve to teach deviant behavior to novices. To some extent, every adolescent peer group teaches its members some kinds of deviance, since rebellion against the standards of parents, teachers, and the establishment is an integral part of the adolescent stage of life.

Ironically, sociologists have noted that many institutions which are supposed to function in our society to correct deviance

18. Richard A. Cloward and Lloyd E. Ohlin, *Delinquency and Opportunity* (New York: Free Press, 1960), p. 38.

19. Claude Brown, *Manchild in the Promised Land* (New York: Macmillan, 1965).

are actually schools which teach the new "students" deviant behavior and transmit a deviant subculture. Older prisoners teach the young inmates more refined methods of committing their crimes; they also teach them how to behave like a criminal and how to see the world the way a criminal does. The same is true to some extent of a mental institution; there the role behavior of a mentally ill person tends to be reinforced by the subculture of the institution.

Of course, no one is ever exposed only to the teaching of deviance; the institutions and mechanisms which teach conformity reach everyone. Members of delinquent gangs who are taught by the older gang members how to steal a car are also taught by their parents, their teachers, the policeman on the beat, the comic books they read, and the programs they watch on television, that car theft is morally and legally wrong, and that if they steal a car, they will be caught and punished. A basic goal of the sociologist who studies deviance is to find out why it is that deviants learn and enact deviant behavior rather than conforming behavior.

In observing criminal behavior, Edwin G. Sutherland proposed a theory called *differential association*,[20] which may be usefully applied to all deviant behavior. Basically, Sutherland stated that people are socialized by different groups, each of which presents ideas that are favorable or unfavorable to various activities. The different groups may not agree on what is favorable and unfavorable; indeed, their ideas may actually compete with each other. Thus educational institutions teach students that they should compete with one another to obtain A's, whereas student peer groups teach members that they should not work too hard or appear too eager to succeed. A person will accept, or internalize, the ideas which he has the most contact with, or the ones taught by the groups

Many inmates of our "correctional" institutions receive not rehabilitation, but an education in the fine points of criminal behavior. By confining older experienced criminals together with relative beginners, our prisons may inadvertently promote the very kinds of deviant behavior that they seek to eliminate. Isolation, overcrowding, and the lack of effective counseling, educational, or rehabilitative programs may create an environment where prisoners are confirmed in their deviance, rather than helped to overcome it. *(Danny Lyon, Magnum)*

which are most important to him. If a person internalizes ideas favorable to deviant actions, he will act in a deviant way.

A somewhat different approach to the social cause of deviant behavior uses role theory as its basis.[21] Deviant behavior may serve to express, or to support or protect a person's

20.   Edwin H. Sutherland and Donald R. Cressey, *Principles of Criminology*, 7th ed. (Philadelphia: J. B. Lippincott, 1966), chap. 7.

21.   See Erving Goffman, *The Presentation of Self in Everyday Life* (New York: Doubleday, Anchor, Paper, 1959).

role, which in many cases is a role that is culturally approved. The physical violence and taking of risks that are inherent in many kinds of crime can express a male role in societies that define masculinity in such terms. An example of protective deviance might be the man who lies, forges a check, or embezzles from his office, to maintain or protect his role of respectable citizen of the community.

The role supported may also be a deviant role. Once a deviant accepts a deviant role and thinks of himself as a deviant, he may continue to commit deviant acts simply to maintain this self-image. A member of a teen-age delinquent gang may steal a car he does not want or fight another boy with whom he has no real quarrel, simply to support the deviant role in which he has cast himself. He is committed to deviance in the same way that most people are committed to conformity—that is his role.

TOPIC

3 THE DEVIANT CAREER

It would probably be impossible to find a human being on the face of the earth who had not at some time in his life failed to conform to some social rule; everyone has committed some act of deviance. There is, however, a great difference between committing one, or even several, acts of deviance, and becoming the kind of person labeled by society as deviant.

In the preceding topic, we have looked at some of the various causes of acts of deviance. How can an act of deviance lead some people into a deviant career, that is, into a life built around playing the role of the social deviant? In most cases, an act of deviance has no long-range consequences, and the individual who commits it immediately returns to the group of conformists. What is the difference between these people and the ones whose initial act or acts of deviance lead to a deviant career?

Sociologists have isolated three important steps or factors which are part of an individual's progress toward a career of social deviance. The first step is the observation or perception of the individual act of deviance, either by a significant number of other people, or by people whose attitudes are of importance to the particular individual. The second step is the labeling of this individual as deviant (meaning someone who is different from "us") by the observing others. The third step is the deviant individual's joining a deviant group or subculture which will give a measure of social support to his deviant behavior. When all three of these conditions have been met, the chances are very great that the individual will be unable to abandon his deviant behavior and return to conformity; in other words, he will have a deviant career.

PERCEPTION OF DEVIANCE

An act of social rule breaking which is known only to the deviant may have few social consequences for him, even though it is performed regularly. An example might be the man who steals a few things from the corner store each week. Such action breaks both a legal and a moral rule, but so long as no one else finds out, the man will not become what society calls a deviant. The same is true of offenses that are known only to a few sympathetic people. A pregnant teen-ager whose parents react to the situation understandingly, and who has an immediate abortion, will not be socially defined as a deviant either; her actions remain a well-kept secret. This does not mean that such acts will not have a personal and emotional effect on the people involved—only that there will be minimal social consequences for them.

For an act of deviance to have social consequences for the deviant it must be visible. The number of people who know about the act need not be large; the important thing is who knows about it. For example, if an employee of a store steals money from the cash register and is seen by only one person, a young customer who says nothing about it to anyone, the employee will probably suffer no consequences for that act of deviance. But if the one person to see him take the money is his boss, then the situation is quite different. Yet even in this case, an important factor in the outcome of the situation may be who else and how many other people his boss tells. He may call the police or tell everyone in the store that the man had to be fired because he was a thief. This makes the man a perceived deviant. If the employer fires the man but keeps the reason a secret and takes no legal steps to prosecute him, the man still has a good chance of returning to conformity—of escaping the deviant label as a result of that particular action. The actions of the employer would depend to some extent on how clearly he had seen the deviant act—did he actually catch the employee with his hand in the register, or did he just deduce who it must have been?—and his strength of conviction that the man really is a deviant.

It does sometimes happen that a person

who has, in fact, behaved in a conforming way is labeled deviant. People may be suspected of offenses which they did not commit; they may be taken into police custody without ever being charged with a crime; and they may even on occasion be convicted in a court although innocent of the offense. Being called a deviant is not the same as being a deviant. Just as one may commit a deviant act and have it go unnoticed, one may be accused of deviance without having actually broken a rule.

Several studies have attempted to determine the extent of socially invisible deviance, and have found it to be amazingly widespread. James Wallerstein and Clement Wyle gave over 1,600 randomly selected people a list of forty-nine acts which under New York State law are criminal offenses resulting in jail terms of at least a year's length. They found that 99 percent of the respondents admitted to at least one of the offenses, and that the average number of offenses committed by men was 18 and by women, 11.[22] It is often said that almost everyone breaks at least one law every day. It is probably a safe conclusion that most deviant acts go undetected.

"Official" perceptions of deviance are reported in figures released by police departments, the FBI, and other government agencies. It is important to interpret these statistics with care. When the police department releases figures showing that 1,625 murders were committed in New York City last year, they are referring only to known murders. Many others, the "successful" and unperceived ones, never appear in the official statistics. Similarly, when we are told that 9,610 were arrested on narcotics charges in a twelve-month period we cannot conclude either that all those people are drug addicts (because of the possibility of errors of perception) or that those are all the drug addicts

22. James S. Wallerstein and Clement J. Wyle, "Our Law-abiding Law-Breakers," *Probation* 25 (March–April 1947):107–112.

in the city (because of the many addicts who may go undetected). We may use the official statistics together with other information to make inferences about the actual extent of deviance, however; the statistics also tell us a great deal about the perception and processing of deviants by the agencies of social control.

LABELING THE DEVIANT

Once a deviant offense becomes visible, the next step is the social labeling of the person who committed it as deviant. The deviant is typed: placed in a social category which carries a standardized, negative identification. In extralegal situations, labeling may result in a public reputation of "nut," "junky," "queer," or "bum," or whatever term fits the situation. When the act of deviance breaks the law, labeling means that the person may be called a criminal in addition to whatever reputational label covers his specific crime. Being publicly labeled a deviant is probably the most significant step in the deviant career. As soon as a person is thus labeled, his entire set of social relationships undergoes a change. He is no longer treated as a student, or plumber, or father, or church member, he is treated as a deviant. Labeling can be so significant for the individual that even if he never actually committed the deviant acts implied by the label, the social consequences may still be the same.

Howard Becker has pointed out that the status of deviant tends to be a master status, one which dominates all others and thereby determines a person's general status. This is an indication of how significant the deviant label may be for the deviant. Becker says:

One will be identified as a deviant first, before other identifications are made. The question is raised: "What kind of person would break such an important rule?" And the answer is given: "One who is different from the rest of us, who cannot or will not act as a moral

human being and therefore might break other important rules." The deviant identification becomes the controlling one.[23]

Yet deviance is not always a master status, and the rank of a deviant's other statuses can influence the extent to which he is labeled deviant. A good example can be seen in the case of Grover Cleveland. During Cleveland's first campaign to become President of the United States, his opponent revealed that he had fathered an illegitimate child, an act of deviance that was viewed more seriously then than it is today. Yet because Cleveland had the high status of an important public official, no sanction was applied beyond the momentary public scandal of disclosure, and he went on to be elected President. There is some evidence to show, on the other hand, that a person of low social status is more likely to be given a deviant label, or to be given it sooner, than one of high social status.[24] The relationship between a person's social status level and the chances of his being labeled a deviant points up the fact that perception and labeling are processes which must be clearly distinguished from one another. Labeling is based on deviant acts which first must be perceived, but whether or not a label is applied and made to stick also depends upon certain characteristics of the labeler, whether, for example, he is a person of high rank in an official position.

In some cases, the label given will be something other than "deviant." In cases where the deviance is generally thought to be due to inability, rather than lack of desire, to conform, the label may be "sick" or "moron" or "mentally disturbed." Several sociologists have pointed out that these labels may actually have no fewer social consequences for the individual than that of deviant. Cohen says in this connection:

23. Howard Becker, *The Outsiders*, pp. 33–34.

24. Guy B. Johnson, "The Negro and Crime," *The Annals of the American Academy of Political and Social Science* 217 (September 1961) :93–104.

The tendency to think in terms of sickness rather than wickedness and vice is generally regarded as more kindly, compassionate, and humanitarian. However, it should be noted that the sick role, especially if the sickness is "mental," is also a disvalued role, and not accepted complacently. There are many people who would rather be regarded as bad or morally imperfect than as mentally ill.[25]

Little research has been done on the role of the labeler of deviant behavior until recently. In 1965 Wayne La Fave published a book on his study of the way in which police decide whether or not to arrest and charge a suspect. He reported that in many cases where the police are fully convinced of the suspect's guilt, he is nevertheless not arrested. Sometimes this is due to a desire to avoid labeling the suspect as a deviant in the hope that he might still return to conformity.[26] Another study of labelers, reported by Becker in *The Outsiders,* explains how and why the Federal Bureau of Narcotics purposely campaigned during the mid-1930s to label the marijuana user a deviant.[27]

When a person is labeled as deviant, he is typically rejected and isolated by society. The isolation and rejection may be physical, if the deviant is sent to a jail or mental hospital or some other kind of corrective institution, or it may be social. This social response may be necessary, but we should not overlook the consequences for the deviant individual, which may not always be those we intend.

There may be a drastic reduction in the deviant's opportunity to achieve normal gratifications such as friendship, love, family life, and an adequate income through legitimate or socially approved means. Many of his acquaintances may fail to recognize him, or to respond to his overtures of friendship. His

family, wife, or girl friend may react by withdrawing some measure of the trust and affection they formerly felt and displayed toward him. Once officially labeled, the criminal deviant may be kept from many job opportunities, because people are reluctant to hire criminals for responsible positions.

The result of these actions is often to push the deviant further into deviance and extend it to other areas of his life. For example, the drug addict is forced to steal to support his habit; the ex-convict returns to theft because he cannot find employment. The labeled deviant must also turn to other deviants to make friends, because the conforming people are likely to reject his overtures of friendship. In work, friendship, and outlook, the person who is labeled a deviant slowly begins to organize his whole life around the deviant role.

These changes in a deviant's social status are usually accompanied by changes in his self-image. He learns to think of himself as a deviant, and to present himself to the world in that role. He learns the secondary characteristics of the deviant role, such as dressing in certain ways, or using a special kind of slang or a vocabulary known only to other deviants. The more clearly he sees himself as a deviant and defines himself that way in the framework of his other social relationships, the more he is treated as a deviant. Soon, even people who do not know of his reputation, who have never heard about his acts of deviance, recognize him as a deviant because of the social role he plays.

Labeling can be viewed as another example of the self-fulfilling prophecy. Once a person is labeled as a deviant, all his subsequent social experiences tend to push him farther and farther in the direction of deviance. It is very difficult, after this cycle is set in motion, for the deviant to break out. The accompanying abridgment is a painfully clear illustration of that problem. Marsh Ray tells of the experiences of heroin addicts who manage to break their drug habit and yet find that they

25.   Albert K. Cohen, *Deviance and Control,* p. 37.
26.   Wayne R. LaFave, *Arrest: The Decision to Take a Suspect into Custody* (Boston: Little, Brown, 1965).
27.   Howard Becker, *The Outsiders,* pp. 41–78.

are still regarded by their family and friends and local community as junkies and as unreliable persons, liable to break other important social rules, in other words, as deviants. Their inability to rid themselves of the label, regardless of their behavior, often pushes them back to their drugs and their deviance, because the conforming society denies them any reward for their struggle to return to conformity.

JOINING THE DEVIANT GROUP

The third and final step in a deviant career is to join, and identify with, a group of other deviants. Some deviants never take this step, although they may continue their deviant activities, and be subject to labeling as a deviant. Examples are the physician drug addict, the white collar criminal (the embezzler or pilferer), the check forger: the so-called "aristocrats" of the criminal world. Such people are to some degree protected by their high status, or, because their deviance does not entail contacts with other criminals, they are able to reconcile their specific deviance with an otherwise conformist social existence. The white collar criminal may find another job through an influential relative; an addicted physician can obtain his own supplies of heroin.

But for many deviants, membership in an organized deviant group is the logical outcome of a deviant status. The group serves two important functions for the individual. The first is that it makes his daily life much easier.

When one moves into a deviant group . . . he learns to carry on his deviant activity with a minimum of trouble. All the problems he faces in evading enforcement of the rule he is breaking have been faced before by others. Solutions have been worked out. Thus, the young thief meets older thieves who, more experienced than he is, explain to him how to get rid of stolen merchandise without running the risk of being caught.

Every deviant group has a great stock of lore on such subjects and the new recruit learns it quickly.[28]

The second function of the group is that it serves as a source of emotional and social support for the deviant individual. Within the group, no one will condemn him for his deviance. The other members will sympathize with his viewpoint on the rule and the enforcers of the rule; they will understand his actions. The group satisfies his need for acceptance. It also eases the personal strain of his relationship with society at large, because together the group develops explanations for, and rationalizations of, their behavior. They may assert, for example, that they actually have "better" standards of conduct than the normal world; or that the normal world is full of hypocritical deviants anyway, and at least they are honest about it; or that they cannot help the way that they behave and therefore should not be blamed for it; or that they are really only the victims of prejudice and discrimination. These explanations of the deviant group are substituted for the harsher ones which the normal society makes of their deviation, thereby relieving them of a great burden of guilt and self-hatred. Group membership helps to justify and support the individual's deviance.

Thus, joining a deviant group makes one even more likely to continue in a deviant pattern of behavior. The deviant learns ways to minimize the social and psychological consequences of his deviance, possibly even to construct a life around his deviant status that provides a satisfactory number of social gratifications. He therefore feels less pressure to return to conformity. Joining a deviant group also serves to reinforce the individual's self-image as a deviant; as one girl put it, she only realized she was a drug addict when she noticed that she no longer had any friends who were not addicts.[29] Identifying with a

28. Howard Becker, *The Outsiders*, p. 39.
29. Howard Becker, *The Outsiders*, p. 38.

deviant group is taking a significant step away from conforming society.

DEVIANT SUBCULTURES

Deviant groups often have well-developed subcultures. The rationalizations, or justifications, that we spoke of earlier represent the formation of new values to replace those of conventional society. Special ways of dressing and talking conform to a distinct set of norms. Because the group members often have had the same kind of experiences in dealing with the wider society, they also develop a common way of regarding it and relating to it.

An example of a well-developed subculture is that of the homosexual in many of the larger cities in this country. Homosexuals, especially males, have certain norms of dress; there are even a number of stores which cater especially to their tastes. They have routine procedures and well-established meeting places which help them locate each other. They even have their own formal organizations, such as the Mattachine Society, which prints booklets explaining to members how to cope with possible legal problems and how to combat the prejudice, discrimination, and isolation which the conforming world will probably display toward them because of their known status of deviant. And, perhaps most important of all, they have developed a complete set of justifications for homosexuality. They have, in fact, become so well and strongly organized that they have to some degree succeeded in changing the attitude of society toward their deviance. One hundred years ago, homosexuality was regarded as a dreadful sin; then it came to be a rather distasteful vice. In the last several decades it has been reclassified as a kind of illness, perhaps not even too serious at that. And today there is a segment of the "straight" population that regards homosexuality as simply a matter of personal preference.

Many other deviants also have subcultures. There is one for narcotics addicts; a hippie subculture for those who deviate from many

The Hell's Angels, although largely a West Coast-based organization, often travel extensively in motorcycle "packs." Members have been implicated in a number of violent crimes, and the gang has received national notoriety. They sometimes claim to be "policing" an area where they believe that official police protection is inadequate. *(Photo by Ken Heyman)*

socially approved goals such as the work ethic; a subculture of delinquent gangs for young boys; one for prostitutes, and one for pickpockets. A growing number of studies have recently appeared on deviant subcultures. These studies are important, not only because they help us understand the pressing social problems of deviance and the deviant, but also because they give us many new insights into the nature of social life.

One deviant subculture which has recently attracted much attention is that of organized crime. Those engaged in organized crime are

Homosexuals in large cities have formed a well-developed subculture; in some cities they have become so well organized that they are campaigning successfully to change society's attitude toward their deviance. (Photo by Fred McDarrah)

naturally reluctant to come under close observation, by sociologists or anyone else. However, on the basis of the information that has been assembled on known syndicate members, it appears that their subculture is an interesting example of the limitation of deviance to only one area of life. Their principal point of deviance from normal society, at least for top officials in organized crime, seems to be in the area of what constitutes acceptable business dealings and methods of doing business. Apart

from that, they lead very conformist lives; most other deviant acts are carried out for them by others. They have nice houses in the suburbs, wives and children, and quiet family social lives. They send their children to college and marry them off in big church weddings. It is quite common, when a man is publicly identified as being a member of the syndicate, for his neighbors all to be quoted as saying that they cannot believe it, he is such a nice man and a good neighbor. Yet as a group these men are perceived as members of a well-organized deviant subculture and are labeled deviant.

The existence of deviant subcultures makes the continued existence of deviance highly probable for its members. To return to conformity, the deviant must often be willing not only to discontinue his acts of deviant behavior, but also to give up an entire style of life. It must be realized that the social control of deviance will be most successful if we offer the deviant some viable alternative to his own subculture. We too often think of the deviant as a person who has "nothing to lose," and therefore we cannot understand why he does not want to try to return to conformity no matter how difficult that may be for him. In reality, the deviant may have a great deal to lose by abandoning his deviance, such as recognized status within a structured group and subculture.

MARSH B. RAY
The Cycle of Abstinence and Relapse Among Heroin Addicts

Abridged with permission of The Macmillan Company from "The Cycle of Abstinence and Relapse Among Heroin Addicts," in *The Other Side*, ed. Howard S. Becker. © Copyright by The Free Press of Glencoe, a Division of The Macmillan Company, 1964.

Introduction

This paper is the result of a lengthy research project on narcotics addicts under-

taken by Marsh Ray, who teaches sociology at State University of New York. The chief discovery Ray made is that addicts are often unable to become conformists because society is unwilling to view them as conforming rather than deviant. The paper illustrates how powerful an impact labeling can have on a deviant career.

Those who study persons addicted to opium and its derivatives are confronted by the following paradox: a cure from physiological dependence may be secured within a relatively short period, and studies indicate that use of these curative drugs does not cause psychosis, organic intellectual deterioration, or any impairment of intellectual function. But despite these facts, addicts display a high rate of relapse. On the other hand, addicts continually and repeatedly seek cure.

This paper reports on a study of abstinence and relapse in which attention is focused on the way the addict orders and makes meaningful the objects of his experience, including himself as an object, during the critical periods of cure and relapse, and the related sense of identity or of social isolation the addict feels.

Secondary status characteristics of addicts

The culture of addiction contains a loose system of organizational elements, including a special language, certain artifacts, a commodity market and pricing system, a system of stratification, and ethical codes. In addition to these direct links to the world of addiction, becoming an addict means that one assumes a number of secondary status characteristics in accordance with the definitions society has of this activity. Some of these are found in federal and local laws and statutes, others are defined by the stereotype thinking of members of the larger society about the causes and consequences of drug use.

The addict's confinement to correctional institutions has specific meanings which are reflected in the attitude the rest of society, and other addicts, has toward him. Additionally, as his habit grows and the demands for drugs get beyond any legitimate means of supply, his own activities in satisfying his increased craving give him direct evidence of the criminal aspects of his identity. He then begins to apply criminal slang to his activities and experiences. Thus shoplifting becomes "boosting," the correctional settings become "joints," and the guards in such institutions become "screws."

The popular notion that the addict is somehow psychologically inadequate is supported by many authorities in the field. In addition, support and definition is supplied by the very nature of the institution in which drug addicts are usually treated, since even the names of these institutions define addiction as a mental illness. For example, one of the clinics for the treatment of addicts in Chicago is located at Illinois Neuropsychiatric Institute, and the connotations of Bellevue Hospital, another treatment center for addicts, are socially well known. Also the composition of the staff in treatment centers contributes to the image of the addict as mentally ill, for the personnel are primarily psychiatrists, psychologists, and psychiatric social workers. How such a definition of self was brought forcefully home to one addict is illustrated in the following quotation:

> When I got down to the hospital, I was interviewed by different doctors and one of them told me, "You now have one mark against you as crazy for having been down here." I hadn't known it was a crazy house. You know regular people [nonaddicts] think this too.

Finally, as the addict's habit grows and almost all of his thoughts and efforts are directed toward supplying himself with drugs, he becomes careless about his personal appearance and cleanliness. Consequently nonaddicts think of him as a "bum" and, because he persists in his use of drugs, conclude that he lacks "will power," is perhaps "degenerate," and is likely to contaminate others. The addict is aware that he is judged in these terms, and while he may attempt to reject them, it is difficult if not impossible to do so when much of his own experience serves to reinforce them.

The inception of cure

An episode of cure begins in the private thoughts of the addict rather than in his behavior. These deliberations develop as a result of experience in specific situations of social interaction that cause the addict to experience social stress, to develop some feeling of alienation from or dissatisfaction with his present identity.

I think that my mother knew I was addicted because she had heard rumors around the neighborhood. Around that time [when he first began to think about a cure] she had been telling me that I looked like a "bum" and that my hair was down the back of my neck and that I was dirty. I had known this too but had shoved it down in the back of my mind somewhere. She used to tell me that to look like this wasn't at all like me. I always wanted to look presentable and her saying this really hurt. At that time I was going to college and I wanted to look my best. I always looked at myself as the clever one—the "mystery man"—outwitting the dolts. I always thought that no one knew, that when I was in my room they thought I was studying my books when actually I wasn't studying at all.

After mother said those things I did a lot of thinking. I often used to sit around my room and think about it and even look at myself in the mirror and I could see that it was true. What is it called? When you take yourself out of a situation and look at yourself? Self-appraisal? I guess that's it. Well I did this about my appearance and about the deterioration of my character. I didn't like it because I didn't want anything to be master over me because this was contrary to my character. I used to sit and look at that infinitesimal bit of powder. I felt it changed my personality somehow.

I used to try staying in but I would get sick. But because I had money, when the pain got unbearable, at least to me it was unbearable, I could go out again. I wanted to be independent of it. I knew then that if I continued I would have to resort to stealing to maintain my habit and this I couldn't tolerate because it was contrary to my character. The others were robbing and stealing but I couldn't be a part of that. I first talked with my uncle about it because my mother was alive then and I thought she would crack up and maybe not understand the

problem. I didn't want to be reprimanded; I knew I'd done wrong. I had been through a lot and felt I wanted to be rid of the thing. He was very understanding about it and didn't criticize me. He just talked with me about going to the hospital and said he thought this would be the best way to do it.

But the social and psychological prerequisites for abstinence need not precede physical withdrawal of the drug. It is frequently the case that following the enforced withdrawal that begins a period of confinement in a correctional institution or hospital, the addict engages in self-debate in which the self emerges as an object and is brought under scrutiny.

On occasion, the addict group itself, rather than the non-addict society, provides the experience that motivates the addict to abstain, although the non-addict world and its values are still the reference point. An addict who had been addicted for several years and had had several forced cures describes such an experience:

When I first started using we were all buddies, but later we started burning each other. One guy would say, "Well, I'll go cop [buy drugs]. Then he'd take the bread [money] and he'd never come back. I kicked one time because of that. I didn't have no more money and I got disgusted. First I started to swear him up and down but then my inner conscience got started and I said maybe he got busted [arrested]. Then I said, "Aw, to hell with him and to hell with all junkies—they're all the same." So I went home and I tried to read a couple of comic books to keep my mind off it. I was very sick but after a couple of days I kicked.

While the above situation may not be typical, it illustrates the same process to be observed in the other examples—a disruption of the social ordering of experience that has become familiar, a calling into question of the addict identity, and the rejection of this identity and the values associated with it.

The addict self in transition

The addict who has successfully completed withdrawal now enters a period which might best be characterized as a "running struggle" with his problems of social identity. He could not have taken such a drastic step had he not developed some expectations concerning the nature of his future social relationships. His anticipations concerning these situations may or may not be realistic; what happens is that he has them and that the imagery he holds regarding himself and his potentialities is a strong motivating force in his continued abstinence. Above all, he desires reinforcement by others of his newly developing identity, and in his interactions with them, he expects to secure it.

In the early phases of an episode of cure, the abstainer is unsure about where he stands in addict and non-addict groups, and in discussions of addiction and addicts, he may indicate his ambivalence through his alternate use of the pronouns "we" and "they." Later the ex-addict indicates his non-membership in the addict group through categorizations that place addicts clearly in the third person, and place his own addiction and matters pertaining to it in the past tense. For example, he is likely to preface a remark with the phrase, "When I was an addict . . ." But of equal or greater importance is the fact that the ex-addict who is successful in remaining abstinent relates to new groups of people, participates in their experience, and to some extent begins to evaluate the conduct of his former associates (and perhaps his own when he was an addict) in terms of the values of the new group.

I see the guys around now quite often and sometimes we talk for a while but I don't feel that I am anything like them anymore and I always leave before they make up [take drugs]. I tell them, "You know what you are doing but if you keep on you'll just go to jail like I did." I don't feel that they are wrong to be using but that I'm luckier than they are because I have goals. It's funny, I used to call them squares for not using and now they call me square for not using. They think that they are hip and they are always talking about the old days. That makes me realize how far I've come. But it makes me want to keep away from them, too, because they always use the same old vocabulary — talking about squares and being hip.

During the later stages of the formation of an abstainer identity, the ex-addict begins to perceive a difference in his relations with others, particularly with members of his family. Undoubtedly their attitudes, in turn, undergo modification and change as a result of his apparent continued abstinence, and they arrive at this judgment by observing his cleanliness and attention to personal neatness, his steady employment, and his re-subscription to other values of non-addict society. The ex-addict is very much aware of these differences in attitude.

Lots of times I don't even feel like I ever took dope. I feel released not having to be dependent on it. I think how nice it is to be natural without having to rely on dope to make me feel good. See, when I was a junkie I lost a lot of respect. My father wouldn't talk to me and I was filthy. I have to build up that respect again. I do a lot of things with my family now and my father talks to me again. It's like at parties that my relatives give, now they are always running up to me and giving me a drink and showing me a lot of attention. Before they wouldn't even talk to me. See, I used to feel lonely because my life was dependent on stuff and I felt different from regular people. See, junkies and regular people are two different things. I used to feel that I was out of place with my relatives when I was on junk. I didn't want to walk with them on the street and do things with them. Now I do things with them all the time like go to the show and joke with them and I go to church with my uncle. I just kept saying to myself that junkies are not my people. My relatives don't say things behind my back now and I am gaining their respect slow but sure.

The process of relapse

Relapse occurs when the ex-addict redefines himself as an addict. When his social expectations and those of others with whom he interacts are not met, social stress develops and he has to re-examine the meaningfulness of his experience in non-addict society and in so doing question his identity as an abstainer.

Readdiction most frequently occurs during the period immediately following the physical withdrawal of the drug—the period described earlier as a time of running struggle with identity problems for the ex-addict. It is at this point, when the old values and old meanings he experienced as an addict are still immediate and the new ordering of his experience without narcotics is not well established, that the ex-addict seems most vulnerable to relapse. But addicts do not always relapse on first contact with members of the old group. In fact, there is nothing to indicate that addicts relapse only as a result of association. Instead, contacts may go on for some time, during which the ex-addict carries on much private debate, feeling at one point that he is socially closer to addicts and at another that his real interest lies in future new identities on which he has decided. Typically he may also call to mind the reason he undertook cure in the first place and question the rationality of relapsing. The experiences of a voluntarily committed addict illustrate this kind of internal debate.

> At the hospital, this one kid who was a friend of mine came to me one night and said, "Let's get out of here." So I went and checked out too. Then I got to thinking, "I don't want to go home yet—I'm still sick—and what did I come down here for anyway." So I went up and got my papers back from the officer and tore them up. Then I found this kid and told him that I was staying and he said, "Oh we knew you

> weren't going to do it—we knew you'd chicken out." Then I went back and put my papers through again. I felt they were trying to put me down.
>
> When we got out I could have had a shot right away because one of these guys when we got to town said he knew a croaker who would fix us up, but I didn't go with them. I didn't care what they thought because I got to figuring that I had went this far and I might as well stay off.
>
> When I got home I stayed off for two months but my mother was hollering at me all the time and there was this one family in the neighborhood that was always chopping me up. I wanted to tell this woman off because she talked all right to my face but behind my back she said things like she was afraid I would turn her son on because I was hanging around with him. She would tell these things to my mother. I never turned anybody on! She didn't know that but I wanted to tell her. Finally I just got disgusted because nobody wanted to believe me and I went back on.

While the ex-addict's interaction with addict groups may cause him to question the value of abstaining, experiences with non-addict groups also play a vital role. The addict has previously established a certain status for himself in the eyes of non-addicts who know him—members of his family, social workers, law enforcement officers, physicians, and so forth. These non-addicts indicate to him his degree of membership in their group and his rights to participation there—for example, the right to be believed when he says he has quit.

During the early phases of an episode of cure, the ex-addict has very definite expectations concerning how he should be treated and defined. He shows them his desire for acceptance of his new identity and finds it socially difficult when he sees in the conduct of others a reference to his old identity as an addict.

> My relatives were always saying things to me like "Have you really quit using that drug now?" and things like that. And I knew that they

were doing a lot of talking behind my back because when I came around they would stop talking but I overheard them. It used to burn me up.

On the other hand, the non-addicts with whom he has experience during this period have their own expectations. Based in part on the stereotypic thinking of non-addict society concerning addiction, in part on unfortunate previous experiences with him, they may exhibit some skepticism about his cure and express doubts about his future.

The social psychological meaning of relapse

Relapse requires that the individual re-orient himself to the market conditions surrounding the sale of illicit drugs. He must reestablish his sources of supply and, if he has been abstinent for very long, he may have to learn about new fads and fashions in drug use. But the ex-addict's re-entrance into the social world of addiction has much deeper meanings too. It requires a recommitment to the norms of addiction, and limits the degree to which he may relate to non-addict groups and their values and standards. It demands participation in the old ways of organization and as a consequence, the readoption of the secondary status characteristics of addiction. He again shows a lack of concern about his personal appearance and grooming. Illicit activities are again engaged in to get money for drugs, and as a result the possibility of more firmly establishing the criminal aspect of his identity becomes a reality.

The social consequence of these experiences and activities is the re-establishment of the sense of social isolation from the non-addict group and a new sense of the meaningfulness of the social world of addiction. The ex-addict who relapses is thus likely to comment, "I feel like one of the guys again," or "It was like coming home."

While repeated relapse on the addict's part may convince him that "once a junkie, always a junkie" is no myth but a valid comment on his way of life, every relapse has within it the genesis of another attempt at cure. From his excursions, however long, into the world of non-addiction, the relapsed addict carries back with him an image of himself as one who has done the impossible — one who has actually experienced a period when it was unnecessary to take drugs. But these are not his only recollections. He recalls too his identification of himself as an abstainer, no matter how tentatively or imperfectly this may have been accomplished. He thinks over his experiences in situations while he occupied the status of abstainer and speculates about the possible other outcomes of these situations had he acted differently.

> Now and then I'm given to rational thinking or reasoning and somehow I had a premonition that should I remain in Chicago much longer, shoplifting and doing the various criminal acts I did to get money for drugs, plus the criminal act of just using the drug, I would soon be in jail or perhaps something worse, for in truth one's life is at stake each day when he uses drugs. I reflected on the life I had known in Kansas City with Rose in contrast to the one I had returned to. I didn't know what Rose thought had become of me. I thought that more than likely she was angry and thoroughly disgusted and glad that I was gone. However, I wanted to return but first thought it best to call and see what her feelings were.

Reflections of the above kind provide the relapsed addict with a rich body of material for self-recrimination and he again evaluates his own conduct in terms of what he believes are the larger society's attitudes towards addicts and addiction. It is then that he may again speculate about his own potential for meaningful experiences and relationships in a non-addict world and thus set into motion a new attempt at cure.

Conclusion

The feelings expressed by heroin addicts reveal how complex the labeling process is. Two types of labeling are described here: the labeling of self by self and the labeling of self by others. Interestingly enough, the second type of labeling has more power and influence over the deviant careers of the addicts.

One of the most significant points on the breaking of heroin addiction is when the addict changes his self-label; at a certain

point he refers to addicts as "they" instead of "we," a concept which helps him avoid drug use. But the ex-addict expects his change in behavior and identification to be mirrored by a change in other people's perceptions of him; the way others think of him has great importance. (Ray refers to the role that non-addict groups play as "vital.") Both the addicts quoted by Ray blamed the failure of non-addict groups to change their label of the ex-addict as a prime cause for their relapse into drug use.

TOPIC

4 SOCIAL CONTROL

We have suggested that some degree of deviance goes hand-in-hand with the goal of social regulation by laws and norms. Therefore, every society which has rules must at the same time develop some mechanisms of social control to ensure that the rules are followed. There are two basic ways of controlling deviance. One is to exert external pressures on individuals to conform; this involves applying the wide variety of formal and informal social sanctions. The other is to make the controls internal, so that an individual is motivated to do the thing that is in conformity with the norm. Both internal and external mechanisms of social control will be examined in this topic. In conclusion, we will also look at the problem of reintegrating the ex-deviant into conforming society.

INTERNALIZED CONTROL OF DEVIANCE

Internalization occurs when an individual accepts the norms of the social group and integrates them into his own personality. It is one aspect of the socialization process dis-

cussed in chapter 4. Once a social rule has been successfully internalized, the individual continues to observe it even when no one is watching to see that he does.

Internalization should be distinguished from a fear of the consequences of getting caught in a deviant act, which is a response to the external controls which society applies. When the social norms have been successfully internalized you refrain from stealing someone else's money not because you are afraid the police will arrest you and send you to jail but because you think stealing is wrong; your conscience acts as an internal social control mechanism.

Internalization is by far the most effective means of social control of deviant behavior. Because most social roles have been internalized, the incidence of actual deviant behavior is very low. All people have some deviant impulses, but they are for the most part rejected or they lead only to a few isolated deviant episodes rather than forming part of a continual pattern of deviance. An individual may have lied to parents, or teachers, or friends; he may have stolen a record, a book or a scarf from a store; he may have cheated an employer by taking a day off from work, or by failing to do the work he has been instructed to do and then putting the blame on someone else. In most cases, such experiments lead to remorse, guilt, and a strain on the individual's image of himself as a respectable person, and he therefore abandons the behavior.

When internalization is successful an individual may continue to conform to a social norm even when the necessity which produced the social norm has disappeared. A good example of this can be seen in the American attitude toward work. We regard productive work as a positive good, and work is an important social necessity for a production-oriented society like ours. The work ethic is also followed because productive work is usually a personal necessity; most of us must work to make the money we need to live on. There are, however, certain cases in which the personal benefits of work are reduced —yet the internalized rule still compels the individuals to work. For example, in a study designed to investigate the effects of a guaranteed annual income, the Office of Economic Opportunity gave income subsidies to a group of about 1,300 families, all of which had incomes under $5,000 a year. The OEO made up the difference between whatever the family earned and $5,000. If the family was able to earn $4,500, then they only got five hundred dollars; if they earned nothing, they were paid $5,000. They were not required to work, or even to try to find work; all they had to do was report their income and collect their subsidy.[30] There was no longer any economic incentive for these families to work, since they could live in a manner above their usual standard of living merely by collecting their subsidy; yet the results of the study showed that 53 percent of the families showed an increase

in earned income during the program. (A similar but unsubsidized group, the control group, showed an increase in only 43 percent of the families.) Only 29 percent showed a decrease in earned income (the figure for the control group was 31 percent).

Strung through all the interviews is evidence of a strong commitment to the work ethic. One man's comment seems to summarize a general feeling: "I feel most people prefer to work, or at least the greatest percentage do. It should be essential to the success of a program like this that it be tied to work if the individual is not disabled or old." One recipient in the Paterson area said he got a job, even though he knew his payments would go down, because it would improve his overall financial status. Another recipient declared: "It's an honor to work."[31]

This study indicates how well the social norm of doing productive work has been internalized, and how effective that internalization is in regulating behavior.

EXTERNAL MECHANISMS OF SOCIAL CONTROL

External controls over deviant behavior consist of the elaborate set of social sanctions, found in every society, which we discussed in chapter 3. Breaking the rules results in certain pressures to conform or punishments inflicted by other individuals or by society at large. In some cases the norms and the sanctions are *formally* stated, through laws and organizational rules which specify rewards or punishment for conformity or violation; in other cases they are *informally* understood, and enforced through personal acts such as praise or ridicule.

Informal social control mechanisms

The application of informal social sanctions is one of the main functions of the primary group. In this intimate and emotion-laden setting, the chances are very good that

30.   Fred J. Cook, "When You Just Give Money to the Poor," *New York Times Magazine,* 3 May 1970.

31.   Fred J. Cook, pp. 111–112.

There is little proof that the traditional "hard labor" punishment is necessarily an effective preventive measure against crime. However, many prisons, either due to lack of money or to belief in the deterrent value of punishment, still maintain a kind of "chain gang" approach. As yet, rehabilitative approaches, resting on the belief that criminal behavior can be corrected or cured, are largely in the experimental stages. *(Danny Lyon, Magnum)*

such control will be successful. The primary group, such as the family or a friendship group, has the opportunity to observe acts of deviance and the circumstances under which they are committed. Thus they can deal sensitively with the problem. The negative sanctions used range from a gesture of disapproval to rejection from the group or even physical punishment. For most people, primary group negative sanctions are very adequate deterrents to deviant behavior.

The primary group is probably the oldest agent of social control, but it is not the only informal one. A work group, an organization, or even those people who happen to be in close proximity at the time the offense is committed may act as agents of social control

by applying certain sanctions. A boss may speak to an employee about the affair the employee is carrying on with his secretary; a teacher may threaten to report to the police a student she has caught taking drugs unless he promises to stop; the elderly lady down the block may scold the neighborhood children for ganging up on one little boy.

In all the examples we have just given, the person who applied the sanctions felt some responsibility for taking such a step because of the social role he or she occupied in relation to the deviant. In some cases, however, there is no clear-cut responsibility for punishing deviance. Take the case of a fellow worker on the same level as the man who is having the affair with his secretary. He may very well share with the boss the conviction that such behavior is immoral and unsuitable, and possibly dangerous to the whole organization in a number of ways (such as causing the man and his secretary to be inefficient in their work, or causing outsiders to label the whole company an immoral organization). However, because the relationship between these two men is not that of employer and employee but of co-workers and friends, this man will hesitate to take steps to sanction the offender. As a co-worker, he may very well need the help and support of the offender on many occasions, and therefore he is reluctant to alienate him. Albert Cohen explains another reason sanctions might not be applied in such a case:

It may not be only a fine and noble thing to bring to justice a total stranger, it is also relatively painless. But to do the same to somebody to whom we are tied by the bonds of solidarity and friendship is to incur the hostility of somebody whose good opinion we have come to value.[32]

So the feeling of group solidarity may operate in two conflicting ways. One is that the group wishes to have the deviant behavior stopped, because it is a threat to solidarity; the other is that group members are restrained by that very sense of solidarity from applying sanctions to a deviant fellow member. Cohen suggests that the members of a close-knit group will tend to protect the deviant except under three conditions: (1) when the deviant behavior is highly visible to outsiders; (2) when the deviant can be easily or completely identified with the group; and (3) when the group is liable to incur severe sanctions itself as a result of the behavior of the individual deviant.

Formal social control mechanisms

Informal sanctions can be extremely effective, but they have their limitations. One

is that the sanctions may be so vaguely defined that they do not serve as a deterrent, because the deviant does not really know what punishment, if any, he will be given. Another is that personal feelings, relative social statuses, feelings of group solidarity and many other considerations enter into informal situations. Lack of desire to apply the sanctions, or lack of power to do so, may hinder social control.

Society has created many organizations and positions specializing in the process of social control. These special positions include policemen, judges, prison guards, and lawyers. Legislators, social workers, ministers, and doctors also exert social control as a part of their duties. The network of such formal positions has tended in modern times to replace the informal social control networks which prevailed in simpler and less complex societies. Social control has thus become more impersonal over time, but possibly also more rational and objective.

A number of sociologists have called attention to the fact that formal means of social control are subject to many of the same adjustments to circumstance and other social forces as are informal means. Richard Cloward investigated the relationship of prison guards to prisoners and reported on the way in which guards bargain with the inmates: by "forgetting" to enforce some of the rules they get the prisoners' cooperation in observing others. Likewise, they may give preferential treatment to certain kinds of rule breaking.[33] The deals that a prosecuting attorney may offer to a suspect are another example of this phenomenon. The attorney agrees to drop some of the charges if the suspect will plead guilty to others, or to drop most of the charges if he will cooperate with the prosecution in proving others involved to be guilty. Although

32.   Albert K. Cohen, *Deviance and Control*, p. 91.

33.   Richard A. Cloward, "Social Control in the Prison," in *Theoretical Studies in Social Organization of the Prison* (New York: Social Science Research Council, 1960), pp. 20–48.

CRIMES IN THE UNITED STATES, BY TYPE: 1960 TO 1971

Year	Total	Violent crime*				Total	Property crime*		
		Murder and non-negligent man-slaughter	Forcible rape	Robbery	Aggravated assault		Burglary	Larceny, $50 and over	Auto theft
1960	286	9	17	107	153	1,734	900	507	326
1965	384	10	23	138	213	2,553	1,266	794	493
1966	426	11	26	157	233	2,846	1,392	897	557
1967	496	12	27	202	254	3,316	1,611	1,049	655
1968	590	14	31	262	283	3,887	1,835	1,274	778
1969	657	15	37	297	308	4,357	1,956	1,528	872
1970	733	16	38	348	331	4,848	2,177	1,750	922
1971	810	18	42	386	365	5,185	2,368	1,875	942

*In thousands, except as indicated.

Statistical Abstract of the United States, 1972, p. 143.

Although crime rates in the United States have continued to rise, it is sometimes difficult to tell how much the reported increase represents actual fact, and how much of it reflects improved reporting. Nonetheless, there is no question that the crime problem has reached serious proportions. Some authorities believe that the motives for most crimes are economic. Many violent crimes against people, such as robbery, mugging, kidnaping and sometimes assault and murder, are incidental to property crime and are committed to obtain money or property.

this kind of behavior may be unfair and in some cases leads to rule breaking on the part of the enforcer, it is also a successful kind of social control.

There is much discussion and disagreement at present about the effectiveness of the formal means of social control and the prevalence of deviant acts. "Law and order" has become a popular issue, with many people claiming that deviance, especially criminal deviance, is far outstripping our present ability to apply formal means of control. Others argue that the rise in crime rates, as contained in official statistics, is mainly due to the increased effectiveness of the formal agents of social control—that they are now perceiving and apprehending a higher percentage of deviants. According to this point of view, the crime rate is increasing not because more crimes are being committed, but because more are included when the crime rate is estimated. But most experts hold that

there has been a real increase in some crime, notably armed robbery and automobile theft. A reasonable explanation for this rise in crime is that social circumstances are changing so that our society is generating more of the kinds of situations which produce deviance; for example, the widespread availability of addictive drugs, the increased sense of deprivation fostered among the poor by the persistent portrayals of the "good life" in the mass media. In addition, the crime rate is high because today a higher percentage of our population is in those youthful stages of life which generate the greatest amount of deviance.

Much of the discussion and controversy about the effectiveness of social control agents relates to the definition of "control" of deviance. If control is defined as making the deviant abandon his behavior and return to conformity, then most would argue that our formal means of control are highly unsuccess-

CRIME RATES IN WESTERN NATIONS: 1966

Nation	Murder	Sex Offenses	Larceny	Total
Italy	2.59	13.30	498.6	960.93
France	2.56	30.80	935.41	1,924.10
Great Britain	.35	1.32	931.50	1,538.00
United States	6.10	13.70	1,773.80	1,921.70

Rates are the number of crimes per 100,000 population.

SOURCES: Interpol, *International Crime Statistics: 1956-66 (Saint Cloud, France:* 1967); Home Office, *Criminal Statistics for England and Wales, 1966* (London: 1967); U.S. Federal Bureau of Investigation, *Uniform Crime Reports, 1966* (Washington, D.C.: 1967).

Because of differences in the way crimes are defined and reported in different countries, it is dangerous to leap to conclusions from figures like these. For example, it is possible that the American definition of larceny labels more actions as criminal than the Italian definition, causing the great difference in the larceny rates of the two nations.

ful. However, if control is defined as the perception and labeling of deviants, and their removal from the general society in cases where their deviance may prove harmful to other individuals, then our control system would receive a higher rating of efficiency. Many who pursue deviant careers do in fact spend much of their time isolated in some institution, such as a prison or a mental hospital. When an individual labeled a criminal deviant is released from a prison, he may be watched more closely than the average citizen for a brief time; for example, he may be required to visit a parole officer or a social worker. But surveillance of serious criminals in the United States is less strict than in most European countries where criminals are registered nationally and are denied immigration from one country to another.

REINTEGRATING THE DEVIANT INTO SOCIETY

If we define the social control of deviance in such a way as to include the return of the individual to conforming behavior, then we are faced with a much greater problem than is presented by the mere isolation of deviant individuals. There is even evidence for believing that the two goals may be mutually exclusive, that isolation of deviants serves only to confirm them in their deviance, working against the possibility of a return to conformity.

Certainly the formal means of controlling deviance have proven very inadequate in helping the deviant to return to a conforming pattern. Of course, we must remember that by the time formal mechanisms of control are invoked, a deviant individual has probably already proved somewhat resistant to control by internalized means and by informal external ones. He is well on his way to a deviant career when the police or the courts get his case. Moreover, since the police or courts act as agents of labeling as well, their very involvement in his case becomes a factor leading him to a career of deviance, as we saw in topic 3.

In recent years many governmental and private agencies have instituted experimental programs which try to correct deviant behavior rather than merely isolate it. Although there have been efforts to turn existing prisons into true corrective institutions, most of these are acknowledged failures. More successful has been the development of new types of correctional institutions such as model prison farms; however, these seldom deal with the difficult hard-core deviant cases.

Much of the focus of the current programs is on the crucial period of readjustment to non-institutional life. One such program is the half-way house, for those released from prisons and mental institutions. Ex-inmates may stay there for six months to a year after release. They are helped to find legitimate jobs; they receive counseling through the most difficult period, when their efforts to conform are not yet recognized by the rest of the community and they are still labeled deviants; their families may also be counseled on how to help the individual and how to cope with their own attitudes toward him. These efforts rely heavily for their success on the sense of group support from others in the program, but the participants also are encouraged to make friends outside, to hasten their re-identification with the conforming or normal world.

Such programs, and the similar ones that are currently being established for ex-drug addicts and juvenile delinquents, may offer some hope of breaking the cycle of the deviant career, and substituting for it a cycle of social integration and conformity. Of much greater importance in the long run, however, are broad programs of social reform leading to the reduction of poverty, discrimination, poor housing, broken homes, and the many other factors which have long been associated with high rates of criminal deviance.

TOPIC

5 THE SOCIAL EFFECTS OF DEVIANT BEHAVIOR

We have so far concentrated on deviance in terms of the individual deviant: the causes of deviant acts, the deviant career, and the control of the deviant. An equally significant consideration is the effect of deviance on the society as a whole. What happens to society when citizens fail to pay their parking tickets, or when men beat up and rob people on the street? We generally think first of the effects that are negative or disruptive—what sociologists call dysfunctions. We will also discuss some positive functions which are not so well recognized or understood.

In discussing the social effects of deviance, it is useful to distinguish between deviance and social disorganization, which are sometimes spoken of as if they were the same thing. *Social disorganization* refers to the disintegration or breakdown of the institutionalized structures of a social system. An organized society can tolerate a great deal of deviance without becoming seriously disrupted. Only when deviance is practiced by large numbers of people over long periods, or when it undermines belief in the value of basic social institutions, or when it generates conflict that cannot be contained, does it lead to social disorganization. Of course, social disorganization is not caused only by deviance—other causes are wars, population change, and technological innovation.

However, the concepts of deviance and social disorganization are closely related; individual acts of deviance may often lead to the breakdown of social structure, and poorly integrated social structures are often a cause of deviance, as we saw in discussing the anomie theory of Robert Merton.

SOCIAL DYSFUNCTIONS OF DEVIANCE

There are several ways in which deviance may upset the regular functioning of society. It is very rare that one act of deviance or the deviance of one person affects the functioning of society, for society can absorb an extensive amount of deviance without great effect. But continual or widespread deviance can be socially dysfunctional.

Deviance can hamper the complex system of interdependence that exists in the human community. All complex social organization requires the cooperation of a number of specialists, and if one or more of those specialists breaks the rules that govern his participation, then the successful operation of the whole system is in danger. A good example might be seen in the army. If, in the middle of a battle, a great number of soldiers begin to break the rules which are supposed to govern their conduct—they fail to follow the orders their officers give them, throw down their guns, and run away—then that army is going to lose the battle. The example of the army also illustrates the principle that the effect of deviance on the social system depends in part on the responsibilities and status of the deviants. If ten privates become deviants, there is relatively little harm done; if it is ten generals, the situation is much more serious.

The presence of deviance in a group can destroy other people's motivation to conform. If all the students taking an examination are aware that one student is systematically cheating on his exam, then they all begin to wonder why they stayed up so late so many nights studying to pass it honestly, in accordance with the rules. Of course, if the cheating student is caught and given a failing grade, then the value of the rules and the system is upheld. But where deviance is successful—meaning that it goes unpunished and achieves its goal—it weakens other people's commitment to conformity. If deviance and conformity are given the same social rewards, then why bother to conform?

Deviance destroys trust in the functioning of the social system. All kinds of social cooperation require a certain degree of trust in other people. People are willing to live together in towns and cities because they trust their neighbors not to attack them as soon as they appear on the street. They do business together on a contract system because they trust the other person to fulfill his obligations. A democratic system of government is possible only if we trust the elected or appointed officials to act in the public interest. Social organization is possible only when we can depend on the honesty and good will of the other people in the system.

Of course, deviance is always recognized as a natural part of every social system, and to some extent all relationships, and the workings of all organizations, are hedged with certain protections against deviance in others. For example, our government is set up so that the various branches can check each other's actions, because we assume that some officials may break the rules or put their own interests above those of the public; for the same reason, we try to maintain an uncensored press. We put locks on our doors because we do not trust our neighbors. Business contracts include clauses that specify the penalties for work that is faulty or not completed.

So some distrust of others can be built into the system without having any serious effect on its functioning. However, this is only true up to a point. People may stay behind the locked doors of their apartment or house all night, but in the morning they must leave it and go to work or to the grocery store. If people begin to be afraid to go out because they fear the deviance of others, then the successful operation and continuation of the community is in danger.

It has often been assumed and feared that pornography leads to sex crimes. However, some recent studies indicate that sex-crime offenders tend to have significantly less experience with pornographic materials than do most non-offenders. The question of whether open dissemination of pornography may not result, on the other hand, in more subtle harm, which society cannot afford to ignore, is much more difficult to study scientifically and is the subject of widespread public discussion. *(Photo by Geoffrey Gove)*

SOCIAL FUNCTIONS OF DEVIANCE

The existence of some recognized deviance can also serve to help the operation of the social system, in the following ways.

(1) Deviance sometimes serves to clarify social rules and define them for the non-deviant members of a social group. Occasionally no one in the group is really aware of what the rules are until they see someone else breaking them. The group reaction on that occasion defines the rule. For example, a fraternity might have a rule stating that cleanliness is expected in the fraternity house. But cleanliness is a rather ambiguous term; the members might not know exactly what is expected. But if one fraternity brother has a messy room and is not defined as a deviant, whereas another leaves his dirty dishes

strewn about the kitchen and is so defined, the members of the fraternity become aware of just what cleanliness does and does not mean to the group.

Also, since many rules are very general it is necessary for people to see how the rules will be applied to specific cases. It is, for example, the duty of the courts to decide whether a particular law applies to a particular situation, and in some cases even these specialists are not certain of the answer. However, once the application of a rule is specified, the rule can serve as a more accurate guideline for everyone.

(2) Deviance may increase group solidarity. The community may be brought together by its disapproval of the deviant. G. H. Mead said, "The attitude of hostility toward the

lawbreaker has the unique advantage of uniting all members of the community in the emotional solidarity of aggression."[34] Group members find that they share a common attitude toward the deviant, and in many cases they are also required to take some common action to control or suppress his deviance. This has the effect of increasing the cohesion of the group. It may also serve to increase the group's value to the conforming members, because they have, through their actions in the group's defense, invested more emotion and self-identification in it.

It should be noted that the group may occasionally unite on behalf of the deviant; this too increases group solidarity. The group may wish to protect one of its members from the consequences of his deviance, or to help him in returning to conformity. Both these actions assert the value of the group, because members feel that preserving the group intact is worth considerable trouble and effort.

(3) Deviance may serve to bring needed changes to the social system. This is the hope of those who practice nonconforming deviance. On occasion change becomes a reality. Because of the deviant actions of certain individuals, the rest of the group may be brought to realize that a certain rule is a bad one, or one that contradicts other more important rules; then the rule is changed. This has been the case in the civil disobedience campaign begun by Martin Luther King, Jr.

34. George Herbert Mead, "The Psychology of Punitive Justice," in *Sociological Theory: A Book of Readings,* 2d ed., ed. Lewis A. Coser and Bernard Rosenberg (New York: Macmillan, 1964), p. 596.

The rule breaking of large numbers of black Americans called the nation's attention to the unfairness of certain existing laws requiring or allowing their segregation, with the result that the laws were changed. Nonconforming defiance can perform a similar service in organizations which are sometimes hemmed in by hundreds of inherited rules having no relevance to current circumstances. Deviance, the ignoring of some of these rules, may prove to simplify and expedite the work of the group by demonstrating that these rules can be broken with good result.

(4) Deviance makes conformity seem more desirable. This, of course, is true only in cases where the deviance is unsuccessful and is given some kind of punishment. When everyone conforms, conformity is taken for granted and therefore cannot be considered any special virtue. However, when a deviant is punished all those who did not deviate are rewarded by their avoidance of punishment and their gratifying feeling of "doing the right thing." If a person never breaks a rule, but sees others breaking it without being punished, his faith in the rule is diminished. When the rule breaker is punished, the conformist's desire to adhere to the rule is strengthened.

These points suggest that deviance may have some value both to the individual and to society, and it is important for us to understand the intricate, complex, and sometimes beneficial relationship that exists between deviance and the broad system of social regulation.

SUMMARY

Human social life depends on the willingness of individuals to follow certain rules and to regulate their behavior in accordance with certain norms. Although society attempts to enforce conformity with the rules through various mechanisms of social control, it is

inevitable that on certain occasions, for a variety of reasons, some people will break some of the rules: they are going to be deviant. Because of the difficulty of determining average or functional behavior, any definition of deviance must be relative to social circumstances. Sociologists have distinguished several major types of deviance: 1) The *aber-*

rant deviant is one who basically accepts the validity of the rules but breaks them for some personal advantage. He is distinguished from the *nonconforming deviant* who breaks a rule because he thinks it is a bad one. 2) When the rule or regulation which is broken does not represent the sentiments of the system's members, deviance may be *socially approved.* Otherwise deviance is obviously *socially disapproved.* 3) An insane or ill person may break rules because he is *unable to conform.* On the other hand, a person who *fails to conform* although he is capable of doing so must accept personal responsibility for his act. 4) The consequences are also different for *individual deviance* than for a person who is acting as a party to *group deviance.*

No genetic factors have been positively established as causes of deviance, but many have been investigated. Another large area of research focuses on the psychological causes of deviance. According to the *frustration-aggression theory* deviance is a form of aggression toward society produced by frustration resulting from unfulfilled needs. Sociologists believe that certain social situations produce pressures toward deviance, and some regard deviance as an individual's attempt to adapt to his social environment rather than as something inherently pathological. Robert K. Merton has hypothesized that when an individual is blocked from achieving socially prescribed goals in socially approved ways the result is social strain or anomie. An individual may adapt to this situation through *innovation,* by accepting the goals and rejecting prescribed means of achievement; *ritualism,* or rejecting the goals but accepting the means; *retreatism,* or rejecting both goals and means; or *rebellion,* substituting new goals and means.

In order to become deviant, an individual usually must have access to an opportunity structure, such as a delinquent street gang, where deviance can be learned and reinforced. Often "corrective" institutions such as prisons and mental institutions will actually transmit a deviant subculture, reinforcing and refining the individual's deviant behavior. The theory of *differential association* hypothesizes that a person is socialized by many different groups but will internalize the ideas with which he has most contact or that are taught by groups that are particularly important to him. Deviant behavior may also serve to protect a person's culturally approved role, or it may support a deviant role by maintaining a deviant individual's self-image.

In order to build a *deviant career* an individual first commits an offense that is perceived by a number of other people, or by people whose attitudes are particularly important to him. Once his offense becomes visible the deviant is labeled or typed, placed in a social category which carries a standardized, negative identification. Typically this label becomes his master or principal social status, and the individual is rejected and isolated by society. As a consequence he may be pushed further into deviance, and he may begin to define himself as a deviant. Finally an individual may seek emotional and social support by joining and identifying with a group of other deviants. These groups often have well-developed subcultures based on a set of common experiences in dealing with the larger society. At this point a return to conformity becomes extremely difficult because the deviant must give up his established self-image and an entire style of life.

Society relies heavily on internalization of social norms and values in attempting to control deviance. It also uses external means of control through informal sanctions applied by the primary group, and through formally stated laws and organizational rules that specify rewards and punishments. Although formal means of control are successful in labeling and isolating deviants from the general society, they are notably unsuccessful in making deviants abandon their behavior and return to conformity. Isolation and labeling often serve to perpetuate deviant behavior and make reintegration into the normal or conforming world particularly difficult.

Poorly integrated social structures are often a cause of deviance. Individual acts of deviance may lead to social disorganization if they are practiced by large numbers of people over long periods, or if they undermine belief in the value of basic social institutions and trust in other people, or if they generate conflict that cannot be contained. On the other hand, recognized deviance can also benefit the social system by clarifying social rules for all members of society, by uniting members of a community through disapproval of the deviant, by pointing up unfair or unworkable social norms and thus bringing needed changes to the social system, or by dramatizing the undesirable consequences of unsuccessful deviance and thereby making conformity seem more desirable.

GLOSSARY

Anomie   A social condition in which there are relatively few values to guide the individual, or in which the values are confused and unclear. (page 500)

Deviance   The process of breaking the rules or norms of a group or society. (page 490)

Formal social control mechanisms   Systems of formally established laws and rules, and the means of enforcing them, which specify rewards for those who conform to them and punishments for those who violate them. (page 519)

Informal social control mechanisms   Systems of informal rules and codes enforced through personal actions such as praise and ridicule. (page 517)

Internalization   An individual's acceptance of the norms of a social group or society as part of his own personality. (page 516)

Social control   A process by which restrictions are imposed on individual behavior in order to motivate people to conform to the norms of a group or society. (page 489)

Social disorganization   The disintegration or breakdown of the institutionalized structures of a social system. (page 522)

SUGGESTED READINGS AND RELATED RESOURCES

I   READINGS IN SOCIOLOGY

Becker, Howard S., ed. *The Other Side*. New York: Free Press (Paper), 1967. This collection of articles by various sociologists discusses the relationships between deviance and society, with particular emphasis on the responses of nondeviants to deviant behavior. The book could serve as a good reader for many of the topics covered in chapter 12.

_____. *The Outsiders*. New York: Free Press, 1963. Becker asserts that deviance is created by society when certain acts are defined as deviant. From this perspective he examines a group of marijuana users and a deviant occupational group and discusses the process of social control.

Clinard, Marshall B., ed. *Anomie and Deviant Behavior*. New York: Free Press, 1964. From the point of view of this collection of essays, deviance is not a result of biological or psychological factors, but is caused by society's inability to provide the means for some people to achieve the goals or rewards of the society. These people deviate to try to obtain those goals or rewards.

_____. *Sociology of Deviant Behavior*. Rev. ed. New York: Holt, Rinehart & Winston, 1963. Clinard discusses social norms in modern society and analyzes types of deviance which occur in urbanized societies. He also dissects several kinds of deviance, from murder to white collar crimes.

Cloward, R., and L. Ohlin. *Delinquency and*

Opportunity. New York: Free Press, 1960. In discussing the formation of delinquent gangs, Cloward and Ohlin develop the anomie theory of deviance; from their point of view delinquency arises because of the lack of opportunities to fulfill society's goals through legitimate means.

Cohen, Albert K. *Delinquent Boys: The Culture of the Gang*. New York: Free Press, 1955. This book focuses on delinquency as a subculture, and includes a great deal of useful empirical data.

———. *Deviance and Control*. Englewood Cliffs, N.J.: Prentice-Hall, 1966. Cohen offers a concise survey of types and theories of deviance; an excellent book for the beginning student.

Erikson, Kai T. *Wayward Puritans: A Study in the Sociology of Deviance*. New York: John Wiley, 1966. This scholarly and entertaining study recounts some notable examples of deviant behavior in history.

Jessor, R., T. Graves, R. Hanson, C. Robert, and S. Jessor. *Society, Personality, and Deviant Behavior*. New York: Holt, Rinehart & Winston, 1968. From a study of the drinking problems of residents of a small town, these researchers attempt to arrive at a broad theoretical understanding of the causes for deviant behavior. They emphasize the social-psychological aspects of deviance.

Matza, David. *Delinquency and Drift*. New York: John Wiley, 1964. Matza views delinquency as a youthful experiment that is part of the process of maturation. He finds that some subcultures purposely or inadvertently encourage such experimentation, and that most delinquents "drift" out of crime when they are older.

Merton, Robert K. *Social Theory and Social Structure*. Rev. ed. New York: Free Press, 1967. Merton perceives the root cause of deviant behavior as anomie; he develops this theory in studying different aspects of America's social structure. Important references to deviance are found on pp. 371–384 (major causes of deviance); pp. 60–82 and 357–368 (the functions of deviance); and in his section on "Social Structure and Anomie," pp. 121–123 and 131–161.

Merton, R. K., and Robert A. Nisbet, eds. *Contemporary Social Problems*. 2d ed. New York: Harcourt Brace Jovanovich, 1966. This collection of essays by major sociologists offers an excellent overview of major personal, social, and cultural causes and forms of deviance and social disorganization in the United States today.

Rushing, William A., ed. *Deviant Behavior and Social Processes*. Chicago: Rand McNally, 1969. The essays in this reader cover several criminal and noncriminal forms of deviance. Most of the articles emphasize the social processes involved in becoming deviant or maintaining a deviant life style.

Thrasher, Frederic M. *The Gang*. Abr. ed. Edited by James F. Short. Chicago: University of Chicago Press, 1963. This book is the result of a study of the major gangs in Chicago; it analyzes the gang as a subculture in society, with its special role assignments, normative systems, and political structures.

Articles and Papers

Bordua, David. "Delinquent Subcultures: Sociological Interpretations of Gang Delinquency." *Annals of the American Academy of Political and Social Science* **338** (November 1961):119–136.

Clark, A. L., and Jack P. Gibbs. "Social Control: A Reformulation." *Social Problems* **12** (Spring 1965):398–415.

Coser, Lewis A. "The Functions of Deviant Behavior and Normative Flexibility." *American Journal of Sociology* **68** (1962):172–182.

Esseltyn, T. C. "Prostitution in the United States." *Annals of the American Academy of Political and Social Science* **376** (March 1968): 123–135.

Gibbons, Don C. "Crime and Punishment: A Study in Social Attitudes." *Social Forces* **47**, 4 (June 1969):391–397.

Globetti, Gerald. "The Use of Alcohol Among High School Students in an Abstinence Setting." *Pacific Sociological Review* **12**, 2 (Fall 1969): 105–108.

Goldman, Nathan. "Social Breakdown." *Annals of the American Academy of Political and Social Science* **373** (September 1967):156–179.

Jaco, E. Gartly. "Attitudes Toward and Incidence of Mental Disorder: A Research Note." *Southwestern Social Science Quarterly* **38**, 1 (1957):27–38.

Kitsuse, John I. "Societal Reaction to Deviant Behavior." *Social Problems* **9**, 3 (Winter 1962): 247–256.

McCluggage, Marston M., and Jackson E.

Bauer. "Drinking Patterns of Kansas High School Students." *Social Problems* **5**, 4 (Spring 1958): 317–326.

Scheff, Thomas J. "Stereotypes of Insanity." *New Society,* 9 March 1967, pp. 348–350.

Schwartz, M. "Delinquency Research and the Self-Concept Variable." *Journal of Criminal Law, Criminology and Police Science* **58**, 2 (June 1967): 182–190.

Shibutoni, Tamotsu. "Reference Groups and Social Control." In *Human Behavior and Social Processes,* edited by A. Rose. Boston: Houghton Mifflin, 1962.

Snyder, Charles Royce. "Inebriety, Alcoholism, and Anomie." In *Anomie and Deviant Behavior: A Discussion and Critique,* edited by Marshall B. Clinard. New York: Free Press, 1964.

Yablonsky, Lewis. "The Delinquent Gang as a Near Group." *Social Problems* **9** (Fall 1961): 108–117.

Yablonsky, Lewis, and John Irwin. "The New Criminal: A View of the Contemporary Offender." *British Journal of Criminology* **5**, 2 (April 1965): 183–190.

II   RELATED RESOURCES
Nonfiction

Conger, John J., and W. C. Miller. *Personality, Social Class and Delinquency.* New York: John Wiley, 1966. Conger and Miller relate such variables as residential area, personality traits, and intelligence to the occurrence of juvenile delinquency.

Endleman, S., ed. *Violence in the Streets.* Chicago: Quadrangle Books (Paper), 1968. This book is a collection of essays on the origin and forms of violence, its dissemination by mass media, and the role of the police in relation to it.

Gerassi, John. *The Boys of Boise.* New York: Collier (Paper), 1968. This book documents the homosexual subculture of Boise, Idaho, and the hysterical reaction of the city's residents to a scandal which arose from this subculture. It constitutes a strong case against present laws regarding homosexuality.

Klein, M., ed. *Juvenile Gangs in Context.* Englewood Cliffs, N.J.: Prentice-Hall, 1967. For those students interested in reading further in the area of original research on delinquency.

Short, James F. *Gang Delinquency and De-linquent Subcultures.* New York: Harper & Row (Paper), 1968. This collection of essays, by men in various social science disciplines, surveys various factors which give rise to deviant gangs.

Fiction

Baldwin, James. *Another Country.* New York: Dell, 1965. Rufus, a young black man, is involved in the worlds of jazz, drugs, and homosexuality. The narrative of his experiences in these subcultures is vivid and revealing.

_____. *Go Tell It on the Mountain.* New York: Dell, 1963. The novel portrays a boy growing up in a deviant religious group.

Burroughs, William. *Naked Lunch.* New York: Grove Press, 1962. Burroughs, a former drug addict, has written a portrait of the drug addict and his obsession with supplying himself and avoiding arrest. The book contains some vivid descriptions of hallucinatory experiences brought on by drugs.

Genet, Jean. *Thief's Journal.* Translated by Bernard Frechtman. New York: Grove Press, 1964. Written by a member of both the thief and homosexual subcultures, the journal describes both worlds as reversed and sometimes extreme versions of respectable middle-class culture.

O'Neill, Eugene. *Long Day's Journey into Night.* New Haven, Conn.: Yale University Press (Paper), 1961. In this autobiographical play, O'Neill describes a family in which the mother is addicted to drugs, and the father and brother are caught in varying degrees of alcoholism.

Films

The Boys in the Band. Mart Crowley, 1970. Various aspects of the homosexual subculture which has developed in the United States are portrayed in this film about a party given by and for a group of homosexuals in New York City.

Easy Rider. Dennis Hopper, 1969. This film reveals how some young people today have deviated from the dominant American culture and developed a subculture, or counterculture, which incorporates a different life style and, frequently, the use of drugs.

Midnight Cowboy. John Schlesinger, 1969. The two leading characters of this story are deviants; the film shows how their need to survive both thwarts and perpetuates their deviance.

13. Collective Behavior

*In one sense, all the subject matter of sociology
is the study of collective behavior, if we think of
the term in its literal meaning. But in sociology this
phrase is used in a more specific and precise
way.* Collective behavior *is the behavior of a group
of people responding to a common influence or
stimulus in fairly temporary, unstable, and
unstructured situations. Collective behavior
tends to be emotional and unpredictable, and
irregular in occurrence. However, it does show some
pattern or structure, and it is that structure which
sociologists study. According to the
sociological definition, a group of one hundred
college students attending a protest rally falls into
the category of collective behavior, whereas the same
one hundred students attending lectures for the
course they are all taking in art appreciation
does not. In the lecture the students' behavior
is organized or highly structured, but at the rally
it is lacking in structure and stability.*

*Collective behavior includes such social phenomena
as crowds, riots, fads and fashions, public opinion,
and social movements. It is important not only
because of its newsmaking character—riots,
demonstrations, protest movements, and mass
rallies have made many headlines in the 1960s
and 1970s—but also because it is a very
important force in social change. Today's fads may
become tomorrow's customs, and out of the*

*crowds of the present may emerge the
enduring and well-structured social groups of
the future. Many of our present-day institutions,
including our nation itself, started as protest
movements.*

*Collective behavior is related to the informal
patterns of association which arise in
complex organizations (discussed in chapter 5).
Both are rather spontaneous and continuously
changing responses to a structured social situation. Both must be understood if we are to
understand how change occurs in institutionalized social structures.*

*The field of collective behavior is as much a part
of psychology as it is of sociology. The
psychologist studies people's individual
intellectual and emotional responses, and their
motivations, in collective situations. What
interests the sociologist are the social
conditions in which collective behavior occurs,
the elements of collective behavior which are
particular to the group rather than the individual,
and the effects of collective behavior on
other aspects of social life.*

1 THE TYPES AND CONDITIONS OF COLLECTIVE BEHAVIOR

We can bring the nature of collective behavior into sharper focus by comparing it with the behavior of highly organized or structured situations, in which goals and expectations are clear, roles are well defined, and social control mechanisms are successfully operating. For example, the college students in the lecture hall are in a highly organized situation. They are there for a specific purpose—getting an education (or a degree)—which is clear to them and approved by the society at large. The behavior of both professors and students is subject to normative controls, and everyone understands the demands of the role he is to play in the classroom; he also knows what to expect from the others there. The students know that the university can apply a variety of negative sanctions to discourage undesirable behavior in individual students—disciplinary action by the dean or punitive action by the professor in regard to grades.

But at a protest rally, there is a marked absence of social structure and norms to govern behavior. People are brought together in almost haphazard fashion. Reasons for attending may vary widely; some are there to support the cause, others to heckle the supporters, and others to see what's going on or to kill time until the dinner hour. Some of the crowd may be dedicated pacifists, who want to avoid violence at any cost, whereas others may be militant radicals who are hoping for a chance to try out the politics of confrontation. So there is no uniformity of purpose, or even of expectation. Since most people do not attend protest rallies regularly, they have little knowledge of the way the role of protester is supposed to be played, and those who are in charge of the rally may be similarly ignorant about their roles as organizers or supervisors. There may also be some question about how the university or the outside community will respond to the behavior of the demonstrating students and, therefore, an uncertainty about the sanctions which might be applied. If the cause is a popular one, or one the administration also supports, and if the demonstration doesn't seem to threaten the interests of the university, then the students might be praised by their president for their "social conscience." On the other hand, the administration might order the use of tear gas and fire hoses to break up the meeting and later take punitive action, such as suspension, expulsion. probation, or even court action, against those known to have attended. In this situation, individuals have few normative guidelines to direct their behavior and are, therefore, subject to the influences of the crowd and the situation—influences that are very important in collective behavior.

The crowd, which we have used as the prime example thus far and which we shall discuss more fully in topic 2, is often thought of as being synonymous with collective behavior. However, many other important and interesting types of collective behavior exist.

A crowd is a collection of people who are gathered in one place at one specific time. Other forms of collective behavior erupt from people who are scattered but still reacting to a common stimulus. A *public* is a scattered group of people who share a common interest; a discussion of publics and public opinion will be taken up in topic 3. A *social movement* is a group of people, usually somewhat scattered, who are acting to promote some form of social change. Some examples are youth movements and political reform movements. These are the subject of topic 4.

One form of collective behavior among a scattered group of people is the *business panic,* which reached extraordinary proportions during the stock market crash of 1929. This is a form of collective behavior that may have far-reaching repercussions.

Another kind of collective behavior is a *craze*—an unreasoned rush toward some satisfaction. Like many forms of collective behavior, it is often generated by some serious underlying social dissatisfaction. For example, a craze for some kind of speculative get-rich-quick idea may occur when there is some weakness in the economy such as extensive wage and price fluctuations or a recession. Such a craze developed in England in the early eighteenth century when many people invested large sums of money in real estate in the South Sea Islands. This craze had serious consequences. When the real estate speculation collapsed, a number of men lost all their money and the national economy suffered a recession of several years' duration. A craze is more often trivial and without long-range social effects; in the United States we have had crazes for sitting on flagpoles, for swallowing goldfish, and for writing chain letters, none of which had any lasting effect on our society.

Mass hysteria, one of the least understood forms of collective behavior, is the contagious spread of certain hysterical symptoms such as fainting, delusions, or trances. Certain kinds of religious services, in which the congregation begins to twitch, shout unintelligible words, or perhaps lapse into trances, are really exercises in mass hysteria. Another example of mass hysteria may be the sudden and numerous sightings of flying saucers and various space visitors that occur every time an article or book on the subject is publicized. Recently an interesting study of mass hysteria was conducted by A. J. W. Taylor in New Zealand.[1] He investigated the phenomenon of mass screaming, jumping up and down, and even fainting, which was often displayed by teen-age girls at the concerts given by the Beatles. Taylor was unable to answer conclusively the question of why some people succumb to mass hysteria and others resist, for he found no essential or significant differences between those who screamed and jumped and those who watched more quietly.

Fads and *fashions* are classified as collective behavior because of their temporary nature and their mass appeal. We often think of both fads and fashions as trivial, but they can play serious parts in social life.[2] Either one may be a status symbol, and therefore serve as an integral part of the system of social stratification. Moreover, as Thorstein Veblen has shown, fashion can serve as an index to the values and attitudes of the society.[3] The abridgment by Marshall McLuhan in chapter 3 illustrated how fashion in the 1960s reflected a change in attitudes toward sensuality. Fashion is often a "customary" departure from custom; that is, it is an attempt to depart from what is customary, to be new and different but at the same time it usually remains within the bounds of accepted styles of dress.[4]

1. A. J. W. Taylor, "Beatlemania—A Study in Adolescent Enthusiasm," *The British Journal of Social and Clinical Psychology* 5 (1966):81–88.

2. See Rolf Meyersohn and Elihu Katz, "Notes on a Natural History of Fads," *American Journal of Sociology* 62, no. 6 (May 1957):594–601, for a full discussion of the birth and death of fads.

3. Thorstein Veblen, *The Theory of the Leisure Class* (New York: Viking Press, 1967).

4. See Edward Sapir, "Fashion," in *Encyclopedia of the Social Sciences* (New York: Macmillan, 1937), p. 140.

Interpersonal relations are at a minimum in a casual crowd. People may spontaneously gather together in large numbers for a variety of reasons: to catch a glimpse of a passing public figure, to watch a building under construction, or a house on fire. Regardless of what captures attention, crowds often develop a common mood. The feeling of anonymity, and heightened stimulation and suggestibility may encourage people to express certain emotions, impulses, and sometimes hostilities that they are normally restrained from expressing. In this case crowds have gathered on Wall Street in front of the Sub-Treasury building during the stock market crash in 1929. *(World Wide Photos)*

CONDITIONS OF COLLECTIVE BEHAVIOR

Since collective behavior takes so many forms, it is difficult to generalize about the social conditions which encourage or cause it. As a starting point, Ralph Turner has noted that "by the nature of the definition of the field, collective behavior occurs only (but not always) when the established organization ceases to afford direction and supply channels for action."[5] The following conditions have been singled out as particularly basic for generating collective behavior, although they do not all have to be present at one time, nor is each necessarily associated with all forms of collective behavior.[6]

Conflicting values

Conflicting values and norms are often a precondition of collective behavior. The series of riots in black neighborhoods of large cities such as Detroit and Los Angeles during the sixties demonstrated this clearly. The average resident was faced with a conflict between the value of abiding by the law and the value of maintaining ethnic group solidarity with those who were rioting. This puts the individual in the position of having to make a decision

5. *Handbook of Modern Sociology,* ed. Robert E. L. Faris (Chicago: Rand McNally, 1964), p. 392.

6. For a slightly different scheme see Ralph H. Turner and Lewis M. Killian, *Collective Behavior* (Englewood Cliffs, N.J.: Prentice-Hall, 1957), chap. 2.

about his behavior in the face of two equally compelling values; due to this ambiguity he becomes susceptible to the influence of momentary needs and mass example.

Conflicting values and norms also may result from rapid social change or the introduction of a foreign culture. The move to the city, for example, can be an unsettling experience for people who have been raised in a rural area. The many new ways of life and thought are difficult to integrate with the old. Values such as loyalty and patience, which may have been highly prized in the rural tradition, clash with the urban values of competitiveness and economic achievement.

Breakdown in mechanisms of social control

We discussed social control in the last chapter as a continuing function of every social system. When the mechanisms of social control weaken and seem to be breaking down people may lose confidence in the social system and some may attempt to reform or restructure it. This is the case with vigilante groups, who "take the law into their own hands" when they feel that some injustice has not been officially corrected.

The breakdown in social control may occur because the formal agents of social control — such as the police and the courts — perform their roles inadequately, or it may occur because the informal mechanisms of social control no longer function well. The breakdown of informal controls is characteristic of some urban neighborhoods, for example, where there are few watchful eyes of neighbors safeguarding the streets, and where families lose control of their own children.

Social deprivation

In normal circumstances, an individual is able to work out patterns of behavior that offer him certain gratifications and he is reasonably contented with life. He may be looking for security, or for an opportunity for self-expression, or for a sense of belonging; society has taught him that he will generally achieve these gratifications if he behaves in certain specified and socially approved ways. Under conditions of social deprivation, an individual is denied these normal channels of gratification, causing him frustration, insecurity, and disenchantment. Social deprivation can result from a variety of circumstances: poverty, discrimination, religious persecution, defeat in war, and unemployment are but a few examples. These conditions are likely to lead an individual to seek outlets for his frustrations in crowds, mobs, and other forms of collective behavior. For any sort of collective behavior to develop out of social deprivation, however, there must also be a belief that better conditions may be possible as a result of collective action.

Normlessness

Some situations are so new or occur so infrequently that few norms have developed to cover them. For example, there are almost no norms to govern behavior of people involved in a shipwreck (except perhaps "women and children first") or an avalanche, because these are not things which we expect to have to cope with.[7] On the other hand, the death of a family member or a loved friend is fully covered by institutionalized norms. Although it is a situation that occurs only a few times to each individual, it is a common human situation and one which everyone expects to face at some time. In contrast, examples of situations in which there is relative "normlessness" are those in which the individual's normal ties to social structure are loosened — at vacation resorts, rock festivals, and public gatherings. The condition of being temporarily away from familial and occupational role attachments is quite conducive to collective behavior.

It is interesting to note that even in times of disaster or social disruption (if the situa-

---

7. An interesting analysis of the social behavior that results in such circumstances is Walter Lord's book on the sinking of the *Titanic*. Walter Lord, *A Night to Remember* (New York: Holt, Rinehart & Winston, 1955).

tion continues over a period of time), behavior can become patterned by norms. In England, during World War II, the first bombing raids on London led to much unstructured collective behavior as people poured out of their homes and into the bomb shelters for protection throughout the night. But as the raids continued, norms evolved. A certain degree of informality of dress was established as acceptable attire for the bomb shelter—bathrobes, slippers, or even bare feet. Hair could be uncombed, or put up in curlers, although neither would be acceptable on the street the following morning. It was considered bad manners not to share some degree of cameraderie with the others in the shelter, but people were also granted a certain voluntary invisibility for the pursuit of personal relationships and intimacies. A whole set of regulations finally governed behavior in the shelters; when the same group of people had to adapt regularly to the same situation, they found it desirable to bring order and routine into their lives—to develop social structure.

TOPIC 2 CROWDS

*C*rowds are temporary groupings of people physically close together with a common focus or interest. People collect in crowds for many reasons. In an essay published in 1939,[8] which has stimulated much of the recent work on collective behavior, Herbert Blumer made the important distinction between an *expressive* crowd and an *acting* crowd. An expressive crowd is interested in expressing feelings—the release of tension without any other purpose. The acting crowd, on the other hand, is concerned with acting out, focusing on an external goal or objective. Acting crowds are often hostile to the existing social order.

Another distinction can be made between socially acceptable and antisocial crowds. Most crowds are acceptable to society. People may gather to see a football game, or to attend a revival or a play, or to watch a parade. There are crowds at sales, on the beaches in the summer, and at rock festivals. None of these has antisocial purposes and most of them have some recognizable patterns of order, usually constructed around the activity of the crowd. But any aggregation of people may develop into a crowd which displays antisocial behavior. The crowd that is simply watching an exciting soccer game may turn into a rioting mob, leaving scores of people dead. A question of great interest to sociologists is what makes it happen— how does an orderly crowd become a hostile mob? In this topic, we will look at the various types of crowd behavior, and also discuss some of the reasons crowds may become antisocial.

SOCIALLY ACCEPTED CROWD BEHAVIOR

Some forms of crowd behavior are actually encouraged by society as being functional or useful. One social benefit is that they provide

8. Herbert Blumer, "Collective Behavior," in *Principles of Sociology,* ed. R. E. Park (New York: Barnes & Noble, 1939), pp. 221–282.

Mass political rallies are designed to stimulate feelings of solidarity. However, the expressions of enthusiasm often become stereotyped. Many aspects of our national political conventions, for example, have become part of a ritual display. The hats, banners, the songs and even the speeches often seem more of a public relations show than an expression of genuine feeling. *(Eliott Erwitt, Magnum)*

opportunities for emotional expression and release. For example, most primitive cultures have some sort of periodic festival, celebrating the harvest or some great military victory, or a day of religious significance. On such occasions the people try to gather as large a crowd as possible, and so they may invite tribal members from miles around, perhaps also the residents of neighboring villages. This celebrating crowd indulges in a variety of activities—dancing, drinking, feasting, singing, shouting, competing in games and tests of skill, even (in the Trobriand Islands) making love. This whole community experience serves as a kind of emotional release. It is one which the people are not normally free to obtain individually because such rambunctious behavior in the ordinary course of events would be frowned on as disruptive. Some anthropologists have theorized that such festivities are especially important in a culture which customarily calls for a great deal of repression of emotion; as an illustration they cite the Indian tribes of the American Southwest, who occasionally relieve the emotional stoicism that is demanded in daily life with bouts of unrestrained emotionalism, usually associated with some religious ceremony such as a rain dance or a peyote rite.[9]

In our culture, there are also certain kinds of gatherings that serve this purpose of emotional expression or release. At football games, the spectators are free to sing and shout without incurring the kind of social disapproval such behavior would merit in an isolated instance. The crowd conditions actually encourage this behavior, by reducing the inhibitions that normally suppress it. The example of others, increased willingness to accept suggestions from others, the anonymity and impersonality of the crowd, the unstructured situation, all contribute to this effect. This phenomenon is referred to by some sociologists as emotional *contagion*. Contagion of emotional expression can also be seen at conventions, homecoming weekends, large parties, and revival meetings, all of which are approved by society.

A second kind of social benefit of crowd behavior is the building of a sense of social integration on the part of the participants. To be with a large group, all of whom affirm one's own attitudes or beliefs, strengthens the individual's identification with the group or the society. It is, for instance, significant that those who attended the rock festival near Woodstock, New York, in the summer of

9.   Ruth Benedict, *Patterns of Culture*, 2d ed. (Boston: Houghton Mifflin, 1959), pp. 78–79.

1969, went back home speaking of a "Woodstock nation." Many of these people had previously felt themselves to be alienated or isolated adherents of a minority subculture; in a crowd of 500,000 they discovered a sense of social belonging. Not everyone would classify this particular example as a benefit to the wider society, but it nonetheless was probably of some benefit to the participants, and a good case may be made for its social value on the grounds that a sense of belonging to a social group of any kind may be preferable to widespread alienation.

Governments sometimes sponsor rallies or mass meetings to attract crowds for the purpose of building this feeling of social belonging. This practice is especially noticeable in wartime, and helped nations on both sides during World War II to unify the populations. Other political examples are the annual May Day parades in the Soviet Union, and the crowds that gather (or are gathered) to hear the public speeches of Fidel Castro. Official use of this tactic calls for a certain degree of assurance about the political climate of the nation, for the crowd could turn into a mob that would take action against the government. It is characteristic of unpopular governments that they prohibit or suppress large public gatherings for fear of just such an occurrence. Thus, the British Government tried to prohibit the gathering of colonial Americans before the American Revolution, and the slaveholders in the South prohibited meetings of more than three slaves.

Not all of the crowd behavior which is accepted by society can be termed truly beneficial; some such behavior might be more accurately called neutral. This is especially true of passive or casual crowds, where a minimum of emotional involvement and action is called for from crowd members. We see this in the kind of crowd that is essentially an audience, where there is little interaction among individuals in the crowd. Another kind of neutral crowd is one made up of people pursuing the same activity at the same time,

without needing the crowd as a support or catalyst for the activity. Crowds in parks and other recreational facilities, the crowd at a bargain sale on Washington's Birthday, the people waiting in line to vote on Election Day—these crowds are an accidental by-product of the individual's freedom of choice and action. In chapter 2 we referred to this crowd situation as *recurrent aggregative behavior,* one of the most loosely structured of all forms of social interaction. No particular social benefit accrues to a crowd of shoppers gathered at a sale. The crowd gathers simply because a large number of people want to take advantage of the opportunity of the sale. Yet there is also nothing in the situation that is antisocial, for hunting a bargain is a socially approved activity.

As the population of the world increases steadily, the neutral crowd will become a regular feature of daily life, as it already is for the people who live in large cities like New York and Tokyo. They are used to shopping, eating, riding the subway, and seeing a movie along with a large crowd of other people. Sociologists, and also behavioral psychologists, are interested in the effects of this kind of crowd on the individual, but not much solid information has as yet been obtained on the subject.[10]

ANTISOCIAL CROWD BEHAVIOR

Crowd behavior is called antisocial when its goals are the destruction or disruption of the prevailing social order, especially through the infliction of damage, injury, or death, or the impairment of the freedom of others. Collective antisocial behavior usually involves an acting rather than a passive or expressive crowd. There are two principal types of such action: the mob action and the riot action.

10. A biosociologist's view of this question is contained in Desmond Morris, *The Human Zoo* (New York: McGraw-Hill, 1969). A purely sociological viewpoint regarding the effects of living in crowd conditions can be found in Lincoln H. Day and Alice Taylor Day, *Too Many Americans* (Boston: Houghton Mifflin, 1964).

The assassination of Dr. Martin Luther King sparked a new militancy in many blacks who had previously been faithful proponents of nonviolent resistance. Here, the plane bearing the civil rights leader's body is hailed with a Black Power salute, symbol of a disillusioned, angry mood among blacks. For many, organizations that advocated aggressive or violent solutions provided an outlet for the increased frustration and stress felt by members of the black community. *(Burk Uzzle, Magnum)*

A *mob* can be defined as a crowd which is trying to accomplish or cause an antisocial act of aggression. Usually, such groups have leaders, and the group action is often quite structured. However, mob action still falls within the definition of collective behavior because it is temporary and unstable; the nucleus of planners or leaders must recruit the followers from a crowd; and the influences of collective behavior become a strong factor in the motivation of individuals who join. Lynchings, fire-bombings, effigy-hangings, and the terroristic activities of groups like the Ku Klux Klan or the Hell's Angels are examples of mob action.

A *riot* is a violently aggressive and destructive mob, often characterized by a lack of goals or direction. Although some of the rioters may have specific goals in mind, such as the destruction of homes or businesses owned by unpopular individuals, most act out deep and general resentment and hatred. The collective outburst usually involves an attack on groups that are disliked, looting and destruction of property, and a general flouting of authority.

SOME DETERMINANTS OF RIOTS AND MOB ACTIONS

Those who participate in either a riot or a mob action are typically under great psychic and social stress. For it to be a cause of community action the stress must be widespread; it may be due to conditions of poverty, war, the fear of restrictive or repressive actions by the government, or some great social change to which the community has not yet adjusted. For example, rioters are frequently members of a racial or ethnic group that has been discriminated against. Furthermore, participating individuals generally feel that there is no quick or certain remedy to their problem in sight, and moreover, that the power structure (the establishment) either cannot or will not listen to their complaints. This was the case in the Watts race riot of 1966; the blacks felt that the municipal government had no serious intention of assisting them in their fight for social and economic equality. In other words, rioters are people with grievances for which there appear to be no solutions and no legitimate outlets.

This underlying social stress is then often heightened by the individual's awareness that there are formally organized groups that advocate some kind of aggressive response to the stress situation; this creates a corresponding awareness of violence or aggression as a possible outlet, perhaps even a solution. For example, the riots that occurred in black communities during the second half of the decade of the sixties can be traced in part to the prior existence of such groups as the militantly reorganized Student Nonviolent Coordinating Committee (SNCC) and the Black Panthers. This does *not* mean that rioters were members of these organizations, or that they incited anyone to riot: it merely means that they indicated to the general black community that aggressive responses to problems of discrimination were conceivable.

In nearly all cases of either riots or mob actions, there seems to be some specific precipitating event which rouses the emotions of the group. It is this event which makes the crowd decide to retaliate aggressively against a person or property. Sometimes the precipitating event is meaningful, and symbolizes an underlying conflict. Sometimes the event, and the victim at hand, are simply the focus of displaced emotion and blame.

A major factor in riot behavior is the emotional contagion that spreads through assembled crowds such as those who may be waiting to hear more news about the precipitating event.[11] People in crowds become more open to suggestion, both from spoken remarks and underlying meanings. Social controls are weakened by the pressure and anonymity of the crowd, which create a temporary release from the usual sense of personal moral responsibility. People respond imitatively to the observed and/or reported actions of others. In this regard the actions of the crowd leaders are especially important.

Secondary factors include such things as hot weather, which causes tempers to rise (and may also drive people out on the streets to seek a breeze, thus setting the stage for the collection of a crowd), and idleness and boredom, which make people eager to investigate "what's going on." The Allport abridgment in this topic contains a list of factors that are commonly associated with incidents of racial violence.

THE ROLE OF RUMOR

A *rumor* is a widespread report that is unsubstantiated in fact. It often serves to provoke, or to increase, antisocial collective behavior. Rumor must be distinguished from lack of communication, for the rapid spread of rumor may very well be due to effective communication. The term rumor refers not to a method of its communication, but to its content. Under crowd conditions, it becomes difficult to check the source and accuracy of the information one receives, and thus to evaluate it, and so rumors are acted on as if they were true information. Rumor often arises because of a lack of information. People want to know what is happening, and so the rumor fills that need. Rumor may also be created as a rationalization or justification for emotional excesses and collective behavior.

Let us analyze a specific example of the role of rumor in a crowd situation. The following quotation comes from the Report of the Na-

11. For a discussion of emotional contagion, see Kurt Lang and Gladys E. Lang, *Collective Dynamics* (New York: Thomas Y. Crowell, 1961), pp. 221–229.

tional Advisory Commission on Civil Disorders; it concerns the rioting in Newark, New Jersey, in the summer of 1967:

On Saturday, July 15, [Director of Police Dominick] Spina, received a report of snipers in a housing project. When he arrived he saw approximately 100 National Guardsmen and police officers crouching behind vehicles, hiding in corners and lying on the ground around the edge of the courtyard.

Since everything appeared quiet and it was broad daylight, Spina walked directly down the middle of the street. Nothing happened. As he came to the last building of the complex, he heard a shot. All around him the troopers jumped, believing themselves to be under sniper fire. A moment later a young Guardsman ran from behind a building.

The Director of Police went over and asked him if he had fired a shot. The soldier said yes, he had fired to scare a man away from a window; that his orders were to keep everyone away from windows.

Spina said he told the soldier: "Do you know what you just did? You have now created a state of hysteria. Every Guardsman up and down this street and every state policeman and every city policeman that is present thinks that somebody just fired a shot and that it is probably a sniper."

A short time later more "gunshots" were heard. Investigating, Spina came upon a Puerto Rican sitting on a wall. In reply to a question as to whether he knew "where the firing is coming from" the man said: "That's no firing. That's fireworks. If you look up to the fourth floor you will see the people who are throwing down these cherry bombs."

By this time four truckloads of National Guardsmen had arrived and policemen and troopers were again crouched everywhere looking for a sniper. The Director of Police remained at the scene for three hours, and the only shot fired was the one by the Guardsman.

Nevertheless, at six o'clock that evening two columns of National Guardsmen and state troopers were directing mass fire at the Hayes Housing Project in response to what they believed were snipers.[12]

We see here the essential elements of the operation of rumor in a crowd situation. First of all, we note that the rumor was spread by the effective network of the National Guard and state police systems, through their radios and walkie-talkies. Secondly, we see that the rumor was something which the listeners expected to hear; in the situation of the race riot, it was easy to believe that they were being fired on from inside the project apartments. This particular rumor was a half-truth: it was true that a shot was fired, and that a shot-like noise was heard, but it was not true that it was sniper fire. Last and most important of all, we see that reason and true information did not serve to dispel the rumor. Although the Director of Police explained what had happened to the men, they continued to believe that they were under fire, and acted accordingly. There is reason to believe that rumor cannot be contradicted until the collective situation which caused its birth is dissolved.

12. Report of the National Advisory Commission on Civil Disorders (New York: Bantam Books, 1968), pp. 3–4.

GORDON W. ALLPORT
Racial Violence

Abridged from Allport, *The Nature of Prejudice*, 1954, Addison-Wesley, Reading, Mass. pp. 57–63.

Introduction

The book from which the following excerpt is taken is a careful and scholarly analysis of both the causes and the results of prejudice; in this particular section, Allport discusses the conditions that lead to actual physical attack on a minority group. Though based on studies made several decades ago, his conclusions have been borne out by more recent investigations and are still highly relevant today. Perhaps the most illuminating section of the work is Allport's examination of the role that rumor plays in such antisocial group behavior.

Conditions of physical attack

It is apparent that under certain circumstances there will be a stepwise progression from verbal aggression to violence, from rumor to riot, from gossip to genocide. In cases where violence breaks out, we can be fairly certain that the following steps have prepared the way.

(1) There has been a long period in which the victim group has been typed. People lose the power to think of them as individuals.

(2) There has been a long period of verbal complaint against the victimized minority. The habits of suspicion and blaming have become firmly rooted.

(3) There has been growing legal discrimination.

(4) There has been some outside strain on the society. They have suffered from economic privation, a sense of low status, irritation due to political developments — such as wartime restrictions, or fear of unemployment.

(5) People have grown tired of their own inhibitions, and are reaching a state of explosion. Irrationalism comes to have a strong appeal. People distrust science, democracy, freedom. Down with minorities!

(6) Organized movements have attracted these discontented individuals. They join the Nazi Party, or the Ku Klux Klan, or Black Shirts. A mob may serve their purpose in case no formal organization exists.

(7) From such a formal or informal organization the individual derives courage and support. He sees that his irritation and wrath are socially sanctioned. His impulses to violence are thus justified by the standards of his group — or so he thinks.

(8) Some precipitating incident occurs. What previously might have been passed over as a trivial provocation now causes an explosion. The incident may be wholly imaginary or it may be exaggerated through rumor. (For many people who participated in the Detroit race riot, the precipitating incident seems to have been a wildly circulating rumor to the effect that a Negro had seized a white woman's baby and tossed it into the Detroit River.)

(9) When violence actually breaks out, the operation of "social facilitation" becomes important in sustaining the activity. To see other equally excited persons in a condition of mob frenzy augments one's own level of excitement and behavior. One finds his personal impulses heightened and his private inhibitions lessened.

These are the conditions required to remove the normal brakes that exist between verbal aggression and overt violence. They are likely to be fulfilled in regions where the two opposing groups are thrown into close contact; for example, at bathing beaches, in public parks, or at boundaries of residential districts.

Hot weather favors violence, both because it increases bodily discomfort and irritability, and because it brings people out of doors where contact and conflict can occur. Add the idleness of a Sunday afternoon, and the stage is well set. Disastrous riots do, in fact, seem to start most frequently on Sunday afternoons in hot weather. The peak of lynchings is in the summer months.

The participants in fist fights, gang fights, vandalism, riots, lynchings, pogroms, it has been noted, are predominantly youthful. It seems unlikely that young people are more frustrated in their lives than older people, but presumably they do have a thinner layer of socialized habit between impulses and their release. Youth too has the agility, the energy, and the risk-taking proclivity required for violence.

In America the two most serious forms of ethnic conflict are riots and lynching. The chief difference between them is that in a riot the victims of attack fight back; in a lynching the victim cannot do so.

Riots and lynching

Most riots occur where there has been some rapid change in the prevailing social situation. There has been an "invasion" of a residential district by Negroes, or members of a certain ethnic group have been imported as strikebreakers, or there has been a rapid rise in immigrant population in an unstable region. None of these conditions alone produces riots. There must also be a prepared ground of previous hostility and well-formed ideas concerning the "menace" of the particular group that is attacked.

It has been noted that rioters are usually drawn from lower socioeconomic classes, as well as from the youthful age level. To some extent this fact may be due to the lesser degree of discipline (self-control) taught in families of these classes. To some extent it may be due to the lower educational level which prevents people from perceiving correctly the true causes of their miserable conditions of living. Certainly the crowdedness, insecurity, and deprivations of existence act as direct irritants. In general, rioters are marginal men.

A riot may conceivably be based on a realistic clash of interest. When a large number of impoverished Negroes and equally impoverished whites are competing for a limited number of jobs, it is easy to see that rivalry is genuine. Insecurity and fear make the individuals both irritable and angry. But even in so realistic a situation we note the essential illogicality of regarding only the man of the *other* race as a threat. One white man takes a job away from another white man as surely as does a Negro. The chances are, therefore, that

the conflict of interests between ethnic groups is not wholly realistic.

The origins of a riot, therefore, lie in the prior existence of prejudice strengthened and released by the chain of circumstances reviewed in the preceding section. After a riot has broken out the resulting pandemonium has no logic. In the Harlem riot of 1943 the precipitating incident was apparently an "unfair" arrest of a Negro by a white policeman. The racial protest, however, took a nonracial form. Hot, tense, rebellious Negroes went wild. They looted, burned, destroyed stores owned by Negroes, and damaged Negro property as well as property owned by whites. Of all the forms of physical hostility a riot is the least directed, the least consistent, and therefore the least logical. It can be likened only to the blind temper tantrum of an angry child.

Lynchings occur chiefly when discrimination and segregation are firmly entrenched and where they are customarily enforced by severe intimidation. There is an additional essential condition — a low level of law enforcement in the community. The fact that lynchings are not prevented, that lynchers are seldom apprehended, and almost never punished, reflects the silent acquiescence of police officials and courts. The entire process, therefore, partakes of a "social norm" — and cannot be explained entirely in terms of the mental life of the lynchers.

This whole macabre practice depends to a considerable extent upon cultural custom. Among marginal and uneducated men of certain localities there has existed the tradition of the man hunt (not unlike the tradition of the coon hunt). To "get your nigger" has been a permissible sport, virtually a duty. When excitement grows high in the course of a lynching it is taken for granted that there will be looting and destruction of Negro homes and businesses. Not infrequently furniture from Negro homes is used as firewood for burning the victim's body. It seems like a sound idea to teach *all* the niggers a lesson at the same time.

The essential role of rumor

We may state as a dependable law that no riot or lynching ever occurs without the aid of rumor. Rumor is found to enter into the pattern of violence at any or all of its four stages.

(1) The gradual building up of animosity preceding a violent outbreak is assisted by stories of the misdeeds of the hated out-group. One hears particularly that the minority in question is itself conspiring, plotting, saving up guns and ammunition. Also the customary run of ethnic rumors takes a spurt, thus reflecting the mounting strain. One of the best barometers of tension is the collection and analysis of ethnic rumors in a community.

(2) After preliminary rumors have done their work, new rumors may serve as a call to rioting or lynching parties. They act like a bugle to assemble the forces. "Something is going to happen tonight by the river." "They'll catch that nigger tonight and whale the life out of him." If alert to the situation, the police may use these "marshalling rumors" to forestall violence. During the summer of 1943 in Washington, D.C., rumor had it that large numbers of Negroes were planning an organized uprising on the occasion of their parade scheduled for a certain day. Such a rumor was almost certain to bring out an opposing army of hostile whites. But by taking a firm public stand in advance of the event, and by providing adequate protection for the Negro marchers, the police were able to forestall the threatened clash.

(3) Not infrequently a rumor is the spark that ignites the powder keg. Some inflammatory story flies down the street, becoming sharpened and distorted at each telling. The Harlem riot was spread by means of an exaggerated story to the effect that a white policeman had shot a Negro in the back (the truth of the episode was much milder). A dozen wild rumors bruited around Detroit were the immediate touch on the trigger of overcharged passions. But for months before the fateful Sunday, Detroit had been fed on racial rumors. One tale to the effect that carloads of armed Negroes were heading for Detroit from Chicago had even been broadcast over the radio.

(4) During the heat of the riot rumor sustains the excitement. Particularly puzzling are the stories that appear based on hallucination. Lee and Humphrey tell how at the peak of the violence in Detroit, police received a telephone report from a woman who claimed to have witnessed with her own eyes the killing of a white man by a mob of Negroes. When the squad car reached the scene the police found a group of girls playing hopscotch and could find no trace of violence nor any support for the woman's story. Other citizens, as excited as she, no doubt believed the tale and spread it.

Let us turn back for a moment to the suggestion that rumor provides a good barometer of group tension. In themselves, of course, rumors are mere words, expressions of verbal hostility. One hears them directed against Catholics, Negroes, refugees, government officials, big business, labor unions, the armed services, Jews, radicals, various foreign governments, and many other out-groups. The rumors without exception express hostility and give a reason for the hostility by featuring some objectionable trait.

Anti-Semitic rumors were collected in great quantities during the war. Many of them took some such form as the following:

West Coast draft boards have refused to draft any more men until the Jewish boys in New York, Philadelphia, and Washington, deferred by Jewish draft boards, are drafted.

All the officers at Westover are Jews. It

is almost impossible for gentiles to get any of the higher offices in that air field.

The Associated Press and the United Press are both controlled by Jews and therefore we cannot believe anything they say pertaining to Germany or Hitler who knows what really ought to be done to the Jews.

Stories derogatory to Negroes are somewhat less numerous. Of 1,000 rumors collected and analyzed in 1942, 10 percent were anti-Semitic, 3 percent anti-Negro, 7 percent anti-British, and about 2 percent each against business and labor. The armed forces accounted for 20 percent, and the administration for 20 percent. About two-thirds of all rumors were directed against some out-group. Most of the others expressed deep-seated fears concerning the course of the war.

Thus rumor seems to offer a sensitive index for the state of group hostility. The discrediting of rumors may provide one means—probably a minor one—of controlling group hostility. During the war "rumor clinics" in newspapers attempted this service, and probably did succeed in making people aware of some of the dangers involved in rumor-mongering. It is doubtful, however, that the mere exposure of a rumor changes any deeply rooted prejudices. What it does at most is to warn those of mild or negligible prejudice that wedge-driving rumors in wartime or in peacetime are not in the best interests of the nation.

Conclusion

The causes of riots and mob actions are highly complex. However, contrary to popular opinion, such episodes of collective behavior are not irrational; they are patterned and, therefore, ultimately predictable. Social scientists have gathered a substantial amount of scientific information about riots during the past few years, but we are still a long way from being able to predict their occurrence with any accuracy.

TOPIC

3 PUBLIC OPINION

For collective behavior to occur, personal proximity or face-to-face contact is not necessary. The kind of group called a public may exhibit various features of collective behavior. As we have noted, a public is a scattered group of people who have a common interest or are affected by some event or activity. An example might be the people who watch a television program at the same time.

Although some members of a public may be organized—for example, voters may be registered Democrats, and moviegoers may be members of the John Wayne Fan Club—more typically they are not organized. This means that it is difficult to determine exactly who comprises the membership, or how numerous it is. Yet in spite of its vague or amorphous composition, a public is not unimportant or powerless. We may not know exactly who supports the Democratic ticket, but after an election is over we know that the next President will be a Republican if the Democratic public is too small. In the same way, John Wayne's fans may be faceless and uncounted, but it is their "votes" at the box office that make him a star and convince the studios to keep making pictures in which he appears.

Mass media—newspapers, magazines, radio, and television—help to create publics and then serve as a cohesive force to maintain them. For example, according to sociological research conducted by Wilbur Schramm, the extensive television coverage of President Kennedy's assassination was a vital factor in maintaining the stability and solidarity of the nation and American society in that time of emotional crisis.[13] Winston Churchill's radio broadcasts to the British people during the darkest and most uncertain days of World War II had much the same integrating effect.

These examples illustrate several basic characteristics of most publics. The members of a public have some interest or opinion in common; they have some way to register or express their opinions; their opinions may exert some influence over the actions of others; and the public usually is temporary and continually changing. A public is also quite dispersed and it will be generally unorganized, although there may be some organization at its "core."

The attitudes and opinions about an issue held by a public are called *public opinion*. Sociologists have concentrated their attention on three aspects of public opinion: the way it is formed, the way it is influenced, and the way it is measured.

FORMATION OF PUBLIC OPINION

There has long been uncertainty about the exact process by which public opinion is formed. It would seem reasonable to assume that public opinion is a direct expression of

basic values and societal attitudes, but in fact close connection is not always present. Public opinion can be shown to fluctuate widely and rapidly, whereas basic value orientations, laid down early in childhood, remain relatively constant all through life. Also, very different public opinions are often based on the same basic value, a further indication that opinions and values are not always directly linked. Take the example of the war in Vietnam. In spite of very different opinions about the policies the United States should follow regarding the war, the value of peace was widely shared by Americans. Those in favor of each of the different possible courses—increasing the pace of war, continuing the status quo, gradually withdrawing our troops, or immediately ceasing all military actions there—all based their appeals on the American people's desire for peace. Opinions, unlike basic values, are greatly affected by the pressure of specific situations.

A number of sociological studies show that the formation of public opinion is determined by social background and group membership.[14] Members of certain groups, such as Unitarians, or executives of American Telephone and Telegraph, tend to hold similar opinions on certain issues. So do members of the same social class and those of the same ethnic background. Of course, everyone belongs to more than one group and social category, and some groups are more effective than others in framing public opinion. The strength of the group in this regard will depend on such factors as its purpose and organization and the extent of the allegiance individuals feel toward the group. Membership in the Catholic church might be a considerable influence in an individual's opinion about the dispensing of birth-control devices and information, but have much less influence on his opinion regarding the election of a senator

13. Wilbur Schramm, "Communication in Crisis," in *The Kennedy Assassination and the American Public: Social Communication in Crisis,* ed. Bradley S. Greenberg and Edwin B. Parker (Stanford, Calif.: Stanford University Press, 1965).

14. See Herbert Blumer, "Public Opinion and Public Opinion Polling," *American Sociological Review* 13 (October 1948):542–549.

who will vote on this issue when it appears before Congress. Some groups make a great effort, by means of lobbies and advertising campaigns, to exert an influence over the formation of opinion, whereas others consider such activity beyond the limits of their functions and purposes.

The concept of *reference group* has been developed to refer to those groups or social categories which are especially significant to an individual in helping to define his beliefs, attitudes, and values.[15] The individual need not be a member of his reference group; it may be a group or category which he aspires to join and, therefore, identifies with. For example, a salesman and his wife who live in Detroit and would be classified as middle class think of themselves not in terms of their present social environment, but of the one they hope to inhabit in five years, when he has been promoted and works in the main office in New York. Their reference group is thus the upper-middle-class subculture in the urban Northeast, and their opinions will be as much influenced by this subculture as they will be by the middle-class Midwest subculture to which they presently belong. In general, however, a person's main reference groups are the most important social groups or categories to which he belongs. In our society, most adult males are highly influenced by their occupational group and economic class.

Another important agent of opinion formation is the influential individual. Every community has certain *opinion leaders* who exert more than their share of influence over the formation of public opinion. The leaders may differ according to the area of interest involved—one person may be an opinion leader in consumer activities, and another in political affairs—but these people can be isolated and identified. Elihu Katz and Paul Lazars-

feld, in a study reported in their book *Personal Influence,* found that in some instances personal influence was the single most important factor in the formation of opinion.[16]

INFLUENCING PUBLIC OPINION: PROPAGANDA AND CENSORSHIP

There are many individuals and groups who would like to manipulate public opinion. Manufacturers and merchants want to sell things, politicians want to be elected, and governments want the support of the populace. How can they influence public opinion in their favor? Two principal means of deliberately influencing public opinion are propaganda and censorship.

Propaganda is a term which has more than one meaning. It was originally applied to the teaching of any unified body of doctrine and had no particularly unfavorable connotations. Religious and political groups used it to describe the education of potential and new members. But gradually it has come to mean any calculated attempt to influence beliefs, choices, or opinions, in a way that encourages prejudice for or against a person, group, idea, or object. According to this definition, both advertising and public relations fall within the category of propaganda, as well as the more obvious political maneuvers that we immediately associate with the word. Today we distinguish propaganda from education. Education involves the cultivation of one's ability to judge or decide for himself. Propaganda involves the concealed or secret manipulation of the ideas of others.

Propaganda is most successful when its goals are limited and short-range—the changing of one particular opinion. Look at the example of the Volkswagen advertising campaign which changed our country's attitude toward that car; once disliked for its association with Nazi Germany (where it was designed), the VW became an accepted part of

15. See Muzafer Sherif, "Reference Groups in Human Relations," in Muzafer Sherif and M. O. Wilson, *Group Relations at the Crossroads* (New York: Harper & Bros., 1953), p. 206.

16. Elihu Katz and Paul Lazarsfeld, *Personal Influence* (New York: Free Press, 1955).

Outdoor signs and billboards that are so grotesque, so poorly placed or spaced — so many miles of ugly. We've learned to live with it, even laugh about it. Until, one day, it's our oak tree they're chopping down. Our view that's being blocked.

America, the beautiful. Our America. The crisis isn't in our cities; the crisis is in our hearts. With a change of heart, we can change the picture.   **AIA/American Institute of Architects**

Write your name and address on this page. Send it to AIA, 1735 New York Avenue, N.W., Washington, D.C. 20006. We'll forward it to your Senator asking him to support sign control laws.

This appeal, designed to enlist our support in a movement to eliminate billboards, clearly illustrates several propaganda techniques. It is directed at our self-interest: "our oak tree" and "our view"; and it associates outdoor signs with the defilement of "our beautiful America": an unimpeachable symbol. (The Atlantic, *September, 1970, p. 33*)

the American scene. Another example is the Army's campaign to make the universal draft acceptable even in peacetime. Propaganda which attempts to change more basic beliefs tends to be much less successful.

Most propaganda is based on some emotional appeal, and may use a variety of techniques to accomplish its aims. Propaganda often plays on the fears and anxieties of the public, then offers the reassurance of its point of view. For example, Hitler's government

played on the German fear of economic collapse, and then offered the Nazi political philosophy as the way to avoid it. Another technique is to associate the propaganda's view with some previously held value, or some valued person, organization, or symbol, as when a bakery says its pies are just like the ones mother used to bake. Propaganda also takes care to represent its doctrines as popular ones. In many cases, propaganda techniques are a calculated attempt to provoke the kind of emotional contagion which was discussed above in connection with crowds.

Propaganda tries to influence opinion by giving a one-sided or partisan interpretation of a situation, but *censorship* exercises its influence by limiting the amount of information on the subject or situation made available to the public. Every government exercises some degree of censorship over its citizens. In our country, materials which might affect the formation of attitudes toward sex and morality have been censored—as, for example, in the prohibition of obscene pictures, books, and plays. Censorship has also been exercised on information of a military nature. Whether this censorship has been due to the requirements of national security or to a desire to hide policy blunders is a current source of controversy, sparked by the publication of the Pentagon Papers.

We usually think of censorship as a government action, but it can be unofficial as well. The mass media exercise a constant though perhaps mild form of censorship in their choice of which news to cover; many people suspect that the choice is sometimes due to a desire to influence public opinion. And censorship is exercised by business and industry—as, for example, when they suppress their knowledge of hazards or weaknesses of their products.

Both propaganda and censorship raise complex moral questions. Whether or not the ends they serve should be their justification, to what extent a government should engage in them, and whether spotlighting them can render them less harmful—these are questions often hotly debated in public life. Because of the growing capacity of modern governments to use propaganda and censorship, we should expect this debate to become even more important as time goes on.[17]

MEASURING PUBLIC OPINION

The quantitative measurement of public opinion through polls, questionnaires, interviews, and preference surveys is a relatively recent invention which has become very important to modern business and government. Businesses use opinion polls to test markets and to determine how to sell products. Governments find it useful to measure public opinion continually to determine the attitudes of the people toward government policies, to discover the people's needs and desires, and to help make decisions about future courses of action. Politicians use opinion polls to guide their campaigns and to help them get elected; perhaps the best known use of public opinion measurement is for the prediction of election results. The measurement of public opinion on political and social matters also has news value; the Gallup, Harris, and Roper polls regularly report their findings through the mass media.

Public opinion polling is an application of one of the most important methodological tools in the social sciences—the *sample interview survey*. Through this interviewing technique, social scientists are able to develop reasonably accurate information about many aspects of social life, such as religious behavior, economic patterns, interaction within organizations, and political behavior.

17.   Joseph T. Klapper, *The Effects of Mass Communication* (New York: Free Press, 1960), pp. 1–7.

4 SOCIAL MOVEMENTS

We have defined collective behavior as relatively unstructured and spontaneous action involving numbers of people. Collective behavior may sometimes be just a minor deviation or eccentricity, a momentary response to a set of social and psychological pressures. It can also be the forerunner of major changes in the social system. A concerted and deliberate attempt to alter the society through collective action is called a *social movement*. Social movements usually have some degree of organization, and they have an obvious sense of direction; but they still exhibit a basic lack of structure, which classifies them as a kind of collective behavior.

We might consider social movements as a kind of social experiment. If the action is unsuccessful, or proves to be obviously disadvantageous to individuals or to society, it will be discouraged or discontinued. This was the case with the temperance movement to abolish alcoholic drinks, for example. However, if the action proves successful or effective, it may be permanently incorporated into the social system. This was the case with the Protestant Reformation.

This is the sense in which collective behavior is sometimes referred to as "institutions in process" or "seedbeds for the generation of groups and organizations." From one perspective all social structure and change stems from collective behavior, because all structure originally derives from nonstructure and all organized groupings have developed from loose aggregates of people.

Contemporary America has seen the creation of a number of social movements—civil rights, antiwar, drugs-rock-youth, women's liberation, political radicalization, to name a few. Some people simply lump them all together as "the movement," meaning a total change in the society. It is interesting to note that most of these movements, such as the civil rights movement, are accompanied by numerous episodes of collective behavior of many different types, such as sit-ins, demonstrations, riots, marches, and rallies.

We can identify four principal characteristics of a social movement. They are: (1) a new perspective, such as an altered conception of the proper role of the government, or of the role of women or the status of black people; (2) a kind of idealism, which sustains the individual members of the movement and helps them remain loyal to their abstract concept of change during the difficult periods when the movement encounters resistance from the present social system; (3) a commitment to activism, which convinces people that they can and should "do something" about the situation which they want to change; and (4) a pluralistic form of organization. It is extremely rare for a social movement not to have more than one formal association organized for its support. The black civil rights movement is typical in this respect; think of the variety of organizations which are participating in it. They include the Southern Christian Leadership Conference, which advocates nonviolent resistance in the tradition of Gandhi; the Black Panthers, who favor militant resistance; the National Association for the Advancement of Colored People (NAACP), which urges peaceful cooperation with whites; the Black Muslim church, which is organized around a theological focus; and the Urban League, oriented toward employment opportunities—to name only some of the largest and best known organizations. Although

The civil rights movement entered a new stage in the late 1950s with the success of the Montgomery, Alabama, bus boycott led by Martin Luther King. Blacks, impatient with the older techniques of legal and legislative action, were ready for a commitment to activism. King seized on this new mood to develop organized dedication to the principles and techniques of nonviolent direct action. *(UPI)*

these organizations all share the same goal of black equality, there is a great variety in choice of means, philosophical orientation, and specific short-range goals. The contemporary social movement among Mexican-Americans for full equality is described in the abridgment by Joseph L. Love in this chapter.

THE LIFE CYCLE
OF SOCIAL MOVEMENTS

Although social movements differ widely, it is possible to describe a general life cycle for them. Rex D. Hopper has postulated that revolutionary movements typically have four stages.[18]

The *preliminary stage* is marked by a great restlessness in the society, antagonism between various groups, and inefficient and insufficient efforts to deal with these problems.

18. Rex D. Hopper, "The Revolutionary Process: A Frame of Reference for the Study of Revolutionary Movements," *Social Forces* 28 (March 1950):207–279.

The people who are affected, who are restless and discontent, will not have any focus for their energy. Any leaders who emerge at this time are likely to be agitators.

The second stage is the *popular stage*. At this point, the discontented individuals become aware that others share their discontents and they see that united action, or a social movement, is possible. The type of leader who is most likely to emerge at this stage is the prophet or reformer. The prophet speaks with a sense of authority and confidence, and he can sway the mass with his vision of the future. The reformer focuses the mass on specific problems and solutions.

In the third or *formal stage* the excitement of the mass is formalized. Ideologies are developed which help to give the movement direction and cohesion; values and goals become clarified. At the same time the movement develops an organizational structure with a hierarchy of leaders, a set of policies, and programs of action. In this period, the statesman is the most effective leader.

In the final stage of the social movement, the *institutional stage,* the social movement becomes an accepted and more or less permanent part of society. The idealism and fervor of the members are dulled or lost, and decision making within the movement becomes marked by political process and deliberation. The administrator-executive proves to be the most effective leader at this stage.

Not all social movements are successful; but almost every social movement has some effect, for whenever social problems become large enough to breed movements, they must be taken into account in some fashion. Success comes when the programs or policies or perspectives of the social movement become institutionalized. Those movements which are successful generally tend to follow the life cycle just discussed. Take, for example, Protestantism. It began as a series of undirected responses to great social changes of the time, changes which the Catholic church seemed unwilling to acknowledge and for which the church would offer no supportive mechanisms. There were numerous episodes of unrest and collective behavior in crowds. Then a few brilliant ideologies and leaders appeared, Martin Luther foremost among them, and a social movement was born. The visible outcome was the establishment of a number of Protestant sects which are now fully institutionalized religions, but Protestantism also had far-reaching effects on aspects of culture other than religion.

JOSEPH L. LOVE
La Raza

From "La Raza: Mexican-Americans in Rebellion" in trans-*action,* Feb. 1969, pp. 35–41. Published by permission of Transaction, Inc. from trans-*action,* vol. 6, February 1969. Copyright © 1969 by Transaction, Inc.

Introduction

Among the important social movements in the United States in the 1960s was one initiated by the Mexican-Americans in search of a more equal share of the nation's prosperity. One part of this movement was a group of agricultural workers in California, led by Cesar Chavez, who struck against the California grape growers. A less well-known branch of this movement is the Alianza Federal de Mercedes in New Mexico. The Alianza, part of the whole movement of equality for la raza (the Mexican-American "race"), demanded the return of land taken from the Spanish residents by American settlers, and they even adopted certain tactics used by the militant faction of the black power movement to try to enforce this demand. This excerpt is from a longer paper analyzing the movement of la raza. Joseph L. Love explains both the underlying factors of social discontent which caused the movement and the precipitating incidents that sparked it.

In early June, 1967 a group of Spanish-speaking Americans who call themselves the Alianza Federal de Mercedes (Federal Alliance of Land Grants) and claim that they are the legal and rightful owners of millions of acres of land in Central and Northern New Mexico, revolted against the governments of the United States of America, the State of New Mexico, and Rio Arriba County, formally proclaiming the Republic of Rio Chama in that area.

On June 5 an armed band of forty or more Aliancistas attacked the Tierra Amarilla courthouse, released eleven of their members being held prisoners, and wounded a deputy sheriff and the jailer.

They held the sheriff down on the floor with a rifle butt on his neck, searched for the District Attorney (who wasn't there), and for an hour and a half controlled the village (population 500). They took several hostages (later released when the getaway car stuck in the mud).

Despite some of the melodramatic and occasionally comic opera aspects of the affair, both the members of the Alianza and the local and state authorities take it very seriously. This is not the first time the Aliancistas have violated federal and state law, attempting to appropriate government property (in October, 1966, for instance, their militants tried to take over Kit Carson National Forest, and to expel the rangers found there as trespassers); nor is it the only time their activities have resulted in violence. In this case the state government reacted frantically, sending in armored tanks, 300 National Guardsmen and 200 State Police. They rounded up dozens of Spanish-speaking persons including many women and children, and held them in a detention camp, surrounded with guns and soldiers, for 48 hours. The raiders got away, but in several days all of them — including their fiery leader, former Pentecostal preacher Reies Lopez Tijerina — were captured.

It has become common to associate these actions of the Alianza with other riots or revolts by poor, dark-skinned, and disaffected Americans — with Watts, Newark, and Detroit. Tijerina himself helps reinforce this impression by occasionally meeting with, and using the rhetoric of, some leaders of the black urban revolt. The fact is, however, that the Alianza movement is really a unique example in the United States of a "primitive revolt," a kind almost always associated with developing nations rather than advanced industrialized countries, and which includes such diverse phenomena as peasant anarchism, banditry, and millenarianism (the belief that divine justice and retribu-

tion is on the side of the rebels and that the millennium is at hand).

As the Aliancistas see it, they are not violating any legitimate law. The territory around Rio Arriba belongs to them. They demand the return of lands — primarily common lands — taken from Hispano communities, most of which were founded in the Spanish colonial era. The members speak primarily of common lands, rather than individual heirs, and define the towns in question as "closed corporations, with membership restricted to the descendants and heirs of the founding fathers and mothers" — that is, themselves.

The Alianza and its actions cannot really be understood without knowledge of its background and leader. First, the people from whom it draws its members and its strength — the Mexican-American minority in the U.S. — and specifically New Mexico; second, the rapid economic changes throughout the area since World War II that have so greatly affected their lives; and last but surely not least the dynamism, determination and charisma of Reies Tijerina, without whom the movement would probably never have arisen.

In the 1960 census Mexican-Americans, though they made up only 2.3 percent of the population of the United States, constituted 12 percent of the population of Texas, New Mexico, Arizona, Colorado and California — almost three-and-a-half million persons.

Generally they are a submerged minority that have only lately begun to articulate their demands. They formed "Viva Kennedy" committees in 1960; since then three Mexican-American Congressmen have gone to the House, and New Mexico's Joseph Montoya sits in the Senate. The end of the bracero program in 1964 opened the way to a successful unionization drive among agricultural workers; and the celebrated "Huelga" strike in Delano, California in 1965 was a symptom of and stimulus to the new awakening. The federal and state poverty programs, and the example of the Negro revolt, have also undoubtedly had their effects.

The Alianza was born in 1963, partly to combat the alienation and isolation of the Hispanos in New Mexico, but specifically to reclaim lands taken from the Spanish-speaking population since 1848. In colonial New Mexico, Spanish officials made land grants of indeterminate size to both individuals and communities in common, and the latter were respected through the era of Mexican rule. When Anglo-Americans began to enter New Mexico in significant numbers in the 1880s, they found it possible to wrest lands from the native inhabitants through legal and financial devices of land taxes, mortgages, and litigation over disputed titles. By 1930, through legal and extralegal means, the Anglos had taken over most of the farming and ranching land in the state, and the state and federal governments had appropriated much of the common lands. The Spanish-speaking population ultimately lost 1.7 million acres of community lands and two million acres in private holdings. The Alianza now demands the return of these lands.

Yet in all probability, the Alianza would not exist but for the efforts of a single man, a leader who devotes his life to his cause, and inspires his followers to do likewise. Reies Lopez Tijerina is a man of rare charisma who is most in his element when haranguing a large crowd. Of average height, he seems to have great physical strength as he grasps a microphone with one sinewy arm and gesticulates artfully and furiously with the other. He sometimes shouts violently as he asks rhetorical questions of his audience in Spanish and gets "Si" and "No" bellowed back in appropriate cadences.

It is no coincidence that Tijerina's style and language recall Pentecostal protestantism. He has been a minister in the Assembly of God, and was an itinerant revival preacher for many years to Mexican-Americans throughout the Southwest.

Unlike the vast majority of his followers, he was not born in New Mexico but in Texas. One of seven children of a migrant farm family, once so desperate that they were reduced to eating field rats, he picked crops and preached in Illinois and Michigan as well as in Texas and Arizona. He did not settle in New Mexico until 1960; and with his five brothers, formed the Alianza three years later.

The quasi-religious fervor of Tijerina has strongly shaped the aspirations and style of the Alianza. However, there is greater emphasis on Old Testament justice than New Testament love.

The Alianza now claims to have 30,000 dues-paying members paying at least $2 a month. A scholar guesses that 10,000 may be closer to the true figure. It seems clear that Tijerina's computation includes sympathizers or at least persons who have only occasionally contributed funds.

As with some sectors of the American Negro movement, the Alianza's programs began with an emphasis on [lawsuits]; and when that failed, frustration and a disposition toward violence emerged.

But the real historical and sociological meaning of the Alianza cannot be solely understood in terms of its current embroilments of recent history in New Mexico. Most of the literature on the movement, so far, has dealt with the spectacular, bizarre, or violent elements involved; but the roots of primitive revolt go far back. Since the enclosure movement began in Europe in the twelfth century, there have been scores of peasant revolts. Many sought the restoration of common lands taken by nobles and gentry.

One student of Mexican-American culture, anthropologist Nancie Gonzalez, writes that ". . . even now [1967] sheep-herding remains an ideal way of life for the

Hispano. . . . Virtually all contemporary accounts by social scientists comment upon the people's stated preference for this occupation." This preference explains why in Tijerina's Utopia the common lands are so highly valued. The Chama region, where the Tierra Amarilla revolt broke out, was principally a sheep-grazing area until after the Second World War.

What has occurred in New Mexico has been a breakdown of the traditional society, the ripping of the fabric of Hispano culture. In 1950, 41 percent of the Spanish-surname population in the state lived in urban areas; but by 1960, 61 percent did. Many of those moving to the cities were ill-prepared for their new way of life. In 1956 one investigator found that 834 out of 981 women in Albuquerque who received Aid to Dependent Children had Spanish surnames.

The legal structures of a modern capitalist society had by the late 1930s wrecked the traditional land-tenure patterns of the Upper Rio Grande. In 1940 Dr. George Sanchez reported that in Taos County "65 percent of the private lands represent land grants which have been subdivided or otherwise lost to the communities and families to which they were originally assigned." Furthermore, "Commercial livestock operators have acquired [the Hispano's] land grants and compete with him for grazing leases and permits on public lands. Exorbitant fees, taxes, and forced sales have crowded him out of his former grazing domain."

Rio Arriba County was one of the areas least affected by the state's economic growth. In 1960 it had the highest percentage of rural non-farm population of all New Mexico's counties (91.3 percent). It ranked high in native-born inhabitants, and low in the percentage of migrants. It had the third lowest median education and the fifth lowest median family income. In Rio Arriba and the other northern counties where the Spanish-speaking population predominates, the average per capita income in 1967 was less than $1,000. Furthermore, according to Governor Cargo, "11,000 of 23,000 residents of Rio Arriba County are on welfare rolls." The 1960 census showed that county with the state's highest rate of unemployment— 15.1 percent—almost three times the state average.

The disintegration of the traditional Hispano community seems well underway, and Tijerina articulates widely shared feelings that his people do not want to assimilate into Anglo culture. He also rejects relief as demoralizing to its recipients, stating again and again, "We will no longer take powdered milk in exchange for justice." Reaction to social disintegration can take many forms, and the Hispanic religious tradition, plus Tijerina's own background as a Pentecostal preacher, have helped channel it into millenarianism. The frequency of millenarianism when belief in and identity with the dominant society are lost has been well documented in sociological literature. The Alianza constitutes an almost classic case.

Yet there is a modern dimension to the Alianza, and this is a direct outgrowth of its appearance in an industrial society with rapid transcontinental communications and ever-vigilant news media. The Alianza fits the requirements of a primitive rebellion or revitalization movement, but its links with urban radical and reformist groups outside New Mexico show its potential for evolving into something more modern. Thus there are two distinct dimensions of the movement—the primitive rural grass-roots constituency on the tributaries of the Upper Rio Grande; and the modern urban nationally connected leadership in Albuquerque.

The ignorance of government officials of the basic nature of the movement is almost monumental. They tend to explain the Alianza away by easy modern clichés. Some find in the references to common lands the spore of modern communism. At the 1967 trial of Alianza leaders, the prosecuting attorney declared, "This is not a social problem we're trying. This is a criminal problem." Even some sympathetic observers have used singularly inappropriate terms, calling Rio Arriba County a "rural Watts."

But Rio Arriba has little in common with Watts. The majority of Aliancistas, the rural grass-roots, are not industrial proletarians but primitive rebels— peasants reacting and striking back in millenarian fashion against the modernization that is tearing their society apart.

Conclusion

The relationship between the causes of a social movement and the goals of that movement is often intriguing. The goal of any movement must be highly meaningful to its members. It must motivate them to expend great effort and at times to withstand great disapproval, even danger. The goal must unify the members of the movement and must appear to be attainable. But often the social conditions that cause the formation of a social movement are only indirectly related to the goals. The underlying social conditions might be so nearly permanent that realistically nothing could change them in the short run. Or, other factors could prevent the social necessities from being translated into realistic goals for the movement. What were the conditions that led to the formation of the Alianza? What were the goals of the movement, and how are the causes and the goals related?

SUMMARY

Although *collective behavior* tends to be emotional, unpredictable, and irregular in occurrence, sociologists have identified certain patterns in the behavior of a group of people responding to a common influence or stimulus in fairly temporary, unstable, and unstructured situations. Collective behavior includes a number of different social phenomena. *Crowds* are collections of people who are gathered in one place at one specific time. A *public* is a scattered group of people who share a common interest. In a *social movement* a group of somewhat scattered people act to promote some form of social change. A serious underlying social dissatisfaction may generate a *craze,* an unreasoned rush toward some satisfaction. *Business panics, fads and fashions,* and *mass hysteria,* the contagious spread of certain hysterical symptoms such as fainting, delusions, or trances, are all classified as collective behavior because of their temporary nature and their mass involvement.

Collective behavior can be generated by various conditions. 1) *Conflicting values* and *ambiguous norms* may leave the individual susceptible to the influence of momentary needs and mass example. 2) *Breakdown in the formal and informal mechanisms of social control* may cause people to lose confidence in the social system and attempt to reform or restructure it. 3) *Social deprivation,* or blockage of normal channels of gratification, may lead an individual to seek an outlet for his frustration in forms of collective behavior that promise better conditions. 4) *Normlessness,* which occurs when a person's normal ties to the social structure are loosened, is also conducive to collective behavior.

People may collect in crowds merely to release tension and express their feelings; or they may be concerned with acting out, with focusing on an external goal or objective. Contagion of emotional expression may occur, for example, at spectator sports events, large parties, conventions, and revival meetings. Society often encourages certain gatherings that promote emotional expression and release, or gatherings—such as mass rallies— that build a sense of social integration among participants. Other types of more passive or casual crowds, although not particularly bene- ficial to society, are also socially acceptable. Audiences, shoppers, or commuters ex- emplify *recurrent aggregative behavior,* one of the loosely structured forms of social in- teraction.

Antisocial crowd behavior which aims at the destruction or disruption of the social order, involves an acting rather than a pas- sive or expressive crowd. *Mobs,* which usual- ly have leaders, try to accomplish specific acts of aggression. A *riot* is a violently aggressive and destructive mob, often characterized by a lack of goals or direction. Typically those who participate in mob action or riots are under some great psychic or social stress. Usually the actions are precipitated by a specific event and they are fed by the emotion- al contagion that may spread through a crowd. Rumors may provoke or increase antisocial collective behavior, or they may be created as a justification for emotional excesses.

Collective behavior may also occur among people who have no face-to-face contact, as among a public. Although a public is tem- porary or continually changing, the members have some interest or opinion in common that can be registered or expressed and that may influence others. Public opinion can fluctu- ate widely, and unlike basic values, is greatly affected by the pressure of specific situations. Public opinion is influenced by social back- ground, and particularly by one's reference groups, those groups or categories that are especially important in helping a person de- fine his attitudes and beliefs. Certain in- fluential people in the community may also serve as opinion leaders. Public opinion may also be manipulated through propa- ganda, a calculated attempt to influence be- liefs or choices by encouraging prejudice for or against a person, group, or idea. Propa- ganda is based on an emotional appeal and provides a one-sided interpretation of a situa- tion. Censorship, in contrast, influences opin- ion by limiting the amount of information available to the public.

Although like other forms of collective be- havior, social movements lack a high degree of structure, they are somewhat more organ- ized and have a deliberate purpose: to alter society through collective action. They usual- ly have a pluralistic form of organization and provide a new perspective, a sustaining ideal- ism, and commitment to activism. Four stages have been identified in the life cycle of social movements: 1) the *preliminary stage* of social dissatisfaction and restlessness; 2) the *popu- lar stage,* when group consciousness develops and leaders emerge; 3) the *formal stage* of organization and policy development; and 4) the *institutional stage,* when the movement becomes an accepted part of society.

GLOSSARY

Business panic Collective behavior among a scattered group caused by a common fear that economic systems are failing. (page 534)

Censorship An attempt to influence public opin- ion by limiting the amount of information on a subject that is made available to a public. (page 550)

Collective behavior The behavior of a group of people responding to a common influence or stimulus in fairly temporary, unstable, and un- structured situations. (page 531)

Contagion The increase of people's willingness to express emotion caused by crowd conditions. (page 538)

Craze A common interest, among scattered people, in an activity which is usually trivial and without long-range social effect. (page 534)

Crowd A temporary grouping of people who are physically close together and who have a common focus or interest. (page 537)

Fads and fashions A departure from what is cus- tomary, in an attempt to be different, which re- mains within the bounds of good taste and manners. (page 534)

Mass hysteria   The contagious spread of certain hysterical symptoms such as fainting, delusions, or trances. (page 534)

Mob   A crowd which is trying to accomplish or cause an antisocial act of aggression. (page 540)

Opinion leader   An individual in a community who exerts more than a normal share of influence over the formation of public opinion. (page 548)

Propaganda   Any calculated attempt to influence beliefs, choices, or opinion. (page 548)

Public   A scattered group of people who share a common interest or who are all affected by some event or activity. (page 534)

Public opinion   Attitudes and opinions that the public holds about an issue. (page 547)

Reference group   A group or social category that is especially important in helping an individual define his beliefs, values, attitudes, and opinions. (page 548)

Riot   A violently aggressive or destructive mob. (page 540)

Rumor   A widespread report that is not supported by fact. (page 541)

Sample interview survey   A method of measuring attitudes, beliefs, or opinions by interviewing a sample of a certain category of people. (page 550)

Social movement   A group of people, usually somewhat scattered and loosely organized, who are acting to promote some form of social change. (page 534)

SUGGESTED READINGS AND RELATED RESOURCES

I   READINGS IN SOCIOLOGY

Barton, Allen. *Communities in Disaster: A Sociological Analysis of Collective Stress Situations*. New York: Doubleday, Anchor (Paper), 1970. Barton examines individual and social responses to collective stress, including natural disasters, man-made disasters (atomic bombing and assassination), and long-term stresses such as depressions and poverty.

Cantril, Hadley. *The Psychology of Social Movements*. New York: John Wiley and Sons, 1963. The causes of collective behavior and the motivations of the participants are the focus of this study by a social psychologist. The book contains many well-documented case studies. Especially interesting is chapter 4, an analysis of the participants in two lynchings.

Ellul, Jacques. *Propaganda: The Formation of Men's Attitudes*. Translated by Konrad Keller and Jean Lerner. New York: Albert A. Knopf, 1965. Ellul proposes a theory that propaganda is useful and necessary to a technological society, that it fulfills important needs for the individual and for governments. He also points out that education can increase susceptibility to propaganda.

Faris, R. E., ed. *Handbook of Modern Sociology*.

Chicago: Rand McNally, 1964. This book can be used as a general source book beyond an introductory sociology text. It has pertinent essays on "Social Effects of Mass Communication" by O. Laren, "Collective Behavior" by R. Turner, and "Social Movements" by L. Killian.

Hartogs, R., and E. Artzt, eds. *Violence, Causes and Solutions*. New York: Dell (Paper), 1970. This book analyzes situations in which revolt and reaction occurred and resulted in violence. It includes studies of the Newark, N.J., and Columbia University revolts, as well as violence in American literature.

Hyman, Herbert H. *Survey Design and Analysis: Principles, Cases and Procedures*. New York: Free Press, 1955. Hyman's book introduces the complexities of sampling, interview or questionnaire construction, implementation of a survey and, briefly, data analysis. Techniques are discussed for dealing with a major problem of all surveys—bias.

Katz, Elihu, and Paul F. Lazarsfeld. *Personal Influence*. New York: Free Press, 1955. Primarily a statistical study of the spread of information through a community, this book opens with an excellent summary of communications theory and research, and a statement of the "two-step flow" theory in which the importance of opinion leaders is stressed.

Klapper, Joseph. *The Effects of Mass Communication.* New York: Free Press, 1960. Klapper writes about the effects and limits of mass media in influencing the values, opinions, and behavior of their audiences.

Lane, Robert. *Political Ideology: Why the American Common Man Believes What He Does.* New York: Free Press, 1962. Lane presents important insights into the psychological and sociological sources of middle- and lower-class beliefs in America. It has been a good source book for undergraduates interested in tracing the origins of their own beliefs and values.

Lazarsfeld, Paul F., Bernard Berelson, and Hazel Gaudet. *The People's Choice: How the Voter Makes up His Mind in a Presidential Campaign.* 3d ed. New York: Columbia University Press, 1968. The electorate of Erie County, Ohio, during the 1940 presidential campaign was the subject of this intensive survey. The age, sex, income, occupation, and numerous other characteristics of the voters were examined along with the effect of campaign propaganda upon their votes.

Schramm, Wilbur, ed. *Mass Communications.* 2d ed. Chicago: University of Illinois Press (Paper), 1969. This comprehensive basic reader on mass communications contains essays by professionals from various academic and service-oriented fields.

Smelser, Neil J. *Theory of Collective Behavior.* New York: Free Press, 1962. Smelser presents a comprehensive theoretical framework for the analysis of collective behavior and shows how that framework may be applied in social research. The theory is notable because it is primarily a sociological, rather than psychological, theory of collective behavior.

Turner, R., and L. Killian. *Collective Behavior.* Englewood Cliffs, N.J.: Prentice-Hall, 1957. This important book provides in greater depth definitions and explanations of topics covered in chapter 13.

Articles and Papers

Blumer, Herbert. "Public Opinion and Public Opinion Polling." *American Sociological Review* **13** (October 1948):542–549.

DeFleur, M. L. "Mass Communication and the Study of Rumor." *Sociological Inquiry* **32** (1962): 51–70.

Hartman, John J., and James A. Walsh. "Simulation in Newspaper Readership: An Exploration in Computer Analysis of Social Data." *Social Science Quarterly* **49**, 4 (March 1969):840–852.

Hopper, Rex D. "The Revolutionary Process: A Frame of Reference for the Study of Revolutionary Movements." *Social Forces* **28** (1950): 270–279.

Kelman, Herbert C. "Processes of Opinion Change." *Public Opinion Quarterly* **25** (Spring 1961):57–78.

Killian, Lewis M. "The Significance of Multiple-Group Membership in Disaster." *American Journal of Sociology* **57** (January 1952):309–313.

Lieberson, Stanley, and A. R. Silverman. "The Precipitants and Underlying Conditions of Race Riots." *American Sociological Review* **30** (December 1965):887–898.

Lincoln, C. Eric. "The Black Muslim Movement." *Journal of Social Issues* **19** (1963):75–85.

Meyersohn, Rolf, and Elihu Katz. "Notes on a Natural History of Fads." *American Journal of Sociology* **62**, 6 (May 1957):594–601.

II RELATED RESOURCES
Nonfiction

Armstrong, Gregory, ed. *Protest: Man Against Society.* New York: Bantam (Paper), 1969. Armstrong has collected several essays which describe, from various perspectives, the protests of the Christians in the first century A.D., the democratic protests in the late 1700s, and the protests of blacks and students in contemporary America.

Connery, Robert H., ed. *Urban Riots: Violence and Social Change.* New York: Random House, Vintage (Paper), 1969. This book deals with the causes and consequences of urban unrest and riots.

Cruse, Harold. *Rebellion or Revolution.* New York: William Morrow (Paper), 1969. Cruse analyzes black unrest as both revolution and rebellion. He also examines the relevance of black writers in America.

Denney, Reuel. *The Astonished Muse.* New York: Grosset & Dunlap (Paper), 1964. Denney writes about popular culture and how it is transmitted through television, movies, advertising, newspapers, and science fiction.

Fanon, Frantz. *The Wretched of the Earth.* New York: Grove Press (Paper), 1968. Fanon develops the idea that revolts and violence by oppressed groups develop out of their exploitation by oppressors and out of the violence in the life of the oppressor.

Innis, Harold, *The Bias of Communication*. Toronto, Canada: University of Toronto Press, 1964. In a clear and provocative manner Innis deals with subjects ranging from bias in the "Publishing Trade" to "Technology and Public Opinion in the United States."

Mailer, Norman. *Miami and the Siege of Chicago*. New York: Signet (Paper), 1968. Mailer describes American protests against the Vietnam War and the violent confrontations of demonstrators and police in Chicago in 1968.

Millett, Kate. *Sexual Politics*. New York: Doubleday, 1970. Kate Millett's book was a product of, and an influence on, one recent social movement, women's liberation.

Silberman, Charles. *Crisis in Black and White*. New York: Random House, Vintage (Paper), 1964. This book is an excellent attempt by a white man to understand and explain the black revolt in the United States.

Skornia, H. *Television and Society: An Inquest and Agenda for Improvement*. New York: McGraw-Hill, 1965. Skornia discusses the problems inherent in business and government control of broadcasting; he includes insightful comments on the effects television and radio have on their listening audiences. He concludes his book with proposals and recommendations for changes in our broadcasting system.

Stapp, Andy. *Up Against the Brass*. New York: Simon and Schuster, 1970. Andy Stapp organized a group called the American Servicemen's Union to promote civil rights for servicemen. In this book he chronicles the group's development from a social movement to a relatively formal organization.

Fiction

Baldwin, James. *Going to Meet the Man*. New York: Dial Press, 1965. The story that gave this collection of short stories its title is about a young boy who witnesses a lynching. The story illustrates how the memory of this incident of collective behavior made emotional adjustments difficult in his adult life.

Clark, Walter Van Tilburg. *The Ox-Bow Incident*. New York: Signet Classic (Paper), 1962. First published in 1940. This tense and emotional novel deals with mob rule and lynchings in the "Old West."

Dickens, Charles. *A Tale of Two Cities*. New York: Oxford University Press, 1960. First published in 1812. In this classic novel about the French Revolution Dickens depicts both the evils of the government before the revolution and the "terrors" during it.

Mailer, Norman. *Armies of the Night*. New York: Signet, 1968. By treating an actual experience as fiction the author recounts his participation in an antiwar march on the Pentagon in 1968, and describes the effects the experience had on him personally.

Warren, Robert Penn. *Night Rider*. 1939. Reprint. New York: Bantam Books (Paper), 1968. Warren vividly describes the activities of the Ku Klux Klan in the South, including specific episodes of collective behavior.

Films

The Battle of Algiers. Gillo Pontecorvo, 1967. This documentary-like film is about the national liberation movement the Algerians waged in the 1950s against the French colonialists.

Fidel. Saul Landau, 1969. Fidel Castro is portrayed as a personality and as a revolutionary leader in this film. Included is footage taken of Fidel and Che Guevara fighting in the mountains during the revolution.

Orphans of the Storm. (Silent). D. W. Griffith, 1921. The French Revolution through the eyes of two orphans whose lives are the subject of this classic film.

Triumph of the Will. Germany, 1936. This is an example of a propaganda film created to support the rise of Nazism in Germany.

14. Community and Economic Change

We usually think of a community as a place: a neighborhood or a town on the map. Sociologists prefer to consider it as a set of patterns of daily interaction that center on residence and work. Historically, there has always been a close connection between man's residential life and his working or economic life. Even today, when rapid mass transportation has allowed work to be separated from the home, the two most important features of community living remain linked. We will discuss them together here, especially how they have evolved and changed.

This chapter and the following one are devoted to a discussion of some of the master trends that are important in creating what we call a "modern" society. Here we focus on social and economic trends; in the next chapter we will look at political trends. Our first topic in this chapter will be the development of community organization and structure from the earliest time up to the period of industrialization. Topic 2 discusses the processes of industrialization and urbanization. In topic 3, we will look at the city and urbanism in the United States in terms of social structure and culture. Topic 4 is devoted to changes in man's working life.

1 THE DEVELOPMENT OF COMMUNITIES

What do we mean by the term *community?* It is one of the most ambiguous terms in sociology, with many different meanings, but here we shall use it to refer to a grouping of people organized around residential units or households and based on daily patterns of interaction. A community may be six houses together in the middle of acres of farmland, sometimes called a hamlet, or millions of people squeezed together into a metropolis. It can be a town of 2,000 or a small neighborhood within a large city. The common elements are that all these groups are based on the residential unit and are organized around patterns and activities that occur on a very regular or daily basis: shopping, schools, work, church, local government, and some forms of recreation.

PREURBAN COMMUNITIES

The earliest humans were probably organized in bands of roving foragers and hunters; they had no stable or settled community because they did not confine themselves to any specific location. This pattern of group life can still be seen in certain nomadic tribes; it is one of the best ways to adapt to an environment with a limited food supply, or a soil that will not sustain planting or grazing for more than a short time. Nomadic communities are typically found in parts of the world where climate limits food supplies, such as the Arctic ice fields and the arid sand deserts of the Middle East and Near East.

Settled communities began with the development of agriculture. It was probably about 10,000 years ago that men first devel-oped the skills of cultivating plants and domesticating animals for food, and thus were able to live in one area for some time. These early settlements were very small, never larger than one or two hundred people, partly because each resident had to work in the fields and therefore needed to be within easy walking distance of his plot of land. All the people who lived in such villages were probably closely related to each other, and the community was primarily organized on a kinship basis. This was the original primary group— primary associations embedded, as Lewis Mumford says, in "birth and place, blood and soil."[1] Archeological traces of such villages have been found all over the world. The evolutionary descendant of this kind of community can still be found in the modern world: the small agricultural villages which exist in nearly every country, including our own. Almost everyone in the village is a farmer who lives off the land, and there is very little specialization of labor.

RISE OF THE CITY

Most experts agree that the most significant factor defining a city or urbanized community is not its size, but the way its residents earn a living. A city has a high concentration of people who do not grow their own food. Cities can arise only where there is a surplus of food grown outside the city, and where there is some way of acquiring that surplus and transporting it from the farm to the city. The need to obtain food in the earliest cities led to the

1. Lewis Mumford, *The City in History* (New York: Harcourt Brace Jovanovich, 1961), p. 14.

Early cities like this one in Peru arose when men learned to produce surplus food; some of the population farmed and provided food for others who specialized in manufacturing and commercial occupations carried on within the city. *(George Holton, Photo Researchers, Inc.)*

development of many new institutions and specialists, such as armies, taxes, and government agents. The freeing of many persons from the task of producing food permitted the development of still other specialists such as the artisan, trader, and religious official.[2] The kinship institutions of the early agricultural communities, with their informal norms and methods of social control, were inadequate for the organization of a community based on non-agricultural specialists who were free to move from place to place if they wanted to.

The new conditions required the development of government, laws, formal mechanisms of social control, and most of the other social institutions which have predominated in man's communities ever since. This fundamental community change is sometimes called the "urban revolution"[3] and is regarded as one of the most significant developments in the rise of civilization.

The earliest towns and cities seem to have appeared along the river banks of the Middle East from 6000 to 5000 B.C. They were not large. Ur, one of the oldest known cities in

2. See Kingsley Davis, "The Origin and Growth of Urbanization in the World," *American Journal of Sociology* 60 (1955): 431.

3. See V. Gordon Childe, *Man Makes Himself* (New York: New American Library, 1952).

the world, is estimated to have contained about five thousand people at the most, and it was large for its day. At this early stage, size was still greatly restricted by poor transportation (the wheel was not invented until around 3000 B.C.) and by the difficulty of earning a living in the city: only a few officials and traders were really needed, and artisans had only very primitive methods of production. These early cities were usually very unstable units; they were easily captured, easily destroyed, quick to revolt against their leaders, and sometimes subject to mysterious collapse and disappearance. In fact, we really do not know why most of the great cities of the ancient world were finally abandoned.

Around 1000 B.C., when iron began to be in widespread use, cities grew noticeably because of this technological innovation, which led to better transportation and improved production. The exchange of ideas and greater interaction between many people in cities began to stimulate new inventions and discoveries – writing and reading, the calendar, mathematics, money, democratic institutions, bronze, copper, and brass – which also helped their growth. Yet even after centuries of growth, no city, with the possible exception of ancient Rome, was able to exceed a population of several hundred thousand. This limitation was due to a number of important factors:

1. Agricultural methods were inefficient; it took at least seventy-five farmers to support one city man.[4]
2. There was no large-scale manufacturing, which is necessary to sustain a large work force.
3. Political and cultural organization was not well developed, and no city was really able to effectively unite a very large population with its diverse languages, religions, and customs.
4. Lack of medical knowledge made large concentrations of people unsafe: epidemics

4. Kingsley Davis, "The Origin and Growth . . . ," p. 429.

of disease commonly killed high percentages of the population.
5. Kinship and feudalism remained strong forms of organization in the countryside, linking people to the land and permitting few to migrate.

Cities were virtually abandoned during the Dark Ages and then were gradually revived during the late Middle Ages (in the eleventh and twelfth centuries). But the great period of urban growth did not come until the eighteenth and nineteenth centuries, when it came as a result of the industrial revolution. In 1377 London, for example, had a population of only 30,000 people; it was close to the million mark by 1800. Sociologist Kingsley Davis says:

In Western Europe, starting at the zero point, the development of cities not only reached the stage that the ancient world had achieved but kept going after that. It kept going on the basis of improvements in agriculture and transport, the opening of new lands and new trade routes, and above all, the rise in productive activity, first in highly organized handicraft and eventually in a revolutionary new form of production – the factory run by machinery and fossil fuel.[5]

THE SOCIAL STRUCTURE OF PREINDUSTRIAL CITIES

Sociologist Gideon Sjoberg has suggested that all preindustrial cities share many common characteristics and are unlike our modern industrial cities in many important respects.[6] We think of the modern city as a community oriented toward industry and commerce, dominated by large impersonal organizations, and subject to constant change and innovation. The preindustrial city, which was the main type of city from about 6000 B.C. to A.D. 1800, shares with the modern city some characteristics, such as a relatively high density of

5. Kingsley Davis, "The Origin and Growth . . . ," p. 433.

6. Gideon Sjoberg, *The Preindustrial City* (New York: Free Press, 1960).

In cities like Istanbul, Turkey, there are still many evidences of the preindustrial city: the city is divided into sections according to occupational and social groups, people often live and work in the same building, and occupational specialization is not very advanced. *(Jim Hubbard, Photo Researchers, Inc.)*

population and great diversity, but in many respects it is much closer in its social structure to rural villages.

Extended family or kinship networks were still the dominant form of social organization in the preindustrial city, although in some cases they had to compete with more modern forms such as government bureaucracies. The class system was a rigid one and social mobility was slight. Industry consisted of the craftsman or artisan working in his home. Government was usually a small ruling clique of the elite: an oligarchy. Social order was based more on class or caste lines than on formalized control such as laws and policemen.

The preindustrial city was usually divided into sections or quarters, for the various occupational and social groups. Government officials and those of high social class lived in one quarter, and those of low social class or foreign origin in another. Metalsmiths, cloth weavers, tailors, saddlers, and all the other artisans had their own districts. Traces of this kind of urban ecological organization can still be seen in street names: in London's Fleet Street where printers and journalists still work and often live as well, and in New York's garment district where one whole industry is jammed together in the space of several city blocks. It is characteristic of the preindustrial city to have little specialization of buildings. People live and work under the same roof; the local store may also be the school, and perhaps a government office as well. There is a corresponding lack of occupational specialization, for the same man buys raw materials, transforms them into manufactured articles, and then sells them to his customers.

Most of the large cities of the world — London, Paris, Rome, New York — were once preindustrial cities, but they have evolved past that stage. There are still some cities in the world today which are mainly preindustrial, such as Mecca in the Middle East and Hué in Vietnam. As the forces of modernization come to these areas of the world, it is probable that they too will change and become industrial, or perhaps even postindustrial, cities.

TOPIC

2 THE PROCESS OF MODERNIZATION

When we say that a society is "modern," we are referring especially to the related phenomena of *industrialization* and *urbanization* and the great changes they have brought to community life. The second of the great natural revolutions of man, the industrial revolution (the first was the urban revolution), began in England in the late eighteenth and early nineteenth centuries. Industrialization has had a striking effect on the growth of cities; it started what might be called a second urban revolution which has led to the huge metropolitan areas and urban-dominated societies of the present day.

Only the nations of western Europe and the United States began to modernize as early as the nineteenth century. Most nations started only recently, and many still remain rural and agricultural societies. In this topic, we will look at the experiences of the Western nations and of the so-called Third World nations — meaning most of the countries of Africa, Asia, and Latin America. We will also discuss the process of urbanization, how it relates to industrialization, and the impact both industrialization and urbanization have had on society.

INDUSTRIALIZATION IN THE WEST

Industrialization in the Western nations was for the most part a long, slow, and sometimes painful process, although compared with the current experience of some developing Third World nations, it seems to have been a relatively smooth social change. Of course, the idea of doing work by machines was not one suddenly conceived in A.D. 1800. Man has been a toolmaker for most of his existence and archeologists have even found evidence of "factories" dating back to the earliest Stone Age period; these were places where knife blades, axes, and arrowheads were made in large quantities, probably for a whole tribe.[7] What was new about industrialization was the speed of manufacture and the uniformity of the product. Technological innovations such as the steam engine and the internal combustion engine were used to provide more power than the unassisted muscle of man or animals could ever give. The idea of uniform, or identical, units of manufacture which were continually reproducible probably began with the printing press, and was developed all

7. James H. Breasted, *The Conquest of Civilization* (New York: Harper, 1938), p. 29.

through the nineteenth century, with the invention of the spinning jenny, the power loom, the die-cast mold, and so on. The assembly line, an innovation of the early twentieth century, speeded up the mechanization of work even more by dividing the manufacturing process into small steps or units which could be repeated over and over with standardized results. The next significant step was automation, the replacement of direct human control over machines with machine control of machines. The most recent advance has been the use of computers, which can plan, order, and check up on most of the operations of the automated machines. Each of these discoveries has removed man one step further from the actual labor of producing goods.

The inventions and ideas that made industrialization possible came into being slowly, each a response to a change initiated earlier. Each innovation brought about great social changes (most of which were barely perceived and rarely understood at the time) affecting family structure, social class and mobility, and sometimes the basic political fabric of the society.

Most experts agree that the industrial revolution began in England in the late eighteenth and early nineteenth centuries. A number of important social factors helped to stimulate its growth. Economic competition in agriculture made it impossible for many small farmers to earn a living and so a large labor force was ready and eager to take work in factories. Improved transportation methods, such as canals, and later the steam locomotive and railroad, made it possible for a factory to be separated from its raw materials and its market by relatively long distances. Thus communities became economically connected to other communities, until the entire nation was involved in one economic network.

The government became increasingly centralized and was therefore able to rise above narrow local interests and bring the country together into a single industrial economy. (Indeed, it was the rising national governments that sponsored improved transportation

The assembly line, an invention of the twentieth century, was an important step in the industrialization of the West, for it speeded up the manufacturing process. But today automation is replacing more and more assembly workers, and new jobs are rapidly appearing in service, rather than manufacturing, areas. *(Burk Uzzle, Magnum)*

networks, thus enabling the establishment of commercial trading on an international scale.) The main function of government was to implement the natural system of supply and demand in the marketplace, rather than to control productivity or wage and price scales. This *laissez-faire* policy (the French words mean "not to interfere") was a marked change from the economic controls and regulations that prevailed before the industrial revolution. The policy allowed individual men to take the initiative to create wealth and provide goods and jobs. The Protestant ethic of self-discipline, hard work, competitiveness, and individual initiative was especially suited to the successful undertaking of capitalistic industrial enterprise.[8]

INDUSTRIALIZATION: THE CONTEMPORARY THIRD WORLD EXPERIENCE

Many nations of the world today, especially in Africa and Asia, are only now starting to

8. Max Weber, *The Protestant Ethic and the Spirit of Capitalism* (London: George Allen & Unwin, 1930).

Unlike the nations of the West, Third World countries cannot develop into fully modernized societies through a gradual evolutionary process. Change is often disjointed as some aspects of life may be revolutionized overnight, while other elements remain just as they have been for centuries. On a visit to Nairobi this Kikuyu tribesman is suddenly confronted with the invention of the double-decker bus. *(Marc and Evelyne Bernheim, Woodfin Camp and Associates)*

undergo the process of industrialization as part of the effort to modernize their societies. Their experience has been quite different from that of the Western world for a number of reasons. The first is that these nations must start with a fully developed form of industrialization. The inventions have been made, the processes developed. In the West, industrialization was the result of a slow evolution from the preindustrial society; for the Third World nations, it comes as a fully developed, conflicting culture, which they must somehow learn to adapt to quickly. They must move from oxcart to airplane in one generation. Their progress can be swift, but because of this speed it also carries the possibility of extreme social disorganization.

A second reason why some of these Third World nations differ in their experience of industrialization is that the values and attitudes of their existing cultures are basically quite different from ours. They have different religious and philosophical beliefs, different attitudes toward work and even toward prosperity. This was pointed up in great detail recently by the Swedish economist and sociologist Gunnar Myrdal in the book *Asian Drama.*[9] As a result of a survey of many countries of the Third World, he concluded that a major handicap to modernization in these countries was a lack of the very attitudes and values which motivated the Western experience. Deeply based traditional values and beliefs are among the most difficult elements to change.

Another major distinction of the Third World experience is the serious problem of overpopulation. Many of the developing nations were overpopulated at the onset of the modernization process, and every step of economic growth has been matched by population growth. This population growth is mainly due to the rapid reduction of death rates caused by medical advances. Among the

9.   Gunnar Myrdal, *Asian Drama: An Inquiry into the Poverty of Nations,* 3 vols. (New York: Random House, Pantheon, 1968).

many problems of overpopulation, perhaps the most serious are food shortages and the constant threat of starvation. Increasing population may also keep per capita (per individual) income unchanged even though total national incomes are rising.

Next, it should be noted that contemporary modernization is almost never a decentralized laissez-faire process, but rather one planned and managed by a relatively strong, centralized government. This is true of both Communist and non-Communist states, though the degree of centralized political control of the economy differs somewhat in each case.

Finally, many of the Third World nations have histories of colonialism, an important factor in the attempt of these nations to modernize. We will discuss colonialism and its effects in the next chapter.

The nations of the Third World are at widely varying stages of economic development. Economists and sociologists have devised developmental models to classify levels of economic growth. These models are often based on three stages of development: premodern, transitional, and modernized, or advanced, implying a more orderly progression than actually exists, for there are many different paths to modernization. Whatever the particular developmental path a nation chooses or is forced to take, however, certain basic conditions have been identified as necessary if economic development is to occur.

Foremost among these conditions is a set of values and attitudes which favors economic growth. The ideology which has emerged most prominently, one that can divert individuals from their traditional patterns and orient them toward material achievement and the future, is nationalism. Other important values which encourage modernization are a belief in productive achievement, the importance of technology, and a rational and scientific rather than traditional approach to problem solving.

Another basic condition is a certain degree of mobility of the productive resources: labor, land, capital, and raw materials. These must be generally available so they can be assembled at strategic times and places, but these resources are sometimes locked up in a traditional social system. This is often the case, for example, in regard to land. In some countries land changes hands only through inheritance. It is usually extremely difficult to break these ancestral ties to land and treat land as something which can be bought and sold. It is also essential to establish money as the basic medium of exchange. Industrialization brings about extreme specialization of occupations and goods, making the barter system (trading with goods rather than money) inoperable; a relatively impersonal medium of exchange, such as paper bills or coins, becomes essential.

Next, there must be a certain degree of social order and stability in economic markets, and in the political system in general. Successful market operations between buyers and sellers require trust and predictability, and the widespread and effective use of sanctions to prevent fraud and ensure that people comply with contracts. Political and civic stability are important to enforce these sanctions and to attract and protect capital investments, especially for facilities such as transportation and communication which require large investments of money.

Finally, we must note the great importance of the city and the business corporation. Few nations are able to achieve high rates of economic growth without the concentration of labor and markets which the city contains. Equally necessary to economic development is the rise of the large business corporation which is able to organize its workers for efficient productivity.

Only one non-Western country has succeeded in becoming a fully industrialized society comparable to those of the West, and that is Japan. For the most part, the early efforts among the Third World nations to industrialize were not very successful. Neither the leaders of the Third World nations, nor the Westerners who introduced them to the

**PERCENTAGE OF LABOR FORCE IN INDUSTRIAL, AGRICULTURAL, AND SERVICE
OCCUPATIONS IN THE WEST, THIRD WORLD, AND EAST: 1970**

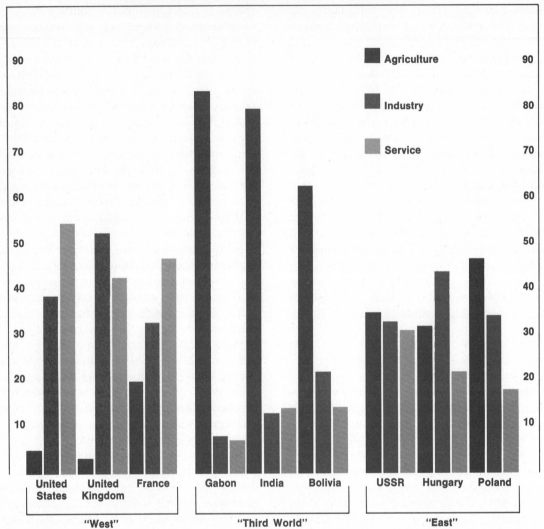

SOURCE: International Labor Office, *Year Book of Labour Statistics* (Geneva, 1972).

Modernization brings a steady decrease in the proportion of workers employed in agriculture. In the Western nations, service occupations are often the largest category; the varied patterns of the graph for the Communist nations indicate that these economies are in transition.

machines and ideas of industrialism, realized the complexities involved in such an undertaking. Everyone had to learn by experience. Factories were built that no one knew how to run; jobs were created that no one was willing to fill; products were turned out which no one wanted to buy. Projects that made good economic sense to the Americans and Europeans who acted as advisers and investors turned out to make no social sense to the local residents. Westerners gave advice on how to double crop production to people who believed that such things were preordained by the gods and beyond man's power to control.

Some of the people they urged to work hard and "get ahead" came from caste societies where social class is fixed at birth.

If the Westerners were naive, so on occasion were officials of the Third World nations. They thought they could bring technological change to their countries and exclude what we know are inevitable social changes. Problems arising from industrialization were sometimes said to be the result of the influence of Westerners, and some nations even took steps to exclude Westerners from the country. But the sociocultural changes, of course, could not be contained.

This is not to say that all industrialized societies will have to be exactly like ours. Industrialization is possible without capitalism, without Protestantism, and without Westernization. Many of our own responses to the experience will not necessarily become universal. Let us turn now to several case studies of economic development in the Third World.

India

India's modernization has been the subject of much sociological inquiry. There the effort to industrialize began mainly after World War II, when Nehru became prime minister. With the aid of foreign capital and technological advice, India began to build factories to make cloth, fertilizer, cement, and other products which would be immediately useful. As they prospered, additional types of industry were established. The products of India's factories are often quite sophisticated: jet planes, antibiotics, large industrial machines. Yet in spite of this rather successful program of industrialization, Indian society today can by no means be called an industrial one. Only 23 percent of the country's total income is from manufacturing including mining;[10] 80 percent of the population still lives in very small villages and on farms where most agriculture is practiced in the traditional way. The average Indian is still very poor; the per capita income

10. *The New York Times Encyclopedic Almanac* (New York: The New York Times Co., 1972).

is $72 a year (compared with $4,140 in the United States). This figure is, however, partly misleading, because many communities still function on a barter economy, another sign that the society is not industrialized.

Even though industrialization has not yet reached the average Indian, it has already begun to affect certain areas of India's culture and social structure. For example, the traditional caste system was greatly weakened as a result of the laborer's opportunity to earn a better wage in the factory than he could have in his caste-determined occupation. As new ways to earn status and wealth emerged, the caste system was undermined, and this change was accelerated by national efforts to change attitudes and laws.

Industrialization has gone hand in hand with urbanization; in fact, the cities are growing faster than the economy's ability to support an urban population, a phenomenon called *overurbanization*. Bombay and Calcutta both have populations of over five million people for the entire urban area. Calcutta is probably the fastest-growing city in the world, and the many grave problems of that city, including starvation, give an indication of the serious effects which can stem from overurbanization.

One factor that has served to soften the impact of industrialization on Indian society is its ancient tradition of cultural pluralism. Indians belong to a number of different races; they speak over 1,650 different languages and dialects; they are divided into groups of hundreds of castes and tribes. They are predominantly Hindu, but there is still a large Moslem minority (which was larger before the partition of Pakistan which created a separate nation for the Moslems). The Indians' strong tradition of cultural pluralism means that in some ways industrialism can be just another subculture, claiming the interest of a minority of the population. It coexists temporarily in peace with a number of other subcultures, but the long-run prospect for industrialization is uncertain.

Despite successful efforts to modernize their economy, industrialization has not basically altered the lives of many Indians. A majority of the population is still engaged in agricultural pursuits, sometimes within sight of fully modernized manufacturing plants. *(Photo Courtesy of United Nations)*

India's most serious problem is overpopulation which, coupled with food shortages, produces the threat of mass starvation. India's economy has shown little real growth since World War II, due to the great increase in population which has kept per capita incomes at about the same level. India's population problem stems in large part from declining death rates, which are due to the introduction of advanced medical technologies. There have been numerous nationwide programs designed to diminish the birthrate, but to date these have not been adequate to the task.

Iran

A somewhat different experience with industrialization can be seen in Iran, a Middle Eastern country which has managed to achieve more widespread modernity than India, without any significant manufacturing industries.

Part of the secret of Iran's success are vast oil and mineral deposits; together these account for nearly a fourth of Iran's total national income. These resources were developed by foreign companies, but Iran's share of the profits has given her the capital needed to undertake many programs of modernization without the direct help of modernized countries.

Modernization began in this country when the present Shah took the throne in 1941, and it has proceeded according to a carefully planned program. The government decided against the building of factories as the first step in this program. Instead, it attempted first to bring modern technology to agriculture. The government built dams for irrigation and power, and established farming cooperatives to purchase modern machinery and serve as a way to learn modern agricultural techniques. Most important of all, the government has focused on land reform. Large landowners have been forced to turn their land over to the government for redistribution, and 15 million farmers, or about 85 percent of the total farm population, now own their own land. This program has been quite successful, and Iran, a country made up mostly of mountains and deserts, now exports many agricultural products to neighboring countries in the Middle East.

As agriculture became more efficient, some farmers were freed to move to the city, and urbanization began. Today about 31 percent of the population lives in cities, and 10 percent of all Iranians live in the capital city, Tehran, which is quite modern. Factories are now being built to produce cement and some metals; Iranian-made cars are on the roads; the famous Persian carpets are being produced in mechanized factories in the city rather than on handlooms in the villages. The per capita income is now about $321 a year.

As might be expected, there have been many basic social and cultural changes. The traditional village structure has been altered, with more power going to younger men who have some education and a knowledge of the new technology. Moslem religion allows a man four wives, but the practice of polygamy has virtually disappeared, except in a few remote desert tribes. The position of women has changed enormously. Formerly severely restricted, they are now allowed to own property, they appear on the street, do their own marketing, and take jobs as secretaries, factory workers, or maids. Opportunities to move into the highest social class have not increased noticeably (as land was taken away from the families of the wealthy elite, many moved into the even more profitable oil business), but a new and rapidly growing middle class now makes up much of the population of Tehran.

Social change has come more quickly in Iran than it has in India, perhaps because the former is a more homogeneous country. The population is 98 percent Moslem, and most of the people speak the same language and are of similar ethnic background. The exceptions are the Turkomans in the north and the desert tribes in the south. Change has been slower for them. Their old-fashioned agricultural methods cannot compete with those of the other farmers, and so they have been forced to abandon their traditional nomadic way of life, settle in country villages where they can get the benefits of government agricultural programs, and try to evolve some pattern of social organization that is better adapted to their new way of life.

URBANIZATION

Kingsley Davis says that statistics show clearly "that urbanization has tended to reach its highest point wherever economic productivity has been greatest—that is, where the economy is industrialized and rationalized."[11] When large factories are built, they attract a labor force to work in them. They also attract other factories and services. For example, automobile factories are usually built near steel mills, clothing manufacturers locate near textile factories, and so on. As the population of factory workers grows, there is more opportunity to sell goods and services to those people. At the same time, the application of industrial methods to agriculture makes it more efficient, so fewer and fewer people are needed in the country. The result is large-scale urbanization.

The cities of western Europe began to grow in the nineteenth century, as industrialization developed there. England's fastest rate of urbanization came between 1810 and 1850; in America it was between 1860 and 1890; in Germany, between 1870 and 1910. By the twentieth century the rate of urbanization in all the Western nations had slowed down, but the world rate has remained high. One estimate is that by the year 2000 at least one-

11. Kingsley Davis, "The Origin and Growth...," p. 435.

FASTEST-GROWING UNITED STATES URBAN AREAS*

Urban area	Projected Growth Increase 1965 to 1975
Fort Lauderdale-Hollywood, Florida	51.9%
Santa Barbara, California	51.5%
San Jose, California	51.4%
Huntsville, Alabama	51.4%
Las Vegas, Nevada	46.6%
San Bernardino-Riverside-Ontario, California	35.2%
West Palm Beach, Florida	34.5%
Phoenix, Arizona	34.2%
Sacramento, California	32.4%
Orlando, Florida	31.2%
Tampa-St. Petersburg, Florida	28.1%
Washington, D.C.	25.9%
Los Angeles-Long Beach, California	25.6%
Lexington, Kentucky	25.2%
Tucson, Arizona	23.8%
Houston, Texas	23.4%
Lubbock, Texas	23.2%
Dallas, Texas	23.1%
Atlanta, Georgia	23.0%
Denver, Colorado	22.5%
Madison, Wisconsin	22.3%
Albuquerque, New Mexico	22.2%
Amarillo, Texas	22.0%

*Percent of increase based upon projected growth, 1965 to 1975
SOURCE: U.S. Bureau of the Census

This list of American cities with high growth rates demonstrates the westward trend of population movement. Note that all these cities, with the single exception of Madison, Wisconsin, are in warm, pleasant climates. The appearance on this list of the cities of Huntsville, Lexington, and Atlanta may indicate a new southeastward trend as many industries relocate in southern states, where land and labor are cheaper.

quarter of all the people in the world will be living in cities of 100,000 or more people. In a study made in 1955, Kingsley Davis reported that the figure at that time was 19 percent.[12] Some nations which are presently urbanizing at a very rapid rate are India, Egypt, Mexico, and Brazil. It is interesting to note that of the 20 largest cities in the world, only a quarter are in Western nations. There are 83 cities in the world with populations over 1 million. Only 18 are in Europe

and 9 in North America. There are 39 in Asia, 7 in the Soviet Union, 7 in South America, and 3 in Africa.[13]

Typically the largest cities are located along the seacoast, on large rivers, or near large deposits of natural resources. Even though airplanes and railroads can now serve to transport raw materials, food supplies, and manufactured products, water transportation is still the cheapest and easiest method in many areas, and accessibility to it continues

12. All the above statistics are from Kingsley Davis, "The Origin and Growth...," pp. 435–436.

13. *The New York Times Encyclopedic Almanac* (New York: The New York Times Co., 1969), p. 362.

to be a factor in urban development. Other environmental factors, such as climate and topography, and the productivity of the surrounding farmland, also influence the growth and establishment of cities.

Cities play a modernizing role not only in stimulating economic growth and development, but also with respect to cultural and social change. The density of population of a city makes certain programs—for example, widespread education—more feasible. Literacy rates almost invariably go up when a country becomes urbanized. Also, mass education is often used to promote nationalistic feeling, which seems so important to the modernizing process.

City life itself, independent of the educational opportunity it offers, may serve to increase nationalism and a national culture. Cities are usually the setting for most social assimilation, for there people must learn to cope with the customs, language, and attitudes of the other residents. Foreign cultures brought there by immigrants, regional cultures of its own society, ethnic subcultures, and rural or provincial cultures all must be partially assimilated into one urban culture.

Cities are almost always the locale of the rising middle class, which was limited to a handful of traders and artisans in the preindustrial period. The modern middle class—the independent businessmen and merchants; those in various professions such as law, teaching, and engineering; and administrators, supervisors, and bureaucrats—is almost entirely dependent on the city and the factory for its existence. A growing middle class is both a major result of modernization and a key element in its continuation.

THE IMPACT OF INDUSTRIALIZATION AND URBANIZATION

In spite of the diversity of conditions in the process of modernizing, and the many paths which countries may take toward modernization, social scientists have identified basic ways in which modernization generally affects a country's culture and social structure. These represent profound and far-reaching changes in social life. The following ten points summarize the major sociocultural impacts:

(1) Economic relationships are separated from other types of social relationships. In preindustrial societies, economic relationships are simply one part of a wide and more encompassing relationship between individuals: typically family members or kinship related people, but perhaps also the parties in a feudal lord-subject relationship, or the members of some important organization, such as a religious one. The industrial system separates economic relationships out of this web, and they come to function independent of other concerns. This is one aspect of the general process known as *differentiation,* in which functions formerly fused in one structure are placed in separate social structures. Thus industrialization usually brings changes in family and kinship structures, and in most cases serves to weaken them.

(2) Economic activities among the labor force shift from agricultural and extractive (for example, mining and fishing, and forestry) to manufacturing and later to service activities.

(3) This is accompanied by the emergence of many new occupational roles; for example, many people leave their old occupations to become skilled and semiskilled factory workers. The problem of learning new skills in "mid-career" is always a difficult one for an adult. In addition there is the constant problem of unemployment as old occupational roles are made obsolete by the new technology.

(4) The specialization of occupational roles makes a whole new layer of activity necessary: administrative organization. The administration consists of managers and supervisors who coordinate and integrate the many specialties, making sure that they mesh together in an efficient and productive way. In time these administrative activities also become specialized, touching off an almost

never-ending cycle of differentiation, integration or coordination, more differentiation, and more integration.[14]

(5) New occupational roles lead to a rise in both geographic and social mobility. New jobs are often in the city, requiring rural families to leave their traditional surroundings and relocate in new surroundings: the process of urbanization. This move to cities and new occupations involves an increase in skills and a rise in income, leading to upward mobility and higher social status.

(6) The existing system of stratification is changed. Wealth and occupation become relatively more important determinants of status, and birth and kinship become relatively less important; that is, ascribed statuses are replaced by achieved statuses based more on merit, and a closed system of social stratification becomes more open. There is often some significant redistribution of power within the society as well. The new power elite may be composed of new faces, or it may be the same individuals who composed the elite in the preindustrial period, organized in new ways.

(7) Because the nuclear family is so much better adapted to the industrial society, the extended kin network becomes seriously undermined, though it never disappears entirely. The very old and the very young, who had been able to contribute certain productive labor under an agricultural or handicraft economic system, become unproductive because they cannot work in highly skilled jobs. Therefore they are no longer economic assets, but liabilities. Women are able to find employment outside the home in large numbers. Their greater independence alters the nature of the husband-wife relationship, which in turn alters the structure and the experiences

14. Neil J. Smelser, *Essays in Sociological Explanation* (Englewood Cliffs, N.J.: Prentice-Hall, 1968), chap. 6.

of family life. The family becomes less of a center for all activities and more of a "home base" to which one returns after a pattern of activities outside the home. Its structure may become more democratic and less authoritarian.

In turn, the informal social control mechanisms of the family and kin network give way under the pressure of the new mobility and freedom. They are superseded by the more formalized procedures of the state: its laws and its agents.

(8) Some religious beliefs give way to secular rationality and science (the process of secularization). As religious beliefs become less important, religion is increasingly separated as an institution from other aspects of life. Religious institutions are disentangled from economic and political institutions and are maintained primarily in conjunction with the nuclear family.

(9) There is a gradual growth of mass communications, mass education, and ultimately mass culture. Advertising, political appeals, and some art forms tend to become standardized, commercialized, and widely distributed throughout the population. This does not necessarily mean that cultural forms degenerate; rather, it means that cultural forms are communicated in new ways and to a wider audience.

(10) In most cases of modernization, there has been a marked development of centralized and bureaucratically organized political power. This differs from the earlier Western experience of laissez-faire which we noted. In addition, a general growth of popular and widespread political participation has occurred, although the form of participation may not always be democratic. Participation may, instead, be manipulated by a single, state political party for its own support.

DANIEL LERNER
Turkey in Transition

Reprinted with the permission of Macmillan Publishing Company from *The Passing of Traditional Society: Modernizing the Middle East,* by Daniel Lerner. © The Free Press, a Corporation, 1958.

Introduction

Lerner's book is one of the best studies of the effect of modernization on traditional society in the Third World nations. This excerpt is taken from the section on Turkey. Lerner divides the Turks into three groups: the moderns, who had already accepted both the technological and the cultural changes of modernization; the traditionals, who had either not been exposed to the changes or had rejected them; and the transitionals, who were actually in the process of modernization, changing their traditional habits and patterns of life. Perhaps of most interest to American readers is the discussion of the traditionals, because their cultural assumptions and attitudes are so far from our own. Lerner helps us understand both the enormous problems of modernization, and the reasons the traditionals are unwilling to undertake it.

From tradition to transition

Most Turkish Traditionals remain contained within their familiar little universe of family, mosque, village. They remain uncurious about the larger world, unresponsive to its occasional impingements — so long as they remain occasional. When the impinging stimuli become too pervasive to be ignored, the Traditionals turn rejective. But once such "instinctive" rejection comes to require defensive verbalization, signifying a need for self-reassurance among the Traditionals, then a process of change is under way. A fine example of how this phase was operating in 1950, in the village of Sakaltutan (near Kayseri), has been described by Paul Stirling:

The villagers do not think of the village as a changing society and children accept their father's point of view more or less without question. Although most of the young men have been to the cities and seen the modern generation of Turkish girls in Western dress about the streets, and been to American films, they state not only to me but to each other that their own customs are better. The only time I heard the opposite view it was greeted with a storm of protest.

Dr. Stirling's account shows how, while tradition still rules, transition gets under way. When people feel obliged to defend tradition they are no longer simple Traditionals unaware of alternatives. So, the "storm of protest" against the exponent of new ways indicates which way the wind was blowing in Sakaltutan. In an earlier period the responsive storm would more likely have taken the form of a chill indifference. Had the offender persisted beyond tolerable limits, he might have been condemned as an idiot or punished as a heretic. In neither case would "most of the young men," as Dr. Stirling reports, have been likely to "state not only to me *but to each other* that their own customs are better." They would have felt no such need for mutual self-reassurance.

In villages that remain Traditional, no voices need be raised to defend traditional ways because no other ways are on the agenda. It is a distinctive trait of Traditional society that it promotes no alternatives to itself; hence the corresponding psychic trait of the Traditional villager is that he lacks "curiosity." The sense of variousness and possibility develops as a specific feature of Modern society, where changes in the daily round of life are frequent, the unexpected may happen at any time, and people must be prepared to make choices. The secular evolution of curiosity as personal trait and social utility is a phase of modernization closely linked to the rise of mass communication — which taught large audiences to ask questions, perhaps more effectively than it taught them to find answers.

At different points in the Turkish interviews, respondents were asked what they would like to know about the world, about various countries, about specific events they had heard of only vaguely. The Moderns, with the Transitionals just behind them, demonstrated an abundant curiosity; there were all sorts of questions they wanted to have answered. The Traditionals, typically, could find few questions to ask. Most of them said that there wasn't anything they cared to know. Some, who wished to be polite to the interviewer, did search out questions to ask. Those were invariably personal, often purely sensory, and clearly derived from immediate concerns of their actual life rather than imaginative curiosity about life elsewhere.

The Traditional's incapacity to establish connections between himself and the larger world is the key to his perspective. His personality has been socially disciplined to constrict imagination to the familiar time-space dimensions of his daily life. Even on the simplest level of generalizing from self to a larger universe, the trained incapacity of the Traditional is evident. All respondents were asked to name "your biggest problem," for example, and there was marked convergence on economic troubles. But when asked later to name Turkey's biggest problem, the Traditionals failed to generalize as compared with the others. Only one of twelve Traditionals was able to connect his personal economic problems with those on the national level. It is fair to say "able" rather than "willing," for most Traditionals simply did not name *any* alternative problem before the nation. Confronted with so awesome a demand upon their capacities, they fell silent altogether.

The consistent incapacity to link oneself to the other world underlay most of the regularly recurring differences among the respondents. At one point (after he had identified the biggest problems facing himself and the nation), the respondent was asked what he would do about these problems if he were the president of Turkey. This is a role-identification question, typically requiring heavy demands upon the self among pre-Modern persons. At another point a simpler demand was made upon empathic capacity: the respondent was asked where he would choose to live if he had to live elsewhere than Turkey. If he refused to imagine living elsewhere, the interviewer probed: "But if you *had* to live elsewhere . . . !" At still another point the respondent was asked how he would feel about living in the United States. The results on these three questions are given in the following tables:

Ability to Imagine	Moderns	Tran- sitionals	Tradi- tionals
. . . being Turkish president	86%	63%	35%
. . . living outside Turkey	94	74	49
. . . living in United States	100	98	74

These figures speak, to a certain point, for themselves. It is at the point where they stop speaking for themselves that the student of Turkish (or human) behavior must ponder them. It makes common sense to reflect that, after all, one cannot reasonably expect to ask an Anatolian (or any other) peasant what he would do as President and get a comprehensive answer. This is obvious upon statement. But it is as a start rather than a conclusion that one needs to take this obvious point. For the figures also show that some Anatolian peasants, although living in the same social setting as their silent peers, *can* answer such questions, i.e., practically all Transitionals and three out of four Traditionals could imagine living in the United States.

This involves nothing less than a personality transformation of major proportions. Perhaps the deepest insight the data give into the gravity of this change is the prevailing dysphoria [dissatisfaction or unhappiness] in the daily round of life among the Traditionals. The feeling that this must be so is expressed by their own Traditional proverb: "Our enemies make us laugh; our friends make us cry." In the world of the Traditionals, the sense of life is dull, heavy, gloomy. "Never have I seen such a colorless, shapeless dump. The main color is gray . . ." wrote the Ankara-bred interviewer Tosun on his first exposure to Balgat. The dysphoric tonality of Traditional life *for those who live it* is documented by another set of questions. One asked simply, and in quite general fashion, whether the respondent felt himself to be "happy or unhappy." Another, much later, asked what his reaction had been to the last piece of news he had received. A third asked what the respondent felt he could do to help solve Turkey's problems. The responses are given here:

	Moderns	Transitionals	Traditionals
Feels unhappy generally	15%	20%	33%
Feels unhappy about last news (i.e., sad, sorry, angry)	39	46	86
Feels unable to help solve Turkey's problems	45	53	86

The complex of gloom condensed by these figures is difficult to reconstruct for those who live in a participant society fashioned in the century of optimism with the ideology of progress. Clarity on how we evaluate this is therefore essential. Nowhere on this page or in this volume is the implication intended that Modernity is utopian or that Americans, as the most modern people in the sense we use this term, are therefore the best and happiest.

Neither by this caveat is the contrary intended. There is simply no net judgment of this order made or needed in this book. What our study underscores is that Modernity and Tradition are even more radically different from each other than is commonly acknowledged, that bridging the difference hinges upon a transformation of personality along with a remaking of institutions, that this modernizing process is underway among a large number of Middle Easterners. Our data on happiness show why so many Middle Easterners are willing to undergo the difficult process of modernization—they simply are too unhappy with the old traditional ways to resist an opportunity to try something new.

Constriction and communication

A first item to note is the response made to the interview situation itself. Balgat [a small Turkish village] illustrates two main ways of responding that are quite characteristic. The Grocer sought to make the interview an occasion for psychic rapprochement with the Modern young interviewer Tosun; he "evidently wished to feel that he is closer with me than he is to the other villagers." Along with this, the Grocer answered all questions freely and fully. The Chief, however, remained wholly disengaged from the urban interviewer—neither friendly, nor hostile, but simply observant and self-contained. He answered questions with regard only to his own interests rather than Tosun's. Hence the Chief, as interviewee, was a man of few words on many subjects and many words on a few subjects.

The intent of these remarks goes beyond their limited relevance to the technique of interviewing. The manner in which persons perceive the interview situation is a datum on their readiness and competence to participate personally in essentially impersonal social enterprises. It is axiomatic among American communication specialists that most Americans are not at all intimidated by opinion surveys which demand their views on great men and great matters well outside their actual experience. The population is accustomed to projecting themselves into strange roles and situations, and they enjoy exercising their skill. Indeed, a more common complaint about opinion polls heard among ordinary Americans is that the pollsters do not get around to them.

The contrast with the social psychology of the interview situation among Turks is striking. How little they perceive the essential impersonality of the situation is clear from the excessive preoccupation of Turkish interviewees with what the interviewers might think of them. With extraordinary frequency, for example, interviewers were thanked profusely for their personal interest. Said one 47-year old illiterate villager after a three-hour interrogation: "You are the nicest *effendi* I have ever known. No other *effendi* has ever cared to know my thoughts on so many things." The meaning of impersonal communication simply has not penetrated in such measure that question-and-answer can be handled, psychologically, as a game.

In participant societies, where the mass media have taught people how to communicate socially without being personally "engaged," the question-and-answer game is played with uninhibited pleasure by the populace. Among Traditional Turks, who have not yet learned the participant style taught by the mass media, the situation of question-and-answer is deadly earnest. Words count for much, we have seen, with the Traditionals; and one does not speak lightly on weighty matters. Consider the following array of responses to the question where one would live if he could not live in Turkey:

> I could not live in any other place. (Why?) Because I love Turkey. (If you were forced to leave Turkey?) I would kill myself. (001: Housemaid, age 25, illiterate, poor)

> God forbid! I would rather die than live somewhere else than in Turkey. (Why?) Because this is our country. (021: Worker, age 30, illiterate, destitute)

> I would rather die than live. I would not want to go anywhere. If all go I would go. If nobody goes I would choose death. (089: Housewife, age 24, illiterate, poor)

> Would not want to live in any other country. I cannot leave my people. Wherever my nation is I want to be there. (If you had to go?) Nowhere. I would rather die. (116: Horsewagon Driver, age 29, illiterate, poor)

> I would rather prefer to die. (127: Farmer, age 58, illiterate, poor) I would rather die. (186: Doctor, age 53, college, moderate)

These respondents exhibit one common trait: they can more easily imagine destroying the self than making the effort to project it beyond the familiar world into the strange. In the foregoing quotations we deliberately chose a wide spread of sociological characteristics (sex, age, occupation, education, economic status) to emphasize that this is a *psychological* trait. But the incapacity to take questions casually, to project "impersonally" into the situations they define, is especially marked in that social setting where Traditionals are the rule.

Consider the 30-year old worker, illiterate and destitute in his village near the Black Sea, who invoked God and death to save himself from the apparently worse fate of imagining himself living elsewhere. He was terrified by the question as to what he would do if he were President of Turkey and again invoked God to preserve him from ever thinking of such a thing. He was less intensely agitated by the question as to what he would do if he were editor of a paper or manager of a radio station; but he still replied, though without seeking aid from the Deity, that it would be "unseemly" for him to imagine himself doing such a thing. Even when asked what he considered the biggest problems facing Turkey, this man, raised in a coastal village across the Black Sea from the Soviet Union, could only reply: "I don't know." By this time he had probably been intimidated and exhausted by the interview situation.

For it is evident that this young man has not been trained to receive, retain, and relay opinions about the world outside his daily round of life. He is not interested in things foreign; when asked what he would like to know about other lands he replied: "Nothing." When asked his impressions of various foreign peoples, he said: "I don't know: they are all infidels." Indeed, in the whole series of questions dealing with mediated news of the world external to his village, the one positive expression was that he sometimes liked to listen to the newspaper being read. Why? "They tell things in a nice way, everything about governors, commandants, officials." When probed further about his interest in these important people, he continued (under continuous stimulation) as follows:

> Yes. They are big. They do big things. (Why do these big things interest you?) They are our leaders. What would happen to us if something would happen to them? (What would happen?) We would all be lost. We could not do a thing without them. (Why not?) They are our masters. We all depend on them.

The Black Sea worker thinks of the newspaper solely as a way of being informed, at appropriate distance, about the doings of "our masters" without whom "we would all be lost." The newspaper for him is no vehicle of opinion, neither for hearing those of others nor for selecting some to make his own. What would a man want with an opinion if his fate is in any case decided for him by those whose proper role it is to decide such matters? Opinion is simply irrelevant in such a perspective. All he wants is a court chronicle of those great men on whom "we all depend."

The Traditional does not participate in shaping public policy; nor does he feel that he "should" (is expected to) participate; nor is he particularly interested in (desirous of) participating. For him enlightenment signifies incuriosity and practical wisdom counsels ignorance. The 58-year old farmer, who was very firm in his conviction that he missed nothing by ignoring the radio, stated the case for constriction very concisely: "Even if I had enough money, I would not buy a radio. (Why?) *I don't like too much news."* He dismissed all imaginative fiction as "nonsense stuff and not real." His interest in media was restricted to but a single category: "I like to listen while my son reads the Korean war news. I get excited and even with my old age I want to go there and fight." The Traditional's only public role is to fight; the rest is not his affair. The 29-year old horsewagon driver echoed these sentiments of the farmer twice his age in a different province. On the question whether he missed anything by ignoring newspapers and radio, he said: "I lose nothing because I am not interested in *things which do not concern me."*

Throughout the Traditional interviews resonates this empty space between the private and the public arenas, this zero or near-zero contact between oneself and the larger world. The Traditional cares nothing, wants nothing, can do nothing about this world.

Conclusion

Lerner points out one of the key problems facing countries on the brink of modernization: the traditionals cannot conceive of or accept a new life style. Imagine trying to motivate a population such as this to move to urban areas, work in factories, and adopt a different value system! The task is incredibly difficult. We often get the impression that economic problems are the main focus of the modernization process — the construction of factories and dams are much in the news. While economic concerns are central, changing the cultural and social orientation of the population is often the most serious obstacle to modernization.

3 URBANISM IN THE UNITED STATES

The broad process of modernization is at a more advanced stage of development in the United States than in most other countries, but it can be studied here to see ways in which modernization affects community and national life. The living patterns of rural areas and small towns have given way to the patterns of large metropolitan areas, where about two-thirds of all Americans now live. Rural cultural values have given way to the culture of urbanism.

SOCIAL CHANGE AND THE COMMUNITY

In the last two hundred years, American community life has been affected by each of the changes brought by the modernization process discussed in the last topic. We have discussed changes in economic activities, in social stratification, and in family, religion, and politics; all of these changes have played a role in shaping contemporary life in the United States. The specific impact of the changes may differ somewhat from place to place, depending upon such factors as the size of the community, its location, its main economic functions, its age and history, degree of dependence on other communities, and so on. These changes have been the focus of much of this book, for they are an important aspect of contemporary American society. We can identify and summarize here some examples of these changes; R. L. Warren has referred to them as the "great change" in American communities.[15]

The modernization process brings about an increasing fragmentation and specialization of

15. Roland L. Warren, *The Community in America* (Chicago: Rand McNally, 1963), chap. 3.

activity and relationships. More and more relationships are separated from the web of community life as a whole or take place in specialized voluntary associations; thus we develop work relationships, play relationships, love relationships, service relationships, and so on. Today a higher proportion of an individual's relationships are secondary and dependent on carefully observed role playing, rather than primary and involving the whole individual.

Social organizations in the community have tended to become more bureaucratic and most have increased in size and scale. Many organizations have expanded beyond the size where it is still possible to tailor job responsibilities and activities to the unique interests and capabilities of the individual workers. Both work and the channels of communication regarding it are made routine and more impersonal. At the same time, the work organization often has a national base, removing it from the effective control of the local community.

Many functions which were once performed in the home, or by volunteers outside the home, have been taken over by businesses or by the government. We have mentioned before that the family has given up many of its former economic functions. Today the family seeks recreation in commercial establishments; schools provide much of the guidance parents used to provide; welfare responsibilities have been taken over in large part by the government. Even the preparation of food is done more and more by profit-making enterprises: by restaurants, food packagers, by producers of TV dinners, and so on.

Communities themselves have become in-

PERCENTAGE OF POPULATION OF THE UNITED STATES LIVING IN URBAN AREAS 1790 - 1970

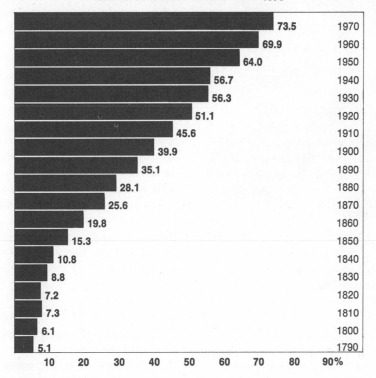

Year	Percentage
1970	73.5
1960	69.9
1950	64.0
1940	56.7
1930	56.3
1920	51.1
1910	45.6
1900	39.9
1890	35.1
1880	28.1
1870	25.6
1860	19.8
1850	15.3
1840	10.8
1830	8.8
1820	7.2
1810	7.3
1800	6.1
1790	5.1

SOURCE: *Historical Statistics of the U.S.* and *Statistical Abstracts of the U.S.*, 1970

Obviously our society is becoming increasingly urbanized with each decade. Yet these statistics can be misleading. They include those who live in suburbs rather than central cities, and they make no distinction between relatively small cities of 15,000 and large ones of several million people.

creasingly interrelated, whatever their size, and dependent on regional and national markets and on centralized political direction by state and federal governments. Just as people can no longer be truly self-sufficient, neither can towns or cities. Nearly every town and city depends on federal or state money to subsidize many educational costs, to build roads, and to provide for old, disabled, and unemployed residents; partly because of this, they are subject to federal or state control. A town may be ordered to build a more modern sewage system, to raise the level of the courses taught in its schools, or to open its municipal swimming pool to citizens of all races. The

extension of government controls means that every community in the United States is dependent on Washington, and through the democratic electoral process, on the other communities that help to elect the legislators and the President.

We have already pointed out certain ways in which the city and rural areas are economically interrelated. Rural areas provide food for the city and a market for some of the city's products; they also help to supply a labor force for city industries. The city, on the other hand, provides manufactured goods and employment opportunities for rural residents, as well as a market for its agricultural produce.

The residents of small towns such as this one in Iowa are correct in thinking their lives somewhat different from those of urban people, but this may slowly change since the mass media that bring them news of cities and the world also tend to impart to rural residents the value and cultural attitudes of the city. (David Krasnor, Photo Researchers, Inc.)

Equally important is the way the city and smaller communities are culturally interrelated. The attitudes of the city tend to dominate those of the small town and rural areas in forming the culture of the society as a whole. This is part of what we mean when we speak of urbanization. It is not just that a certain percentage of the population lives in large cities; it is also that the viewpoint, the culture, and the interests of the city become the dominant cultural interest of the whole society.

Mass communication is both a cause and a carrier of this process. Millions of Americans all over the country read *Newsweek* or *Time* each week, watch the news or other television programs produced by one of the three national networks, and spend Saturday nights at a movie made in Hollywood. All of these are the products of city residents in New York, Los Angeles, Chicago, and Washington, and they tend to impart the values and cultural attitudes of the city rather than those of the country.

An interesting study was made by Arthur J. Vidich and Joseph Bensman in the 1950s of the attitudes of residents of a small town in upstate New York toward cities and city life.[16] They found that the small town residents had a negative concept of the city, and contrasted it in their minds with the virtues — morality, honesty, the American way of life, religious belief, orderly conduct — of their own town. They also conceived of their town as independent of the city, failing to recognize or admit many important areas of their dependency. Vidich and Bensman concluded that these illusions of independence created many strains (both social and personal) in the town; among these were mistrust of outsiders, discontent among local merchants, and failure of the local government to take actions necessary for the town's continued development.

THE CULTURE OF URBANISM

Sociologists have long been interested in studying the unique culture of the city, and how it differs from the culture of rural communities. A great deal of research on the social patterns and attitudes of city dwellers was done in the 1920s and 1930s by sociologists at the University of Chicago, specifically, by Robert Park, Ernest Burgess, Ellsworth Faris, Louis Wirth, and Clifford Shaw. They developed a body of sociological materials relative to urban culture that has had a lasting impact on the field.

The "Chicago school" viewpoint on urban culture is probably best expressed and summed up in an article published originally in 1938 by Louis Wirth, entitled, "Urbanism as a Way of Life."[17] Wirth's thesis is that population size, population density, and population diversity combine to produce a "culture of urbanism." He pointed to certain aspects

16. Arthur J. Vidich and Joseph Bensman, *Small Town in Mass Society* (Princeton, N.J.: Princeton University Press, 1958).

17. Louis Wirth, "Urbanism as a Way of Life," *American Journal of Sociology* 49 (1938):46–63.

of the culture: urbanites "meet one another in highly segmental roles"[18] rather than in total or personal relationships; they have highly specialized work tasks; symbols, such as those of role, occupation, or status become extremely important; formal social control mechanisms are more important than informal ones; many forms of activity are commercialized and bureaucratized; and kinship and family groups play a less important part in social experience. Additional analyses now available, such as those discussed in the last topic, indicate that many of these changes do not necessarily stem from population characteristics alone, but rather from the broader process of modernization.

Wirth, and the Chicago school in general, stressed the difficulties and problems of urban life: anomie and social disorganization, crime, mental illness, manipulative personal relationships, and distrustful responses. Their evaluation of urban life leans toward the negative, for a variety of reasons. The city they were analyzing, Chicago in the twenties and thirties, was in a stage of great stress and disorganization. They were studying mostly the inner-city residents, not those of the outer residential districts or the suburbs. Most of their subjects were urbanites not by choice but because they could not afford to live anywhere else. Moreover, as Maurice Stein has commented:

Many of these sociologists, like the large majority of the population of the time, had spent their early years in small towns. This was the form of community living with which they were most familiar and it provided a frame of reference within which the highly dissimilar features of Chicago social life were perceived and evaluated.[19]

In the last few decades sociologists have modified somewhat this negative view of

Louis Wirth (1897–1952) was a leading figure in the field of urban studies. A student of Robert Park, and later a professor at the University of Chicago, Wirth is best known for his studies of the life and social environment of Chicago residents. His special interest was in the bases of group life within urban communities; he sought the factors that enable men, often strangers to one another, to work together for some common goal. Wirth's best-known works are *The Ghetto* (1928) and the article "Urbanism as a Way of Life" (1938). *(Fabian Bachrach)*

urban culture. First of all, they are discovering that the city embraces a much wider variety of life styles, each with its own subculture, than was once realized. The Chicago school concentrated their studies on only one or two of these. Herbert Gans, a contemporary urban sociologist, has identified five very different life styles that can be found in the typical American central city area.[20] They are:

1. The "cosmopolites" : This group tends to be well-educated, to work in the professions or those industries allied with literature and art, such as advertising,

18. Louis Wirth, "Urbanism as a Way of Life," p. 51.
19. Maurice R. Stein, *The Eclipse of Community: An Interpretation of American Studies* (New York: Harper & Row, 1964), p. 15.

20. Herbert J. Gans, "Urbanism and Suburbanism as Ways of Life: A Reevaluation of Definitions," in *Human Behavior and Social Processes,* ed. Arnold M. Rose (Boston: Houghton Mifflin, 1962), chap. 6.

publishing, designing, and so on. On the average, their incomes are quite high. They choose to live in the city so as to be near its "cultural" facilities; they do not have strong ties to a local neighborhood.

2. The unmarried or childless: They also live in the city by choice, primarily because of its advantages as a place to meet people and to live an active but not home-centered social life. They move frequently, and usually leave the city altogether when they marry and have children. For these people the city is a temporary stopover in their journey to some suburb, and they typically have little sense of commitment to it.

3. The "ethnic villagers": These are the immigrants from other countries who remain largely unintegrated, continuing in many respects the way of life of the rural villages from which they came. In most cases they stay strictly within their own neighborhood and have little interest in, or information about, the rest of the city.

Although they reside in the city, they isolate themselves from significant contact with most city facilities, aside from workplaces. Their way of life differs sharply from Wirth's urbanism in its emphasis on kinship and the primary group, the lack of anonymity and secondary-group contacts, the weakness of formal organizations, and the suspicion of anyone and anything outside their neighborhood.[21]

4. The deprived: These are the poor, the nonwhite, the economically marginal, the divorced mothers of large families. They live in the city because they can find cheap housing in the slums and rooming houses, because welfare payments are usually larger in the cities than they are in rural areas, and because they hope that the city will provide a chance to find employment and improve their economic situation.

5. The "trapped": They are usually old people who cannot afford to move, who are living out their lives on their pensions. They often have lived in the city all their lives. Like the ethnic villagers, they identify strongly with their own neighborhood and seldom leave it.

In virtually every large city of America, these five life styles exist, and it is important to note that they consist of very divergent kinds of city experiences and attitudes toward urban life. For such different patterns to exist side by side as they do, within the same environment, requires a high degree of social organization in the city as a whole. Recent studies of the city have indicated that there is a great deal more organization and structure than the picture of Louis Wirth suggested; they have also tended to emphasize the more positive aspects of urban life. For example, a 1955 study by Scott Greer of two different Los Angeles neighborhoods reported that half the total sample visited relatives at least once a week, undermining the notion put forth by Louis Wirth that the extended family is very weak in the city.[22] In the abridgment in chapter 7, Harold Hodges reported another example of the importance of urban kinship networks, found among the working and lower-class residents of San Francisco. Gans's book, *The Urban Villagers,* is a study of the way a very traditional and agriculturally based style of life, that of rural Italian peasants, has been adapted to the city and yet still maintains intact much of its traditional social structure.[23] Even the once accepted conclusion that city life automatically leads to high rates of mental illness and other forms of pathology has been challenged, though the evidence on this matter is still too incomplete to allow conclusions to be drawn.

21. Herbert J. Gans, "Urbanism and Suburbanism . . . ," p. 309.

22. Scott Greer, "Urbanism Reconsidered: A Comparative Study of Local Areas in a Metropolis," *American Sociological Review* 21 (February 1956):19–25.

23. Herbert J. Gans, *The Urban Villagers* (New York: Free Press, 1962).

Slums are becoming ever greater problems in central cities: poor urban residents are joined by other poor people moving in from rural areas. The cities need to spend more money to provide for the needs of the poor but at the same time income from taxes decreases as the middle class leaves for the suburbs. *(Arthur Tress, Photo Researchers, Inc.)*

PROBLEMS OF OLDER CENTRAL CITIES

From another perspective, however, the central cities have never been more disorganized and problematic than they are today. In recent decades, public attention has been focused on the growing problems of the older American cities, such as Cleveland, Detroit, Washington, D.C., and Boston.

A major part of the problem of the older central cities is physical and economic, a combination of obsolescent physical facilities and a declining tax base. People who move out to the suburbs and then commute to work in the city do not for the most part pay city taxes. But they continue to use many of the city's facilities, such as public transportation, streets and sidewalks, shops, and so on. If the city government tries to solve the financial squeeze by raising its property taxes and utility fees, the end result is usually to drive even more middle-income families out to the suburbs in search of a cheaper place to live and own property. Raising commercial taxes causes business and industry to leave. So the city has to make do with the taxes it already has, and the level of public services, in the face of growing needs, and physical facilities (already old and obsolescent) continues to decline. Outmoded and inadequate transportation facilities cannot be modernized; police protection cannot be provided everywhere that it is needed; and schools cannot afford to hire a highly qualified staff.

Faced with this kind of deterioration, city residents either adapt or leave; and middle-class families have been leaving in great numbers. Those who stay are either the very rich or the poor. The rich can use their money to compensate for the city's problems. They can send their children to expensive private schools instead of to the public ones. They can drive their own cars rather than depend on public transportation. They can hire door-men and private guards to protect their property when police patrols are inadequate. Their wealth can insulate them from many of the problems of the city's decay.

The poor stay because they cannot afford to do anything else. Suburban living requires money for a down payment on a house, and a good credit rating to obtain a mortgage for the rest of the cost. It often means buying a car to get to work, the shopping center, or the children's school. The cost of the move alone is out of reach of most poor families.

The poor who stay in the city are joined by a steady influx of other persons with low incomes who come from rural areas or small towns in search of economic opportunity. This influx of new poor just about replaces, in terms of absolute numbers, the middle-class families who are leaving, so that the total population of central cities is remaining stable or even decreasing slightly. But the new residents have a much greater need for city services, and they cannot afford to pay as much for them. Thus the urban problem is mainly one of rising costs and needs for services in the face of diminishing resources.

Several of the abridgments in earlier chapters deal with living problems in the older central cities. Lee Rainwater's study of a housing project in St. Louis (chapter 7) is an accurate description of many of the problems that affect the inner city. The abridgment by Elliot Liebow (chapter 5) is a portrait of the way of life of the urban poor, large numbers of whom are black.

An increasing amount of federal and state tax money has been made available to help these older cities solve their problems of crime, poverty, and inadequate public facilities and services, but the amount is still far short of what is necessary. This is an area where the knowledge of sociologists can be put to use in public social planning.

THE SUBURBS

Today 37.2 percent of all Americans live in communities which are classified as suburban; 31.4 percent live outside all metropolitan areas, and 31.4 percent live in central cities. Significantly, suburban communities are the fastest growing communities in America; in a few more decades more than half of all Americans will be suburban, if the trend continues.

The *suburb,* a relatively small community adjacent to and dependent on a central city, is a creation of the twentieth century. It was made necessary by rapid urban growth and made possible by the advances in transportation (especially the automobile and mass transport) and by rising personal incomes. The central cities have more or less remained stable in population growth over the last several decades, and many have even declined. Today most of the actual growth of metropolitan areas is taking place in the suburbs. When we say that more and more people in this country are living in cities, we should be saying that they are living in suburbs. Sociologist Philip Hauser says:

Between 1900 and 1950, suburbia accounted for 45 percent of the total gain in metropolitan areas. During the last decade of this period 1940 to 1950, the suburbs contributed 61 percent of the total metropolitan growth, and during the fifties, about 80 percent.

As a result of these growth differentials, the relative size of central city and suburb has,

Suburbs are the fastest growing areas in America. Service centers, such as this shopping center, which grow up at easily accessible places around and within suburbs, are giving serious competition to central city commercial districts. *(Photo by Jane Latta)*

cial establishments and government offices expand their facilities to meet growing demand and begin to appropriate the space which was once residential, thus causing even more overcrowding in residential areas. The solution to this syndrome of problems in almost all cities in modernized countries has been to expand the territorial limits of the city and establish residential areas on its edges. Kingsley Davis has noted that

The outward movement of urban residences, of urban services and commercial establishments, and of light industry — all facilitated by improvements in motor transport and communications — has made it possible for huge agglomerations to keep on growing without the inconveniences of proportionate increases in density. In many ways the metropolis of three million today is an easier place to live and work than the city of five hundred thousand yesterday. Granted that the economic advantages of urban concentration still continue and still push populations in the direction of urbanization, the effect of metropolitan dispersion is thus to minimize the disadvantages of this continued urban growth.[25]

of course, been affected. In 1900 38 percent of the population of metropolitan areas was in suburbia. By 1950, the proportion had risen to 42 percent. In 1960, suburban population constituted 49 percent of metropolitan areas population.[24]

From one point of view, the suburbs are a solution to high population density in cities, which cuts down on the living space available to each individual and is always one of the basic problems a city must face. With high density, public facilities become overcrowded and break down from overuse. Housing becomes expensive and scarce. Commer-

The central city and the suburb are interdependent. The city is dependent on the suburbs for a significant part of its labor force and its retail shoppers; the suburbs are dependent on the central city for employment opportunities, and for many "cultural" and educational facilities. There is a growing movement of central city jobs and facilities to the suburbs, however, along with the people. Industries are moving out, attracted by the open space and the lower taxes. Local shopping centers are giving serious competition to central city commercial districts; local newspapers and radio and television stations make the suburbs less dependent on communications media of the cities. This trend toward

24. Philip M. Hauser, "The Growth of Metropolitan Areas in the United States," in James L. Price, ed., *Social Facts: Introductory Readings* (London: Macmillan, 1969), p. 412.

25. Kingsley Davis, "The Origin and Growth...," p. 436.

ever greater dispersion can be noticed especially in the newest American cities, such as Houston or Phoenix. These cities have minor "downtown" areas; they are actually made up of a connected series of separate residential areas interspersed with offices and shopping centers.

Suburbs tend to be stratified along lines of class and income differences. Some, such as Evanston, Illinois, or Arlington, Virginia, or Stanford, California, have a high percentage of residents with college degrees and large incomes; they are upper-middle-class suburbs. There are even a few upper-class suburbs — perhaps Darien, Connecticut, and Grosse Point, Michigan, would be examples of this type. Others are middle- or upper-lower class in composition. It is interesting to note that suburbs seem to retain their particular character and composition longer than city neighborhoods, which may change class composition fairly quickly.[26] Perhaps the suburbs' greater degree of isolation helps in this regard; so does the fact that property generally must be purchased, not rented, and the price keeps the residents within certain income lines. Building and zoning codes that regulate sizes and types of buildings and uses of property help to reinforce this effect.

We must be careful when we generalize about "suburbia," because suburbs differ greatly in the social climate they provide. Yet much has been written about the special "culture" of suburbia, often by contrast with urban culture. Since the typical suburbanite is married and has children living at home, much of the suburban culture centers around the family. Because suburbs tend to be composed of

26.   Reynolds Farley, "Suburban Persistence." *American Sociological Review* 29 (1964):38–47.

middle- and lower-middle-class people, they are more conservative, both politically and socially. They may also tend to put a premium on "getting ahead," especially in terms of financial success that can be displayed in consumer purchases, but this again is a characteristic of the middle class. Since a move to the suburbs is usually part of the process of moving up socially, it is not surprising that suburbanites display more upward mobility than do those who live in the central city.

We can see that there are some differences between the culture of the city and that of the suburbs, but we must exercise caution in drawing conclusions about the meaning of these differences. It is probably wrong to assume that moving from the city to the suburbs causes one to behave differently. It is more accurate to say that people move to a suburb because its culture conforms to their own, or to their aspirations. They may have behaved much the same way in the city, but there they were a cultural minority; in their suburb they become a majority. A study by Gans supports the idea that even though the city and the suburbs differ somewhat in their culture, the move to the suburbs does not usually mean a significant social change for the individuals who make the move.[27]

The accompanying abridgment by William Dobriner points to many of the values and attitudes characteristic of the middle- and upper-middle-class suburbanite. It is also an interesting study of how these values conflict in many instances with the more rural attitudes of the native townspeople.

27.   Herbert J. Gans, "Effects of the Move from City to Suburbs" in *The Urban Condition,* ed. Leonard J. Duhl and John Powell (New York: Basic Books, 1963), pp. 184–198.

WILLIAM M. DOBRINER
The Natural History of a Reluctant Suburb

From *The Yale Review* 49 (Spring 1960): 399–412. Copyright the Yale University Press.

Introduction

This study discusses the ways in which population changes have affected the social patterns of a small community, and how the institutions of government, religion, and education have changed in response to the changing population. Dobriner's study, and its implications, are especially relevant today, when census figures show that more and more small towns like the one discussed here are being turned, reluctantly or not, into suburbs for the major cities.

The first 300 years

What it means for a long-established village to be suburbanized can be seen from the recent history of a community here called "Old Harbor." It is a real place, in the New England area, on the Atlantic Coast. Over 300 years old, Old Harbor lies at the foot of a curving valley between two green necks of land stretching into the sea. Its history resembles that of many another New England village. In 1662, for example, a "morals committee" of six "respectable" citizens and the minister carefully scrutinized all new settlers who arrived in the community. A newcomer who failed to pass the committee's standards of morality and respectability was asked to leave. So Old Harbor's tradition of skepticism and caution as to the worth of recent arrivals is anchored in over 300 years of experience.

In its early years, Old Harbor served as the nexus of an agrarian and colonial society. The village prospered but remained comparatively changeless in some fundamental ways—it continued to be a Yankee village of industrious merchants, seamen, farmers, and craftsmen. In time more land was cleared, more ships were built, and small but vigorously independent men set up industries and crafts, farms, and homes. Yet the essential ethos of the village remained constant—Yankee, Protestant, independent, cautious, shrewd, calculating, hard working, and conservative.

By the middle of the nineteenth century, in a society where so many persons, traditions, and things were new, Old Harbor had a heritage of 200 years to look back upon. But change was imminent. In 1867 the railroad came to the village and became a serious competitor of marine transportation, and thereafter the harbor declined as a vital force in the village's economy. Even more ominous was the fact that 36.6 miles from the village lay the borders of a city.

The first invaders of Old Harbor were members of the new industrial aristocracy that emerged in the decades after the Civil War. By the turn of the century, Old Harbor had become their carefully guarded preserve. They bought the old farms and cleared away acres for their summer playgrounds and gigantic estates. They fenced off two- and three-hundred-acre parcels and created separate dukedoms populated by communities of servants and laborers.

On the surface, things had not changed much. The old inhabitants kept to themselves. They ran the village as they always had, but supplied the estates with provisions and such services as they were capable of providing. Though there was little basic understanding and compatibility between the "high society" of the nation and the "high society" of the village, the coming of the estates brought a new prosperity to Old Harbor and helped to take up the slack left by the decline of the fishing and whaling industries and the harbor in general.

By the 1930's, the age of the palatial estates, begun seventy-five years earlier, was about over. The huge mansions had served their purpose. They had proclaimed the grandeur of American industrial growth and had bestowed calculated and lavish honor on those who built them. Now they were in the hands of the third generation or had been sold to second and third buyers, and each time a portion of the land had been sliced off in the transaction. In addition, government action unfriendly to the rich in the New Deal decade was making it difficult to maintain huge houses; income and inheritance taxes were forcing the estate holders to sell their property or simply to let the place go to seed. A few were given to educational institutions and one or two more were turned over to Old Harbor

Township as museums or public parks. But there is little contemporary use for a decaying 30-room castle with its entourage of outbuildings, so they wasted away in their crabgrass kingdoms, the gargantuan headstones of an age of excess.

Suburbanites and villagers

After World War II population that had been trapped in the city during the war years exploded into the country neighboring Old Harbor. In ten years, the number of people in this "rural" county passed a million and made it one of the most rapidly growing areas in the United States. In the ten years from 1945 to 1955, Old Harbor Township doubled its population, and the village itself has now absorbed between two and three times the number it had in 1940. In just ten years, a 300-year-old village, with many of the descendants of the original founders still living there, underwent a social shock that wrenched it from whatever remained of the patterns of the past.

As Old Harbor soaks up the steady stream of suburban migrants, it has taken on a physical pattern quite different from the community of twenty years ago. Toward the center of town is the "old village," the nucleus of the "oldtimer" community. There the streets are lined with aging oaks, elms and maples. The houses are comparatively large and reflect the architectural trends of 150 years—authentic and carefully preserved saltboxes and Cape Cods, two-story clapboards or brick Colonials, straight and angular American Gothics, and prissy frivolous Victorians. Each house proclaims an identity of its own. In front of an occasional Colonial or cottage a small sign will read "1782" or "1712."

Out along the periphery of the old village, up on what were farmlands five years ago, out along the land necks reaching toward the bay, down in the cover valleys, and up among the woody ridges, range the dwellings of suburbia. Here among the asbestos shingle or "hand-split shakes,"

the plastic and stainless steel, the picture window, the two-car garages and pint-sized dining areas, the weathered wagon wheel and ersatz strawberry barrel, live the suburbanites in their multi-level reconstructions of Colonial America.

No longer is there enough space in Old Harbor. You can't park your car on Main Street any more; there may not be room in church if you arrive late on Sunday; classrooms are overcrowded; and you have to wait your turn for telephones to be installed in your new house. But these are simply the unsurprising results of sudden growth, and the Old Harborites are on their way to solving many of them. They have built schools and plan more. They are tearing down bits of the old village surrounding Main Street and are putting in parking lots. Some churches are adding wings or erecting entirely new buildings. They have added policemen and fire engines, and have widened the critical streets. The physical problems, in general, are understood and are being coped with realistically.

The fundamental schism between the world of the oldtimers and the world of the newcomers makes a problem that is less obvious but more important and harder to cope with.

In their occupational characteristics, the old settlers range between the middle and upper-middle class. The majority are employed in Old Harbor as merchants, small manufacturers, and businessmen. The rest are mostly white collar people of various persuasions who are employed either in Old Harbor or the neighboring, highly suburbanized county. Less than 20% commute into the central city.

The average villager is middle-aged, married, and probably has two children either finishing high school or going to college. As a group the oldtimers' formal education did not go beyond high school, but they want their children to go to college and they will generally pick one of the better ones. About half of the oldtimers are

Protestant, a third are Catholic, and 7% are Jewish. The Catholic and Jewish populations represent the changes in Old Harbor's ethnic or religious character that began at the turn of the century. The median family income for the oldtimers in 1955 was $6700; roughly $2300 over the national median for that year. Obviously not all oldtimers in Old Harbor are high-school educated, regular church attendants, and securely anchored in the white collar occupations, but enough are to justify the image of the oldtimers as localistic, Protestant, economically comfortable, conservative, and middle class.

The suburbanites are another story. They are a high-income group ($9700 a year) of professional men and executives. Ninety-seven percent arrived in Old Harbor married and almost 94% bought houses there. They average two grade-school children per family. Only a fourth are Roman Catholics; the great majority are Protestants, although a few more Jews have entered the community in recent years. Nearly four out of every ten of the newcomers were born outside the state. Two-thirds have been exposed to a college education. Close to half commute to the central city, and another third are employed in the county adjacent to the city.

Though the villagers are economically comfortable, they are nonetheless rather stationary on the income ladder. They are pretty well frozen into an occupation dead end. The suburbanites, on the other hand, are upward bound—their jobs pay better and carry more prestige than the villagers'. For them the primary world is the metropolitan area. They work there, play there, and their most intimate friends live there. To the villager, Old Harbor represents continuity between generations, stability instead of the city's chaos, and a place of permanence in a universe of bewildering change. The suburbanite sees in the village a weekend away from the advertising agency or the pilot's compartment. He experiences

Old Harbor as a series of isolated, fragmented, unconnected social situations.

Perhaps the greatest single issue separating villager from suburbanite has been the school problem. With the tripling of the school population, Old Harbor has been faced with an intensive building program. Since they are essentially realists in their village microcosm, the oldtimers have reluctantly admitted the need for more schools. But the basic and decisive issue has not been whether to build more schools or not, but what kind of schools to build and what kind of education the children should have.

In their approach to this question, the villagers are traditionalists and conservative. They see a good education as including the basic skills taught by a dedicated but maidenly teacher in a plain school building. The suburbanites, on the other hand, are educational radicals; they are irrepressible spenders and cult-like in their dedication to the cause of modern education. It is an axiom among the oldtimers that the more costly a pending proposition is the more the newcomers will take to it, and they are not entirely wrong.

For the newcomers, anything that is educationally worthwhile must also be very expensive. "After all, you get what you pay for." The villagers, on the other hand, will battle the frills and extravagances and will turn down "excessive" curricular and building proposals. Eventually a compromise is worked out. But in the suburbias of the upper-middle class, education is the cohesive issue around which a consciousness of kind develops among the newcomers. For many, education seems to have taken the place of religion.

While the newcomers have taken over the PTA and infiltrated the school board, the villagers continue to control the churches. Suburbanites usually join the PTA before they become members of a church, though they swell the numbers of those attending religious services. But even in the ranks of the devout, there have been indications of a schism between oldtimers and suburbanites.

This is not the whole story. A few years back, one of the most fashionable churches of Old Harbor made some sympathetic overtures to a purely newcomer religious group—Jews of the Reform group who were conducting their services in an empty store on Main Street. The minister of an old Protestant church offered the facilities of his church to the Jewish newcomers. The Jews happily accepted the offer. This not only brought the two worlds together, but the Protestant and localistic villagers and the Jewish, cosmopolitan suburbanites even sponsored joint functions together. The differences between the villagers and suburbanites are not insurmountable, nor are the two separated by an impenetrable curtain of prejudice and ignorance.

The newcomers have largely ignored the formal political organizations of Old Harbor. The oldtimers fill almost all the political offices, where they serve to balance the limited and self-interested objectives of the civic associations [newcomers' organizations] against the broader needs of the village and the township. But in this capacity the oldtimers are more than oldtimers; they are also politicians. Having learned that the suburbanites are amazingly perceptive on the level of neighborhood self-interest, the politicians throw an occasional sop to the militant civic associations, with an eye to the coming elections. Though the suburbanites are circumscribed in their interests, they are nonetheless organized, and can marshal massive political displeasure at the polls. As a consequence, the villager politicians must somehow walk a tightrope, balancing the political expediency of pleasing the newcomers against their own desire to keep the village what it was.

Conclusion

The important change in Old Harbor was not the increase in population, which was great, but the change in type of resident. The newcomers were far different from the traditional Yankees who preceded them. The main problems in the town resulted from the diverse outlooks of the two groups. In a like manner our central cities are undergoing a great change in type of resident. What are some similarities and differences between the problems faced by this small suburb and those of the large central city?

TOPIC

4 SOME SOCIAL TRENDS IN MODERN ECONOMIES

The economic development of a society creates many kinds of broad social change, as we have seen. In the economic sphere, industrialization and urbanization change the traditional way of doing work, create new places where it is done, develop new jobs, and give employment opportunities to new groups of people. We will discuss these trends in the first section of this topic.

Karl Marx pointed out that the economic in-

WOMEN IN THE LABOR FORCE: 1940 TO 1971

Year	Female Labor Force (1,000)				Female labor force as percent of female population
	Total	Single	Married	Widowed or divorced	
1940	13,840	6,710	5,040	2,090	27.4
1950	17,795	5,621	9,273	2,901	31.4
1960	22,515	5,401	13,485	3,629	34.8
1971	31,681	7,187	19,986	4,508	42.5

Statistical Abstract of the United States, 1972.

The number of working women has steadily increased throughout the twentieth century. The most dramatic rise has been in the number of married women who choose to continue their careers after marriage.

terests of those who own land and factories are always in conflict with the interests of those who work for them. This conflict has been further complicated in modern society by the application of the bureaucratic system of organization to both management and labor. The man who speaks for the company often does not own any share of it, and the man who speaks for the workers may not actually do any productive work in the factory; both are bureaucratic officials. We will take up the changing conditions of labor-management relations in the second section.

The concluding section will be devoted to an examination of the social impact of the technology associated with industrialization and economic development.

THE LABOR FORCE

We use the term *labor force* to refer to those people who work regularly and receive money in exchange for their work. This eliminates most of the very young and the very old; it also eliminates many women who devote themselves to the "nonprofit" occupations of housework and child care. Altogether, the total labor force of the world is now about 1⅓ billion people, not quite half the world's population. It is largely composed of able-bodied men, and about three-fourths of them are engaged in agricultural rather than industrial work. This worldwide average reflects conditions in countries like Burundi, an African nation where 98 percent of the popu-

lation lives in rural areas, or Laos, with 85 percent of the population living in rural areas. In technologically advanced countries, such as the United States and Great Britain, the labor force is located mostly in urbanized places and only a very few people still work on the farm—5 percent in the United States and 1.5 percent in Great Britain.[28]

In the United States, the following trends in the composition of the labor force seem especially important:[29]

(1) The labor force is much better educated than ever before. This is partly the result of widespread educational opportunity. It also stems from the demands of modern technology; more and more jobs require education or training. In 1952, the American labor force had completed on the median 10.9 years of school. Just 15 years later the median had increased to 12.3 years. That means that the average American worker is a high school graduate, a fact which by itself says a great deal about the changing patterns of work in this country.

(2) More and more women are entering the labor force. Today about 35 percent of the labor force is female, and about 32 million women, or 30 percent of the female popula-

28. All statistics are from United Nations Statistical Office, *Demographic Yearbook, 1972* (New York: United Nations, 1972).

29. Statistics on the U.S. labor force are from U.S. Bureau of the Census, *Statistical Abstract of the United States, 1971* (Washington, D.C.: Government Printing Office, 1971).

EMPLOYED PERSONS BY MAJOR OCCUPATION GROUP: 1950 TO 1972*

Occupation group	1950	1960	1970	1972
White-collar workers	22,373	28,726	37,997	38,892
Blue-collar workers	23,336	24,211	27,791	27,744
Service workers	6,535	8,349	9,712	11,066
Farmworkers	7,408	5,395	3,126	2,926

*In thousands

Statistical Abstract of the United States, 1972.

Automation and agricultural mechanization have shifted the distribution of our work force. Since 1920, the number of farmers has been drastically reduced, while the number of service workers has nearly doubled. Increases in blue-collar jobs are far exceeded by newly expanded white-collar occupations as machines take over many of the traditional assembly-line tasks, and the need for clerical, technical, and administrative workers grows.

tion, are employed outside the home. Three-fifths of these working women are married. Working wives often contribute substantially to family incomes: half of all families with incomes over $10,000 a year have working wives; in families with incomes below $3,000, only 14 percent of wives are working. A study of the reasons women work showed that it was usually not out of a stark financial need, such as that caused by an unemployed husband, but because the family wanted the money for such things as a second car, the children's education, or a bigger house in a better neighborhood.[30] Other factors involved are the trends toward later marriage, smaller families, and more education for women — these mean that women have more years when they are free to work, and more training to enable them to get jobs with higher rates of pay. As norms and values change to reflect these new circumstances, it is likely that even more women will enter the labor force. However, although the number of women in the labor force is increasing, women are not distributed evenly throughout all kinds and levels of occupations. They are most likely to occupy the low status and low pay positions: only 8 percent of all professional workers are women; only 5 percent of those with incomes over $10,000 a year are women; women exec-

utives are only 4 percent of the total of those employed at that level.[31]

(3) More new jobs are being created in the fields of personal and professional service than in industry. The service occupations include such areas as banking, advertising, the professions, sales, household work, education, and government. More than 50 percent of the labor force in America is now engaged in service occupations and the proportion will be even higher in the future. The United States is the first nation to achieve such a "service economy." A recent estimate of the annual job openings through 1975 shows that the greatest demand will be for stenographers and secretaries, with about 237,000 new openings per year. Second are salespeople, of whom 175,000 more will be needed annually. We will need about 121,000 household workers, 113,000 teachers, and 100,000 hospital attendants. By contrast, we will need only 12,000 new machinists, 900 boilermakers, 6,000 printers and typographers.[32]

One of the main reasons for this shift in job opportunities, of course, is automation. Many tasks in industry which were once done by people are now done by machines. But at

30.　Carl Rosenfeld and Vers C. Perrella, "Why Women Start and Stop Working: A Study in Mobility," *Monthly Labor Review,* September 1965.

31.　Caroline Bird, *Born Female* (New York: David McKay, 1968), pp. 82–83.

32.　*The New York Times Encyclopedic Almanac* (New York: The New York Times Co., 1972) p. 653.

the same time, because of industrial expansion, new jobs are created for those who service industry: employment agencies, banking houses and insurance firms, computer services and so on. This trend will almost certainly increase as time goes on. Many companies today employ unnecessary industrial workers, because social pressures prevent them from firing large numbers of long-time employees; but as these people retire, they will be replaced by machines rather than people.

(4) New occupations and occupational levels are being opened to minority group members. Nonwhite and ethnic minorities are today beginning to occupy a greater proportion of the jobs that require skilled manual labor, and the lower level office jobs. Although they are still overrepresented in low pay and low status jobs and underrepresented at the highest levels, the change is noticeable.

Part of this change is due to social factors such as a general reduction in prejudice and discrimination and increased opportunities for education. Other reasons for the change are directly related to working patterns. For example, in new areas of technology it is easier for all minority group members to obtain jobs. The need for workers makes employers anxious to hire all qualified applicants and patterns of discrimination have not yet been established.

LABOR–MANAGEMENT RELATIONS

Relationships among industry owners, labor, and management have undergone significant change. First, the distinction between owners and managers is one that came with industrialization; before that time production was carried out from start to finish by a single person or family, who also received all the profits from the process. Industrialization created two different groups of bosses: those who were rich enough to afford the machinery and the plant to go into the manufacturing business, and those who managed the business

on a salary. The daily conduct of most businesses today is in the hands of trained professional managers, who are paid a salary and given promotions on the basis of their performance record. At the same time, the amount of capital required in large modern industries is so large that no single "owner" can supply it all, so industries have become "publicly owned" corporations with hundreds or thousands of stockholders. It is now common for many of the employees of a company also to be among its owners, through stock purchasing programs at work.

The most striking trend of the twentieth century in the area of labor is widespread unionization. The fight of workers for the opportunity to form unions began in the early nineteenth century, in the factories. The principal new development in today's unionization movement is that it has spread to nonindustrial workers. For example, agricultural workers are forming unions; the most famous case is the United Farm Workers' union in California, headed by Cesar Chavez, which is trying to improve the wages and working conditions of migrant farm workers. A trend toward unionization of those who work in service fields, even professional ones, is evident. Several teachers' unions exist. Social caseworkers in New York City have formed a union to represent them in their dealings with their employer, the city government. Sanitation workers, mailmen, and transit workers are other examples of government employees who now have strong and effective unions. The specialization and interdependence of urban activities makes large cities especially vulnerable to the effects of strikes by workers in such services as mass transit or garbage removal, and so the union movements there have been quite effective in achieving their goals.

Unionization is in part a response to the bureaucratization of industry. Small, locally owned businesses often have more flexible forms of organization, less rigid ways of doing things. When an organization grows larger it

The unionization movement began in factories in the nineteenth century, but today it has spread to nonindustrial, service, and even professional fields. Workers in these fields are seeking ways to deal with the growing bureaucratization of the organizations in which they work. (*Steve Schapiro,* LIFE Magazine, © *Time Inc.*)

begins to need routine work patterns, and much of its organization and activity may become highly institutionalized, as we discussed in chapter 6. Contact between labor and management becomes limited to the scope of their business roles; their private lives are entirely separated from one another, often in different communities.

In the past, bitter clashes between unionized labor and management were often marked by violence and destruction on both sides. Unionization usually starts as a response to some specific problems or grievances of the workers, and the resulting relationship between unions and management is marked by hostility and fear. However, in time, the union itself becomes a mature organization with a large membership and a bureaucratic pattern of organization. Then its viewpoint tends to move closer to that of the management. Conflicts lessen, and the relationship changes, with each side trying to accommodate the other. Eventually, union–management bargaining can even become ritualized. Generally today it is only when a union is relatively new that bitter conflict or violent conduct characterizes the relationship between labor and management.

THE SOCIAL IMPACT OF TECHNOLOGY

The new technology that developed in the course of industrialization has altered man's personal relationship to his work, still one of the most important (and time-consuming) segments of his life. Karl Marx was one of the first to investigate this change.[33] He theorized that factory technology and the resulting specialization of tasks made the worker feel powerless and alienated. In preindustrial times, the quality of the end product depended entirely on the worker's skill in his craft, his judgment, and his experience. In a modern factory, quality, speed, and accuracy of production are determined by machines; men perform only a few repetitive tasks—the worker is subordinate to the machine. In an assembly line type of factory, for example, the work moves at an established pace controlled by a machine, and the humans must accommodate themselves to it. Marx concluded that men working under such conditions cannot take any satisfaction in the work itself, nor can they identify themselves with their job or their company. They are merely putting in the time and effort needed to earn a living.

Marx's view was widely accepted for many years, and it is still seen as valid for many kinds of industrial work. It is particularly applicable to jobs on an assembly line. These, however, constitute only a small fraction of the manual labor jobs in the United States—about 5 percent—and an even smaller fraction of all industrial jobs.

Several recent trends have served to reduce the workers' alienation which was so widespread in Marx's time. First, automation and other new technologies have made industry so efficient that a smaller labor force can produce a larger output. Only about 40 percent of today's labor force actually works in industry. Many workers have been freed from the repetitive tasks of the factory or the drudgery of hard manual labor; they now work in service positions, where individual skills and attitudes are of much greater importance. A television repairman, for instance, has ample opportunity for the exercise of his own judgment, and the use of his own initiative. His work provides many satisfactions, including that of seeing his work immediately appreciated by the customer whose set is restored to working order. Second, even industrial workers today are likely to have some degree of responsibility in their work. For example, in certain kinds of automated processes the worker operates a number of control boards and instrument panels which give him a feeling of control and involvement quite different from that of the assembly line worker.

Changing technology and job situations are not the only reasons for changes in the relationship of men to their work. The increasing bureaucratization of modern businesses has also affected this relationship. There are few people, even at the executive level, who really have a clear conception of exactly how their work fits into the total work of the company, or who see the actual results of their own work. With specialization of labor, so many are involved in any one project that no one can say, "This is mine; I made it." Many people never see, perhaps never even know about, the end product of their labor. Some administrators and supervisors—the proverbial bureaucrats—do not even do much productive work, which is one reason they are inclined to measure their performance in terms of memos written or phone calls made, or some other concrete and visible work product. This effect of specialization, on all levels, is one which business today is seeking ways to combat.

So far, we have concentrated on the way modern technology has affected man's relationship to his work. We should also look at the way it has affected the structure of his society. The attitudes, the habits of thought, the kinds of behavior that men learn at their jobs carry over into other fields. Also, many of the products of modern technology influence the way we live—the telephone, television, computers, all affect our daily lives.

For example, communication between people exists on a much wider scale than was formerly possible. Modern communication

33. See Karl Marx and Friedrich Engels *The Communist Manifesto* (Baltimore: Penguin Books, 1969).

media are so swift and efficient and extensive that no one is isolated, no matter where or how he lives. People on the farms in Iowa know all about the battles in the Middle East, the debates in Washington, and the new styles in Paris and New York. Upper-class people who have never been near a slum in their lives find out what life there is like by watching a television documentary or reading a magazine. Partly for this reason there has been an increase in social awareness and perhaps political participation. This same communication has expanded the scope of our knowledge and made us more education-oriented. Scientists say there have been more discoveries made in the last forty years than in all previous years of man's history.

Partly due to our great technological successes, the notion of progress is deeply embedded in our culture. We assume that a better way to do things will be continually invented and that answers to our problems will be discovered. We accept many kinds of change easily if we see it as progress, an attitude incomprehensible to people who live in a tradition-bound agricultural society. As a consequence of our acceptance of change, technological innovation acquires a certain degree of inevitability—if something can be done it is done. A highly industrialized society includes many people working on the research and development of new products. Once they work out a new product, there is a strong pressure to go ahead with its manufacture; the fact that it can be done makes it desirable to do. As our technological ability increases, many new moral issues will be raised for our society to face. Examples of possible problems are those raised by organ transplants, by the synthesis of genetic material, and by the freezing of dead people to await future regeneration.

SUMMARY

Settled *communities,* groupings of people organized around residential units and based on daily patterns of interaction, began with the development of agriculture about 10,000 years ago. Originally, they were small settlements organized in terms of kinship ties or primary associations. As technological advances promoted the development of food surpluses and improved methods of transportation, an increasing number of people were freed from the task of food producing, and agricultural communities underwent a basic transformation: specialization and the development of new institutions and more formal mechanisms of social control replaced the more informal kin-based structural networks. This urban revolution was further stimulated by the development of iron and the extension of trade networks; but the growth of urban populations was still limited by relatively inefficient agricultural methods, the absence of large-scale manufacturing, poorly developed political and cultural organization, poor health conditions, and the persistence of traditional kin and feudal ties. Although the *preindustrial city* had a relatively high population density and great diversity, it did not develop extensive occupational and geographical specialization; social control was maintained through a rigid class or caste system rather than through a formalized legal system.

"Modern" societies dominated by huge metropolitan areas are the product of *industrialization* and *urbanization.* In the West mass production was stimulated by technological innovations such as the steam engine and the internal combustion engine, by improved methods of transportation, and by the availability of a large labor force. Centralized government helped to implement the natural system of supply and demand in the marketplace through a *laissez-faire* policy, and capitalistic enterprise was encouraged by the Protestant ethic of self-discipline, hard work, competitiveness, and individual initiative. More recently automation and the use of computers have again transformed the production process, and many other aspects of our society as a consequence.

Many nations in the Third World are today just beginning to modernize. While industrialization in the West evolved slowly, these societies must adapt quickly to a fully developed culture that conflicts with many of the existing values and beliefs in non-Western societies. Overpopulation, the absence of centralized political controls, and a history of colonialism in these areas create further problems. Sociologists have identified a number of basic conditions necessary for economic development: a set of values and attitudes favoring economic growth, availability and mobility of productive resources, economic and political stability, concentration of labor and markets in cities, and efficient business corporations. However, modernization has not followed an identical pattern in all societies. In India urbanization has outstripped industrialization, creating serious food shortages. Iran, in contrast, has relied on vast oil and mineral deposits to achieve widespread modernization without industrialization. In general, however, urbanization is greatest where the economy is industrialized and rationalized. Cities in turn play a modernizing role by promoting mass education, cultural pluralism, and the growth of a middle class.

In spite of the diversity of existing conditions, social scientists have identified a number of ways in which modernization affects a country's culture and social structure: 1) economic relationships are separated from social relationships; 2) economic activities shift from agricultural and extractive to manufacturing and service areas; 3) new occupational roles emerge; 4) specialization necessitates administrative organization; 5) geographic and social mobility increase; 6) stratification systems are increasingly based on wealth and occupation, on achieved rather than ascribed status; 7) the kin network is limited more to nuclear family

ties and social control becomes more formalized; 8) religious activity becomes more limited and other social institutions become secularized; 9) there is a growth of mass communication, education, and mass culture; and 10) usually political power becomes more centralized and bureaucratized.

All of these trends are well developed in contemporary American society, transforming us from a nation of isolated and independent small communities to an urbanized culture in which activities and relationships are increasingly fragmented and specialized. Within a typical American city, a rich diversity of life-styles can be found: 1) the well-educated "cosmopolites" who are drawn to the city's cultural facilities; 2) the unmarried and childless who will eventually have families and move to the suburbs; 3) the "ethnic villagers" or unassimilated immigrants; 4) the deprived who are drawn by cheap housing, welfare, and the hope of employment; 5) the "trapped" old people who identify strongly with their neighborhood and cannot afford to move out.

Increasingly, our older central cities are confronted with rising costs in meeting the growing needs for public services and various facilities; simultaneously, they are faced with diminishing economic resources as middle-class families try to escape urban deterioration by fleeing to the suburbs. While the population of central cities has remained stable or declined over the past few decades, the suburbs, small communities adjacent to and dependent on the central city, have grown enormously. The suburbs tend to be composed of middle- and lower-middle-class people who are relatively conservative and whose life-styles center around the family. Suburban communities are highly stratified along class and income lines, however, and differ greatly in the social climate they provide.

Economic development has had a broad social impact on our country. The labor force is much better educated and includes a greater number of women. As production has become more automated more new jobs have been created in the personal and professional service fields than in industry. New occupations and opportunities are being opened to minority group members. Unionization has increased, particularly in the service and professional fields, partly in response to the bureaucratization of industry. Automation and bureaucratization have changed the relationship of men to their work. New technology has freed many workers from the repetitive tasks of the factory or the drudgery of hard manual labor. Mass communication has expanded the scope of our knowledge and increased our social awareness. Finally, our technological successes have committed us to the notion of progress, a goal that we pursue relentlessly and sometimes with unintended consequences that raise serious moral questions.

GLOSSARY

Community A grouping of people organized around residential units and based on daily patterns of interaction. (page 564)

Differentiation The process in which functions formerly fused into one social structure develop into new and separate social structures; the systems of the society become more specialized. (page 577)

Industrialization Changes in methods of production, and in economic and social organization, which result from the introduction of power-driven machinery and the factory system. (page 568)

Labor force That part of the population which is able to work, including those actually working full- or part-time and those unemployed but seeking employment. (page 597)

Overurbanization A situation in which people move to cities at a faster rate than the economy can support. (page 573)

Suburb A relatively small community that is part of an urbanized area; it is adjacent to and dependent on a central city. (page 590)

Urbanism Patterns of culture and social structure which are characteristic of cities. (page 586)

Urbanization 1. The movement of people from rural to urban areas, and the resulting increase in the proportion of a population that resides in urban rather than rural places. (page 568) 2. The spread of urban patterns of cultural and social structure. (page 576)

SUGGESTED READINGS AND RELATED RESOURCES

I READINGS IN SOCIOLOGY

Burgess, E., and D. Bogue, eds. *Contributions to Urban Sociology.* Chicago: University of Chicago Press, 1964. This is a collection of the best of the Chicago school of urban sociology.

Gans, Herbert. *The Levittowners: Ways of Life and Politics in a New Suburb.* New York: Random House, Pantheon, 1967. In this study of a new suburb, Gans traces the emergence and development of local institutions. He concentrates especially on the evolution of a political system and how it was used in mediation between various citizen groups involved in planning the community.

Greer, Scott A. *The Emerging City: Myth and Reality.* New York: Free Press, 1962. In this attempt to formulate a new frame of reference for the study of cities, Greer shows how politics, economics, demography, stratification, and individual personalities fit into the urban structure, and how the urban structure relates to the larger society.

Gutman, Robert, and David Popenoe, eds.

Neighborhood, City, and Metropolis: An Integrated Reader in Urban Sociology. New York: Random House, 1970. A comprehensive collection of important articles in the fields of urban and community sociology.

Hauser, Philip M., and Leo Schnore, eds. *The Study of Urbanization.* New York: John Wiley and Sons, 1965. This reader includes essays describing economic, geographic, and political studies of individual cities, and four essays which summarize current research in comparative urban studies.

Hoselitz, Berthold F., ed. *The Progress of Underdeveloped Areas.* Chicago: University of Chicago Press, 1966. Experts from an extremely broad range of fields have contributed papers to this collection, which focuses on industrialization and economic growth. Topics include methods of training a population for industrial occupations, culture lag, and the effects of industrialization upon the personalities of workers and upon the international market.

Jacobs, Norman. *The Origin of Modern Capitalism and Eastern Asia.* Hong Kong: Hong Kong University Press, 1958. Jacobs has investigated the basic social values of China and Japan to try to explain why Japan developed industrial capitalism and China did not. The author maintains the position that institutions are based on social values.

Kerr, Clark, et al. *Industrialism and Industrial Man.* 2d ed. New York: Oxford University Press, 1964. This book contains a careful analysis of the cultural conflicts which may arise from industrialization. Labor–management relations in newly modernizing nations and techniques for developing a labor force are examined, and suggestions are given for minimizing disruptive changes in the lives of the workers.

Lerner, Daniel. *The Passing of Traditional Society: Modernizing the Middle East.* New York: Free Press, 1964. Through a detailed description of the process of modernization in each of the major Middle-Eastern nations, Lerner explains how some of the most important cultural characteristics distinctive to each country have affected the process of modernization. He places special emphasis upon the effects of the mass media as an agent of change.

Lynd, Robert S., and Helen M. Lynd. *Middletown.* New York: Harcourt Brace Jovanovich, 1929. In an ambitious study of the "interwoven trends that are the life of a small American city," the Lynds describe the occupational structure, economics, home and family life, socialization, leisure-time activities, religious life, politics, and community activities of Muncie, Indiana.

———. *Middletown in Transition: A Study in Cultural Conflicts.* New York: Harcourt Brace Jovanovich, 1937. This follow-up study of Muncie 10 years later notes the changes that had taken place, or were taking place, as a result of the 1930s Depression.

Mumford, Lewis. *The City in History.* New York: Harcourt Brace Jovanovich, 1961. Mumford traces the development of cities in the West, considering their forms and their functions for society. He also looks optimistically at some of the possibilities for cities in the future.

Reissman, L. *The Urban Process: Cities in Industrial Societies.* New York: Free Press, 1964. Reissman writes about urbanization and industrialization, from a perspective which criticizes existing sociological approaches for their oversimplification of theories about life within the city.

Seeley, J. R., R. A. Sim, and E. W. Loosley. *Crestwood Heights.* New York: John Wiley (Paper), 1967. This book is the result of a five-year study of a suburb. It provides insight into the life styles and daily lives of the suburbanite, and the researchers develop a theory about the culture of suburban life.

Shepard, Jon M. *Automation and Alienation.* Cambridge, Mass.: M.I.T. Press, 1970. Shepard's hypothesis is that the less specialized a job is, the less alienated the worker will be. His study compared office and factory workers, analyzing such factors as the kind of freedom and control they had, the degree of self-involvement, how meaningful their jobs were to them.

Sjoberg, G. *The Preindustrial City.* New York: Free Press (Paper), 1960. Sjoberg analyzes preindustrial cities and societies from a sociological perspective.

Smelser, Neil J. *Social Change in the Industrial Revolution.* Chicago: University of Chicago Press, 1959. Smelser traces the process of differentiation of occupations and its effects upon social structure. His study is based on historical data of the British cotton industry and the family economics of its laborers.

Sobin, Dennis P. *The Future of the American*

Suburbs: Survival or Extinction. Port Washington, N.Y.: Kennikat Press, 1971. The author discusses the misconceptions and controversies surrounding the decreasingly functional suburbs.

Stein, Maurice. *The Eclipse of Community.* Princeton, N.J.: Princeton University Press, 1960. Stein critically analyzes the problems and future of American community life by drawing upon the major sociological studies of communities done in the last fifty years.

Vidich, Arthur J., and J. Bensman. *Small Town in Mass Society: Class, Power and Religion in a Rural Community.* Rev. ed. Princeton, N.J.: Princeton University Press (Paper), 1968. From the point of view of Vidich and Bensman, the small town way of life is strongly influenced by urban and mass culture and is therefore not the "polar opposite" of city life.

Warren, R. *The Community in America.* Chicago: Rand McNally, 1963. In this book, Warren analyzes the changing pattern of American community life and attempts to define characteristics common to many different types of American communities.

————, ed. *Perspectives on the American Community.* Chicago: Rand McNally, 1966. In this reader, basic approaches to community studies are discussed, and the various structures and processes of three main types of communities are analyzed.

Wilensky, Harold L., and Charles N. Lebeaux. *Industrial Society and Social Welfare.* New York: Russell Sage Foundation, 1958. Wilensky and Lebeaux have studied the consequences of industrialism and capitalism for workers, stressing such problems as unemployment, family disorganization, and delinquency. They point out how the modern welfare system grew up in response to these problems.

Wirth, Louis. *Louis Wirth on Cities and Social Life.* Edited by Albert J. Reiss, Jr. Chicago: University of Chicago Press, 1964. This collection of papers on various aspects of urban studies includes: the effects of mass communication; "Urbanism as a Way of Life"; the nature and importance of community; racial and ethnic group problems; and rural–urban differences.

Articles and Papers

Bell, Daniel. "Notes on the Post-Industrial Society." *The Public Interest* 1, 6 (Winter 1967) and 2, 7 (Spring 1967).

Bendix, Reinhard. "Industrialization, Ideologies and Social Structure." *American Sociological Review* 24 (October 1959).

Davis, Kingsley. "The Origin and Growth of Urbanization in the World." *American Journal of Sociology* 60 (1955).

Gans, Herbert J. "Urbanism and Suburbanism as Ways of Life: A Re-evaluation of Definitions." In *Human Behavior and Social Processes,* edited by A. Rose. Boston: Houghton Mifflin, 1962.

Greer, Scott. "Urbanism Reconsidered: A Comparative Study of Local Areas in a Metropolis." *American Sociological Review* 21 (February 1956):19–25.

Gusfield, Joseph R. "Educational Institutions in the Process of Economic and National Development." *Journal of Asian and African Studies* 1, 2 (April 1966):129–146.

McKeown, James E. "Research Implications of the Platonistic and Aristotelian Concepts of Community." *American Catholic Sociological Review* 19, 1 (March 1958):35–44.

Seeley, John R. "The Slum: Its Nature, Use and Users." In *Neighborhood, City and Metropolis,* edited by R. Gutman and D. Popenoe, pp. 285–296. New York: Random House, 1970.

Theodorson, George A. "Acceptance of Industrialization and Its Attendant Consequences for the Social Patterns of Non-Western Societies." *American Sociological Review* 18 (1953):477–484.

Wirth, Louis. "Urbanism as a Way of Life." *American Journal of Sociology* 49 (1938):46–63.

II RELATED RESOURCES
Nonfiction

Brodersen, Arvid. *The Soviet Worker.* New York: Random House, 1966. This examination of the interaction between labor and the government, in a system where the state is a major industrial force, provides an interesting contrast to our Western system.

Cox, Harvey. *The Secular City.* Rev. ed. New York: Macmillan, 1966. An eminent theologian, Cox points out the virtues of urban life in the process of making a contribution to Christian theology. He sees the city as a place of maximum opportunity.

Duhl, L., ed. *The Urban Condition.* New York: Basic Books, 1963. In this collection of essays edited by psychiatrist Leonard Duhl, the emphasis is on the effect of urbanization and industrialization upon mental health and social functioning.

Form, William H., and Delbert C. Miller. *Industry, Labor and Community*. New York: Harper and Bros., 1960. This study focuses upon the relationships between economic institutions and other institutions within the communities of industrialized societies.

Galbraith, John Kenneth. *The Affluent Society*. Boston: Houghton Mifflin, 1958. This well-known economist suggests that an economic theory based upon scarcity of goods is not workable for an affluent society. He proposes a new theory that takes account of changing economic conditions.

Green, Constance. *The Rise of Urban America*. New York: Harper & Row, 1965. In this concise and readable book, Green writes about urban life in America from an historical perspective.

Handlin, Oscar, and John Burchard. *The Historian and the City*. Cambridge, Mass.: M.I.T. Press and Harvard University Press, 1963. This book is a collection of essays by historians interested in the nature, problems, and future of the city.

Jacobs, Jane. *The Death and Life of Great American Cities*. New York: Random House, 1961. Miss Jacobs points to a number of inadequacies in current city planning practices, which she says are destroying cities. She proposes alternative ways of dealing with today's urban problems.

Lyford, Joseph P. *The Airtight Cage: A Study of New York's West Side*. New York: Harper & Row, 1966. Lyford finds a glaring lack of neighborhood or community organization in Manhattan's upper West Side which, he states, results in a lack of any real power in city government for the residents.

Starr, Roger. *Urban Choices: The City and Its Critics*. Baltimore: Penguin Books (Paper), 1968. Starr attempts to relate social values to the decisions made by urban governments and to the way in which urban residents interact with each other.

Weaver, R. C. *The Urban Complex*. New York: Doubleday, Anchor (Paper), 1966. The former Secretary of the Department of Housing and Urban Development gives some practical advice about today's urban crisis.

Wood, R. *Suburbia: Its People and Their Politics*. Boston: Houghton Mifflin (Paper), 1958. Wood studies the life styles and politics of suburban residents. He stresses the faith suburbanites have in communities of limited size and their suspicions of "big city" politics and way of life.

Fiction

Cornelisen, Ann. *Torregreca*. New York: Dell (Paper), 1969. This book vividly describes the way of life in a small town in southern Italy, from the people's superstitions to their great determination to live.

Dickens, Charles. *Hard Times*. Greenwich, Conn.: Fawcett (Paper), 1966. First published in 1854. Dickens describes the crises and hardships of industrialization in nineteenth-century England, and the effect on the people who had to adjust to urban living.

Lins Do Rego, Jose. *Plantation Boy*. New York: Alfred A. Knopf, 1966. Do Rego describes the social consequences of the industrialization of agriculture in northeast Brazil.

Miller, Henry. *The Air-Conditioned Nightmare*. New York: Avon, 1945. Miller levels his acid pen at American technology and its dehumanizing effects upon individuals.

Roth, Henry. *Call It Sleep*. New York: Avon (Paper), 1964. First published in 1934. This book is about an immigrant boy's family and their struggle to adjust to and survive life in New York City.

Wilson, Edmund. *Memoirs of Hecate County*. New York: Signet, 1961. This revealing look at suburban life in the northeastern United States shows how some of the residents were torn between the culture of the city which they had left and that of the local residents.

Yglesias, Jose. *The Truth About Them*. New York: World Publishing, 1971. A novel about a Spanish-Cuban family and an account of the settling, flowering, and destruction of a community.

Films

Far from the Madding Crowd. John Schlesinger, 1968. This film depicts the lives of English villagers during the nineteenth century. It is adapted from a story by Thomas Hardy, first published in 1874.

In the Heat of the Night. Norman Jewison, 1967. This film is set in a small Mississippi town, where a young black detective from a northern city is intimidated by the local sheriff, both because he is a Negro and because he has achieved a certain status in the "big city."

15. Politics and Power

A basic feature of all modern societies is the assumption by government of more and more responsibility for the direction and control of the society. The major trends of the twentieth century, such as urbanization and industrialization, have resulted in a high degree of social and cultural diversity, in complex economic and social interdependence, in internal tensions, and also in disorganization stemming from rapid social change. Centralized group decision making has, therefore, seemed both necessary and inevitable. This is true for all types of economic or political systems: capitalistic or communistic, totalitarian or democratic.

The increasing importance of government has led to the development of the specialized area of sociology called political sociology; in the last several decades it has become one of the leading fields of sociological study. Political sociology focuses on the relationship between broad social structure and the political institutions of a society; the subject matter and methodology are drawn from both sociology and political science. The word "politics" is commonly used to refer to the maneuvers of candidates at election time and of political officeholders, but to the social scientist the word has a broader meaning. Politics *means the acquisition and use of power, especially within the context of the institution of the state and its government. So a political sociologist will study not only the activities of politicians, but the broad functions of political institutions, such as the influence our form of government exerts on education, religion, or economics.*

1 POWER, AUTHORITY, AND THE STATE

Politics is the process in which some individuals and groups acquire power and exercise that power over others. The state is the primary institution through which political power is exercised. Various political organizations regulate the political process. The need for such regulation stems from the basic conflict between the abundance of the people's desires and interests and the scarcity of resources and other valuables; if the varied interests of social groups and individuals were always compatible, political institutions would be unnecessary.

POWER

There are many forms and degrees of power. In chapter 7, we distinguished between personal power (or the individual's power to control the circumstances of his own life) and social power (the ability to control the actions of others, even against their own wishes). In this chapter, we are interested primarily in the varieties and dynamics of *social power,* especially that held by the state.

An analogy has been drawn by the sociologist Marvin E. Olsen between power in the social sphere and energy in the physical world. Dr. Olsen says:

Wherever we look we observe its [energy's] effects, and all activities are in one sense an expression of it. We talk freely about the uses of energy and power, but when we attempt to specify more precisely what either of these phenomena is, we encounter difficulties. The main reason is that neither energy nor power can be directly observed or measured. Their existence, nature and strength can only be inferred from their effects.[1]

An individual acting alone may exercise social power; for example, a woman named Madelyn Murray waged a successful one-woman campaign to maintain the separation of church and state by banning prayers in the public schools. More frequently, however, power is exercised by an individual acting on behalf of a group.

We can also distinguish between power used directly and power used indirectly. When a boss tells an employee whether or not he may have a raise, the boss is using power directly. Sometimes, however, a man's action goes through intermediate stages before having an impact. For example, when the president of United States Steel decides to make a change in the price of his products he may set off a chain reaction of other price adjustments for products made from steel, that will eventually reach the wallets of both workers and consumers. He is using power indirectly. We say that power is exercised positively when it is used to promote the achievement of some goal; when it prevents an achievement or event from taking place, we say it is used negatively.

Power may be used in a great variety of ways, but the tactics for asserting power remain basically the same in most situations. Three basic kinds of pressure may be used to persuade people to comply with some-

1. Marvin E. Olsen, *The Process of Social Organization* (New York: Holt, Rinehart & Winston, 1968), p. 172.

one's wish. First, one may offer an advantage or a desired object or social condition as a reward for compliance. A mother offers her children a snack of homemade cookies and chocolate milk in return for good behavior on a shopping trip; the workers in a tire factory are offered a large Christmas bonus for lowering the rate of absenteeism and increasing the rate of production; the supporters of a successful candidate for president are offered jobs in the new administration.

In the second kind of pressure, one may threaten a disadvantage or punishment in response to noncompliance. The football player who breaks training rules knows he will be fined or benched; a husband who has lost the week's grocery money in a poker game expects to incur his wife's anger; the critics of a dictator must beware of capture and jail.

Third, one may manipulate information, or values, attitudes, and feelings. Walter Cronkite and Eric Sevareid exercise power because their comments on the daily news are accepted as authoritative by millions of Americans. Fidel Castro is able to convince his countrymen, through political speeches, of the accuracy of his own estimate of Cuban economic problems and their solution.

How successfully an individual exerts these pressures and wields power depends on the degree to which he possesses some or all of certain social assets. These include wealth, occupational prestige, knowledge, and persuasive skills. Many of these bases of power were discussed earlier in chapter 7.

AUTHORITY

Sociologists classify power in two different ways, based on the social circumstances surrounding its use. When power is used in a way that is generally recognized as socially right and necessary, then it is *legitimate power.* When power is used to control others without the support of social approval, then it is referred to as *illegitimate power.*

This distinction has important implications for our discussion of the state.

When power is legitimate, it is called *authority,* and is socially accepted as right, proper, and necessary. Authority, then, denotes control over others which is socially accepted, even when that control may infringe on the wishes of those subject to it. When gangsters demand and receive protection money from a shopkeeper by threat of violence, they are using illegitimate coercive power; when government agents demand and receive a sales tax from the same shopkeeper, they are using legitimate coercive power or authority.

Those given the right to use legitimate power are said to be in positions of authority. Their authority is strictly limited according to the role definitions of the position. A policeman has the authority to write a traffic ticket or arrest a speeder, but he does not have the right to convict a criminal. A judge, who cannot give tickets, has the authority to try criminals. But the use of power is not limited to those in positions of authority; moreover, persons in authority do not always limit their use of power by staying within the limits of legitimacy. Illegitimate power is often exercised by persons both in and out of authority. Striking examples are contained in the book *Power and Morality: Who Shall Guard the Guardians,* by Pitirim A. Sorokin and Walter Lunden.[2] The authors have assembled significant evidence indicating that in many modern governments persons in high political positions have engaged in behavior that their society defines as "criminal."

Although it is possible to exercise a relatively high degree of power illegitimately, this usually requires secrecy and great discretion, since if such power comes to public attention, attempts will be made to restrict or prevent its use. Most powerholders seek to have their power legitimated, if possible,

2. See Pitirim Sorokin and Walter Lunden, *Power and Morality: Who Shall Guard the Guardians* (Boston: Porter Sargent, 1959).

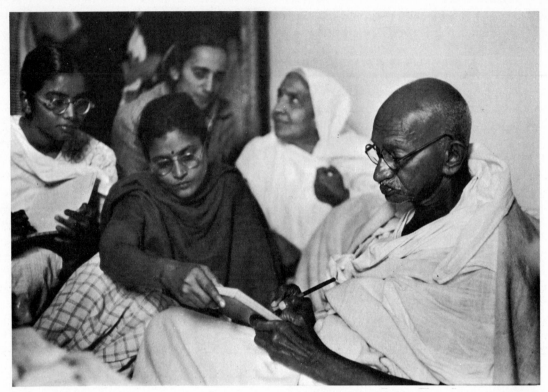

Gandhi, one of the great charismatic figures of the twentieth century, was both a political and religious leader. His followers called him Mahatma, meaning "great soul." As the leader of India's movement for independence, he developed the tactics of collective civil disobedience and passive resistance. His methods have served as a model for many groups that have sought social reform, including the civil rights movement in this country. *(Cartier Bresson, Magnum)*

so that they can exercise it free of such restrictions and limitations.

Legitimation of power comes from many different sources. Sometimes legitimacy is granted through formal procedures such as constitutions and elections; often it is informally or indirectly granted through failure to oppose an action. Max Weber classified the main sources of social authority, or legitimate power, into three major types.[3] They are:

(1) *Traditional authority,* or that conferred by custom and accepted practice. In a monarchy, the power of the head of the government is legitimated by his birth; he is the king because his father was the king. In an-

cient Chinese society, it was believed that the ruling elite (called the mandarins) received their authority to rule by a heavenly order that permitted them to govern the rest of China in accordance with the ethical rules of the prevailing religion, Confucianism.

(2) *Charismatic authority,* which is the authority generated by the personality or personal appeal of some individual. The leaders of many movements—George Washington, Martin Luther King, Jr., and Fidel Castro—are examples of people who have held charismatic authority.

(3) *Legal bureaucratic authority,* or that which rests upon rules that are rationally established. This type of authority is exemplified by elected and appointed government officials, company executives, and any officer

3. Max Weber, *From Max Weber: Essays in Sociology,* ed. and trans. H. H. Gerth and C. Wright Mills (New York: Oxford University Press, 1946), pp. 196–252.

of a formal organization. In America, legitimation of political authority is based on the
ultimate consent of the people through such
"rational" mechanisms as the Constitution
and popular elections.

In most societies all three types of authority are represented, although one type
usually predominates, as legal bureaucratic
authority does in the United States. Pope
John XXIII is an example of a man whose
authority came from all three sources. As a
man of God, a priest, he had traditional authority; as the head of a large and complex
religious institution, the Roman Catholic
church, he had legal bureaucratic authority;
and as a man of wisdom and great magnetism,
he had charismatic authority as well. Even
in states that are based on the legitimation
of legal bureaucratic authority, political leaders are usually most successful when they
combine that authority with some authority
of the charismatic kind; it helps them get
elected, and it also helps them win fuller cooperation for their policies. This can be seen
in modern times, for example, in the political
careers of Winston Churchill, Charles de
Gaulle, and John Kennedy.

THE STATE

Some legitimate authority is found in almost every group or organization. But it is
the state "that successfully claims a monopoly
over the legitimate use of coercion and physical force within a territory."[4] Thus the state
as an institution has the supreme power in a
society. The institution of the state dictates
when, where, and how much physical force
may rightfully be used, although, for the
most part, physical force is only used as a last
resort. (Legitimate power is usually restrained
power.) The power of the state is put to use
primarily to resolve conflicting interests in
the society and to achieve collective goals.
We have mentioned that in political sociology,

4.   Robin Williams, Jr., *American Society: A Sociological Interpretation* (New York: Alfred A. Knopf, 1960),
p. 233.

the term state is used to mean the political institution, and is distinct from the *government,*
which is the group of individuals who actually
exercise the powers that are invested in the
state. The state may continue while many different governments rise and fall.

In primitive societies, the state was not a
separate and distinct institution. The functions of the state were closely joined with
other functions of the society: religion,
economy, education, art, sometimes even
propagation. Often all institutions and most
activities were regulated by the same person. He was not only tribal chief or village
headman, but also religious and cultural leader
and chief educator. But the historical trend
has been toward making each of the important social functions relatively independent
and separate — or differentiated — and giving
the authority in each area to separate individuals, trained for their particular position.

The modern state is a specialized institution; though its functions are quite broad
and central, its powers are by no means all-
inclusive. For example, artistic production
is rarely a function of the state any more,
although censorship of such production, on
the grounds of political or moral content,
may still be. Many nations have not gone as
far as the United States in the separation of
church and state, and they continue to have
an official religion. But in most of these nations the head of state is no longer the chief
religious leader; it is not Queen Elizabeth or
the Prime Minister who directs the activities
of the Church of England, but the Arch-
bishop of Canterbury. Also, few modern
countries try to make religious belief or observance of any sort compulsory. The economy, too, is clearly separated from the state,
with its own separate organizations such as
corporations, banks, and stores. However,
in modern industrial society, the state has a
growing power to manage and control the
economy, such as regulating the money supply
or setting wage and price guidelines.

What, then, are the functions of the mod-

Robert M. MacIver (1882–1970) was born in Scotland and educated in England, but taught for many years in the United States and today is considered the first American political sociologist. He is noted for his ability to synthesize materials from a variety of sources, including classical scholars, and to apply these materials to contemporary problems. His major books are *Community* (1917), *Social Causation* (1942), and *The Web of Government* (1947).

ern state? Three stand out as the most significant. First is the establishment and enforcement of formal norms of behavior that are considered necessary for the social order and welfare. The state acts to protect life, limb, and property rights of its citizens from the consequences of other citizens' actions. Traffic regulations, laws against murder or assault, the inspection of public buildings for their fire safety, zoning regulations which place restrictions on the development of property and thus keep neighboring property values from being depreciated are ways in which the state protects the citizens. And if these laws and regulations are broken, and one person does harm to another's person or property, then it is the obligation of the state to act as the guilty party's prosecutor, judge, and punitive agent. This authority is delegated to the state by the people in the society; however, as we noted above, some limitation on its use is always inherent in the granting of the authority.

Second, the state protects the society from outside enemies. The state maintains an army and provides its weapons and equipment. Certain procedures are agreed upon for recruiting or drafting soldiers to serve in the army, and for calling the army into combat. Once again, the state's power must be legitimated by social approval of its use, and if a government undertakes a war without legitimation, it is in serious political trouble.

Third is the planning, financing, regulating, and operation of certain activities that are important for the general welfare of the society and its citizens. This may include the allocation and conservation of important natural resources; the building, maintenance, and operation of public transportation systems; the regulation of agricultural and industrial activities; and the redistribution of income through taxes and other programs. This is the state function which has expanded so markedly in modern times; previously most states lacked the resources to do much in this broad area, and perhaps the function was less necessary. The complex nature of modern societies seems to require much centralized planning, coordination of activities, and achievement of collective goals if these societies are to remain efficient and stable. The government is the only organization large and powerful enough to do the job.

2 POLITICAL DEVELOPMENT AND MODERNIZATION

Modernization always has a major impact on the political development of societies. Modernization brings changes in many aspects of social structure, which then lead to changes in the structure of the state and political process; or the pattern may be reversed, with political changes leading to other social changes.

THE CREATION OF NATIONS

The oldest kind of political unit is that based on kinship: the family and the clan. As societies grew larger and more complex, clans joining together developed the tribal form of organization. Although still mainly embedded in the kinship network, tribal organization led to the first rudimentary specialization of political functions.

As populations continued to increase, family political organization no longer proved workable. Peoples from various clans, tribes, races, and cultures began to live near each other, forming towns and cities; populations were so large and diverse that the exercise of power had to become more impersonal and specialized. The old system of kinship-based political control, which depended on daily personal interaction among people who had known each other literally for generations, broke down as geographical mobility increased. When strangers replaced kin or fellow tribesmen as neighbors, new political institutions were necessary. The increased specialization of political control included: separate occupations of political leadership, such as mayor; establishment of separate institutions for social control, such as the police force and the courts; and the creation of formal bodies of laws.

In time, the city-state emerged as the most effective form of organization to achieve physical and economic protection. From about 1000 B.C. until the end of the Middle Ages in about A.D. 1500, the city-state was the dominant form of political organization in the Western world. These preindustrial city-states were usually organized into feudal estates: rigid social strata based on land ownership. The governmental powers of the city-state also extended into the surrounding farmlands that supplied the city with food. Even the so-called "empires," such as those of the Romans or the Persians, were little more than a string of loosely assembled city-states held together by a constant show of military might and numerous political concessions. The "fall" of these empires did not usually mean that these cities were destroyed; instead they resumed functioning as autonomous city-states, freed from the necessity of paying tribute to some foreign overlord, but also perhaps lacking the protection, trade, institutions, and technology brought by the empire.

The rise of the city-state did not in all cases mean the end of clan or family political organization. Often the two coexisted; sometimes they conflicted. An example of a family organization that was incorporated into a city-state organization is the Medici family. The Medici were political, social, and cultural leaders of the city-state of Florence, Italy, from 1434 to 1537. Hereditary monarchies such as those in England or Belgium, are another example of a family organization that was superimposed on a more impersonal state.

The welding together of neighboring city-states to form a nation did not begin to occur until around the fifteenth century. Louis XI made France a nation by annexing several neighboring provinces; King Ferdinand and Queen Isabella created the nation of Spain by their marriage, which brought the two largest provinces, Aragon and Castile, under their joint rule. The development of nation-states (nationhood) depends on a number of social and political circumstances. There must be a geographical definition of a country, coupled with the ability to defend it. This is one reason nationhood came early to England, a small island. There must be some method of trade and communication throughout the entire nation; here technological advances help to speed up a nation's political development. There must be some significant degree of social integration. Different linguistic and ethnic groups must have a sense of mutual loyalty and usually a language in common; older political organizations, such as those of the family or the independent city-state, must be made subordinate to the national organization. Each of these factors leads to and is to some extent created by a strong central government.

The emergence of the nation-state is one of the most important developments of the modern world. National states, and the associated loyalties and beliefs of nationalism, have become powerful motivating and organizing forces in the urban-industrial period. They have been central both to the rise of complex, technologically oriented societies as well as to international antagonisms of the gravest sort.

THE COLONIAL EXPERIENCE

The first true nations emerged in western Europe, in those societies which had strong monarchies and a high degree of technological progress. By 1500, England, Spain, France, Portugal, and Russia had all achieved nationhood. These European nations, and others which were established somewhat later, such as Holland and Belgium, then began the highly competitive commercial and political process known as colonialism. Basic to colonialism was the wish to discover new trade sources in the untraveled lands beyond Europe and the Mediterranean. Some of the expeditions these countries sent out into Asia, Africa, and the Americas were designed mainly for trade exploration. The famous voyages of Columbus are an example: he was looking for information about trade routes, not new lands to conquer. Other expeditions were also for trade: for example, the Portuguese sent trading expeditions to West Africa early in the fifteenth century; they did the same to India, and also China.

But in most cases, where the Europeans discovered lands with societies that were not technologically advanced, they moved in to stay. The new land became a colony; its government was either directly or indirectly dictated by the conquering nation; and it was run primarily for the benefit of the colonizers. From 1500 to 1900, colonization was literally a worldwide activity. The Dutch were in New Amsterdam (New York), southern Africa, Java, Ceylon, Formosa, and the East Indies; the French were in Canada, Madagascar (off the African coast), Indochina, and Haiti; the Spanish colonized the Philippines, Cuba, Florida, and Mexico, and most of South America. Although some colonies began to fight for, and win, their independence in the eighteenth century, the process of establishing, or conquering, colonies continued until well into the twentieth century.

Because colonization went on for so many years in so many parts of the globe, there are not many countries outside of Western Europe that have not at one time or another been colonies. Among the problems faced both by colonies and colonizers were: the cultural clash between the native society

The Dutch and English settlers who colonized South Africa have not only deprived all non-whites of any political participation but have also institutionalized an elaborate system of racial separation and subordination known as apartheid. The color bar separates the small white minority from the country's 2 million persons of mixed ancestry, half a million Asians, and 15 million Bantu peoples. Non-Europeans are assigned to segregated and inferior public and private facilities by law, and they are required to carry pass books for identification and permission to work in "European areas." *(Paul Conklin, Monkmeyer)*

and the European newcomers (which we discussed in chapter 3); the establishment of patterns regulating relationships between dominant and minority groups; and the creation of workable and acceptable institutions of political control.[5]

The colonizing power has the choice of maintaining the state organization of the original society or of establishing a new one. In cases where the Europeans found a strong state, they were often content to install their

5.   A useful source for the study of colonialism is Rupert Emerson, *From Empire to Nation: The Rise to Self-Assertion of Asian and African Peoples* (Cambridge, Mass.: Harvard University Press, 1960).

own men as chief officials, or to make the head of the local government responsible to the European government, or some representative of it, such as a governor general. The Dutch colonization of Indonesia followed this pattern. This policy, sometimes called indirect rule, tended to support the original social and political institutions and to minimize the influence of the European nation. Indirect rule worked well when the colony was desired chiefly as a source of raw materials, or as a trading station or military base.

However, if the colony was to serve as a market for goods or a manufacturing center, and if the existing political institutions were weak or undermined by internal conflict, then the European colonizer generally chose to establish direct rule. The new state was usually modeled after that of the colonizing nation, using the same kind of political process and legal system. This is the way the British colonized our own country. They set up British-style legislative bodies and courts, and in place of a monarch, a governor who was the representative of the British government.[6]

Obviously, under either direct or indirect rule, many institutions of the original society are either destroyed or made unworkable because of the new circumstances. Even with the best of intentions, colonialism is a policy that exploits the natural and human resources of the colony for the benefit of the conqueror or colonizer.

In many cases minerals and other natural resources in the colonized country were taken to the colonizing nation for processing into finished products. The colonial people thus lost both the resources and the great profits which were derived from their processing. Paternalism and the "white man's burden" approach of colonialism caused many native peoples to develop strong feelings of subservience and inferiority. These feelings prevented or retarded their development of the self-initiative and desire for achievement so necessary for modernization. Colonialism was most repressive where paternalism was infused with racism, as in the African nations. Furthermore, the elite of the colonial countries were often educated abroad, usually in the colonizing country, where they learned a cultural pattern quite different from their own. This sometimes led them to reject the culture and the people of their own country and even to remain abroad permanently, leaving their native countries without leadership.

Yet history and experience show that colonization is not a purely negative political force in the colonized countries. Colonialism can in some cases, especially where there is direct rule, serve to encourage nationalism by laying the groundwork for the national experience. Among the contributions which colonialism can make to the prenational society are:

(1) Establishing boundaries to the country, giving it a name and an identity. Some nations were quite literally not even on the map until they became colonies. When the European colonizers made a country a physical unit, this opened up the possibility that the country would become a political unit, or a state.

(2) Creating a centralized social organization that binds together the various parts of the country. The Europeans applied the techniques that they had learned as government officials of a modern nation-state to the administration of the affairs of their colonies. They created networks of transportation and communication, centralized controls of the economy, and at least the rudimentary machinery of national governments. Although the colonial political institutions may be rejected when independence comes, they provide a model of state organization.

(3) Training and education of the native population. In the period of the greatest colonial expansion, no European country had a large enough population to be able to staff the governments of all its colonies; therefore, it had to rely on the natives of the colonies. Schools, and even colleges, were set up in the colony, or talented, promising young men were often sent back to Europe for education and training. This system provided many countries with leaders:[7] India's former leader, Mahatma Gandhi, for example, studied in London for several years.

(4) Promoting nationalistic feeling. Because the Europeans saw the country as a

6. For an analysis of the way that British colonialism aided American independence, see Clinton Rossiter, *The First American Revolution* (New York: Harcourt Brace Jovanovich, 1956), chaps. 4 and 5.

7. See Immanuel Wallerstein, *Africa: The Politics of Independence* (New York: Random House, Vintage, 1961).

In the developing nations of the Third World, traditional customs often conflict with modern, Western approaches. In order to effect change in local values and attitudes, governments often try to enlist the support and understanding of native leaders. Here, a health worker in a Ghana village asks the witch doctor for permission to spray the huts with DDT. *(Marc and Evelyne Bernheim, Woodfin Camp and Associates)*

whole, so in time did the natives. As the natives' pride and loyalty to their nation grew they began to share a dislike of the colonial intruder. This dislike of a common enemy united the country, encouraged a feeling of nationalism, and usually led to a struggle for independence from the colonizer.

THIRD WORLD NATION-STATES

The last several decades have seen the emergence of many new nations. In Africa and Asia, old colonial names and boundaries have been changed, resulting in the creation of new countries such as Botswana, Burundi, and Malaysia. All over the Third World, countries that were colonies or protectorates are becoming independent nations. The political experience of these nations is different from that of most European countries, partly because they had to win their independ-

ence by revolution or through the exercise of international politics. Today's new nations also are undergoing the process of social and economic modernization in a way quite different from the West, as we discussed in chapter 14. They must suddenly adapt to very advanced technologies, cope with serious problems of overpopulation, and adjust to a foreign system of values.

Certain political problems seem to be common to emerging Third World nations:

(1) The problem of the conflict of older patterns of political organization with that of the modern state. This is especially true of the predominantly preindustrial nations of Africa, where tribal organization is still predominant. In most cases, the traditional bases of authority are in conflict with the new rational ones, with the result that neither functions effectively to decide who will legiti-

mately acquire and exercise power. The highly personal patterns of tribal organization must rapidly give way to the impersonal bureaucratic type of organization of the modern state; people must learn to transfer their loyalty from the personal and emotion-laden family group to the more abstract organizations of bureaucracy. Intensive resocialization is required.

(2) The problem of the rising expectations of the people which results from an introduction to economic and technological modernization. Limitations and hardships which were taken for granted as inevitable are suddenly seen as just a form of backwardness, and there is a new awareness of possible alternatives. Modern medicine can bring longer life and better health; modern factories can provide salaries and labor-saving devices; modern bureaucratic social organization can create the opportunity to escape the restrictions of lower-class life. This rise in expectations also has a political base. People expect that achieving nationhood and a strong central government will quickly solve many of their problems of underdevelopment and powerlessness. These unrealistic expectations are often encouraged by the propaganda of both capitalistic and communistic countries trying to win the new nation's friendship; they sometimes exaggerate the effects that a new dam or factory, donated to win political friendship, will have on the development of the country.

(3) The problem of the need for effective leaders. The new nation needs people who can fill the government offices created, people who have been educated and trained for such responsibility. In some cases, the colonial government may have filled that need; this was true of India, for example, under the colonial rule of the British. Many African and Asian nations, however, lack the educational facilities to train bureaucratic officials. This means that the new states may be ineffectively governed for some time, until experience and increased educational opportu-nities can provide people with the needed skills. Sociologists have observed that in times of great social change, when existing institutions are weak or ineffectual, personal and charismatic leadership serves as a very important basis for political organization. Or, to use Weber's terminology, in the process of modernization, traditional authority is weakened or made irrelevant and legal-bureaucratic authority has not yet become fully accepted as a social value. Charismatic authority, therefore, becomes quite significant as a source of legitimation and leadership. Examples of this kind of leadership can be seen in several modernizing nations. Nasser in Egypt and Castro in Cuba are examples of the maintenance of authority in large part by means of stirring speeches, emotional appeal, and a personal aura of leadership.

(4) The problem of conflict between the needs and wants of the people and the long-range plans or programs of the leaders. As a result of rising expectations and political propaganda, the people are led to believe that modernization will provide quick answers to the problems of hunger, poverty, and low status. On the other hand, their leaders, with a more sophisticated grasp of the social and economic changes that must be made, may prefer to begin with programs which do not immediately benefit the wage earner and consumer, such as heavy industry, transportation, and the development of sources of power.

This problem is made more serious by antagonism toward government in general. In order to make the necessary changes, it almost always seems desirable to have a strongly centralized and authoritarian type of government. The people of developing nations are usually accustomed to personal and family loyalty, however, and often find it difficult to deal with a distant and bureaucratic government.

Many of these people view the government not as a source of help but as a potential danger to their traditional way of life. The benefits of proposed changes, such as a system of taxes or a universal draft, are hard to visualize, but the disadvantages of losing part of one's income or an eldest son are immediately apparent. The fear and suspicion of the people is directed not against the abstraction of the government but against the political figures who head the government. This creates serious political instability.

(5) The problem of the global competition between capitalism and communism. These two major ideologies of the twentieth century, in their struggle for power and supremacy, have made many developing Third World nations an arena for competition. Their political and economic maneuvers affect the development of emerging nations in a way that the leaders of these countries cannot control. Wars are started, political leaders rise and fall, and governments succeed or fail because of the currents of global politics among the powerful nations.

PATHS OF POLITICAL DEVELOPMENT

In discussing political development it is useful to distinguish between political change that is *evolutionary,* meaning that it develops out of existing trends and institutions, and that which is *revolutionary,* meaning that it is a kind of change which seeks to destroy existing institutions of political power and replace them with new ones.

A good example of evolutionary change is seen in India. From 1763 until 1947, India was a colony of the British. Resistance to British rule began to be organized by Gandhi in the 1920s, and it eventually became so strong that the British granted India its independence after World War II. As an independent nation, India kept many of the political institutions established there by the British. The parliamentary system of government, the legal system and the bulk of the laws themselves, even many domestic policies such as the abolition of the caste system date back to the period of British rule. But change

has come, in foreign policy especially, and in the working of the political process to accommodate India's racial and cultural diversity.

Evolutionary change, by working with established social and political institutions, provides a measure of continuity and helps to soften the effects of new ideas, attitudes, and institutions. However, evolutionary change is not always possible; those who held the official power in the old state may not be willing to let go without a struggle. In that case, the path of political development may be a revolutionary one.

Revolution is a word used so often today that it is practically meaningless. We hear television commercials about the "revolution" in laundry detergents; political figures of both the extreme right and extreme left claim that America is in the midst of a revolution right now. But revolution has a specific meaning in a sociopolitical context, and it is not a term that can usefully be applied either to soap or to a sit-in. Revolution refers to any large-scale change in the leadership and political institutions of a society and a successful restructuring of those aspects of society by the new ruling group.

Most changes of political leadership are not revolutionary. In democracies there is provision for legal means of changing leaders when they lose the confidence or support of the public; they are voted out of office. In totalitarian governments, changes of leadership may be brought about by internal struggles among the group of ruling elites. This happened in the Soviet Union when Nikita Khrushchev fell from power, and earlier when there was a power struggle to decide Stalin's replacement. Dissension among ruling elites is also a frequent occurrence in Latin American countries, where heads of state are often deposed by a *coup d'état,* in which one leadership group forcefully overthrows another. In all these situations, the change centers on the leadership only; in a true revolution, the entire structure of the government itself is changed.

The revolutionary situation involves certain basic social conditions. There must be an awareness of the inequities in the way desirables, including social power, are distributed; moreover, there must also be a strong awareness that some other method of distribution is possible.[8] Poverty or powerlessness alone does not cause revolution; the people must have the feeling that such a condition could and should be avoided. This dual awareness must be widespread throughout society, for regardless of myths, revolution is not something carried out by a small group of radicals; it is a collective action of a large mass of people. Small radical groups may, however, serve to spread the awareness of existing unfairness and possible solutions throughout the larger public. Revolutionary leaders are rarely themselves members of the most deprived classes; they tend to be well-educated members of the middle class who are motivated by a combination of idealism and the desire to achieve higher status and greater freedom personally.

For revolution to occur, there must also be a weakness in, or breakdown of, the existing political institutions and the governing elite. Sometimes the old officials have already lost the power to govern effectively and the revolution is just an open recognition of that fact. Revolutionaries do not always have to seize power violently because in many cases the old government has already lost it. Revolutionaries do restructure the old political institutions, and seek to get the new structures legitimated as quickly as possible.

The life cycle of revolutionary movements as examples of collective behavior was discussed in chapter 13. The political development of most revolutions, like the life cycle, seems to follow a general pattern.[9] After the overthrow of the government, there is a period of experimentation and a struggle for power among various revolutionary groups. In the case of the Russian and French revolutions, this period of struggle and uncertainty lasted for a number of years and caused more bloodshed than did the original overthrow of the government. Radicals of various ideological groups rise to power, taking advantage of the uncertainty and fear of the general public during this period of transition. Only those who are fully committed, highly disciplined, and thoroughly determined can remain in the political arena for any reasonable length of time. They fight for "control" of the revolution, seeking to establish the new state in accordance with their own beliefs. They also fight the more moderate leaders who are looking for compromises which will enable the society to begin the task of rebuilding. In the end, the extremes are usually rejected: compromises are made with older institutions and social norms.

Revolutions never accomplish as much as they set out to; the resistance of habit, custom, and tradition is always harder to overcome than anyone had recognized. Yet the history of national development in the last several centuries is closely linked with revolution. The French, American, Russian, and Chinese revolutions have had profound effects on the course of the modern world.

8. Crane Brinton. *The Anatomy of Revolution* (New York: Random House, Vintage, 1960), p. 35.

9. Crane Brinton, *The Antomy of Revolution,* chap. 3.

3 POLITICS AND SOCIAL STRUCTURE IN THE UNITED STATES

The United States is a country with a great diversity of races, languages, subcultures, and life styles. Yet this nation is one of the oldest constitutional democracies in the world; as a nation-state it has had a remarkably long life, though not without considerable stress and tension, including a bloody civil war. How has this political stability and freedom been maintained in a nation so filled with conflicting interests and discord? The best answer to this question may lie in our tradition of political pluralism. *Political pluralism* is a social pattern in which power is divided up among a number of groups, each of which represents a significant set of interests or values. Thanks to this tradition, we seem to have avoided the dangers of extreme concentrations of power. Yet there is also a high enough degree of unity in American political attitudes to offset the equally serious danger of fragmentation of power, which can lead to ineffectiveness and instability.

POLITICAL PLURALISM

Political pluralism is at the very basis of personal freedom, since freedom depends on a wide possibility of choices and the counterbalance of powers that pluralism represents. But there are many other positive functions of pluralism which often go unnoticed.

The sociologist Seymour Martin Lipset suggests that "multiple and politically inconsistent affiliations, loyalties, and stimuli reduce the emotion and aggressiveness involved in political choice."[10] In a society where many different politically powerful groups exist, the chances are very great that a single individual will belong to more than one of these groups. For example, John Smith may be a registered member of the Democratic party; he may also be a member of a labor union; perhaps he also belongs to a veterans' organization such as the Veterans of Foreign Wars (V.F.W.) or to a fraternal society like the Elks or the Masons. In each one of these groups, he hears a slightly different political message. This means that he himself is already aware that there may be more than one way of looking at the issue, that legitimate conflicts of attitude or interest may take place. Thus he may be more tolerant, less certain that there is one and only one answer to the question. Both Robert Dahl and Talcott Parsons have observed that in a pluralistic system, members of a majority group holding political power tend to be protective of the rights of political minorities. According to Dahl: "If most individuals in the society identify with more than one group, then there is some positive probability that any majority contains individuals who identify for certain purposes with the threatened minority."[11] Parsons suggests

10. Seymour Martin Lipset, *Political Man: The Social Bases of Politics* (New York: Doubleday, Anchor, 1959), p. 77.
11. Robert A. Dahl, *A Preface to Democratic Theory* (Chicago: University of Chicago Press, 1956), p. 104.

Alexis de Tocqueville (1805–1859) was a politician and a writer, not a sociologist. In the early nineteenth century the French government sent de Tocqueville to the United States to study the American penal system, but he broadened his study into an overall analysis of American society. He was particularly interested in American political systems and how they affected the larger social system. The book he published as a report on his visit, *Democracy in America* (1835), is considered one of the most insightful sociological studies ever made of our country. *(Culver Pictures, Inc.)*

that in times of great or deep political differences, members of the political majority may eventually come to defend those who differ from them politically but share other interests.[12]

The American two-party system seems to act as a preserver of pluralism. Since there are so many different groups holding some degree of political power, it is clear that each of the two parties is not a unified group, but a coalition of various interests. We can see in both the Republican and the Democratic parties a constant struggle for power within

12. Talcott Parsons, "Voting and the Equilibrium of the American Political System," in *American Voting Behavior* (New York: Free Press, 1959), p. 93.

the party, as it tries to accommodate the left wing and the right wing, the farmer and the city dweller, the rich man and the poor man. At election times, each party must look for the broadest possible base of support, which means that it must be tolerant of many political minorities and sympathetic toward their views.

In a country that has many political parties, hard and fast ideological and political lines tend to develop, with each party jealously guarding its own beliefs and treating the others with hostility. This tends to divide the country into small intolerant groups and to paralyze the democratic process. For example, the Dominican Republic has a population of 4 million and twenty-four different political parties. In such cases, the parties are so deeply divided that they cannot combine even to defeat a common enemy, which is one reason such countries often end up as dictatorships rather than democracies.

American pluralism is also reinforced by the specific organization of our national government. Elected officials represent a geographical territory rather than just a social class or political party. Some countries allocate seats in the legislature to the various parties, on the basis of their size, and each party then holds its own election to choose the representatives. In the United States, senators and congressmen represent geographical districts or states, which ordinarily means that they must reconcile many different viewpoints. In addition, our government is set up as a system of interlocking balances and interest groups. The House and the Senate compete for power in the legislative branch of the government; and the three branches – legislative, judicial, and executive – serve as checks and balances on each other. This prevents power from becoming too centralized and helps to keep open many different channels to the central apparatus of decision making.

Analysis of current American political attitudes indicates that the trends toward

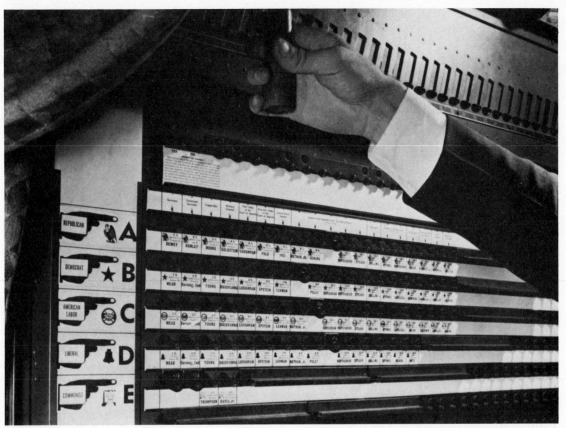

Theoretically, every citizen in a democratic nation should be interested in government and act effectively. However, compared to other nations, the number of Americans who participate in the electoral process is relatively low. The complexities of modern politics are often incomprehensible to many citizens. In particular, low income, low education, and second class citizenship lessen the sense of involvement in public affairs and depress voter participation. *(UPI)*

urbanization, mass education, and increased and rapid communication may also help to promote democratic stability and freedom. They serve to increase the tolerance of diversity which is associated with political pluralism. Studies have indicated that the lowest degree of political tolerance is found among those who are the most isolated: residents of very small towns or farms, and those who work at jobs that limit their contact with others.[13] Such people are more likely to have extremist political attitudes and to be intolerant of dissent.

13. Samuel A. Stouffer, *Communism, Conformity and Civil Liberties* (New York: Doubleday, 1955), p. 139.

POLITICAL ATTITUDES AND POLITICAL BEHAVIOR

People's behavior and attitudes in political affairs are closely linked to their behavior in other areas and to their position in the social structure. The study of politics has come increasingly to rely on the methods and approaches of sociology for this reason.

Political participation

The level of political participation in the United States is not particularly high. In recent presidential elections, an average of about 60 percent of eligible voters have turned out at the polls.[14] Who does vote? Many different studies have indicated that the factors which tend to be associated with a high level of voting activity are: high income, extended education, white collar occupation, long-term residence in the community, marriage, and membership in social organizations. Men vote more regularly than women, and whites more than blacks. It is not surprising that the factors influencing political participation are very similar to those we have mentioned as influencing social participation in general; political behavior is simply one form of social participation. The less socially isolated an individual is, or the more ties he has to groups, the more likely he will be to vote and participate in politics in general. The roles of citizen and of social participant seem to go hand in hand. It is also evident that the characteristics of voters tend to be those of the higher social classes, while nonvoters display characteristics of low social status.[15]

The differential rates of voting participation among low and high status groups has important implications for a democratic society. The poor, and the members of low status groups are almost always underrepresented; moreover, as Lipset mentions,

The combination of low vote and a relative lack of organization among the lower-status groups means that they will suffer from neglect by the politicians who will be receptive to the wishes of the more privileged, participating, and organized strata.[16]

This phenomenon has led to many recent attempts to organize the poor, the nonwhite, and other lower status groups into political pressure groups; examples are the National Welfare Rights Organization, and the community action programs established as part of the war on poverty.

Political party membership

A study of party affiliations over a century of American history suggests that certain class distinctions greatly affect choice of party membership. One study made of election polls between 1936 and 1960 indicates that the farther down the ladder of income and occupational status the voter stands, the greater the likelihood of Democratic party affiliation.[17] Other studies have shown that business and professional men are most likely to belong to the Republican party, and that among corporation executives there is also a correlation between size of the business and party allegiance; 69 percent of the executives of small firms (under 100 employees) were Republicans, while the figure rose to 84 percent for firms of over 10,000 workers.[18] This trend of Democratic membership for lower-class individuals and Republican membership for the upper classes was noticed, at the turn of this century, by historians, most notably Charles Beard, and it is supported by popular images.[19] In 1958, the Gallup Poll asked Americans for their picture of the typical Democrat. The answers included "a friend . . . average person . . . someone who thinks of everybody . . . an ordinary person . . . works for his wages." The picture of the typical Republican was "better class . . . well-to-do . . . wealthy . . . big businessman . . . money voter."

An exception to this general line of division can be found among the well-educated individuals who are not in business occupations. Artists and writers, actors and professors, and some of those in "creative" businesses like advertising and publishing,

14. *New York Times Encyclopedic Almanac 1970* (New York: New York Times, 1969), p. 156.

15. Morris Janowitz and Dwaine Marvick, *Competitive Pressure and Democratic Consent,* Michigan Governmental Studies, no. 32 (Ann Arbor: University of Michigan Press, 1956), p. 26.

16. Lipset, *Political Man,* p. 227.

17. Lipset, *Political Man,* p. 303.

18. Lipset, *Political Man,* p. 305.

19. Quoted in V. O. Key, Jr., *Politics, Parties and Pressure Groups,* 4th ed. (New York: Crowell, 1958), p. 235.

PARTICIPATION IN 1970 NATIONAL ELECTIONS, BY POPULATION CHARACTERISTICS

Characteristic	Persons of voting age	Percent reporting they voted	Percent reporting they did not vote
TOTAL	120,701	54.6	45.4
Sex:			
Male	56,431	56.8	43.2
Female	64,270	52.7	47.3
Color:			
White	107,997	56.0	44.0
Black	11,472	43.5	56.5
Age:			
21-24 years	12,594	30.4	69.6
25-34 years	24,666	46.2	53.8
35-44 years	22,390	58.1	41.9
45-64 years	41,477	64.2	35.8
65 years and over	19,138	57.0	43.0
Residence:			
Metropolitan	43,337	55.3	44.7
Nonmetropolitan	22,550	53.2	46.8
Education:			
8 years or less	29,174	43.4	56.6
9-11 years	20,290	47.1	52.9
12 years	42,927	58.4	41.6
More than 12 years	28,311	65.7	34.3
Employment status:			
Employed	71,548	57.2	42.8
Unemployed	3,235	41.2	58.9
Not in labor force	45,919	51.5	48.5
Family income:[1]			
Under $3,000	9,238	42.0	58.0
$3,000-$4,999	12,302	45.0	55.0
$5,000-$7,499	19,393	48.0	52.0
$7,500-$9,999	19,549	55.3	44.7
$10,000 and over	37,987	66.2	33.8
Not reported	6,323	53.9	46.1

[1] Covers persons 21 years of age and over in primary families

Statistics indicate that the highest rate of voting is shown by white males who live in cities, are employed, have high incomes, and are between 45 and 64 years of age.

SOURCE: U.S. Department of Commerce, Bureau of the Census, *Current Population Reports*, series P-20, nos. 192, 228. Abridged from *Statistical Abstract: 1972*, p. 374.

tend to be Democrats.[20] There is also a faintly discernible tendency toward liberalism in the very upper class that leads some of its members to join the Democratic rather than the Republican party. Some examples are Franklin D. Roosevelt and the Kennedy brothers.

20. Paul F. Lazarsfeld and Wagner Thielens, Jr., *The Academic Mind* (New York: Free Press, 1958), pp. 14–17.

In recent years, there has been a movement of the well-educated away from both parties and into the ranks of the independent voters. Although earlier studies showed that independent voters were often poorly informed and politically apathetic, current studies indicate that in a significant number of cases, the independent voter is relatively well informed on the issues involved in a campaign and chooses his candidates on the basis of their positions in regard to the issues. There is evidence that young people vote independently more often than their parents; it remains to be seen whether this indicates the existence of a new type of political awareness that will be basically nonpartisan, or whether it is a simple age difference and these young people will affiliate themselves with a party as they grow older.

Political attitudes

When political attitudes and opinion ranging from "conservative" to "liberal" are considered separately from the question of party membership, a slightly different picture emerges. In terms of economic policies, the lower and working classes tend to be more liberal than the higher classes. They are more likely to support "liberal" measures such as welfare and social security payments, government controls of the economy, and graduated income taxes. However, in areas other than economic policy, the lower and working classes are generally much less liberal in their attitudes. In areas such as civil liberties and international policy, their views tend to be conservative. For example, they favor the curtailment of certain civil liberties for some dissident groups, and the isolation of America from international ties and alliances.[21]

In general, the lower-class social outlook may be termed an authoritarian one, in specifically political terms. Lipset suggests that the experience of the lower-class individual produces

A tendency to view politics and personal relationship in black and white terms, a desire for immediate action, an impatience with talk and discussion, a lack of interest in organizations which have a long-range perspective, and a readiness to follow leaders who offer

demonological interpretation of the evil forces (either religious or political) which are conspiring against them.[22]

The amount of education a person has seems to be influential in determining whether or not he will have liberal attitudes regarding civil liberties and international policy. Studies have indicated that the relative liberalism of the middle class in this area is due more to their higher level of education than to their higher incomes. However, there is also evidence to show that those individuals with higher incomes are less likely to favor liberal economic policies;[23] in regard to economic attitudes, income is a more important determinant than education.

REPRESENTATIONAL DEMOCRACY AND POLITICAL ELITES

The type of political system we have in the United States is called a representational democracy. Every adult citizen has a vote to choose the leaders and decision makers in government, and anyone who can demonstrate some degree of popular support (a certain number of signatures on a petition, for example) and meet a few qualifications of age and citizenship, may put himself forward as an election candidate for leadership and office holding.

Every citizen of a certain age may cast his vote freely (though in practice this freedom has sometimes been restricted, such as in the cases of sex and racial discrimination), and every vote carries equal weight; that is the essential meaning of a democracy. Yet once the officials are elected, the average citizen plays only a small part in the political process; his elected representative acts in his behalf. Citizens may offer their opinions on an issue or a policy, but the official is not obligated to listen to them. He is relatively

21. Morris Janowitz and Dwaine Marvick, "Authoritarianism and Political Behavior," *Public Opinion Quarterly* 17 (1953): 195–196.

22. Lipset, *Political Man*, p. 115.

23. Mabel Newcomer, *The Big Business Executive* (New York: Columbia University Press, 1955), p. 49.

free to use his own judgment, even when it runs against the wishes of the people who elected him. He must remain reasonably responsive to his constituency, however, under threat of being defeated in the next election.

Our form of government inevitably creates a small group of people, both elected and appointed officials of the government, and others in "high places," who hold a large measure of political power over the rest of the population. This centralization of power is magnified by the complexity and hierarchical nature of modern governmental organization. Some sociologists, notably C. Wright Mills in his book *The Power Elite*,[24] regard this small group as relatively cohesive, with many common perspectives and interests, and somewhat unresponsive to the electorate. Looked at in this light, democracy in America is a form of elite rule, which is periodically sanctioned by the voters in public elections. A member of the elite may occasionally be voted out, but by and large, the group remains very stable.

Other sociologists, while agreeing that those who hold political office do indeed constitute an elite, feel their power is much less absolute than may be imagined and that there is little evidence to indicate that they are self-perpetuating oligarchies. In this view, there are many constraints on the actions of elites, the most important of which may be the actions of counter-elites: the many powerful organizations and interest groups which are characteristic of a pluralistic society. This view is similar to the one expressed by the Italian sociologist and economist, Vilfredo Pareto, in the late nineteenth century. He theorized that social stability and freedom depend on the "circulation of elites": the free access to the ruling class of men of ability and talent and the continuing flow of these men through the power centers of society, preventing any one group from obtaining a monopoly

Vilfredo Pareto (1848–1923) was influenced by his early training in mathematics and engineering to take a somewhat mechanistic view of social organization. He saw society as a rational system for achieving goals which was occasionally interrupted by irrational factors. Pareto was one of the first grand theorists of social systems; modern sociologists reject his broad hypothesis but value many of his insights into the nature of social change and stratification. His major work has been translated from Italian into English under the title *Mind and Society: A Treatise on General Sociology* (1916).

on the sources and exercise of power.[25]

It is fair to say that America's founding fathers saw this nation as one that would be run by a governing elite. However, their rhetoric has proved more influential than their intentions, and the idea of government "by the people" has been strongly embedded in our political attitudes. The kind of state which was organized under our Constitution has been adaptable to changes in the direction of greater mass participation.

One of the most important questions fac-

24.   C. Wright Mills, *The Power Elite* (New York: Oxford University Press, 1956).

25.   Vilfredo Pareto, *Mind and Society: A Treatise on General Sociology* [*Mattato di sociologia generale*], trans. A. Livingston and A. Bongiorno (1916; English trans., New York: Dover Publications, 1935).

ing our country today is whether or not the state can continue to make itself responsive to the demands for wider participation in the face of increasing centralization of power. As Dwight D. Eisenhower noted at the end of his presidency, the increasing concentration of power in the hands of the military-industrial complex is a source of potential danger to American freedom. The need for a strong centralized government and the pressures of international politics have combined to encourage the concentration of power beyond that envisioned by the framers of our Constitution.

PARTICIPATORY DEMOCRACY

The term *participatory democracy* was used by the political philosopher Herbert Marcuse to describe the trend toward greater involvement of the entire population with the processes of politics and the working of the government.[26] The demand for participatory democracy is evident today in a number of different areas. The desire for neighborhood control of public institutions such as the schools and the police department; the requests of students, welfare recipients, and residents of public housing

projects for a larger voice in the agencies or organizations that control so many of the circumstances of their daily lives; the explicitly stated intention of government programs to acquaint members of low status groups with the mechanics of democratic self-government and to encourage political participation are all signs of growing interest in participatory democracy.

There are certain dangers as well as benefits in widespread or mass participation in politics. Democratic processes require the learning of certain skills, such as the evaluation of issues and policies, compromise, and the protection of the rights of minorities. The sudden inclusion of large numbers of people who lack these skills into the political system of a democracy could seriously threaten its stability. Participatory democracy can also be inefficient: as the number of competing interests increases, the longer it takes to make decisions. A modern state would find it virtually impossible to operate entirely on the basis of participatory democracy.

A great issue of the coming decades will be how to achieve a balance between widespread political participation, local decision making, and popular control, on the one hand, and the realities and requirements of a highly complex, centralized, and technical political system, on the other.

26. Herbert Marcuse, *One Dimensional Man: Studies in the Ideology of Advanced Industrial Society* (Boston: Beacon Press, 1964), p. 57.

PAUL LAZARSFELD, BERNARD BERELSON, AND HAZEL GAUDET
The Political Homogeneity of Social Groups

Abridged from *The People's Choice*, by Paul F. Lazarsfeld, Bernard Berelson, and Hazel Gaudet (New York: Columbia University Press, 1944), pp. 137–149.

Introduction

A classic study of the way American voters decide how to vote in national political cam-

paigns was made during the 1940 election by Lazarsfeld, Berelson, and Gaudet. The two candidates for president in that year were Wendell Willkie and Franklin D. Roosevelt, who was running for his third term in office. It was a hotly contested campaign. These three sociologists made a careful and thorough study of the attitudes of voters in Erie County, Ohio, before, during, and after the election. They sampled opinion at every fourth house and from this sample drew up a representative group of 3,400 people to study in depth. The focus

*of their investigation was how the voter
makes up his mind. This section deals
with the effects of socialization, both in
the family group and in formal organizations, on voter attitudes and
preferences.*

Repeatedly in this study we found indications that people vote "in groups."

Slightly more than half of Erie County
voters were Republican. This was true for
the total population of the county, as well
as for the different groups of 600 people
included in our study. If, then, we had taken
the name of every hundredth person from an
alphabetical list of all county residents,
we would have found, again, that slightly
more than half were Republicans.

But suppose now we had proceeded differently, had picked a score of Republicans
at random, and had asked them to name as
many friends, neighbors, and fellow workers
as they could remember. If we then asked
the people assembled on this list for whom
they intended to vote, the proportion of
Republicans would have been considerably
higher than it was for the county as a whole.
And, conversely, if we had started with a
score of Democrats and had asked them to
name their associates in the different spheres
of their lives, we would have found a considerably lower proportion of Republicans
on this list than we found in the county.

This represents another formulation of our
statement that voting is essentially a group
experience. People who work or live or play
together are likely to vote for the same
candidates.

Two kinds of evidence may be provided
for this general statement. On the one hand
we can study directly the political homogeneity of such groups as fraternal organizations, churches, sports clubs, as well as the
family and similar institutionalized groups.
On the other hand, we can use an indirect
approach. People who have certain characteristics in common are more likely to belong
to the same groups. We know from general

observation, for instance, that people
tend to associate with others of their own
age rather than with people considerably
older or younger than themselves. If we find
then that there are marked differences in
voting between various age groups, we
would have inferential evidence that people
who have closer contacts with each other
are more apt to vote alike.

The political structure of the family

The family is a group particularly suited
to the purposes of our study, because here
living conditions attain a maximum of similarity and because mutual contacts are more
frequent than in other groupings.

In August we found 344 panel members
who had made up their minds as to how
they would vote, and who also had another
eligible voter living in the same household.
At that time, 78 percent of these other
eligible voters intended to vote for the
same candidate as did the respondent, 20
percent were uncertain, and 2 percent disagreed with the respondent in his choice of
candidate. The situation changed little when
it came to actual voting. After the election,
only 4 percent of the 413 panel members
who voted claimed that someone in their
families had voted differently from themselves. It is interesting to observe
incidentally, that the extent of disagreement
increased slightly toward the end of the
campaign.

We can explore the interrelationships of
influence within the family in somewhat
greater detail. Among husbands and wives,
both of whom had decided to vote, only one
pair in 22 disagreed. Among parents and
children, one pair in 12 disagreed, the gap
of a generation increasing differences in life
and outlook. Agreement was least—as all
the jokes emphasize—among "in-laws" living
in the same household. One pair in five
showed disagreement on party alignment.

The almost perfect agreement between
husband and wife comes about as a result
of male dominance in political situations.

At one point of the study we asked each respondent whether he had discussed politics with someone else in recent weeks. Forty-five of the women stated that they had talked the election over with their husbands; but, of an equal number of randomly selected men, only four reported discussions with their wives. If these family discussions play as important a role for husbands as they do for wives, then we should get approximately the same number of reports on the interchange of political ideas from both sexes. But only the wives are aware of the political opinions of their husbands. Men do not feel that they are discussing politics with their wives; they feel they are telling them. And, as we can see from the following quotations, the wives are willing to be told:

"On previous interviews, I hadn't given it any thought, but it is close to election and I guess I will vote Democratic and *go along with my husband.*"

"My husband has always been Republican. He says that if we vote for different parties there is no use in our voting. So *I think I will give in this year and vote Republican. . . .*"

It appears that not only the color of opinion, but the whole level of interest is contagious from one family member to another. Of the men who had a vote intention and great interest in the election, only 30 percent claimed that their wives did not intend to vote, or did not know for whom. For men with less interest, the figure is 52 percent.

If the relationships between father and daughter or between brother and sister are studied, we find a similar dominance of the male in political matters.

In addition, the political homogeneity of the family may extend over several generations. Our panel members were asked, "Do you consider that your family (parents, grandparents) have always been predominantly Democratic or predominantly Republican?" Fully three-fourths of the respondents with vote intentions in September followed the political lead of their families. Here are examples of two *first voters* who

took over the family pattern at the very beginning of their voting careers:

"Probably will vote Democratic because *my grandfather will skin me if I don't.*"

"If I can register I will vote Republican because *my family are all Republicans so therefore I would have to vote that way.*"

These young voters, one a man and the other a woman, provide excellent illustrations of family influence. Neither had much interest in the election and neither paid much attention to the campaign. Both accepted family tradition for their first votes and both are likely to remain in line with that tradition. In the first case, there is even a hint that family sanctions are used to enforce the decision. Thus are party voters born.

Now, what of the exceptional cases in which disagreement does occur within the family? A number of respondents agreed with the young voter just quoted, that political conformity is the price of domestic peace. There was evidence of a good deal of tension in families which could not reach an agreement.

One girl reported in June she intended to vote for the Democratic party because she "liked the Democratic candidates better than the Republicans." She "read an article in Collier's about the Republican candidates and didn't think they sounded very interesting." She "felt Roosevelt did a good job as president" and approved the third term. The girl's parents, however, favored the Republican candidate and this was the source of much conflict. The girl's mother told the interviewer: "She just does it to be opposite. I have always felt that *her views were just revolt against tradition and the stuffy ideas of her parents.*"

The respondent finally broke down and voted for Willkie, explaining, *"My father and friends* thought it would be a good idea not to have Roosevelt for a third term because he would be too much of a dictator."

It is reasonable to expect that with such pressure toward homogeneity, people with unhomogeneous family backgrounds will be more uncertain about their own political affiliations.

Less than 3 percent of voters in families homogeneous in August changed their vote intention during the rest of the campaign. But if there were some relatives who were undecided almost 10 percent of the respondents shifted between August and October. And in the small group of families in which there was definite disagreement, 29 percent of the respondents went through at least one change in position.

And when the people in families not homogeneous in their vote intentions did change their minds, they changed toward the party favored by the rest of the family. Fully 81 percent of the members of Republican families who were originally undecided were pro-Republican in October; and 71 percent of those in Democratic families later came out for Roosevelt. Whatever the reason, whether honest conviction or family loyalty, the family molded their votes — and as a result the family became politically more homogeneous as the campaign wore on.

Again, if all the family members were undecided about their vote intention in August, 63 percent of the respondents from these families were still undecided two months later. But if anyone in the family had reached a decision in August, the proportion of respondents remaining undecided two months later was only 48 percent. In other words, the person who lives in a family where members have decided their intention is much more likely to make up his own mind before Election Day than is the person who lives in a family where no one has a clear cut vote intention.

The family, then, provided a very definite climate of political influence. All of its members are inclined to vote in the same way, and in those cases where there is disagreement, the tension of the situation leads the family members to make some adjustments. It is usually the women who

so adjust, and it is from them that we get most of the references to family discussions as sources of change.

There is no reason why other social groups should not be studied in the same way. The higher level of political tension created during the campaign gives us an opportunity to find out how this political homogeneity of social groups comes about. It is to some of the finer aspects of this process that we now turn.

The role of formal associations

Our sample was too small to make feasible a study of specific organizations. But we can distinguish between those people who belong to formal organizations and those who do not. There are two general findings with regard to membership in these formal organizations which are as applicable to Erie County as they are to other American communities which have been studied before. In the first place, we find that the members of any given organization are recruited from fairly similar socio-economic levels. Secondly, people on the lower SES (socio-economic status) levels are less likely to belong to any organizations than the people on high SES levels.

With these two results in mind, what differences between members and non-members of such organizations does our main thesis lead us to expect? We anticipate that on each SES level the social predisposition of organization members will be more strongly activated than is that of those people on the same SES levels who are not just subject to the "molecular pressures" of the associations. This, we must realize, will be possible only so long as the comparison is carried out on each separate SES level.

Although the proportion of Republicans is generally great on high SES levels, the Republican trend is still stronger among those who join various associations. Why? Is it not likely that simply meeting more often with other persons, even in organizations not ostensibly concerned with politics,

brings about a greater activation of predispositions?

Politically, then, formal associations have
a class character. They facilitate the transformation of social characteristics into
political affiliations. But, conversely, our
results show that the prestige values within
the organizations may, in the case of minority
members, operate to develop affiliations
which are opposed to the predispositions
of these members.

Bringing opinions into line

One final observation demonstrates that
during the campaign social groups imbue
their individual members with the accepted
ideology of the group. By and large, people
who intend to vote for a certain party agree
with its main tenets. Republicans do not
approve of the third term, have a high opinion
of Willkie, think that business experience
is more important than government
experience, etc. Democrats feel the other
way around on all these issues. But in the
middle of the campaign, in August, there were
still a number of people who had an inconsistent attitude pattern. There were, for
instance, 33 Republicans who felt that
government experience is more important
in a president, and 30 Democrats who
thought that business experience would be
more desirable. In the course of the campaign there was a tendency toward consistency. More than half (33) of the people
just mentioned achieved harmony between
vote intention and opinion on this specific
question by October. But how did this come
about? Did people finally join the party which
conformed to their ideas or did they take
over the prevailing opinion of the political
group to which they belonged? The answer is
very clear-cut. Thirty retained their party
allegiance but changed their vote intention
to fit their theory.

This is consistently true for whatever
specific opinion we take. Inconsistencies
are reduced, but in such a way that people
stick to their vote intention and start to

think about specific issues in the way the
majority of their fellow partisans do. These
results fit very well into what we have said
before. If a person's vote intention is to a
great degree a symbol of the social group to
which he or she belongs, then we should not
be surprised that people iron out inconsistencies in their thinking in such a way as
to conform to the group with which they live
from day to day. In a way, the content of this
chapter can be summarized by saying that
people vote, not only *with* their social group,
but also *for* it.

Vote decision as a social experience

How may we explain the fact that social
groups are politically homogeneous and that
the campaign increases this homogeneity
still more? There is, first, the fact that
people who live together under similar
external conditions are likely to develop
similar needs and interests. They tend to see
the world through the same colored glasses;
they tend to apply to common experiences
common interpretations. They will approve
of a political candidate who has achieved
success in their own walk of life; they will
approve of programs which are couched in
terms taken from their own occupations and
adapted to the moral standards of the groups
in which they have a common "belonging."

But this is only part of the picture. There
may be many group members who are not
really aware of the goals of their own group.
And there may be many who, even if they
were aware of these goals, would not be
sufficiently interested in current events to
tie the two together consciously. They
acquiesce to the political temper of their
group under the steady, personal influence
of their more politically active fellow citizens.
Here again, we find the process of activation
by which the predisposed attitudes of some
are brought out by the influence of others.

Conclusion

*An interesting question is how many of
our ideas and attitudes are really "ours,"*

and how many of them were given to us or "forced" on us by others. Voting behavior is especially useful for studying the effects of socialization on attitudes, because the expression of the attitude is so clear; it is usually Democrat, Republican, or not voting

at all. Lazarsfeld's study reveals the great extent to which our political attitudes are influenced and shaped by important groups around us. In this respect political attitudes are little different from our attitudes and beliefs in general.

TOPIC

4 MASS SOCIETY AND TOTALITARIANISM

In this book, we have characterized the American political system as one dominated by political pluralism and representative democracy. However, some observers of the American scene contend that other models of sociopolitical order, especially *mass society* and *totalitarianism,* better represent this country.

We call mass society a "model," because it is not an actual description of an existing society; instead it is a concept that identifies certain current tendencies in societies and suggests what it would be like if they were carried to the logical extreme. Totalitarianism is also a model, but it is an extreme which a few societies have very nearly put into practice.

Both mass society and modern totalitarianism are rooted in, and caused by, the powerful social trends we have already discussed —urbanization, industrialization, bureaucratization, and centralization of power and social control. Therefore, these models are frequently used in the study and analysis of twentieth-century societies, including our own.

MASS SOCIETY

The two basic conditions of the *mass society* are a weak governing elite and a highly

volatile mass of citizens. As the processes of modernization undermine the traditional social ties of family, church, local community, and primary groups, people develop a strong sense of alienation, anomie, and powerlessness. Although social and economic roles are highly specialized and differentiated, individuals themselves rarely have an opportunity to distinguish themselves from others in the mass. This leads to an increasing sense of isolation; people feel that they are related to one another only through their common tie to the distant central authority, the state.

A major feature of the social structure of mass society is the absence of strong medium-sized organizations that can serve to mediate between the individual and the state. The small groups in the society, such as a family, are too weak to be able to influence social events; the large organizations that dominate political and economic life, such as the federal government and business corporations, are too large, distant, and complex to be responsive to individual needs or wants. In a pluralistic society, the gap between these two levels of organization is filled by medium-sized organizations, such as labor unions, professional organizations, and voluntary associations. These serve as the means for

Activist dissenters in our society have often accused the government of using arbitrary police power to curtail public opposition to its policies. The government in turn has charged radical groups with being undemocratic and using illegal methods of protest. Confrontations often involve each side accusing the other of fomenting violence and undermining the public interest. *(Burk Uzzle, Magnum)*

individuals to exert some influence on the centralized power. In a mass society, these mediating organizations are either nonexistent or ineffectively weak.

The centralized power of the mass society is contained in huge organizations run by a small and closed group of elite individuals; these organizations dominate all the major social activities of the society. However, the power of the individuals in this governing elite is unstable and inconsistent. Because their elite status tends to cut them off from the masses, they have difficulty maintaining order, recruiting new leaders, mobilizing support for their policies, and legitimating their authority. Their only channel of communication with the rest of the citizens is the mass media. They are continually open to arbitrary and extreme pressures of mass movements and all forms of collective be-

havior. The structure of mass society encourages such movements, for they are the principal means by which the masses can influence the central authority.

In a mass society, the government and the electorate are thus locked into a system of great instability, with a high potential for violent social and political change. The elites are dominated by unpredictable popular pressures; the masses are subject to manipulation by the elite through the mass media and pressures from their fellow citizens in the form of mass movements.

The foremost theoretician of mass society is William Kornhauser, whose book, *The Politics of Mass Society,* is a classic in the field. One conclusion that Kornhauser draws about mass society is that "this kind of social arrangement leaves society vulnerable to antidemocratic movements based on mass support."[27] He suggests that a very likely outcome of the instability of mass society is the emergence of a totalitarian regime.

TOTALITARIAN SOCIETY

A *totalitarian society* is one in which the state assumes total control over all social organization. It is not a new concept, for example, a number of Roman emperors aspired to establish a totalitarian state. But only in the twentieth century has it become a real possibility, because never before have the means for total control been available. With modern communication, and with technological advances in methods of monitoring conversations, surveying behavior, and recording activities and utterances, the complete control of an entire nation is nearly possible. There have been several actual societies which have come very close to achieving the reality of a totalitarian state: Hitler's Germany and Stalin's Russia are two prime examples.

No conventional government organization can hope to exert the control necessary in this type of society; therefore, the state must establish extragovernmental controls as well. An effective totalitarian state will set up an official political party, the arena for most of the political process. It trains, chooses, and legitimates the ruling political elite. No other party is allowed to organize; attempting to form one is classified as an act of treason. In Hitler's Germany, for example, the Nazi party was the one and only channel of political power.

27. William Kornhauser, *The Politics of Mass Society* (New York: Free Press, 1959), p. 100.

The state also creates an official ideology, a total world view which tells people how to behave, what to believe in, and when and how to act in any given situation. Nationalism usually plays an important part in this ideology, for people's patriotic love of their country serves to blind them to its totalitarianism. Other ideologies, such as fascism or communism, may also be included. Rival world views are suppressed. Religious groups are persecuted and the creations of artists and intellectuals are censored by the state.

The totalitarian state manages the economy, the communications media, and all forms of groups or associations. Its power is legitimated through the use of force, not by any kind of consent, although the state may go through the formal motions of elections to maintain the appearance of having legitimation by consent. A totalitarian state must also be a police state; those who disagree with state policies are executed, imprisoned, or exiled.

The totalitarian state is unquestionably efficient in achieving certain kinds of social goals, especially those of an industrial society. Nazi Germany and Stalinist Russia had high rates of industrial production and succeeded in modernizing their economies with amazing rapidity. This kind of success helps the totalitarian state win the compliance of the population. But the cost in human suffering and lack of freedom is high, higher than most people would willingly choose to pay. Moreover, to the extent that a totalitarian society succeeds in establishing total control of the people, it also succeeds in destroying the vitality and creativity that are necessary for the society's continued existence.

SUMMARY

Centralization of the decision making and regulatory institutions of society has been made necessary and inevitable by the growing diversity and interdependence that characterize modern societies. In all types of political and economic systems, the state has assumed greater power in coordinating the varied and conflicting interests of its citizens. Power can be used directly or indirectly, positively or negatively by applying pressure through the promise of rewards, the threat of punishment, or by manipulating information, attitudes, or feelings. When power is used in a way that is recognized as socially right or *legitimate,* it is called *authority.* Max Weber has classified the main sources of social authority or legitimate power into three major types: 1) *traditional authority,* or that conferred by custom and accepted practice; 2) *charismatic authority,* generated by the personal appeal of an individual; and 3) *legal bureaucratic authority,* which rests upon rules that are rationally established. The institution with supreme legitimate power or authority in society is the state. In primitive society the state was closely integrated with broad and diverse social functions. However, in modern society the state is a specialized institution which functions primarily to establish and enforce formal norms of behavior that are considered necessary for the social order and welfare, to protect the rights of individual citizens, to protect the society from outside enemies, and to plan, finance, regulate, and operate activities that are important for the general welfare.

Modernization has an important impact on the political development of societies. Political changes are both a cause and a consequence of other social changes. As societies became larger and more diverse, the old system of kinship-based political control which depended on daily personal interaction broke down. More impersonal and specialized political forms evolved based on specialized leadership roles, separate institutions for social control, and formal bodies of law. In the Western world, the *city-state,* often organized in terms of feudal estates or rigid social strata based on land ownership, gradually emerged as the dominant political form. In the fifteenth century neighboring city-states were welded together to form nations in various parts of Europe. The development of

politically centralized nations was made possible by the existence of geographically defined countries that could be defended, that were internally united by channels of trade and communication, and were socially integrated to some degree.

The first true nations to appear in western Europe emerged in those societies which had strong monarchies and a high degree of technological progress. These nations conquered and imposed their government on numerous societies throughout Asia, Africa, and the Americas. Where the local government was strong and the colony was used chiefly as a source of raw materials, the colonizers maintained the existing state organization and ruled indirectly. Where political organization was weak and the colony served as a market for goods or as a manufacturing center, Europeans established their own system and ruled directly. In either case, many of the colonial societies' original institutions were destroyed and the colonized nations were placed in a subservient position. Yet colonialism did help to establish boundaries in the colonized nations, created centralized social organizations, sometimes trained and educated the population, and helped to unify colonial peoples by promoting a sense of nationalism. Today as the Third World countries are undergoing the process of social and economic modernization, they share certain political problems: 1) conflict between older patterns of political organization and those of the modern state; 2) rising expectations which cannot adequately be met; 3) the need for effective leaders; 4) conflict between the needs and wants of the people and the long-range plans of the leaders; and 5) competition between the advocates of capitalism and communism. Political change and development in these areas is occurring both through revolution and evolution. *Evolutionary change* works with established social and political institutions and provides a measure of continuity to ease the transition from the old to the new social order. However, when such a process is not possible, transformations may be precipitated through *revolution,* a large-scale restructuring of the leadership and political institutions of a society. For revolution to occur, people must be aware of the inequities they suffer and of alternatives to their present condition; existing political institutions must also be weak.

Despite a diversified population, we have maintained political freedom and stability in the United States through a tradition of *political pluralism,* a social pattern in which power is divided among many different groups, each of which presents a significant set of interests. Political pluralism is supported by the fact that Americans are often members of a number of different politically powerful groups and therefore accept conflicts of interest as legitimate. Pluralism is also reinforced by the American two-party system and by a governmental organization based on separation of powers and a system of checks and balances.

Political participation and voting patterns often reflect our system of stratification, with the lower classes generally participat-

ing less and therefore being underrepresented. *Representative democracy,* as we practice it, contributes to the creation of political elites. Sociologists disagree on the extent to which this elite is dispersed or forms a concentrated and self-perpetuating oligarchy. Increasingly, however, people are demanding a greater involvement in the political process, or a more *participatory form of democracy.* It is very difficult to find the proper balance between local decision making and popular control on the one hand, and the requirements of a highly complex, centralized, and technical political system on the other.

Some social scientists have described America as tending toward a *mass society* or a *totalitarian state.* Mass society, characterized by a weak government, a highly volatile mass of citizens, and the absence of strong mediating organizations, is a highly unstable system with a potential for violent upheaval. Totalitarian society, in which the state assumes total control over all social organization, may successfully achieve a number of social and economic goals, but the cost of human suffering and loss of freedom is usually very high.

GLOSSARY

Authority Power that has been made legitimate, that is, socially accepted as right, proper, and necessary. (page 611)

Charismatic authority Authority generated by the personality or personal appeal of some individual. (page 612)

Coup d-état A change of government in which one leadership group forcefully overthrows another. (page 621)

Evolutionary change Political change that develops out of existing trends and institutions. (page 621)

Government The group of individuals who exercise the powers invested in the state. (page 613)

Illegitimate power Power used without the support of social approval. (page 611)

Legal bureaucratic authority Authority which rests upon rationally established rules. (page 612)

Legitimate power Power used in a way that is generally recognized as socially right and necessary. (page 611)

Mass society A society in which there is a weak governing elite and a highly volatile mass of citizens who feel a sense of alienation, anomie, and powerlessness. (page 635)

Participatory democracy Involvement of the entire population of a society with the processes and workings of the government. (page 630)

Political pluralism A social pattern in which power is divided among a number of large groups, each of which represents a significant set of interests or values. (page 623)

Politics The acquisition and use of power, especially within the context of the institution of the state and its government. (page 609)

Revolutionary change A kind of political change that seeks to destroy existing institutions of political power and replace them with new ones. (page 621)

Social power The ability to control the actions of others, even against their own wishes. (page 610)

State The social institution which has the su-

preme power in a society; it has a monopoly on the legitimate use of coercion and physical force. (page 613)

Totalitarian society A society in which the state assumes total control over all social organization. (page 637)

Traditional authority Authority conferred by custom and accepted practice. (page 612)

SUGGESTED READINGS AND RELATED RESOURCES

I READINGS IN SOCIOLOGY

Almond, Gabriel A., and James S. Coleman, eds. *The Politics of the Developing Areas.* Princeton, N.J.: Princeton University Press, 1960. The work of a committee, this study attempts to develop a comprehensive framework for the analysis of political and economic systems.

Bendix, Reinhard. *Nation-building and Citizenship: Studies in a Changing Social Order.* New York: John Wiley, 1964. Using the history of Western political systems as a frame of reference, Bendix tries to plot the past and probable future growth of the emerging non-Western nations.

Bottomore, T. B. *Elites and Society.* New York: Basic Books, 1964. Bottomore compares classical and contemporary theories of elites to theories of class structure, and shows how the former have related to ideologies of democracy and egalitarianism.

Campbell, Angus, et al. *The American Voter.* New York: John Wiley, 1960. This examination of the participation of Americans in government looks at the impact of party identification, at the effect government policies and economics have on political preferences, and at the effect electoral behavior has on politics.

Dahl, Robert A. *Who Governs?* New Haven: Yale University Press, 1961. This study of the patterns and distribution of influence in the city politics of New Haven, Connecticut, stresses the importance of political pluralism in community level politics.

DeWitt, Robert L. *Public Policy in Community Protest.* Toronto: University of Toronto Press, 1970. This monograph focuses on a small group of fishermen off the Newfoundland coast and their reactions to government policies. It is an interesting study of how an isolated culture adapts to industrialization.

Etzioni, Amitai. *The Active Society.* New York: Free Press, 1968. This book is an example of macrosociology. Etzioni forecasts that more social planning will be used to help institutions adapt more readily to mushrooming technology, industrialization, and bureaucratization. He also predicts a greater degree of centralization in some sectors of modern societies and an increasing concern with social welfare, focusing on the importance and uses of social planning.

Gans, Herbert. *People and Plans: Essays on Urban Problems and Solutions.* New York: Basic Books, 1968. Gans discusses various topics concerning modern urban areas, from the problems of the inner city to the suburbs and the coming of new towns.

Gouldner, Alvin W., and S. M. Miller, eds. *Applied Sociology.* New York: Free Press, 1965. This collection of articles presents some of the practical uses organizations and communities have made of sociological knowledge and research.

Horowitz, Irving Louis. *Three Worlds of Development: The Theory and Practice of International Stratification.* New York: Oxford University Press, 1966. Horowitz makes historical comparisons of political and economic development in Eastern, Western, and Third World nations to demonstrate some general principles of national development.

Kornhauser, William. *The Politics of Mass Society.* New York: Free Press, 1961. This book discusses the theory of mass society, drawing on other political and social theories, as well as a wide range of empirical data.

Lipset, S. M. *Political Man: The Social Bases of Politics.* New York: Doubleday, Anchor (Paper), 1960. In a major contribution to political sociology, Lipset discusses such topics as the form and content of Western democracies, voting patterns, and party politics.

MacIver, Robert M. *The Web of Government.* Rev. ed. New York: Free Press, 1965. In an extensive examination of the nature of government, MacIver discusses its historical development from the family to the state, the processes of change, and the dynamics of international relations. He sets up a typology of governmental forms and discusses the nature of authority and law.

Mills, C. Wright. *Power, Politics and People.* New York: Ballantine (Paper), 1963. This collection of essays by Mills covers such topics as the structure of political power and elites in the United States, the social consequences of political action by the major American political groups, and the formation of public opinion through the mass media.

Nisbet, Robert A. *Community and Power.* New York: Oxford University Press, 1962. Nisbet states that with the centralization and ascendancy of the mass society, the community is becoming less important as a source of social power. The individual, left on his own, is becoming alienated, and nationalism is replacing the values of personal autonomy and pluralism.

———. *Tradition and Revolt.* New York: Random House, 1968. In these historical and sociological essays, Nisbet analyzes the historical conflict between "traditionalism" and modernization, from the end of the eighteenth century to contemporary times.

Odegard, Peter. *Political Power and Social Change.* New Brunswick, N.J.: Rutgers University Press, 1966. Odegard discusses the concepts of permanence and change in social and political structures, the development of pluralistic societies, and concludes with a chapter on the "use and abuse of political power."

Pareto, Vilfredo. *The Rise and Fall of the Elites.* Totowa, N.J.: Bedminster Press, 1968.

First published in 1901. This concise essay spells out Pareto's classical theory of the circulation of elites.

Articles and Papers

Bierstedt, Robert. "The Problem of Authority." In *Freedom and Control in Modern Society,* edited by Morroe Berger, Theodore Abel, and Charles Page. New York: Van Nostrand, 1954.

Bittinger, Desmond W. "An Examination of the Socio-Political Economic Effect of the 'Concept of History' on a Nation's Outlook and Endeavor." *American Journal of Sociology,* December 1963, pp. 81–91.

Davies, James C. "Toward a Theory of Revolution." *American Sociological Review* 27 (February 1962):5–19.

Dyckman, John W. "Social Planning, Social Planners and Planned Societies." In *Neighborhood, City and Metropolis,* edited by R. Gutman and D. Popenoe, pp. 896–909. New York: Random House, 1970.

Etzioni, Amitai. "Toward a Theory of Societal Guidance." *American Journal of Sociology* 73, 2 (September 1967):173–187.

Frankel, Jesse. "Towards a Decision-making Model in Foreign Policy." *Political Study* 7, 1 (February 1959):1-11.

Greer, Scott, and Peter Orleans. "The Mass Society and the Parapolitical Structure." *American Sociological Review* 27, 5 (October 1962):634–646.

Gusfield, Joseph R. "Mass Society and Extremist Politics." *American Sociological Review* 27, 1 (February 1962).

Hobbs, Daryl Jerome. "A Comment on Applied Sociological Research." *Rural Sociology* 34, 2 (June 1969):241–245.

Janowitz, Morris, and Dwaine Marvick. "Authoritarianism and Political Behavior." *Public Opinion Quarterly* 17 (1953).

Key, William H., and Louis A. Zurcher. "The Overlap Model: A Comparison of Strategies for Social Change." *Sociological Quarterly* 9, 1 (Winter 1968):85–96.

Parsons, Talcott. "The Distribution of Power in American Society." In *Structure and Process in Modern Society,* by Parsons. New York: Free Press, 1960.

Rankin, R., and Eugene A. Quarrick. "Personality and Attitude Toward a Political Event."

Journal of Individual Psychology **20**, 2 (November 1964):189–193.

Spinrad, William. "Power in Local Communities." *Social Problems* **12** (Winter 1965):335–356.

II   RELATED RESOURCES
Nonfiction

Brinton, Crane. *The Anatomy of Revolution.* New York: Random House, Vintage (Paper), 1962. First published in 1938. Brinton compares the various stages of the revolutions in France, America, and Russia, analyzing the changes they brought about.

Castro, Josue De, et al. *Latin American Radicalism: A Documentary Report on Left and Nationalist Movement.* New York: Random House, Vintage Books (Paper), 1969. The authors write about left-wing groups which are working to remove foreign powers from their countries and to bring about social change.

Clark, Kenneth B., and Jeannette Hopkins. *A Relevant War against Poverty.* New York: Harper & Row, Harper Torchbooks (Paper), 1969. Clark and Hopkins study community action programs and the social change which they have brought about.

Dahrendorf, Ralf. *Class and Class Conflict in Industrial Society.* Stanford, Calif.: Stanford University Press, 1959. Dahrendorf discusses political order and stability in modern society from the point of view of class and class conflict.

Heilbroner, Robert L. *The Future as History.* New York: Harper & Row, 1960. Heilbroner, an economist, discusses the main currents of modernization and the directions in which they seem to be taking Western nations.

Klapp, Orrin. *Symbolic Leaders: Public Dramas and Public Men.* New York: Minerva Press (Paper), 1968. Using case histories of such diverse public figures as Martin Luther King, Jr., Richard Nixon, Nelson Rockefeller, Marilyn Monroe, and the New York Mets, Klapp analyzes the significance these leaders had for the structures of our rapidly changing society.

Sigmund, Paul E., ed. *The Ideologies of the Developing Nations.* New York: Praeger (Paper), 1963. This collection of essays analyzes the ideologies and political leaders of the anticolonial revolutions that have occurred and are occurring in nations undergoing modernization.

Fiction

Ruark, Robert. *Uhuru.* New York: Fawcett, 1969. A newly independent African nation is the setting for this novel about politicians struggling to build a working political structure from the shambles left by the departing colonial powers.

Warren, Robert Penn. *All the King's Men.* New York: Bantam, 1966. Willie Stark, the main character of this novel, rises through the political ranks to become governor of his state. Along the way he has become expert in the use of graft, payoffs, and even less savory arts, and has amassed the power of a near dictator.

Films

Advise and Consent. Otto Preminger, 1962. This film is based on Allen Drury's novel of the same name and portrays the political and personal struggles for power that go on in the nation's capital.

La Chinoise. Jean-Luc Godard, 1968. In a quasi-documentary style, Godard satirically portrays the new political youth from the perspective of a member of the youth movement.

The Last Hurrah. John Ford, 1958. This film portrays the pressures and struggles for power in big-city machine politics and the life of a man who ran such a machine.

16. Social and Cultural Change

In the first four chapters of Part III we have been
discussing the major social trends in modern
societies: urbanization, industrialization, and the
growth of centralized political direction and control.
We have also looked at two major social phenomena
which are both consequences and primary sources of
social and cultural change: deviance and collective
behavior. In this final chapter we shall summarize
the major overarching theories which have been
developed in the social sciences to explain sociocultural change. These include theories about which
specific factors seem most important as generators
of change, several "grand" theories which have
been developed to explain change throughout world
history, and a reemerging theoretical orientation
toward change: sociocultural evolution.

The question of where modern societies are
headed now that they have become urbanized and
industrialized is discussed in topic 2. Many
sociologists feel that a new sociocultural order is
emerging, called posturban-industrial society. This
new order has its own distinctive set of social
problems, most of which are now rapidly becoming
matters of public concern. One central feature of
posturban-industrial societies is the great importance
of social planning: collective attempts to guide
sociocultural change in desired directions. This is
the subject of discussion in the final topic of the
book. It is especially suitable as a closing topic
because it represents a major way in which sociological knowledge can be a constructive force in the
modern world.

TOPIC

1 THEORIES OF SOCIOCULTURAL CHANGE

Sociocultural change has long been a subject of great interest to sociological theorists because it provides the answers to many questions about human history. There has recently been an upsurge in interest in this field because it holds the key to understanding man's future. The theories range from detailed explanations of specific social or cultural factors which are regarded as especially important in causing change, to systematic and abstract theories which attempt to pull together all available knowledge directed toward establishing the broad trends, fluctuations, and cycles in the development of human societies. We shall focus first on the major change factors.

FACTORS OF CHANGE

Social scientists have identified a variety of factors that cause social and cultural change, ranging from the dedicated efforts of a single individual, as in the case of Sequoya's invention of a written language for the Cherokees, to the effects of some natural cataclysm, such as a volcanic eruption that buries fertile farm land under tons of rocky lava and forces the inhabitants of the area to learn new ways of providing food for themselves. However, both these examples are extremes, and they occur only rarely. A much more common factor of change, and one which has received widespread scientific study, is *technology*—the knowledge and tools man uses to manipulate the environment.

The technological factor

Advances in technology often seem to be irresistible. As soon as man learns how to do

something, it is put into practice, whether or not the moral and social implications have been understood or even considered. These changes bring about responding changes in the culture, some of them very far-reaching, which may not be observed or analyzed until many years later.

In the last few decades, we have seen many examples of the impetus toward change furnished society by technology. The development of the atomic bomb, the isolation of the human gene, the trips to the moon, the transplantation and replacement of human organs—all these have been recently undertaken with surprisingly little consideration or planning regarding their long-range effects. Their developers were mainly interested in whether or not they were possible and what their more immediate short-range benefits would be. Yet each one of these feats could possibly lead to hundreds of dramatic changes in our culture.

The only one of the technological changes listed above that has had time to effect noticeable changes in our culture is the invention of atomic weapons, for it has been nearly twenty-five years since their power was demonstrated to the world. What changes can we attribute to this one technological advance? There has been a change in the structure and orientation of our army, as technological experts have become increasingly necessary. More importantly, there has been a change in the basic attitude of the whole world toward war, which is viewed with increasing fear and dread since the consequences would be so dire. Because everyone realizes there is no shelter even for noncombatants in a nuclear war, a greater recognition of the need for

Cultures vary greatly in the degree to which they can accept and incorporate new technological inventions. These traditional wind-driven junks will be used in Asian societies for many years, because they are closely linked to other aspects of Asian culture, and because the economic structure necessary to support fully mechanized systems of transportation (which include the helicopter) does not yet exist. *(René Burri, Magnum)*

peace is evident all over the globe (with a consequent increase in internationalism). At the same time, a sort of fatalism has pervaded our attitude toward the future, for the end of the world is no longer an unimaginable disaster but a daily possibility. We might, therefore, call many social changes—more widespread political involvement, a reluctance to defer plans and pleasures for the unknown future, a large antiwar movement—in part the results of this one technological change.

It is interesting to note how often technological changes exert pressure on a society to move in the direction in which it is already going. For example, the recent discovery of birth control pills clearly brought about changes in sexual norms, all in the direction of greater permissiveness. Yet that change was already slowly evolving even before the discovery was made. The pill merely speeded up the rate of evolution. We must remember that technology takes place not in a vacuum,

but in the setting of the particular culture of which it is a part.

An important American theorist of technological determinants of change was William F. Ogburn, who devised a theory called *cultural lag*.[1] Ogburn suggested that most changes occur first in the material aspects of a culture. The nonmaterial aspects of the culture, the system of knowledge and beliefs, norms and values, must then adjust to accommodate the new material advance; it is that period of adjustment which is called cultural lag. It is, of course, possible for the change to occur the other way and for the nonmaterial change to come first, but Ogburn felt that this is a less frequent occurrence. One important qualification of Ogburn's theory of cultural lag must be made; it is impossible for the

1. William F. Ogburn, *Social Change with Respect to Culture and Original Nature,* rev. ed. (New York: Viking, 1950).

material advances to proceed very far ahead of the nonmaterial changes. Material inventions result from the development of nonmaterial ideas; man invents what he sees a use for. An electronic computer is a meaningless object to an Australian aborigine.

The economic factor

There is a school of thought, associated particularly with Karl Marx, that attributes most social change and social movements to underlying economic factors. In this view, the prime motive for human action is the necessity for food, clothing, and shelter, and the employment which can provide these necessities. The Marxian hypothesis is that within a society, the social classes are constantly in conflict for economic reasons, and it is that conflict which produces social change.[2] Marxist communism believes that ultimately the conflict will be won by the working class; but one can accept the importance of economic motives in social change without necessarily agreeing with this particular interpretation of social trends.

Marx has contributed much to sociology by focusing attention on economic explanations for social change and the pressures of class conflict (Marx's views on this subject were discussed in chapter 7). There were economic motives involved in the rise of Protestantism, in both the practice of slavery and the Civil War that ended that practice in America, and in the French Revolution of the late eighteenth century. In all of these instances, analysis of the economic factors of change is vital to an understanding of the situation. But many sociologists hold that the Marxist view is in error in insisting that economic factors are the *only* forces of social change. A more widely held position in American sociology is that religious beliefs, social norms, political ideologies, cultural symbols, and other such social and intellectual

creations may often have more influence over men's actions than do economic necessities.

The ideological factor

The classic analysis of the thesis that the predominating beliefs, values, or ideological commitments of a society are an important factor of social change was that undertaken by Max Weber. His study was in regard to the social and economic changes that resulted from the new ideas and attitudes of Protestantism.[3] Weber suggested that it was the Protestant values in the areas of work, savings, and worldly prosperity that encouraged the development of capitalism in the societies of England and America. (Weber's work on the Protestant ethic was discussed in chapter 10.) Weber later traced a similar connection between the ethical beliefs of Confucianism and the kind of bureaucratic, contractual social system which flourished in China for many centuries.[4] In our own times, we have seen how ideological conversions, such as that of Russia from feudalism to communism, may bring about corresponding changes in social structure and cultural content of a society. In Russia and Communist China, even the work of artists and writers is largely dictated by ideological commitments.

Diffusionism

Another important source of cultural change is exposure to other cultures. Because it is a kind of change that comes from outside the society rather than inside, it sometimes causes a dramatic and dangerous upheaval. This kind of cultural change is of particular interest today, because it is happening in many countries all over the world.

There are a number of examples of the confrontation of two cultures, or the spread-

---

2. Karl Marx and Friedrich Engels, *The Communist Manifesto* (Baltimore: Penguin Books, 1969).

3. Max Weber, *The Protestant Ethic and the Spirit of Capitalism,* trans. Talcott Parsons (New York: Charles Scribner's Sons, 1958).

4. Max Weber, *The Religion of China* (New York: Free Press, 1951).

ing of a culture into new groups, a process called *cultural diffusion*. It happens in wartime, when the troops of one country land in another, as happened when American soldiers landed in the Pacific and later when they occupied Japan. We will read about such a confrontation in Margaret Mead's abridgment, where she describes what happened to the culture of a small New Guinea island when it was exposed to Western culture through the American and Australian armies. It is interesting to note that in this example we see again the irresistibility of technological progress, for it was the Manus (the New Guinea tribe) who changed more than the Americans. Yet Americans have also changed as a result of their contact with other societies. Since the introduction of the jet airliner, when extensive travel became relatively cheap and could be compressed into a two-week vacation, millions of Americans have been to other countries, particularly European ones, and the results are evident in our increased consumption of wine, greater interest in well-designed European furniture and automobiles, and the abundance of recipes for Swiss fondue and beef bourguignon in magazines like *Family Circle*. It is difficult to believe that a program on good French cooking, like Julia Child's or Graham Kerr's, could ever have attracted a national audience twenty years ago.

The process of acquiring the culture of a different group or society is called *acculturation*. Acculturation can serve as a means of stimulating great growth and development in both the cultures involved; for example, think of the benefits that many countries received when Alexander the Great, in the course of his conquest of the known world, spread Greek culture from Egypt to India. Yet it can also spell disaster to a culture, because the changes could come faster than the culture could absorb or cope with them — too fast for any selectivity or direction to be exercised over them.

Diffusionism as a general theory of cultural change was quite popular in the early twentieth century. It suggested that all cultural change was the result of contact between different cultures, that every innovation of culture was born only once and then spread from its birthplace to other cultures. This idea has been largely discredited, due partly to evidence of similar customs or technology in two cultures that could not possibly have had any contact with each other. But the processes of diffusion and acculturation still remain as important sources of change in many different situations.

GRAND THEORIES OF SOCIOCULTURAL CHANGE

In the first half of the twentieth century several extremely wide-ranging theories of sociocultural change, or "philosophies of history," emerged. Although for the last several decades social scientists have turned away from these grand syntheses in favor of more detailed and empirical approaches, there is some evidence that the trend is now turning back — that many social scientists are again trying to comprehend the "big questions" of the human experience. In any event, these theories stand as great monuments to the powers of the human mind. The three most widely known theories formulated by scholars are those of Oswald Spengler, Arnold Toynbee, and Pitirim A. Sorokin.

Spengler

Oswald Spengler (1880–1936) was a German historian; his most famous work was *The Decline of the West,* the first volume of which was published in 1918.[5] Spengler looked on societies as if they were living organisms. Each one has a birth or beginning; a period of childhood in which it develops rapidly; a maturity, which is its "Golden Age"; a long and slow decline, during which social forms become more important than content; and a final period of disintegration, relatively rapid,

5. Oswald Spengler, *The Decline of the West* (1918; reprint ed., New York: Modern Library, 1965).

which is analogous to the death of an organism. Spengler studied eight different societies, and traced this same life cycle in each. As the title of his work suggests, Spengler believed that Western civilization is now in its period of slow decline, leading to eventual disintegration. He pessimistically declared that the process was unalterable, that we could do nothing to stop it. Although few contemporary sociologists agree with all of Spengler's views, his philosophy of history continues to generate much interest more than fifty years after its publication.

Toynbee

Like Spengler, Arnold Toynbee (1889–   ) is an historian who interprets the history of social development. Toynbee is English; the name of his major work is *A Study of History*.[6] He too sees the development of society as a cyclical process, but as one that can be repeated many times over, and he is decidedly optimistic about the outcome of the modern age. Toynbee said that each cycle begins with a "challenge" of some sort — initially the challenge to make a living from the land, later the social challenges of man's adjustment to his fellow men. Each challenge is met by a "response"; if the response is successful, the society survives and the process continues on to the next round; if the response is an unsuccessful one, the society is destroyed by the unmet challenge. Toynbee views the cycle of challenge and response as a kind of progress toward a perfect civilization. Some critics have noted that there is a significant element of ethnocentrism in Toynbee's social theory, for he assumes that modern Western, and especially English, society is the greatest yet achieved.

Sorokin

Pitirim A. Sorokin (1889–1968) was a Russian-American sociologist who also wrote a multivolumed sociological interpretation of history; his is called *Social and Cultural Dynamics*.[7] Sorokin's interpretation is largely based on a detailed, partly quantitative comparison of a large number of cultures. He suggests that there are two basic types of culture. One he calls sensate, and in it human interaction and symbolic expression are primarily designed to gratify the senses. Its art is pictorial; its philosophy is based on what can be learned or perceived through the senses (science). The other cultural type is ideational, meaning that it appeals most to the mind or the soul. Ideational art is abstract; ideational philosophy is based on faith and belief (religion). Sorokin says that all societies alternate between sensate and ideational cultures. The alternation is not necessarily regular or cyclical, but it does occur over and over again. In this view, sensate culture begins to develop as an inevitable reaction to a highly organized ideational culture, and vice versa. Sorokin's theory has provoked much debate and controversy among sociologists. It is most often criticized for its failure to provide an explanation of why and how cultures change in specific terms; why is it "natural" for a society to begin to change away from its main cultural theme, and why is it that the change must always be back and forth between only two alternatives? Despite these objections, Sorokin's work must stand as a landmark of sociological scholarship.

SOCIOCULTURAL EVOLUTION

After years of decline and neglect, the concept of social evolution has again become an important orientation in sociology. The notion of evolution appeared throughout the work of the founding fathers of sociology, but in the last fifty years American sociologists have concentrated on building sociology as a science, and have not been concerned with developing such broad and quite speculative theories. The theories of evolution try to

6. Arnold Toynbee, *A Study of History*, 12 vols. (1935–1961; reprint ed., New York: Oxford University Press, paper, 1962–1964).

7. Pitirim A. Sorokin, *Social and Cultural Dynamics* (New York: American Book, 1941).

answer the question, "How have societies changed throughout history and where are they headed in the future?" The rebirth of concern for evolutionary thought is due to a general growing concern with large-scale, international problems. The Third World nations are seeking guidelines for rapid and widespread modernization; there is growing concern about the future of the Western societies; and within sociology there is a trend toward macrosociology and the comparative study of whole societies.

The theory of sociocultural evolution holds that over time cultures and societies change and develop from simpler to more complex forms.[8] Unlike the "grand" social theorists discussed in the last section, who held that cultures and societies go through continual cycles of growth and decay, challenge and response, the evolutionists point to important trends that seem to continue in roughly one direction, without repeating themselves or turning back. These master trends build on themselves, so previous changes are retained and influence future changes.

Some examples of evolutionary trends are:

1. The increased ability of societies to master the environment. In other words, the increased *technological development* of societies.
2. More social and cultural activities and functions are being created, and individuals or groups are increasingly specializing in one or more of these activities. This increased diversity and specialization is known as *social differentiation*.
3. The units of societies (such as individuals, groups, organizations, and governments) are becoming more and more dependent on one another; each unit relies more on other units to help it perform its task. Sociologists say there is increasing *functional interdependence*.

8. See, for example, Talcott Parsons, *Societies: Evolutionary and Comparative Perspectives* (Englewood Cliffs, N.J.: Prentice-Hall, 1966) and Gerhard Lenski, *Human Societies* (New York: McGraw-Hill, 1970).

Pitirim A. Sorokin (1889–1968) was a prolific writer whose interests ranged from art to revolution. He is best known for his theoretical works, which analyze and compare the cultural and social structure of various societies, both past and present. However, he also undertook many investigations in specialized areas of research. His writings provide a conceptual basis for much of sociology's present-day research, and at Harvard, where he founded the sociology department and taught for many years, many of the leading contemporary sociologists were his students. Sorokin's best-known work is *Social and Cultural Dynamics* (1937–1941), a multivolumed study which examines sociocultural change throughout history. (*Culver Pictures, Inc.—Bachrach*)

Modern scholars who study such master trends are careful to avoid some of the mistakes of the past. They do not suggest that these trends necessarily lead to progress in the sense of increased human happiness. They do not believe that all societies must pass through the same fixed stages; there are many paths of development. They do not believe that these trends are inevitable, but consider them to be subject to a certain degree of control and modification by man. Finally, they would hold that trends might in the future reverse their direction. For example, large segments are apparently tending to become more alike, rather than more diverse — the opposite of the trend of social differentiation. We see this in the breakdown of regional sub-cultures in America, in the standardization of culture fostered to some extent by the mass media, and in the gradual reduction of class, ethnic, and religious differences.

MARGARET MEAD
New Working of Old Themes

Introduction

In 1932, Margaret Mead made a study of the natives of one of the Admiralty Islands in New Guinea, the Manus. Her book, Growing Up in New Guinea, *is an anthropological classic. Some years later, she heard that as a result of contact with the American and Australian troops who were stationed in the Admiralty Islands during World War II, there were great changes in the culture which she had studied. So she returned and did another study of the Manus, published in 1956 as* New Lives for Old. *In this selection Margaret Mead compares some interesting differences in the way two groups of the Manus adapted to the New Way (Western culture). She compares the adaptation of the "middle-aged" men in their thirties, who actually instituted the change, and that of the younger men in their twenties, who were thrust into the New Way during early adolescence.*

When the young middle-aged men in their early thirties succeeded in building their New Way, they were doing two things which were wholly congruent with their child-hood rearing. In the first place, they were copying reality as they had experienced it, rearranging a series of elements — the British law court and government, the Church and its emphasis on the soul, the American Army and its system of interpersonal relations, the Western world's type of housing, clothing, marriage, etc. They had watched how people moved in these situations, listened to the judge as he held a hearing, listened to the priests as they preached from the chancel steps, listened to the tone of voice of the Americans who abandoned huge amounts of property so easily and yet went to such pains for one another. They caught the spirit, the style, the movement involved in these institutions — what a school was, what taxes were meant for, what participation in a meeting really was — by active identification with those whom they saw going through the forms and rituals of civilization. In the second place, they showed a continued rejection of the traditional adult way of life which they had learned from their elders to hate and chafe under. Neither activity was new in form; only the content was new. They had experienced a highly systematized culture which they had learned to dislike. They built, along imitative lines, a new highly systematized culture which contained substitutions and corrections for the rejected elements — arranged marriage, exploitation of young men by their elder male relatives, taboo restrictions between relatives-in-law, slavery to acquiring forms of native money which were only useful for increasing the turnover within the system, clothes and houses which differentiated from the work of the white man. They constructed a new set of social forms congenial to them, building a world which was like the world they had learned to escape to, and unimaginatively reproducing the form of something which they perceived as a pattern. They had had the opportunity to see how the Americans lived within the Western system, and they set to work to reproduce the system.

In this reproduction there was all the surge of excitement, of discovery, of newness. These were men who had from childhood avoided their future mothers-in-law, who had lain embarrassed and inert under the mats on the platforms of canoes because of the presence nearby of their affianced wives, who in the early days of their marriages had had to treat their wives, whom they had not chosen, with avoidance and embarrassment. So they were experiencing the full force of the change in expectation, the relaxation of being able to live in a world free from already experienced taboos. This sense of release, of newness, of weights lifted off the shoulders and doors opened where only barriers had been anticipated, provides the conditions of zest and ardour with which human beings adapt to a new situation, as immigrants to a country where their footsteps are no longer dogged by political police, as women who walk the streets with bared faces in a land where only yesterday all women were veiled, even, in situational terms, as discharged servicemen who, after a long period of rigid discipline, are free again as civilians to treat every man whom they meet on his merits. It is this zest which patterns and allocates the energy needed to build a new society, to build a whole village at once or sit attentively through meetings which drove on through many hours of unaccustomed clumsy deliberation. It is because the people who do these things are the *same* people that they receive such a sense of freedom from the change.

The great problem then becomes how the sense of a dearly won and so valuable freedom is to be incorporated in the next generation, in the children who now play on safe beaches, less rigorously trained to care

for property now that objects are no longer so breakable and difficult to replace and parents are not so economically driven. The results will also be different because it is not merely a matter of parents transmitting to their children their own sense of release and freedom but because the generation who were late adolescents at the time of the change have to be taken into account.

These young men in their early twenties represent a particularly difficult problem because the war cut them off from both the continuing teaching they would have received from the Mission and from the ordinary sort of long term work for the European in which their elders had been schooled. They were just reaching adolescence when the Japanese occupation started, and very few of them were old enough to do much work for the Americans. Their knowledge of Neo-Melanesian is inferior to that of the older men, and they do not have the same sense of free communication with Europeans which their elders learned as work boys. Their encounter with the Mission after the war was brief and stormy, and in their first experiences with the return of Australian civil government there were many negative aspects—unsympathetic patrol officers who made fun of the New Way or ordered the beautiful gateway made with such effort to be destroyed. The only Australian communities they have known at all have been post-war communities, put together with a patchwork of wartime salvage materials, and a harassed set of terribly overworked post-war officials faced with a thousand new problems and trying to cope with a group of people who were defined as subversive.

These young men can hardly remember the pre-war world, at home or abroad. They were the generation who with no preparation at all for any relation to women except the old highly patterned ones—freedom to tease and jest with a cross-cousin, respectful dependence on a mother and sister, avoidance of all affinal females—were now suddenly told to form the new kind of marriages, walk about with their wives in public, "enjoy" their wives' company.

It was in this group that one found men with the most rigid ideas, who wore their clothes, not with the practised nonchalance of an American on leave, but stiffly, as a kind of cult uniform. These were the men who recoiled from pictures showing people in the old costumes, pictures over which the older men and women (who had worn them) laughed with amusement. "These appear unpleasant in my eyes," said Peranis Cholai, stiffly. "I see nothing good here," said Peranis Kiapin, coldly. This group also had the poorest memories of their childhood and much worse memories for their childhood playmates and elders than had people ten and fifteen years older. They were definitely children of the new order, clinging to it rigidly, almost angrily, and without the flexibility and resiliency of their elders. They had had, in fact, the same early childhood as the older men, but had lacked the kind of late childhood and adolescence in which the older men's habits of companionship and friendliness, and so their capacity to feel free, had been born. They were stiff and difficult fathers, with less tenderness and indulgence toward their children than the older or much younger men. In them could be seen clearly the first effects of a far-reaching change: the new life, which the older men embraced with a depth of thankfulness that was never completely gone from their voices, has become to them something barely attained, thin, brittle, likely to be destroyed by inimical forces, something to defend in anger, and to live by rote. They were the ones who got into complications with their parents-in-law, demanding as a right that their in-laws "talk and eat and laugh with them," in sharp contrast to the tender smile on the middle-aged Raphael's lips as he had looked at his diminutive mother-in-law and said, "And once I would not have been allowed even to say her name,

and now she can be here with us and help us eat the delicious scrapings of the feast cooking pot."

There was one man in Peri, Karol Manoi, who contained within himself the whole series of attitudes which were otherwise seen embodied in different generations. He would shift from a mood of gay relaxed companionship in which every muscle softened to the ukulele that he played with delight, every posture expressing a sense of freedom and ease, to a mood of rigid, watchful, unadventurous determination "to get it right," in which his clothes (which a few minutes before fitted him like his own skin) seemed to crawl up his neck till his collar was too high, his sleeves too short—the whole an unbecoming and unaccustomed uniform— his brow furrowed with anxiety and his mind become hampered by his certainty that there was a right answer and he didn't know what it was. An hour later he might have shifted to an active, competent man dealing with some problem, turning his house into a reception center for the sick, or discussing with glowing eyes how Paliau had insisted so skillfully in court that men who had been told to obey the Japanese could not later be tried for having done so. But, while the memory of such a flexible, intelligent conversation was still fresh in my eyes, there would be another shift. Karol, looking as savage and tense as a leopard, every muscle subtle with a rage which was designed to destroy, or if not destroy, to punish terribly, would be walking across the square, a stick in hand, and I knew that he had caught someone doing something for which he felt he had a right to be angry. The uninhibited rage of his father, which he had experienced in his muscles when he was a small boy, was now combined with the moral fury of an official of the New Way, ready to pounce on the two luckless women who had "stolen" two coconuts. And it might be only two days later that he was off gambling, hoping to retrieve the money which he had "borrowed" without proper authority.

It was both painful and exciting to watch his very good mind struggle with these shifts, trying to work out what had got into him that made him see a thing one way on one occasion and quite differently on another. Hauled into a village "court" for beating his wife because she had refused to make their child limeade, he repeated over and over: "Here in court when she repeats it as evidence, it sounds like something of no moment. Here she says, 'I only asked the child, "Is it your lime?"' in just an ordinary voice. The wind of the saying is different. But before, when I heard it, when she said it to our son, it sounded very different. I know it was different. It sounded as if he was not her child." And the local "judges," with minds less complicated than his, wrinkled their brows in perplexity. What did all this talk about the wind being different—he didn't even have a word to express what he meant—have to do with the quarrel?

Characteristically Karol did not know to which age group he belonged. One minute he was playing a ukulele with the schoolboys, the next flying into a rage and impounding their ukuleles because no one had volunteered to run a message for him as head of the village. Nor did he know on whose side he was. He and John Kilipak had been enemies and rivals ever since he had been instrumental in getting John Kilipak's adored younger half-brother put into prison—a case where Karol Manoi had been pursuing private and personal family goals of his own. John Kilipak and he were usually on terms of formality, each chipping away at the other whenever possible. Yet, when Karol acting as "judge" saw John Kilipak

sorely pressed and endangered by the possibility that his violent mistress, angry at the way the evidence was going, would say something irrevocable in "court," it was Karol who slipped in a device for giving the angry woman a chance to score off everyone and go away somewhat appeased. A temporary complete identification with John Kilipak possessed him and he responded intelligently, expertly, to save the man who was actually so very much like himself, but less violent and less complex in his moods and identifications.

Karol Manoi bridged the gaps between his dead father, his own age mates—the generation who had made the New Way—and his juniors, who adhered to the New Way with such stiff, anxious rigidity, and the schoolboys, who were the beneficiaries of the greater joy in work and song which was the heritage of the New Way. Also he had something of the intelligent flexible mind of Paliau, the rigid apocalyptic religious ideas of Lukas Banyalo, and the reactive criminal potentialities for adultery, gambling, and graft, which the New Way also provided. His personality summed up the conflicts between the old and the new, and the people of Peri themselves vacillated about him, one minute following his lead, the next, angry and sullen, or baffled and perplexed.

Conclusion

Diffusion is a predominant factor of socio-cultural change for most "primitive" societies today. But there is widespread variation in the adaptability of different societies, and of different persons in each society. In this abridgment Margaret Mead shows us how a person's age or stage of life affects how receptive he is to cultural change.

2 POSTURBAN-INDUSTRIAL SOCIETY

Today, most of the nations of the world are in the process of that form of social evolution which we have called modernization. Since the rate of change has been accelerated by recent technological advances, we can expect many of these nations to reach our present level in the next several generations—perhaps fifty or seventy-five years. It seems safe to predict that by the beginning of the twenty-first century, the world will, for the most part, have passed through the early and difficult transitional period of modernization at least. In the meantime, however, the presently advanced nations may have entered an era as different from the industrial period as the industrial was from the preindustrial. There is some evidence, in fact, that the United States and several other countries have already entered this new era.

THE POSTURBAN-INDUSTRIAL PERIOD

What may be called the posturban-industrial[9] period will probably be characterized by the following factors:

(1) The services will continue to expand and eventually dominate the economy. Both agricultural and industrial production can be made more efficient by modern techniques, especially those of automation. In the United States today, it takes less than half the total labor force to produce our food and goods; that figure will be reduced even more in the future and the great majority of people will be employed in jobs of a service or a professional category.

A service economy is very different from an industrial economy in ways which we have discussed briefly in earlier chapters. Work organizations are often smaller and more personalized; there is often less emphasis on profit making and competition, and greater room for personal initiative and growth.[10] Consider, for example, how a government office is a different work environment from a factory.

(2) In the industrial period, workers were of blue collar status, but the postindustrial period labor force will be made up almost entirely of white collar, middle-class workers. This is of course a trend closely related to the growth of service jobs. Automation and mechanization remove people from the direct work of production, and at the same time they increase the demand for administrators, supervisors, and bureaucrats—all the white collar occupations.

(3) The society's greatest need will be for intellectual and technical knowledge. Most problems will require highly technical solutions and education will be a much valued commodity. The key occupations will be those of the scientist and highly educated specialist, rather than the business entrepreneur of the industrial period.

(4) Many forms of labor, including the labor of learning and communicating, will be changed or replaced by automation and com-

9. See Daniel Bell, "Notes on the Post Industrial Society," *The Public Interest* 1, 6 (Winter 1967), and 2, 7 (Spring 1967).

10. See Victor Fuchs, "The First Service Economy," *The Public Interest* 2 (Winter, 1966).

puterized systems. The computer has been the most significant technological invention in recent years, and it will affect almost every aspect of life.

(5) The public (government owned or controlled) sector of the society will grow even larger in importance and include a greater number of jobs; for all intents and purposes it will become merged with the private sector. When an economy becomes as sophisticated and complex as is the modern industrial economy, the need for supervision increases, and generally this must be supplied by government. More and more people will be employed by the various government agencies, especially those which deal with social services, the regulation of industry, and the protection and maintenance of the physical and social environment. Government will dominate the period, as business dominated the industrial period; politics will replace the market in first importance. Centralized political direction will lead the economy and the society.

Community structure

In the postindustrial period of development, community structure changes also. Just as the factory town and the industrial city were the main community units of the industrial period, so the residential suburb is the main community unit of the posturban era. As we have noted, the suburb represents in part a move away from the city and high density urban way of life; it is a low density community oriented toward the automobile for easy and rapid transportation. These low density residential communities are clustered together in supermetropolitan areas sometimes called *megalopolises*.

With such a pattern of residential living, we will probably see more and more separation of people and families according to life style and stage of life. For example, in the densest part of the city, we will have the young adults, the single, and the rich, and on the fringes of the inner city the "hard core" poor. Located in various suburbs, divided according to

Suburbia has been called a clustering of "little boxes made of ticky-tacky." The bedroom suburb is becoming the dominant community form in postindustrial society. It is characterized by low density, automobile-oriented transportation systems, sociocultural homogeneity, and a lack of community focus. These kinds of areas are extending ever farther into the outlying countryside, a phenomenon sometimes dubbed "urban sprawl." *(Elliott Erwitt, Magnum)*

class and age, will be the family-oriented middle classes and upper-lower classes. In separate retirement communities will dwell many of the nation's rapidly growing group of senior citizens. This represents a living pattern radically different from the more "balanced" communities of earlier eras.

Such separation will encourage the development of rather distinct life styles for each of these groups. Therefore the cultural pluralism which currently characterizes our society may become even more marked than it is now. It will also become more widespread than it is today, for many areas, such as large stretches of the Midwest, are still quite homogeneous. Among various groups a new set of competing interests may arise based not on earning power and financial security, as in the industrial era, but on, for example, the very different life styles and consumption patterns of family-oriented persons versus singles, or young versus old.

SOCIAL PROBLEMS OF TOMORROW

All these changes in society will inevitably lead to new social problems, though they may be quite different from those of the industrial period. Difficulties will be created by the large amount of leisure time available for everyone. Both the labor force and those who do household chores are being freed of many hours of work by machines. But often, neither education nor social norms have thus far adequately provided the individual with ways to utilize this time so that it will be both socially approved and individually satisfying.

Because widespread bureaucratization is still a recent development, we have not yet learned to cope with it successfully, to make it responsive to individual needs and desires. The conflict between personal needs and bureaucratic demands will be of increasing public concern. For example, student revolts represent in part a reaction to the bureaucratization of education.

Many of the traditional social relationships and structures which give meaning and support to individual personalities and lives —

broad family networks, institutional religions, strong neighborhoods — will become less obtainable or relevant, and so new ones must be invented or adapted to take their place. This problem is one reason for the current and rapidly growing interest in activities ranging from sensitivity groups to communes.

As yet, we have not changed our attitudes to take into account the growing role of the public sector, that is, government and politics. We fear government interference and control but also recognize that public intervention is necessary and even desirable in many areas. In addition, there is a great need for more established patterns for public decision making. This problem has shown up vividly during strikes by public employees. How should they be resolved? Do public employees even have the right to strike? No one has yet established a way to deal with such aspects of the growing responsibility of the government and its employees.

The increasing amount of communication between people and groups leads to the dangers of a communications overload. Obviously, none of us has time to pay attention to all the information being communicated in printed matter, television, and radio; we must learn to select what is of importance to us, and reject the rest. In a growing degree, the same is true of knowledge. No one can hope to learn everything, because there is far too much to learn, so we must first learn how to choose what to learn.

The provision of personal freedom and privacy in a tightly interwoven, centrally controlled, technological society will always be a problem. For example, the government increasingly needs personal information to guide the society, but this may conflict with the individual's desire to maintain his privacy and independence.

Most of these problems and issues arise from, or are closely related to, national economic abundance. Some of the age-old human problems — poverty, unemployment, economic instability — are problems of scarcity, and may be alleviated, if not solved, by national mate-

Isolation and alienation of the individual have become problems of major concern in our affluent, complex, and impersonal social order. As work organizations have become larger and more bureaucratic and the traditional family, religious, and neighborhood networks have become less viable, individuals are often left without the emotional supports that deep immersion in group life can provide. *(Burk Uzzle, Magnum)*

rial abundance. But we should guard against the idea that material abundance will bring a problem-free world. In the industrially advanced nations abundance may be achieved, and distributed reasonably evenly, within this generation, but complex problems of a new sort will doubtless arise. It is also quite possible that further advancement of the modernized countries will be seriously hampered by the needs of the developing countries, to say nothing of major environmental holocausts.

In any event, it seems reasonable to speculate that among the most important of the problems that will continue far into the future will be those of finding individual meaning and a sense of creative growth and achievement in a highly formal, complex, impersonal, technical, and centrally controlled social order.

ALVIN TOFFLER
The Modular Man

Specified excerpts from "People: The Modular Man," pp. 86–100, from *Future Shock* by Alvin Toffler. Copyright ©1970 by Alvin Toffler. Reprinted by permission of Random House, Inc.

Introduction

Toffler describes the Modular Man in his book, Future Shock, *as capable of only temporary interpersonal relationships. These relationships have been characterized as fragmented, superficial, limited, and func-tional. According to Toffler, "We have created the disposable person.... Rather than entangling ourselves with the whole man, we plug into a module of his personality." Modular Man and the environment that has created him are described in the following abridgment.*

Each spring an immense lemming-like migration begins all over the Eastern United States. Singly and in groups, burdened with sleeping bags, blankets and bathing suits, some 15,000 American college students toss aside their texts and follow a highly accurate homing instinct that leads them to the sun-bleached shoreline of Fort Lauderdale, Florida. There for approximately a week, this teeming, milling mass of sun and sex worshippers swims, sleeps, flirts, guzzles beer, sprawls and brawls in the sands. At the end of this period the bikini-clad girls and their bronzed admirers pack their kits and join in a mass exodus. Anyone near the booth set up by the resort city to welcome this rambunctious army can now hear the loudspeaker booming: "Car with two can take rider as far as Atlanta . . . Need ride to Washington . . . Leaving at 10:00 for Louis-ville . . ." In a few hours nothing is left of the great "beach-and-booze party" except butts and beer cans in the sand, and about $1.5 million in the cash registers of local mer-chants—who regard this annual invasion as a tainted blessing that threatens public sanity while it underwrites private profit.

What attracts the young people is more than an irrepressible passion for sunshine. Nor is it mere sex, a commodity available in other places as well. Rather, it is a sense of freedom without responsibility. In the words of a nineteen-year-old New York co-ed who made her way to the festivities recently: "You're not worried about what you do or say here because, frankly, you'll never see these people again."

What the Fort Lauderdale rite supplies is a transient agglomeration of people that makes possible a great diversity of temporary interpersonal relationships. And it is pre-cisely this—temporariness—that increasingly characterizes human relations as we move further toward super-industrialism. For just as things and places flow through our lives at a faster clip, so, too, do people.

The cost of "involvement"

Urbanism—the city dweller's way of life—has preoccupied sociology since the turn of the century. Max Weber pointed out the obvious fact that people in cities cannot know all their neighbors as intimately as it was possible for them to do in small com-munities. Georg Simmel carried this idea one step further when he declared, rather quaintly, that if the urban individual reacted emotionally to each and every person with whom he came into contact, or cluttered his mind with information about them, he would be "completely atomized internally and would fall into an unthinkable mental condition."

Louis Wirth, in turn, noted the frag-mented nature of urban relationships. "Characteristically, urbanites meet one another in highly segmental roles . . ." he wrote. "Their dependence upon others is confined to a highly fractionalized aspect of the other's round of activity." Rather than becoming deeply involved with the total personality of every individual we meet, he explained, we necessarily maintain super-ficial and partial contact with some. We are interested only in the efficiency of the shoe salesman in meeting our needs: we couldn't care less that his wife is an alcoholic.

What this means is that we form limited involvement relationships with most of the people around us. Consciously or not, we define our relationships with most people in functional terms. So long as we do not become involved with the shoe salesman's problems at home, or his more general hopes, dreams and frustrations, he is, for us, fully interchangeable with any other sales-man of equal competence. In effect, we have applied the modular principle to human relationships. We have created the disposable person: Modular Man.

Rather than entangling ourselves with the whole man, we plug into a module of his personality. Each personality can be imagined as a unique configuration of thou-sands of such modules. Thus no whole person is interchangeable with any other. But certain modules are. Since we are seeking only to buy a pair of shoes, and not the friendship, love or hate of the salesman, it is not necessary for us to tap into or engage with all the other modules that form his personality. Our relationship is safely limited. There is limited liability on both sides. The relationship entails certain accepted forms of behavior and communication. Both sides understand, consciously or otherwise, the limitations and laws. Difficulties arise only when one or another party oversteps the tacitly understood limits, when he attempts to connect up with some module not relevant to the function at hand.

Today a vast sociological and psychological literature is devoted to the alienation presumed to flow from this fragmentation of relationships. Much of the rhetoric of existentialism and the student revolt decries this fragmentation. It is said that we are not sufficiently "involved" with our fellow man. Millions of young people go about seeking "total involvement."

Before leaping to the popular conclusion that modularization is all bad, however, it might be well to look more closely at the matter. Theologian Harvey Cox, echoing Simmel, has pointed out that in an urban environment the attempt to "involve" oneself fully with everyone can lead only to self-destruction and emotional emptiness. Urban man, he writes, "must have more or less impersonal relationships with most of the people with whom he comes in contact precisely in order to choose certain friendships to nourish and cultivate ... His life represents a point touched by dozens of systems and hundreds of people. His capacity to know some of them better necessitates his minimizing the depth of his relationship to many others. Listening to the postman gossip becomes for the urban man an act of sheer graciousness, since he probably has no interest in the people the postman wants to talk about."

Moreover, before lamenting modularization, it is necessary to ask ourselves whether we really would prefer to return to the traditional condition of man in which each individual presumably related to the whole personality of a few people rather than to the personality modules of many. Traditional man has been so sentimentalized, so cloyingly romanticized, that we frequently overlook the consequences of such a return. The very same writers who lament fragmentation also demand freedom—yet overlook the unfreedom of people bound together in totalistic relationships. For any relationship implies mutual demands and expectations. The more intimately involved a relationship, the greater the pressure the parties exert on one another to fulfill these expectations. The tighter and more totalistic the relationship, the more modules, so to speak, are brought into play, and the more numerous are the demands we make.

In a modular relationship, the demands are strictly bounded. So long as the shoe salesman performs his rather limited service for us, thereby fulfilling our rather limited expectations, we do not insist that he believe in our God, or that he be tidy at home, or share our political values, or enjoy the same kind of food or music that we do. We leave him free in all other matters—as he leaves us free to be atheist or Jew, heterosexual or homosexual, John Bircher or Communist. This is not true of the total relationship and cannot be. To a certain point, fragmentation and freedom go together.

All of us seem to need some totalistic relationships in our lives. But to decry the fact that we cannot have *only* such relationships is nonsense. And to prefer a society in which the individual has holistic relationships with a few, *rather than* modular relationships with many, is to wish for a return to the imprisonment of the past—a past when individuals may have been more tightly bound to one another, but when they were also more tightly regimented by social conventions, sexual mores, political and religious restrictions.

This is not to say that modular relationships entail no risks or that this is the best of all possible worlds. There are, in fact, profound risks in the situation.... Until now, however, the entire public and professional discussion of these issues has been badly out of focus. For it has overlooked a critical dimension of all interpersonal relationships: their duration.

The hurry-up welcome

Continuing urbanization is merely one of a number of pressures driving us toward greater "temporariness" in our human relationships. Urbanization, as suggested earlier, brings great masses of people into close proximity, thereby increasing the actual number of contacts made.... Geographical mobility not only speeds up the flow of places through our lives, but the flow of people as well.

The increase in travel brings with it a sharp increase in the number of transient, casual relationships with fellow passengers, with hotel clerks, taxi drivers, airline reservation people, with porters, maids, waiters, with colleagues and friends of friends, with customs officials, travel agents and countless others. The greater the mobility of the individual, the greater the number of brief, face-to-face encounters, human contacts, each one a relationship of sorts, fragmentary and, above all, compressed in time. (Such contacts appear natural and unimportant to us. We seldom stop to consider how few of the sixty-six billion human beings who preceded us on the planet ever experienced this high rate of transience in their human relationships.)

If travel increases the number of contacts —largely with service people of one sort or another—residential relocation also steps up the through-put of people in our lives. Moving leads to the termination of relationships in almost all categories. The young submarine engineer who is transferred from his job in the Navy Yard at Mare Island, California, to the installation at Newport News, Virginia,

takes only his most immediate family with him. He leaves behind parents and in-laws, neighbors, service and tradespeople, as well as his associates on the job, and others. He cuts short his ties. In settling down in the new community, he, his wife and child must initiate a whole cluster of new (and once more temporary) relationships.

Here is how one young wife, a veteran of eleven moves in the past seventeen years, describes the process: "When you live in a neighborhood you watch a series of changes take place. One day a new mailman delivers the mail. A few weeks later the girl at the check-out counter at the supermarket disappears and a new one takes her place. Next thing you know, the mechanic at the gas station is replaced. Meanwhile, a neighbor moves out next door and a new family moves in. These changes are taking place all the time, but they are gradual. When you move, you break all these ties at once, and you have to start all over again. You have to find a new pediatrician, a new dentist, a new car mechanic who won't cheat you, and you quit all your organizations and start over again." It is the simultaneous rupture of a whole range of existing relationships that makes relocation psychologically taxing for many.

The more frequently this cycle repeats itself, of course, in the life of the individual, the shorter the duration of the relationships involved. Among significant sectors of the population this process is now occurring so rapidly that it is drastically altering traditional notions of time with respect to human relationships.

. . . . John Barth has captured the sense of turnover among friendships in a passage from his novel *The Floating Opera:* "Our friends float past; we become involved with them; they float on, and we must rely on hearsay or lose track of them completely; they float back again, and we must either renew our friendship—catch up to date—or find that they and we don't comprehend each other any more." The only fault in this is its unspoken suggestion that the current upon which friendships bob and float is lazy and meandering. The current today is picking up speed. Friendship increasingly resembles a canoe shooting the rapids of the river of change. "Pretty soon," says Professor Eli Ginzberg of Columbia University, an expert on manpower mobility, "we're all going to be metropolitan-type people in this country without ties or commitments to long time friends and neighbors. . . ."

Monday-to-Friday friends

One reason to believe that the trend toward temporary relationships will continue is the impact of new technology on occupations. Even if the push toward megalopolis stopped and people froze in their geographical tracks, there would still be a sharp increase in the number, and decrease in the duration of relationships as a consequence of job changes. For the introduction of advanced technology, whether we call it automation or not, is necessarily accompanied by drastic changes in the types of skills and personalities required by the economy.

Specialization increases the number of different occupations. At the same time, technological innovation reduces the life expectancy of any given occupation. "The emergence and decline of occupations will be so rapid," says economist Norman Anon, an expert in manpower problems, "that people will always be uncertain in them." The profession of airline flight engineer, he notes, emerged and then began to die out within a brief period of fifteen years.

A look at the "help wanted" pages of any major newspaper brings home the fact that new occupations are increasing at a mind-dazzling rate. Systems analyst, console operator, coder, tape librarian, tape handler, are only a few of those connected with computer operations. Information retrieval, optical scanning, thin-film technology all

require new kinds of expertise, while old occupations lose importance or vanish altogether. When *Fortune* magazine in the mid-1960's surveyed 1,003 young executives employed by major American corporations, it found that fully one out of three held a job that simply had not existed until he stepped into it. Another large group held positions that had been filled by only one incumbent before them. Even when the name of the occupation stays the same, the content of the work is frequently transformed, and the people filling the jobs change.

Job turnover, however, is not merely a direct consequence of technological change. It also reflects the mergers and acquisitions that occur as industries everywhere frantically organize and reorganize themselves to adapt to the fast-changing environment, to keep up with myriad shifts in consumer preferences. Many other complex pressures also combine to stir the occupational mix incessantly. Thus a recent survey by the US Department of Labor revealed that the 71,000,000 persons in the American labor force had held their current jobs an average of 4.2 years. This compared with 4.6 years only three years earlier, a decline in duration of nearly 9 percent.

"Under conditions prevailing at the beginning of the 1960's," states another Labor Department report, "the average twenty-year-old man in the work force could be expected to change jobs about six or seven times." Thus instead of thinking in terms of a "career" the citizen of super-industrial society will think in terms of "serial careers. . . ."

Any change in job entails a certain amount of stress. The individual must strip himself of old habits, old ways of coping, and learn new ways of doing things. Even when the work task itself is similar, the environment in which it takes place is different. And just as is the case with moving to a new community, the newcomer is under pressure to form new relationships at high speed. Here, too, the process is accelerated by people who play the role of informal integrator. Here, too, the individual seeks out human relationships by joining organizations—usually informal and clique-like, rather than part of the company's table of organization. Here, too, the knowledge that no job is truly "permanent" means that the relationships formed are conditional, modular and, by most definitions, temporary.

Conclusion

Toffler concludes that, in contrast to *fragmented relationships, totalistic relationships result in a lack of individual freedom—* *"To a certain point, fragmentation and freedom go together." Pressures that create the Modular Man will increase with* **the** *rise of the posturban-industrial order. "'Pretty soon,' says Professor Eli Ginzberg of Columbia University, . . . 'we're all going to be metropolitan type people in this country without ties or commitments to long time friends and neighbors.'" Toffler agrees with Ginzberg but goes on to warn that a wish for a return to only totalistic relationships is a wish to return to the imprisonment of the past. Modular Man, up to a point, may be necessary.*

TOPIC 3 SOCIAL PLANNING

Where it was once felt that societies were at the mercy of impersonal forces and trends, it is now thought that man can exert some effective control over his physical and social environment. This changed attitude has been in part the result of necessity. The complexities and interlocking dependence of modern social systems require central guidance and control to keep them functioning smoothly and effectively. And because of the great advances in knowledge and technology, as well as the existence of large and powerful organizations, modern societies now have the capacity to make and implement collective social decisions. This new attitude toward social change also reflects an element of human choice; people have chosen social planning as a tool to help achieve common goals and values.

OBJECTIVES OF SOCIAL PLANNING

The general goal of all social planning is to "improve" society, but the definition of improvement differs, depending on the underlying values of the social system. For example, in American society, we might define improvement as an increase in efficiency, or a widening of democracy. But "efficiency" and "democracy" are abstractions; to attain these values, social planners must decide on concrete and specific goals and courses of action.

The short-range objective of social planning is to manipulate the social environment in some way that will enhance or change some designated value. Men can plan to change the structure of important institutions; for example, a society can alter the bureaucracy of the government to make it more responsive to

Social planning is essential in today's rapidly changing, complex, and interdependent world. While technological innovations often create new social problems, they also can, through social planning, provide solutions. Medical advances, for example, have dramatically lowered death rates and thereby contributed to explosive population growth, particularly in underdeveloped areas. However, we have also developed the technology to control birth rates. Efforts to check population growth often start with local family planning clinics, such as this one in Deoli, India, that make birth control devices, medical information, and counseling available to a large number of people. *(Photo Courtesy of United Nations)*

the problems of its client-citizens, or make changes in the laws governing marriage or divorce, or punishment for crime. Social planning may also try to manipulate the material goods of society, by allocating housing on the basis of need rather than ability to pay, or by putting more desks in elementary schools. In America, social planning in the last several decades has especially focused on the relationship between the population and the natural resources; we irrigate some land for farming, set aside some for wildlife preserves and recreation areas, and try to clean our rivers and prevent them from turning into polluted sewers. But social planning in this country increasingly deals with social as well as environmental concerns—poverty, education, family welfare, and mental health.

LIMITATIONS OF SOCIAL PLANNING

Amitai Etzioni is a leading observer of the recent trend toward large-scale guided social change, or what he calls "societal guidance." He suggests that many modern societies are becoming "active societies," ones which seek to be "masters of themselves."[11] Yet not

11. See Amitai Etzioni, *The Active Society* (New York: Free Press, 1968).

everyone embraces this goal with enthusiasm; the concept of centralized government planning evokes many negative responses. This is especially true in democracies such as the United States which have capitalistic economies and historic doctrines of *laissez-faire* in the political and economic arenas. People fear that the great concentration of power may be misused, that social planning may serve to further the interests of elite individuals or groups, rather than the common good of society. The experience of some societies, such as Nazi Germany and Stalinist Russia, has shown that social planning can serve the interests of a totalitarian state as well as those of a democracy, that it can be used to curtail individual freedom of choice. Modern democracies face the great challenge of learning to keep centralized power restrained and guidance responsive.

APPLICATIONS OF SOCIAL PLANNING

It is interesting to note that the tools and concepts of planning have so far had their greatest impact in the private business sector. Every large corporation has a man, or a department, in charge of planning the company's future. The planners devise alternate courses of action, collect relevant knowledge about the possible effects of each course, and suggest choices. After a decision has been made, they collect feedback on its success and effectiveness. It is such planning that has allowed mining and oil companies to develop new sites, that has encouraged the development of new products such as fluoridated toothpaste, and has allowed cigarette manufacturers to branch out into other products, such as foods and beverages, to offset declining sales in the face of cancer research.

It is partly in response to this development in private industry that planning has now spread to the government agencies. Some of America's large business corporations exercise a virtually monopolistic control over certain segments of the economy; the government has had to develop methods of planning and guidance so that it could remain powerful enough to guard public interests. The federal government has borrowed both ideas and men from successful large corporations, as it tries to utilize the tools of planning and decision making for the general public welfare.

An excellent illustration of social planning in action is the Tennessee Valley Authority, a broad program of change undertaken in the 1930s. The Tennessee Valley had many serious problems; its inhabitants were among the poorest people in a depression-struck country. Poor farming and lumbering practices were causing massive soil erosion; yearly floods destroyed what few crops there were; and navigation on the Tennessee River was difficult. Although there was a sizable labor force in the area, no industry would move in because power supplies were limited. These conditions kept the residents both poor and isolated from the outside world. A plan was drawn up to combat these problems, and it was passed into law in 1933, amid a storm of protest about "socialism" and threats to free enterprise.

The primary objectives of the plan were the improvement of navigation, flood control, the development of artificial fertilizer, promotion of a system of agriculture using this fertilizer and conserving the soil, and the development and distribution of hydroelectric power.

In general, the TVA met with success in achieving these objectives. Erosion has been checked on more than a million acres of farmland. Hundreds of millions of trees have been planted to help retain existing soil. A series of artificial lakes and dams has made the Tennessee River navigable and provides inexpensive electricity to the Valley.

From these accomplishments came a concrete improvement in the daily lives of Valley residents. Incomes went up as farmland grew richer and floods no longer wiped out crops. Many industries moved into the Valley, creating more new jobs. Increased prosperity, in

Corporate planning has helped to provide the United States with the world's highest per capita rate of automobile ownership; traffic planning has generated the world's most extensive freeway network. But the United States falls significantly behind other modern societies in the amount of land use planning which is practiced. This cartoon suggests a possible future result. *(Drawing by Franklin © 1968 The New Yorker Magazine, Inc.)*

conjunction with TVA-established clinics, has raised the health level of the local population. Recreation areas attract both residents and tourists. Of course, the TVA encountered many problems along the way, and the plan did not succeed perfectly. But it is an encouraging example of the effectiveness of social planning.

SOCIOLOGY IN ACTION

Social planning is in one sense the application of social scientific knowledge to help solve social problems. In the studies of the early sociologists, such as Comte, there was a heavy stress on the applications of soci-ological knowledge. In fact, many of the sociologists in the late nineteenth and early twentieth century were really disguised social reformers, who sought to change society through their knowledge of its workings. But the lack of success of these early efforts, together with the lack of hard knowledge, discouraged this point of view, and in reaction, sociologists turned more to research and to the development of sociology as a science. In the last several decades, sociology has once again begun to seek practical applications of its knowledge, and the pure and applied branches of the discipline work more closely together to contribute to the solution of social problems.

ROBERT A. DAHL
Politics of Urban Planning
In New Haven

Excerpted from *Who Governs?* by
Robert A. Dahl, pp. 130–137.
Copyright © 1961 by Yale University.
Reprinted by permission of Yale
University Press.

Introduction

*In the late 1950s, Robert Dahl made a
case study of the course of urban redevelopment in New Haven, Connecticut.
In this excerpt, he analyzes one element of
that successful program—the creation of a
Citizens Action Commission which was to
advise and help the mayor and his city
planners.*

What was the function of the Citizens
Action Commission? [Mayor] Lee described
the CAC this way:

> We've got the biggest muscles, the biggest
> set of muscles in New Haven on the top
> C.A.C. . . . They're muscular because they
> control wealth, they're muscular because
> they control industries, represent banks.
> They're muscular because they head up
> labor. They're muscular because they
> represent the intellectual portions of the
> community. They're muscular because
> they're articulate, because they're
> respectable, because of their financial
> power, and because of the accumulation of
> prestige which they have built up over the
> years as individuals in all kinds of causes,
> whether United Fund, Red Cross, or
> whatever.

The members had been shrewdly selected
to represent many of the major centers
of influence or status in the community.
Its membership included three bankers; two
men from Yale; John Golden, the Democratic national committeeman and hitherto
the acknowledged leader of the New Haven
Democratic party; the president of the State

CIO Council and the secretary-treasurer of
the State Federation of Labor; four of the
city's most prominent manufacturers; the
president of an investment firm; the board
chairman of the leading power company;
the manager of a large chain store; the
Italian-American president of a construction company; an elder statesman of the
Jewish community; a partner in one of the
leading law firms; and four individuals who
had special status in housing, welfare,
education, and industrial development.
In addition to the Citizens Action
Commission itself, there were six special
committees; these in turn had nearly
thirty subcommittees. Altogether the
Commission and the committees had over
four hundred members, drawn mainly from
the educated, activist, middle-class segments
of the community, the very people who
ordinarily shunned direct participation
in partisan politics.

Except for a few trivial instances, the
"muscles" never directly initiated,
opposed, vetoed, or altered any proposal
brought before them by the Mayor and his
Development Administrator. This is what
the men on the Citizens Action Commission themselves said:

A banker said:

> Well, I think the decisions would be
> brought up first by the technical staff to the
> Mayor. The Commission would pass
> them on the general policy level . . . then
> the decision would be made by the Board of
> Aldermen on the recommendation of the
> Mayor.
> *Did you have to modify their proposals
> very often?*
> Well, they usually came up pretty well
> developed, but we oftentimes would slant
> the way we felt the business community
> would react to certain things and the way
> we felt the approach should be made. I think
> that our function was to—*we were a selling
> organization.*

The president of a large industrial firm said:

The CAC helps set the atmosphere in the community so they're receptive to these things the city administration is trying to do. So, therefore, the city administration is not shoving things down the community's throat. It's selling them to the community, through the CAC.
Have you, for example, done any selling?
Oh yes, oh yes.... Talking to friends of mine, talking at meetings of the Manufacturers' Association...
Do you talk individually or do you give speeches, or what?
Mostly individual. I've never given a speech on the subject.

An executive in a utilities firm:

Have there been any cases where the CAC has modified the proposals that have been put forth since you've been on it?
I can't recall any.

A lawyer:

Who would you say was important in making that decision? [*To extend the Oak Street Connector*] Well, the matter was taken up by the Mayor at a meeting of the Citizens Action Commission. It was discussed and debated around and we agreed with the Mayor. He got his information, of course, from the traffic commission, from the engineers, from the Redevelopment Agency and all the others and he passed it on to us. We represent the group through which these decisions are filtered. I've often felt the group as a group is inadequate in the sense that *we don't really initiate anything as far as I can recall. We haven't yet initiated anything that I know of.* We discuss what has been developed by the Redevelopment Agency or the City Planning Commission or one of the other groups. The Mayor or somebody from one of these groups presents it to us and we discuss it, we analyze it, we modify some of it, we change—
Could you give me an example of some case where you modified or changed some proposal? Well, I don't think that I can

give you an example of anything where I can say that the Commission actually changed a proposal.

A lawyer:

Do you know of any cases where proposals that have been brought forward from the city administration have been altered by the CAC or the people on the redevelopment agency? No I can't say that I do. I can't think of any that would fall into that description.

To see the members of the CAC and its action committees as policy-makers is, however, to miss their real role. The elaborate structure of citizen participation, it must be remembered, did not grow up spontaneously; it was deliberately *created* by Mayor Lee. Its functions in urban redevelopment seem to have been roughly equivalent to those performed by the democratic rituals of the political parties in making nominations for public office; citizen participation gave legitimacy and acceptability to the decisions of the leaders, created a corps of loyal auxiliaries who helped to engender public support for the program and to forestall disputes.

The importance of the CAC in assuring acceptability for the redevelopment program can hardly be overestimated. The mere fact that the CAC existed and regularly endorsed the proposals of the city administration made the program appear nonpartisan, virtually nullified the effectiveness of partisan attacks, presented to the public an appearance of power and responsibility diffused among a representative group of community notables, and inhibited criticisms of even the most daring and ambitious parts of the program as "unrealistic" or "unbusinesslike." Indeed, by creating the CAC the Mayor virtually decapitated the opposition. The presence of leading bankers, industrialists, and businessmen—almost all of whom were Republicans—insured that any project they agreed on would not be attacked by conservatives; the presence of two of the state's most distinguished labor leaders and the participation of well-known liberal Democrats like the Dean of the Yale Law School meant that any proposal they accepted was not likely to be suspect to liberals. To sustain a charge of ethnic or religious discrimination would have required an attack on distinguished representatives of these groups.

A Republican banker on the CAC summed up a prevalent view among the members of the CAC itself.

> It [the CAC] has to exist to get the combined community in back of something of this nature. In other words, if the city administration tried to put this over as a political effort it would meet, obviously, right away, serious objections, because it would become a political football.

The aura of nonpartisanship helped to gain acceptance for redevelopment and its consequences—not all of which were immediately beneficial—and at the same time did no harm to the political career of Mayor Lee [a Democrat]. The leaders of the Republican party were presented with a dilemma which they never quite knew how to meet. Because the Mayor was building his political career on the success of redevelopment, the Republicans could not damage him without attacking either redevelopment or his role in it, but because everything in the redevelopment program was endorsed by Republican notables to attack the Mayor was to alienate established sources of Republican electoral and financial support.

The appointment of over four hundred people to the various action committees gave urban redevelopment a broad and heterogeneous set of subleaders it might otherwise have lacked. The members of these committees initiated no key decisions; they were auxiliaries. They were recruited because they were thought to be favorably pre-disposed toward certain aspects of redevelopment and renewal; they were counted on to form a group of loyal supporters who would help enlist a community following. Like the main CAC itself, the action committees drew on diverse segments of the community. There was an action committee on industrial and harbor development consisting mainly of businessmen, architects, and lawyers, and a second on the central business district, traffic, and parking, that was drawn from the same sources; there was one on housing, and another on health, welfare, recreation, and human relations, made up in great measure of social workers, liberals, clergymen, Negro leaders, housing officials, and religious leaders; a fourth on education consisted mainly of teachers, members of the Board of Education, school administrators, PTA heads, and housewives; and a small committee on the metropolitan area consisted of leading lawyers, town planners, and architects. Most of the action committees rarely met; many members failed to attend the few meetings there were. The actual effects of membership on the CAC or on action committees is unknown, but it seems reasonable to conclude that many people who might otherwise have been apathetic or even opposed to the program were provided with at least a weak tie of loyalty.

It would be carrying the parallel with political parties too far to say that the democratic ritualism of the CAC and its action committees provided a means for the orderly settlement of conflicts among the leaders for, as we have seen, no significant conflicts ever arose within the CAC or between the CAC and the city administration. Yet the fact that no conflicts appeared is itself significant. For the men on the CAC were too important in their own right, too knowledgeable, and too independent to be merely tools of the Mayor. There is no indication in the interviews that the Mayor and the redevelopment officials significantly altered or even tried to alter the kinds of criteria the men on the CAC brought to their judgments; probably the most the Mayor and redevelopment officials could do was to show how, given these criteria, the proposals made sense. One of the most conservative Republicans on the CAC, a banker, evidently saw no inconsistency between redevelopment, which, of course, depended on federal funds, and his opposition to "giveaway programs," foreign aid, and social security.

> I think there's altogether too much money given away and I don't know where it's going to come from as the thing snowballs. ... We are undermining the moral fibre of the whole country. Nobody has to do anything, and I've never seen a country yet, or read of one, that didn't fall apart after they went so far, and that's where I think we're headed.

But as for redevelopment the same respondent said that the Chamber of Commerce

> felt that something had to be done here, it couldn't be done by private interest, it couldn't be done by public entirely, and it couldn't be political. And as a result of that, when Mayor Lee did come into power, he took this over and he's, I think, done a marvelous job with it. ... I'm thoroughly convinced that if we're going to have a city, and it's going to be a shopping area, that something had to be done. Something is being done now. ... Here's a dream that we've had for a long time and we're very happy to see it be culminated in this final action that's been taken.

Another banker said:

> If taxes are going to remain high and there is going to be a social program in the United States and if ... there's no other way—if we can't stop it—if personal income taxes cannot be reduced, why there's only one thing to do and that is to devise ways

and means so that we can share in it. That's pretty selfish. I'm not interested in building a highway through Montana or ... a TVA down South, and I'd like to see some of those dollars come back into Connecticut so that we can enjoy some more benefits.

A labor leader who emphasized the "universal support" of union members and officials for the program was asked whether there had been "any criticism or concern over the large role of the business interests in the program." He replied:

> No ... nobody seems to be bothered by that because I think everybody wants a prosperous community and because in the long run I think everybody feels— that is, most everybody feels—that they benefit in one way or another by a prosperous community, even if it just means a better economic atmosphere. ... And there's another factor here that's probably important. The building trades, the most conservative element in the labor movement, even more conservative than the teamsters ... the building trades benefit directly from the program, and so they are enthusiastic towards it and have even made contributions to the CAC committee itself. ... On the other end of the scale from the conservative building trades, the more sophisticated trade union leaders (and they don't number as many as they did some years ago, when idealism was much stronger than it is today) have been completely taken with the program because of the concern of the program leaders with the human relations aspect of it. So, for different reasons, we have a pretty good cross section of real interest of the labor leadership and the labor movement in general.

It would be unrealistic in the extreme to assume that these men could have been persuaded to lend their support to just any proposal. The task of the Mayor and the Development Administrator was to persuade them that a particular proposal satisfied their own criteria of judgment, whether these were primarily the criteria of businessmen concerned with traffic and retail sales, trade union leaders concerned with employment and local prosperity, or political liberals concerned with slums, housing, and race relations.

Thus, properly used, the CAC was a mechanism not for *settling* disputes but for *avoiding* them altogether. The mayor and the Development Administrator believed that whatever received the full assent of the CAC would not be strongly opposed by other elements in the community. Their estimate proved to be correct. And the reason was probably not so much the direct influence over public opinion of the CAC collectively or its members individually, as it was that the CAC *was* public opinion; that is, its members represented and reflected the main sources of articulate opinion in the political stratum of New Haven.

Conclusion

This is a significant example of the role of citizens in social planning. Though social planning is becoming an increasingly important function of government at local, state, and federal levels, it is by no means solely a job for bureaucrats and civil servants. The important contribution of this commission was a political one; it legitimated the programs which the city was to undertake.

SUMMARY

In identifying and analyzing factors that cause sociocultural change, social scientists have focused on technology, economics, ideology, and the process of diffusion. Advances in the knowledge and tools used to manipulate the environment frequently effect far-reaching sociocultural changes that may not be immediately apparent. William F. Ogburn has suggested that changes in the material aspects of a culture are followed by a *cultural lag,* a period of adjustment between the new technological or material advances and the knowledge, beliefs, norms, and values of a culture. Technological innovations of course result from the development of nonmaterial ideas, and consequently reflect the existing level and direction of cultural development.

Marxian theorists have attributed most social change to underlying economic factors: change results from competition among social classes for basic economic necessities and social resources. Max Weber, in contrast, maintained that change occurred first in the ideas and attitudes of a culture and secondarily in the economic area. The rise of the Protestant ethic, for example, made possible the development of capitalism in England and America. Sociocultural change can also occur when two societies come into contact and certain elements spread or *diffuse* from one culture to the other. *Acculturation,* the process of acquiring the culture of a different group, may stimulate growth and development, or it may destroy a culture that is unable to absorb the rapid and extensive changes initiated by contact.

Oswald Spengler, Arnold Toynbee, and Pitirim A. Sorokin all developed "grand" theories to explain sociocultural change throughout human experience. Spengler regarded societies as living organisms that are born, develop, mature, and inexorably disintegrate. More optimistically, Toynbee has proposed a cycle of challenge and response. Progress continues as long as a society can successfully meet its challenges. Sorokin believed that change occurs as societies alternate between sensate and ideational forms of culture. Sensate culture, based on gratification of the senses, develops as an inevitable reaction to a highly organized ideational culture that emphasizes the mind or soul. In time, the process is reversed.

Most modern theorists have abandoned such broad and necessarily speculative designs, and many now favor the view that societies change and develop from simpler to more complex forms, continuing in roughly one direction without repeating themselves or turning back. Modern evolutionists have focused on the increased *technological development* of societies, the *social differentiation* that occurs as societies become more diversified and specialized, and the *functional interdependence* that develops among the units of society. However, these changes do not necessarily lead to increased human happiness, nor do they occur universally and irresistibly. The trend toward social differentiation, for example, is opposed by the homogenization of culture in America.

The posturban-industrial period of social development that follows modernization is characterized by several factors. As a service economy comes to dominate industrial production, work organizations become smaller and more personalized; there is less emphasis on profit making and competition; there may be greater room for personal initiative and growth. The labor force is dominated increasingly by white collar workers and highly educated specialists rather than by blue collar workers and business entrepreneurs, and many forms of labor are replaced by automation and computerized systems. As the need for regulation of industry and for protection and maintenance of the physical and social environment increases, the public sector merges with the private sector and centralized political direction leads the economy and society. In the postindustrial period the factory town and industrial city are replaced by low density suburban residential communities clustered together in supermetropolitan areas or *megalopolises*. The new pattern of residential living is characterized by increasing segregation of people and families in terms of life style, class, and age, and consequently by greater cultural pluralism. These changes will inevitably lead to new problems as individuals seek meaning and a sense of creative growth and achievement in a highly formal, complex, impersonal, technical, and centrally controlled social order. We must learn how to make use of the large amounts of leisure time available to us, how to make bureaucracies responsive to individual needs, how to provide supportive social relationships and structures, how to make government both responsive and efficient, and how to ensure personal freedom and privacy.

The complexities and interlocking dependence of technologically advanced and highly organized social systems make central guidance and planning both essential and possible. Effective social planning depends on a centralized government that is both restrained and responsive to the needs of its citizens. In utilizing the tools of planning and decision making for the general public welfare, the government has borrowed both ideas and men from private industry. The TVA provides an encouraging example of the effectiveness of social planning.

GLOSSARY

Acculturation The acquiring of the traits of another culture by an individual or group. (page 649)

Cultural diffusion The process by which culture traits spread from one group or society to another. (page 649)

Cultural lag A situation in which some parts of a culture (usually material culture) change at a faster rate than other parts (usually nonmaterial). (page 647)

Functional interdependence The process in which units of a group or society become increasingly dependent on the other units in that system in order to function. (page 651)

Social differentiation The process in which systems and units of a society or culture become more diverse and specialized. (page 651)

Social planning The attempt by a group or society to guide social change to achieve predetermined goals. (page 664)

Sociocultural evolution The view that, over time, cultures and societies develop and change from lower and simpler forms to higher and more complex forms. (page 650)

Technological development The increased ability of societies to master the environment. (page 651)

Technology Knowledge directed toward practical applications in the physical and social world. (page 646)

SUGGESTED READINGS AND RELATED RESOURCES

I READINGS IN SOCIOLOGY

Dahl, Robert A. *Who Governs?* New Haven: Yale University Press, 1961. This study of the patterns and distribution of influence in the city politics of New Haven, Connecticut, stresses the importance of political pluralism in community level politics.

Etzioni, Amitai. *The Active Society.* New York: Free Press, 1968. This book is an example of macrosociology. Etzioni forecasts that more social planning will be used to help institutions adapt more readily to mushrooming technology, industrialization, and bureaucratization. He also predicts a greater degree of centralization in some sectors of modern societies and an increasing concern with social welfare, focusing on the importance and uses of social planning.

Malinowski, Bronislaw. *The Dynamics of Cultural Change.* New Haven: Yale University Press, 1945. Culture is viewed by this early anthropologist as the vehicle that carries on social organization. He studied culture mainly from the point of view of its functions.

Odegard, Peter. *Political Power and Social Change.* New Brunswick, N.J.: Rutgers University Press, 1966. Odegard discusses the concepts of permanence and change in social and political structures, the development of pluralistic societies, and concludes with a chapter on the "use and abuse of political power."

Parsons, Talcott. *Societies: Evolutionary and Comparative Perspectives.* Englewood Cliffs, N.J.: Prentice-Hall, 1966. This is a somewhat difficult book, but in it Parsons presents a framework and conceptual scheme for the study of social organization and change from an evolutionary perspective.

Redfield, Robert. *The Primitive World and Its Transformations.* Ithaca, N.Y.: Cornell University Press, 1953. Redfield's study is one of a series in which the effects of modernization upon primitive cultures is analyzed. Redfield sees the technological order becoming progressively more important than the moral order as societies move from isolated tribe to peasant society to civilization.

Warren, R. *The Community in America.* Chicago: Rand McNally, 1963. In this book, Warren analyzes the changing pattern of American community life and attempts to define characteristics common to many different types of American communities.

Articles and Papers

Bell, Daniel. "Notes on the Post-Industrial Society." *The Public Interest* **1**, 6 (Winter 1967) and **2**, 7 (Spring 1967).

Dyckman, John W. "Social Planning, Social Planners and Planned Societies." In *Neighborhood, City and Metropolis,* edited by R. Gutman and D. Popenoe, pp. 896–909. New York: Random House, 1970.

Etzioni, Amitai. "Toward a Theory of Societal Guidance." *American Journal of Sociology* **73**, 2 (September 1967):173–187.

Key, William H., and Louis A. Zurcher. "The Overlap Model: A Comparison of Strategies for Social Change." *Sociological Quarterly* **9**, 1 (Winter 1968):85–96.

II RELATED RESOURCES

Nonfiction

Clark, Kenneth B., and Jeannette Hopkins. *A Relevant War against Poverty*. New York: Harper & Row, Harper Torchbook (Paper), 1969. Clark and Hopkins study community action programs and the social change which they have brought about.

Handlin, Oscar, and John Burchard. *The Historian and the City*. Cambridge, Mass.: M.I.T. Press and Harvard University Press, 1963. This book is a collection of essays by historians interested in the nature, problems, and future of the city.

Hunter, Guy. *Modernizing Peasant Societies: A Comparative Study in Asia and Africa*. New York: Oxford University Press, 1969. Hunter discusses how the importation of institutions from technologically oriented countries to agriculturally undeveloped countries results in cultural upheaval.

Jacobs, Jane. *The Death and Life of Great American Cities*. New York: Random House, 1961. Miss Jacobs points to a number of inadequacies in current city planning practices, which she says are destroying cities. She proposes alternative ways of dealing with today's urban problems.

Rosenberg, Bernard, and David M. White. *Mass Culture*. New York: Macmillan, 1957. A provocative examination of the contributions (for good or ill) of advertising, television, movies, and magazines to Western culture, and a conceptual formulation of the meaning of "mass culture."

Roszak, Theodore. *The Making of a Counter Culture*. New York: Doubleday, 1969. Roszak looks at the culture which young people are forming within, but in opposition to, the dominant American culture and examines the reasons for its formation.

Weaver, R. C. *The Urban Complex*. New York: Doubleday, Anchor (Paper), 1966. The former Secretary of the Department of Housing and Urban Development gives some practical advice about today's urban crisis.

Fiction

Greene, Graham. *The Quiet American*. New York: Bantam Books, 1957. Greene writes of a young American diplomat who has recently graduated from Harvard and describes his first extracultural experience; he sharply portrays the diplomat's self-righteous and innocent response to the culture of French Indochina.

Kazantzakis, Nikos. *Zorba the Greek*. New York: Simon & Schuster, 1952. An educated Englishman, transplanted to rural Greece, is at first repelled by the culture, later attracted to it, and finally influenced by it. His experiences are instigated and guided by a Greek named Zorba.

Nordhoff, Charles, and James Norman Hall. *Pitcairn's Island*. New York: Pocket Books, 1962. This novel reconstructs the history of the *Bounty* mutineers. Cut off from their civilization, the mutineers attempt to create a new society on an unknown island by combining elements of British and Tahitian culture.

Films

The Savage Innocents. Nicholas Ray, 1961. This drama portrays the culture shock sustained by a Western official and an Eskimo when they meet.

GLOSSARY

Acculturation The acquiring of the traits of another culture by an individual or group.

Achieved status A position in society which can be gained by an individual's own achievements.

Age-specific birthrate The number of live births per 1,000 women of a specified age group.

Age-specific death rate The number of deaths per 1,000 persons in a specified age group of a population.

Age-specific marital fertility rate The number of live births per 1,000 married women of a specified age group.

Amalgamation The biological merging of an ethnic or racial group with the native population.

Annihilation The process by which a dominant group causes the deaths of minority group members in large numbers.

Anomie A social condition in which there are relatively few values to guide the individual, or in which the values are confused and unclear.

Anticipatory socialization The learning of the beliefs, values, and norms of a role or group as preparation for taking on the role or joining the group.

Applied research Research designed to provide answers for the solution of some immediate practical problem.

Apprenticeship A type of socialization in which a new member of an organization observes and copies the role of an established member.

Ascribed status A position in society to which members are assigned by criteria beyond their control, usually parentage, age, and sex.

Assimilation The process by which a minority group is absorbed into the dominant society.

Authoritarian structure An organizational structure in which the leadership exerts broad control over the members.

Authority Power that has been made legitimate, that is, socially accepted as right, proper, and necessary.

Basic research Research designed to build knowledge of fundamental facts, processes, and phenomena.

Beliefs Ideas men hold about the natural or supernatural world which are not supported by objective or factual evidence.

Bureaucracy A large-scale type of organization in which various functions are separated and carried out by special highly trained individuals, departments, or bureaus; which is organized by formal rules; and which is coordinated and controlled by a hierarchical chain of command.

Business panic Collective behavior among a scattered group caused by a common fear that economic systems are failing.

Caste A closed social grouping based on heredity that determines its members' social relationships, prestige, and place of residence; was found principally in India.

Censorship An attempt to influence public opinion by limiting the amount of information on a subject that is made available to a public.

Census The counting and collection of data about a population, usually involving a count of every person.

Census tract A small subdivision of an urban area, usually including from 3,000 to 6,000 people, which is created to make easier the tabulation and analysis of population data.

Centralization The concentration of economic, governmental, and service functions.

Charismatic authority Authority generated by the personality or personal appeal of some individual.

Church A stable and institutionalized organization of religious believers.

Clan A large kinship group whose members inhabit one geographical area and believe they are descended from a common ancestor.

Class conflict Hostility between classes due to their different interests.

Class consciousness Recognition of a system of social stratification and of one's location within it; awareness of some shared goals or interests in common with other members of the same status group.

Class divisions The perceived and real differences between the classes of a society.

Coercion The relationship in which one person or group forces its will on another.

Collective behavior The behavior of a group of people responding to a common influence or stimulus in fairly temporary, unstable, and unstructured situations.

Community (1) A relatively small cluster of people centered around individual residences and places of work and based on daily patterns of interaction.

(2) Any group of people who share common interests or traditions and who have a strong feeling of solidarity (or "sense of community").

Community control The ability of members of a community to influence the actions of public institutions serving their neighborhoods.

Competition The process of social interaction in which individuals or groups struggle with one another to attain the same goal; their primary concern is directed toward the object or goal which is being sought rather than toward each other.

Concentration The ecological process in which individual and social units tend to cluster where conditions are favorable.

Conflict The process of social interaction in which two or more persons struggle with one another for some commonly prized object or value.

Conformity Behavior that is in accord with the norms of a social group or society.

Contagion The increase of people's willingness to express emotion caused by crowd conditions.

Controlled migration Free migration which takes place under government restrictions.

Conversion A sudden change in values and then behavior, caused by one experience or set of experiences.

Cooperation The relationship in which people or groups engage in joint action in order to promote common interests or shared goals.

Coup d'état A change of government in which one leadership group forcefully overthrows another.

Craze A common interest, among scattered people, in an activity which is usually trivial and without long-range social effect.

Crowd A temporary grouping of people who are physically close together and who have a common focus or interest.

Crude birthrate The number of live births per 1,000 persons in a population within a given period, usually a year.

Crude death rate The number of deaths per 1,000 persons in the population during a given period, usually a year.

Cultural diffusion The process by which culture traits spread from one group or society to another.

Cultural lag A situation in which some parts of a culture (usually material culture) change at a faster rate than other parts (usually nonmaterial).

Cultural pluralism The social pattern in which the dominant group allows newcomers to achieve full participation in society, without discriminating against them, and at the same time allows them to maintain many of their cultural and social differences.

Cultural relativity The principle that a culture must be judged on its own terms and not in comparison to another culture.

Cultural survival A culture trait that has survived after its original function has disappeared.

Culture 1. The system of values and meanings shared by a group or society, including the embodiment of those values and meanings in material objects.

2. The way of life of a social group; the group's total man-made environment or social heritage.

Culture trait The simplest significant unit of a culture.

Decentralization The dispersion of economic, governmental, and service functions.

De facto school segregation Segregation of schools due to the residential patterns of minority groups.

Deferred gratification pattern The postponing of immediate pleasures in order to better prepare for later life.

De jure school segregation Segregation of schools based on law.

Democratic structure An organizational structure in which the members participate in decision making.

Demography The study of population size, composition, and distribution, and patterns of population change.

Denomination One of a number of religious organizations considered socially acceptable by a society.

Deviance Behavior that does not conform to the norms of a social group or society.

Differentiation The process in which functions formerly fused into one social structure develop into new and separate social structures; the systems of the society become more specialized.

Discrimination Unfair or unequal treatment that is accorded to people or groups.

Dispersion The scattering of population and social units; the opposite of concentration.

Dysfunction A function that has a negative effect. (see *Function*)

Ecclesia A church which is integrated with other social institutions and embraces almost all members of a society.

Ecological segregation The process in which certain areas of a city become specialized in type of land use, services, or population.

Ecology The study of the interrelationships between organisms and their environment.

Ecosystem (or **ecological complex**) The web of interrelationships between living things and their environment.

Education A set of processes specifically and purposely directed toward inducing learning.

Egalitarian family A form of family organization in which the husband and wife regard each other as equal in authority and privileges.

Esteem The favorable evaluation that a person receives from others concerning his own unique qualities, or how well he performs a certain role.

Ethnic group Any group which is socially distinguished from other groups, has developed its own subculture, and has a shared feeling of peoplehood.

Ethnocentrism The attitude that one's own culture or group is by nature superior, and the evaluation of another culture in terms of one's own culture.

Evolutionary change Political change that develops out of existing trends and institutions.

Exchange A relationship in which one person acts in a certain way toward another in order to receive a reward or return.

Expressive relationship A social relationship which is valued for its own sake.

Expulsion A form of exclusion in which minority group members are forced to leave the country.

Extended family A family unit that consists of a nuclear family plus one or more relatives living together.

Fads and fashion A departure from what is customary, in an attempt to be different, which remains within the bounds of good taste and manners.

Family group A relatively permanent group of two or more people who are related by blood, marriage, or adoption, live together, and cooperate economically.

Family of orientation The family into which an individual is born and in which the major part of his socialization takes place.

Family of procreation The family formed by an individual when he marries and has children.

Fecundity The potential capacity of the females of a population to have children. This figure represents an estimate of the maximum number of births biologically possible in the population.

Fertility The frequency of births in a population.

Folkways Social norms that are approved of and accepted by a society but not considered to be morally significant and not strictly enforced.

Forced migration Compulsory transfer of people from one region or country to another.

Formal organization An organization in which formal structures predominate.

Formal social control mechanisms Systems of formally established laws and rules, and the means of enforcing them, which specify rewards for those who conform to them and punishments for those who violate them.

Formal structure An organizational structure which consists of a specific and formally stated set of rules and regulations that define the activities of the members.

Free migration The movement of peoples motivated by an individual desire for adventure or a search for improved living conditions and social circumstances.

Function The effect one unit of a culture or a society has on another unit or on the society as a whole.

Functional interdependence The process in which units of a group or society become increasingly dependent on the other units in that system in order to function or perform their tasks.

Functionalism An approach or orientation toward studying social and cultural phenomena.

Generalized other A generalized conception an individual has of the expectations and attitudes of a group or society; this conception is incorporated into his personality and helps to determine his behavior.

Government The group of individuals who exercise the powers invested in the state.

Group consciousness An awareness of belonging to a group and having a sense of group identity.

Ideological primary group A primary group in which the members are mainly united by a common ideology.

Ideology A system of beliefs about the social world which is strongly rooted in a specific set of values and interests.

Illegitimate power Power used without the support of social approval.

Impelled migration The movement of people from one country to another due to social conditions, wherein the individual may choose not to leave.

Industrialization Changes in methods of production, and in economic and social organization, which result from the introduction of power-driven machinery and the factory system.

Infant mortality rate Age-specific death rate for infants under the age of one.

Informal organization An organization in which informal structures predominate.

Informal social control mechanisms Systems of informal rules and codes enforced through personal actions such as praise and ridicule.

Informal structure An organizational structure consisting of personal relationships which develop spontaneously as members interact.

Instinct Complex behavior patterns which are biologically inherited and typical of all animals in a given species.

Institution A formal and stable way of carrying out an activity or function that is important to a society.

Instrumental relationship A social relationship which is merely a means to some other end.

Integration The fusion of minority and majority groups which takes place through the spreading and sharing of cultural and social traits.

Internalization An individual's acceptance of the norms of a social group or society as part of his own personality.

Invasion A process involving the movement of one type of population or land use into an area already occupied by a different type of population or land use.

Knowledge Ideas or information about the existing world which are supported by objective or factual evidence.

Labor force That part of the population which is able to work, including those actually working full- or part-time and those unemployed but seeking employment.

Laws Standardized and formalized norms which regulate human conduct.

Learning The process by which an individual's thoughts, feelings, and behavior are changed as a result of new experience.

Legal bureaurcratic authority Authority which rests upon rules that are rationally established.

Legitimate power Power used in a way that is generally recognized as socially right and necessary.

Life chances The probability that an individual will attain or fail to attain important goals and experiences in life.

Life table A statistical table that presents the death rate and life expectancy of each of a series of age-sex categories over a period of time.

Macrosociology The study of large-scale social systems and relations between these systems.

Magic A set of actions, usually highly ritualistic, that are believed to bring about some desired change in the environment.

Mass hysteria The contagious spread of certain hysterical symptoms such as fainting, delusions, or trances.

Mass society A society in which there is a weak governing elite and a highly volatile mass of citizens who feel a sense of alienation, anomie, and powerlessness.

Master status The status which dominates others and thereby determines a person's general status level in the case of status inconsistency.

Material culture All man-made physical objects.

Matriarchal family A form of family organization in which the mother is dominant.

Megalopolis A concentration of two or more metropolitan areas which have grown and spread until they overlap one another.

Microsociology The study of small-scale social systems and social relationships.

Migration The movements of individuals or groups from one geographical area to another.

Minding A hypothetical communication between the "I" and the "me" in the social psychological theory of George Herbert Mead.

Minority group Any recognizable ethnic, racial, or religious group in a society which suffers some disadvantage due to prejudice or discrimination.

Mob A crowd which is trying to accomplish or cause an antisocial act of aggression.

Monotheism The belief that there is only one god.

Mores Social norms that provide the moral standards of a group or society and which are strictly enforced.

Multibonded group A group organized around more than one major set of values and goals.

Nation-state A powerful multibonded group which combines a strong central government with a common territory, usually a common language, and a strong feeling of group identity.

Natural area A territorial area with some common unifying characteristic which emerges through ecological processes.

Neonatal mortality rate Age-specific death rate for infants under one month of age.

Norms, social A rule or standard which defines what people should or should not do, or think, or feel in any given social situation.

Nuclear family A unit of family organization consisting of a couple and their children.

Opinion leader An individual in a community who exerts more than a normal share of influence over the formation of public opinion.

Organization A social group that has been deliberately and consciously constructed in order to seek certain specific goals.

Overurbanization A situation in which people move to cities at a faster rate than the economy can support.

Panel study A method of measuring opinion or attitude change; the same people are repeatedly interviewed over a period of time.

Participatory democracy Involvement of the entire population of a society with the processes and workings of the government.

Participatory (positive) socialization A method of socialization which emphasizes the participation of the child and the use of rewards and positive sanctions.

Partition The political reorganization of a country along racial, ethnic, or religious lines.

Patriarchal family A form of family organization in which the father is dominant.

Peer group A grouping of individuals of the same general age and having approximately the same social position.

Personal power The ability to control one's own

life.

Personality An organized system of behavior, attitudes, beliefs, and values characteristic of an individual.

Political pluralism A social pattern in which power is divided among a number of large groups, each of which represents a significant set of interests or values.

Politics The acquisition and use of power, especially within the context of the institution of the state and its government.

Polyandry A form of polygamy in which a wife has more than one husband at the same time.

Polygamy Marriage which involves more than one husband or one wife at the same time.

Polygyny Form of polygamy in which a husband has more than one wife at the same time.

Polytheism The belief that there is more than one god.

Population Any category of people selected for a study of attitudes, values, beliefs, or opinions.

Prejudice Judging of people, things, or situations on the basis of preformed stereotypes or generalizations.

Prestige The favorable evaluation and social recognition that a person receives from others.

Primary group A group, usually relatively small, durable, and unspecialized, in which primary relationships predominate. The members of a primary group have a strong sense of group identity.

Primary relationship A personal, emotion-laden, and not easily transferable relationship which includes a variety of roles and interests of each individual. It involves free and extensive communication and the interaction of whole personalities.

Primitive migration Movement of a population to follow food sources.

Primordial primary group A primitive group, such as a peasant village or folk community, which is united by common biological, cultural, and neighborhood ties, and in which membership is not voluntary.

Propaganda Any calculated attempt to influence beliefs, choices, or opinion.

Public A scattered group of people who share a common interest or who are all affected by some event or activity.

Public opinion Attitudes and opinions that the public holds about an issue.

Race A subgroup of the human species characterized by physical differences which result from inherited biological characteristics.

Reference group A group or social category that is especially important in helping an individual define his beliefs, values, attitudes, and opinions.

Religion A system of beliefs and practices concerning ultimate reality and the sacred.

Religious officialdom Full-time workers in a religious organization.

Religious ritual Formalized behavior, usually of a symbolic nature, oriented toward the sacred.

Repressive (negative) socialization A method of socialization which emphasizes obedience and the use of punishment and other negative sanctions.

Resocialization A process involving a radical change, in both role behavior and values, to a new way of life which is inconsistent or incompatible with the former one.

Revolutionary change A kind of political change that seeks to destroy existing institutions of political power and replace them with new ones.

Riot A violently aggressive or destructive mob.

Role (1) A set of expectations and behaviors associated with a specific position in a social system (social role).
(2) The way an individual personality tends to react to a social situation (individual role).

Role, prescribed A role as defined by cultural standards; the set of behaviors expected for all occupants of a status or position; an ideal role.

Role conflict Incompatibility between two or more roles that an individual performs in a given situation; also called role incompatibility.

Role distance The maintenance of psychological distance between an individual's personality and his role.

Role performance A role as it is actually played by the occupant of a social position.

Role set A complex set of roles associated with a single status or position.

Role strain A feeling of conflict or stress caused by inconsistent demands of a single role; also called role inconsistency.

Rumor A widespread report that is not supported by fact.

Sacred, The A culture trait or object which is set apart from everyday life and which evokes great respect and reverence.

Sample A part of a population that is considered to be representative of the population as a whole.

Sample interview survey A method of measuring attitudes, beliefs, or opinions by interviewing a sample of a certain category of people.

Sanction A reward (positive sanction) or penalty (negative sanction) directed at a person or group to encourage or discourage certain types of behavior.

Science An approach to the problem of human knowledge which utilizes quantifiable and objective methods.

Secondary relationship A relationship which is specialized, relatively unemotional and impersonal, and involving a limited aspect of one's personality. The participants in a secondary relationship are usually quite interchangeable.

Sect An exclusive group of religious believers which tends to ignore or repudiate the established order and place emphasis on faith and fervor.

Secularization A trend in which many aspects of life become increasingly separated from religious or spiritual connections or influences.

Segregation The establishment of separate residential areas, services, and other facilities to which people are involuntarily restricted on the basis of racial, ethnic, or religious characteristics.

Self That aspect of an individual's personality which consists of his awareness and feelings about his own personal and social identity.

Self-fulfilling prophecy A false belief regarding a social situation which, because one believes it and acts upon it, actually becomes true.

Self-segregation A process by which a minority group somewhat willingly tries to keep itself separated from the dominant society.

Sense of cultural identity Awareness of an identity with attitudes, values, and experiences shared by members of one's group or society.

Separatism A form of self-segregation in which a minority group aspires to set up a totally independent society of its own.

Sex ratio The number of males per 100 females in a specified population.

Significant others Those people who have the greatest influence on an individual's evaluation of himself and on his acceptance or rejection of social norms.

Social categories An aggregate of people who are not organized into a social group but who share certain socially important characteristics.

Social class (or **status grouping**) A grouping of persons with similar status levels and some degree of similarity of behavior and values.

Social control The process by which limits and checks are put upon the individual's behavior and people are motivated to conform to the norms of a group or a society.

Social disorganization The disintegration or breakdown of the institutionalized structures of a social system.

Social estate (or **social order**) A social grouping whose members share a common social rank; less rigid and closed than a caste but more closed than a class. Usually associated with medieval European feudal society.

Social interaction The basic social process involving communication through language and gestures. Through the exchange of meanings individuals affect each other's behavior and mental states.

Social mobility The movement from one status to another, either upward, downward, or horizontal. This can be measured intergenerationally (one generation to another) or intragenerationally (within an individual's own lifetime).

Social movement A group of people, usually somewhat scattered and loosely organized, who are acting to promote some form of social change.

Social organization Same as social structure.

Social planning The attempt by a group or society to guide social change to achieve predetermined goals.

Social power The capacity to control or influence the actions of others, whether they wish to cooperate or not.

Social relationship A reciprocal (two-way) pattern of interaction between two or more people that continues over a period of time so that a relatively stable set of social expectations develops.

Social structure The orderly or patterned way that people and groups relate to one another.

Social system A set of persons or groups who are interacting, are dependent on one another, and are somewhat integrated. The set is conceived of as a social unit distinct from the particular individuals who compose it.

Socialization The process by which the culture of a group or society is taught to, and instilled or internalized in, the individuals who live in that group or society.

Society (1) The type of social grouping that includes the most functions and is most complex and dominant. It has the highest degree of self-sufficiency of all social systems.

(2) A complex web of social relationships.

Sociocultural evolution The view that, over time, cultures and societies develop and change from lower and simpler forms to higher and more complex forms.

State The social institution which has the supreme power in a society; it has a monopoly on the legitimate use of coercion and physical force.

Status (1) A position in a social system that carries with it a set of rights and responsibilities.

(2) A ranked position in a social system.

(3) A person's general or total social standing in society.

Status consistency The general tendency for people in any given quarter of one status ranking to be in the same quarter of other status rankings.

Status hierarchies The order in which statuses are ranked.

Status inconsistency A combination of statuses, embodied in one person, which are of unequal ranking.

Status symbol A conspicuous possession, style of dress, manner of speech, etc., which denotes that its owner belongs to a particular status level.

Strata (or **stratification levels**) A unit or category in a status hierarchy.

Stratification A social pattern based on ranking individuals and social positions according to the distribution of the material and emotional desirables which society has to offer.

Structural mobility Vertical mobility resulting from changes in the social or economic system.

Subculture The culture of a segment of society, such as a social group.

Suburb A relatively small community that is part of an urbanized area; it is adjacent to and dependent on a central city.

Succession The replacement of one type of occupancy of an area by another type; the completion of the process of invasion.

Symbol A thing that stands for or suggests something else by reason of association.

Symbolic interactionism A social psychological theory that stresses the importance of communication through language and gestures in the formation and maintenance of personality and social relationships.

Task-oriented primary group An informal group that operates within a complex, formal organization, mainly for the benefit of the group members.

Technological development The increased ability of societies to master their environment.

Technology Knowledge directed toward practical applications in the physical and social world.

Totalitarian society A society in which the state assumes total control over all social organization.

Totemism A complex of beliefs organized around a totem, an object worshipped as a god and an ancestor.

Traditional authority Authority conferred by custom and accepted practice.

Training A type of socialization to an organization which teaches specialized skills and the organization's values and norms.

Tribe A social grouping which consists of two or more clans or other kinship groupings inhabiting a common territory and which has a form of government somewhat differentiated from the family system.

Unibonded group A group organized around a single major set of values and goals.

Urbanism Patterns of culture and social structure which are characteristic of cities.

Urbanization (1) The movement of people from rural to urban areas, and the resulting increase in the proportion of a population that resides in urban rather than rural places.

(2) The spread of urban patterns of culture and social structure.

Value (1) An abstract and generalized conception of what is good, beneficial, desirable, and worthwhile.

(2) A desired object or goal.

Voluntary association An organization which is freely organized by individuals for the pursuit of some common interest; usually members are unpaid volunteers and there are few formal control mechanisms.

Wealth All the economic assets of a society — the material products, land and natural resources, and productive labor services.

NAME INDEX

SUBJECT INDEX